LATIN AMERICAN
POLITICS AND DEVELOPMENT

LATIN AMERICAN POLITICS AND DEVELOPMENT

EIGHTH EDITION

Edited by

Howard J. Wiarda, *University of Georgia*

Harvey F. Kline, *University of Alabama*

WESTVIEW
PRESS

A MEMBER OF THE PERSEUS BOOKS GROUP

Westview Press was founded in 1975 in Boulder, Colorado, by notable publisher and intellectual Fred Praeger. Westview Press continues to publish scholarly titles and high-quality undergraduate- and graduate-level textbooks in core social science disciplines. With books developed, written, and edited with the needs of serious nonfiction readers, professors, and students in mind, Westview Press honors its long history of publishing books that matter.

Find us on the World Wide Web at www.westviewpress.com.

Every effort has been made to secure required permissions for all text, images, maps, and other art reprinted in this volume.

Westview Press books are available at special discounts for bulk purchases in the United States by corporations, institutions, and other organizations. For more information, please contact the Special Markets Department at the Perseus Books Group, 2300 Chestnut Street, Suite 200, Philadelphia, PA 19103, or call (800) 810-4145, ext. 5000, or e-mail special.markets@perseusbooks.com.

Designed by Jack Lenzo

Library of Congress Cataloging-in-Publication Data

Latin American politics and development / edited by Howard J. Wiarda, University of George, Harvey F. Kline, University of Alabama.—Eighth edition.
     pages cm
  Includes bibliographical references and index.
  ISBN 978-0-8133-4904-6 (pbk.)—ISBN 978-0-8133-4905-3 (e-book) 1. Latin America—Politics and government. I. Wiarda, Howard J., 1939– II. Kline, Harvey F.
  F1410.L39 2014
  320.98—dc23
                                        2013025394

10 9 8 7 6 5 4 3 2 1

CONTENTS

PART III

The Political Systems of Central and Middle America and the Caribbean   305

TABLES AND MAPS

ACRONYMS

ALADI	Latin American Integration Association
GATT	General Agreement on Tariffs and Trade
GDP	gross domestic product
GNP	gross national product
IADB	Inter-American Development Bank
IAF	Inter-American Foundation
IMF	International Monetary Fund
ISI	import-substitution industrialization
NAFTA	North American Free Trade Agreement
NGOs	nongovernmental organizations
OAS	Organization of American States
USAID	US Agency for International Development

PREFACE TO THE EIGHTH EDITION

The first edition of this book was published in 1979, the second in 1985, the third in 1990, the fourth in 1996, the fifth in 2000, the sixth in 2007, the seventh in 2010, and now the eighth in 2014. The issues we have sought to examine in all eight editions include why Latin America is different from the United States, why it lagged behind economically and politically, how societies cast historically in a medieval, dependent, and semifeudal mode have gone about achieving modernization and development, what paths of national development the distinct countries of the area have followed (evolutionary or revolutionary; authoritarian, Marxist, or democratic; capitalist, socialist, or statist), and what developments and difficulties of democracy have been encountered in the area. These are large, meaty issues; their importance goes beyond the geographic confines of Latin America.

Each of the eight editions of the book has reflected the major dynamic changes occurring in Latin America itself. The decade of the 1970s was a period of authoritarianism and repression, and human rights abuses in much of the region, all of which resulted in interpretations about the area—corporatism, dependency theory, and bureaucratic authoritarianism—that reflected scholars' pessimism about Latin America's future. Following this, the 1980s was a period of democratization throughout Latin America, with greater optimism about the area's political future (even though the economic prospects continued to be poor) and newer interpretations that stressed transitions to democracy.

In the early 1990s there was considerable agreement between the United States and Latin America on goals for the region (labeled the "Washington consensus"): democracy, economic liberalism, and free trade. By this point most of the authoritarian regimes of the area had given way, and with the collapse of the Soviet Union, Marxism-Leninism had become less attractive; democracy and liberalism therefore seemed the only viable option. But by the end of the 1990s and continuing into the twenty-first century, although democracy, economic reform, and freer trade were still high on the agenda, a number of cracks had appeared in the prevailing consensus. Democracy was still limited and not working well in quite a few countries: much of Latin America had achieved electoral democracy but not liberal or participatory democracy. Economic reform continued, but the neoliberal agenda had resulted in widespread unemployment and privation in many countries. Trade barriers continued to fall in Latin America, but in the United States protectionist political pressures prevented new trade initiatives. Meanwhile, Latin America moved increasingly away from the United States and followed a more independent policy.

While Latin America has gone through political and economic ups and downs over this period of more than fifty years, its society has been massively transformed. These are no longer the "sleepy," "backward," "underdeveloped" countries of cartoon and movie stereotypes. Since 1960, Latin America as a whole has gone from 70 percent rural to 70 percent urban and from 70 percent illiteracy to 70 percent literacy. The old two-class society is giving way, a new middle class is emerging, and poverty is slowly being reduced. These figures reflect the massive social changes under way throughout the area as well as the transformation from a peasant-agricultural economy to a more modern, industrial, and diversified one.

In the mid-1970s seventeen of the twenty countries were authoritarian, but today nineteen of the twenty (all except Cuba, and even there changes are likely soon) are democratic—incomplete democracies, but certainly better than the human-rights-abusing regimes of earlier decades. Economically, quite a number of the countries are booming, with miraculous or nearly East Asian–level growth rates, but others are still mired in underdevelopment. At the same time a host of new issues—rising crime and insecurity, drugs, gangs, social inequality, and globalization—have come to the fore. So, as always, Latin America reflects a mixture of successes and failures, of traditional and modern features, of mixed and often crazy-quilt regimes in an always changing, dynamic context.

No longer a group of backward, underdeveloped countries, Latin America is one of the most exciting regions of the globe for the comparative study of economic, social, and political change. In previous decades the choice of developmental models seemed wide open, representing diverse routes to modernization, but by now the route of democracy and mixed economies seems the main one conceivable, although with great variation still among the countries of the region. But populist regimes dedicated to redistribution have also come to power. In most countries the state plays a major role in the economy, and the private sector is weaker than in the United States. Virtually every social, economic, and political issue, process, and policy present in the world can be found in Latin America. It thus remains an exciting, innovative, ever-changing, and endlessly fascinating living laboratory for study, travel, and research.

Not only is Latin America an interesting area to study, but it has also become increasingly important to the United States. After Canada, Mexico is now the United States' second-largest trading partner in the world. Hispanics have become the largest minority in the United States and are voting in increasing numbers. On a host of new, hot issues—including drugs, trade, immigration, tourism, energy, investment, the environment, democracy, and human rights—the United States and Latin America have become increasingly intertwined and interdependent. Yet conflict persists in US relations with Cuba, Venezuela, and other countries. At the same time, both Europe and Asia are increasing their trade with and interest in Latin America and, as a result, are often competing with the United States for influence. So is Iran.

This book offers in its introduction a broad, regionwide overview of the patterns and processes of Latin American history, politics, society, and development. It then proceeds to a detailed country-by-country treatment of all twenty Latin American countries. Major countries such as Argentina, Brazil, Chile, Colombia, Cuba, Mexico, Peru, and Venezuela receive extended coverage, and the smaller countries receive complete but somewhat briefer treatment. Each country chapter is written by a leading specialist in the field. To facilitate comparisons between countries we have asked each of our authors to use a common outline and approach as far as it is feasible. We emphasize throughout both the unique features of each country and common patterns and processes. Instructors thus have maximum flexibility in the selection of which countries to study and which themes or developmental models to emphasize.

Latin American Politics and Development has throughout its previous editions emerged as one of the most durable yet innovative texts in the field, and we hope that this eighth edition will intrigue new students of Latin America as it has stimulated two generations of earlier ones. Many of these students have now gone on to careers in business, academia, private agencies, or foreign policy; it is always rewarding to meet, hear from, or run into these former as well as current students. We hope that some of our enthusiasm for the subject continues to rub off on them.

The editors wish to thank their wives and families, for whom this book has over the years become almost another addition to the household. Thanks also to our contributors, both new and old; in each edition we have tried to bring in new faces, new ideas, and more women and minority contributors. Finally, we wish to thank acquisitions editor Anthony Wahl of Westview Press for encouraging this new edition and shepherding it through the publication process.

Howard J. Wiarda
Harvey F. Kline

PART I

The Latin American Tradition and Process of Development

Howard J. Wiarda
Harvey F. Kline

I

THE CONTEXT OF
LATIN AMERICAN POLITICS

Profound social, economic, cultural, and political transformations are sweeping through Latin America, affecting all institutions and areas of life. Accelerated economic and social change, democratization, and globalization are having an impact on all countries, often incompletely and unevenly. Latin America, however, still has abundant poverty, malnutrition, disease, poor housing, and the worst distribution of income in the world; its economic and political institutions often fail to work well or as intended; and social and political reforms are still strongly needed. However, at least some of the countries—generally the larger, more stable, and richer ones—are making what appears to be a definitive breakthrough to democracy and development, and many of the small nations are modernizing as well.

We speak of "Latin America" as if it were a single, homogeneous region; however, the area is exceedingly diverse. Because of this diversity, we need to understand each country individually as well as the common patterns. While the Latin American countries share a common basis in law, language, history, culture, sociology, colonial experience, and overall political patterns that enables us to discuss the region in general terms, we also recognize that each country is different and becoming increasingly more so. Unity amid diversity is a theme that runs throughout this book, so in Part I we survey the general patterns before moving on to the individual countries in Part II.

Throughout Latin America's history its leaders and people have debated their heritage and future, particularly between Western and non-Western; feudal, capitalist, and socialist; First World (developed nations) and Third World (developing ones); and evolutionary or revolutionary change. Conflict over these issues has often delayed development.

Now at last a consensus seems to be emerging, namely, democracy in the political sphere; a modern, mixed, and in some cases social-democratic economy; and greater integration with the rest of the world. Authoritarianism seems to be on the decrease

3

in Latin America, although when the economy declines and instability results, the authoritarian temptation is still often present. Marxism-Leninism is similarly in decline, even while social democracy and populism are still attractive options for many political leaders. More and more of Latin America is becoming middle-class and centrist. The old extremes are no longer attractive, and the range of political and economic options has narrowed.

Driving these changes are democratization, economic development, and globalization. Democracy is overwhelmingly the preferred form of government of Latin America, even though democracy does not always work well or quickly enough, it takes forms that are often different from that of the United States, and it is still threatened by upheaval, corruption, and vast social problems. Globalization affects Latin America in all areas of life: culture (movies, television, and music), society (behavioral norms), politics (democracy), and, above all, economics. Latin America is now part of a global market economy. It has little choice but to open its markets to global trade and investment.

With the Cold War over and the war on terrorism concentrated elsewhere, there is little foreign aid, and Latin America can no longer play the superpowers against each other. Instead it must have private investment and become globally competitive or else it will sink. If a country deviates very far from the path of democracy or free markets, that all-important investment will simply go elsewhere. All political leaders and economic sectors in Latin America now recognize these hard facts, even though they may still rail against them in populist fashion or disagree on the precise balance between authority and democracy, statism and open markets, and unfettered capitalism and social justice. The Latin American countries vary greatly in how they manage development policy, and they are still debating their choices about the basic model to follow.

As Latin America has become more democratic and its economies more open, it has, in its own way, balanced outside pressures and domestic, often traditional ways of doing things. Modernity and tradition frequently exist side by side in Latin America—the most traditional agricultural methods alongside the most modern skyscrapers—reflecting the mixed, often transitional nature of Latin American society. Patronage considerations often remain as important as merit and electoral choice. Moreover, as democracy has come to the area, it has frequently been a more centralized, executive-centered form of democracy rather than one of separate and equal executive, legislative, and judicial branches. At the same time, despite privatization and neoliberalism, the state has remained a strong force in the economic and social programs, closer to the European tradition than to the US laissez-faire model. Thus modernization in Latin America has represented a fascinating blend of US, European, and historically Latin American ways of doing things.

A QUICK SNAPSHOT

For the purposes of this book, Latin America consists of eighteen Spanish-speaking countries, one Portuguese-speaking country (Brazil), and one French- or Creole-speaking country (Haiti). Including South America, Central America, Mexico, and the Caribbean islands, it encompasses eight million square miles (twenty-one million square kilometers), about one-fifth of the world's total land area. Its population is about 550 million, almost twice that of the United States. The former Dutch and British colonies in the area are also interesting and worthy of study, and although they are part of the geographic region of Latin America, they are not culturally, socially, religiously, or politically "Latin" American. For this reason, they are not included in this book.

The social and racial composition of Latin America is exceedingly diverse and complicated. At the time of Columbus's arrival in America in 1492, some areas (Mexico, parts of Central America, Andean South America) had large numbers of indigenous people, whereas other areas did not. Even today assimilation and integration of indigenous people into national life remain among the great unsolved problems of these countries. Where there were few Indians or they died out and where the climate was right for plantation agriculture (such as in the Caribbean islands, northeast Brazil, and some coastal areas), large numbers of African slaves were brought in. White Europeans formed the upper class, and Indians and blacks were slaves, peasants, and subsistence agriculturists. In these areas social and race relations were then written mainly in terms of relations between whites and blacks; on the rest of the mainland the major socioracial components remained white and Indian. The cultures of the Spanish colonies in the Caribbean and the Portuguese one in Brazil, because of the African influence, were often different from those in the other Spanish-speaking countries. In some countries all three major racial strains (Indian, black, white), as well as Asian and Middle Eastern, are now present.

In contrast to North America, where the colonists took their wives and families along with them to settle and farm, the conquest of Latin America was viewed as a military campaign (no women initially), and widespread miscegenation between whites and Indians, whites and blacks, blacks and Indians, and all of their offspring took place right from the beginning. Hence a mulatto (white and black) element in the Caribbean and Brazil and a mestizo (white and Indian) element in the mainland countries of the Spanish empire emerged, with endless social and racial gradations based on skin color, hair texture, and facial features. Although there is racial prejudice, because of these many variations and gradations Latin Americans tend not to typecast people as "black," "white," or "Indian" based solely on color, as North Americans do. Indeed, in many of the Central American and Andean countries of South America, one is considered an *indio* or *indigena* mainly if he or she dresses like a native American and speaks a native language other than Spanish. Moving to a city, wearing Western clothes, becoming educated, and speaking Spanish probably mean that the person would no longer be called an "Indian," even though there has of course been no change in the person's ethnic background.

The racial situation in Latin America is generally more fluid and permeable than it is in the United States; in addition, higher education, wealth, and particular styles of dress and comportment tend to make one "whiter." Because being viewed as whiter is pragmatically seen by most Latin Americans as being easier and/or better, it has long been hard to launch Indian or black rights or power movements, although this is changing as well. Endlessly fascinating, racial/social relations in Latin America are very different from those in the United States.

Richard C. Williamson, in *Latin American Societies in Transition,* suggests that in broad ethnic terms the countries of Latin America could be classified into four major groups (although many countries have regional variations):

1. Countries in which a mestizo population dominates
2. Countries overwhelmingly European in character
3. Countries with conspicuous Indian groupings, generally inhabiting the highlands
4. Countries dominated by African admixtures[1]

The first group of countries includes the South American countries of Venezuela and Colombia, as well as Nicaragua, El Salvador, Honduras, and Panama in Central America, and Mexico. The predominantly European countries are Argentina, Chile, Uruguay, and Costa Rica, and the countries with large Indian groups are Guatemala, Ecuador, Peru, Bolivia, and Paraguay. Finally, the countries dominated by African admixtures are Brazil and the Caribbean countries of Cuba, the Dominican Republic, and Haiti.

The economies of the area are similarly diverse. A few countries (Argentina, Brazil, Uruguay, Venezuela) have vast, rich agricultural lands comparable to the US Midwest, while in most of the others subsistence agriculture has predominated. Because of climate, few countries, except those in southern South America, can grow the kind of grains raised in more temperate climates; hence sugar, coffee, cacao, and fruits have predominated. Mexico and the larger South American countries have considerable mineral wealth and some have oil, but others have few natural resources and are likely to remain poor, regardless of whether they call themselves capitalist or socialist. Based on their resources, some countries—generally the bigger ones with large internal markets (Argentina, Brazil, Chile, Colombia, Mexico, Panama, Uruguay)—are "making it" in the global economy and becoming competitive with the most efficient countries. Several Latin American countries are doing moderately well economically and improving their condition. A handful of countries, however (Bolivia, Paraguay, El Salvador, Guatemala, Haiti, Honduras, Nicaragua), are not doing well at all and are mired at the lower end of the rankings with the world's poorest nations.

The Latin American countries differ not only in people and economics but also in terms of geography. The continent contains the world's second-highest mountain range (with peaks over twenty thousand feet [six thousand meters]), the Andes, which runs like a spine up and down the Pacific Coast. Latin America also has some of the world's largest river systems (Amazon, Orinoco, Plate), but few of these connect major cities with agricultural areas or provide the internal transportation networks formed by the rivers and Great Lakes of North America. In many countries mountains come right down to the sea, leaving little coastal land for settlement and agricultural development. Much of the interior land is similarly unsuitable for cash crops, and although some countries have iron ore, few have coal, thereby making it difficult to produce steel, one of the keys to early industrial development. Hence, although nature has been kind to Latin America in some resources, it has been stingy in others, and even though a few countries are resource-rich, others are stunningly poor. The rise of commodity prices has helped benefit the resource-rich countries, but those prices could fall again—boom and bust.

One of the most startling features of South America is the vast Amazon basin, stretching nearly two thousand miles (thirty-two hundred kilometers) in all directions. Largely uninhabited until recently, the Amazon rain forest produces upward of 40 percent of the world's oxygen supply. Environmentalists seek to preserve this area, but Brazil and other countries on its perimeter see the Amazon's resources as the keys to their future development. Note from the map in Part II that most of South America's great cities are located on the ocean coast; only in recent decades have efforts been made to populate, develop, and exploit the vast interior.

Geographically, Latin America is a land of extremes: high mountains that are virtually impassable, lowlands that are densely tropical and also difficult to penetrate, and such extremes of heat, rainfall, and climate that living and working can be difficult. Latin America largely lacked the resources that the United States had during its great march to modernization in the nineteenth century, one of the key reasons it lagged behind. The mountainous, chopped-up terrain made internal communications and transportation difficult, dividing Latin America into small, isolated villages or regions, making national integration extremely difficult. Only now, with the advent of modern communications and transportation, have the Latin American countries begun to become better integrated and develop their vast potential.

THE ECONOMIES

The Latin American economies were founded on rapacity and exploitation. Under the prevailing economic theory of mercantilism, colonies such as those of Spain and Portugal existed solely for the benefit of the mother countries. The considerable gold, silver, and other resources of the colonies were drained away by the colonial powers. Latin America was cast in a position of dependency to the global powers. Ironically, Latin America's precious metals little benefited the mother countries but flowed through Spain and Portugal to England and Holland, where they helped launch the Industrial Revolution. As in the Americas, in Europe the north then forged ahead while the south fell further behind.

The most characteristic feature of colonial Latin America was the feudal or semi-feudal estate, patterned after the European model, with Spaniards and Portuguese as the overlords and Indians and blacks as peasants and slaves. Even after independence, Latin America remained mainly feudal; only slowly did capitalism and an entrepreneurial ethic develop. Under feudalism, the land, wealth, and people were all exploited; there was almost no effort to plow back the wealth of the land into development or to raise living standards. In accord with the feudal ethic and then-prevailing values, the total social product was fixed, and people had a duty to accept their station in life. Land, cattle, and peasants, then as now, were to the wealthy elites symbols of status and power and not necessarily to be used for productive purposes. The whole system was imperialistic and exploitive. However, the economic situation of the colonies varied considerably: the Caribbean islands and northeast Brazil were areas of large-scale sugar plantations, and Mexico, Central America,

Colombia, Peru, Bolivia, and other areas of Brazil were valued for their mineral wealth, while Argentina, Uruguay, and other farm areas were settled later because at the time there were better ways than agriculture to get rich quick.

Once the readily available precious metals were exhausted, the vast territory of Latin America was divided up among the Spanish and Portuguese conquerors, mostly into huge estates that were the size of US states or counties and resembled medieval fiefdoms. Along with the land came the right to exploit the Indian labor living on it. Each Spanish and Portuguese conquistador could live like a feudal noble: haughty, authoritarian, exploitative, and avoiding manual labor. These large estates were mainly self-sufficient, with their own priests, political authority (the landowners themselves), and social and economic life. Few areas in Latin America (Chile and Costa Rica come closest) were founded on the productive, family-farm basis that the New England colonies were.

It was only in the last half of the nineteenth century that these feudal estates began to be converted into more capitalistic enterprises producing more intensively for a world market as well as home consumption. Sugar and tobacco in the Caribbean, bananas and coffee in Central America and Colombia, rubber in Brazil, and beef, hides, and wool in Argentina and Uruguay were the new crops being produced for profit. The old feudal estates began to modernize and become export-oriented enterprises. Foreign investment further stimulated this conversion process. Latin America went through the first stages of economic development, but in the process many Indians and peasants were exploited even more than in the past or pushed off their communal lands onto the infertile hillsides. The result was class polarization and, in Mexico, a violent revolution in 1910.

Production for the export market resulted in an economic quickening throughout Latin America that led to further growth later on, but it also brought Latin America into the world economy for the first time, with both positive and negative consequences. Greater affluence led to greater political stability and new economic opportunities from roughly the 1890s to the 1930s, but it also made Latin America subject to global economic forces over which it had no control. Particularly in countries where 60 percent or more of export earnings depended on one crop, if that crop (for instance, sugar, coffee, or bananas) suffered a price decrease on world markets, the entire national economy could go into a tailspin. This is precisely what happened with virtually every price fluctuation in this period, especially during the 1929–1930 world market crash, when not only did the bottom drop out of all the Latin American economies but their political systems collapsed as well. Almost every country of the area had a military coup d'état associated with the Depression; Colombia and Mexico were exceptions.

Industrialization began in Latin America in the 1930s precisely because the countries had inefficient export earnings to purchase imported manufactured goods and therefore had to produce them on their own. Most of the heavy industry—steel, electricity, petroleum, and manufacturing—was established as state-owned, reflecting the weakness of entrepreneurialism and the history of mercantilism. This system was called state capitalism in order to distinguish it from the laissez-faire capitalism of the United States. It was the beginning of Latin America's large but often bloated, inefficient, and patronage-dominated state sector.

Table 1.1   Indices of Modernization in Latin America, 2008

Country	Population in millions	Population growth rate*	GNI per capita	GDP growth rate*	Inflation*	Life expectancy***	Infant mortality****
Argentina	39.88	1	7,200	7	20	75	16
Bolivia	9.68	2	1,460	6	10	66	57
Brazil	191.97	1	7,350	5	6	73**	22
Chile	16.76	1	9,400	3	0	78	9
Colombia	44.53	1	4,660	3	8	73	20
Costa Rica	4.53	1	6,060	3	12	79	11
Cuba	11.25	0	..	..	..	78	7
Dominican Republic	9.84	1	4,390	5	10	72	38
Ecuador	13.48	1	3,640	7	8	75	22
El Salvador	6.13	0	3,480	3	6	71**	24
Guatemala	13.68	2	2,680	4	9	70	39
Haiti	9.78	2	660	1	9	61	76
Honduras	7.24	2	1,800	4	10	70	24
Mexico	106.35	1	9,980	2	7	75	35
Nicaragua	5.68	1	1,080	4	17	73	35
Panama	3.39	2	6,180	9	9	76	23
Paraguay	6.23	2	2,180	6	7	72	29
Peru	28.84	1	3,990	10	1	73**	20
Uruguay	3.33	0	8,260	9	9	76	14
Venezuela	27.94	2	9,230	5	31	74	19
Latin America	**565.29**	**1**	**6,780**	**6**	**8**	**73**	**26**

Source: World Bank. World Development Indicators 2009. http://ddp-ext.worldbank
.org/ext/dd[re[prts/ViewSharedReport?REPORT ID=9147&REQUEST TYPE=VIEWAD
VANCED, December 15, 2009
    * Annual percentage.
   ** 2008 data.
  *** Life expectancy at birth in years (2007).
 **** Mortality rate, under five, per one thousand live births (2007).

During World War II and the postwar period Latin America developed rapidly
on the basis of this model of import substitution industrialization (ISI). However,
growing demand for new social programs outstripped countries' ability to pay for
them, and then came the massive oil price increases of the 1970s and the debt crisis
of the 1980s. Latin America was unable to pay its obligations, and many countries
slipped into near bankruptcy. Economic downturn again helped produce political
instability in the 1960s and 1970s, as it had in the 1930s.

In the 1990s and continuing into the new millennium, the Latin American economies began to recover, but in many countries growth was anemic and debt continued to be a burden. Nevertheless, there was recovery throughout the region and

many countries began to reform their economies. In an effort to become competitive in the global economy many countries sold off inefficient public enterprises, opened previously protected economic sectors to competition, emphasized exports, and sought to reduce or streamline inefficient bureaucratic regulation. They also tried to diversify their economies internally and sought a wider range of trading partners. However, their reform efforts often produced mixed results, because although it was economically rational to reduce the size of the state, such reductions conflicted with social justice requirements and the political patronage demands of rewarding friends and supporters with cushy state jobs.

Chile, Brazil, and Mexico were the chief leaders and beneficiaries of the new free market economic policies. Several countries did moderately well as middle-income countries, but others remained poor and backward, as shown in Table 1.1. Then the global economic crisis of 2009 brought renewed pressures for state-led growth.

CLASSES AND SOCIAL FORCES

During the colonial period Latin America was structured on a fundamentally two-class basis. There was a small white Hispanic or Portuguese elite at the top and a huge mass of Indians, black slaves, and peasants at the bottom, with almost no one in between. The two-class system was a reflection of feudal Spain, with its medieval Christian conception of each person being fixed in his or her station in life, and of slavery. This strict social hierarchy was assumed to be immutable and in accord with God's ordering of the universe; in Latin America the rigid class structure was further reinforced by racial criteria. Over time, as miscegenation progressed, a considerable mixed-race population emerged, with these mulattos and mestizos often forming a small middle class.

The onset of economic growth in the late nineteenth century and industrialization in the twentieth century eventually gave rise to new social forces, although for a long time it did not change the basic two-class structure of society. In the early stages of modernization in the nineteenth century a new business-commercial class began to emerge alongside the traditional landed elite, but this new class thought like the old elite, intermarried with it, and adopted the same aristocratic, haughty ethos. Similarly, as a large middle class of shopkeepers, small-business owners, government workers, and professionals began to emerge in the 1930s and thereafter, it too acquired conservative attitudes, disdained manual labor, and often allied with a repressive military to prevent left-wing and lower-class movements from acquiring power. Emerging new social movements were co-opted by the elites and the two-class society was generally preserved.

During the 1930s, as industrialization began, a working class also developed in Latin America; by the 1950s and 1960s peasant groups were being mobilized, and in the 1970s and thereafter women, indigenous elements, community and neighborhood groups, and other social movements and civil society also organized. At first the elite groups (oligarchy, church, army) that had long dominated Latin America tried either to co-opt these groups as they had others in the past or to send the army out to repress, kill, and intimidate them. The carrot-and-stick strategies of co-optation and repression worked when these new groups were small, heading off revolution or even democracy and enabling the old power structure to survive. However, as the labor movement, peasant elements, and other civil society groups grew in power, the old techniques of co-optation and repression proved less successful. These processes then produced a variety of outcomes in Latin America: dictatorships in some countries, democracy in others, revolution in still others, and in most either alternation between rival alternatives or simply a period of muddling along.

Latin America today is much more pluralistic and democratic than before. There is still an old, landed, oligarchic class in most countries, but it has been largely supplanted by business, banking, industrial (including agro-industrial), and commercial groups. There is now a larger middle class that, depending on the country, may comprise 20 to 50 percent of the population. In many countries the business and middle classes, rather than the old oligarchies, dominate. These groups tend to favor a stable democracy both because it serves their interests and because the global international community now demands it.

Since 2003 there has been rapid economic growth in most Latin American countries. Higher overall income plus some redistribution of it have led to higher percentages in the middle-income sector of most countries. A recent analysis by World Bank economists concludes that from 2003 to 2012, the percentage of people in extreme poverty (earning US$4–10 per day) shrank to 38 percent. If one assumes that about 2 percent of the Latin American population is "rich," meaning earning more than US$50 a day, that means the middle-income sector is the remaining 30 percent. Another 30 percent are poor but not in extreme poverty.

The important conclusion from this analysis is that the extremely poor are no longer the majority; rather, it is the group "sandwiched between the poor and the middle class . . . who appear to make ends meet well enough so as not to be counted among the poor but who do not enjoy the economic security that would be required for membership in the middle class," a group that might be best called "the vulnerable."[2] Important questions, considered in Chapter 3, include whether this middle sector has become a "middle class" (stable, prosperous, peaceful, democratic) in any sense and how this still vulnerable sector might have changed its politics.

At lower class levels important changes are occurring as well. Labor is organizing, peasants are mobilizing and sometimes marching on private lands, and new neighborhood and community groups are forming. Protestantism is growing, especially evangelical groups; women's organizations, racial and ethnic groups, and many nongovernmental organizations (NGOs) are becoming more active. At the grassroots many of these civil society groups have organized to get things done, often bypassing the traditional political parties, bureaucratic agencies, and patronage systems. In many countries, however, there are rivalries between these newer, more pluralistic civil society groups and the traditional, patronage-dominated ones. We must also remember that Latin America's pluralism is still more limited than the chaotic hurly-burly of US interest group pluralism, still more state-controlled, and therefore less participatory and democratic. The number of plural groups is small, the elites and/or the state still try to co-opt and control them, and interest group lobbying, as seen in the US system, is often absent. Nevertheless, Latin America is sufficiently pluralistic that it is harder now to govern dictatorially, and that means a stronger base for democracy's survival.

CHANGING POLITICAL CULTURE

Political culture—the basic values and ideas that dominate in a society—varies from country to country and from region to region. Political culture provides a composite view of a society's beliefs as represented by its religious orientation, historical experience, and standard operating procedures. Political culture can be determined and analyzed using literature, music, other elements that shape the general culture, and, most important, public opinion surveys. In speaking of political culture we want to avoid stereotyping; at the same time, when carefully used, the concept can be an important explanatory tool. Remember also that political culture may change (usually slowly) over time, there may be two or more political cultures within a given society (elite versus mass, left versus right), and the diverse views and orientations that compose political culture may be in conflict.

Whereas the political culture of the United States is mainly democratic, liberal (believing in the classic freedoms of the Bill of Rights), and committed to representative government, that of Latin America has historically been more elitist, authoritarian, hierarchical, corporatist, and patrimonial. Latin American elitism stems from the Iberian tradition of nobility, the feudal landholding system, and a powerful tradition in Spanish-Portuguese political theory that holds that society should be governed by its "natural" elites. Authoritarianism in Latin America derived from the prevailing elitist power structure, biblical precepts and medieval Christianity's emphasis on top-down rule, and the chaotic and often anarchic conditions in Latin America that seemed to demand strong government.

The notion of a hierarchy among people thus derived from early Christian political ideas as well as the social and power structure of medieval Spain and Portugal, which was carried over to Latin America. God was at the top of this hierarchy, followed by archangels, angels, and so on down, until one reached humankind. Rulers received their mandate from God; land, cattle, military prowess, and high social and political status were similarly believed to derive from the "Great Chain of Being," God's unchanging design for the universe. Proceeding down through society, one eventually reached workers and peasants, who had some, though limited, rights. In the New World, Indians and Africans were thought to be barely human. After a long debate, the Roman Catholic Church decided that Indians also had souls; as a result, they were given to Spanish conquerors in *encomiendas,* through which they would work for the Spanish, who had the duty of "civilizing" and "Christianizing" the less-fortunate Indians. The church fathers initially decided, on the other hand, that Africans did not have souls and could therefore be enslaved, having no rights at all. It is obvious that this hierarchical conception is profoundly inegalitarian and undemocratic.

Another feature of Latin American political culture and institutions is corporatism, or the organization of the nation's interest groups under state regulation and control rather than on the basis of freedom of association. The main corporate groups in Latin America have been the church, the armed forces, the landed and business elites, and more recently the trade union movement, peasants, women, and indigenous elements. Corporatism, which is largely unknown in US politics, is a way of both organizing and controlling interest group activity. Corporatism is thus often associated with authoritarianism and an illiberal society, and it reinforces the other undemocratic traits previously mentioned.

One other feature of traditional Latin American society and politics that has continued into the present is patronage. Historically in Latin America this has been based on a system of mutual obligation: a favor for a favor. This is also a quasi-feudal concept with its roots in Greek and Christian philosophy: if I give you a gift, then you owe me a gift in return. Patronage manifests itself in various ways, including votes in return for gifts or money, votes in return for a government job, friends or relatives rewarded with government contracts, special access to those with good connections, and sometimes whole programs or government offices doled out in return for critical political support. At high levels patronage verges on or is corruption; at low levels it constitutes the "grease" that keeps the machinery of government working. Patronage is inherently uneven and undemocratic: some are patrons or godfathers, others are humble petitioners.

These features of historical Latin American political culture—elitism, authoritarianism, hierarchy, corporatism, and patrimonialism—remained largely intact over three centuries of colonial rule and became deeply embedded in the region's customs and political processes. However, when Latin America became independent in the nineteenth century, a new political culture based on representative institutions emerged, even while the old political culture remained strong. The result was two political cultures, one authoritarian, the other nascently liberal, existing side by side and vying for dominance throughout the nineteenth century and into much of the twentieth. The two political cultures also had different social bases: the more traditional one was centered in the church, the landed elite, the military, and the conservative peasantry, with the newer, liberal one concentrated in urban areas among intellectuals, students, the emerging middle class, and some business elements. With no single political culture dominant (unlike the situation in the United States after the Civil War, when the liberal-democratic ethos definitively triumphed), Latin American politics was often unstable and torn by frequent civil war between the two ways of life.

A third tradition—socialist, Marxist, social-democratic—emerged in the 1930s, particularly among students, trade unionists, and intellectuals. Some of these groups favored a full-scale Marxist-Leninist regime, others wanted a socialist redistribution of wealth, and still others advocated only greater social welfare. The common themes of these groups included a strong role for the state in directing change, a leftist ideology, and anti-US nationalism. Fidel Castro, the Nicaraguan Sandinista revolution, and Hugo Chávez galvanized these leftist groups, which in the past often looked to the Soviet Union and/or China for support. However, the collapse of the Soviet Union and of Marxist-Leninist movements and regimes worldwide led to a severe drop in support for Marxist solutions, although in an updated social-democratic or populist form it may be possible for the left to come back to power.

Meanwhile, the historical political culture, or at least some of its aspects, is fading. No one believes anymore that one must stay poor and one's children must have bloated bellies because God or St. Thomas has willed it that way and one must accept one's station in life. The older notions of authority, hierarchy, and elitism, although still often present, are no longer the dominant political culture. At the same time, the groups that were the strongest proponents of the traditional political culture (the church, the landed oligarchy, the army, the conservative peasantry) either are chang-ing internally or are losing influence. However, patronage and patrimonialism seem as strong as ever.

Latin America has modernized, democratized, and become part of the global economy. It is no longer the same Latin America portrayed in earlier editions of this book. Rising literacy, urbanization, social change, immigration, globalization, and democratization are all changing the appearance and culture of Latin America. Polls tell us that 60, 70, or even 80 percent of the public in most countries support democratic rule, and none of the other alternatives (authoritarianism or Marxism-Leninism) has much support. It may be that the historical conflict over political culture in Latin America is finally ending and that the democratic option with a modern and social-democratic mixed economy has finally emerged as triumphant.

Yet these same polls show that Latin Americans want an effective government, one that delivers real social and economic reform. Democracy and economic liberal-ism (or neoliberalism) are still weak and unconsolidated in Latin America, and they could still be upset in some of the weaker and poorly institutionalized countries. Moreover—and this is what makes Latin America so interesting—the form that democracy takes there is often quite different from democracy in the United States. It is more organic and centralized, with still-powerful features of patronage and corporatism. Latin America now has formal, electoral democracy; whether it has genuinely liberal democracy may be quite another thing. Although the changes have been vast, the continuities from Latin America's past remain strong.

AN ASSESSMENT

Latin America's geography, economic underdevelopment, dependency conditions, socioracial conditions, and traditions of political culture have historically retarded national unity, democracy, and development. However, the great forces of twentieth- and twenty-first-century change—urbanization, industrialization, modernization, democratization, and now globalization—are breaking down historical barriers and altering the foundations of traditional Latin American society. Latin America is ex-periencing many of the same revolutionary transformations that the United States, Western Europe, and Japan went through in earlier times. Latin America has com-menced the process, but here the period is much more telescoped and the outcome is still likely to be a great variety of political systems rather than some pale imitation of the United States. To us that is healthy, invigorating, challenging, and interesting.

Although the changes have been immense and often inspiring, many problems still remain. Poverty, malnutrition, and malnutrition-related disease are still en-demic in many areas; too many people are ill-housed, ill-fed, ill-educated, and just plain ill. Wages are too low, economies and democracies are often fragile, and the gap between rich and poor is greater than in any other area of the world. Political systems can be corrupt and ineffective, the standards of living of the rural and urban poor are woefully inadequate, and crime, violence, drug activity, and general per-sonal insecurity are increasing. Frequently social and economic change occurs faster than political systems can handle it; fragmentation, ungovernability, and collapse are still lurking.

Three recent changes also command special attention. The first is the dramatic shift to democracy in all but one country (Cuba). The second is the new movement in economic policy toward a modern economy, reform of the state, export-led growth, and integration. Some of these economic reforms are still weak and limited, and in some countries where democracy is fragile and has not been consolidated, these changes still could be reversed. Nevertheless, the degree of progress over the previous two decades is often breathtaking.

The third profound change is the impact of globalization on Latin America in all its dimensions (cultural, political, technological, economic), which has broken down the region's traditional isolation and forced all countries to become integrated into the modern world, mostly for good but damaging to marginal groups such as small farmers.

There is, overall, strong economic, social, and political reform, a growing realization that Latin America must take charge of its own future, and a great eagerness to enter the modern global community of developed nations. Later chapters detail which countries have made this great leap forward, examine how they have done so, and consider the successes, failures, and future prospects of all the Latin American nations.

2

THE PATTERN OF
HISTORICAL DEVELOPMENT

Whereas the United States was founded during the seventeenth and eighteenth centuries, when modernization was beginning (capitalism, liberalism, pluralism, the Enlightenment, the Industrial Revolution), Latin America was founded in an earlier time, when feudal and medieval practices and institutions still held sway. If the United States was "born free," Latin America was "born feudal," and these differences still account for many of the contrasts between the two areas. To a degree unknown in the United States, Latin America has long been dominated by a political, social, and economic structure that had its roots not in modernity but in medievalism. Much of Latin America's recent history involves the efforts to overcome or ameliorate that feudal past. Because this feudal legacy remains so strong, because the heavy hand of ancient history hangs so oppressively over the area, we must come to grips with Latin America's past to understand its present and future.

Latin America is not just a product of its own history, however. It was also exploited and pillaged by the colonial powers. Spain, Portugal, England, France, Holland, and most recently the United States all exploited and took advantage of Latin America. Colonialism and imperialism devastated the area. At many levels and throughout history Latin America was brutalized, exploited, and robbed of its resources. It was an isolated dependency of the great powers, an exploited periphery kept apart from global modernizing movements, a region with a history of suffering.

THE CONQUEST

The conquest of the Americas by Spain and Portugal was the extension of a reconquest of the Iberian Peninsula that had been occurring in the mother countries for the preceding seven centuries. In the eighth century AD the armies of a dynamic, expansionist Islam had crossed the Strait of Gibraltar from North Africa and conquered most of present-day Spain and Portugal. In the following centuries the Christian forces of Spain and Portugal had gradually retaken these conquered lands, until the last of the Islamic Moors were driven out in 1492, the same year that Columbus arrived in America. Because of the long military campaign against the Moors, which was also a religious crusade to drive out the Islamic "infidels," Spanish and Portuguese institutions tended to be authoritarian, intolerant, militaristic, and undemocratic. These same practices and institutions were carried over to Latin America.

The conquest of the Americas was one of the great epic adventures of all time; its impact was worldwide. The encounter with the New World vastly expanded humankind's knowledge, exploration, and frontiers, led to a period of prolonged European world dominance, and helped stimulate the Industrial Revolution. It also led to the brutalization, death, and isolation of much of the indigenous population.

At the time of Columbus's landing in America there were only three million indigenous people in all of North America but some thirty million in Latin America. The Indians in Latin America were often organized into large civilizations—Aztec, Maya, Inca—of five to seven million people each, as compared with the generally small tribal, nomadic basis of most North American Indians. Whereas in North America the Indians were often eliminated, pushed farther west, or confined to reservations, in Latin America the large numbers and organization of indigenous groups called for a different strategy. The Spanish tactic was usually to capture or kill the Indian chiefs, replace them with Spanish overlords, and rule (and enslave) the Indian populations by dominating their own power structure, meanwhile seeking to Christianize, Hispanicize, and assimilate them into European ways. That has been the strategy for over five hundred years, but recently Indian groups in such countries as Mexico, Guatemala, Colombia, Ecuador, and Bolivia have been raising the issue of indigenous rights and seeking new degrees of autonomy from the nation-states that Spain and Portugal left in their wake.

The degree of colonial influence varied from place to place. The first area to receive the impact of Spanish colonial rule was Hispaniola, an island in the Caribbean that later was divided between the two independent countries of Haiti and the Dominican Republic. Here Spain carried out its first experiments in colonial rule: a slave plantation economy, a two-class and caste society, an authoritarian political structure, and a church that served as an arm of the conquest. But Hispaniola had little gold and silver, and as the Indian population was decimated, largely by disease, Spain moved on to more valuable conquests.

Next came Cuba and Puerto Rico, but when the scarce precious metals and Indian labor supply were exhausted there also, Spain moved on to conquer Mexico and explored Florida and the North American Southeast. The conquest of Mexico by Cortés was fundamentally different from the earlier island conquests. First, Spain found a huge Indian civilization, the Aztecs, with immense quantities of gold and silver and a virtually unlimited labor supply, and second, Mexico's huge mainland territory finally convinced the Spaniards that they had found a new continent and not just scattered islands on the outskirts of Asia. Mexico therefore became a serious and valuable colony to be settled and colonized by Spain, not just a way station en route to somewhere else.

From Mexico Cortés's lieutenants fanned out to conquer Central America and the North American Southwest. In the meantime, Balboa had crossed the Isthmus of Panama to gaze out upon the Pacific, and other Spanish conquistadores had explored both the east and west coasts of South America. From Panama in the 1530s the Pizarro brothers, using the same methods Cortés had used in Mexico, moved south to conquer the vast Inca Empire, which stretched from southern Colombia in the north through Ecuador and Peru to Chile in the south. Meanwhile, Portugal had gained a foothold on the part of Brazil's coast that sticks out toward Africa. Other Spanish explorers spilled over the Andes from Peru to discover and subdue Bolivia and Paraguay and sailed all the way downriver to present-day Buenos Aires, which had been explored in the 1530s but was not settled until the 1580s. Meanwhile, Chile, where the Indian resistance was especially strong, was conquered in the 1570s, and other previously unconquered territories were then explored and subdued.

In less than a hundred years from the initial discovery, Mexico, the Caribbean, Central America, and all of South America, east to west and north to south, had been conquered. Spain had most of the territory; Portugal had Brazil. It was a remarkable feat in a short period of time, especially when one considers that it took North American settlers almost three hundred years to cross the continent from the Atlantic to the Pacific.

COLONIAL SOCIETY: PRINCIPLES AND INSTITUTIONS

The institutions that Spain and, less aggressively, Portugal brought to the New World reflected the institutions that had developed in the mother countries during their centuries-long struggles against the Moors and their efforts to form unified nation-states out of disparate social and regional forces. These institutions included a rigid, authoritarian political system, a similarly rigid hierarchical class structure, a statist and mercantilist economy, an absolutist church, and a similarly closed and absolutist educational system.

In the New World the Spanish and Portuguese conquerors found abundant territory that they could claim as feudal estates, enormous wealth that enabled them to live like grandees, and a ready-made "peasantry" to exploit, in the form of the indigenous Indian population or imported African slaves. The men who accompanied Columbus and other explorers to the New World were often the second or third sons of the Spanish and Portuguese aristocracy, and under Spanish law they were prohibited from inheriting their fathers' lands, which went to the first sons. But in the New World they could acquire vast territories and servants and live like feudal overlords. The oligarchies of Latin America, then as now, were haughty, aloof, authoritarian, and disdainful of manual labor and those forced to work with their hands. The aristocratic ethos and power structure has been a very powerful force in Latin America even to this day.

The institutions established by Spain and Portugal in Latin America reflected and reinforced the medieval system of the mother countries. At the top was the king, who claimed absolute power; his authority came from God (divine-right monarchy) and was therefore unquestionable. Below the king was the viceroy (literally "vice king"), similarly with absolute power and serving as the king's agent in the colonies. Below the viceroy was the captain-general, also absolute within his sphere of influence; next came the landowner or *hacendado*, who enjoyed absolute power within his own estate.

The economy was feudal and exploitative; the wealth of the colonies, in accord with the prevailing mercantilism, was drained off to benefit the mother countries and not used for the betterment of the colonies themselves. Similarly, the social structure was basically feudal and two-class, with a small group of Spaniards and Portuguese at the top, a large mass of Indians and Africans at the bottom, and almost no one in between. Democracy cannot be based on such a strict two-class structure, which was not only social and economic but also racist.

The Roman Catholic Church reinforced royal authority and policy in the colonies and was similarly absolutist and authoritarian. Its role was to Christianize and pacify the indigenous population and thus serve the crown's assimilationist polices. Some individual clergy sought to defend the Indians against enslavement and maltreatment, but the church was primarily an arm of the state. Intellectual life and learning, monopolized by the church, was scholastic, based on rote memorization, deductive reasoning, and unquestioned orthodoxy.

It is not surprising that Latin America was founded on this feudal-absolutist basis in the early sixteenth century; that was before the onset of modernization, and most countries were still organized on that basis. What is surprising is that this system lasted so long: through three centuries of colonial rule, only slightly modified by the Latin American independence movements, and on into the twentieth century. Most Latin American countries are still struggling to overcome this feudal past.

In contrast, by the time the North American colonies were established, the back of feudalism had been broken in England and Holland, and hence the thirteen colonies that would later form the United States were organized on a more modern basis. By that time the idea of limited government rather than absolutism had emerged, the Protestant Reformation had destroyed the older religious orthodoxy and given rise to religious and political pluralism, the Industrial Revolution was occurring, mercantilism was giving way to commerce and entrepreneurship, the scientific revolution was breaking the hold of the old scholasticism, and a new multiclass society was beginning to emerge. Founded on these principles and changes, North American society was modern from the start, whereas Latin America continued to be plagued by feudalism. These differences also explained why from the beginning the United States was destined to forge ahead while Latin America lagged behind. Table 2.1 summarizes these contrasting foundations of US and Latin American society.

Spanish and Portuguese colonial rule lasted for over three centuries, from the late fifteenth through the early nineteenth century. It was a remarkably stable period, with few revolts against the colonial system, a testimony to its efficiency even if it was unjust. However, in the late eighteenth century the first serious cracks began to appear in this monolithic colonial structure. Under the impact of the eighteenth-century Enlightenment, ideas of liberty, freedom, and nationalism began to creep in; the examples of revolutions in the United States (1776) and France (1789) also caused tremors in Latin America. In addition, the rising Latin American commercial class sought to break the monopolistic barriers of Spanish mercantilism so as to trade freely with other countries. One of the main sources of independence sentiment was the growing rivalry between creoles (people of Spanish background born in the colonies) and peninsulars (officials sent out by the Spanish crown to govern the colonies). The creoles had growing economic and social influence, but the

Table 2.1   Contrasting Foundations of Latin and North American Society

Institutions	Latin America, 1492–1570	North America, Seventeenth Century
Political	Authoritarian, absolutist, centralized, corporatist	More liberal, early steps toward representative and democratic rule
Religious	Catholic orthodoxy and absolutism	Protestantism and religious pluralism
Economic	Feudal, mercantilist, patrimonialist	Emerging capitalist, entrepreneurial
Social	Hierarchical, two-class, rigid	More mobile, multiclass
Educational and intellectual	Scholastic and deductive	Empirical

peninsulars monopolized all administrative positions. Denied the political power to go along with their rising prominence, many creoles began to think of doing away with the inconvenience of Spanish colonialism and moving toward independence.

The immediate causes of Latin American independence were precipitated by events in Europe. In 1807–1808 the forces of Napoleon Bonaparte invaded the Iberian Peninsula, occupied both Spain and Portugal, ousted the reigning monarchs, and placed Napoleon's brother Joseph on the Spanish throne. The Latin American creoles opposed this usurpation of royal authority by Napoleon's army and, operating under longtime medieval doctrine, moved to hold power until the legitimate king could be restored. This was, in effect, an early declaration of independence. A few years later Napoleon's forces were driven from the peninsula and the Spanish and Portuguese monarchies restored. However, when the Spanish king accepted the principle of limited monarchy and a liberal constitution, the conservative creoles in Latin America moved for independence.

The independence struggles in Latin America waxed and waned for nearly two decades before succeeding in the 1820s. The first revolt in Argentina in 1807 was quashed by Spanish authorities, but independence fervor was also growing in Colombia, Mexico, Venezuela, and other countries. Independence sentiment waned for a time after 1814, when the Spanish monarchy was restored, but resumed again in 1820 as a result of the king's shortsighted policies.

Simón Bolívar, the "George Washington of Latin America," led the struggle against Spanish forces in Venezuela, Colombia, and Ecuador. José San Martín liberated Argentina, then crossed the Andes to drive the Spanish forces from Chile. The key to the independence of the rest of South America was Lima, Peru, one of the most important Spanish viceroyalties and home of a sizable Spanish garrison. Bolívar came south overland and San Martín north by ship, and in the key battle of Ayacucho they defeated the royalist forces, ending Spanish authority in South America. The other main viceroyalty was Mexico City, but by 1821 independence forces were in control there also. Once Mexico was freed, Central America, as part of the same viceroyal administration, was liberated without much actual fighting. By 1824 all Spanish forces and authority had been removed from mainland Latin America. The two exceptions were Cuba and Puerto Rico, which remained Spanish colonies until 1898; for all of the nineteenth century their nationalism was frustrated by the lack of independence, which would also shape twentieth-century politics on the two islands.

Haiti and Brazil were special cases as well. In Haiti a successful slave revolt in 1795 drove out the French colonial ruling class, destroyed the plantations, and established Haiti as the world's first black republic, unloved and unwelcomed by the rest of the world (including the United States), which still practiced slavery. Haiti's economy went into decline, and its political system since then has alternated between repressive dictatorships and chaotic upheaval.

Brazil was a different story. When Napoleon's troops occupied Portugal, the royal family fled to Rio de Janeiro, making them the first reigning monarchs to set foot in Latin America. In 1821 the king, Dom João, was called back to Lisbon, but he left his son Pedro in charge of the kingdom of Brazil. The following year Pedro too was called back to Portugal, but he refused to go and declared Brazil an independent monarchy. Thus Brazil gained independence without the upheaval and destruction of the other countries and was a monarchy for the first seventy years of its existence. Brazil escaped the tumult that soon enveloped its Spanish-speaking neighbors.

The independence movements in Latin America had almost all been conservative movements of separation from the mother countries rather than full-scale social or political revolutions. Led and directed by the white, aristocratic, creole elite, they were aimed at holding power for the deposed monarch and defending the old social hierarchy. After they later became movements for independence, they retained their elitist, conservative orientation. When social revolution raised its head, it was either isolated and despised, as in Haiti, or brutally repressed, as in Mexico, where large-scale Indian protest had been part of the independence struggle.

The same conservative orientation was present in the laws, constitutions, and institutions established in the new republics. The franchise was extremely limited: only literates and property owners (less than 1 percent of the population) could vote, if and when there were elections. Thus the feudal landholding and class system was kept intact, before and after independence. The church was given a privileged position, and in most countries Catholicism remained the official religion. However, a new, similarly conservative power force was added: the army, which replaced the crown as the ultimate authority and became almost a fourth branch of government. Although Latin America adopted constitutions modeled after that of the United States, checks and balances, human rights, and separation of powers existed mostly in theory. The laws and constitutions of the new Latin American states enshrined the existing power structure and perpetuated paternalistic, top-down, elite rule.

During the more than three hundred years of colonial rule, Latin America had no experience with self-government, lacked infrastructure, and had none of the civil society or "web of sociability" (neighborhood, community, religious, civic, and social groups) that nineteenth-century theorist Alexis de Tocqueville identified with US democracy. With independence the Latin American economies also went into decline, and the social structure was severely disrupted. It should not be surprising, therefore, that after independence Latin America fell into chaos and that the disintegrative forces set loose by independence continued. The former viceroyalty of New Granada split up into the separate nations of Colombia, Ecuador, and Venezuela; the viceroyalty of Rio de la Plata divided into the separate countries of Argentina, Paraguay, and Uruguay; and the Central American Confederation disintegrated into the small "city-states" (too small to be economically viable) of Guatemala, El Salvador, Honduras, Nicaragua, and Costa Rica. Within the new nations further fragmentation and confusion occurred. Only Brazil under its monarchy and Chile under a stable oligarchy escaped these divisive, disruptive, and disintegrative early postindependence forces.

Deprived of their Spanish markets but still lacking new ones, many of the countries slipped back to a more primitive barter economy, and living standards plummeted. Similarly, the old Spanish/Portuguese social and racial categories were formally abolished in most countries but were resurrected informally; at the same time, the levels of education, literacy, integration, and assimilation were so low (in many countries the majority of the population did not speak the national language, participate in the national economy, or even know that they were part of a nation-state) that pluralist and participatory democracy seemed only a distant dream. In the absence of political parties, organized interest groups, civil society organizations, or well-established institutions of any kind, the Latin American countries sank into dictatorship or anarchy, usually alternating between the two. Internationally Latin America was isolated and cut off from the modern Western world. Hence the immediate postindependence period, from the mid-1820s until the mid-1850s, was in most countries a time of turbulence and decline.

EARLY STIRRINGS OF MODERNIZATION

By the 1850s a degree of stability had begun to emerge in many Latin American countries. Some of the more vexing questions of early independence—sovereignty and borders, federalism versus unitarism, church-state relations—had been resolved. By this time also, the first generation of postindependence dictators (Juan Manuel de Rosas in Argentina, Antonio López de Santa Anna in Mexico) had passed from the scene. Agriculture began to recover; a degree of order returned.

With increased stability at midcentury came foreign investment and greater productivity. The first banks in the region were chartered. British capital invested in the area provided a major stimulus for growth. New lands were opened to cultivation, and new exports (sugar, coffee, tobacco, beef, and wool) began to restore national coffers. The first highways, railways, and port facilities were built to transport exports to foreign markets. The telephone and telegraph were introduced. The opportunities available in Latin America began to attract immigrants from Europe, who often brought knowledge and entrepreneurial skills with them. They opened small shops and started farms, and they prospered; often this new wealth intermixed with older landed wealth.

As Latin America's prospects began to improve, the area attracted other investors: France, Germany, Italy, and, most important, the United States, which began to replace England as the largest investor in the area. These changes, beginning at midcentury but accelerating in the 1870s and 1880s, represented the first stirrings of modernization in Latin America after nearly four centuries of stagnation. They brought prosperity for the landed and business elites and stimulated the growth of a middle class, but often peasant and Indian elements were left behind or had their lands taken from them for the sake of greater production for global markets.

Economic growth also increased political stability, although not in all countries. Three patterns may be observed. The first, in Argentina, Brazil, Chile, Peru, and other countries, involved the consolidation of power by an export-oriented landed oligarchy whose leaders rotated through the presidential palace over a thirty- to forty-year period. The second, in Mexico, Venezuela, and the Dominican Republic, involved the seizure of power by strong authoritarian dictators, no longer the simple caudillos of the past but leaders who provided both long-term stability and development. A third pattern emerged slightly later, in the first decades of the twentieth century, in the smaller, weaker, resource-poor countries of Central America and the Caribbean. It involved US military intervention and occupation and the carrying out by the Marines of many of the same policies as the order-and-progress oligarchs and dictators: pacification, infrastructure development (roads, communication, port facilities), and overall nation building.

Two subperiods are discernible here. The first, 1850 to 1890, established the pre-conditions for Latin America's takeoff: greater stability, banks, investment, population increase, and infrastructure development. The second, 1890 to 1930, was the economic takeoff itself, the most stable and prosperous period in Latin American history. Under more stable regimes and exporting for the first time for a world market, Latin America began its development process, not at the rapid rate of the United States and Europe during the same period, but slowly and steadily.

Although Latin America's development was often impressive, it came under non-democratic leadership: oligarchs, order-and-progress dictators, and US military occupations. Hence the potential for future problems was present amid the growing prosperity. Three applecarts were upset even before the 1930s market crash caused the entire edifice to come crumbling down. In 1910 the order-and-progress dictator Porfirio Díaz was overthrown in Mexico, precipitating a bloody ten-year social revolution out of which Mexico's present political system emerged. In 1912 in Argentina and in the early 1920s in Chile a rising middle class challenged and eventually wrested political power from the old oligarchs. These changes in some of the more advanced countries of Latin America provided a foretaste of what would occur in the other countries in later decades.

UPHEAVAL AND RESTRUCTURING

When the stock market crashed in the United States in 1929 and in Europe the following year, the effects were global. The bottom dropped out of the market for Latin America's exports, sending the economies of the area into a tailspin and crashing their political systems as well. Between 1930 and 1935 there were governmental overthrows in fourteen of the twenty Latin American countries, not just the usual substitution of one colonel for another but real transforming revolutions. The immediate causes of this collapse were economic, but deep-rooted social and political issues were also involved. By this time Latin America had a business class, a middle class, and a restless trade union movement, but power was still monopolized by the old landowning oligarchs, and something had to give. The chasm between traditional holders of power and the new social and political forces clamoring for change had grown wider; the new forces were demanding change and democratization, while the older elites clung to their privileges at all costs. The 1930s Depression was the catalyst that collapsed the prevailing political as well as economic structure.

Once Humpty Dumpty (the Latin American political systems) had fallen off the wall, the question was how to put him back together again, and a variety of solutions were tried. This is an important turning point to remember because this is the time when most of our country-by-country analyses begin. Some countries, after a brief interruption in the early 1930s, reverted to restoring oligarchic rule. In others new, tough dictatorships (Fulgencio Batista in Cuba, Anastasio Somoza in Nicaragua, Rafael Trujillo in the Dominican Republic, Jorge Ubico in Guatemala) brought the new business and middle classes into power and stimulated development, but under authoritarian auspices. (It is getting ahead of the story only a little bit to note that all these countries with brutal right-wing dictatorships produced left-wing revolutions later on.) Mexico replaced the old regime with a one-party authoritarian-corporatist regime that monopolized power for the next seventy years.

In Argentina and Brazil the regimes of Juan Perón and Getúlio Vargas, respectively, borrowed some semifascist features from Mussolini's Italy in an effort to bring labor unions into the system even while imposing strict controls over them. Other countries borrowed selectively from European corporatism and fascism while maintaining a democratic facade. Populism was still another option, whereas other countries—Chile and Uruguay followed by Costa Rica, Colombia, and Venezuela—moved toward democracy. The revolutionary alternative (as in Cuba) came later.

The 1930s were thus, in the words of David Collier and Ruth Berins Collier, a "critical juncture" in Latin American history, a period in which various alternative developmental models —authoritarian, quasi-fascist, populist, single-party, democratic—were tried out and came to power in various Latin American countries.[1]

Some countries rotated among several of these options or tried to combine them. Many countries are still strongly shaped by the choices made and the directions taken during this period. The Depression years of the 1930s and the war and postwar years of the 1940s were thus a time of both uncertainty and upheaval; although the old, stable, oligarchic order had come crashing down, what would replace it was not altogether clear, and eighty years later it is still not clear in quite a number of countries.

As the demand for their products rose again during World War II, the Latin American economies began to recover from the devastation of the Depression; they were also stimulated by industrialization. The postwar period continued this economic growth, enabling some countries to move toward greater prosperity and democracy while others continued under dictatorship. Although gradual economic growth was occurring throughout the region in the 1940s and 1950s and stimulating further social change, the political systems of Latin America remained divided, full of conflict, and often unstable.

A key turning point in the region and in US–Latin American relations was the Cuban revolution of 1959. Cuba became the first openly socialist country in Latin America, the first to ally itself with the Soviet Union, and the first to openly turn its back on the United States. The revolution initiated improvements in health care, education, and other social programs, although over time its economic policies proved a failure and its political system was hardly democratic (see Chapter 17 for details), but here we are concerned with Cuba's broader, regionwide impact.

First, Cuba added a new model to the Latin American landscape, one that stood for armed revolution and a Marxist-Leninist political structure. Second, the Cuban revolution divided and thus hurt the prospects for democratic development and social reform in Latin America by splitting the reform groups into pro- and anti-Castro factions. Third, although the Cuban revolution forced the United States to pay closer attention to Latin America (through such schemes as the Peace Corps and the Alliance for Progress), it skewed US policy by making the prevention of "another Cuba" (a Marxist-Leninist state allied with the Soviet Union and housing missiles aimed at the United States) virtually the only goal of that policy. This was the "lesser evil" doctrine: when faced with the choice between a usually wobbly Latin American democracy that believed in freedom even for leftists and a tough anti-Communist military regime, the US government almost always opted for the military regime. But the policy polarized Latin America even more and led in the 1960s and 1970s to a series of civil conflicts and wars that tore several countries apart.

After a brief democratic interlude in the late 1950s and early 1960s, by the late 1960s and throughout the 1970s Latin America had succumbed to a new wave of militarism. By the mid-1970s fourteen of the twenty countries were under military authoritarian rule, and in three others the military was so close to the surface of power that authoritarianism ruled even if civilians were still technically in office. That left only Colombia, Costa Rica, and Venezuela as democracies, and even they were elite-directed regimes.

The causes of this throwback to military authoritarianism were basically two: economic and political. By the 1960s Latin America's economies had become less competitive in global markets, the strategy of import substitution industrialization (ISI) was not working, the terms of trade had turned unfavorable (it cost Latin American more exports of sugar, bananas, coffee, or other items to pay for its imports than before), and the economies of the area could not pay for all the programs its citizens were demanding. Politically, the 1960s were a period when workers, peasants, and left-wing guerrillas were all mobilizing; the traditional wielders of power felt threatened by the mass mobilization and thus turned to the army to keep the lower classes in check. This was called bureaucratic authoritarianism—rule by the institutional armed forces and their civilian supporters, as distinct from the caudillos of the past.

By the late 1970s the steam had gone out of most of these military regimes, and Latin America began to reverse course and return to democracy. The armed forces had often proved just as corrupt and inefficient at running governments as their civilian predecessors, they were notorious human rights abusers and thus despised by their own people, and the international community (led by the United States) put pressure on them to return to their barracks. There followed one of the most amazing transformations in Latin American history. By the turn of the millennium nineteen of the twenty Latin American countries were ruled by the "third wave" of democratization, which affected the entire world and surely constituted one of the most significant events of the late twentieth century.

Many of these new democracies are still weak and not very well institutionalized. Crime and drugs are tearing some countries apart. They lack strong and independent legislatures, judiciaries and court systems, bureaucracies, political parties, interest groups, and local governments. They are often not very effective in carrying out public policies. They are referred to as "electoral democracies" (formal elections are held) but not "liberal democracies," in the sense of being open, pluralistic, and egalitarian. Many regimes in the area are still partial or limited democracies, designations that indicate links to Latin America's past. Nevertheless, even partial democracies are better than no democracies at all. No one doubts that an important breakthrough has been made, and certainly the human rights situation in virtually every country is far better now than it was two or three decades ago.

A FRAMEWORK FOR THINKING

The 1930s was a critical juncture—a key turning point, maybe *the* key turning point—in Latin American history. In that period (give or take a decade or two depending on the country), Latin America's old oligarchic, feudal, and medieval social, economic, and political structures began to collapse, in some cases giving way altogether, in others hanging on but in attenuated form. What replaced the old order was then uncertain and often unstable, frequently alternating between one type of regime and another. But there could be no doubt that Latin America had begun a profound transformation leading to modernization. At present, after decades of confusion and upheaval, what seems finally to be emerging is a system of democracy and a mixed economy; however, this process is still incomplete, shows many continuities with Latin America's past, and remains fragile.

As we begin to probe more deeply into Latin America's political institutions and processes, and as we go through the country-by-country analyses, readers should keep in mind the following framework for assessing the changes occurring: how much has changed in each country, what are the emerging patterns, and what outcomes are likely? This approach not only will give us a deeper understanding but also is fundamental to the comparative analysis that is at the heart of this book.

Changes in Political Culture

Until the 1930s Latin America still was often feudal and medieval in its thinking, but then education increased, literacy expanded, and first radio and then eventually television, VCRs, and the World Wide Web brought new ideas even to the most isolated areas. The old fatalism and passivity faded, people were mobilized, and new and challenging ideas (democracy, socialism) arose. The Catholic Church, long a supporter of the traditional political culture, began to change; Protestantism as well as secular ideas made strong inroads. The fundamental beliefs, ideas, and orientations by which people order their lives began changing. So in each country we will want to know among which groups these ideas are changing, how deep and extensive the changes are, and what impact a changing, more democratic, and more participatory political culture has had on institutions and policy.

Economic Change

Latin America's economies are now more diversified toward business, industry, services, manufacturing, tourism, mining, and agro-industry and no longer rely on the subsistence and plantation agriculture of the past. The economies are larger, more complex, and integrated into world markets. Most of them are now moving away somewhat from the statism and mercantilism of the past toward a system of open markets, freer trade, greater efficiency, less corruption, and neoliberalism. These changes are creating greater affluence (although the wealth is unevenly distributed), creating new jobs and opportunities, and giving new dynamism to the economies of the area. However, there are also lags and uneven development, with some groups and countries doing much better than others. In addition, all of these changes, both positive and the negative, carry important political and policy implications that vary from country to country.

Social Change

The economic changes just outlined have also accelerated social change. The old landed oligarchy is giving way to a more diverse panoply of business, industrial, commercial, banking, and other new elites. A sizable middle class has grown up in every country, ranging from 20 to 50 percent of the population, and its size and political orientation help determine whether democracy survives. Labor unions have organized, peasant groups are mobilizing, and employed urban slum dwellers are becoming politicized. In addition, there are new women's groups, community organizations, civil society organizations, and indigenous movements. Some of the older groups such as the church and the military are also undergoing change (becoming more middle-class and less elitist), and Roman Catholicism is being challenged in many countries by Protestant evangelicalism, which often involves quite different values and attitudes toward work and the role of family. In a forty-year period Latin America has gone from mostly rural to more than two-thirds urban. All these social changes and the far greater social pluralism force us to ask whether political pluralism (which usually means democracy) can be far behind.

Political Institutions

Along with the transformations in Latin America's political culture, economy, and society have come changes in political institutions. First, political parties in most countries tend to be better organized, with a real mass base and real programs and ideology, as compared with the small, personalist, and patronage-based parties of the past, which still exist in some countries. Second, reflecting the greater societal pluralism, there are far more interest groups, NGOs, and civil society organizations than ever before whose agendas need to be satisfied—although US-style lobbying is still seldom practiced in Latin America. Third, government agencies and institutions are being forced to modernize, increase efficiency, reduce corruption, and deliver real goods and services. Elections have become more honest and are recognized as the only legitimate route to power; legislatures, court systems, the police, and local government are all being modernized in various ways.

Public Policy

Not only are Latin American political processes and institutions modernizing, but so are public policy programs. In the past, governments in Latin America had few functions, but now government is being called upon to provide a host of new public policy programs in the areas of agrarian reform, family planning, education, economic development, the environment, housing, health care, and dozens of others. Moreover, with an aroused population, these programs are demanded as a matter of course, and governments in this new era of democracy have to deliver or they will be voted out. Rather than jobs, patronage, and handouts, public institutions in Latin America are called upon to provide public goods and services. But patronage and special favoritism still operate.

The International Environment

For centuries Latin America was isolated from the rest of the world, but now it is becoming closely integrated into it politically, culturally, and economically. Globalization has come to Latin America. Politically Latin America is becoming democratic, and if a country deviates from that course, the full weight of international sanctions comes down on it. Culturally Latin America is being swept up in the world political culture of jeans, rock music, Coca-Cola, and consumerism; values, especially those of young people, are becoming like those everywhere else (democratic, less authoritarian, less religious, less traditional). Economically Latin America is now a part of the global economy, with mostly good consequences (increased trade, commerce, jobs, affluence) but sometimes negative ones (currency uncertainties, fluctuating market demand, capital flight). Latin America can no longer choose among very many other economic options because foreign aid is meager and no other country is about to bail it out. It must join the global economy, compete with everyone else, and adopt some degree of economic reform. It must do so not just because outside pressures force it to but also because its own businesspeople, middle classes, and governments recognize that they have no other choice.

All of these long-term modernizing and globalizing changes have had a profound effect on Latin America, but they vary between countries, within institutions, and even between individuals, all of which continue to show complex mixes of traditional and modern attitudes and practices. As the twenty-first century moves along we will want to know in general for the region and for individual countries just how democratic they are. Have the societies modernized sufficiently to provide a firmer basis for pluralism and democracy? How successful are the new reforms in favor of free trade and open markets, and will they pay off in terms of improved living standards? How strong are political parties, interest groups, and government institutions? Now that the Cold War is over, can US–Latin American relations be put on a normal, more mature basis, and what of Latin America's relations with the rest of the world? These are some of the crucial questions that this book tries to answer.

In the next three chapters we examine the nature and role of interest groups and political parties in Latin America, describe government institutions and public policy, and analyze the overall political process and how it is changing. In the rest of the book we then examine individual countries to see how they conform to these overall patterns.

3

INTEREST GROUPS
AND POLITICAL PARTIES

Latin American political parties and interest groups are involved in the current conflict in the area between its corporatist past and a newer system based on pluralism and democracy. Since the beginning of the 1990s the conflict has been between two different views of what the political rules of the game should be. On one side are new forces that desire majority rule, human rights, and freedom of association. On the other side are those that favor traditional ways of doing things, where the emphasis was often on creating an administrative state above party and interest-group politics, and in which such agencies as the church, the army, the university, and perhaps even the trade unions were often more than mere interest groups, forming a part of the state system and inseparable from it.

Of particular importance is the nature of relationships between the government and interest groups. Although these traditionally ranged from almost complete governmental control to almost complete freedom, as under liberalism, the usual pattern involved considerably more state control over interest groups than in the United States, and this helped put interest group behavior in Latin America in a different framework than was the case in the United States. As Charles Anderson has suggested, at least until the 1980s Latin America never experienced a definitive democratic revolution—that is, a struggle resulting in agreement that elections would be the only legitimate way to obtain public power.[1] In the absence of such a consensus, political groups did not necessarily work for political power by seeking votes, the support of political parties, or contacts with elected representatives. The groups might seek power through any number of other strategies, including coercion, economic might, technical expertise, and controlled violence. Any group that could mobilize votes was likely to do so for electoral purposes, but since that was not the only legitimate route to power, the result of any election was tentative. Given the varying power of the competing groups and the incomplete legitimacy of the government itself, the duration of any government was uncertain. Political competition was a constant, virtually permanent struggle and preoccupation.

Further, group behavior in Latin America was conditioned by a set of unwritten rules, called by Anderson the "living museum." Before a new group could participate in the political system, it had to demonstrate both that it had a power resource and that it would respect the rights of already existing groups. The result was the gradual addition of new groups under these two conditions but seldom the elimination of the old ones. The newest, most modern groups coexisted with the oldest, most traditionalist ones, often leading to gridlock.

A related factor was the practice of co-optation or repression. As new groups emerged as potential politically relevant actors, already established actors (particularly political parties or strong national leaders) sometimes offered to assist them in their new political activities. The deal struck was one mutually beneficial to each: the new group gained acceptance, prestige, and some of its original goals, and the established group or leader gained new support and increased political resources. In some circumstances, new groups refused to be co-opted, rejecting the rules of the game. Instead, they took steps indicating to established groups and leaders that they might act in a revolutionary fashion against the interests of the established elites. In the case of a group that violated the ground rules by employing mass violence, for example, an effort was made by the established interests to repress the new group, either legally by refusing it legal standing or in some cases through the use of violence. Most commonly, such repression proved successful, and the new group disappeared or atrophied, accomplishing none of its goals. The general success of repression made co-optation seem more desirable to new groups, because obtaining some of their goals through co-optation was preferable to being repressed. In a few cases the established political groups failed to repress the emergent groups, and the latter came to power through revolutionary means, proceeding to eliminate the traditional power contenders. These are known as the true, genuine, or social revolutions in Latin America and include only the Mexican Revolution of 1910–1920, the Bolivian Revolution of 1952, the Cuban Revolution of 1959, and the Nicaraguan Revolution of 1979. Examples of the reverse process—utilization of violence and repression to eliminate the newer challenging groups and to secure in power the more traditional system—were Brazil in 1964 and Chile in 1973. Both led to the elimination of independent political parties, student associations, and labor and peasant unions as power groups.

Before the late 1980s we viewed the politically relevant groups of Latin America in this context of a historically patrimonial, corporative, and co-optive tradition. Since then, with the movement toward liberal democracy, some individuals and groups have favored the new regime while other people and organizations have preferred the historical one, and throughout Latin America there has been conflict between the new supporters of democracy and the supporters of the traditional system. Peru and Guatemala hold special interest in this regard, as both are cases where presidents tried to govern within the old, unwritten rules rather than the new, written ones incorporated in constitutional and democratic precepts.

THE TRADITIONAL OLIGARCHY

After independence three groups, what can be called the nineteenth-century oligarchy, were predominant in Latin America: the military, the Roman Catholic Church, and the large landholders. Through the process of economic growth and change new groups emerged: first commercial elites; later industrial elites, students, and middle-income sectors; then industrial labor unions and peasants; and most recently groups representing indigenous people, women, consumers, nongovernmental organizations, and many others. Political parties have existed throughout the process. Particularly since the end of the nineteenth century, the United States has been a politically relevant force in the domestic politics of the Latin American countries. During the Cold War years of conflict with Communist countries (1945–1989), the US government seemed most interested in keeping Latin America out of the enemy camp; today, in the absence of international enemies, US governmental concerns have more to do with free trade, drugs, democracy, and human rights.

The Armed Forces

During the wars for independence, the Spanish American countries developed armies led by a great variety of individuals, including well-born creoles, priests, and people of humbler backgrounds. The officers did not come from military academies but were self-selected or chosen by other leaders. Few of the officers had previous military training, and the armies were much less professional than armies today.

Following independence, the military element continued as one of the first important power groups. The national army was supposed to be preeminent, and in some countries national military academies were founded in the first quarter century after independence. Yet the national military was challenged by other local or regional armies. The early nineteenth century was a period of limited national integration, with regional subdivisions of the countries often dominated by local landowners or caudillos, charismatic leaders who had their own private armies. One aspect of the development of Latin America was the struggle between the central government and its army on one hand and the local caudillos on the other, with the former winning out in most cases. One of the unanswered questions about Latin American politics even today is the extent to which outlying areas of the countries, in the mountains or jungles, are effectively covered by the laws made in the national capitals.

The development of Brazil varied somewhat from the norm because Portugal was the colonizing power and because of the lack of a war for independence. The military first gained prominence in the Paraguayan War (1864–1870). Until 1930 the Brazilian states had powerful militias, in some cases of comparable strength to the national army.

Although Latin American militaries varied in the nineteenth century, two general themes applied. First, various militaries, including the national one, became active in politics. At given times they were regional or personal organizations; at others, they were parts of political parties that were participants in the civil wars frequently waged between rival factions. However, national militaries also often played the role of a moderating power, staying above factional struggles and preferring that civilians govern, but taking over power temporarily when the civilians could not rule effectively. Although not emerging in all countries, this moderating power was seen in most, especially in Brazil, where, with the abdication of the emperor in 1889, the military became the chief moderator in the system.

As early as the 1830s and 1840s in Argentina and Mexico, and later in the other Latin American countries, national military academies were established. Their goal was to introduce professionalism into the military, requiring graduation rather than elite family connections for officer status. These academies were for the most part successful in making entry to and promotion within the officer corps proceed in a routinized manner, and by the 1950s Latin American officers were named generals, with potential political power, only after a career of some twenty years.

Through professionalization the military career was designed to be a highly specialized one that taught the skills for warfare but eschewed interest in political matters. Being an officer would supposedly absorb all an individual's energy, and officers' functional expertise would be distinct from that of politicians. Civilians were to have complete control of the military, which would stay out of politics. However, this model of professionalism, imported from Western Europe and the United States, never took complete root in Latin America. In the absence of strong civilian institutions, the military continued to play politics and to exercise its moderating power, and coups d'état continued.

By the late 1950s and early 1960s a change had occurred in the nature of the role of the military in Latin America. The success of guerrilla revolutions in China, Indochina, Algeria, and Cuba led to a new emphasis on the military's role in counterinsurgency and internal defense functions. In addition, Latin American militaries—encouraged by US military aid—began to assume responsibility for civic action programs, which assisted civilians in the construction of roads, schools, and other public projects. The new professionalism, with its emphasis on counterinsurgency, was a product of the Cold War and may have been more in keeping with Latin American political culture than the old professionalism had been. Military skills were no longer viewed as separate or different from civilian skills. The military was to acquire the ability to help solve national problems that might lead to insurgency, a task that was in its very essence political rather than apolitical. The implication of the new professionalism was that, besides combating active guerrilla factions, the military would ensure the implementation of social and economic reforms necessary to prevent insurgency if the civilians proved incapable of doing so. The new professionalism in Latin America led to more military intervention in politics, not less.

The end result of this process was bureaucratic authoritarianism, the rule of the military institution on a long-term basis.[2] Seen especially in Argentina, Brazil, Chile, Peru, and Uruguay, this new form of military government involved the institution as a whole—not an individual general—and was based on the idea that the military could govern better than civilians. The bureaucratic authoritarian period, during which the military often governed repressively and violated human rights, lasted from the mid-1960s through the late 1970s.

Since the 1980s the Latin American militaries have begun transitions to constitutionalism, subservience to civilian control, and support of democratically elected presidents. The transformation has had its difficulties, with militaries supporting a president who dismissed congress and the courts (Peru), playing a key role in overthrowing a president who attempted the same maneuver (Guatemala), putting down coups d'état against chief executives (Venezuela), helping civilian groups to depose unpopular presidents (Ecuador), and failing to intervene even though key elements of public opinion and the US ambassador apparently favored getting rid of the elected president (Colombia). The Latin American militaries are now in the process of learning the new role of support for civilian democracy.

Table 3.1   Patterns of Civil-Military Relations in 2000

Military control	Military tutelage	Conditional military subordination	Civilian control *
None as of 2000 (with the possible exception of Guatemala)	Ecuador El Salvador Guatemala Venezuela	Bolivia Brazil Chile Colombia Dominican Republic Honduras Nicaragua Paraguay Peru	Costa Rica Mexico Haiti Panama Argentina Uruguay

Source: Peter H. Smith, *Democracy in Latin America: Political Change in Comparative Prospective* (New York: Oxford University Press, 2005), 103.
*Grouped in this way because of structural variations.

It has always been difficult to compare the Latin American militaries cross-nationally. Similarly, trying to distinguish "civilian" and "military" regimes was a difficult task at best and sometimes a meaningless one. Often military personnel temporarily resigned their commissions to take leadership positions in civilian bureaucracies or as government ministers. Frequently they held military and civilian positions at the same time. In some cases an officer resigned his commission, was elected president, and then governed with strong military backing. In almost all instances, coups d'état were not just simple military affairs but were supported by groups of civilians as well. It was not unheard of for civilians to take a significant part in the ensuing governments. Sometimes civilians actually drew the military into playing a larger political role. In short, Latin American governments were often coalitions established between certain factions of the militaries and certain factions of civilians in an attempt to control the system.

We suggest that several dimensions of military involvement in politics be considered in the chapters about individual countries that follow. First is whether the military still forcefully removes chief executives, an activity that now has become a thing of the past in most countries. The second is the extent to which military leaders have a say in nonmilitary matters. Although in the past generals have protected their large-landowner friends and relatives, that phenomenon may also be passing. The last is the extent to which the role of moderating power still obliges the military to step in and unseat an incompetent president or one who has violated the rules of the game.

Considering this very complicated question, Peter Smith classified Latin American countries into four types:

1. Military control
2. Military tutelage: in the case of a crisis of the civilian government, the armed forces supervise civilian authorities and play key roles in decision making

3. Conditional military subordination: the armed forces keep careful watch over civilians, protecting military prerogatives
4. Civilian control

Smith's classification of the Latin American countries is shown in Table 3.1.[3]

Besides the degree of military influence in the political system, several other interrelated questions should be kept in mind. These include the reason for military involvement in politics, what the results of military rule were, and how the military was internally divided. The military was one of the traditional pillars of Latin American society, with rights, responsibilities, and legal standing that can be traced back to colonial times. This meant the military played a different role than it did in the United States. Although this seems to be a matter of the past, the cases of Peru (1992), Guatemala (1993), and Honduras (2009) show that in some countries the generals still play very important roles in politics.

The Roman Catholic Church

All Latin American countries were nominally Catholic, although the form of that religion varied from country to country. The Spanish and Portuguese came to "Christianize the heathens" as well as to seek precious metals. In areas with a heavy concentration of indigenous peoples, religion became a mixture of pre-Columbian and Roman Catholic beliefs. To a lesser degree, Catholicism later blended with African religions, which also existed on their own in certain areas, especially in Brazil and Cuba. Religion in the large cities of Latin America is similar to that in the urban centers of the United States and Western Europe, while in the more isolated small towns, Roman Catholicism is still of fifteenth-century vintage.

The power of the church hierarchy in politics also varies. Traditionally the church was one of the main sectors of Spanish and Portuguese corporate society, with rights and responsibilities in such areas as care for orphans, education, and public morals. Beginning in the nineteenth century some laypeople wanted to strip the church of all its temporal power, including its lands. Generally speaking, the conflict over the role of the church ended in most countries by the first part of the twentieth century.

Between the 1960s and the 1980s the church changed, especially if by "church" we mean the top levels of the hierarchy that control the religious and political fortunes of the institution. These transformations were occasioned by the new theologies of the previous hundred years, as expressed through various papal encyclicals, Vatican II, and the conferences of the Latin American bishops at Medellín, Colombia, in 1968 and Puebla, Mexico, in 1979. Significant numbers of bishops (and many more parish priests and members of the various orders) subscribed to what was commonly called liberation theology. This theology stressed that the church was of and for this world and should take stands against repression and violence, including the demeaning and life-threatening institutionalized violence experienced by the poor of the area. Liberation theology also stressed the equality of all believers, laypeople as well as clerics and bishops, as opposed to the former stress on hierarchy. The end result, in some parts of the region, was new popular-level churches with lay leadership and only minimal involvement of priests.

It would be a mistake to assume that all, or even most, members of the Latin American clergy ever subscribed to liberation theology. Many believed that the new social doctrine had taken the church more into politics than it should be. Some were concerned with the loss of traditional authority that the erosion of hierarchy brought. The various countries of Latin America differ substantially in church authority and adherence of the bishops to liberation theology.

As a result of these changes, the clergy is no longer uniformly conservative; rather, its members differ on the role that the church should play in socioeconomic reform and on the nature of hierarchical relations within the church. At one extreme of this conflict is the traditional church elite, usually with social origins in the upper class or aspirations to be accepted by it, still very conservative, and with close connections to other supporters of the status quo. At the other end of this conflict are those priests, of various social backgrounds, who see the major objective of the church as assisting the masses to obtain social justice. In some cases these priests have been openly revolutionary, fighting in guerrilla wars. Other priests fall between these two extremes of political ideology, and still others favor a relaxing of the rigid hierarchy, giving more discretion to local parish priests.

Liberation theology had its critics outside of Latin America. The Congregation for the Doctrine of the Faith, headed by German cardinal Joseph Ratzinger (later Pope Benedict XVI), strongly opposed certain elements of liberation theology. In both 1984 and 1986 the Vatican officially condemned liberation theology's acceptance of Marxism and armed violence. In 1985 Leonardo Boff, a Brazilian leader in the liberation theology movement, was "condemned to 'obsequious silence' and was removed from his editorial functions and suspended from religious duties." While some argue that liberation theology weakened as the Marxist world disappeared, it did not disappear. In mid-2007 the Vatican strongly criticized the work of the Jesuit father Jon Sobrino, who was born in Spain but had been working in El Salvador since the 1980s. The Congregation for the Doctrine of the Faith warned pastors and all other Catholics that Father Sobrino's work contained "erroneous or dangerous propositions."[4]

The church still participates in politics to defend its interests, although in most cases its wealth is no longer in land. Certain church interests are still the traditional ones: giving religious instruction in schools, running parochial high schools and universities, and occasionally attempting to prevent divorce legislation and to make purely civil marriage difficult. At times the church has been a major proponent of human rights, especially when military governments deny them. A touchier issue has been that of birth control, and in most cases the Latin American hierarchies have fought artificial methods. However, in the face of the population explosion many church officials have assisted in family planning clinics, turned a blind eye when governments have promoted artificial methods of birth control, and occasionally even assisted in those governmental efforts.

Some analysts feel the Roman Catholic Church in Latin America is no longer a major contender. They argue that on certain issues its sway is still considerable but that the church is no longer as influential politically as the army, the wealthy elites, or the US embassies. Modernization, urbanization, and secularism have also taken their toll on church attendance and the institution's political power. However, that has not prevented church leaders from making statements in recent years in opposition to abortion and same-sex marriage.

On March 13, 2013, Jorge Mario Bergoglio, an Argentine Jesuit whose parents were of Italian background, was elected the 266th pope of the Roman Catholic

Church. Choosing the name of Francis, he is the first pope from Latin America. It is too soon to know how he might change the church.

In recent decades Protestant religious groups have grown rapidly in Latin America. In some countries Protestants constitute 25 to 35 percent or more of the population; in Guatemala a Protestant general became dictator for a time. The fastest-growing of these sects were the evangelical ones, not the older mainline churches. Protestantism was identified with a strong work ethic, obliging its members to work hard and save. Until recently, however, the Protestant groups have generally not become politically active.

Large Landowners

In all the countries of Latin America save Costa Rica and Paraguay, the colonial period led to the establishment of a powerful group of individuals who had received large tracts of land as royal grants. With the coming of independence these landowners wielded more influence than before and developed into one of the three major power groups of nineteenth-century politics.

This was not to say that they operated monolithically; in some cases they were pitted against each other. In recent times such rifts have remained among the large landowners, usually along the lines of crop production. However, the major conflict has been between those who have large tracts of land and the many landless people. In those circumstances the various groups of large landowners tend to coalesce. In some cases there is an umbrella organization to bring all of the various producer organizations together formally; in other cases the coalition is much more informal.

In the 1960s the pressures for land reform were considerable, both from landless peasants and from foreign and domestic groups who saw this type of reform as a way to achieve social justice and to avoid Castro-like revolutions. In some countries, such as Mexico, land reform had previously come by revolution; in others, such as Venezuela, a good bit of land had been distributed by the government to the landless; in still others, the power of the landed, in coalition with other status quo groups, led to merely the appearance of land reform rather than actual changes. In some of the Latin American countries, especially those in which the amount of arable land is limited and the population has exploded, the issue of breaking up large estates will continue for the foreseeable future.

Since the 1960s, with Latin America rapidly urbanizing, the rural issue has become less important. The traditional landowners still dominate in some countries, but in others power has passed to newer commercial and industrial elites. Although land reform may still be necessary in some areas, with large percentages of the population moving to the cities many of the main social issues have become urban rather than rural.

OTHER MAJOR INTEREST GROUPS

Commercial and Industrial Elites

Although not part of the traditional oligarchy, commercial elites have existed in Latin America since independence; one of the early political conflicts was between those who wanted free trade (the commercial elites and allied landed interests producing crops for export) and those who wanted protection of nascent industry (industrial elites with allied landed groups not producing for export). In recent decades the strength of these commercial and industrial groups has steadily grown.

With the exception of Colombia, the real push for industrialization in Latin America did not come until the Great Depression and World War II, when Latin America was cut off from trade with the industrialized world. Before those crises industrial goods from England and the United States were cheaper, even with transportation costs and import duties, than locally produced goods.

Between the mid-1930s and the mid-1980s, Latin American countries experienced industrialization of the import substitution type—that is, producing goods that formerly were imported from the industrialized countries. This was the case in light consumer goods; in some consumer durables, including assembly of North American and European automobiles; and in some other heavy industries such as cement and steel. Because import substitution necessitated increased foreign trade to import capital goods, there was no longer much conflict between commercial and industrial elites: Expanded trade and industrialization go together.

Since the 1980s neoliberal presidents in Latin America have been pushing for more foreign commerce in a world with trade barriers that are lower or do not exist at all. In this internationalization of the Latin American economies, foreign trade is of utmost importance. Hence so are the commercial elites. Mexico entered a free trade association with the United States and Canada in 1994 through the North American Free Trade Agreement (NAFTA), Central America and the Dominican Republic entered into a similar association with the United States in 2005 through the Central American Free Trade Association (CAFTA), and in separate agreements Colombia and Peru began free trade agreements with the United States in 2011. The goal is to have a free trade association covering all of the Americas, from Alaska to Tierra del Fuego.

A complicating factor is the industrial elite's relationship with the landed elite. In some countries, such as Argentina, the early industrialists were linked to the landed groups; later, individuals who began as industrialists invested in land. The result was two intertwined groups, a marriage of older landed and newer moneyed wealth, with only vague boundaries separating them and with some families and individuals straddling the line. All these groups were opposed to agrarian reform.

Industrialists and commercial elites, who are strategically located in major cities of Latin America, are highly organized in various chambers of commerce, industrial associations, and the like. Generally they favor a status quo that profits them. They are often the driving forces in Latin American economic development; for this reason and because they are frequently represented in high official circles, no matter what government is in control, they are very powerful. Neoliberalism and globalism have made these groups even more essential to the functioning of the economy, and hence also to the political system.

The Middle Sectors

With economic growth the percentage of Latin Americans who are in the middle class has increased, with some suggesting that a majority of Mexicans are now in that group. Although the Latin American countries began independence with a basically two-class system, there have always been individuals who fell statistically into the middle ranges, neither very rich nor abjectly poor. These few individuals during the nineteenth century were primarily artisans and shopkeepers; later this group included doctors and lawyers. The emergence of a larger middle sector was a twentieth-century phenomenon, associated with urbanization, technological advances, industrialization, and the expansion of public education and the role of the government.

All of these changes necessitated a large number of white-collar, managerial workers. New teachers and government bureaucrats constituted part of this sector, as did office workers in private businesses. In addition, small businesses grew, particularly in the service sector of the economy. Many of these new non-manual-labor professions have been organized, including teachers, small-business owners, lawyers, and government bureaucrats. Military officers, university students, political party officials, and even union and peasant group leaders are usually considered middle class.

The people who filled the new middle-sector jobs were the product of social mobility, with some coming from the lower class and others "fallen aristocrats" from the upper class. Their numerous and heterogeneous occupations temporarily impeded the formation of a sense of common identity as members of a middle class. Indeed, in some of the Latin American countries this identification has yet to emerge.

In those countries of Latin America in which a large middle-sector group first emerged, certain generalizations about its political behavior can be made. In the early stages of political activities, coalitions tended to be formed, with groups from the lower classes against the more traditional and oligarchic groups in power. Major goals included expanded suffrage, the promotion of urban growth and economic development, a greater role for public education, increased industrialization, and social welfare programs.

In the later political evolution of the middle sectors the tendency was to side with the established order against rising mass or populist movements. In some cases the middle-class movements allied with landowners, industrialists, and the church against their working-class partners of earlier years; in other cases, when the more numerous lower class seemed ready to take power on its own, the middle sectors were instrumental in fomenting a middle-class military coup, to prevent "premature democratization" (a democratic system that the middle sectors could not control).[5]

Because the status of the middle class varies greatly in Latin America, a number of factors should be considered when reading the chapters about individual countries, including the size of the middle-income group, its cohesion and relationships with political parties, and the degree of self-identification as members of a "middle class." Only time will tell whether the middle sectors will serve as a new, invigorated social base for democracy or whether they will continue to ape and imitate the upper class and thus perpetuate an essentially two-class and polarized social structure.

Labor Unions

From its inception, organized labor in Latin America has been highly political. Virtually all important trade union groups of the area have been closely associated with a political party, strong leader, or government. On some occasions labor unions have grown independently until they were co-opted or repressed. In other cases labor unions have owed their origins directly to the efforts of a party, leader, or government.

Latin American unionism was influenced by ideological currents that came from southern Europe, including anarchist and Marxist orientations. In addition, three characteristics of the Latin American economies favored partisan unionism. First, unions came relatively early in the economic development of the region—in most cases earlier than in the United States and western Europe. Second, the labor pool of employables has been much larger than the number who can get the relatively well-paid jobs in industry. An employer in that situation could almost always find people to replace striking workers unless they were protected by a party or by the government. Finally, inflation has been a chronic problem in Latin America, making it important for unions to win the support of other political groups in the continual renegotiation of contracts to obtain higher salaries, which often need governmental approval.

The Latin American legal tradition required that unions be officially recognized by the government before they could bargain collectively. If a group could not obtain or retain this legal standing, it had little power. Labor legislation, in addition, varied greatly, including codes mandating that labor organizers be employed full-time by the industry they were organizing, limiting the power of unions that lacked leaders who were paid full salaries to spend part of the working day in union activities. This was only one of the many governmental restrictions placed on labor unions.

Some union organizations were co-opted by the state; others remained outside the system. Key questions to consider when reading the country chapters include the extent to which workers are organized, how the labor code is used to prevent or facilitate worker organization, the nature of the relationships between labor and the political parties or between labor and the government, and the extent to which unions have been co-opted or repressed. Are the unions a declining or growing interest in Latin America?

Peasants

The term *peasant* refers to many different kinds of people in Latin America. Some prefer the Spanish term *campesinos* (people who live in the *campo*, the countryside) rather than the English term with its European-based connotations. The major groups of campesinos, who vary in importance from country to country, include indigenous groups who speak only their native language or who are bilingual in that language and Spanish; workers on the traditional haciendas, tilling the fields in return for wages or part of the crops, with the owner as a patron to care for the family or, more frequently, a manager-patron who represents the absentee owner; workers on modern plantations, receiving wages but remaining outside of the older patron-client relationship; individuals with a small landholding, legally held, of such a size that a bare existence is possible; people who cultivate small plots but have no legal claim to that land, perhaps moving every few years after the slash-and-burn method and the lack of crop rotation deplete the soil; and those who have been given a small plot of land to work by a landowner in exchange for labor on the large estate.

What all of these campesinos have in common, in the context of the extremely inequitable distribution of arable lands in Latin America, is a marginal existence due to their small amount of land or income and a high degree of insecurity due to their uncertain claims to the land they cultivate. It was estimated in 1961 that more than 5 million very small farms (below 30 acres, or 12 hectares) occupied only 3.7

percent of the land, while, at the other extreme, 100,000 holdings of more than 1,500 acres (607 hectares) took up some 65 percent of the land. Three decades later, the situation had changed little. At least eighty million people still lived on small landholdings with insufficient land to earn even a minimum subsistence, or they worked as agricultural laborers with no land at all. For many of these rural people their only real chance of breaking out of this circle of poverty was to move to an urban area, where they faced another—in some ways even worse—culture of poverty. For those who remained on the land, unless there was a dramatic restructuring of ownership, the present subhuman existence was likely to continue. Moreover, as commercial agriculture for export increased in many countries, the campesinos were increasingly shoved off the fertile lands into the sterile hillsides, where their ability to subsist has become more precarious.

Rural peasant elements have long been active in politics, but only recently as independent, organized interest groups. The traditional political structure of the countryside was one in which participation in national politics meant taking part in the patronage system. The local patrons, besides expecting work on the estate from the campesino, expected certain political behavior. In some countries this meant that the campesino belonged to the same political party as the patron, voted for that party on election day, and, if necessary, served as cannon fodder in its civil wars. In other countries the national party organizations never reached the local levels, and restrictive suffrage laws prevented the peasants from participating in elections. In both patterns, for the peasants there was no such thing as national politics, only local politics, which might or might not have national party labels attached to the local person or groups in power.

This traditional system still exists in many areas of Latin America. However, since the 1950s signs of agrarian unrest and political mobilization have been more and more evident. In many cases major agrarian movements were organized by urban interests: political parties, especially those of the Marxist left. Some of these peasant movements were based in revolutionary agrarianism, seeking to reform and improve the land tenure system and to significantly reform the entire power structure of the nation. They employed strategies that included the illegal seizure of land, the elimination of landowners, and armed defense of the gains thus achieved. Less radical were the movements that sought to reform the social order partially through the elimination of a few of the most oppressive effects of the existing power structure, but without threatening the power structure as such.

The United States

Another important power element in Latin American politics is the United States. This influence usually has been seen in at least three interrelated ways: US governmental representatives, US-based private business, and US-dominated international agencies. The US government has been interested in the area since Latin America's independence. Its first concern, that the new nations not fall under the control of European powers, led to the Monroe Doctrine in 1823. Originally a defensive statement, the doctrine was later changed through various corollaries to a more aggressive one, telling the Latin Americans that they could not sell strategically located lands to nonhemispheric governments or businesses and that the United States would intervene in Latin America to collect debts owed to nonhemispheric powers (the Roosevelt Corollary).

At various times the US government has set standards that had to be met before full diplomatic recognition was accorded to a Latin American nation. This de jure recognition policy, most memorable in the Wilson, early Kennedy, and Carter administrations, favored elected democratic governments, exclusion of the military from government, and a vision of human rights that should be applied in Latin America. At other times the United States has pursued a de facto recognition policy, according full diplomatic standing to any government with effective control of its nation's territory.

The US ambassador to a Latin American country usually has impressive powers. This ambassadorial power typically has been used to support or defeat governments, to focus Latin American governmental policy in certain directions, and to assist US-based corporations in various countries. One ambassador to pre-Castro Cuba testified that he was second only to the Cuban president in influence in the country. In Central America during the 1980s a number of US ambassadors played this strong proconsular role, as did the ambassador to Colombia during the government of Ernesto Samper (1994–1998), because of the Colombian president's suspected ties to drug groups.

From their early beginnings, particularly in sugar and bananas, US-based corporations in Latin America have grown dramatically. In addition to agribusiness, corporations later entered the extractive field (petroleum, copper, coal, iron ore), retailing, the services industry (accounting firms, computer outfits), and communications (telephones, telegraphs, computers). The most recent kind of US corporation introduced to Latin America was the export-platform variety—that is, a company that takes advantage of the low wages in Latin America to produce pocket calculators in Mexico or baseballs in Haiti, mainly for export to the industrialized world.

US corporations in Latin America often enter into the politics of their host countries. Some of the instances have been flagrant: bribing public officials to keep taxes low or threatening to cut off a country's exports if certain policies were approved by its government. However, most political activities of US corporations currently are much less dramatic. Almost always Latin Americans in the host countries buy stock in the US corporations that operate there, and locals hold high managerial positions in them. US businesses purchase Latin American corporations, the leaders of which then work for the new owners. The result is that the US corporation develops contacts, obligations, and political influence similar to those possessed by domestic interest groups. In the 1980s the business climate improved as Latin American governments rescinded restrictions on maximum profits and repatriation. Once again US capital began to flow into the area, something that continues until the present.

Most foreign-aid and international lending organizations have been dominated historically by the United States. These agencies, especially active during the 1960s, when aid to Latin America began in large quantities, include the US Agency for International Development (USAID), which administers most US foreign aid; the World Bank; the International Monetary Fund (IMF); the Inter-American Development Bank (IADB), and a variety of others. The World Bank and the IMF are international agencies, results of post–World War II agreements between the countries of the West. However, the representation of the United States on the governing boards of both has been so large (based on the amount of money donated to the agencies) and the convergence of interests of the two with those of the US government has been so great that they can be considered US-oriented groups. So can the IADB. Contrary to the wishes of Latin American leaders who wanted a lending agency less dominated by the United States, in effect the IADB cannot lend to countries if the US government does not want it to. Economic development has been a central goal of the Latin American states for the past fifty years, and because loans for that development have come predominantly from USAID, the World Bank, and the IADB, with those loans contingent many times on a monetary policy judged healthy by the IMF, the officials of these four groups have much influence in the day-to-day policies of the governments of the area.

This power of the lending agencies was probably greatest during the 1960s, and then again during the debt crisis of the 1980s. USAID had most leverage or "conditionality" during the existence of the Alliance for Progress, a foreign-aid program initiated by the Kennedy administration that attempted to change Latin America dramatically in a decade. Even though it failed, it did lead to large loans from the US government, substantial progress in some fields, and much influence for the local USAID head in the domestic politics of some Latin American countries. The Alliance for Progress was terminated by the Nixon administration. Further, the power of the World Bank waned in the wake of the crisis of the industrialized economies of the West following the Arab oil embargo of 1973–1974 and with the growing power of OPEC. Then the private banks, recycling petrodollars, filled many of the needs of the Latin American countries. However, with the debt crisis of the 1980s, the IMF and its Bretton Woods partner the World Bank regained much of their lost power.

The influence of US-directed and -oriented groups—diplomatic, business, foreign-assistance—in Latin America is considerable. This does not mean that the power has been equal in all the Latin American countries. When a Latin American country is strategically important to the United States and when US private investors have established a large investment in the economy (such as in Cuba before Castro), US elements are extremely powerful in domestic Latin politics. This does not mean that the United States cannot have considerable influence in domestic politics in distant countries with relatively little private investment by US corporations, as the example of Allende's Chile showed. With the end of the Cold War, US foreign policy interest in Latin America, with the exception of a few countries, waned; private transactions are now more important than official ones.

NEW GROUPS

Many new groups have appeared in Latin America in recent decades. Three of particular importance are indigenous groups, women's groups, and nongovernmental organizations (NGOs).

Indigenous Groups

Indigenous peoples constitute about 8 percent of the total population of Latin America, or an estimated forty million people. In some four hundred distinct groups, they are concentrated in southern Mexico, parts of Central America, and the central Andes of South America. In these states they make up between 10 to 70 percent of the population. Some individual language groups have more than one million members. A dozen groups have more than a quarter million members, in total making up some 73 percent of the indigenous population of the region. Finally, two groups have less than one thousand members.

In the 1970s Indian populations in Latin America began to mobilize politically in unprecedented ways to protect their lands and cultures from the increasing influence of multinational companies, colonists, the state, and other intruders. In the 1980s they placed a greater emphasis on the recuperation of ethnic identities and the construction of a pan-indigenous cultural identity. Contemporary Latin American indigenous organizations seek equal status for their cultures, forms of social organization and laws to advance their interests, and the means to facilitate and control their economic development. Their ultimate goal is the transformation of what they view to be a discriminatory, homogeneous state into a "plurinational state," one whose institutions reflect the cultural diversity of society. In the 1990s seven Latin American states—Bolivia, Colombia, Ecuador, Mexico, Nicaragua, Peru, and Paraguay—recognized a milder version of this claim, declaring their societies "pluricultural and multiethnic." At the same time many individuals of indigenous background continue to follow the traditional assimilationist strategy of seeking to integrate themselves into Hispanic culture.

The main component of rising indigenous nationalism is the struggle for territorial, political, economic, and cultural autonomy. Until 1987 only the Kuna of Panama enjoyed what could be described as territorial and political autonomy. In 1987 the Nicaraguan government established two multiethnic autonomous regions to accommodate claims of the Miskitu and other smaller groups, who had joined the anti-Sandinista counterrevolutionary guerrilla movement supported by the United States. Although the autonomous regions were largely a failure in terms of indigenous peoples' aspirations, their establishment inspired indigenous organizations throughout Latin America to make similar claims.

Only Colombia's indigenous population has achieved politico-territorial autonomy. The 1991 Colombian constitution elevated indigenous reservations to the status of municipal governments; recognized indigenous traditional leaders as public authorities and, with some restrictions, indigenous customary law as public and binding; and provided guaranteed representation in the national senate. The governments of Bolivia, Ecuador, Guatemala, and Mexico considered some type of politico-territorial autonomy arrangements following constitutional reforms or peace agreements with armed groups concluded in the 1990s.[6]

The most notable cases of members of indigenous groups taking part in national politics were the election of Alejandro Toledo in Peru in 2001 and the election of Evo Morales in Bolivia in 2006. While the Toledo presidency was troubled (see Chapter 10), the Morales presidency is still a work in progress (see Chapter 14).

Women's Groups

Women in Latin America are making progress in ascending to leadership positions in government, politics, and civil society. A 1999 study concluded that although their numbers remain low, the percentage of women in national congresses and cabinets in Latin America (15 and 11 percent, respectively) is second only to that seen in the Nordic countries of Europe (36 and 35 percent) and is higher in congresses but lower in cabinets than in the United States (12 and 21 percent).[7]

More (and more-politicized) women's groups emerged in the 1970s and 1980s, playing a prominent role in the struggles against authoritarian rule, raising hopes that the return to democracy would generate greater opportunities for women in the region. The consolidation of democracy was expected to promote greater participation of women in the formulation and execution of laws governing their lives. From 1994 to 2004 women's participation rose, on average, from 9 to 14 percent in the executive branch (in ministerial positions), from 5 to 13 percent in the senate, and from 8 to 15 percent in the lower house or unicameral parliament.[8] In that decade women's presence in the public spheres of the economy and society also grew. Such growth is a reflection of social changes such as women's entry into the labor force, rising educational levels, and changing attitudes about the role of women. Most notably, five women were elected presidents in their countries: Violeta Barrios de Chamorro in Nicaragua in 1990, Mireya Moscoso de Gruber in Panama in 1999, Michelle Bachelet in Chile in 2006, Cristina Fernández de Kirchner in Argentina in 2007, and Dilma Rousseff in Brazil in 2010.

Figures on women's representation in politics show that their opportunities to exercise leadership are greater outside the main centers of power, in the lower levels of organizational hierarchy, outside the capital city area, and in less powerful governmental agencies. For example, in the judicial branch of government, women make up 45 percent of trial judges but only 20 percent of judges at the appellate court level, and virtually zero at the supreme court level.

One important consequence of women's organizing has been the adoption of quota laws, intended to increase women's representation in political office. After pressure from organized women's groups, Argentina, Bolivia, Brazil, Costa Rica, the Dominican Republic, Ecuador, Panama, and Peru have passed national laws requiring political parties to reserve 20 to 40 percent of candidacies for women. Of course, that women are nominated does not necessarily mean that they are elected. Colombia enacted a law making it mandatory that mayors have women as one-third of their appointed officials, a law that is not always followed.

Despite the growth of women's representation, the women's movement has appeared to some observers to be increasingly fragmented and to have lost its visibility and capacity for political intervention. The obstacles to women's full participation in Latin American democracies and economies stem from women's weaker social position, traditional gender roles and the cultural expectations and stereotypes built around these roles, and blatant sex discrimination. Few Latin American countries have made efforts to make motherhood and work compatible. No Latin American country has a comprehensive child care policy. Although most countries have laws requiring businesses that employ twenty or more women to have on-site day care facilities, these laws are rarely enforced. Pregnancy discrimination is widespread in the region, some companies requiring a pregnancy test or a sterilization certificate as a condition of employment. Some fire women once they become pregnant. Although both actions are against the law, once again the laws are seldom enforced. Although cultural changes coming from women's improving position will help erode such discriminatory barriers, this is likely to happen only in the very long run.

Nongovernmental Organizations

Nongovernmental organizations (NGOs), a newer type of group, are increasingly important actors in Latin American politics. Although some are specific to individual countries, others are based on a general theme and have offices in many Latin American countries. Some NGOs are transnational, with headquarters in one country and activities in many countries. Amnesty International, the Environmental Defense Fund, and the Red Cross are transnational NGOs that have influenced recent events in Latin America. Local NGOs are shaping contemporary politics too. For example, NGOs are providing community services in Mexico, raising racial consciousness in Brazil, extending credit to poor people in Colombia, defending indigenous peoples in Bolivia, and asserting women's rights in Argentina. Unlike interest groups, NGOs do not focus their activities exclusively on governments. They also work to change the policies of international institutions such as the World Bank, the practices of private businesses and entire industries, and the behavior of individuals and society as a whole.[9]

POLITICAL PARTIES

In Latin America political parties have often been only one set of groups among several, probably no more (and perhaps less) important than the army or the economic oligarchy. Elections were not the only legitimate route to power, nor were the parties themselves particularly strong or well organized. They were important actors in the political process in some of the more democratic countries, representing the chief means to gain high office. But frequently in other countries the parties were peripheral to the main focal points of power and the electoral arena was considered only one among several. Many Latin Americans have viewed political parties as divisive elements and hence they are not held in high esteem. This increasingly seems to be the case in recent years as candidates use the mass media rather than parties to get elected.

Many of the groups described earlier in this chapter have often joined into political parties in their pursuit of governmental power. As a result, there have been a myriad of political parties in the history of Latin America. Indeed, someone once quipped that to form a political party all you needed was a president, vice president, secretary-treasurer, and rubber stamp. (If times were bad, you could do without the vice president and the secretary-treasurer!) Peter Smith shows that during the period of democracy since 1978 there have been more political parties in most Latin American countries than there were during the 1940–1977 period.[10] Nevertheless, there have been certain characteristics common to parties, although the country chapters that follow show great national variation.

The first parties were usually founded by elite groups in competition with other factions of the elite. Mass demands played only a small role, although campesinos were sometimes mobilized by the party leaders, often to vote as they were instructed or to serve as cannon fodder. In many cases the first cleavage was between individuals in favor of free trade, federalism, and anticlericalism (the liberals) and those who favored protectionism for nascent industry, centralism, and clericalism (the conservatives). In most countries these original party divisions have long since disappeared, replaced by other cleavages.

With accelerating social and economic change in most countries of Latin America, the emergence of new social strata in the 1920s and 1930s led to the founding of new political parties. Some of these attracted the growing middle sectors, which were quite reformist in the early years but later changed as they became part of the system. In other cases new parties were more radical, calling for a basic restructuring of society and including elements from the working classes. Some of these originally radical parties were of international inspiration; most of the countries have had Communist and socialist parties of differing effectiveness and legality. Other radical parties were primarily national ones, albeit with ideological inspiration traceable to Marxism.

One such party, founded in 1923 by the Peruvian Víctor Raúl Haya de la Torre, was the American Popular Revolutionary Alliance (APRA). Although APRA purported to be the beginning of a new international association of like-minded democratic-left individuals in Latin America, this goal was never fully reached. At the same time, inspired by Haya and APRA, a number of similar national parties were founded by young Latin Americans. The most successful APRA-like party was Democratic Action (AD) in Venezuela, but many of the same programs have been advocated by numerous other parties of this type, including the Party of National Liberation (PLN) in Costa Rica and the National Revolutionary Movement (MNR) in Bolivia, as well as parties in Paraguay, the Dominican Republic, Guatemala, Honduras, and Argentina. Only in Venezuela and Costa Rica did the APRA-like parties come to power more than temporarily, and in a much less radical form. They favored liberal democracy, rapid reform, and economic growth. In most cases the APRA-like parties were led by members of the middle sectors, and they received much of their electoral support from the middle and lower classes. APRA came to power in Peru in 1986, although founder Haya was no longer living.

A newer group of political parties was the Christian-Democratic ones, particularly successful in Chile, Venezuela, Costa Rica, Nicaragua, and El Salvador. These parties often call for fundamental reforms but are guided by church teachings and papal encyclicals rather than Marx or Engels, even though they are nondenominational and open to all. The nature of the ideology of these parties varies from country to country.

Other parties in Latin America have been based on the leadership of a few people or even a single one, and hence do not fit into the neat party spectrum just described. Quite often the caudillo was more important than the program of a party. This tradition was seen in Brazil, where Getúlio Vargas founded not one but two official political parties; in Ecuador, where personalistic parties have been strong contenders for the presidency; and in Communist Cuba, where in the 1960s the party was more Castroist than Communist. In Venezuela former military coup leader Hugo Chávez personalized not only a presidency but an entire change of government structure.

The system of co-optation further complicates the attempt at classification. How is one to classify a political party that is traditional in origin and includes at the same time large landowners and the peasants tied to them, as well as trade union members organized by the party with the assistance of segments of the clergy? How does one classify a party such as Mexico's Institutional Revolutionary Party (PRI), which until the mid-1990s made a conscious effort to co-opt and include all politically relevant sectors of the society?

With the increasing number of popularly elected governments in Latin America in the 1990s, political parties generally became more important than before. Democracy exists only if there is real competition between candidates, and throughout the world political parties have been the organizations that have presented such rival candidates. However, in some Latin American countries (Peru and Venezuela, for example) political parties are held in such low esteem that attempts have been made to have democracy without parties. In addition, as pointed out in Chapter 5, political parties have less importance when countries move to delegative democracy.

In addition to the traditional questions posed about parties in Latin America (the number of major parties, their programs and policies, the nature of electoral laws, the relationships between parties and the military), we need to ask questions posed in democracies all over the world. How are parties funded? Do they come up with programs and follow them after the elections? Are voters well informed about political party activities by the mass media? Are those countries that are trying to have democracy without parties having any success?

CONCLUSIONS AND IMPLICATIONS

The preceding discussion has indicated that there have been many politically relevant groups in Latin America and that they use various means to secure and retain political power. Yet at least two other themes should be introduced that tend to complicate the picture.

First, it should be noted that the urban poor outside the labor unions have not been included in the discussion. This shows one of the biases of the system. Since traditionally a necessary first step in attaining political relevance is being organized, potential groups, especially poorly educated and geographically dispersed ones such as peasants and the urban poor, face difficulties in becoming politically relevant because they have trouble organizing themselves or being organized from the outside. The same applies to the new "vulnerable" sector described in Chapter 1. The poor and the vulnerable tend to be the weakest groups in politics, although in most countries they are numerically the largest.

Second, not all politically relevant groups fall into the neat categories of this chapter. Anthony Leeds's research in Brazil has shown (at least in small towns, probably larger cities, and even perhaps the whole nation) a politically more relevant series of groups to be the patronage- and family-based *panelinhas* ("little saucepans").[11] The same kinds of informal family-based networks exist in other countries. These groups are composed of individuals with common interests but different occupations—say, a doctor, a large landowner, surely a lawyer, and a government official. The panelinha at the local level exercises control at that level and endeavors to establish contacts with the panelinha at the state level, which might have contacts with a national panelinha. Of course, at the local level there are rival panelinhas, with contacts with like-minded ones at the state level, which in turn have contacts in the national patronage system as well. As is generally the case with such patrimonial-type relations, all interactions (except those within the panelinhas themselves) are vertical, and one level of panelinha must take care to ally with the winning one at the next higher level if it wants to have political power.

Similar research in other countries has revealed a parallel pattern of informal, elitist, familial, patronage politics. Whether called the panelinha system, as in Brazil, or the camarilla system, as in Mexico, the process and dynamics are the same. The aspiring politician connects himself with an aspiring politician at a higher level, who is connected with an aspirant at a yet higher level, and so forth, up to an aspiring candidate for the presidency. If the person in question becomes president, the various levels of camarillas prosper; if he remains powerful without becoming president, the camarillas continue functioning in expectation of what will take place at the next presidential election; but if the aspiring candidate is disgraced, is dismissed from the official party, or dies, the whole system of various levels of camarillas connected with him disintegrates. The camarilla system operates outside of but overlaps the formal structure of groups and parties described here.

This discussion of panelinhas and camarillas raises the question of whether US-style interest groups and political parties are operating and are important in Latin America, or if they are operating in the same way. The answer is that they are and they aren't. In the larger and better-institutionalized systems, the parties and interest groups are often important and function not unlike their North American or European counterparts. However, in the less institutionalized, personalistic countries of Ecuador, Paraguay, and Central American nations (and even behind the scenes in the larger ones), family groups, cliques, clan alliances, and patronage networks frequently are more important, often disguised behind the appearance of partisan or ideological dispute. One must be careful, therefore, not to minimize the importance of a functional, operational party and interest-group system in some countries, while recognizing that in others it is often the less formal network through which politics is carried out.

4

GOVERNMENT MACHINERY, THE ROLE OF THE STATE, AND PUBLIC POLICY

Neither the classic Marxian categories nor the theory of liberalism gave more than secondary importance to the role of the state. In the Marxian paradigm the state or governmental system is viewed as part of the superstructure, which was shaped, if not determined, by the underlying structure of class relations. In the liberal model the state was generally conceived as a referee, umpiring the competition among interest groups while not itself participating in the game— a kind of black-box intermediary into which the inputs of the system go in the form of competing interests and pressures and from which come outputs or public policies. Neither of these two classic models adequately explains the Latin American systems.

In Latin America the state historically held an importance that it lacks in the classic models. The state was viewed as a powerful and independent agency in its own right, above and frequently autonomous of the class and interest group struggle. Whether in socialist regimes such as Cuba's or capitalist ones such as Brazil's, it was the state and its central leadership that largely determined the shape of the system and its developmental directions.

The state did not merely reflect the class structure but rather, through the control of economic and political resources, itself shaped the class system. The state was viewed as the prime regulator, coordinator, and pacesetter of the entire national system, the apex of the Latin American pyramid from which patronage, wealth, power, and programs flowed. The critical importance of the state in the Latin American nations helps explain why the competition for control was so intense and sometimes violent.

Related to this was the contrasting way citizens of North America and Latin America tended to view government. In North America government has usually been considered something of a necessary evil requiring elaborate checks and balances. Political theory in Iberia and Latin America, in contrast, viewed government as good, natural, and necessary for the welfare of society. If government was good, there was little reason to limit or put checks and balances on it. Hence, before we fall into the trap of condemning Latin America for its powerful autocratic executives, subservient parliaments, and weak local government, we must remember the different assumptions on which the Latin American systems are based.

With the neoliberal changes of the 1990s and at present, there has been a change in the procedures about which most of Latin American politics revolve. The fundamental issues are still who controls the state apparatus and the immense power, patronage, and funds at its disposal, and the ongoing efforts of the states or strong presidents to expand their power. However, now there are also issues of how much of the old corporatist structure will be retained, if any; how neoliberal or civil society dominates the political and economic systems; and how the historically powerful role of the state can be harmonized with the new demands for limited government, privatization, and democracy.

THE THEORY OF THE STATE: CONSTITUTIONS AND LEGAL SYSTEMS

After achieving independence early in the nineteenth century, the Latin American nations faced a severe legitimacy crisis. Monarchy was a possibility (and some nations did consider or experiment briefly with monarchical rule), but Latin America had just struggled through years of independence wars to rid itself of the Spanish imperial yoke, during which monarchy had been discredited. Liberalism and republicanism were attractive and seemed the wave of the future, but Latin America had no prior experience with liberal or republican rule.

The solution was ingenious, though often woefully misunderstood. The new nations of Latin America moved to adopt liberal and democratic forms while at the same time preserving many of the organic, elitist, and authoritarian principles of the colonial tradition. The liberal and democratic forms not only provided goals and aspirations toward which society could strive but also helped present a progressive picture to the outside world. But these principles were circumscribed by a series of measures, authoritarian in content, that were truer to the realities and history of the area and to its existing oligarchic power relationships.

Virtually all the Latin American constitutions have provided for the historical three-part division of powers among executive, legislative, and judiciary. However, in practice the three powers are not coequal and were not intended to be. The executive is constitutionally given extensive powers to bypass the legislature, and judicial review until recently has been largely outside the Latin American legal tradition. The same kinds of apparent contradictions exist in other areas. Although one part of the constitution may be devoted to civilian institutions and the traditional three branches of government, another may give the armed forces a higher-order role to protect the nation, preserve internal order, and prevent internal disruption. However, the legislative branch is now increasing in power in many countries.

The same is true of human rights. Even though all the Latin American constitutions contain long lists of human and political rights, these same constitutions also give the executive power to declare a state of siege or emergency, suspend human rights, and rule by decree. The same applies to privilege. Although one section of the constitution may proclaim democratic and egalitarian principles, other parts may give special privileges to the church, the army, or the landed elites, and even while representative and republican precepts are enshrined in one quarter, authoritarian and elitist ones are legitimated in another. Increasingly, however, human rights and democratic precepts are being incorporated into Latin American basic law.

None of this is meant to imply approval of human rights violations or of overthrows of democratic governments; it is only to point out how these have often been perceived differently in Latin America. Hence, the real questions may concern the degrees of military intervention or limits on legislative authority and how and why these actions are taken. It has not simply been a matter of the military usurping the constitution, because it was often the constitution itself that gave the military the right—even the obligation—to intervene in the political process under certain circumstances. Similarly, when human rights violations are reported, we must understand this within the Latin American constitutional and legal tradition as well as our own. Human rights have not been conceived as constitutional absolutes, and frequently there is a constitutional provision for their suspension. Recently, however, human rights as well as democracy in Latin America are being viewed more and more according to universal standards.

The most important issues of Latin American politics involve the dynamics of change and process from both the Latin American and global perspectives. We cannot understand the region if we look only at the liberal and republican side of the Latin American tradition while ignoring the rest, nor should we simply condemn some action from the point of view of the North American constitutional tradition without seeing it in the Latin American context. If the civil and military spheres are not strictly segregated, as in the US tradition, then what are their dynamic relations in Latin America, and what are the causes of military intervention? If strict separation of powers is not seen in the same light in Latin America and if the branches are not equal, what are their respective powers and interrelations? If hierarchy, authority, and special privilege have long been legitimate principles along with democracy and egalitarianism, then how are these reconciled, glossed over, or challenged—and why? And how are these relations all changing as Latin America enters a more democratic era?

The Latin American constitutions are misunderstood in another way that has to do with their sheer number. Focusing on the number of constitutions (some countries have had thirty or more) ignores the fact that in most of the countries a new constitution is generally promulgated whenever a new amendment is added or when a major new interpretation requires official legitimization. The facts are, first, that the Latin American constitutional tradition has been far more stable than the number of constitutions implies, and, second, that in most countries of the area there are only two main constitutional traditions, one more centralized and even authoritarian and the other liberal and democratic, with the trend now increasing toward the democratic side. The many constitutions, then, generally signify the repeated alternations between these two basic traditions, with some variations.

These perspectives on the constitutional tradition also provide hints as to the distinct legal tradition of Latin America. Whereas in the United States laws and constitutions are based on a history and practice derived from British common law, those of Latin America derive from a code-law tradition. This difference has several implications. Where the US legal system is founded on precedent and reinterpretation, the Latin American codes are complete bodies of law, allowing little room for precedent or judicial reinterpretation. The codes are fixed and absolute, embodying a comprehensive framework of operating principles. And, unlike the common-law tradition with its inductive reasoning based on cases, enforcement of the codes implies deductive reasoning: one begins not with facts or cases but with general truth (the codes or constitution), and then one deduces rules or applications for specific circumstances from this truth.

Although it is important not to overstress the point, and although mixed forms exist throughout Latin America, an understanding of the code-law system and its philosophical underpinnings carries us a considerable distance toward understanding Latin American behavior. The truths embodied in the codes, constitutions, and the deductive method have their origins and reflection in the Roman, medieval, and Catholic scholastic tradition. The authoritarian, absolutist nature of the codes also finds reflection in (and helps reinforce) an absolutist, historically authoritarian political culture. The effort to cover all contingencies with one code or to engage in almost constant constitutional engineering to obtain a "perfect" document tends to rule out the logrolling, compromise, informal understandings, and unwritten rules that lie at the heart of US or British political culture. Because courts and judges, in their role as applicators and enforcers of the law rather than creative interpreters of it, are bureaucrats and bureaucratic agencies, they do not enjoy the respect their counterparts in the United States do, thus making judicial review and even an independent judiciary difficult at best. These precepts and practices are changing as Latin America becomes more democratic and as US legal precepts are incorporated into Latin American law.

EXECUTIVE-LEGISLATIVE-JUDICIAL RELATIONS

Power in the Latin American systems has historically been concentrated in the executive branch, specifically the presidency. Terms such as *continuismo* (prolonging one's term of office beyond its constitutional limits), *personalismo* (emphasis on the person of the president rather than on the office), and, particularly, *machismo* (strong, manly authority) are all now so familiar that they form part of our own political lexicon. The present-day Latin American executive is heir to an imperial and autocratic tradition stemming from the absolute, virtually unlimited authority of the Spanish and Portuguese crowns. Of course, modern authoritarianism has multiple explanations for its origin (a reaction against earlier mass mobilization by populist and leftist leaders, the result of stresses generated by modernization, and the strategies of civilian and military elites for accelerating development) as well as various forms (caudillistic and more institutionalized arrangements). In any case, the Latin American presidency has long been an imperial presidency in ways that no president of the United States ever conceived.

The formal authority of Latin American executives is extensive. It derives from a president's powers as chief executive, commander in chief, and head of state, as well as from the broad emergency powers to declare a state of siege or emergency, suspend constitutional guarantees, and rule by decree. The presidency has been a chief beneficiary of many twentieth-century changes, among them radio and television, concentrated war-making powers, and broad responsibility for the economy. In addition, many Latin American chief executives serve simultaneously as heads of state and presidents of their party machines. If the potential leader's route to power was the army, the president also has the enormous weight of armed might for use against foreign enemies and domestic foes. Considerable wealth, often generated because the lines between private and public wealth are not so sharply drawn as in North American political society, may also become an effective instrument of rule.

Perhaps the main difference lies in the fact that the Latin American systems, by tradition and history, are more centralized and executive-oriented than those in the United States. It is around the person occupying the presidency that national life swirls. The president is responsible not only for governance but also for the well-being of society as a whole and is the symbol of the national society in ways that a US president is not. Not only is politics concentrated in the office and person of the president, but it is by presidential favors and patronage that contracts are determined, different clienteles are served, and wealth, privilege, and social position are parceled out. The president is the national patron, replacing the local landowners and caudillos of the past. With both broad appointive powers and wide latitude in favoring friends and those who show loyalty, the Latin American president is truly the hub of the national system. Hence, when a good, able executive is in power, the system works exceedingly well; when this is not the case, the whole system breaks down.

Various gimmicks have been used to try to limit executive authority. Few have worked well. These range from the disastrous results of the experiment with a plural executive (nine-person government by committee) in Uruguay to the varied unsuccessful efforts at parliamentary or semiparliamentary rule in Chile, Brazil, Cuba, and Costa Rica. Constitutional gimmickry has not worked in limiting executive rule because it has been an areawide tradition and cultural pattern that is in effect, not simply some legal article. Spreading democracy in Latin America is now forcing most presidents to work within a constitutional framework.

The role of the congress in such a system has not historically been to initiate or veto laws, much less to serve as a separate and coequal branch of government. The congress's functions can be understood if we begin not with the assumption of an independent branch but with one of an agency that historically has been subservient to the president and, along with the executive, a part of the same organic, integrated state system. The congress's role was thus to give advice and consent to presidential acts (but not much dissent), to serve as a sounding board for new programs, to represent the varied interests of the nation, and to modify laws in some particulars (but not usually to nullify them). The legislature was also a place to bring some new faces into government as well as to pension off old ones, reward political friends and cronies, and ensure the opposition a voice while guaranteeing that it remained a minority. In recent years, however, the congress in several Latin American countries has acquired newfound power and autonomy.

In some countries (Chile, Colombia, Costa Rica) the congress has long enjoyed considerable independence and strength. A few congresses have even gone so far as to defy the executive—and gotten away with it. In 1992–1993, congresses in both Brazil and Venezuela removed the president from office for fiscal improprieties. The congress may serve as a forum that allows the opposition to embarrass or undermine the government, as a means of gauging who is rising and who is falling in official favor, or as a way of weighing the relative strength of the various factions within the regime.

Many of the same comments apply to the courts and court system. First, the court system has not historically been a separate and coequal branch, nor was it intended or generally expected to be. Many Latin American supreme courts would declare a law unconstitutional or defy a determined executive only at the risk of embarrassment and danger to themselves, something the courts have assiduously avoided. Second, within these limits the Latin American court systems have often functioned not entirely badly. Third, the courts, through such devices as the writ of *amparo* (Mexico and Argentina), popular action and *tutela* (Colombia), and *segurança* (Brazil), have played an increasingly important role in controlling and overseeing governmental action, protecting civil liberties, and restricting executive authority even under dictatorial regimes.

The court system had its origins in the Iberian tradition. The chief influences historically were Roman law, Christianity and the Thomistic hierarchy of laws, and the traditional legal concepts of Iberia, most notably the Siete Partidas of Alfonso the Wise. In Latin America's codes, lists of human rights, and hierarchy of courts, the influence of the French Napoleonic Code has been pronounced. In the situation of a supreme court passing judgment (in theory at least) upon the constitutionality of executive or legislative acts, the US inspiration is clear. At present the courts in various countries are increasing in power and beginning to assert themselves, but they often face problems of incompetence, corruption, and lack of adequate training.

It should be remembered, however, that what has made the system work is not so much the legislature or judiciary but the executive. Formally institutionalized limits on executive power, as in the usual checks and balances, are still not extensive and frequently can be bypassed. More significant has been the informal balance of power within the system and the set of generally agreed-upon understandings and rules of the game beyond which even the strongest of Latin American presidents goes only at severe risk to his regime's survival. Nevertheless, the growing importance of congress and courts in many countries is a subject for further study.

LOCAL GOVERNMENT AND FEDERALISM

Federalism in Latin America emerged from exactly the reverse of the situation that existed in the United States. In the United States in 1789 a national government was reluctantly accepted by thirteen self-governing colonies that had never had a central administration. In Latin America, by contrast, a federal structure was adopted in some countries (Argentina, Venezuela, Mexico, Brazil) that had always been centrally administered.

Although these four nations were federal in principle, the central government reserved the right to "intervene" in the states. As the authority of the central government grew during the 1920s and 1930s, its inclination to intervene also increased, thereby often negating the federal principle. Over a long period these major countries were progressively centralized, with virtually all power concentrated in the national capital. Nevertheless, the dynamics of relations and tensions between the central government and its component states and regions, which still have some independent autonomy, make for one of the most interesting political arenas. Recently there have been pressures to decentralize, but in all countries the central state remains dominant.

The Latin American countries are structured after the French system of local government, with virtually all power concentrated in the central government and its ministries, and authority flowing from the top down. Local government is ordinarily administered through the ministry of interior, which is also responsible for the national police. Almost all local officials historically were appointed by the central government and served as its agents at the local level.

Local governments have almost no power to tax or to run local social programs. These activities are generally administered by the central government according to a national plan. This system of centralized rule is also a means of concentrating power in oftentimes weak and uninstitutionalized nations.

Yet even though the theory has been that of a centralized state, the reality in Latin America has always been somewhat different. The Spanish and Portuguese crowns had difficulty enforcing their authority in the interior, which was far away and virtually autonomous. With the withdrawal of the crown early in the nineteenth century, centrifugal tendencies were accelerated. Power drained off into the hands of local landowners or regional caudillos, who competed for control of the national palace. With a weak central state and powerful centrifugal tendencies, a strong de facto system of local rule did emerge in Latin America, contrary to what the laws or constitutions proclaimed.

Thereafter, nation building in Latin America often consisted of two major tendencies: populating and thus "civilizing" the vast empty interior and extending the central government's authority over the national territory. Toward the end of the nineteenth century, national armies and bureaucracies were created to replace the unprofessional armed bands under the local caudillos, national police agencies enforced the central government's authority at the local level, and the collection of customs duties was centralized. Authority became concentrated in the central state, the regional isolation of the *patria chica* broke down as roads and communications grids were developed, and the economy was similarly centralized more under the direction of the state.

In most of Latin America the process of centralization, begun in the 1870s and 1880s, is still going forward. Indeed, that is how development is often defined throughout the area. A developed political system is one in which the central agencies of the state exercise control and regulation over the disparate and centrifugal forces that constitute the system. In many countries this process is still incomplete, so in the vast interior, in the highlands, in diverse Indian communities, and among some groups (such as landowners, large industrialists, the military, and big multinationals), the authority of the central state is still tenuous. Even today isolated areas (especially those in the rugged mountains or tropical jungles) often have little governmental presence. Local strongmen—sometimes guerrillas or drug traffickers—may be more powerful than the national government's representatives. Indeed,

the efforts of the central government to extend its sway over the entire nation constitute one of the main arenas of Latin American politics. Conversely, the local units
(be they regions, towns, parishes, or Indian communities) still attempt to maintain
some degree of autonomy. Centralization and decentralization are often going forward at the same time.

FOURTH BRANCH OF GOVERNMENT:
THE AUTONOMOUS STATE AGENCIES

One of the primary tools in the struggle to centralize power in Latin America from
the 1930s to the 1980s was the government corporation or the autonomous agency.
The growth of these agencies in many ways parallels that of the "alphabet agencies"
in the United States, giving the central government a means to extend its control
into new areas. These agencies became so large and so pervasive that they could be
termed a separate branch of government. Some Latin American constitutions even
recognized them as such.

The proliferation of these agencies was such that in some countries they numbered in the hundreds. Many were regulatory agencies, often with far broader powers than their North American counterparts, with the authority to set or regulate
prices, wages, and production quotas. Others administered vast government corporations, among them steel, mining, electricity, sugar, coffee, tobacco, railroads, utilities, and petrochemicals. Still others were involved in social programs: education,
social security, housing, relief activities, and the like. Many more participated in the
administration of new services that the state had been called upon to perform, such
as national planning, agrarian reform, water supplies, and family planning.

The purposes for which these agencies were set up were diverse. Some, such as
the agrarian reform or family planning agencies, were established as much to please
the US government and to qualify a country for US and World Bank loans as they
were to carry out agrarian reform or family planning. Others were created to bring a
recalcitrant or rebellious economic sector (such as labor or the business community)
under government control and direction. Some were used to stimulate economic
growth and development, to increase government efficiency and hence its legitimacy, or to create a capitalist structure and an officially sanctioned entrepreneurial
class where none had existed before. They also enabled more job seekers to be put on
the public payroll.

The common feature of these myriad agencies was that they tended to serve as
agents of centralization in the historical quest to "civilize" and bring order to what
was, in the past even more than now, a vast, often unruly, nearly empty territory
with strong centrifugal propensities. The growth of these agencies, specifically the
government corporations, meant that the degree of central state control and even
ownership of the means of production increased significantly as well. As a result, it
is a fundamental mistake to think of the Latin American economies as private-en-
terprise-dominated systems. It is not just Cuba that had a large public sector; in fact,
all the Latin American economies were heavily influenced by the state.

This phenomenon had important implications. It meant that the stakes involved
in the issue of control of the central government, with the vast resources available,

were very high. It also implied that very rapid structural change was readily possible. In countries where between 40 and 60 percent of GNP was generated by the public sector and where so much power was concentrated in the central state, the transformation from a state-capitalist to a state-socialist system was relatively easy and could happen almost overnight (as in Cuba, Ecuador, or Venezuela). All that was required was for a left or socialist element to capture the pinnacles of these highly centralized systems.

The growth of all these centralized state agencies had another implication deserving mention. Although established as autonomous and self-governing bodies, the state corporations had in fact become heavily political agencies. They provided a wealth of sinecures, a means to put nearly everyone on the public payroll. They were giant patronage agencies by which one rewarded friends and cronies and found places for (and hence ensured the loyalty or at least neutrality of) the opposition. They also became centers of corruption, often on a massive scale. Depending on the country, 30 to 50 percent of the gainfully employed labor force worked for the government. Many of the agencies were woefully inefficient, and the immense funds involved provided nearly endless opportunities for private enrichment from the great public trough. In performing these patronage and spoils functions, the state agencies preserved the status quo because large numbers of people—indeed, virtually the entire middle class—were dependent upon them for their livelihood and opportunities for advancement. It is not surprising that a significant part of the debt problems faced by many Latin American countries came from state agencies—not the national governments—receiving foreign loans.

Today the Latin American countries are trying to solve the problems of corruption, inefficiency, and overcentralization. With the neoliberal reforms of the 1990s governments reduced the number and role of decentralized agencies. Many that were in productive activities were privatized. In the process the benefits for poorer people in the countries have been reduced, as well as the number of jobs available to be passed out to political supporters. But in the recent economic downturn these state agencies have again been increased in size.

5

THE STRUGGLE FOR DEMOCRACY
IN LATIN AMERICA

In the preceding chapters we have made reference to how Latin America became more democratic after the late 1970s. While we maintain that position, it is important to draw attention to the characteristics of democracy, a term that is really quite complex, and to the difficulties that Latin American countries have had in achieving and maintaining constitutional governments. In this chapter we discuss the ongoing conflict between three models of government in the area: the traditional "living museum" form discussed in Chapter 3, liberal democracy, and a combination of the two called "delegative democracy," a form of populism that at its extreme might better be considered to be semiauthoritarian instead of democratic.

THE DEMOCRATIC WAVE

The 1980s brought remarkable change to the world in general and to Latin America in particular. Communism collapsed in the Soviet Union, which then had elections and disappeared as a political system replaced by a smaller Russia. In some countries of Asia and Africa dictatorships disintegrated and elections ensued. In Latin America the changes might have seemed less dramatic, although in the 1980s military dictatorships ended in Brazil, Ecuador, Bolivia, Argentina, Uruguay, Chile, and several of the Central American countries.

In Nicaragua internationally monitored elections saw the defeat of the candidate of the ruling Sandinista Party; even more remarkable, that revolutionary party allowed the opposition candidate, Violeta Barrios de Chamorro, to take office. In Panama, with the assistance of an armed intervention by the United States, strongman Manuel Antonio Noriega fell and the previously elected Guillermo Endara occupied the presidency. Finally, in Paraguay, Alfredo Stroessner—longest in power of the Latin American caudillos—fell to a military coup, and the coup leaders immediately called for elections. In 2013, of the twenty Latin American countries, only Cuba did not have a democratically elected chief executive, which seemed to suggest that democracy had finally arrived as the dominant political system in Latin America.

THE LATIN AMERICAN CONTEXT FOR DEMOCRACY

As the democratic wave came ashore in Latin America, difficulties arose from six sources: the Iberian tradition and history, the misuse of "democracy" before the 1980s, pockets of underdevelopment, serious inequities of income distribution, the aftereffects of recent civil wars, and the absence of governments that could effectively implement policies for the nation as a whole.

The Iberian Tradition and History

Constructing and maintaining a democracy is not an easy matter anywhere. As the Latin American countries faced a possible democratic future, difficulties arose from a political tradition unfavorable to limited government, as shown in Chapters 1 and 2.

It might be anticipated that the groups that benefited from the old system would resist democracy, and if Latin American history of the 1980s and 1990s is any guide, the two major groups uncomfortable with the new rules of the game were the military and the economic elite. Although evidence suggested that the civilian elites now saw democracy as the best hope for stability, it still seemed possible that if elected governments in Latin America faced serious economic difficulties, some members of the military would think of the traditional way of disposing of misbehaving governments—the military coup. There were two attempts to overthrow the elected president of Venezuela in the early 1990s, and the *New York Times* reported in January 1994 that many Brazilians were ready for the military to return to power because of economic problems and rampant corruption among civilian politicians. With the passing of each year the probability of a military coup seemed lower. However, in the first five years of the new millennium coups occurred in Ecuador, Bolivia, and Paraguay.

Previous Misuse of Democracy

Some Latin American countries called themselves "democracies" before 1989, although they were not in fact. Various Latin American dictators, including Anastasio Somoza Debayle in Nicaragua and Rafael Trujillo in the Dominican Republic, had already shown that a nice electoral facade could make a country appear to be democratic.[1]

Within a cultural tradition that favored strong leadership more than institutional constraints on power, the region has often had elections without having democracy. Historically this came about for four basic reasons: the limitation of suffrage on gender, educational, or economic grounds; the restriction of voting rights of parties opposing the one in power; the limitation of the power of the elected executive by some other body, usually the military or foreign governments and multilateral institutions; and excessive executive power. But even if those four conditions are taken care of, a consolidated democracy means much more than elections.

In the first case, suffrage was sometimes restricted by either literacy or property ownership. Of course, in many countries the landless and uneducated tended to be indigenous people, blacks, mulattos, and mestizos, but there were also many whites who had the misfortune to fall into that category. As for the question of female suffrage, enfranchisement of women tended to come later in Latin American countries than in the United States. However, by the 1960s there were no Latin American countries in which suffrage was not at least theoretically open to all.

Second, many Latin American countries denied the vote to some on the basis of political loyalties. At times this has been done by not allowing members of one political party to vote while allowing members of another the prerogative to vote more than once (Colombia in the 1950s). In other cases the ability to vote as one pleases was constrained when the voting process was watched closely by the military (Venezuela in the early 1950s). Likewise, there have been instances when press freedoms were so restricted that opposition parties could not effectively get their views out to the electorate (Nicaragua and El Salvador in the 1980s; the opposition to Hugo Chávez stated that the same happened in 2012 in Venezuela).

Third, there were countries in which all citizens apparently had the right to vote and there were few constraints on any candidate during the electoral process. However, afterward the elected president's policy options were greatly restricted by the military. Hence in the 1960s the Guatemalan military allegedly informed President Julio César Méndez Montenegro that he could do anything that did not affect either the military or the large landowners. In the 1990s the Sandinistas in Nicaragua placed similar restrictions on Violeta Barrios de Chamorro, protecting Sandinista labor unions and the military upon agreeing to let her take the presidency after her election in 1990. Sometimes the constraint might come from a foreign government or international organization.

In addition, while internally very democratic in some ways, some Latin American governments were constrained in their economic policies, especially those having to do with foreign businesses, by the US government, the World Bank, the IMF, or the combination of the three. The most notable instance in the 1970s was the government of Salvador Allende in Chile.

After the 1990s the outside constraints had more to do with the continuation of democracy. In 1992, for example, the United States reduced aid to Peru after President Alberto Fujimori suspended the congress and the judicial system. This policy was tempered in the new millennium, especially after terrorism became a priority of the US government. However, the Organization of American States (OAS) used its influence at times to maintain democracy, as seen in the cases of Ecuador and Paraguay. The Inter-American Democratic Charter, passed by the OAS in 2001, recognized that the countries of the region might confront critical political situations that could lead them to request OAS intervention. After assessing the situation, representatives of the OAS member states can collectively take the necessary diplomatic initiatives, with the support of the general secretariat, to prevent or confront an alteration of the constitutional regime, thus protecting or restoring democratic institutions.

Another aberration of democracy in some elective governments was the excessive power of the president, with no real separation of powers or checks and balances. Hernando de Soto and Deborah Orsini analyzed decision making in Peru before the presidency of Alberto Fujimori (although their analysis could have described other Latin American countries as well), commenting that "the only element of democracy in Peru today is the electoral process, which gives Peruvians the privilege of choosing a dictator every five years." Once in power, the president made decisions in a vacuum, enacting 134,000 new rules and regulations over a period of five years (or about 106 a day), with no checks on his power.[2] The gridlock of this system led Fujimori to disband congress and the courts in 1992, leading to international condemnation for ending "democracy." Guatemalan president Jorge Serrano tried to do the same in 1993, although in this case he failed because of a lack of support from the armed forces, which removed him from power. Both cases show that even though excessive executive power detracts from democracy in Latin America, on occasion chief executives have attempted to increase their already overwhelming power.

Traditionally almost all Latin American countries had constitutional ways for the president to acquire more power. These stipulations allow presidents to decree policy in a "state of siege" or "state of emergency," in many cases without conferring with the congress or having the decrees subject to judicial review. Although the democratic idea of limited power is found in the constitutions of Latin America, so also are means for the chief executive to rule with almost unlimited authority.

Pockets of Underdevelopment and Inequities of Income Distribution

Although very modern in many ways, all Latin American countries have large pockets of people living in abject poverty. The neoliberal economic changes—including the end of protective tariffs, the privatization of state-owned industries, and the reduction of support for the poor—that occurred in the area in the last decade of the twentieth century increased, at least in the short run, the number of poor people, particularly through the unemployment that resulted when previously protected industries went bankrupt. In addition, some people with slightly higher living standards, such as owners of small businesses and bureaucrats, opposed further change because they benefited from the traditional state-capitalist economic system.

These socioeconomic inequalities seemed to some to make democracy unlikely in Latin America. Robert Wesson, for example, after listing the problems of ethnic divisiveness, low standards of living, disdain for politics, a weak or unfree press, poorly organized and narrow parties, unfair elections, politically powerful armies, weak institutions of higher education, traditions of strong leadership, the paternalistic state, and clientelist politics, argued that "one basic condition may account for most of the rest, and it is probably a sufficient condition to explain the difficulty of democracy in Latin America, although by no means the sole cause. This is inequality, the separation of the rich from poor or top from bottom, of educated from ignorant or illiterate, or refined and proud elite from despised masses."[3] The difficulty that this inequality creates for democracy is that "to expect the cultured and well-off would accede to major social changes because they are outnumbered and outvoted in elections of dubious honesty by the ignorant and impoverished—many of whom are undernourished and diseased—is unrealistic. That would require a society of saints with an unlikely degree of loyalty to democratic principles."[4]

Ironically, since neoliberals see democracy and economic reform as interdependent, the poor and others who benefited from the mercantilist system may use the new democratic political regime to elect presidents and members of national congresses who are opposed to neoliberalism. This happened in the elections of Hugo Chávez in Venezuela, Evo Morales in Bolivia, and Daniel Ortega in Nicaragua, among others.

The Legacy of Civil Wars

In many Latin American countries thousands have died in recent civil wars. Tension exists between conflict and consensus in any democracy, by its nature a system of institutionalized competition for power. As Larry Diamond argues, "Hence the paradox: Democracy requires conflict—but not too much; competition there must be, but only within carefully defined and universally accepted boundaries. Cleavage must be tempered by consensus."[5] Many Latin American countries have suffered years of civil war before learning this lesson. Nowhere has the problem of conflict been more serious than in Mexico (although not since the 1920s) and Colombia, where there have been bloody civil wars between parties. Other countries have had civil wars at the beginning of their independent history but then moved on to less violent modes of competition. In the 1960s Marxist guerrilla groups chose armed conflict instead of electoral competition, and the resulting civil wars created a series of related problems for Latin American democracies.

It is especially difficult for a democratic government to deal with revolutionaries who have different ethical standards. As Gustavo Gorriti has argued about countries with guerrilla challenges, "a well-planned insurgency can severely test the basic assumptions of the democratic process. While they provoke and dare the elected regime to overstep its own laws in response to their aggression, the insurgents strive to paint the very process they are trying to destroy as a sham. If ensnared in such perverse dynamics, most Third World democracies will find their legitimacy eroding, and may eventually cease to be democracies altogether."[6] Democracy is abandoned altogether when a government under this pressure becomes involved in a "dirty war." A number of countries have had such wars, in which thousands of people have been murdered or simply "disappeared"—Argentina and Chile in the 1970s, El Salvador and Guatemala in the 1980s, Peru in the 1980s and 1990s, and for at least the last fifty years in Colombia. In these cases the government, or at least the military, has been involved. Once the dirty war is over and democracy is restored, the question becomes to what extent violators of human rights in the previous period should be punished. Punishing the guilty (from the military, predominantly) may in turn threaten the democracy. As did Raúl Alfonsín in Argentina, many civilian presidents may pardon putative violators of human rights rather than risk making the military subsequently so angry as to intervene again.

Although during the 1960s most Latin American countries faced guerrilla threats, by 2013 only in Colombia were they still numerous. The Marxist guerrilla group Sendero Luminoso (Shining Path) still existed in Peru, but with much less importance than before, and guerrillas still were present in the southern part of Mexico. Where civil wars have only recently ended, the difficult task is to achieve consensus among erstwhile enemies. As has become apparent in El Salvador and Colombia, even though a government may grant amnesty to guerrillas, the people who suffered at their hands may not be ready to forgive and forget.

Lack of Ability to Govern

As Charles Tilly has argued, "No democracy can work if the state lacks the capacity to supervise democratic decision making and put its results into practice."[7] Although the degree of state weakness varies in Latin America, few governments have been able to enforce their decisions throughout their countries. As relatively poor countries with serious problems of transportation and communication, many Latin American countries have never been able to ensure the rule of law for the entire nation. Although they might be quite democratic in the way in which their leaders are elected and their laws are written, at best those elements govern only the major cities.

This weakness of government was exacerbated in Latin American countries with the emergence of the drug trade in the 1970s. Especially affected in this regard were Colombia, Peru, Bolivia, and Mexico. In Peru the Sendero Luminoso along with the drug traffickers of the Upper Huallaga Valley destabilized politics for ten years. Mexico, given its size and apparent stability, at times seemed less affected. However, its location makes it a transit point to the United States, and drug interests have infiltrated its government as much as they have in Colombia. By 2008 Mexican drug groups had replaced Colombian ones as the chief suppliers to the market in the United States. Conflict between rival groups made murder and kidnapping rates in Mexico sadly reminiscent of those in Colombia in the 1980s.

THE PERIOD OF DEMOCRACY SINCE 1978

At no time in history have the Latin American countries had elective presidents as frequently as they have since the democratic wave began in 1978. However, this does not mean that liberal democracy has arrived in all the Latin American countries. In addition, delegative democracy has replaced the liberal variety in some countries.

Liberal Democracy

Elections are not the only criterion for liberal democracy, with Philippe Schmitter and Terry Lynn Karl suggesting the ten characteristics shown in Table 5.1.[8] First, constitutionally elected officials must effectively control government decisions. Second, the elections for those officials must be frequent and fair. Coercion cannot exist on a large scale if the criterion of free elections is going to be met. Third, almost all adults must have the right to vote in these elections, and fourth, they must have the right to run in them. There must be no danger in either voting or running for public office.

Fifth, citizens must have the right to express themselves about politics without fear of punishment. Sixth, they also must have the right to seek alternative sources of information, and such sources must exist and be protected by law. This suggests that the media must be allowed to publish and broadcast, unlike many cases in the past when states of siege or emergency have led to censorship.

Seventh, citizens must have the right to form independent organizations and groups, including political parties, civil societies, and interest groups. The stipulation of "independent" suggests that the government should not favor certain interest groups over others (as was characteristic of the groups that had been successfully co-opted), and should neither reward some with financial assistance nor punish others by using violence against them.

Table 5.1 Characteristics of Liberal Democracy

1. Constitutionally elected officials must effectively control government decisions.
2. The elections for those officials must be frequent and fair.
3. Almost all adults must have the right to vote in these elections.
4. Almost all adults must have the right to run in them.
5. Citizens must have the right to express themselves about politics without fear of punishment.
6. Citizens must have the right to seek alternative sources of information, and such sources must exist and be protected by law.
7. Citizens must have the right to form independent organizations and groups, including political parties, civil societies, and interest groups.
8. Officials who are elected must be able to govern constitutionally without the veto power of unelected officials, such as the military.
9. Officials must be able to act independently without outside constraints.
10. Power must not be controlled by one branch of government alone; rather, there should be a system of checks and balances.

Source: Philippe C. Schmitter and Terry Lynn Karl, "What Democracy Is . . . And Is Not," *Journal of Democracy 2*, no. 3 (Summer 1991): 75–88.

Eighth, the officials who are elected must be able to govern constitutionally without the veto power of unelected officials, such as the military. Ninth, the same officials must be able to act independently without outside constraints. Tenth, power must not be controlled by one branch of government alone; rather, there should a system of checks and balances.

In addition, some argue that a full democracy should also have a considerable degree of egalitarianism, a sense that all people are full citizens, not victims of class, racial, or gender discrimination. Such a democracy should offer a sense of participation, social and economic programs that are more or less just, and a certain civic consciousness that all people deal with each other in fair, impartial, and just ways. So although some of the Latin American countries may have the institutional apparatus of democracy, in many respects they are still far from having democratic societies.[9]

A democracy is considered "consolidated" when people see it as the only game in town. This means that no matter how bad things get, the only option is to behave in a democratic way—that is, wait for the next election, contact representatives in government, and use (if available) other constitutional methods such as recall elections. It does not mean occupying key roads and bridges (as happened in Argentina in 2000–2002), using the military to overthrow a president who is disliked (Ecuador several times in the first decade of the new millennium), or using economic power to get rid of a president or at least pressure him to change policies (Venezuela in 2002).

Chile, Uruguay, and Costa Rica are the only three Latin American countries who have met these criteria during the entire period, although Argentina, Brazil, the Dominican Republic, and Mexico after the 2000 presidential elections have made notable progress toward that ideal.

Delegative Democracy

The recent wave of democratization in Latin America demonstrates a paradox. On one hand, there have been more elective presidents in more nations than ever before. For the first time there is near universal suffrage. But on the other hand, democratic practices have been limited and shallow. Scholars have come up with descriptors such as "low-intensity democracy" and "schizophrenic democracy." The most common, however, has been "delegative democracy." All suggest that the initial euphoria surrounding the demise of military dictatorships has changed to a growing dissatisfaction regarding the ambiguous character and quality of new civilian regimes.[10]

Guillermo O'Donnell's idea of a delegative democracy includes four major characteristics (see Table 5.2). First, the president is "the embodiment of the nation and the main custodian of the national interest, which it is incumbent upon him to define." Second, "what he does in government does not need to bear any resemblance to what he said or promised during the electoral campaign—he has been authorized to govern as he sees fit."

Third, "since this paternal figure has to take care of the whole nation, it is almost obvious that his support cannot come from a party; his political basis has to be a *movement*, the supposedly vibrant overcoming of the factionalism and conflicts that parties bring about. Typically, and consistently, winning presidential candidates in [delegative democracies] present themselves as above all *parties*, i.e., both political parties and organized interests. How could it be otherwise for somebody who claims to embody the whole of the nation? In this view, other institutions—such as congress and the judiciary—are nuisances that come attached to the domestic and international advantages of being a democratically elected president."[11]

While such executive domination is far from new in Latin America, in the first decade of the new millennium liberal democracies became delegative ones in Venezuela (Hugo Chávez), Bolivia (Evo Morales), Ecuador (Rafael Correa), and, perhaps to a lesser degree, Colombia (Álvaro Uribe). In all cases necessary constitutional changes were accepted by the voters through referendums or by the national congress through constitutionally mandated procedures.

Some scholars, however, think that the governments are not "democratic" in any way, not even a delegative one. In a study of Venezuela and Paraguay Paul Sondrol argued that calling them "democracies" with modifiers failed to capture their authoritarian nature and the unlikelihood that they would become democracies over time.[12]

These are, Sondrol says, democratically disguised dictatorships, a particular regime type whereby formal democratic institutions both mask and legitimate de facto authoritarian political control. They have four major characteristics: (1) blocking mechanisms that limit electoral transfers of power, (2) democratic trappings and weak institutionalization, (3) a policy disconnect between economic and political liberalization, controlled and manipulated by regime elites, and (4) limits to civil society empowerment.

Sondrol concludes that Venezuela's Hugo Chávez represented the new type of revolutionary, messianic strongman, elected by citizens "with eyes wide open." Voters were "alienated by traditional politics and lured by simple, appealing, populist solutions to cut through the red tape of confusing, corrupt, and tedious pluralist

Table 5.2   Guillermo O'Donnell's Characteristics of Delegative Democracy

1. The President is the embodiment of the nation and the main custodian of the national interest, which it is incumbent upon him to define.
2. What he does in government does not need to bear any resemblance to what he said or promised during the electoral campaign; he has been authorized to govern as he sees fit.
3. Since this paternal figure has to take care of the whole nation, it is almost obvious that his support cannot come from a party; his political basis has to be a movement, the supposedly vibrant overcoming of the factionalism and conflicts that parties bring about.
4. In this view other institutions, such as congress and the judiciary, are nuisances that come attached to the domestic and international advantages of being a democratically elected President.
5. Accountability to those institutions or to other private or semiprivate organizations appears as an unnecessary impediment to the full authority that the president has been delegated to exercise.

Source: Guillermo O'Donnell, "Delegative Democracy?" Kellogg Institute Working Paper #192 (April 1993), http://kellogg.nd.edu/publications/workingpapers/WPS/172.pdf, 7.

politics." Therefore, "perhaps it is time to stop thinking in terms of the 'democratic transitions' paradigm, and to start calling these semi-dictatorships what they really are." The fourth consecutive election of Venezuelan president Hugo Chávez in October 2012 suggested that Sondrol is correct, while Chávez's death from cancer in 2013 showed the inherent weakness of a regime built on one person.

CONCLUSIONS

As the following chapters of this book demonstrate, in many Latin American countries the old system of "living museum" politics, liberal democracy, and delegative democracy coexist. Some of those countries might best be called semiauthoritarian. To the extent that the living museum system exists, the paradigm suggested by Charles Anderson (and presented here in Chapter 3) is still useful. If liberal democracy, delegative democracy, or semiauthoritarianism has become the dominant system, new paradigms for interpreting Latin America must be developed. In assessing which system prevails in a country, the factors presented in Tables 5.1 and 5.2 will be helpful.

Two concerns should be kept in mind as one evaluates the politics of the Latin American nations. First, the systems are very dynamic, with change occurring constantly. A valid conclusion made on one date might soon change. Second, judgment about the factors in Tables 5.1 and 5.2 is very difficult; many times sources in the United States do not include adequate information, and in Latin American sources (many are readily available on the Internet) often information from both governments and oppositions is intentionally reported incorrectly.

Both concerns were clearly shown in Honduras in mid-2009. On the face of it the country abandoned liberal democracy and returned to the living museum system when the military overthrew President Manuel Zelaya. Both the United Nations and the Organization of American States condemned this, while the Obama administration called for Zelaya's return to office. Some even called this a "return to banana republic politics."

This case might seem straightforward: a president who had been elected in a liberal democracy tried to change his country to a delegative democracy, just as Chávez had in Venezuela or Correa in Ecuador. The military as the representative of the living museum system took over power.

However, the matter was not quite that simple. The Honduran constitution limited a president to a single four-year term; Zelaya wished to remain in power and change the country into a delegative democracy. He wanted to have a "consultation"—a vote of the people. The electoral commission denied him that right, and the supreme court declared such a vote to be unconstitutional. Nevertheless, President Zelaya ordered the armed forces to organize the consultation. They refused and instead overthrew him. After the supreme court removed him from his post, the congress, following the constitution, elected Roberto Micheletti as the new president.

The Honduran case demonstrates the fragility of democracy in some Latin American countries. It also shows that aspects of the living museum model—a strong executive and military intervention—could reappear.

Notes

CHAPTER 1

1. Robert C. Williamson, *Latin American Societies in Transition* (Westport, CT: Praeger, 1997), 127.

2. Francisco H. G. Ferreira, Julian Messina, Jamele Rigolini, Luis-Felipe López-Calva, Maria Ana Lugo, and Renos Vakis, *Economic Mobility and the Rise of the Latin American Middle Class* (Washington, DC: World Bank, 2013), 1–2.

CHAPTER 2

1. David Collier and Ruth Berins Collier, *Shaping the Political Arena: Critical Junctures, the Labor Movement, and Regime Dynamics in Latin America* (Princeton, NJ: Princeton University Press, 1991).

CHAPTER 3

1. Charles W. Anderson, *Politics and Economic Change in Latin America: The Governing of Restless Nations* (New York: Van Nostrand, 1967), especially Chapter 4.

2. See David Collier, ed., *The New Authoritarianism in Latin America* (Princeton, NJ: Princeton University Press, 1979).

3. Peter H. Smith, *Democracy in Latin America: Political Change in Comparative Prospective* (New York: Oxford University Press, 2005), 103.

4. On Boff: http://leonardoboff.com/site-eng/lboff.htm. On Sobrino: Congregation for the Doctrine of the Faith, "Notification on the Works of Father Jon Sobrino, SJ," 2006, *Zenit: The World Seen from Rome*, www.zenit.org/article-19147?l=english (accessed August 10, 2013).

5. José Nun, "The Middle Class Military Coup," in *The Politics of Conformity in Latin America*, ed. Claudio Véliz (London: Oxford University Press, 1967), 66–118.

6. This section is based on Donna Lee Van Cott, "Latin America: Indigenous Movements," *Encyclopedia of Nationalism*, vol. 2 (San Diego: Academic Press, 2000).

7. Mala N. Htun, "Women's Political Participation, Representation, and Leadership in Latin America," Women's Leadership Conference of the Americas issue brief, www.iadiaglo .org/htunpol.html (accessed September 22, 1999).

8. Mayra Buvinic and Vivian Roza, "Women, Politics and Democratic Prospects in Latin America," Inter-American Development Bank, December 2004.

9. This section is based on suggestions from Dr. Vanessa Gray.

10. Smith, *Democracy in Latin America*, 176.

11. Anthony Leeds, "Brazilian Careers and Social Structure: A Case History and Model," *American Anthropologist* 66 (1964): 1321–1347.

CHAPTER 5

1. Mario Vargas Llosa, "The Culture of Liberty," in *The Global Resurgence of Democracy*, ed. Larry Diamond and Mark F. Plattner (Baltimore: Johns Hopkins University Press, 1993), 86.

2. Hernando de Soto and Deborah Orsini, "Overcoming Under-Development," *Journal of Democracy* 2, no. 2 (Spring 1991): 106.

3. Robert Wesson, *Democracy in Latin America: Promise and Problems* (New York: Praeger, 1982), 125.

4. Ibid., 130–131.

5. Larry Diamond, "Three Paradoxes of Democracy," *Journal of Democracy* 1, no. 3 (Summer 1990): 49.

6. Gustavo Gorriti, "Latin America's Internal Wars," *Journal of Democracy* 2, no. 1 (Winter 1991): 86–87.

7. Charles Tilly, *Democracy* (Cambridge: Cambridge University Press, 2007), 15.

8. Calling anything with elections "democracy," despite fraud, was labeled "electoralism" by Philippe C. Schmitter and Terry Lynn Karl, "What Democracy Is . . . And Is Not," *Journal of Democracy* 2, no. 3 (Summer 1991): 78.

9. A study of Latin America that added other criteria to the institutional ones of democracy was Jorge I. Domínguez and Abraham F. Lowenthal, eds., *Constructing Democratic Governance: Latin America and the Caribbean in the 1990s* (Baltimore: Johns Hopkins University Press, 1996).

10. Kenneth M. Roberts, *Deepening Democracy? The Modern Left and Social Movements in Chile and Peru* (Stanford: Stanford University Press, 1998), 1.

11. Guillermo O'Donnell, "Delegative Democracy?" Kellogg Institute Working Paper 192 (April 1993), http://kellogg.nd.edu/publications/workingpapers/WPS/172.pdf, 7.

12. Paul Sondrol, "Semi-Authoritarianism in Latin America," http://citation.allacademic .com//meta/p_mla_apa_research_citation/0/9/8/8/8/pages98880/p98880-1.php, 1–2.

Suggested Readings for Chapters 1–5

Anderson, Charles. *Politics and Economic Change in Latin America: The Governing of Restless Nations*. New York: Van Nostrand, 1967.

Burkholder, Mark, and Lyman Johnson. *Colonial Latin America*. New York: Oxford University Press, 2002.

Bushnell, David, and Neill Macauley. *The Emergence of Latin America in the Nineteenth Century*. New York: Oxford University Press, 2002.

Camp, Roderic. *Democracy in Latin America*. Wilmington, DE: Scholarly Resources, 1999.

Collier, David. *The New Authoritarianism in Latin America*. Princeton, NJ: Princeton University Press, 1980.

Collier, David, and Ruth Collier. *Shaping the Political Arena: Critical Junctures, the Labor Movement, and Regime Dynamics in Latin America.* Princeton, NJ: Princeton University Press, 1991.

Dominguez, Jorge, and Abraham Lowenthal. *Constructing Democratic Governance.* Baltimore: Johns Hopkins University Press, 1996.

Evans, Peter. *Dependent Development.* Princeton, NJ: Princeton University Press, 1979.

Gwynne, Robert, and Cristóbal Kay, eds. *Latin America Transformed.* London: Arnold, 1999.

Kryzanek, Michael J. *U.S.-Latin American Relations.* Westport, CT: Praeger, 2008.

Langley, Lester. *The Americas in the Modern Age.* New Haven, CT: Yale University Press, 2005.

Levine, Daniel. *Religion and Politics in Latin America.* Princeton, NJ: Princeton University Press, 1981.

Lewis, Paul. *Authoritarian Regimes in Latin America.* Blue Ridge Summit, PA: Rowman and Littlefield, 2005.

Lorrain, Felipe, and Marcelo Selowsky. *The Public Sector and the Latin American Crisis.* San Francisco: ICS Press, 1979.

Loveman, Brian. *Por La Patria: Politics and the Armed Forces in Latin America.* Wilmington, DE: Scholarly Resources, 1999.

Malloy, James. *Authoritarianism and Corporatism in Latin America.* Pittsburgh: University of Pittsburgh Press, 1977.

McClintock, Cynthia. *Revolutionary Movements in Latin America.* Washington, DC: US Institute of Peace Press, 1998.

McDonald, Ronald, and Mark Ruhl. *Party Politics and Elections in Latin America.* Boulder, CO: Westview Press, 1989.

Needler, Martin. *The Problems of Democracy in Latin America.* Lexington, MA: Lexington Books, 1987.

Pastor, Robert. *Democracy in the Americas.* New York: Holmes and Meier, 1989.

Peeler, John. *Building Democracy in Latin America.* Boulder, CO: Lynne Rienner, 1998.

Skidmore, Tom, and Peter Smith. *Modern Latin America.* New York: Oxford, 2001.

Smith, Peter. *Democracy in Latin America.* Oxford: Oxford University Press, 2005.

Veliz, Claudio. *The Centralist Tradition in Latin America.* Princeton: Princeton University Press, 1980.

Wiarda, Howard J. *Authoritarianism and Corporatism in Latin America—Revisited.* Gainesville: University of Florida Press, 2004.

———. The *Soul of Latin America.* New Haven, CT: Yale University Press, 2001.

Wynia, Gary. *The Politics of Latin American Development.* Cambridge: University of Cambridge Press, 1990.

PART II

The Political Systems of South America

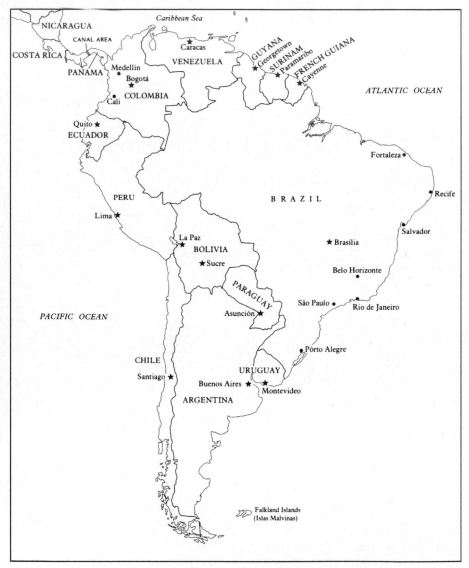

SOUTH AMERICA

6

ARGENTINA IN THE TWENTY-FIRST CENTURY

Linda Chen

INTRODUCTION

As the second-largest economy in South America, just after Brazil, Argentina is an interesting study in economic policy making and weak political institutionalization. The country ushered in the twenty-first century in political and economic turmoil. The neoliberal reforms of the 1990s had failed and Argentina's economy was in free fall. By the end of 2001, Argentina had experienced a succession of three presidents and defaulted on its external debt of US$93 billion, at the time the largest sovereign default in history. Political stability returned in 2003 with the election of Peronista Néstor Kirchner, who succeeded in arresting the economic decline by refusing to adhere to International Monetary Fund prescriptions. Under his administration, the economy grew, a number of social welfare bills were enacted, and a political dynasty that included his wife, Cristina, was in the making. In the 2007 elections, Néstor stepped aside in favor of his wife, who easily won the presidential elections. Were it not for Néstor's untimely death from a heart attack in 2010, he might very well have run for another term as president. Instead, Cristina Fernández de Kirchner easily won reelection in 2011.

HISTORICAL BACKGROUND

Argentina's history has been shaped by conflict and division. The period after independence from Spain was characterized by conflicts over whether Argentina should

BOLIVIA

Pocitos

JUJUY

San Salvador
de Jujuy

SALTA

Salta

San Miguel de Tucumán

TUCUMÁN
CATAMARCA

Catamarca

La Rioja

LA RIOJA

SAN JUAN

San Juan

Mendoza

San
Luis

SAN
LUIS

MENDOZA

Bardas Blancas

NEUQUÉN

Zapala

Neuquén

San Carlos de Bariloche

CHUBUT

SANTA CRUZ

Ushuaia

PACIFIC
OCEAN

CHILE

Río Pilcomayo

PARAGUAY

FORMOSA

Río Bermejo

CHACO

Santiago
del Estero

Resistencia

SANTIAGO
DEL ESTERO

SANTA
FE

Río Salado

CÓRDOBA

Córdoba

Santa Fe

Villa María

Río Cuarto

Junín

BUENOS AIRES

Santa Rosa

LA PAMPA

Río Colorado

Bahía Blanca

Río Negro

RÍO NEGRO

Viedma

Río Chubut

Rawson

Comodoro Rivadavia

Caleta Olivia

San Julián

Río Gallegos

BRAZIL

Formosa

Posadas

Puerto Iguazu

MISIONES

Río Alto Paraná

Corrientes

CORRIENTES

Río Paraná

Uruguay

Paso de los Libres

ENTRE
RÍOS

Paraná

Concepción del Uruguay

Rosario

Ibicuy

URUGUAY

Buenos Aires

La Plata

Río de la Plata

Azul

Tres
Arroyos

Mar del Plata

Necochea

ATLANTIC OCEAN

Falkland Islands (Islas Malvinas)
(Administered by U.K.,
claimed by Argentina)

0   100   200   300   400   500 Miles

0   100 200 300 400 500 Kilometers

ARGENTINA

have a centralized government centered on Buenos Aires and free trade, as represented by Bernardino Rivadavia and his Unitary Party, or a decentralized system whereby the interior provinces would be free to run their own affairs under a system of federalism. Resolution of this conflict would take place under Juan Manuel de Rosas, who established a federalist system with Buenos Aires as its center. A powerful rancher who represented the cattle interests of the interior, Rosas ruled with an iron fist and personified the image of the caudillo (military strongman) that characterized power relations in Latin America in that era. He was ousted in 1852 by a combination of rebellious rival caudillos and exiles.

From 1852 to 1916, Argentina was governed by a liberal oligarchy that adopted a constitution patterned closely after that of the United States. Its liberal principles included the separation of powers, checks and balances, the right to private property, and guarantees of freedom of speech and of the press. It also encouraged the immigration of Europeans. In practice, the liberal oligarchy controlled electoral outcomes and governed by fraud and corruption. Economically, foreign trade grew rapidly, and the profits were plowed into domestic developments: roads, bridges, ports, and public education. New methods of agriculture were adopted, cattle breeding and pasturage were improved, and new lines of production were introduced, including grain growing and sheep raising. Foreign capital invested in the railroads, telephone and telegraph lines, gas and electric power, refrigerated steamships, modern meatpacking, and modern sanitation. With the commercial boom also came an increase in banking, insurance, and construction. The port of Buenos Aires became one of the busiest in the world, and the city was transformed from a dull colonial outpost into a modern European-style capital whose broad boulevards and imposing buildings reminded travelers of Paris.

The twentieth century saw the rise of mass politics in Argentina as the agricultural oligarchy's political dominance was contested by the emergence of urban middle-class sectors and a huge working-class population, fueled by immigration mostly of southern European descent. By 1914, Argentina's population had mushroomed to 7.8 million; Buenos Aires had grown to a city of 1.5 million, with fully half of the population being foreign-born. New political parties formed (the most prominent of which was the Radical Civic Union, UCR), a universal suffrage law was passed, the secret ballot was instituted, and labor unions representing socialist, syndicalist, and anarchist persuasions proliferated. The UCR, representing middle-class business interests, would dominate the politics of Argentina from the early twentieth century through the Great Depression. The rise of urban middle-class interests would clash with growing labor union activism.

The era of the Great Depression and the 1930s brought profound changes to Argentina. With the economic dislocation brought about by declining demand and prices for Argentina's commodity exports, the political situation destabilized. Responding to oligarchic interests and their own sense of nationalist pride, a new political era began for Argentina as the military entered domestic politics and a new political phenomenon, Peronism, seized the day.

The Peronista Watershed

The political scene in Argentina in the early 1940s was dominated by the external events of World War II. The army, many of whose officers were German-trained, supported an alliance with the Axis powers. A group of high-level officers conspired to implant a government modeled after Mussolini's fascist regime in Italy. Calling themselves the Group of United Officers (GOU), they successfully took power in 1943. Among its members was a little-known army colonel named Juan Domingo Perón. When the events of World War II made it clear that the Axis powers were losing, the military establishment in power began a search for an exit strategy.

Meanwhile, in 1943 Perón had asked to take over the management of the Secretariat of Labor and Social Welfare. Previously he had served as minister of war, a position he used to build a support base within the army. As minister of labor, Perón began to settle disputes in labor's favor. He reversed long-standing antilabor legislation and actively promoted legislation to improve workers' lives. Old-age pensions, accident and health insurance, annual paid vacations, factory safety codes, and minimum-wage and maximum-hours legislation were all expanded and enforced. A number of trade unionists were given positions in his ministry; others were freed from jail. Employers who had fought the creation of labor unions were now forced to accept them. Perón's support base among labor grew.

Some within the military began to view Perón's policies with alarm. The conservative elites and industrial groups were also resentful and suspicious of Perón's courting of workers. The growing opposition to Perón led a group of officers to oust him from his government post and put him under arrest on a naval base in the La Plata River. What happened next is still the stuff of Peronista legend. Labor unions and workers' organizations mobilized to protest Perón's jailing. Thousands of workers descended on the capital, Buenos Aires, and converged on the Plaza de Mayo demanding Perón's release. Not having an alternative, the military finally agreed to let Perón go. On October 17, 1945, Perón appeared on the balcony of the Casa Rosada (Government House), gesturing in victory to the thousands of workers cheering him. It was clear that the working classes had forced their way into the political arena. The Peronista era had begun.

The election of 1946 passed the mantle of power and legitimacy to Perón. In the run-up to the election Perón founded his own political party, the Labor Party, which organized his many supporters under his leadership. He had the solid support of the labor unions, many of which had formed within the past three years; factions of the military, from whose ranks he came; and the Catholic Church, which Perón had promised would retain its right to control education and to prevent divorce legislation. The Conservative Party, landed elites, urban industrialists, middle-class radicals, and an array of socialists and communists were opposed to Perón. Nevertheless, Perón's victory in the 1946 election was decisive: 1,479,517 votes for the Labor Party compared to 1,220,822 for the opposition Democratic Union, a coalition of anti-Peronista interests. Perón's allies also swept the two houses of congress, the provincial governorships, and all but one of the provincial legislatures.

Perón came to power with a number of factors in his favor. He had won a fair and open election with the support of a broad coalition of groups, including elements of the military and the Catholic Church. The state treasury was full, as Argentina had been able to capitalize on the sale of supplies to the Allies during World War II. Furthermore, international prices for food and agricultural raw materials were rising relative to industrial goods. His development policies focused on the expansion of basic industrialization, growth in social welfare benefits, a certain redistribution of wealth, and the promotion of nationalism.

Perón continued to pursue his pro-labor policies by promulgating legislation covering all aspects of workers' lives. Real wages and fringe benefits went up. Under the Secretariat of Labor and Social Welfare, Perón created an extensive network for the administration of labor affairs. He gradually concentrated labor matters under the General Direction of Labor and Direct Social Action (DGTASD). All aspects of labor relations, including collective bargaining, labor law enforcement, union registrations and dues, workplace conditions, and employer-union conflicts, came under the purview of the DGTASD. To ensure labor compliance with Peronista policies, the General Confederation of Labor (CGT) was given a monopoly of control over labor unions. The CGT was the only legally recognized labor confederation in the country, and any other union that wished to be legally recognized had to fall under its control and oversight. In classical corporatist fashion, the CGT was the vehicle by which Perón transmitted his policies down to labor's rank and file.

Perón's pro-labor policies were part of his economic project to further industrialization. Profits from the agricultural sector were transferred to the industrial sector. Agriculturalists were forced to sell all their commodity exports to a government agency, the Argentine Institute for Production and Trade (IAPI), at government-set prices. The idea was for IAPI to buy at the lowest possible price and then sell the goods on the world market at the highest possible price, with the profits used to finance industrialization.

Perón's industrial project sought to expand import substitution industrialization. To that end, he nationalized the central bank, the railroads, and the telephone, electricity and gas, and urban transport services. The state began development of the aviation and steel industries. Compensation for the nationalizations came from state treasury funds, leading to a severe depletion of state funds for promoting industrialization beyond light manufactured goods. As a result, capital-intensive industrialization never really took off. Parallel to the CGT controlling labor, Perón set up the General Economic Confederation (CGE) to represent industrialists, merchants, and agriculturalists.

Perón's political style was clearly populist, as he continued to direct his words and deeds to the working classes. With his wife, Eva Duarte Perón, Perón sought to elevate the working classes from their historical second-class status. Evita, in particular, served as an effective interlocutor between Perón and the people. Her own biography, emphasizing her illegitimate birth, her upbringing in a dusty provincial town, and her rise to political fame, served as an inspiration to millions of working-class and poor Argentines. Adopting a glamorous style, Eva Perón took an active part in dispensing social welfare funds to the working classes and the poor.

Perón's populism, though, had its authoritarian side. Soon after taking office he renamed the Labor Party the Peronista Party, so as to solidify his own personal power base. He and his allies set about purging Argentine politics and society of anyone who opposed Perón, whether independent-minded labor leaders or newspaper publishers. Political parties other than the Peronista Party were harassed and repressed. Perón used censorship and outright strong-arm tactics to reinforce his power. Political corruption was endemic, as the Peróns surrounded themselves with relatives and friends, many of whom saw access to the Peróns as an invitation to seek personal and material gain. In many ways, Peron's authoritarianism resembled that of a modern-day caudillo.

From 1946 to 1949 the Peronista project produced economic growth and a substantive improvement in people's lives. The real income and quality of life of Argentine workers and the middle classes increased, and for all the loathing the economic elites expressed toward Perón, they did not suffer much under his redistributive policies. Regardless, industrialization did not lead to sustained economic growth, and by 1950 the state treasury was running out of money to continue supporting the inefficient state-run industries and expanded social welfare programs. When Eva Perón died from cancer in 1952, Perón's decline began.

Facing pressure from a deteriorating economic situation, Perón sought even greater controls over society. He attacked the Catholic Church, an early Perón supporter, when it refused to canonize his wife as a saint despite popular demonstrations on her behalf. Then the clergy provoked a confrontation when it began to organize Christian Democratic trade unions in competition with Peronista unions. Perón went on the attack, forbidding religious processions and expelling priests. Street clashes escalated until finally, on the night of June 16, 1955, Peronista fanatics set fire to several downtown churches, including the cathedral and the archbishop's palace. Meanwhile, anti-Peronista opposition had been growing in the military. The navy had always been a center of resistance, but now the army, one of Perón's main pillars of support, was restive as well. Its professionalism was insulted by mandatory courses in Peronista political indoctrination at the military academy, and the regime's new program of encouraging sergeants and enlisted men to join the Peronista Party caused the officers to fear that their own men would be encouraged to spy on them. With the Catholic Church and important factions of the military allied against Perón, a military coup, led by General Eduardo Lonardi, forced Perón from office in September 1955. Perón initially took refuge in Paraguay and ultimately made his way to Spain. The first Peronista experiment was over.

The legacy Perón left Argentina in 1955 was of expanded group interests vying for political power. The Peronista Party–supported labor unions and working classes competed for political power with agricultural elites, the armed forces, urban middle-class interests, and industrialists. To the state he left a huge bureaucracy with responsibilities to nationalized industries and social welfare programs. To the economy he left a depleted state treasury and a shaky industrial base. Perón had not destroyed the power of the traditional economic elites, nor had his government gained enough strength to check their power. Rather, the next eighteen years would see attempts to defeat Peronism, all of which would fail at high social and political cost.

Peronism in Exile

The period from 1955 to 1973 was one of political and economic turmoil. The military regime that came to power in 1955 sought to de-Peronize Argentine society by outlawing the Peronista Party and attacking the labor unions that were its stronghold. In 1958 the military called elections but the Peronista Party was prohibited from fielding candidates, so the civilian government elected under the Radical Civic Union failed to establish its legitimacy. A military coup in 1966 did little to bring an end to Peronism, especially as Perón continued to assert his influence from exile in Spain. The military called elections in 1973, still prohibiting the participation of Perón. To circumvent the ban on Péron, his trusted secretary, Héctor Cámpora, ran for president. He prevailed, and a few short months later he resigned to pave the way for Péron's return to the presidency. However, Péron could not manage the disparate forces that had emerged during his time in exile. He summarily rejected the Montoneros, students who had agitated for his return by using urban guerrilla tactics; labor union leaders who had built power bases independent of Péron were wary of his intentions; and sectors of the military became increasingly concerned with his erratic decision making. Perón's death in 1974 ushered in further domestic chaos as his widow, Isabel, took over the helm of government but was unable to govern. On March 26, 1976, to most Argentines' relief, Isabel Perón was removed from power in a military coup.

Military-Sponsored Terror

The coup of March 1976 heralded a return to military rule, though it would be a departure from past military interventions. Calling its mission the "Process of National Reorganization" (El Proceso), the military junta, made up of representatives of the army, navy, and air force, with Army general Jorge Rafael Videla as its head, committed itself to ending the political chaos and to setting the economy on a stable course. It was not enough to rout the guerrilla forces that had plagued Argentine society for the past decade; what was needed was to attack the root causes of Argentina's political instability. According to the military junta, Argentina's woes went beyond the problems of Peronism and an intransigent labor movement. To the military junta, the entire fabric of Argentine life had been contaminated by leftist subversion, leading to a society rent by chaos and corruption. The solution was a concerted campaign to purge Argentina of those subversive elements and to reassert the "true" values of Argentine life. One of the self-proclaimed mottos of the military junta was "Tradition, Family, and Property," a slogan borrowed from the ultraconservative Catholic organization Opus Dei, which was popular with some in the military. The Argentine Catholic Church hierarchy became a staunch supporter of the junta.

The Catholic Church's role during the dirty war came under new scrutiny in 2013 with the selection of Argentine cardinal Jorge Mario Bergoglio as pope. Allegations persist that, as head of the nation's Jesuit order during that period, he allowed the kidnapping of two priests who later would be tortured. He is also alleged to have known about the practice of disappearing the babies born of women who were incarcerated. Both allegations have been vehemently denied by the Vatican, but they point to the continuing legacy of the dirty war in contemporary times.

The methods used by the military junta are by now famous. Green Ford Falcons with no license plates, driven by nondescript men, sped through the streets of Buenos Aires both day and night in search of specific individuals believed to be subversives. Illegal detention centers were set up all over the country, equipped with both sophisticated and primitive means of torture. Basic civil liberties were severely restricted as Argentine society found itself gripped with fear and terror as a result of the military junta's actions. All groups representing civil society (political parties, labor unions, civic associations) were repressed and their leadership went underground.

Although no sector of Argentine society was immune from this war against sub-version, the hardest hit were the working classes, students, labor activists, and ur-ban professionals. The phrase "the disappeared ones" entered the Argentine lexicon, signifying people who were taken by shadowy forces. Most of the disappeared were never found (all told, an estimated thirty thousand people lost their lives this way between 1976 and 1983), although mass graves filled with skeletons that show signs of violent death, such as bullet holes, bashed-in skulls, and broken bones, are still uncovered periodically in Argentina today. In addition to torture victims dumped in mass graves, some people were burned alive in ovens, and others were thrown into the La Plata River in the hopes that their bodies would be eaten by sharks, though some remains ended up on the banks of the river. Among those who were disappeared were pregnant women. It is estimated that approximately four hundred babies were born in captivity to women who were subsequently killed after giving birth. The babies were adopted by the families of military men or were sold on the black market. The whereabouts of these children of the disappeared continue to be an issue in contemporary Argentina.

Although all sectors of Argentine society were repressed, it is noteworthy that a group of women whose children were disappeared organized to defy the military jun-ta's policies. The Mothers of the Plaza de Mayo captured the imagination of the inter-national media beginning in 1977, when a few brave women decided to demonstrate publicly against the repressive policies of the regime. Covering their heads with white scarves and holding up placards with pictures of their missing children, the mothers held weekly marches around the Plaza de Mayo, calling attention to the regime's human rights abuses. Several of the original founders of the group were themselves disappeared, but the group persevered and became an important voice in ensuring that the human rights abuses of the junta would not be ignored once it left power.

Part of the motivation for the repression was the military junta's economic prior-ities. Under the direction of José Martínez de Hoz, Argentina's economy was to be reorganized so as to promote growth, competitiveness, and global integration. To fix the economy, which suffered from too much state intervention and the dominance of trade unions, labor unions needed to be tamed and state-run industries needed to be privatized. In these ways foreign investment could be attracted so as to restart the Argentine economy.

The military junta attacked the central labor confederation, the CGT, and jailed many prominent labor leaders. Factory floors were occupied by military men to co-erce laborers to work. Trade union activity was banned, union elections were dis-rupted by the military, and control over union dues reverted to the government. Organized labor's fortunes were also eroded by the regime's free market policies, which led to the closing of inefficient state-run industries, thereby causing massive unemployment.

The long-term impact of such policies was disastrous. The planned economic growth did not occur, nor was inflation tamed, and by 1980 Martínez de Hoz's days were numbered. As the economic situation took a downturn, the military junta sought ways to maintain power. In 1981 General Videla ceded power to General Roberto Viola, who in turn was replaced by General Leopoldo Galtieri at the end of the year. By this time human rights groups in Argentina and newly radicalized labor unions began to agitate against the military regime. To quell the rising domestic discontent, Galtieri took Argentina into the ill-conceived war against Great Britain for control of the Falklands—or the Malvinas, as the Argentines call this group of islands in the South Atlantic—in the hope that inflaming a long-running conflict with Great Britain would spark nationalist sentiment and rally Argentines toward the regime. What Galtieri did not bargain for was Great Britain's response: it sent its famed naval fleet and Royal Air Force to retake the islands. Argentina's defeat led to the hurried exit of the military junta from political power.

Transition to Democracy

The election of Raúl Alfonsín to the presidency in December 1983 was a watershed event in Argentina's political history. For the first time in a freely contested election the Peronistas did not win. The people's preference for the Radical Civic Union candidate, who himself had been jailed under the military, signaled a desire for a fresh start in Argentine politics, one that was a clear repudiation of past authoritarian regimes. During the electoral campaign Alfonsín vowed to bring El Proceso's top military officers to trial for violating human rights, a promise he made good on once elected. Alfonsín appointed a special investigative commission, whose report, entitled *Never Again,* was used as the basis for the trials held in 1985, when for several months victims and families of victims testified to the extent of the human rights violations. General Videla was handed a life sentence and the other junta leaders were given long prison terms. The military, fully discredited due to its disastrous performance in the Falklands War, had little recourse. However, when courts and prosecutors began to indict lower-level officers, military rebellions occurred. Three such rebellions took place in 1987 and 1988, events that led to the curtailing of the human rights prosecutions. A "full stop" law was enacted that limited the period during which cases could be brought to the courts, all but halting prosecutions against military personnel. A "due obedience" law then exempted from prosecution those who were said to have been just following orders. Human rights organizations, including the Mothers of the Plaza de Mayo, vigorously opposed this legislation.

In the area of the economy, Alfonsín and his team embarked on a number of strategies to curb rampant inflation, which had reached a yearly rate of 6,900 percent by 1985. He introduced a reform package called the Austral Plan that consisted of wage and price freezes, spending cutbacks, and rises in utility rates. Although the plan saw some initial successes, Alfonsín's failure to follow through soon led to a resurgence of hyperinflation. Attempts to fix the Austral Plan came to nothing, and in the 1987 congressional elections the Radical Civic Union candidates were roundly defeated by the Peronistas. Two years later Alfonsín himself left office early due to his government's inability to manage the economic crisis. At the time of his resignation, in June 1989, inflation had roared back to 4,900 percent, the GDP had contracted, real wages had fallen, and the external debt had reached a record US $63,314 billion.

Peronism Without Perón

Carlos Menem, governor of La Rioja province, campaigned in the presidential election of 1989 as an old-fashioned Peronista caudillo, promising to be the champion of the lower classes, but on taking office he shifted his stance so as not to end up like Alfonsín. Instead of populist economics he embraced a very orthodox neoliberal formula, vigorously promoting foreign capital, free trade, and privatization. To keep government spending within budgetary limits, the peso was pegged to the dollar at an exchange rate of one to one, and the treasury was allowed to print only as many pesos as there were dollars in the Central Bank. Called the "convertibility plan," such measures soon brought inflation down to single digits, and economic growth climbed to around 9 percent. However, the social costs of these reforms were high. Thousands of government workers lost their jobs, as did workers in Argentina's inefficient industries. Local companies, long protected from competition, were either bought by foreigners or absorbed into Argentine conglomerates. About a third of the economically active population was officially classified as living in poverty. Menem had thus reinvented the terms of debate with regard to the Argentine economy.

While Menem revolutionized the economy, his style of governance in other ways resembled aspects of Peronista caudillismo. Seeking to maximize his power, Menem sought a number of changes to Argentine institutional arrangements. He expanded the supreme court to nine members from the original five and set about packing the court with his allies. Under pressure from the military, he granted pardons to convicted military leaders. Although these moves enabled Menem to successfully reduce the size of the military from around one hundred thousand to twenty thousand, they gained him the enmity of human rights organizations. He succeeded in instituting legislation that severely weakened the labor movement, including abolishing collective bargaining, enabling employers to have greater flexibility in hiring and firing, and breaking the labor unions' control over social welfare funds. Perhaps Menem's most important political maneuver was to have the constitution amended to allow for his reelection. Instead of a single six-year term, in 1994 the constitution was changed to allow for a four-year presidential term with the possibility of reelection.

Menem's early success in controlling the economic situation and the changes he pushed through meant that he easily won reelection in 1995. However, his administration was increasingly beset by scandals (many related to the sale of state-run industries) and allegations of political corruption. Furthermore, Menem's highly public divorce from his wife, his penchant for consorting with movie stars and celebrities, and his use of family members as political advisors who were accountable to no one further compromised his reputation. As the economic situation began to decline, so did Menem's political fortunes.

The election of 1999 brought about Peronism's defeat once again, this time at the hands of a coalition consisting of the Radical Civic Union and the Front for a Country in Solidarity (FrePaso), the latter was a political party formed in 1994 of disaffected Peronistas and individuals from left-of-center political parties. Fernando de la Rúa, head of the UCR, was elected president on a platform of promising to end political corruption and to ameliorate the suffering of millions of Argentines whose economic livelihoods had been destroyed by the neoliberal policies of the 1990s. The coalition between the UCR and FrePaso was short-lived, however, as their political differences led to a fracturing of the alliance and instability in the de la Rúa coalition. The coalition's economic policy failed to arrest the deepening decline of economic productivity, and poverty rates increased.

By the end of 2001 the political and economic situation was chaotic. De la Rúa resigned from the presidency, thereby plunging Argentina into its worst political crisis since the era of military rule. A succession of three presidents moved through the presidency over a two-week period. The third of these presidents, Peronista politician Eduardo Duhalde, served in the position until 2003.

Kirchner Era

Néstor Kirchner was elected to the presidency in the 2003 elections. The Peronista governor of the small Patagonian province of Santa Cruz, Kirchner enacted economic policies that effectively arrested the decline of Argentina's economy. Kirchner adopted a nationalist stance that rejected the call of the IMF and its allies for Argentina to tackle its external debt as its first priority. Instead, Kirchner declared that the IMF and international creditors needed to wait until Argentina got its internal house in order. Defying the prescriptions of the Washington consensus, Kirchner focused on alleviating the suffering of Argentines by plowing money into social welfare spending. During his four years in office, the Argentine economy averaged 8 percent growth and private consumption increased by 52 percent. Unemployment and poverty rates saw sharp declines, and salaries increased. Kirchner's ability to grow the economy was facilitated by a period of high prices for Argentine exports, especially in commodities, fuels, and processed agricultural products.

Riding a tide of popularity, Néstor Kirchner stepped aside in the 2007 elections to enable his wife, Cristina Fernández de Kirchner, to run for the presidency, which she won. It was widely believed that having Cristina become president would enable the Kirchners to maintain dominance in 2011 and beyond. However, these hopes were dashed with Néstor's untimely death from a heart attack in October 2010. Cristina handily won reelection in 2011.

SOCIETY

Argentina's population of just over forty-two million is overwhelmingly urban (92 percent), with approximately one-third living in the greater Buenos Aires metropolitan area. It is also overwhelmingly of European descent—mainly Spaniards and Italians—and also Roman Catholic, at least nominally. Infant mortality stands at eleven per one thousand live births, life expectancy is seventy-four years for males and eighty for females, and the literacy rate is 97 percent for Argentines fifteen years and older.

Argentina's ethnic mix—97 percent European, 3 percent mestizo or other—is a product of its unusual pattern of settlement. As a colony, it produced little wealth for the Spanish crown and therefore remained sparsely settled. The indigenous population was made up of small, nomadic, hostile tribes that were gradually driven off the pampa by the settlers, down into Patagonia. By the end of the nineteenth century they were practically eliminated. At the same time Argentina's cattle-raising culture required little importation of African slaves to work the estancias. Then in the last two decades of the nineteenth century there was an enormous influx of European migrants, drawn by the attraction of vast tracts of cheap land, that significantly reconstituted the population. Today, in addition to Spanish last names, Italian, French, German, English, Irish, Slavic, Jewish, and Arabic last names are common.

Social structure in Argentina has allowed for movement both upward and downward. The upper classes consist of two kinds of elites. First is the traditional large rancher/farmer *estanciero* elite. Although very wealthy, this is by no means a closed aristocracy. Many successful immigrants joined it during the late nineteenth and early twentieth centuries. Alongside and overlapping with it is the more modern group of bankers, merchants, and industrialists. The two elites mingle socially in the highly prestigious Jockey Club and tend to congregate in the fashionable neighborhood of Barrio Norte in Buenos Aires.

The middle classes range from a very well-to-do upper stratum that is positioned just below the elites to a petite bourgeoisie consisting of small farmers and businesspeople, white-collar professionals, and lower-level bureaucrats. Top military officers, Catholic clergy, lawyers, doctors, and managers of corporations form the upper middle class. Sometimes their control of the government may make some of them as powerful as the elites.

The upper levels of the working classes consist of white-collar workers (*empleados*) and skilled laborers (*obreros calificados*). Skilled laborers often make more money than white-collar workers, but they lack the latter's social status. Empleados go to work in a coat and tie, although they may own only one of each, and they do not get their hands dirty. Obreros, on the other hand, do sweaty work. Most working-class parents dream of getting their children enough education to move them up the social scale from obrero to empleado, if indeed not into the middle class. Below these two groups are the semiskilled and unskilled urban workers, and below them are the unskilled rural workers. Joining them are the members of the informal labor force, or *cuentapropistas*. These are unregistered workers who work, part- or full-time, in economic activities that official statistics do not capture. The ranks of these workers in the informal economy have exploded in the past twenty years, with some estimating that they now constitute nearly half of all workers in the country.

POLITICAL PARTIES AND INTEREST GROUPS

Argentina has essentially been a two-party system since popular elections were introduced in 1912. In the first decade of the twenty-first century, however, it has been the Peronista Party or one of its many factions that has dominated national politics, with the Radical Civic Union, the Peronista Party's historic rival, failing to rebuild after the debacle of Fernando de la Rúa's resignation from the presidency in 2001. The UCR, founded in 1889, had been the party that represented the middle classes. Although it continues to maintain a national institutional structure, it has not shown any signs of revitalization in the past several elections.

It is the Peronista Party (or the Justicialist Party, to use its official title) that has weathered the political and economic misfortunes of the past twenty-five years. Justicialismo's institutional development has been marked by the fact that it began as Perón's personal vehicle. Even so, the party has often been a coalition of various interests. Besides the trade union movement, its membership consisted originally of dissidents from the UCR who liked Perón's statist program as well as right-wing authoritarians with fascist leanings. When Perón granted women the vote, Evita Perón helped form a women's wing of the party. Translated into practical terms,

Justicialismo was a version of the corporatist state, in which businesspeople, farmers, laborers, professionals, and students were required to belong to officially sanctioned organizations. Its highly regulated economy aimed at national self-sufficiency and encouraged the growth of three powerful interests that became the permanent basis for the Peronista coalition: a highly centralized trade union movement, a class of rent-seeking capitalists living off state subsidies and protection, and a large government bureaucracy. In the 1970s the left-wing Montonero guerrillas added themselves temporarily to the Peronista coalition, so ideologically its supporters spanned the entire political spectrum, from extreme left to extreme right. In the 1990s President Carlos Menem moved the Justicialist Party decisively to the right with his neoliberal program, alienating a large number of working-class supporters.

President Néstor Kirchner resurrected some traditional populist rhetoric during his term in office, but at the same time he did not fully reverse Menem's neoliberal reforms. Kirchner did, however, pay more attention to the social needs of the population and challenged international lending agencies to be more cooperative. Cristina Fernández de Kirchner has largely followed the same trajectory. Elected to office first in 2007, she was reelected in 2011 with 54 percent of the vote. Many analysts interpreted this win as indicating wide public sympathy for her because of the untimely death of her husband. However, the fact that her electoral coalition, called the Front for Victory, managed to gain an absolute majority in both chambers of congress, having lost that majority in the 2009 by-elections, seems to indicate that support for her may run deeper. Much of Fernández's campaign rhetoric of unity and dialogue appealed to middle-class sectors who had grown increasingly alienated by Menem's authoritarian proclivities. A large student movement, dubbed "La Cámpora" (for a former president, Héctor Cámpora, who supported the Montoneros in the 1970s), is an important base of Fernández's support. Managed by her son, Máximo, the Cámpora movement has achieved dominant status in Fernández's second term.

While Peronism and its various legacies are a constant in contemporary Argentine party politics, it is perhaps the importance of personality that best describes the trajectory of elections. It is charismatic personality, rather than well-honed policy platforms, that wins elections, enabling politicians to promote their own agendas with little regard for party discipline. Losing candidates rarely retain the coalitions that supported their candidacies. In 2003, Néstor Kirchner ran for the presidency by mobilizing a faction of the Justicialists, which became known as the Front for Victory, against two other Peronista rivals. His election enabled him and his wife to continue to build a coalition revolving around their policies and personalities. With the election of Cristina Fernández in 2007 and 2011, Kirchnerism appears to be the dominant political discourse in Argentina today, and *personalismo* continues to dominate Argentine national politics.

GOVERNMENT, STATE POWER, INSTITUTIONS

Though revised, the 1853 constitution is still basically the law of the land. It was modeled after that of the United States and provides for a federal republic with twenty-three provinces and a federal district. The national government is divided into three branches: the executive, a bicameral congress, and a judiciary. There is a strict separation of powers and a classic system of constitutional checks and balances. The constitution also contains a lengthy section outlining citizens' rights and guarantees, including the rights to petition, assembly, free speech, and freedom of the press. Freedom of religion is guaranteed, as is the right to own private property. An individual may not be arrested without a warrant, may not be forced to testify against him- or herself, and has a right to a lawyer and to a speedy and fair trial. The sanctity of the home and personal privacy are protected rights.

There is often a wide gap, however, between the written constitution and how Argentina actually is governed. For example, rights and guarantees may be suspended in times of emergency. Serious domestic conflict or the threat of a foreign attack may be used by the president to justify declaring a state of siege. Although the president is supposed to obtain the senate's approval, which is given only for a limited period of time and only for specific purposes, in practice both dictatorial and democratic governments have found it relatively easy to evade these restrictions, especially if the president has a congressional majority.

By the same token, Argentina's federal system is a great deal more centralized than a formal reading of the constitution would indicate. The federal government has specific, enumerated powers; the provinces are left with unspecified "reserve" powers, which in practice are quite whittled down. Provinces are referred to in the constitution as "the natural agents of the federal government, to see that the laws of the land are obeyed." Federal law and treaties always trump provincial law. The real sources of the provinces' weakness, however, are their financial dependence on the federal government and the latter's right to intervene in a province to maintain order. Concerning finances, the provinces are restricted in their ability to levy taxes. By contrast, the federal government has the revenues derived from the port of Buenos Aires and other, mostly indirect, taxes. What's more, given the widespread practice of tax evasion, even those are hardly sufficient to cover its responsibilities, so there is little left over for revenue sharing with the provinces. As for the federal government's power of intervention, this frequently has been abused. Citing electoral fraud or financial mismanagement, past presidents have often replaced opposition governors or provincial legislators with their own handpicked people.

Despite the tripartite division of powers at the national level, the president dominates the political system. Neither congress nor the courts have developed as powerful, independent institutions. At various times both have been abolished, suspended, or ignored. Even under democratic rule, a president whose party enjoys a comfortable majority in both houses of congress usually has no trouble getting any legislation passed.

Congress consists of two houses, a senate and a chamber of deputies. Each of Argentina's twenty-three provinces has three senators, as does the federal district of Buenos Aires, for a total of seventy-two. Since 2001, they have been directly elected for six-year terms, with one-third of the seats up for reelection every two years. The chamber of deputies is based on population, and it currently has 257 members, directly elected for four-year terms, with one-half up for reelection every two years. Seats are distributed on the basis of proportional representation.

The Argentine congress historically has been weak, and during the present era of democracy dating from 1983 it has delegated a great deal of power to the executive in the form of emergency powers, which have enabled the president to enact budgetary and regulatory laws without congressional oversight. Very few politicians appear to make a career out of serving in congress, and the result is that its institutional capabilities are quite underdeveloped. There are few experienced legislators in the congress, committees are weak, technical expertise is low, and oversight bodies are ineffectual. Legislation may originate in either house, except for bills that deal with taxes or appropriations, which must start in the chamber of deputies. Bills must pass both houses, after which they go to the president for approval. If she signs them, they become law, but if she vetoes them in whole or in part (she has a line-item veto), only a two-thirds majority of both houses can override her.

The president and vice president are directly elected by the voters for a four-year term. The president may be reelected once. The president's patronage powers are wide-ranging: judges, ambassadors, cabinet officers, and the top military posts require senate approval, but lower administrative officials are appointed by the president alone. Beyond that, the president is charged with seeing that the laws are faithfully executed, acting as commander in chief of the armed forces, and opening each annual session of congress with a state-of-the-union message.

The real source of the president's dominance lies in certain extraordinary powers, which presidents traditionally have interpreted in such a way as to overwhelm the other branches of government. First, there is the state-of-siege power, which can temporarily release a president from constitutional restraints. Second, the power to intervene in the provinces has enabled presidents in the past to cancel the mandates of their opponents. Third, the president may issue rules and instructions that are "urgent and necessary" for the execution of the laws. This innocuous phrase has been the source of presidents' increasingly common use of executive orders to bypass the regular legislative process. Some of the most controversial economic reforms of the Menem administration were put into effect in this way. Nor does the congress usually act as a watchdog over such overexpansion of executive power. For President Néstor Kirchner, coming to office in the midst of one of Argentina's worst economic crises enabled him to demand—and obtain—from congress extraordinary emergency powers to issue legally binding decrees.

PUBLIC POLICY: THE DOMINANCE OF THE ECONOMY

The dominant issue in Argentine policy making is the economy. Argentina has a sophisticated economy based on plentiful natural resources (especially oil), a highly skilled labor force, an efficient export-oriented agricultural sector, and a great variety of industries. Its exports consist mainly of wheat, corn, soy, beef, and oilseeds. Argentina's chief trading partners are Brazil, the United States, and Italy. In 1991 it joined Brazil, Paraguay, and Uruguay to form a regional trading bloc called the Common Market of the South (MERCOSUR), which has proved to be an important boost to foreign trade. Economic growth in the early 1990s averaged between 6 and 8 percent a year, following a period in the 1980s of economic contraction and hyperinflation. Unfortunately, that period also left Argentina saddled with a huge foreign debt that continues to plague the Argentine economy. Structural problems, international crises, and domestic policies all worked to undermine Argentina's ability to grow and prosper, and consequently the Argentine recovery of the early 1990s did not last. By the late 1990s the economy was in recession, and the years from 2000 to 2002 saw the Argentine economy contract and economic crises take hold. The situation began to improve starting in 2003 as the administration of Néstor Kirchner managed to arrest Argentina's decline and steer the country onto the road to recovery.

Traditionally Argentina's economy was characterized by the dominance of large estancias in the countryside and small businesses in the towns and cities. Naturally there were many exceptions to this general rule. Small and medium-sized farms and ranches produced profitably for the market, and there were even well-off tenant farmers. In certain industries, such as automobiles, pharmaceuticals, and rubber—really, any large enterprise requiring heavy capital inputs and advanced technology—big foreign companies dominated. The state was in control of basic or militarily strategic industries, including energy, transportation, mining, armaments, and utilities. Often that meant direct ownership and management by the armed forces. The domestic private sector therefore tended to concentrate on manufacturing light, nondurable consumer goods, such as food products, textiles, home furnishings, and small appliances. In addition, domestic private capital controlled most wholesale and retail commerce, as well as the service sector. With a few notable exceptions, these locally owned private companies were small, employing fewer than ten people on average. Many simply worked with their own, unpaid family members. In short, Argentina had an urban economy of mainly small capitalists, what is known as a shopkeeper society.

This society began showing signs of breaking down in the 1960s. Argentine industry was inefficient, and its products were therefore costly and often shoddy. Protected by tariffs and manipulated exchange rates, however, it had a captive market to exploit. Because most people lived in the cities and depended directly or indirectly on this industry, politicians hesitated to challenge it. The money to support public services came mainly from sales taxes, tariffs on foreign goods, and tariffs levied on Argentina's agricultural exports. The tariffs were greatly resented by the farmers and ranchers, but because those groups were only a minority of the population, they were unable to change the policy. Nonetheless, these added costs were pricing Argentine beef and grains out of world markets, and as a consequence, the government's treasury began running low on foreign exchange.

By the 1980s Argentina was in a real crisis: deeply in debt, with banks and businesses failing, agriculture stagnant, and capital fleeing the country. Population trends added to the crisis. As in many other socially advanced countries, Argentina's birthrate had fallen greatly, to a little over 1 percent—not enough to replenish its population. Young people with skills were leaving for Europe or the United States, while the elderly and retired were becoming an increasingly large portion of the population. A slight increase of women in the workforce helped to alleviate the situation somewhat, but with the growing recession and unemployment, there was little incentive to seek regular work. On the other hand, the informal economy—where people worked for below minimum wage, evaded social security payments and payroll taxes, and flouted most other labor laws—grew rapidly. By the end of the 1990s this sector was believed to account for at least 60 percent of all economic activity, although no records exist to prove that assertion.

Following the election of Carlos Menem to the presidency in 1989, the old system came under full-scale attack. The Peronista orthodoxy that supported state-dominated economic policy making was no longer viable, especially as the socialist model was collapsing in the Soviet Union and elsewhere. Menem's economics minister, Domingo Cavallo, instituted a set of neoliberal reforms that sought to insert Argentina into the global economy on terms promoted by the United States and international lending agencies.

The impact on Argentina's urban middle and working classes was devastating. Stripped of protection and subsidies, many small businesses disappeared, gobbled up by larger foreign and domestic companies. Within a few years the shopkeeper society was transformed into one dominated by large private conglomerates. Because these were capital- rather than labor-intensive, unemployment rose in the working classes as well, especially among women and youth.

The linchpin of Menem's neoliberal economic project was the "convertibility plan," which, as we have seen, pegged the peso's value to the dollar. While early results from the convertibility plan were positive and international creditors and lending agencies were impressed, the structural flaws in such a plan began to become visible after 1994. The overvaluation of the Argentine peso meant that Argentine goods were not competitive on the world market. This plan also depended on access to available credit, a situation that would turn sour after the Mexican financial crisis of 1994 caused a shrinking of external investment. With these problems exacerbated by political corruption, infighting in Menem's government, profligate spending by the provincial governments, and the chronic problem of tax evasion, by the end of the 1990s the Argentine economy was headed toward crisis.

Argentina's debt default of 2001 plunged the country into economic and political chaos. Neoliberal reforms were in a shambles. The next two years saw the unprecedented contraction of the economy and severe impoverishment of the Argentine population. Between 1999 and 2002 the GDP shrank by 20 percent, unemployment reached record highs of 18 percent, and over 50 percent of the population saw their lives descend into poverty. International lending agencies all but abandoned the country.

The election of Néstor Kirchner to the presidency in 2003, however, effectively brought a halt to Argentina's economic decline. In a departure from and perhaps rejection of the Washington consensus, Kirchner reasserted the role of the state in managing economic policy and promoted a nationalist-tinged argument for economic recovery. In what is often referred to as "neodevelopmentalism," Kirchner sought to prioritize social welfare spending along with the continued need for global integration. During his four-year term, Argentina's economy rebounded. Economic growth averaged 9 percent per year and private consumption increased by 52 percent. Unemployment and poverty rates saw sharp declines, with the jobless rate declining from a high of 20 percent in 2002 to 9 percent in 2007 and poverty rates falling from a high of 50 percent in 2002 to 27 percent by the end of 2007. Kirchner also resuscitated collective bargaining among labor unions, and workers saw a rise of 70 percent in real wages. Without a doubt, the economic reforms he pushed forward brought much relief to millions of Argentines. Kirchner's ability to carry out such drastic reforms was facilitated by a period of high prices for Argentine exports, especially in commodities, fuels, and processed agricultural goods. The Argentine peso also enjoyed relatively favorable terms on global exchange markets. Tax revenues rose and foreign investment began to flow back into the country. Kirchner also succeeded in renegotiating Argentina's foreign debt on positive terms for Argentina.

Cristina Fernández de Kirchner's election in 2007 coincided with the global downturn in the economy. In her first year in office Fernández did battle with the agricultural export sectors in her quest to raise tax revenues—a fight that she lost. Inflation began creeping into the economy and export prices began to decline. Fernández's decision to take over billions of dollars of private pension funds set off new concerns about the government's fiscal solvency. In addition to the pension funds, Fernández embarked on a series of nationalizations, including Aerolineas Argentinas and the oil company YPF, in which the Spanish firm Repsol had a majority interest. Many outside analysts see Fernández's policies as a turn toward protectionism. Import controls put in place in early 2012 have only reinforced this perception.

As Argentina entered the second decade of the twenty-first century, the economy appeared headed for another inflationary cycle. Cristina Fernández, as did her husband before her, has manipulated the official government statistics on inflation. The National Statistics and Census Institute (INDEC) is widely believed to be disseminating false numbers so as to hide the extent of inflation, with the government reporting inflation at around 10 percent whereas most private analysts put the rate at twice that. Other indicators that the government numbers are misleading are eroding salaries and the resulting public demonstrations of discontent. In September 2012, tens of thousands of Argentines turned out in the streets of Buenos Aires and elsewhere, banging pots and pans over dissatisfaction with shrinking salaries, declining public services, the crisis of public safety, and an overall deterioration of everyday life. A general strike in November 2012 signaled that the labor movement was also unhappy with Kirchner's policies. Argentina's economy may be heading into another crisis.

DEMOCRATIC STABILITY

It is worth noting that when Argentina experienced its severe economic crisis of 2000–2002, the military was not called back to assume power, nor did it even suggest its willingness to do so. In a country that saw its share of military coups throughout the twentieth century, the lack of any serious discussion of a military solution speaks well to how far Argentina's democracy has advanced. That being said, the decade-long administrations of Néstor Kirchner and Cristina Fernández de Kirchner present a very mixed record on the health of Argentine democracy.

Néstor Kirchner's election to the presidency in 2003 engendered a number of political reforms that in many ways strengthened Argentina's political institutions and civil society. He reformed the supreme court by overturning the changes made by former President Carlos Menem, who had packed the court with political cronies. Kirchner forced the resignation of six of the nine justices and replaced them with respected jurists. He eventually reduced the supreme court back to its original five members as a show of support for the supreme court's independence. A major commitment of his presidency was the repeal of amnesty laws that had all but shut down prosecutions of military leaders from the 1976–1983 era of military rule, a period of unprecedented human rights violations. In a move long called for by the human rights community, Kirchner had the pardons of the military leaders annulled, which paved the way for new trials. Prominent human rights organizations saw their years of hard work vindicated and the legitimacy of their demands recognized by the government. Additionally, Kirchner appeared to respect civil liberties, allowed for clean elections, and built greater public trust in the government. He served out his entire term in office, a feat that is noteworthy considering the long history of civilian presidents forced from office early by either military coup or economic crisis.

On the negative side, Néstor Kirchner, like his predecessors, concentrated power in the executive. After the legislative elections of 2005, which gave him huge majorities, he strong-armed congress into granting him vast discretionary authority over budget decisions with the "superpowers" law. He abolished open primaries (which had been in effect since 2002) for the nomination of presidential candidates. He used his power to intervene in the once independent state statistical agency, IN-DEC, by firing technocrats and manipulating the procedures by which inflation was measured. Finally, in a blatant attempt to prolong his presidency, Kirchner had his wife run for the presidency in 2007. The plan was for Fernández to retake the presidency in 2011 (as she did) and then for Kirchner to run for election in 2015. But then came Kirchner's untimely death.

Cristina Fernández de Kirchner was elected in 2007 very much on the popularity of her husband's economic policies. Her contributions to democratic viability have veered from social progressivism to authoritarianism. During her first presidency, Fernández sponsored a program, Asignación Universal por Hijo (roughly translated as Universal Benefit for Children), that gave cash payments to poor families to ensure that their children went to school and had the proper vaccinations. This program was designed to both lift families out of poverty and provide children with education and health care. Approximately five million children are covered under this program, and data from its first year indicated that poverty rates had declined. Another progressive social policy Kirchner endorsed was the legalization of gay marriage, which occurred in 2010. Both of these policies created the hope that civil rights (the right to an education and the right to marry) would strengthen the social fabric of Argentine society.

The push for legalizing gay marriage, however, put her in direct conflict with Cardinal Bergoglio (now Pope Francis). He called the reforms "evil," to which Kirchner replied that the cardinal was engaging in "medieval" thinking. However, when Bergoglio became pope in 2013, Kirchner congratulated him on his new post and attended the installation ceremony. Despite their differences, President Kirchner, like most Argentines, feels the naming of an Argentine pope, the first from the Americas, will redound well to Argentina's global stature.

On the negative side, Kirchner's reelection in 2011 has resulted in a display of more authoritarian impulses. She continuously turns to the student movement, La Cámpora, for advice, eschewing her cabinet. Cultivated by the Kirchners as a way to build political support and managed by their son, La Cámpora has gained greater importance and influence in Kirchner's second term. A number of high government positions have gone to members of La Cámpora, stirring controversy among the more traditional allies of the Kirchners.

Perhaps her most troubling authoritarian move was to go after several media conglomerates that began to criticize her and her husband's policies. Initially introduced in 2009, the media law was designed to break up the oligopolies that had long existed in the Argentine media sector by restricting the number of media licenses per company and allocating greater shares of these to the government and other entities. While on its face this law appeared to support greater openness and access to the media, it was clear from the beginning that the Kirchners were targeting the Clarín media group, a former ally of the Kirchners that had become critical of the increasing heavy-handedness with which the Kirchners wielded national power. The conflict with Clarín became personal when the government sought to compel the adopted children of Clarín's owner, Ernestina de Noble, to undergo DNA tests in order to discover whether they were illegally adopted children of the disappeared.

In 2011, Cristina Fernández extended her attacks on the media by declaring the production of newsprint to be a public interest, thus allowing the government to intervene in its pricing and supply. Its focus was on Papel Prensa, the largest newsprint producer in the country, owned by Clarín and the conservative newspaper La Nacíon. An earlier report, issued in 2010, directed the secretary of human rights to investigate whether the acquisition of Papel Prensa by Clarín and La Nacíon during the military dictatorship was in any way connected to human rights violations committed during that time. These conflicts with the media continue to be played out in Argentina.

The increasing intolerance of dissent by the press and others, the growing importance of the youth movement La Cámpora, and Fernández's increasing self-isolation are reminiscent of how other presidents have governed Argentina. These authoritarian tendencies may become more pronounced as economic growth starts to stall, thereby jeopardizing the democratic gains the country has made.

GLOBALIZATION AND FOREIGN RELATIONS

Argentina's foreign policy has reflected the twenty-first-century trend among Latin American countries of emphasizing independence from the United States and closer relations with governments of the region. Argentina was a founding member of MERCOSUR, which has seen a significant increase in trade among its member countries. Néstor Kirchner maintained friendly relations with Venezuela's leftist president Hugo Chávez, Brazil's Lula da Silva, and the government of Cuba. Safeguarding national sovereignty in the face of external pressures continues to be a popular refrain of the Fernández administration. Her administration's nationalization of the oil company YPF, in which a Spanish firm had a majority interest, has garnered criticism from the European Union. At the same time, Kirchner reignited a dispute with Great Britain over the control of the Falkland Islands, a move interpreted as an attempt to distract Argentines from the deteriorating economic situation at home.

The dominant issue of the past decade has been the aftermath of the 2001 default. Argentina's default on its US $63 billion external debt in that year plunged the country into economic and political chaos. The Néstor Kirchner administration responded with policies that prioritized alleviating the suffering of Argentines over the demands of the IMF and external creditors for debt restructuring. With the advantage of high commodity prices and a stable peso, Kirchner succeeded in arresting the decline of the domestic economy, all the while driving hard bargains with the IMF and external creditors to pay down Argentina's debt. Confounding the predictions of most of the international financial community, Kirchner's policies resulted in a remarkable economic recovery for Argentina, with growth rates averaging 8 percent a year during his four years in office. By 2005, Argentina had paid off its debt to the IMF, which itself had received scathing criticism for the way it handled the Argentine debt crisis. Argentina also subsequently negotiated a steep haircut on most of its debt to private creditors, although a few holdouts continue to demand full payment.

This militancy toward the IMF and the international lending community has not come without its costs. Argentina has had difficulty accessing credit, and interest rates are phenomenally high. It continues to be pilloried by the leading financial media giants, who are brutal in their criticism of the protectionist turn that appears to be taking hold in Argentina. Legitimate criticisms over the doctoring of economic statistics and the increasing authoritarianism of the Kirchner administration dominate international coverage of Argentina. As a global player, the country continues to suffer credibility issues.

PROSPECTS FOR THE FUTURE

Since its transition to democracy in 1983, Argentina has experienced periods of political stability marked by free and open elections, the smooth transition of power from one political party to another, and, after some initial tensions, the military's willingness to subordinate itself to civilian control. In many ways it continues to be a robust democracy, with a politically engaged civil society, respect for civil liberties and human rights, and continued national support for democracy. Despite these gains, Argentina remains a country where the health of the economy plays a disproportionate role in the functioning of political institutions. These institutions are often subordinated to the will of an ever powerful presidency; the rules of the political game change with every crisis, and policy making becomes erratic. With a slowdown in the Argentine economy expected in the near future, Argentine democracy is likely to face new challenges.

Suggestions for Further Reading

Auyero, Javier. *Flammable: Environmental Suffering in an Argentine Shanty Town*. New York: Oxford University Press, 2009.

Bonner, Michelle. *Sustaining Human Rights: Women and Argentine Human Rights Organizations*. University Park: Penn State University Press, 2007.

Cleary, Matthew, and Susan Stokes. *Democracy and the Culture of Skepticism: Political Trust in Argentina and Mexico*. New York: Russell Sage Foundation, 2006.

Epstein, Edward, and David Pion Berlin, eds. *Broken Promises? The Argentine Crisis and Argentine Democracy*. Lanham, MD: Lexington Books, 2006.

Fiorucci, Flavia, and Marcus Klein, eds. *The Argentine Crisis at the Turn of the Millennium: Causes, Consequences and Explanations*. Amsterdam: Aksant, 2004.

Helmke, Gretchen. *Courts Under Constraints: Judges, Generals, and Presidents in Argentina*. New York: Cambridge University Press, 2004.

Levitsky, Steven, and Maria V. Murillo, eds. *Argentine Democracy: The Politics of Institutional Weakness*. University Park: Penn State University Press, 2005.

Lopez-Levy, Marcela. *We Are Millions: Neo-Liberalism and New Forms of Political Action in Argentina*. London: Latin America Bureau, 2004.

Nouzeilles, Gabriela, and Graciela Montaldo. *The Argentina Reader: History, Culture, and Politics*. Durham, NC: Duke University Press, 2002.

Spiller, Pablo, and Mariano Tommasi. *The Institutional Foundations of Public Policy in Argentina*. New York: Cambridge University Press, 2007.

Tedesco, Laura. *The State of Democracy in Latin America: Post-Transition Conflicts in Argentina and Chile*. New York: Routledge, 2004.

Veigel, Klaus. *Dictatorship, Democracy, and Globalization: Argentina and the Cost of Paralysis, 1973–2001*. University Park: Penn State University Press, 2009.

Wright, Thomas. *State Terrorism in Latin America: Chile, Argentina, and International Human Rights*. Lanham, MD: Rowman and Littlefield, 2007.

_7

BRAZIL: A UNIQUE COUNTRY

Iêda Siqueira Wiarda

By the second decade of the twenty-first century, Brazil had become a regular feature in most financial journals as well in most international news media. Not only did the country now boast its first woman president, Dilma Rousseff, but it had positioned itself as a major economic and global power. Possibly, at long last, the country's motto, "Order and Progress," would reflect its reality. Its current status was buttressed by several factors that distinguished it from other Latin American countries—its size, actually larger than the continental United States; its culture, based on Portugal rather than Spain; its racial mix, predominantly European and African; and its trade relations with all continents.

Yet it is good to remember that this "country of the future," in the words of Stefan Zweig, has many times seen promises and disappointments, especially in the rhythm of everyday life, away from the headlines. But even here, amidst the travails of life, the uniqueness of Brazil is likely to surprise even sophisticated researchers—the vast panorama of Brazil's multifaceted resources, both human and geographic, and an unexpected history intriguing because of its uniqueness in Latin America. It is thus incumbent on us to examine Brazil's cultural and political underpinnings as we begin to assess whether this giant of a country, richly endowed in so many ways, will ever be able to obtain what it senses it deserves: respect and weight within world councils.

Brazil covers nearly half of South America and is the fifth-largest country in the world. Given its size, it is not surprising that Brazil has distinct regions and that Brazilians from each of them enjoy touting their state of origin as the best. Historically, its population ranges from those living at the level of the Stone Age to those who are comfortable in the great metropolises of the world. Throughout this largest Portuguese-speaking country in the world, the language is surprisingly uniform. Different accents are detectable, but Brazilians of all classes, colors, and regions understand

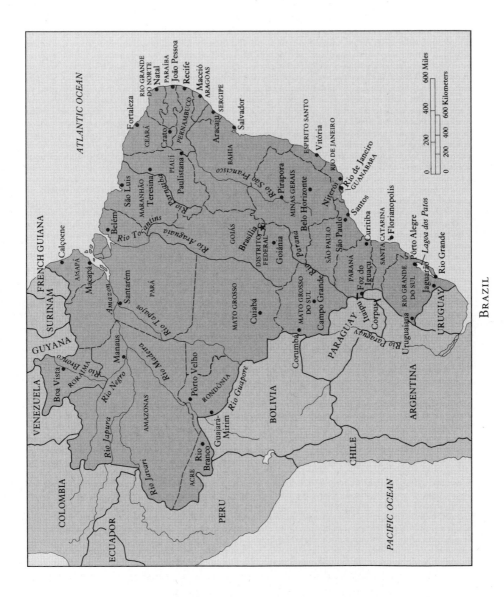

BRAZIL

each other. Thus, although Brazil faces many complex problems, a high degree of cultural integration remains a major source of strength. It is indeed "a country of all," as former president Lula da Silva proclaimed.

Brazil's 4,500-mile (7,242-kilometer) Atlantic coast facilitates trade with the world. Its population of over two hundred million (fifth-largest in the world), concentrated along that coast, has now slowed its growth to around 1 percent per year, giving the country a relatively low population density in comparison to other countries. Most of its citizens live on 10 percent of the land, in a zone 200 miles (322 kilometers) wide bordering the Atlantic from Fortaleza to the Uruguayan border. The country shares borders with all South American countries with the exception of Ecuador and Chile. Controlling the world's sixth-largest market-based economy, Brazil was an economic miracle from the mid-1960s until the economic disaster of the 1980s. The hyperinflation of the early 1990s was tamed by the ambitious "Real Plan" of the latter part of that decade. In 2013 inflation was estimated to be around 10 percent.

Globalization has meant that Brazil's products can be found everywhere, from orange juice, coffee, bran and oils, soybeans, cocoa, and beef to transport equipment and parts, metallurgical products, and airplanes. Brazilian engineers and technicians supervise and complete major construction projects in Africa and the Middle East. São Paulo's stock exchange, Bovespa, is quoted in the business sections of most newspapers. The Internet and the World Wide Web have enmeshed the country with the rest of the world, as seen in the linkages formed between international human rights groups and the country's indigenous councils.

With globalization, Brazil has divested itself of its long-held protectionist garb. More liberal and flexible interpretations of 1988 constitutional restrictions have served as inducements for greater foreign capital participation. Under President Fernando Henrique Cardoso (1995–2003), Brazil strengthened its economic ties with Argentina, Paraguay, and Uruguay under the Common Market of the South (MERCOSUR; MERCOSUL is its Portuguese acronym), in which Chile and Bolivia became associate members. Early in 2005 Brasília was the site of a South American and Arab country summit, another indication that President Lula had gone beyond traditional ties to Portuguese-speaking African countries in establishing connections with Muslim countries as well as China.

A heightened economic and international profile gave Brazilians a renewed sense of direction and cause for nationalistic pride. But this sense was tempered by the realization that the riches of Brazil have not yet been fully and humanely explored and that corruption seems still rampant. The country's entrepreneurs, among the most highly paid in the world, have not turned their abundance to the improvement of some of the most impoverished people on the face of the earth.

In short, Brazil is now a major player in the economic and strategic worlds, but social and political problems persist and fester. The promise of democracy and reform, so firmly made when power passed into civilian hands after decades of military regimes, has not delivered a better life for many Brazilians. As Brazil celebrated five hundred years of existence in 2000, its citizens began to ask about their past and speculate about their future. It is to history and to speculations about the political and international future that this chapter is devoted. Do we have reasons to consider Brazil a unique country?

HISTORY, BACKGROUND, POLITICAL CULTURE

Mainland Brazil stretches across three time zones, and the Atlantic archipelago of Fernando de Noronha lies in a fourth. Most of the country's landmass is east of the United States; the Equator crosses Brazil's northern border, and the area south of Rio de Janeiro is outside the tropical zone. Mountains, geologically old and not very high, moderate the climate, and nights are relatively cool. Rainfall is generally plentiful, but precipitation in the northeast is irregular, and that region, plagued by drought, is the poorest in Brazil.

Some twenty mountains are higher than 5,000 feet (1,524 meters), but none is as high as 10,000 feet (3,048 meters). Half of the country is a plateau running from 500 to 3,000 feet (152 to 914 meters) above sea level. The Amazon carries more water into the ocean than any other river in the world; the immense watercourse can be plied by oceangoing vessels as far as Peru, and many of its tributaries are navigable by major ships. Despite not having inland bodies of water as large as the Great Lakes, Brazil contains one-fifth of the world's fresh water. For a country that has only recently found much oil, it is fortunate to have great hydroelectric potential (it commands the world's second-largest hydroelectric power plant, at Itaipú); less fortunate is the fact that the country's overall energy production is considered inefficient and expensive compared with that of other countries.

Brazilians usually divide their country into five regions: north, northeast, southeast, south, and west-central. The north, stretching across the northern third of Brazil, is the largest (42.07 percent of the area) and least-populated region. It is dominated by the Amazon and is an area of legendary wealth and potential, mostly still untapped. Manaus and Belém are the major cities in the largest rain forest in the world.

The northeast, with 18.2 percent of the land and 30 percent of the population, occupies the eastern bulge and is notorious in recent years for recurring droughts and human hardship. It is tropical in climate and has a narrow coastal plain where traditional crops such as sugarcane and cacao have been grown for centuries. It is a region of old Portuguese names and proud political traditions. However, poor and far away from the center of power, it is often labeled Brazil's Bangladesh.

The densely populated southeast, with a mild climate and abundant rainfall, represents 10.86 percent of the national territory and close to half of the nation's population. It has long been the political and economic center of the country, contributing to more than 60 percent of the country's GNP. Large numbers of impoverished northeasterners as well as immigrants from Japan, Italy, and Lebanon have come to São Paulo and often prospered, making that city and the state the cosmopolitan heart of Brazil. Industry in this region has attracted millions. The rugged highlands, mined for gold and precious and semiprecious stones in colonial days, are now mined for high-grade iron ore and other minerals.

The south, stretching from Paraná to Rio Grande do Sul, has attracted a large number of north European immigrants. Containing 16 percent of the population, the south occupies 6.79 percent of the national territory. Important agriculturally and the home of national political leaders such as President Getúlio Vargas and General Ernesto Geisel, the south was for decades a haven for separatist ideas. The climate is temperate, with occasional frosts that damage the coffee crop.

The west-central region includes the states of Mato Grosso (North and South), Goiás, and the federal district. This region has grown tremendously since the establishment of Brasília as the country's capital in 1960 and the development of lucrative agribusiness. Rainfall is sometimes sparse, and the climate is tropical to mild in the highlands. In the north the region resembles the Amazon area, with dense forests and heavy rains, but its savannas are ideal for cattle raising. Some rivers flow north toward the Amazon, whereas others run south to the Plata Basin. With 22.08 percent of the territory and about 10 percent of the country's population, the west-central region is now contributing relatively more (slightly over 8 percent) to GNP. It is reminiscent of the American Far West, with extensive cattle ranches, sparse population, and a wealth of minerals.

The southeast and the south have been the undisputed economic and political heartland for decades. São Paulo, a state with a population larger than Argentina's, has a GDP second only to Mexico. The northeast is the proverbial land of history, poverty, and drought. The north is the land of jungle and promise, and the west-central region is the brash political center and a growing home for agribusiness. What links these varied regions is the Portuguese language and a national communications grid. Railroads are scarce, highways are somewhat less so, and rivers are used when not interrupted by falls. Airplanes now link most cities throughout the country, as do television, the telephone, the Internet, and radio.

Brazil's history sets it apart from Spanish America. Brazil can be said to have existed before the Portuguese explorer Pedros Álvares Cabral first landed there in 1500. In 1494 the pope, in an attempt to avoid disputes between the empires of Spain and Portugal, divided the South American continent into an eastern portion, to belong to Portugal, and a larger western portion, to belong to Spain. The Tordesilhas Line had granted Portugal only the easternmost bulge of today's Brazil, but Portuguese and later Brazilian explorers pushed the line westward to the present borders. Seldom did land wars erupt between the Portuguese and the Spanish colonizers and their heirs. Often expansion occurred naturally as Brazilian pioneers went beyond the line to settle new land and populate new areas, and their offspring moved farther west. Thus from the beginning of its history, Brazil's concept of a "living frontier" has been a unique aspect of its existence as a nation and has defined the character of its relations with other South American countries.

In the very early decades, the Portuguese seldom ventured beyond a few scattered outposts on the Atlantic shore. Portugal, in contrast to Spain, was more interested in its lucrative trade with India than in exploring a primitive land where early promises of gold and precious stones had gone unfulfilled. The only attraction of the new colony seems to have been a red wood that produced a brilliant red dye. From this red wood—the color of glowing coals, and thus named *brasil* wood in Portuguese— came the name of Brazil. In the middle of the sixteenth century the French twice tried to settle near present-day Rio de Janeiro and were driven off, but their bold challenge proved to be the catalyst to Portugal's interest, and João III finally decided that he needed to secure Cabral's discovery. The king parceled out the coastline in the form of fourteen royal grants (*capitanias*) to wealthy Portuguese. The *capitanias* gave Brazil its first formal shape and laid the basis for the country's enduring federalist tradition.

The *capitanias* grew slowly and became less stagnant as the Portuguese started raising sugarcane later in the sixteenth century. Sugar, however, required a great deal of labor in its production, and Brazilian Indians were not well suited to the strenuous labor, preferring death to slavery. The Portuguese therefore captured blacks at trading posts along the African coast and took them to tend the sugarcane fields and refineries. Over the next three centuries, more than three million young blacks were forcibly brought to the colony. Intermarriage between Portuguese, Indians, blacks, and the growing number of Brazilians (i.e., Portuguese subjects born in Brazil) was not uncommon, and the basis for Brazil's racial mixture was established.

Jesuit missionaries attempted to protect the indigenous people by gathering them into villages organized around a church, with the aim of Christianizing and educating them. Although the missionaries' intentions may have been good and they did save the Indians from enslavement and slaughter, most of the Indians died from European diseases to which they lacked immunity, such as smallpox, measles, tuberculosis, and the common cold. Their unique culture was largely lost or slowly blended with the culture of the far more numerous blacks and whites. Today fewer than five hundred thousand Indians remain in Brazil.

A sense of Brazilian national identity first emerged with the expulsion of the Protestant Dutch. For two decades they controlled the northeastern coast, but Portuguese and Brazilians drove them out in 1654, a triumph for the Catholic Church and for a Portuguese Brazil. The event that brought about the opening of the interior was the discovery of gold and precious and semiprecious stones just before the beginning of the eighteenth century. In Minas Gerais (literally "general mines"), the development of the interior was given a major impetus by the exploits of the daring *bandeirantes*, mostly pioneers from São Paulo. These descendants of Portuguese and Indians traveled in bands and brought along flags (*bandeiras*), families, cattle, and Indian slaves. Cruel and energetic, they ventured far from the coast and established the first settlements of the present-day states of Goiás and the two Mato Grossos. Diamantina, in central Minas Gerais, is now almost unknown outside of Brazil, but at one time it was the diamond capital of the world. It was these early mining towns that saw the first stirrings toward independence from Portugal, tragic and abortive attempts to emulate the North American independence movement and the republican form of government.

Brazil's independence came about differently than that of its Spanish neighbors. While South American countries rebelled against Spain and eventually formed separate republics, Brazil stayed intact, and its "war" of independence hardly merits that label. Brazil owes its independence to the fact that Napoleon's army invaded Portugal in 1807 and, under British pressure and protection, the Portuguese court moved to Brazil. João VI enjoyed the colony so much that he raised it in rank to a kingdom within the Portuguese Empire and stayed in Rio de Janeiro long after the Napoleonic threat was past. When the British finally persuaded him to return to Lisbon, he left his son Pedro I as his regent. Shortly afterward, in 1822, Dom Pedro proclaimed Brazil's independence, and the Portuguese prince became the country's first monarch.

After this rather uneventful independence, Brazil experienced minor civil wars, slave rebellions, and attempts at secession, including some in the south in favor of a republican form of government, but the former Portuguese colony managed to survive intact. The best explanation is that Brazil, in contrast to the rest of Spanish America, did not struggle through a protracted and divisive war of independence. The Portuguese House of Bragança ruled until 1889.

The easy separation from the colonial power and the long period of relative stability gave Brazil a strong feeling of national unity and nearly a century of enlightened rule. It can be argued that it was the farsightedness of Brazil's second emperor, Pedro II, that brought his reign to a close. His daughter's approval of the abolition of slavery in 1888 robbed Pedro II of the crucial support of the landed gentry, and shortly thereafter a republic was proclaimed and the heartbroken king went into exile.

Other forces, many of them fostered by the deposed king's policies, helped bring about the republic. A greater opening to the world made it possible for the Brazilian elite to become familiar with democratic and republican forms of government elsewhere, and a trip by the emperor to the United States, fully reported back home, made educated people familiar with the thriving republic to the north. Younger military men were becoming increasingly politically involved and restless under the emperor's rule. Brazil's war against Paraguay, which lasted from 1864 to 1870, was fought with a mixture of pride and shame, because it pitted a giant against a determined but extremely weak opponent. Paraguay was ruined for decades by the consequences of the war, and even though Brazil and its allies, Argentina and Uruguay, were victorious, the war was expensive and divisive for them.

The war debt, the doubts about the war itself, a desire for greater say in the form of government, and the abolition of slavery converged to make change a foregone conclusion. While Pedro II was personally respected, the overthrow of the monarchy came as a surprise to most Brazilians. Benjamin Constant and Marshal Floriano Peixoto, who represented disaffected military elements, engineered it with the crucial blessing of Marshal Deodoro da Fonseca, a longtime friend and supporter of Pedro II. On November 15, 1889, the Republic of Brazil was proclaimed. The emperor departed for Europe with his family and a few friends, refusing to accept the substantial compensation that the revolutionaries offered.

Pedro's long reign provided Brazil with decades of stability, but at the turn of the century the country was almost empty, its sparse population mostly illiterate and divided into a minuscule rich elite, a large poor class, and a nearly nonexistent middle class. The freed people were hardly better off than they had been as slaves. Wealthy Brazilians sent their sons to Europe, mostly to France, to get an education, because Pedro II's legendary love of learning had not been translated into the establishment of even a basic educational system. The few schools that did exist were run by the Catholic Church and offered only a rudimentary education to the children of the elite.

From 1889 to today the form of government has been that of a federal republic, but Brazil has never had a truly federal system. The president has traditionally been stronger than governors or mayors, checks and balances have not always applied, and the republican system itself has been tempered by a degree of authoritarianism. The 1988 constitution attempted to give greater power to congress. Although the 1992 impeachment of the first president to be democratically elected seemed to indicate new congressional authority, the corruption surrounding major congressional leaders in the 1990s and 2000s ran counter to constitutional intentions. In reality, the possibility of impeachment for corruption remains alive, but it reflects less congressional power than the weakness of the party system.

The military, a power behind the throne during the monarchy, is still influential, and between 1964 and 1985 it governed the country with very few challenges. Revealingly, the latent powers of the military to intervene were not fully eliminated in the liberal constitutional charter of 1988. In the 1990s political turmoil and the weakness of congresses, presidents, and political parties caused many Brazilians to look again to the military as the ultimate stabilizer, though it was to the credit of the military that it did not take advantage of the situation to reenter the political arena, as it did in the chaos of 1964.

The middle class has expanded, especially since the 1930s, but it cannot compete in terms of sheer political and economic power with the military and economic elites. The poor still form the largest group, and they have gained some welfare protection since the 1930s. The 1988 constitution extended and expanded many of their protections and welfare entitlements, but many promises remained solely on paper. The 1993–1994 constitutional revisions focused on the plight of the poor pragmatically and tried to find the money to implement social justice provisions. The lingering economic gap is somehow bridged, even transcended, by Brazil's vibrant culture. Television viewers worldwide are familiar with the spectacular pageant of carnival in Rio de Janeiro, in which the most daring and imaginative (as well as expensive) displays are staged by slum dwellers. Popular music, similarly highlighted during carnival, reaches many countries in toned-down versions of samba and bossa nova transformed into the all-pervasive Muzak. Brazilian movies compete well in world festivals and in box office appeal, television shows are technically advanced and innovative, and a great many *novelas* (soap operas) are routinely seen in Portugal, in Lusophone Africa, and throughout Spanish America and Spain itself.

From an international perspective, one can consider Brazil the cultural center of the Portuguese-speaking world, because of its vastly superior number of writers, actors, painters, and artists in comparison with other Lusophone countries. Jorge Amado, whose works fictionally depicted life in Bahia and the northeast, saw several of his novels, among them *Gabriela* and *Dona Flor*, become bestsellers and then movies in the United States. The visual arts are noteworthy; some of their best-known representatives reflect the ethnic mix of the country. Candido Portinari's murals in São Paulo portray the suffering of northeastern migrants and urban poor; the paintings of Manabu Mabe, another *paulista*, are viewed around the world. The cities of Salvador and Ouro Preto feature some of the hemisphere's best examples of baroque architecture by early artisans. Brasília is known for its futuristic design, and its architecture has been emulated in all continents.

Sports, particularly soccer, occupy an important position in Brazil. Life comes to a stop when the world soccer competition takes place every four years, and politicians vie with each other to show their devotion to a winning team. The country was chosen to host the World Cup in 2014.[1] Volleyball, water sports, track and field, basketball, car racing, and tennis are other major sports in which Brazilians have done well in international meets. A love of *novelas,* a penchant for emotional and earthy sambas, a cynical approach to religion and other ponderous matters, and a perennial optimism in the face of daily disappointments seem to characterize the Brazilian personality. In the words of Elizabeth Bishop, a Pulitzer Prize–winning writer who made Brazil her home for decades:

> Brazilians are very quick, both emotionally and physically. Like the heroes of Homer, men can show their emotions without disgrace. Their superb futebol players hug and kiss each other when they score goals, and weep dramatically when they fail to. Brazilians are also quick to show sympathy. One of the first and most useful words a foreigner picks up is *coitado* ["poor thing"]. . . . [There is the great] Brazilian belief in tolerance and forbearance . . . [with] the greatest tolerance . . . extended to love, because in Brazil that is always the most important emotion. Love is the constant element in almost every news story, street scene, or familiar conversation.[2]

Few Brazilians would quarrel with the poet's understanding of their soul.

When Bishop wrote, she had in mind a mostly rural country; by the 2000s more than 75 percent of the population had become urban. The growth has been spectacular; it has aided economic development and brought more people to work in the great and expanding industries, but it has also created serious social and political problems. The major cities are chronically short of funds to provide even the most rudimentary services, such as water and sewer. Yet various attempts to lure the peasants back to the land have been dismal failures.

Whether in the cities or in the countryside, four major groups make up the Brazilian population: the indigenous Indians; the Portuguese, who began colonizing in the sixteenth century and who again came in large numbers after their own "revolution" in the 1970s; Africans, brought as slaves to work on the plantations and in the mines; and the various European, Middle Eastern, and Asian immigrants who have settled since the middle of the nineteenth century, particularly in the southeast, where they have made São Paulo one of the most cosmopolitan cities in the world. The states of Santa Catarina and Rio Grande do Sul have been havens for waves of German immigrants. It is conservatively estimated that about five million Europeans settled in Brazil between 1875 and 1960, and millions of Japanese and Middle Easterners have come to Brazil to find a land of opportunity. These immigrants struggled for a long time but eventually succeeded beyond all expectations. Many highly placed politicians, professionals, and entrepreneurs are second- and third-generation hyphenated Brazilians. Most immigrant families have become fully integrated, having adopted the Portuguese language and often the Catholic religion as well. The sense of being Brazilian is strong; ethnic strife is minor, and when it does occur openly it is not condoned officially and is ridiculed and condemned by the media.

Most Portuguese explorers came without their families and intermarried with Indians and later with African slaves. Thus, although the basic ethnic stock of Brazil was once Portuguese, miscegenation and the subsequent waves of immigrants have resulted in a rich ethnic and cultural heritage. Traditionally, Brazilians are adamant in denying any racial or ethnic prejudice. It is true, however, that the farther one progresses up the socioeconomic and political ladder, the whiter one is likely to be (although not necessarily carrying a Portuguese name, as presidential candidate Paulo Maluf and presidents Juscelino Kubitschek and Ernesto Geisel attest). By the same token, attempts to organize black movements have not been very successful, and, perhaps revealingly, the labels used in these attempts are not Portuguese but imported, and the leadership is as likely to be foreign as it is Brazilian.

The Indians have been far less fortunate than the blacks or the immigrants. Located mainly in the northern and western border regions and in the upper Amazon Basin, they are considered an endangered group. Their numbers have been declining for years, but recently increased contact with the outside world, the expansion of agribusiness, and road projects have accelerated the process. Although the government has programs to establish reservations and to provide assistance, it has promoted or at least condoned the expansion of roads, mining, and commerce onto hunting and tribal lands, with disastrous results for the dwindling numbers of indigenous people. Tragic stories of farmers and miners despoiling Indian villages are not unusual. Meanwhile, the efforts of private groups and the Catholic Church to help the Indians survive are subject to controversy, and many Brazilians feel that the Indians should "integrate."

The fact that the few Indians who have survived at times cannot communicate in Portuguese has not helped their cause, because the Indian languages are wholly foreign to the vast majority of Brazilians. In fact, Portuguese is one of the main strands that hold the overwhelming majority of Brazilians together. It is true that Brazilians who live near the borders can communicate in Spanish and that educated Brazilians know English (North American–Brazilian cultural centers are popular, and a knowledge of English is avidly sought as a key to professional, business, and social betterment), but Portuguese is the language of Brazil.

With the economic recession of the early 1990s, some professionals went to the United States, Portugal, and Japan seeking better opportunities, only to find themselves unwelcome aliens; many returned to their native country disillusioned. With the advent of Internet and global communications, most groups have established links with similar ones in the United States, Europe, and Asia.

Another main cultural strand is the Roman Catholic Church, but this largest Catholic country in the world is one in which Catholic tenets have traditionally been lightly respected and in which the number of religious vocations has never been high. Protestant churches, notably charismatic and fundamentalist ones, have grown tremendously in recent years, especially among the poorer urban dwellers. By now, Protestants have their own informal *bloque* or faction in congress. Many Brazilians, even if nominally Catholic, are devoted to various spiritualist and voodoo rituals. There are Jewish groups mostly in Rio de Janeiro and São Paulo; Moacyr Scliar, a well-known novelist and essayist from Porto Alegre, wrote extensively on Brazil's Jewish community and its role in national life. Overall, religious tolerance is the norm, and persecution for one's beliefs has been rare, although the Catholic Church is accorded a special place in religious festivals, family traditions, and everyday life.

INTEREST GROUPS, PARTIES, AND POLITICAL ORGANIZATIONS

With its size and economic, political, and regional diversity, it is not surprising that Brazil has always had a variety of interest groups, parties, and organizations, but this variety has become more pronounced in recent decades. Because Pedro II's empire represented stability and provided for a great deal of freedom, the transition from monarchy to republic in 1889 did not bring about an outcropping of popular groups overnight. Indeed, the republic emerged as a continuation of oligarchic rule, one in which the landed interests were the most powerful, the states of São Paulo and Minas Gerais continued their preeminence, and the top military officers exerted the moderating power (*poder moderador*) that the emperor had represented. Outstanding civilians such as the great jurist Rui Barbosa were sometimes brought to the fore, and it was he, rather than the military leaders, who wrote the decree that brought about the separation of church and state in 1890.

World War I brought the first major challenge to Brazilian rulers. The loss of European markets was disastrous; farmers were unable to sell their crops, and only toward the end of the European conflict did trade improve somewhat as the warring nations sought to import foodstuffs. Brazil officially opted to side with the Allies in 1916, and this choice helped the country's trade situation, but even this improved trade was not enough to cure festering problems. The coffee plantations, which had supplanted the sugar plantations as the major exporters, were overproducing, and prices continued to drop. More ominous was that the southern states, which long had felt alienated from Rio de Janeiro, were becoming more restless, and the old dream of secession persisted.

Issues of civilian-military relations were a constant source of aggravation to people in and out of government. Although civilians managed to keep the military out of the presidency, discontent within the army was a concern for all presidents. The impact of the Great Depression was acutely felt early on in Brazil as exports continued to drop. Influential Brazilians, powerful farmers, and young military officers began to look for a forceful president as the 1930 election approached. Their attention focused on Getúlio Vargas, a popular governor from the southern state of Rio Grande do Sul. Feeling that he had enough military and popular support to succeed, Vargas and his followers moved by train toward the capital. Support grew as he traveled north, and when he reached Rio de Janeiro, Vargas was able to assume power with a minimum of force.

Between 1930 and his resignation in 1945 Vargas ruled with a combination of cunning, ever-changing political coalitions, a vaguely corporatist *estado novo* concept, and a brand of populism that endeared him to many Brazilians, who called him "the father of the poor." With little regard for rules, Vargas instituted extra-constitutional policies and programs and was not averse to ruthless suppression of those who opposed him. Power was centralized, and federalism, already weak, was practically abolished when he used his powers to intervene in the states, appointing his own choice of governors. Education became centralized and controlled, censorship was imposed, and the legislative assembly was not convened. Although many of Vargas's decrees were softened in their application, other policies he instituted were to have lasting effects. His social security system, a novelty in Brazil that made him very popular with workers, still forms the core of today's social welfare system. He garnered a great deal of support from nationalists of different political stripes with extensive nationalization of economic institutions and natural resources. Characteristically calling himself "apolitical," he presided over a regime that lacked a coherent ideology and even political parties. He counted on the support of labor but made sure it had little independent strength.

During World War II, after some initial hesitation, Brazil joined the Allied side in 1942 and contributed troops and officers, who saw action in Italy alongside US forces. The United States was allowed to use Brazilian bases in the northeast, and the country prospered because of the great demand for its products. Yet World War II, fought for the preservation of democracy, had the unsurprising effect of calling into question Vargas's authoritarianism. In October 1945 military officers, responding to popular demands for a freer system, stepped in and sent Vargas home to Rio Grande do Sul. The second republic, with a former minister of war, General Eurico Gaspar Dutra, as president, was ushered in during January 1946.

In September 1946 a new constitution was adopted, and although it guaranteed free elections and civil liberties, it preserved the greatly enlarged executive built up by Vargas and his centralized institutions. President Dutra continued investments in public works and further expanded the health and transportation systems. Inflation, however, was a constant menace. Brazil expected greater trade and economic help from the United States, especially in view of Brazil's role in World War II, but these expectations were disappointed. Even more disappointing was that the massive Marshall Plan for the economic reconstruction of Europe was not paralleled in Latin America.

Vargas was popularly elected to the presidency in 1951 as the candidate of the Labor Party, but he no longer commanded the respect or affection he had enjoyed during his earliest years in power. He had lost much of his popular appeal and was unable to deal with economic problems any more successfully than had Dutra. Charges of corruption involved some of his closest associates, and when one of his aides appeared to have been directly involved in an assassination attempt against an opposition journalist and in the death of an air force major, the armed forces seemed to be prepared to push Vargas to resign. Faced with the possibility of a coup, or perhaps in an effort to avoid possible bloodshed, Vargas committed suicide.

The election of 1955, in which Juscelino Kubitschek was chosen as president and Vargas's former minister of labor João Golart vice president, was made possible by the military's willingness to use its *poder moderador* to guarantee that the duly elected officials could take office. Kubitschek, who had been one of the most popular governors of Minas Gerais, vowed to give Brazil "fifty years of progress in five," and in many ways he fulfilled his promise, but at a heavy price. He pushed for the hasty completion of hydroelectric plants and a variety of public works; the establishment of several new universities, medical schools, and economic institutions; and the opening of major highways and airports. He launched Brazil's automobile and aircraft industries and built the long-planned new capital, Brasília, in the central state of Goiás. All of these projects could be justified as serving as the building blocks for a modern Brazil, but they were pushed too hastily and involved tremendous cost overruns. By the time he left office Kubitschek was still a very popular man, but inflation had become a major burden. The successful presidential candidate in 1960, Janio Quadros, a former mayor and governor of São Paulo, ran on a pledge to balance the budget, end inflation, protect Brazil from foreign greed, curb corruption, and launch an independent foreign policy.

Quadros was elected with the largest plurality in the history of Brazil, but he ran afoul of congress and alienated some of his strongest supporters with his aloof and erratic behavior. He pushed for measures designed to reform exchange controls, end consumer subsidies, and curtail the printing of worthless money, but these measures took away much of his support among the poor people and others most negatively affected. He publicly praised the Soviet Union, even though little trade was possible between the two countries and a Communist system held little appeal for most Brazilians. He pinned a medal on Fidel Castro, even though it was common knowledge that the Cuban dictator had just presided over a period of terrorism and indiscriminate killings. And Quadros exhibited a number of eccentricities, among them wearing a uniform and requiring others around him to wear them as well in order to ward off "germs."

His economic measures were not working, his popularity evaporated, and his peculiarities led people to believe he was unstable. No longer adulated as a savior, he resigned abruptly and left Brazil before completing a year in office. His irresponsible tantrum would cost Brazil's democracy dearly.

Quadros's vice president, João Goulart, had been picked for that position almost as an afterthought and because it was felt he would bring to the ticket whatever remained of the old Vargas machine. Goulart, like Vargas, was from the south, a landowner and a politician with close ties to labor. At the time of Quadros's resignation, Goulart happened to be in the People's Republic of China. Politicians favorable as well as unfavorable to him counseled that he return to Brazil by a slow route so that the military, congress, and other influential groups could work out a compromise that would enable him to become president. The eventual compromise created the post of prime minister who would share power with Goulart (and be close to the people who most objected to him), and Goulart became president.

Almost from the very start the relations among the president, the military, and the old-line politicians were strained. Goulart prevailed in getting rid of the prime minister, but this was a Pyrrhic victory. For the people who were already suspicious of his intentions, it confirmed their fear that Goulart wanted to become a second Vargas, only more so: more populist, more to the left, and more demagogic. His economic policies proved more inflationary than beneficial. And, unable or unwilling to control his one base of support, the unions, he allowed strikes and threats of strikes to become a daily occurrence. For many Brazilians, who traditionally had opted for their flag's motto, "Ordem e Progresso" (order and progress), the spectacle of a demagogic president unable to provide at least a measure of economic and political certainty engendered a longing for a more stable president.

Much has been written about US involvement in the coup that eventually drove Goulart from the presidency. A fair appraisal would conclude that many North Americans felt uneasy about the turn of events. This uneasiness was compounded by Goulart's vague, inflammatory threats against "foreign powers" and by the suggestion that some of his advisors may have had links to Brazil's small Communist Party. However, to conclude that the United States engineered the coup is to be blind to the realities of Brazilian traditions and politics in 1964. The United States probably knew about the coup and did not discourage it. For a variety of good and not-so-good reasons, the US embassy was supportive of the people who wanted to get rid of Goulart. After all, a number of highly placed North Americans in Brazil were close friends of influential Brazilians who were active in the opposition, especially those in the military.[3]

The actual unraveling is beyond dispute. The final catalyst came from Goulart himself when he undermined military discipline by siding with groups of mutinous soldiers. With the growing middle class already bitter because of inflation and the daily uncertainties caused by strikes, the military was urged to fulfill its constitutional duty to act as the *poder moderador* and make sure that "order and progress," as well as discipline, prevailed. Unhappy governors of powerful states such as Minas Gerais joined with generals in insisting that Goulart resign or face the prospect of a protracted civil war.

The "revolution" of March 31, 1964, was virtually bloodless. There was practically no support for Goulart, and even his base, the labor unions, failed to rise in his favor. Most political leaders regarded military rule as the only alternative to strikes, mutinies, and daily chaos. The army chief of staff, Marshal Humberto Castelo Branco, was chosen as president. A quiet, intellectual man, he sincerely believed that his term in office would be a mere transition to another, more reliable civilian president. But Castelo Branco was in the minority among his fellow officers, most of whom—along with a great many civilians in Brazil—felt otherwise and thought that the country needed a strong "apolitical" government. The military was destined to rule Brazil for more than twenty years, and even in the liberal 1988 constitution, its traditional power as a moderating force was not eliminated.

Castelo Branco himself never doubted that he had acted constitutionally. The 1946 constitution had given the armed forces the responsibility of maintaining law and order and ensuring the normal functioning of government. In the military men's eyes—as in the eyes of many Brazilians—the civilian president had violated his own mandate and trampled on the constitution.

Whatever the debate about the constitutionality of the military takeover, there was little anticipation of what came after the coup. Instead of a transitional regime, the military consolidated its power. Even those politicians who had initially sided with the officers were banned from politics or sent into exile. The popular Kubitschek was among those who were proscribed. At first political parties were considered unnecessary or a nuisance, and thus the thirteen that did exist were abolished. Eventually the military saw the need to promote a more "popular" image, and two political organizations, the pro-government National Renovating Alliance (ARENA) and the opposition Brazilian Democratic Movement (MDB), were formed under government auspices. As their names indicated, they were coalitions of parties and ideological factions rather than political parties in the US sense.

For a time, especially between 1968 and 1972, the military leaders in power were prone to disdain any effort at democratization. Their idea seems to have been to provide an economic miracle that would, in turn, expand the economic pie and eventually the number of pieces that could be given away to the populace. The emphasis was on technocratic rather than political advice, on economic development rather than preparation for democracy and popular participation. Censorship was the order of the day; the regime in power was not hesitant to show who was boss, to use threats and outright brutality if it felt they were needed to "sanitize" the system. Among those leading small guerrilla groups against the military was a young woman from Minas Gerais, Dilma Rousseff.

As long as economic expansion continued and inflation was kept fairly low, demands that the military give up power were muted, but the oil shock of 1973 changed the situation. Coming from outside the country and completely out of the control of the government, the skyrocketing oil prices meant drastic changes in the economic forecasts. The economic miracle was no more, the pie was no longer growing, and the people who were demanding more than the merest of crumbs were becoming less intimidated and more vocal. With the economy faltering, the military leaders saw the wisdom of moving for an *abertura*, an opening toward resumption of democratic forms.

Under an administration-sponsored bill, congress abolished the two-party system, and a multiparty system was put in place. Five parties were recognized under the reorganization law; two of them were continuations of those allowed previously. The opposition MDB became the Brazilian Democratic Movement Party (PMDB), based in part on the old Brazilian Labor Party (PTB) and a few smaller political groupings, as well as whatever remained of the more progressive elements of President Dutra's Social Democratic Party (PSD). In its new incarnation, the PMDB counted among its supporters the expanding urban middle class, intellectuals, and workers. Its program called for greater control of the economy, income redistribution to help disadvantaged groups in society, full political democracy, and direct elections.

The pre-1964 PTB suffered much infighting in its attempt to regain its preeminence, and out of the struggle emerged the Democratic Workers' Party (PDT). The PDT was most active in the state of Rio de Janeiro, where it was led by Governor Leonel Brizola. He was closely associated by family, state, and political ties with Goulart, sought to model the party on the European social-democratic parties, but most observers saw the PDT as a personalistic vehicle for the ambitious governor rather than an ideological one. Another party in search of the labor vote was the Workers' Party (PT), which competed primarily with the PMDB and the PDT for the votes of industrial workers and for the ideological backing of urban intellectuals.

The Liberal Front Party (PFL) was led by former vice president Aureliano Chaves of Minas Gerais, who split from the PSD in the 1984 presidential campaign to support the PMDB and fellow *mineiro* presidential candidate Tancredo Neves. In fact, most of the PFL, which in 1985 became a junior partner in José Sarney's democratic alliance, was composed of politicians who had been elected in 1982 on the Democratic Social Party ticket but who had subsequently broken away from that party to support Neves. Though it had capable young leaders, the PFL nonetheless fared poorly in the 1986 election, giving rise to the joke that it was a party of great leaders and a tiny following. Its modest strength lay in small rural enclaves, and this support worked to its disadvantage in a country increasingly urban and urban-oriented.

Sarney himself had been one of the original PFL leaders before he formally joined the PMDB to become Neves's new running mate. The PMDB-PFL coalition enabled Neves to upset most predictions and defeat the government-backed PSD opponent, Deputy Paulo Maluf of São Paulo, in 1984. Neves commanded a wide margin in the electoral college and was a popular, grandfatherly figure. He had accomplished the nearly impossible task of assembling a variety of ideological groups intent upon replacing the military and launching a democratic system. For its part, the military had stacked the game to favor Maluf but, faced with the popularity of Neves, opted to accept Neves as someone too politically cunning to attempt radical progress without a good measure of order. All prognostications came to naught when Neves fell fatally ill on the eve of his inauguration.

With Neves near death, the specter of a military coup or the passing of the presidency to Ulysses Guimarães, the congressional leader, were only two of many possibilities. But Guimarães, a longtime opposition leader, could not count on the goodwill of the military, and vice-president-elect Sarney had been a former president of the pro-military Democratic Social Party. After a great deal of political maneuvering, Sarney was confirmed as the new president. He had the support of the PSD and the PFL, but he was not a popular figure. The military did not fully trust him because he had switched sides instead of supporting its candidate, Maluf; the democratic forces that had so enthusiastically supported Neves could not forget that Sarney had been added to the ticket as a last-minute gesture toward people who had supported the military but were now willing to jump onto the civilian bandwagon.

Opposition to Sarney came mainly from the left, from the PDT and the PT. The PDT mixed populism and machine politics; the PT had been an umbrella for a variety of socialist groups, based on unions and on the Catholic Church's liberation theology wing. Both the PDT and the PT assumed that worsening economic problems would bring them victory. Their calculations backfired because of the short-term maneuvers of the president and his supporters. The early success of the economic Cruzado Plan, launched in February 1986, buoyed Sarney's popularity and ensured an easy victory for those aligned with him. But the Cruzado Plan proved to be an ephemeral respite and had to be abandoned shortly after the 1986 elections.

By 1988 Sarney no longer could hide the economic debacle or buy or influence many voters. In the November election for mayors and municipal assemblies, Sarney's policies were overwhelmingly rejected. Sarney and the old-line politicians were the great losers, and the undisputed great winner was the PT. It could be said that the 1988 election, in which an unpopular and arguably illegitimate government paid the price for an inflation rate of more than 700 percent in the preceding year, socialist Luís Inácio da Silva (better known as Lula) became a serious candidate for the presidency in 1989.

The 1989 contest proved the volatility of a large, young, and inexperienced electorate. More than twenty candidates waged a vigorous campaign. Some of them were old political names. Some represented the new forces of organized labor and liberation theology; Lula probably found his greatest strength here, along with a young former governor of one of Brazil's smallest states, Fernando Collor de Mello.

Disdaining to affiliate himself with any major party, Collor came out of nowhere to lead the race. He survived the first ballot contest and narrowly edged out Lula in the runoff elections in December 1989, 53 percent to 47 percent. Collor had come to prominence when he led a campaign, as governor of Alagoas, against highly paid civil servants. He turned this campaign into a national crusade against corruption and incompetence. His vigorous denunciation of Sarney struck a responsive chord among Brazil's poorest, the rural population, and business people fed up with the state's dominance of the economy. With the backing of the powerful Globo news network, Collor succeeded in undermining Lula's appeal. Most of Brazil's intellectuals supported Lula and agreed with his Marxist prescription for curing the country's ills. Collor called for a vague modernizing and restructuring of the economy.

Collor (a young president, forty years of age) promised to bring back some order and progress to the economically troubled nation. His program included cutting the inflation rate, which ran at a record 1,800 percent in 1989; prosecuting tax evaders; cutting the number of ministries in half; and selling money-losing state companies. He hoped that foreign creditors would not take the 1988 constitutional restrictions too seriously but would be willing to swap their debt titles for shares in Brazilian companies and that the debt could be renegotiated so that debt service payments could be capped at US$5 billion a year. To enact even a portion of this ambitious plan, Collor needed the cooperation of a powerful and hostile congress. Lula and other disappointed presidential hopefuls counted on increasing their supporters' share of the congressional seats in the October 1990 elections. In a factionalized congress, much of it bitterly frustrated by Collor's victory, the goal was not greater order and progress but more chaos and confrontation.

As fate would have it, Collor played into the hands of his enemies and thoroughly disgraced himself even in the eyes of those who had supported him. By early 1992 it became clear that the president—who had come into government under the banner of austerity and probity—was deeply enmeshed in a scandal of corruption and favoritism. Slowly but surely, the congress undertook an unprecedented impeachment process, and by December 29, 1992, Collor was removed from the presidency in disgrace. In his place, Itamar Franco, the physical, political, and generational antithesis of Collor, became president.

The specter of a coup lurked in the wings. The military had been uneasy over Collor's proposal to abolish the National Information Service (SNI), Brazil's foreign and domestic intelligence agency, and to shut down Brazil's nuclear program. Two small Communist parties, illegal during the military regimes, were eager to discredit the youthful Collor and the avuncular Franco, but with the dissolution of the former Soviet Union, these parties were having a hard time justifying their own existence. At most, thirty thousand Communists were said to exist in Brazil; of far greater relevance was the fact that social-democratic ideas and ideals were embraced by a large percentage of the population. A small Green Party objected to Collor's development plans, but a wide variety of ecologically minded groups took advantage of the worldwide forum provided by the proceedings of the 1992 Earth Summit, which garnered a great deal of praise for the Collor government's ability to host a major international gathering.

Overall, the exuberant political ferment of the 1980s had some positive results. Since 1985, Brazilians, regardless of their ideological leanings, have fully participated in vigorous partisan politics, informed by media reporting that reflects a broad range of political views and ideologies. The two dozen or so political parties would eventually coalesce into three to five major fronts or umbrella organizations that fit into the pattern of right, center, and left, with Brazil's political center being considerably to the left of the US one. Less speculative are polling results from the 2000s that showed increasing disenchantment with all political parties and politicians, so much so that those vying for leadership roles are careful to stress their

"independent" and nonpartisan credentials. Thus, the name of the PMDB, if literally translated, is Party of the Brazilian Democratic Movement, but its adherents
stress "movement" rather than "party."

In summary, the political system is notable for the fragmentary nature of parties;
governments struggle to keep their own supporters in line. For a time, during the
years 2003–2005, the PT, which had a minority in both houses of congress, was
able to obtain the support of center-left parties and particularly the powerful centrist
PMDB. With the tainting of several ministers and congresspeople in the growing
corruption scandal of mid-2005, the president found it ever harder to push for his
party's agenda in congress.

In addition to the political parties, a number of interest groups compete for popular support. Some of these groups predate the latest democratic openings and go
back to the Vargas era, when the president subsidized and assisted such groups in
exchange for political support. Among those groups was labor, whose members first
banded together in mutual aid societies in the very early years of industrialization.
However, it was not until Vargas's first term as president, in the late 1930s and early
1940s, that these workers were organized into unions that received benefits from the
government while avoiding strikes and other destabilizing tactics. Labor rights and
social security provisions were provided at the price of collaboration or apathy.

After the 1964 coup the military abolished the largest labor confederation, the
General Workers' Command (CGT), which had been a major supporter of Goulart,
who himself had been a labor minister under Vargas. Under all the military administrations, the labor unions were strictly controlled and subject to government intervention. Union leaders were chosen by the government to ensure industrial peace
because it was essential to the military's plan for attracting domestic and foreign
investment that labor not agitate for raises or go out on strike.

While the economy was booming in the late 1960s and early 1970s, coinciding
with the most stringent military controls, the system of state-imposed industrial
peace worked well in that strikes seldom took place, much less succeeded. After
the downturn in the late 1970s labor was not as easily tamed, and about this time
the military itself was beginning to question the wisdom of remaining in power indefinitely. Eventually, new unions and new leaders emerged outside of government
control or with tacit acceptance by the military administration. After the *abertura*
that began in the late 1970s, it was possible to strike even though strikes could still
be ruled illegal. In 1980 metalworkers in São Paulo managed to shut down the powerful automobile industry for several weeks. Their leader, Lula, was jailed, but the
strike showed that workers were again willing to take risks. From this fairly successful strike action emerged the new PT, the Workers' Party, which remained the
most coherent opponent of the government. It took an anticorruption stance and espoused state-led economic development; but it continued to be plagued by internal
strife and charges of corruption.

Brazilian businesspeople, either as individuals or through their organizations,
encouraged or welcomed the 1964 coup. They had reason to fear Goulart's increasing sympathy for labor's demands; they disliked the general economic and political
uncertainty, which made investment planning difficult if not impossible. Their euphoria over getting rid of Goulart was short-lived, because the military proceeded to

consolidate the government's role in the economy. Military and civilian technocrats moved into various new economic areas without consulting the private sector, and the old tradition of having the government protect weak companies was rendered obsolete by the government's determination to achieve economic growth as fast as possible. Foreign companies were lured to invest in Brazil, often at the expense of less-efficient Brazilian enterprises, and the lowering of tariffs made it easier to import certain items than to produce them at home. Tax collection was tightened, and thus another traditional way of financing business was removed. Growing disappointment with and even resentment of the military made businesspeople, for their own reasons, ready to welcome and support the *abertura* just as the workers and old-line politicians were doing.

Business support for an end to the military regime coalesced with that of other groups that had challenged the authoritarian system. One of these groups was the Catholic Church. Brazil is the most Catholic country in the world in terms of the number of church members, and the church has a special position as an interest group. In contrast to many Spanish-speaking countries in Latin America, Brazil has not experienced long and bitter fights in relation to the church. The first republican constitution in 1891, under the inspiration of positivism, took away the church's special privileges without causing major trauma. For decades after the advent of the republic, the Brazilian Catholic hierarchy concentrated on running schools for the Brazilian elite and performing its theological and pastoral duties. Vatican II, between 1962 and 1965, moved the church toward greater involvement in social and political matters. In the 1940s and 1950s a number of lay and Catholic groups became active among students, workers, and political organizations. Vatican II gave a new impetus to this refocusing of the church, and it provided Brazilian theologians with the opportunity to advocate liberation theology and greater attention to the poor.

In the early 1960s this refocusing coincided with President Goulart's call for populist measures such as agrarian reform and expansion of the welfare system. At the time of the 1964 coup the church was deeply divided, with some members of the clergy supporting Goulart and others seeking to undermine him. Some supported his populism, but others saw it simply as a demagogic appeal. Many people feared that the church's growing political involvement would entangle it in matters that were not crucial to it as an institution and as a church. Large parades in the major cities often had the tacit approval and support of the church, with parishioners calling for moral renewal and decrying the chaos of everyday life. In the northeast, priests were among those who helped landless peasants take over large and often unused tracts of land. The reality of a divided church did not help Goulart's cause.

After the advent of the military regime in 1964 this split continued. Many people continued to be wary of what they perceived as the politicization of the church. Others increasingly denounced government repression and accused the military of failing to conform to Brazilian tradition by refusing to return to the barracks and give power back to civilians. By the 1970s much of the Brazilian church hierarchy was behind the effort to organize popular-level Catholic churches, with the goal of obtaining greater social justice and respect for human rights, and the churches were providing sanctuary for striking workers being pursued by the military. With the *abertura*, church leaders and laypeople alike were involved in the formation of political parties and eventually in the drafting of the new constitution. Perhaps not by coincidence, the greater political involvement of the Catholic Church occurred simultaneously with a growing challenge to Catholicism by a variety of Protestant churches, especially the more charismatic and evangelical ones and those concentrating their proselytizing efforts on the poor, the illiterate, and the displaced in urban areas. In addition, it is said that there are more Mormons in Brazil now than in the United States.

Besides the churches, the unions, the military, the business sector, and the political parties, a number of other organizations acted as pressure groups, with varying degrees of success. The Brazilian Order of Lawyers was active during the military regimes in seeking the restoration and enforcement of legal protections. The Brazilian Press Association opposed censorship and publicized the plight of persecuted journalists. A number of women's organizations emerged after the 1975 International Women's Year. The National Student Union, abolished at the time of the coup, continued to operate underground and sometimes even openly. A Green Party has been active. A novelty in Brazil, race-based groups emerged and began to demand real (instead of theoretical) equality for all. With the *abertura* and the holding of elections, literally hundreds of issue-, policy-, and candidate-focused groups emerged and began to compete, although most of them were transitory. More focused and militant African Brazilian groups have coalesced in more recent years. Benedita da Silva Sampaio, a former PT federal senator and vice governor of Rio de Janeiro at the end of the 1990s, was one of the best-known voices for these groups.

The Superior War College (ESG) continued to be influential. Founded in 1949, the ESG has been a center for training military and civilian elites. Somewhat similar to a think tank except that it is sponsored and subsidized by the government, it trained several presidents, including Castelo Branco, Geisel, and the presidential advisor Golbery do Couto et Silva. The ESG's slogan, "Security and Development," became a banner for anti-Communism during the military regimes, but the organization goes far beyond mere anti-Communism. It has been at the forefront of a great deal of sophisticated economic and strategic planning, and because it stresses that it aims to educate and inspire leaders, whether military or civilian, it is likely to remain a formidable institution. Its extensive network of alumni serves as a recruiting source for both government and private enterprises; many male and female ESG alumni are in key policy positions.

GOVERNMENT INSTITUTIONS, BUREAUCRACY, MAIN POLICY ISSUES

Russell H. Fitzgibbon, one of the most astute observers of Latin America, has said that "the organization of the Brazilian political system is largely distinguished by its federalism, which provides a backdrop for the performance of various political functions." It has been said that Brazil is the most federal of Latin America's regimes, but these statements do not mean that it is federal in terms of the US model.

Given the size and diversity of Brazil, federalism made sense to the people who drafted the first republican constitution in 1891. The Rio de Janeiro government was weak and unwilling to challenge powerful regional centers, and although the central government remained vulnerable, for the next three or four decades the states had a great deal of freedom. São Paulo, Minas Gerais, and Rio Grande do Sul showed so much independence that they maintained diplomatic relations with foreign governments, displayed their state flags above the national one, and called their state governors "presidents."

The Vargas era lessened these centrifugal pulls. The 1934 constitution gave preeminence to the national executive, state flags and anthems were abolished, and most economic functions were handled by the national government. Vargas's *estado novo* strengthened and reinforced centralization to the extent that even after his departure in 1945 the national government's powers far outstripped states' rights. During the turbulent and short Goulart years some states began to act on their own, perhaps secure in the knowledge that the federal government had enough other problems and could not worry about states' initiatives. Governor Leonel Brizola of Rio Grande do Sul, without a clear mandate to do so, expropriated US-owned utilities in that state, and an economic development organization in the northeast managed to receive funds directly from the US Agency for International Development (USAID). Military units based in Rio Grande do Sul, Minas Gerais, and São Paulo were crucially involved in the civilian-military coup that deposed Goulart in 1964.

From 1964 to 1985 the military regimes revised the constitution with institutional acts and decrees; sometimes these gave the national executive carte blanche in the restructuring of the government and in the proclamation of all types of policies. The taxing powers of the federal government ensured that all governors and mayors, even those of powerful states and metropolises, would comply with the wishes of the president if they hoped to get any funding for essential services. After the ushering in of a civilian regime, the president still holds a great deal of power: to choose and head a cabinet, to coordinate the actions of ministries, and to select individuals to occupy thousands of positions.

In an attempt to curb some of the presidential powers and to meld federalist and antifederalist impulses, the 1988 constitution became a monstrous hybrid. It promised greater freedom and power to states and local administrations, but it did not truly reverse the decades-old trend toward centralization. It gave congress greater power than ever before and strengthened civil liberties, labor rights, and social benefits. Its proclamation, in October 1988, abolished the authoritarian charter of 1967. It ensured the right to strike, set the voting age at sixteen, abolished censorship, and gave more power and income to state and municipal governments.

Under the new constitution, Brazilians elected a president by direct popular vote, for the first time since 1960, in November 1989. In what turned out to be a major source of domestic and international wrangling, questions concerning the international debt were debated by the entire congress, and the president and the minister of finance were no longer able to settle by themselves on a course to resolve Brazil's international obligations. Since 1992 major amendments have been adopted, mostly pertaining to economic issues. Many of the more restrictive clauses in the constitution have been implemented in a more liberal way so as to make possible both the privatization of state-owned enterprises and a greater influx of foreign investors. However, unless and until the constitution is fully revised, the possibility of interference by federal and/or state government in business ventures is still very much alive, as seen in the actions of a state governor who challenged not only the constitutionality of some contracts but even the payment of government debts. In the political realm, a 1997 constitutional amendment permitted the president and vice president, who are elected for four-year terms, to serve a second consecutive term.

Brazil remains a federative republic composed of twenty-six states and a federal district where the capital of the country, Brasília, is located. Each state has its own government; their structures mirror the federal ones, and the states may exercise any powers that are not reserved for the federal government or assigned to municipal councils. The governor is elected by direct popular vote and the state legislatures are unicameral. The state judiciary similarly mirrors the federal model, and its jurisdiction is defined to avoid conflicts with federal courts. Brazil has some 5,560 municipalities, and their councils handle local affairs.

While the political fighting continued as a daily occurrence, the revision of the 1988 charter has been piecemeal and sporadic. Ambiguity continues to surround the role of the military as the guarantor of the constitutional order. The left complains that the proposed changes further protect large private landowners and undermine the sputtering efforts to distribute plots to landless peasants at a time when 5 percent of the country's population owns half the arable land.

Regardless of the constitutional tinkering and the travails of a disordered democracy, some structural mainstays are not likely to change. Traditionally, Brazilian ministries have been very large bureaucracies with a plethora of subcabinets, councils, and other agencies, many of them powerful in their own right, plus institutes, autonomous agencies, and the like attached directly or indirectly to the ministries themselves. In this bureaucratic maze, personal and political linkages are of great importance and often override considerations of merit, efficiency, or organizational rationalism. Brazilian bureaucracy is notorious for its *papelada* (red tape). Many people are involved, many of them holding contradictory goals and acting according to incompatible policies; one also encounters unpredictability and a penchant for corruption. Antibureaucratic czars have been appointed, to no avail.

Throughout the system, from top to bottom, the sheer dead weight of myriad legal rules and codes that long ago outlived their usefulness remains untouched. The systematic inefficiency and the opportunity for favoritism are not mitigated when presidents, members of congress, and governors themselves routinely appoint cronies and family members to important posts, regardless of their qualifications. Thus, with little relevance to the constitution du jour, only the proverbial ability of the Brazilian bureaucrat to apply a *jeito*—to bend the rules just a little so that the day's business can be transacted—has kept the whole machinery of government from coming to a grinding halt.

A conservative estimate places the federal civil service at about a million people. This figure is meaningless because it does not take into consideration the countless independent and semi-independent bureaucracies and the many civil servants who have more than one full-time job. Presidents Collor, Cardoso, Lula, and now Dilma have applied regimes of austerity and tried to shrink the federal payroll, with some success. Mostly, longtime employees lost one of their many jobs, but the majority of those dropped from the rolls accepted it because they were entitled to generous pensions and retirement benefits. The Foreign Ministry (known as Itamaraty) is one of the better-run ministries, with a reputation for well-trained career officers, some continuity, and relative insulation from political vagaries. It is also the ministry that is least popular, with Brazilians and foreigners alike complaining about its inflexibility and its mind-numbing respect for the most minute and meaningless detail.

Brazil has traditionally had a bicameral legislature, and this tradition remained unchallenged in the 1988 constitution. Although the number of legislators has varied, the usual provision calls for three senators from each state and the federal district, for a total of 81 members. The chamber of deputies, 513 strong, is chosen on a population basis, and favors the least-populated rural states. The chambers have legislative committees, but their staffing patterns vary a great deal, and thus their ability to draft legislation is hard to predict. Throughout history, the president has been the chief legislator, and the legislation proposed by the executive branch has almost always been approved by congress by overwhelming margins. This has been somewhat moderated by the 1988 charter, which gave greater powers to the congress and denied the presidency its former wide decree powers. It was no longer possible for a strong dictatorial president to dismiss the legislature, as had been done in the past. However, reality does not always reflect constitutional provisions. The presidency was weakened when President Collor was impeached for malfeasance; old-timers recalled that his father had, with impunity, killed a fellow senator in chambers. Currently Collor is a senator. Many of the congress's members are tarnished by reports of grand larceny, rampant favoritism, and even the crude elimination of estranged wives and inconvenient enemies.

Under the 1988 constitution the legislature can sanction the president, alter the national budget, and determine international treaties. The text of the constitution was sufficiently ambiguous concerning the power of the congress to make it possible for the legislative branch to assert itself against a president, and vice versa. In the presidential debacle of 1992, with the removal of President Collor, there was little doubt that congress was preeminent. But in reality congressional powers ebb and flow. To obtain the constitutional amendment that allowed for a second presidential term, President Fernando Henrique Cardoso had to barter power and funds with legislators and governors. His initiatives toward fiscal reforms were stymied by congressional objections, but the congress was equally frustrated in obtaining presidential implementation of some of the measures it had adopted. The weakness of the political parties ensures that neither the president nor the representatives will be able to count on the loyalty of most of their partisans.

Even the constitutions have not been proven safe from outright rigging in day-to-day implementation. Thus, the overly long and detailed 1988 charter proved unworkable and was discarded in favor of a shorter version. To the credit of the 1988 charter, one should not forget that under its aegis the first presidential direct election in decades took place, and the president voted into power in that election lost his job when he was implicated in criminal activities. To the Brazilians' surprise—and pride—the removal of Fernando Collor and his replacement by Vice President Itamar Franco were accomplished without bloodshed. The voters in 1993 showed a marked preference for the continuation of the presidential over the parliamentary and monarchical forms of government.

Government structure and policy making have seen both small and major adjustments, but there is a rising skepticism about the benefits of democracy, and a constant despair over the inability of politicians to govern. Yet if one relies on history and tradition as guides, it seems probable that the 1988 constitution, like the others that preceded it, will be "reformed" through its daily encounters with Brazilian realities, just as policy making, regardless of the mountains of regulations and decrees, will ultimately remain at the mercy of the most skilled bureaucrat and the most imaginative Brazilian's *jeito*.

But even a new constitution and the proverbial *jeito* have not been able to ameliorate some of the country's policy issues. On one hand, the risk of armed conflict is low and no guerrilla groups pose a threat. More worrisome are the threats posed by private militias hired by landowners to deter Landless Worker Movement (MST) members from encroaching on their properties or by the very well-armed groups that protect one or more of the many drug lords; a great deal of international attention was focused upon the 2005 killing of an American nun in the Amazon region. A few years earlier, the mayor and some of the citizens of a border southern town celebrated the September 11, 2001, attacks in the United States with fireworks, leading the Brazilian and American governments to surmise that the remote and mostly unguarded locality harbored terrorism sympathizers.

In reality, far more problematic for Brazil is the rising level of crime, especially in major cities such as São Paulo and Rio de Janeiro.[4] The growing incidence of poverty, widening drug abuse, and drug trafficking is often reflected in the kidnapping for ransom of tourists and wealthy Brazilians. The country's police remain badly trained and worse paid, which helps promote corruption and deficiencies in law enforcement.

From a long-term perspective, the policy area that concerns Brazilian governments the most has been the weaknesses inherent in its educational system. Indicators tend to compare Brazil unfavorably to Uruguay and Chile. Presidents Cardoso and Lula promoted greater funding and attention to primary education. At the upper end, Brazil does have an excellent system of public universities, but most students able to meet stringent entrance requirements come from middle- or upper-class families.

Poor health indices reflect poverty, inadequate sanitation, low levels of education, and ecological degradation. The constitution provides for many health benefits, but these mostly remain on paper. More promising has been the government's proactive programs toward Brazil's HIV-positive population, which have been hailed as among the most successful efforts of their kind in the world.

Bolsa Família (Family Purse) was established by Cardoso and his wife, Ruth. This program, which subsidizes school and health services, has been enormously successful, allowing children to stay in school and eventually graduate. Another initiative, recently organized by President Dilma, has opened universities to students from diverse and underserved lower-income families.[5]

THE INTERNATIONAL ARENA

Even in colonial times Brazil's relations with its neighbors were characterized by accommodation (in the sense that Brazil seldom went to war with its neighbors, with the major exception being its war with Paraguay) and expansion (Brazil's borders, initially marked off by the Tordesilhas Line, now contain more than twice as much territory as originally envisaged by the pope, who drew the imaginary line). In more recent years Brazil has been a leader among the Latin American nations and has played a prominent role in security efforts and in economic cooperation within the Western Hemisphere. During World Wars I and II Brazil aligned itself with the Allies, and in the 1940s Brazilian soldiers played a distinguished and decisive role in the Allied victory at Monte Castello, Italy. Many of the generals behind the 1964 coup were involved in that campaign and formed close professional and personal relations with their North American counterparts. Humberto Castelo Branco, who later became president, shared a tent with the American Vernon Walters, and the two men became lifelong friends.

Brazil is a signatory to the Inter-American Treaty of Reciprocal Assistance (the Rio Treaty) and it is a member of the Organization of American States (OAS), which is sometimes headed by a Brazilian diplomat. Brazilian career foreign officers have distinguished themselves in international bodies, and some of them have been chosen to head such organizations, as was the case with the World Health Organization a few years ago. More recently Brazil has given priority to strengthening its ties with other South American states and has become a member of the Amazon Pact and the Latin American Integration Association (ALADI). Former Brazilian president José Sarney and Argentina's Raúl Alfonsín overcame the traditional enmity between their two countries with several understandings and protocols to ensure cooperation in a number of areas, including nuclear armaments and research. Brazil is a charter member of the United Nations and has been an active participant in several of its specialized agencies. It has contributed troops to UN peacekeeping efforts in the Middle East, in the former Belgian Congo (now the Democratic Republic of the Congo), Cyprus, Mozambique, and Haiti. Brazil helped mediate the resolution of the Angolan civil war.

Brazil's booming economy, trade, and international debt have caused it to become increasingly involved in international politics and economics. It is a member of the General Agreement on Tariffs and Trade (GATT), the Committee of Twenty of the International Monetary Fund (IMF), several World Bank organizations, the Inter-American Development Bank (IADB), and many international commodity agreements. The United States, Western Europe, and Japan are the primary markets for Brazilian exports and the main sources of foreign lending and investments. Brazil is the third-largest trading partner of the European Union. Brazil's earlier dependence on imported oil had forced it to strengthen its ties with the oil-producing nations in the Middle East, and a number of barter arrangements were worked out whereby Brazilian technicians and laborers exchanged their expertise and work for oil from Middle Eastern countries, especially Iraq; the Gulf War found thousands of Brazilian contractors stuck in a variety of jobs in Iraq. The discovery of abundant oil in Brazil in 2007 has changed all this. In a pragmatic if not principled way, Brazil has often voted with Arab countries rather than with Israel in international organizations.

Beginning in the 1970s Brazil expanded its relations with black African countries.[6] In 1986 it introduced a proposal at the UN General Assembly to establish a zone of peace and cooperation in the South Atlantic. Because of its own large black population and its long-standing integrationist record, Brazil consistently voted for resolutions calling for the end of apartheid in South Africa. With the democratization of that country, Brazil has joined and might lead in the formation of a South Atlantic security and economic zone.

Brazil has diplomatic relations with most countries in the world, among them the former Soviet Union, all the East European countries, and Cuba. The country's relations with the United States are unique. The United States was the first country to recognize Brazil's independence in 1822. Dom Pedro II admired Abraham Lincoln and visited the United States during the latter's 1876 centennial. President Dwight Eisenhower was given a hero's welcome when he visited Brazil in 1960, and Presidents Franklin Roosevelt and Harry Truman were cordially received. President Jimmy Carter visited in 1978, but at the time there were major strains between the two countries on questions of human rights, and Brazilians were incensed by US attempts to interfere in Brazil's nuclear program. President Ronald Reagan and President Bill Clinton visited Brazil; the latter has maintained warm relations with former president Cardoso. Presidents Lula and Dilma were received at the White House.

In the 1950s and 1960s Brazil was the recipient of about US$2.4 billion in economic assistance from the United States through USAID, the Food for Peace program, and the Peace Corps. During the military administrations the Peace Corps and the Inter-American Foundation (IAF) were accused of interfering in domestic affairs and were told to leave the country; IAF has since resumed its large program there. After 1972 US aid efforts emphasized, among other programs, the training of young Brazilian technicians and social scientists in graduate schools in the United States. In view of Brazil's economic development and its ability to obtain loans and technical assistance from private and multilateral sources, the US assistance programs were phased out in the 1970s. Major USAID activities ceased in 1979, and the Peace Corps ended its work in Brazil in 1980. The Department of State and other US government agencies have small contingents in Brazil that collaborate on science and technology projects; respond to endemic diseases, emergencies, and natural disasters; and may be of technical assistance in family planning efforts.

The United States is no longer Brazil's most important commercial partner; in 2011, the United States accounted for 10 percent of Brazil's exports and 15 percent of Brazil's imports. The trading relations between these two countries have become less friendly since Brazil began actively seeking other partners (notably China) and refused to open its market to US products, particularly certain types of computers. Nationalism and simple tradition reinforced Brazil's insistence on continuing export subsidies and protectionism; nowhere were these clearer than in the 1988 constitutional provisions that actively discriminated against foreign investors and, in effect, closed certain industries to foreign firms. By the 2000s, tradition and protectionism, shaken by the cold realities of tough global competition, were giving way to privatization and a friendlier response to international economic overtures. The Cardoso, Lula, and Dilma administrations have been characterized by a higher international profile. All have vigorously pursued relations with South America and have led to an expansion of the Common Market of the South to include a free trade agreement with Chile (1996), one with Bolivia (1997), and closer relations with Venezuela and

Cuba (2012). All have campaigned for Brazil to become a permanent member of an enlarged UN Security Council and have heightened Brazil's presence in the IADB and the World Bank.

The more formal agreements between Brazil and the United States include a treaty of peace and friendship, an extradition treaty, and a joint participation agreement on communications satellites, as well as scientific cooperation, civil aviation, and maritime agreements. The two countries exchange academic personnel under the Fulbright and other scholarly programs and carry out university cooperation projects. Under the popular Partners of the Americas Program, several US states have active exchanges with their counterparts in Brazil. Increasingly, Brazil has sponsored visits by artistic groups to the United States and other countries to promote better relations and publicize Brazil's cultural achievements.

With respect to Brazil's international debt, there are both encouraging signs and others that do not seem to augur well. On the plus side, in September 1988 President Sarney formally ended the country's nineteen-month-old moratorium on payments on its then US$121 billion foreign debt. At the time the Brazilian president warned that Brazil could not permanently export capital and called on creditors to do their part, just as Brazil was doing its part. Brazil's return to orthodox strategies and its rapprochement with the IMF marked the end of a roller-coaster period of economic experiments that included a wage and price freeze, a promising boom, and the moratorium on payments enacted shortly after the 1986 elections.

The 1988 constitution complicated the picture by giving the congress wide powers to decide on external payments and policies affecting Brazil's relations with international banking institutions. Those developments were but the most recent chapters in the long-simmering dispute between Brazil and its creditors. The oil shocks of the 1970s and 1980s and the world recession that followed were keenly felt in Brazil because of its crucial need to maintain ever-higher levels of exports to finance its economic development. Brazil has sought to work out mutually satisfactory banking relations that would, in effect, let the country stretch out its payments on the interest and count on eventual forgiveness of the huge principal. Not surprisingly, at times during the 1980s US banks felt that they were hostages to Brazil's economy and, worse, Brazil's sense of nationalism. By the 2010s, more investors began to tout Brazil as a good to excellent location for investment, especially after major oil field finds. But the papelada and corruption remained long-term problems.

Many of the 1988 constitutional restrictions have been formally set aside, and the investment climate is more forthcoming. Constitutionally the climate has become more propitious for investment, constitutional guarantees and enticements can do little to dispel the sense that the papelada remains and that corruption is a long-term problem.

In a broader sense, relations between Brazil and the United States have had an uneven track record in the 2000s. Although tensions and disagreements remain on charges that Brazil "dumps" (i.e., sells below cost) such products as steel, both countries became more engaged in day-to-day consultations after Cardoso took office. On the US side, there seems to be a realization that the health of the Brazilian economy is vital to the health of the other South American economies, while on the Brazilian side, given the stiff competition linked to globalization, there has been a corresponding realization that the United States is too big a customer for Brazil to annoy with obsolete nationalistic posturing. But old attitudes do not change easily. In 2010, the presidential aspirants denounced Cardoso and Lula's more liberal economic policies. They echoed the popular sentiment that the United States could help Brazil overcome its economic and international problems but has not done so because it wishes to prevent Brazil from becoming a world power; they also charge that the United States prevented Brazil from acquiring a permanent seat on the UN Security Council. Investments are routinely labeled "Trojan horses" that enrich foreigners at the expense of ordinary Brazilians. This is particularly true in the case of Chinese investments.

Brazil's relations with other North and South American countries have their own uniqueness. Brazil and Mexico agreed in 1983 to complete a barter deal that would provide for the exchange of up to US$1 billion of goods each way. Brazil has concluded agreements for hydroelectric dam systems in the Plata Basin, and the Itaipú Treaty, signed with Argentina and Paraguay, makes Brazil the owner of the second-largest hydroelectric dam in the world. Better relations now exist between Argentina and Brazil after decades of suspicion on both sides. President Sarney advocated a common market between the two countries, and although this idea is probably far from realization, they are trading much more than before, with Brazil exporting a wide variety of manufactured goods to Argentina in exchange for agricultural products. Many of Brazil's capital goods are exported throughout other parts of Latin America as well.

Brazil was never a major partner with the former Soviet Union, but it has remained interested in increasing its exports to that region. The Soviet Union was quite active in promoting cultural exchanges at all levels, and a number of young, promising Brazilians were provided with scholarships to study in Moscow. Overall, Brazil has been pragmatic in the conduct of its foreign affairs. Unless a clear benefit can be derived, Brazilians seldom take the lead. Brazil is content to pursue its own interests without unnecessarily antagonizing the countries it deeply depends on, but it will stand firm when it feels that its nationalism and sovereignty are not being given the attention they deserve. The best example of this was Brazil's strong stand in obtaining nuclear technology from West Germany in the late 1970s in spite of President Carter's insistent and eventually counterproductive pressure.

The overly specific and detailed provisions in the 1988 constitution might have affected Brazil's conduct of foreign policy to a greater extent than they actually did, given Brazil's internal politics and governmental turnovers. It is clear that for the time being and in the prolonged period of transition, congress will have much more to say in this area than before. Once a popularly elected and determined president comes upon the scene, the pendulum may swing again toward the executive as the major player.

CONCLUSION

Brazil's growing sense of its importance and its impact on the world scene goes beyond mere posturing. If the country were not so diverse, so potentially rich, and so culturally integrated, its assertiveness would be empty indeed. Writing in 1987, Robert Harvey, a longtime observer of Brazil, put it best:

> Brazil is the unstoppable colossus of the south; a major regional power already; the first big third-world country knocking on the door of the club of developed democracies; and a potential United States in the next century. . . . Brazil's long-term prospects are glowing; its very bravado is one of the main reasons why it can look forward to the future much as, say, bankers, investors, potential migrants and, not least, governments ought to be looking at Brazil as carefully as their precursors did at the United States in its early maturity . . . Brazil has reached major power adulthood, although not yet the responsibility—and caution—of middle age.[7]

In fact, most observers usually echo this correspondent's conclusions. They agree that despite Brazil's lingering economic and political questions, it is not too rash to predict that the next decades will witness Brazil's rise to an unchallenged status within Latin America, then to a predominant status within the South Atlantic community, and finally to major world power status.

The potential is there, but so also are the burdens of a chaotic and overly bureaucratized system, constitutional arrangements still untried, and a fragile democracy. One military president expressed his misgivings: "The country is doing well, the people not so well." In spite of nearly three decades of democracy, this assessment is still mostly true because although in the 2000s a new order was taking shape, progress has often been slow and fitful.

Indeed, as the country prepared to receive the new pope in July 2013 and to build essential structures for the 2014 World Cup and 2016 Olympics, a number of relatively peaceful demonstrations began and gained momentum throughout the country. What sparked them initially was a small increase in bus fares, but the protests grew and spread. Only when there was violence and property damage did the police or military intervene. Basically the demonstrations were a result of frustration over the return of inflation, poor health care, cost overruns, and, above all, the perception that politicians were corrupt and out of touch. President Rousseff saw her approval rate plummet, even though she set aside US$1.3 billion to improve public transit in Sao Paulo. Would that be enough to quell the discontent, or would Lula succeed her?

Still, it would be premature to label Brazil another banana republic, with intermittent dictatorships. If anything, because Brazil is a maturing democracy, the average Brazilian expects more of the country's leaders and its system. This is the same average Brazilian who is indeed proud of seeing fellow Brazilians reach international pinnacles in sport, culture, and fashion but who also has to deal with the daily indignities of unemployment, corrupt civil servants, a chaotic party system, and inadequate health care and educational institutions. In the second decade of this new millennium, will the average Brazilian see the potential and the reality finally meld into one? Will Brazilians no longer be at one and at the same time among both the poorest and the richest people in Latin America? Time alone will tell, but "Order and Progress" is now more than a centuries-old motto; the uniqueness of the country looks promising.

Notes

1. Larry Rohter, *Brazil on the Rise: The Story of a Country Transformed* (New York: St. Martin's Press, 2011).

2. Elizabeth Bishop, *Brazil* (New York: Time, 1963), 12–13.

3. Much has been written on the issue. One of the best (and shortest) pieces is the analytical article by Glaucio Ary Dillon Soares, "The Rise of the Brazilian Military," *Studies in Comparative International Development* 21, no. 2 (Summer 1986): 34–62. See also Alfred Stepan, ed., *Democratizing Brazil* (New York: Oxford University Press, 1989).

4. Joe Leahy, "Spiraling Drug War Grips São Paulo," *Financial Times*, December 21, 2012.

5. Ricardo Batista Amaral, *A vidaquer é couragem: A trajetória de Dilma Rousseff: a primeira presidenta do Brasil* (Rio de Janeiro: Sextante, 2011).

6. "Brazil's Vast Increase in Arable Land Complicates Ties to the U.S.," *Washington Post*, November 19, 2012; "Brazilian Africa: A New Atlantic Alliance," *Economist*, November 10, 2012, 66–70.

7. Robert Harvey, "Brazil: Unstoppable," *Economist*, April 25, 1987, 3.

Suggestions for Further Reading

Ames, Barry. *The Deadlock of Democracy in Brazil: Interests, Identities, and Institutions in Comparative Politics*. Ann Arbor: University of Michigan Press, 2001.

Baaklini, Abdo. *The Brazilian Legislature and Political System*. Westport, CT: Greenwood Press, 1992.

Baer, Werner. *The Brazilian Economy: Growth and Development*. 5th ed. Westport, CT: Praeger, 1999.

Cardoso, Fernando Henrique, and Mauricio A. Font. *Charting a New Course: The Politics of Globalization and Social Transformation*. Lanham, MD: Rowman and Littlefield, 2001.

Eakin, Marshall C. *Brazil: The Once and Future Country*. New York: St. Martin's Press, 1997.

Font, Mauricio A., and Anthony Peter Spanakos, eds. *Reforming Brazil*. Lanham, MD: Lexington Books, 2004.

Gordon, Lincoln. *Brazil's Second Chance: En Route Toward the First World*. Washington, DC: Brookings Institution, 2001.

Ireland, Rowan. *Kingdom Comes: Religion and Politics in Brazil*. Pittsburgh, PA: University of Pittsburgh Press, 1991.

Roett, Riordan. *Brazil: Politics in a Patrimonial Society*. 5th ed. Westport, CT: Praeger, 1999.

Skidmore, Thomas E. *Brazil: Five Centuries of Change*. New York: Oxford University Press, 1999.

Telles, Edward E. *Race in Another America: The Significance of Skin Color in Brazil*. Princeton, NJ: Princeton University Press, 2004.

8

CHILE: ALTERNATIVE APPROACHES TO DEVELOPMENT

Paul E. Sigmund

What is it about Chile that is so fascinating to the foreign observer? A long (2,600-mile, 4,200-kilometer) "string bean" of a country of nearly seventeen million inhabitants squeezed between the Andes and the sea, it is one of the most important copper producers in the world. It exports fine fruits and wine and has a literate, relatively large middle class. Evidence of its cultural sophistication is the substantial number of world-class Chilean writers and poets, including two Nobel Prize winners. Its topography is varied, ranging from deserts in the north to the fertile 600-mile (966-kilometer) Central Valley, not unlike the valley of the same name in California, and heavily wooded mountains and fjords in the farthest southern regions. Chile's strategic value is limited, except for its control of the Straits of Magellan. None of these factors accounts for foreigners' extraordinary fascination with the country.

Chilean politics is the reason for the great interest. Until the 1973 coup it was one of the oldest constitutional democracies in the world. Since 1833, with only two interruptions—a short but bloody civil war in 1891 and a period of military intervention and plebiscitarian rule between 1925 and 1932—its political system followed regular constitutional procedures, with civil liberties, the rule of law, and periodic contested elections for a bicameral legislature and a directly elected president.

In recent decades successive governments have attempted to implement a variety of approaches to address Chilean underdevelopment. Between 1958 and 1964 a conservative government headed by President Jorge Alessandri tried to resolve Chile's problems of inflation, unemployment, and slow growth by emphasizing market incentives along with government programs in the areas of housing and

PERU

Arica

Iquique

Chuquicamata

Antofagasta

BOLIVIA

PARAGUAY

Copiapó

La Serena
Ovalle • Coquimbo

Valparaíso
★ Santiago

Rancagua
Talca

ARGENTINA

Concepción • Chillán

Angol

Temuco

Valdivia

Osorno

Puerto Montt
Ancud
Castro

Isla de Chiloé

Puerto Aisén

Península de
Taitao

ATLANTIC

OCEAN

PACIFIC

OCEAN

Strait of Magellan

Punta Arenas • Porvenir

Cape Horn

0 100 200 300 400 Miles

0 200 400 Kilometers

CHILE

limited agrarian reform. The Christian Democratic government of Eduardo Frei Montalva (1964–1970) initiated a "Chileanization" program involving a partial takeover by purchase of the US-owned copper mines, adopted a much more radical agrarian reform law, promoted programs to organize and benefit peasants and "marginalized" sectors, and cooperated actively with the US-sponsored Alliance for Progress in attempting to carry out what Frei Montalva called a "revolution in liberty." A three-way election in 1970 led to the victory of Salvador Allende, the candidate of the Marxist-dominated Popular Unity coalition. Allende tried to initiate a "transition to socialism" involving takeovers—sometimes of questionable legality—of industry and agriculture, income redistribution, and accelerated class polarization.

In 1973 the three armed services and the national police (*carabineros*) overthrew Allende, and what had begun as an institutional coup to save democracy from Marxism soon became a personalist dictatorship under General Augusto Pinochet, the head of the army. Pinochet closed down the political system but allowed a group of free-market-oriented economists, many of whom (known as *los Chicago boys*) had been trained at the University of Chicago, to open up what had been a highly protected economy and drastically reduce government intervention in a controversial experiment in economic—but not political—libertarianism. In 1980 Pinochet appealed to Chilean legalism and constitutionalism to legitimate his power by calling and winning a snap plebiscite on a constitution that enabled him to continue in office until 1989 but required another plebiscite on a new mandate for an additional eight years. On October 5, 1988, he lost that plebiscite by a vote of 55 percent to 43 percent.

In the elections that followed, a multiparty, anti-Pinochet coalition (the Concertación por la Democracia) elected a Christian Democrat, Patricio Aylwin, to a four-year term ending in March 1994. He was succeeded by Eduardo Frei Ruiz-Tagle, the son of the former Christian Democratic president. In 2000, after a very close election, Ricardo Lagos from the Socialist Party, the other major partner in the coalition, narrowly defeated the candidate of the conservative coalition. In 2006, another Socialist, Michelle Bachelet, the daughter of an air force general who had opposed the 1973 coup and died in prison, was elected as the first Chilean woman president. The four Concertación presidents successfully combined an open market economy with increasing expenditures on health, education, and social welfare.

In January 2010, Sebastián Piñera from the center-right Party of National Renovation defeated Frei Ruiz-Tagle, ending the twenty-year rule of the Concertación. Piñera became increasingly unpopular during his four-year term, and Michelle Bachelet, his predecessor, seemed almost certain to win the presidential election on November 17, 2013.

The contrasting approaches to development adopted by successive Chilean governments have produced a large and controversial literature. Conservatives, reformists, revolutionaries, and authoritarians have cited the accomplishments and failures of the various Chilean governments in order to defend or attack more general ideological approaches to Third World politics. The Allende experiment in particular has spawned an enormous literature—probably one thousand books in many languages—but the other governments also have both their defenders and their critics.

The Pinochet dictatorship was characterized by a dramatic opening of the economy, accompanied by violations of human rights that drew worldwide attention. The policies of the post-Pinochet democratic governments that have combined economic growth based on private and foreign investment, export promotion, and low inflation with increased social equity and a dramatic reduction in poverty (from 40 percent in 1990 to 13.7 percent in 2006) have been seen as a model for the rest of Latin America.

Citizens of the United States have reason to be interested in Chilean politics because of the deep involvement of the US government in that country between the 1950s and the 1990s. Because Chile had the oldest and, outside of Cuba, the largest Communist Party in the Western Hemisphere, the United States during the Cold War began to attempt to influence its political life. It supported, overtly and covertly, the reformist Christian Democratic regime in the 1960s; opposed, overtly and covertly, the Allende government in the early 1970s; and was ambivalent about the Pinochet regime—repelled by its human rights violations (which led to a cutoff in 1976 by the US Congress of all military aid and sales to Chile) but supportive of Chile's free market approach to development and its willingness to respect its international economic obligations. Beginning in the mid-1980s, for both ideological and pragmatic reasons, the Reagan administration began to promote a democratic transition in Chile and an end to the Pinochet dictatorship. Before the 1988 plebiscite the US Congress went even further, appropriating US$1 million to support free elections in Chile. Since the return of democracy in 1990 US-Chilean relations have improved dramatically, and in 2004, after many years of negotiation, the two countries signed a free trade agreement.

Interest in Chile revolves around three general questions. First, how is it that, in contrast to most other Latin American countries, Chile has been able to develop and maintain pluralist civilian constitutional rule throughout most of its history? Second, why did what appeared to be a strong, stable democracy give way to repressive military rule in 1973, and what was the role of the US government before and after the coup? And third, what lessons can be drawn from the contrasting approaches of recent Chilean governments for achieving a successful combination of democracy, economic growth, and social justice?

POLITICAL HISTORY TO 1973

To answer the first question we must look at Chile's history and political culture and at the self-image held by the Chileans themselves. Most accounts of the origins of Chile's constitutionalism begin with the early postindependence struggles for control of the government between the conservative *pelucones,* "bigwigs," and the more liberal *pipiolos,* "upstarts." After the autocratic ways of "the Liberator," Bernardo O'Higgins, led to his resignation in 1823, a period of conflict ensued that ended with the triumph of the *pelucones* in the battle of Lircay. The 1833 constitution adopted under their auspices created a strong role for the president, who was elected by property holders for a five-year term with the possibility of reelection for a second term, but it also gave the congress a role in approving the budget. To this day Chilean conservatives look back to the 1830s, when Diego Portales established a strong centralized state operating under the rule of law, for a governmental ideal that is still valid. They argue that the strong presidency and state not only continued cultural patterns inherited from the Spanish monarchy but also maintained the rule of Castilian-Basque landowners in a way that prevented the breakdown of authority and military intervention that characterized many other newly independent Latin American states. Others maintain that the development of civilian constitutionalism owes more to the presidency of Manuel Bulnes (1841 1851), the hero of the 1837 war with Peru and Bolivia, than to Portales. Bulnes sharply reduced the size of the army and built up a civilian-based national guard as a counterweight to it; he also strengthened the state bureaucracy so that it provided effective administration and loyalty to the institutions of the state. In addition, he was willing to work with the congress even when it opposed his plans, and he relied on changes in his cabinet in order to keep in touch with elite opinion. Most important, he left office in accordance with the constitutional timetable, even though he was still personally popular.

In the two-term, ten-year presidency of Bulnes's successor, Manuel Montt (1851–1861), the Liberals reemerged, now reinforced by the influx of progressive ideas from the Europe of the liberal revolutions of 1848. As in other Latin American countries, the Liberal-Conservative split focused on centralism versus federalism and the relations between church and state. The federalist tendencies of the Liberals reflected the opposition of the mining interests of the north and the medium-sized landholders of the south to the political dominance of the large landowners of the Central Valley around the capital, Santiago. Revolts against Santiago's domination in 1851 and 1859 were put down, but what Chileans call the Oligarchic Republic (1830–1861) gave way to the Liberal Republic (1861–1891), in which factions of the elite combined and recombined in the congress and the presidency to open the system by limiting the presidency to five years (1871) and abolishing the property requirement for voting (1874). A small but expanding middle class found political expression in the founding in 1861 of the Radical Party, which was committed to Freemasonry, reducing church influence, promoting public education, and establishing universal male suffrage. However, Conservative control of elections in the countryside in what was still largely a rural country meant that the large landowners were able to use electoral democracy to maintain their dominance rather than resorting to military intervention to stem the effects of increased popular participation. Church-state issues, such as who should control clerical appointments, cemeteries, and education, still divided the political class, but after 1859 all groups now agreed on elections and peaceful competition rather than on the use of force to resolve their differences.

The Liberal-Conservative split was papered over during the War of the Pacific (1879–1883) against Peru and Bolivia. Chile's victory gave it a one-third increase in territory involving the rich copper and nitrate areas of the north, but it also led to border disputes with Peru (which were resolved only as late as 1929) and conflict with Bolivia over its loss of access to the Pacific (still an issue today). The victory vastly increased government revenues from export taxes and produced not only a period of economic prosperity but also the beginnings of an inflation problem that was to continue for almost a century. When President José Manuel Balmaceda (1886–1891) began to take measures to end currency depreciation, promote small landholding, and establish state control over the largely British-owned nitrate deposits, he encountered fierce resistance from landowners and foreign interests. When the congress refused to approve his budget he attempted to rule alone, and a civil war ensued in which ten thousand Chileans died, including Balmaceda himself, who committed suicide after his forces were defeated.

The Chilean constitutional system was fundamentally transformed as a result of the 1891 civil war. During the period of the Parliamentary Republic (1891–1920), power passed from the president to the congress, and the center of political attention shifted to the local bases of the notables who controlled the congress. National governments (a total of 121 cabinets between 1891 and 1924) rose and fell, depending on shifting congressional majorities, while weak presidents presided over unstable coalition governments.

Following the end of the War of the Pacific in 1883 a Prussian captain, Emil Körner, was invited to organize the Chilean Academy of War, and he began a program to professionalize the army along Prussian lines. (The goose step and the army's strict hierarchical structure and professionalism mark the continuing effects of the original Prussian influence.) So effective was Körner that Chilean military missions were subsequently invited to train armies in Colombia and El Salvador.

In the economy, nitrate, coal, and copper mining were expanded (by US companies in the case of copper), and labor agitation increased. Labor began to organize, and the massacre of two thousand nitrate workers and their families at Iquique in 1907 became a part of the collective memory of the labor movement. Luis Emilio Recabarren, a labor leader, was elected to the congress in 1906 but was not allowed to take his seat. In 1912 Recabarren founded the Socialist Workers' Party, which in 1921 became the Communist Party of Chile. The expanding middle class found its political expression in the Radical Party, which, in addition to its traditional endorsement of the separation of church and state, began to adopt programs favoring social welfare legislation.

The development of cheap synthetic nitrate during World War I dealt a serious blow to Chilean prosperity, which had been based on mineral exports. The election of 1920 brought to the presidency a new populist leader, Arturo Alessandri Palma. Although Alessandri's supporters secured a majority in the congressional elections of 1924, the congress resisted his proposals for social legislation and labor rights. These proposals were adopted only under pressure from young reformist military men in the galleries—the so-called rattling of the sabers. Alessandri left the country in protest against military intervention but returned the next year to preside over the writing of the 1925 constitution. The constitution provided for a strong president, elected for a six-year term but denied the possibility of immediate reelection. Members of the congress were elected at a different time and for different terms (four years for the chamber of deputies and eight years for the senate). Legislators were elected according to a system of proportional representation that accentuated the proliferation of parties that had already begun to take place. Church and state were separated, and labor and social welfare guarantees were included in the constitution. Chile was thus well ahead of most other Latin American countries in the establishment of the welfare state.

Alessandri resigned three months later, and his successor was forced out by Colonel Carlos Ibáñez, who ruled by plebiscite and decree until 1931. Following a series of short-lived military governments Chile returned to elected governments in late 1932. The military largely withdrew from politics, and four decades of civilian rule ensued.

One of the many unstable governments in the period from 1931 to 1932 was a military-dominated Socialist Republic that lasted one hundred days, from June to September 1932. Marxist intellectuals, students, and military men then joined to form a new leftist party, the Socialist Party of Chile, which was formally established in April 1933. In late 1932 Arturo Alessandri returned as president, but he now followed a much more conservative policy than earlier. The period that followed has been described by some Chilean writers as *el estado de compromiso* (the compromise state)—that is, one in which there was something for everyone and no interest group was directly threatened. The combination of staggered elections and proportional representation meant that it was difficult to get a stable majority for any program, especially if it involved fundamental reforms.

In 1938 Pedro Aguirre Cerda, the candidate of a Popular Front coalition of Radicals and Socialists with Communist support, won the presidential elections. He faced a hostile legislative majority, and the coalition lasted only two years. The Popular Front succeeded in securing the passage of a few social welfare laws, but its principal accomplishment was the establishment of the Chilean Development Corporation (CORFO), which provided the legal basis for a larger state role in the economy. The period from 1938 to 1952 was characterized by the dominance of the Radical Party, which governed through shifting coalitions and policies along with generous patronage to the party faithful. One such shift was from an alliance with the Communists in 1938 to the outlawing of the party by the Radical-sponsored Law for the Defense of Democracy in 1948. (The Communists were legalized again in 1958.)

When the country looked for an alternative to the Radical Party in 1952 it turned to none other than the old military strongman Carlos Ibáñez, who won by a landslide under the symbol of a broom to sweep out the corrupt and ineffective Radicals. Ibáñez did not deliver on his promises, however, and the traditional parties returned to the fray in 1958. A new party, the Christian Democrats, which had been formed by successive reformist splits from the conservatives, made a surprising showing in the 1958 elections. The Christian Democrats divided the centrist vote with the Radicals, while the leftist alliance of the Socialists and Communists came close to electing Salvador Allende as president. Allende was narrowly edged out by Arturo Alessandri's son Jorge, the candidate of the Liberals and Conservatives. (There were no longer any significant differences between the Liberals and Conservatives, since the church-state issue had been settled in 1925, and overlapping rural and urban interests in both parties rendered obsolete the old divisions between the landowner and merchant classes.) The 1958 election, with its three-way split between left, center, and right, marked the beginning of a recurrent problem in Chilean politics—how to get majority support for presidents and parties when the electorate was divided into "the three thirds" (*los tres tercios*).

When it looked as if the 1964 presidential elections might give Allende a chance to win by a plurality in a multicandidate race (and thus, by tradition, to be elected in the congressional runoff), the right threw its support to the charismatic Christian-Democratic candidate, Eduardo Frei Montalva, whose program for a "revolution in liberty" was offered as a democratic response to the challenge of the Cuban Revolution. Frei Montalva won the popular election with the first absolute majority in modern Chilean history—55 percent to Allende's 39 percent. But when he began to implement his program of accelerated agrarian reform, expanded welfare legislation, and higher taxes, the right withdrew its support.

Frei Montalva's reforms had strong US backing inasmuch as they coincided with the aims and methods of the Alliance for Progress, but they ran into congressional opposition (because of staggered elections, the Christian Democrats never controlled both houses) and created inflationary pressures. After a successful first three years Frei Montalva faced an increasingly hostile congress, and in 1969 he had to put down a local military revolt, the first since the 1930s. The right was optimistic that it could win the 1970 presidential elections with Jorge Alessandri, now eligible to run again, since the Christian Democrats had lost support and did not put forward a strong candidate. On the left, meanwhile, the Socialist-Communist alliance backing Allende was broadened to include a left splinter group from the Christian Democrats as well as the main body of the Radical Party (which also had split).

The result was a narrow victory by Allende (36.2 percent, lower than his vote in 1964) over Alessandri (34.9 percent), with the Christian-Democratic candidate a distant third with 27.8 percent. Chile was thrown into a constitutional, political, and economic crisis as the congress, which was over two-thirds non-Marxist, was asked to elect a Marxist as president in the constitutionally mandated runoff between the top two candidates. The crisis was intensified by US covert efforts to create turmoil in the economy and to promote a military coup, and by the assassination by a rightist group of the army's commander in chief. Despite the turmoil that followed and after lengthy negotiations, the constitutional tradition was followed. In November 1970 Salvador Allende became president.

In the case of the Allende government, the pattern of three good years followed by three bad ones that had characterized previous administrations was telescoped into eighteen months for each period. In 1971 the US-owned mines were completely nationalized by a widely supported constitutional amendment (although the compensation procedures, which in most cases amounted to confiscation, immediately got the Allende government into trouble with the United States government and the copper companies); a boom, produced by the granting of large wage raises while price controls were strictly enforced, buoyed the economy; and the Allende coalition received nearly 50 percent support in the municipal elections. However, by 1972 runaway inflation had set in; violence was increasing in the countryside; shortages of foodstuffs and essential goods occurred; and class polarization, encouraged by a government that was trying to broaden its base of support among the lower classes, exacerbated personal and political relations. Using, among other things, legal loopholes created by legislation from the 1932 Socialist Republic, the government took over and "intervened in" or "requisitioned" five hundred firms; consequently, industrial and agricultural production dropped. Further exacerbating the economic problems, opposition-dominated professional and occupational groups (*gremios*) called strikes that paralyzed the country in October 1972 and again in July 1973.

Despite several attempts at negotiations with the Christian Democrats, Allende was not able to work out an agreement with the opposition-dominated congress.

(The left wing of his Socialist Party opposed any agreement, as did the right wing of the Christian Democrats.) By the time the congressional elections of March 1973 took place, "the three thirds" had become two intransigent pro- and anti-Allende blocs. The center-right Democratic Confederation won 55 percent of the congressional vote, compared with 43 percent for Allende's Popular Unity Federation, but the division of the country only intensified. Violence increased as extremists on both sides (the Movement of the Revolutionary Left [MIR] and the rightist Patria y Libertad) carried out assassinations, blackouts, and bombings. To the concerns of the military over the collapse of the economy and the breakdown of law and order (symbolized by a widely circulated picture of a policeman being beaten by a masked and helmeted revolutionary) were added fears of Marxism as the government announced that all schools would be required to give government-mandated courses in socialism.

Yet the army still considered itself to be "professional, hierarchical, obedient, and non-deliberative," as required by the 1925 constitution. The armed forces did not move until the Supreme Court had written open letters to Allende protesting the government's refusal to carry out court orders to return seized property, the congress had passed a resolution accusing the government of habitually violating the constitution and the law, and the other army generals had forced out their constitutionalist commander in chief, Carlos Prats (later assassinated in exile by Chilean intelligence agents).

On September 11, 1973, the army, air force, navy, and national police overthrew the Allende government in a one-day coup that included the bombing of La Moneda, the presidential palace (the traditional symbol of civilian rule), and the suicide of Allende (following the example, which he had often cited, of President Balmaceda in 1891) as army troops stormed the burning palace.

Despite reports, never proven, of CIA involvement in the coup (a 1975 US Senate investigation concluded that between 1971 and 1973 CIA money supported the opposition media, some of the strikers, an extreme-right group, and anti-Allende propaganda among the military), the coup was an authentically Chilean product. The armed forces moved only when it became clear that the civilian politicians were unable to run the economy or to maintain a constitutional consensus and that the military monopoly on the instruments of coercion was being threatened by armed groups. Allende had been able to use the constitution to defend himself against military intervention as long as the economy was functioning and law and order prevailed. But once it appeared that the legality and constitutionalism that Allende had proclaimed as essential to the *via chilena* to socialism no longer existed, the armed forces broke with their tradition of nonintervention. Many factors contributed to the breakdown of constitutional democracy, but the most important ones seem to have been a sharp increase in violence and polarization and the collapse of the economy.

MILITARY RULE

Most observers had assumed that if the armed forces intervened, it would be for a short period during which they would outlaw the Marxist parties, stabilize the economy, and call new elections. They were wrong. It is now clear that 1973 was a turning point in Chilean history. The leaders of the coup—especially General Augusto Pinochet, who used his position as head of the senior branch of the armed services to centralize political power in his hands—were determined to change the pattern of Chilean politics. They spoke of eradicating the "cancer of Marxism," creating a "protected democracy" that would not be subject to the demagoguery of the politicians, and making sure that the breakdown of law and order as well as the threats to national security that occurred during the Allende administration would never be repeated.

Yet as clear as their determination to change Chilean political culture might have been, the specifics of how to do so were not evident at the outset. The leftist parties were outlawed, the Communist Party headquarters was burned, and the other parties were declared "in recess." Thousands of suspected leftists were rounded up, tortured, and in many cases killed. The best-known case is that of Charles Horman, a US citizen. It is the subject of the book and film *Missing,* which accurately portray the atmosphere of postcoup Chile, although the basic thesis of *Missing,* that Horman was killed because "he knew too much" about the US role in the coup, is incorrect. Many of the leaders of the left went into exile or took refuge in foreign embassies. Those who did not were transported to Dawson Island in the frigid south and were later allowed to go into exile as well. The constitution, in the name of which the coup had been carried out, was simply ignored as the government began to function in accordance with a series of decree-laws that gave legislative and constitutional power to the four-person junta and executive power to its head, Augusto Pinochet. At the time of the coup there had been discussion of rotating the presidency of the junta among the armed forces, but it was soon clear that Pinochet intended to stay in that post, and a decree-law in June 1974 made him president of the republic and supreme chief of the nation. The judiciary remained in place and supinely recognized the legal validity of the decree-laws, refusing to issue writs of habeas corpus (*recursos de amparo*) for all but a minuscule number of the thousands who were arrested. A committee of conservative jurists was appointed to revise the constitution, but it worked very slowly and did not report out a draft until five years later.

The effort to remove what the military viewed as the sources of subversion meant not only that the parties that were members of Allende's Popular Unity Federation were outlawed but also that the universities were put under military rectors and leftist professors were purged; the newspapers and magazines of the left were closed (along with the theoretical journal of the Christian Democrats); labor unions, many of which had been Marxist-led, were dissolved; and peasant organizations were disbanded. Foreigners who had been assisting the Allende government were expelled and, in a few cases, tortured or killed. Diplomatic relations were broken with Cuba and the Soviet Union (but not with China, a principal customer for Chilean copper).

The most important change, in terms of its lasting impact on Chilean society, was the opening of the economy carried out under the auspices of *los Chicago boys.* Departing from the usual statist tendencies of the Latin American military, the junta decided to entrust economic policy to a group of free-market-oriented civilian economists, most of whom had received graduate training in economics at the University of Chicago. Reacting to the socialist interventionism of the Allende years, their program called for opening Chile to internal and external competition by relying on private enterprise, competition, and market forces. It removed price controls, reduced tariffs dramatically, expanded exports, moved toward the establishment of more realistic exchange rates, and returned landholdings and businesses that had been illegally seized. The copper nationalization was not reversed both because it had been carried out by a constitutional amendment and because part of the foreign exchange earnings of copper was earmarked for military purchases. At first the program was adopted in a gradual fashion; two years later it was applied in a drastic "shock treatment."

The new regime engaged in campaigns of violence and repression against its enemies. Military missions moved to the north and the south to carry out summary executions of leftists. The report of the National Commission on Truth and Reconciliation in February 1991 and subsequent investigations identified by name 3,197 Chileans who had been killed or had disappeared between 1973 and 1990, most of them victims of "agents of the state or persons in its service." The reports of the National Commission on Political Imprisonment and Torture, chaired by Bishop Sergio Valech, published in 2004 and 2005, listed 28,456 cases, often involving physical abuse, rape, electric shock, and other forms of torture.

The violation of human rights in Chile led to a serious deterioration in relations with the United States, and in 1976 the US Congress imposed a ban on Chilean arms aid and purchases—a ban that was not lifted until 1990. Relations worsened when President Jimmy Carter made human rights a central element of US foreign policy. In the United Nations, reports to the General Assembly about Chile were prepared each year by a special rapporteur, and the UN Human Rights Commission continued to discuss Chilean abuses.

Within Chile, Pinochet managed to transform what had been an institutional coup by the four services into a personal dictatorship. The system of promotions and retirements was altered so that his protégés could remain beyond retirement age while those who were a possible threat to his power could be retired. The intelligence branches of the armed services were consolidated into a single National Intelligence Service (DINA), which established computerized files and conducted a national system of terror. DINA killed General Prats, in exile in Argentina, and wounded Bernardo Leighton, a Christian Democrat with good relations with the left, in Rome. Its most heinous crime was to blow up the car of Allende's former ambassador to the United States, Orlando Letelier, in the heart of Washington, DC. The US investigation that followed led to the extradition and conviction of the immediate perpetrator, a rightist US citizen who had been living in Chile, and continuing pressure on Chile to extradite the higher-ups involved. After the return of democracy the head of DINA, Manuel Contreras, was tried and sentenced to seven years in prison for ordering Letelier's death. After his release he was tried and sentenced to life imprisonment for other human rights crimes.

As a result of the Letelier investigation, Pinochet removed Contreras and reorganized DINA as the National Information Center (CNI), which wielded less independent power than DINA had exercised. In 1978 when General Gustavo Leigh, the air force member of the junta, began to call for more rapid progress toward civilian rule, Pinochet removed him and appointed a low-ranking air force general as his successor. This action led to the resignation or forced retirement of eighteen air force generals. With his triumph over Leigh, Pinochet's personal control of the armed forces was complete.

Meanwhile, the economy, which had suffered a drastic contraction as a result of the shock treatment, was now beginning to be described as the "Chilean economic miracle." From 1977 until 1981 it expanded at rates of 6 to 8 percent a year. With tariff rates down to 10 percent (from an average of 100 percent during the Allende period), cheap foreign imports flooded the country. The exchange rate was fixed at thirty-nine pesos to the dollar, and nontraditional exports such as fruit, lumber, and seafood reduced the share of copper in earning foreign exchange from 80 percent to less than 40 percent. It was possible to take out dollar loans at the overvalued exchange rate, and Japanese cars and scotch whiskey could be purchased more cheaply in Chile than in their countries of origin. It was in this heady atmosphere that a plebiscite was held on a new constitution.

The 1980 Constitution

In late 1978 the Committee for the Study of a New Constitution produced a draft that was submitted to the advisory Council of State, which had been created by Pinochet in 1976. On July 1, 1980, the council submitted a revised draft that proposed a five-year transition, with an appointed congress until 1985 and a full return to civilian rule at that time. In the next month Pinochet and his advisors completely rewrote the transitional provisions of the draft to produce a quite different timetable that would enable Pinochet to remain in power until at least 1990, and possibly until 1997. With only one opportunity for public criticism—a public meeting at which Frei Montalva spoke and leftist slogans were chanted (by CNI agents, some said)—the draft was submitted to a vote on the seventh anniversary of the coup, September 11, 1980, and the government-controlled media announced that it had been approved by a 67 percent vote. Later there were charges that the vote had been artificially inflated in the more remote areas, with more votes reported than there were voters. (The voting rolls had been destroyed after the coup, and there were no independent poll watchers to check on the voting.)

One of the transitional provisions added in July 1980 was that approval of the constitution also constituted election of General Pinochet for an eight-year presidential term beginning March 11, 1981. The transitional articles called for a plebiscite in late 1988 on an additional eight-year term for a presidential candidate nominated by the junta. In the event that the junta candidate lost the plebiscite (as in fact happened), competitive elections for the presidency and for the congress were to be held in late 1989, with the elected government taking office on March 11, 1990.

The 1980 constitution attempted to remedy the defects of the 1925 constitution by providing for the simultaneous election of the president and the congress (thus removing the adverse effects of staggered elections) and establishing a two-round runoff system for the popular election of the president (so that he would have the mandate of a popular majority)—a system that almost certainly would have led to the election of Jorge Alessandri in 1970. The constitution also created a strong constitutional tribunal with the power to "control" (that is, review) the constitutionality of all important laws and to make definitive judgments on all constitutional disputes. The Chamber of Deputies was to have 120 members elected for four-year terms, and there would be twenty-six senators (later increased to thirty-eight), elected for eight-year terms, with half chosen every four years. In addition, all ex-presidents who had served six years were to be senators for life, and there were to be nine appointed senators—two former members of the Supreme Court, one former controller general, one former university rector, one former cabinet member, and one former commander from each of the four armed services. (The posts of nonelected senators were abolished in August 2005, but in the initial years of the transition to democracy they gave the right the power to block government legislation in the upper house.)

The "Modernizations"

With the apparent success of the government's economic policy Pinochet's advisors began to extend the principle of free choice to the area of social policy by means of the so-called modernizations. Labor unions were now permitted, but they were restricted to the local firm or factory, and their right to strike was limited. The National Health Service was reorganized and decentralized, and private health services were authorized to receive payments from the compulsory health insurance deduction, leading eventually to the enrollment of about 30 percent of Chileans in private health plans. Private universities and educational institutions were authorized, and tuitions were raised, which could be financed by low-interest loans that were immediately payable if a student failed or was expelled from the university (e.g., for political activities). Local education was reorganized on the basis of contracts between the municipality and private educational corporations, so teachers ceased to be civil servants and lost tenure rights. Housing policy was reoriented to encourage private contractors to build low-cost housing, and the government provided low-interest loans and grants to the poor only if they had saved enough to make a small down payment.

The most fundamental shift was the privatization of the complicated and bankrupt social security system. A reduction in premiums persuaded Chileans to place their compulsory social security deductions in publicly regulated but private and competitive pension funds resembling the individual retirement accounts (IRAs) in the United States. Unlike IRAs, however, the pension funds replaced rather than supplemented the public social security program. The government still maintained a minimal social security safety net for those people who, for reasons such as poor health or insufficient contributions, could not participate in the system. Over the next several years, however, the government's responsibility for most of the social security program ended.

The "modernizations" and the opening of the economy to internal and external market forces were part of a broader view that was influenced by economically conservative (Latin Americans would call them "neoliberal") thinkers in the United States and Europe. Friedrich Hayek and Milton Friedman visited Chile, and think tanks and publications began to project a vision of a new Chile with a consumer-oriented and prosperous economy like those of South Korea and Hong Kong, gradually moving toward democratic and decentralized politics that would replace the statism and socialism of the past.

In March 1981 when Augusto Pinochet entered the newly reconstructed presidential palace as "constitutional" president of Chile, he was able to feel secure. The original legitimization for the coup (the prevention of a Marxist takeover) was no longer viable, but it had been replaced by a constitution that had the support of the armed forces and of many members of the upper and middle classes—and the new prosperity of the "economic miracle" was even beginning to trickle down to the lower classes as employment and wages began to rise and inflation declined. A state of emergency in various degrees and a limited curfew were still in force, and police roundups in the poor areas and occasional political murders of leftists still occurred. But some opposition magazines and books (although not newspapers or television) were tolerated and the more visible aspects of the repression were no longer evident.

The Protests

The sudden collapse of the Chilean economy in 1982 shattered this optimistic view of the prospects of the regime. External factors such as excessive indebtedness at rising interest rates and a low price for copper exports, combined with internal weaknesses such as an overvalued exchange rate and the existence of underfinanced paper financial empires involving interlocking banks and industries, led to a wave of bankruptcies and widespread unemployment. As unemployment figures rose to include nearly a third of the workforce (including those enrolled in the Minimum Employment Program) Chileans began to engage in public protests against the government for the first time since 1973. Beginning with the copper workers' union in May 1983 and soon joined by the illegal but newly revived parties, the protests escalated monthly until August, when President Pinochet had to call out seventeen thousand members of the regular army to keep order.

Pinochet, however, was able to keep his hold on power by pointing to the timetable outlined in the constitution and appealing to fears of disorder and violence. (The Manuel Rodríguez Patriotic Front [FPMR], a terrorist movement associated with the Communist Party but more committed to violence than the latter, had begun to engage in acts of sabotage, bombings, and blackouts.) In 1986 Pinochet's position was strengthened when large arms deposits destined for the FPMR were discovered and the group carried out an unsuccessful assassination attempt against him.

The 1988 Plebiscite

In contrast to the plebiscite on the 1980 constitution, the 1988 plebiscite was organized well in advance. Laws were published concerning electoral registration, recognition of political parties, and the method of carrying out the plebiscite itself. The problem for the opposition was to decide whether, by participating, they would give implicit recognition to the 1980 constitution, the legitimacy of which they had always questioned. The Communist Party called for a boycott, but later, under pressure from its membership, it permitted its adherents to register. The Christian Democrats eventually complied with the legal requirements for party registration, and the Socialists had it both ways by refusing to seek recognition while registering the Party for Democracy (PPD), which was open to all who opposed the regime.

The conservative parties—the center-right Party of National Renovation (RN) and the pro-Pinochet Independent Democratic Union (UDI)—had already been recognized, and they urged their members to register and vote. The government pressured the military and public employees to do the same. At the beginning of

1988, when it was rumored that Pinochet was urging the junta to call a plebiscite in March, it looked as if he could get a new eight-year term without difficulty. However, several factors turned the situation around.

First, sixteen opposition parties from the center and the left (minus the Communists) formed a unified Command for the No, published a program calling for a return to democracy and an end to ideological proscriptions, and insisted that a democratic government would respect private property and the economic rules of the game. Second, a church-related group conducted a massive registration drive throughout the country, resulting in the registration of 92 percent of the eligible voters by the time the electoral registries were closed. Third, the constitutional tribunal ruled that the opposition must be given access to state-owned television, and fifteen minutes of prime time at lunch and after dinner were given free of charge to the opposition for twenty-seven days. With the assistance of the Center for Free Elections (COPEL) of the Organization of American States and the US National Endowment for Democracy, the opposition developed an effective television campaign as well as poll-watching and vote-counting techniques that made fraud almost impossible. The result was that, despite massive government propaganda arguing that a no vote would mean a return to the chaos and Communism of the Allende period, Pinochet was defeated by a vote of 55 percent no to 43 percent yes on his continuation as president for another eight-year term.

THE RETURN TO DEMOCRACY

On December 14, 1989, Patricio Aylwin, a Christian Democrat who was the candidate of the center-left Concertación por la Democracia, defeated the candidate of the pro-Pinochet parties and took office on March 11, 1990. Pinochet continued as army commander for an eight-year term, as permitted by the transitional provisions of the 1980 constitution. Along with the heads of the other armed services, he also had a seat on the National Security Council and thereafter, as an ex-president, he could be a senator for the rest of his life.

Thanks to their years of exile in Europe and the United States, the Aylwin cabinet contained the largest number of ministers and deputy ministers with graduate degrees of any modern government. The government announced that it would give priority to primary education and job training. Government spending on education doubled between 1990 and 1997. Health spending increased by 75 percent, although substantial qualitative differences between the public and private health care sectors remained. Between 1990 and 1997 foreign investment and exports doubled, and inflation and unemployment dropped to 6 percent. Economic growth averaged 7 percent a year in the same period, with an 11 percent growth rate in 1992. The percentage of the population living in poverty dropped from 39 percent in 1987 to 23 percent in 1994, and the living standards of all groups rose as average wages increased by 22 percent, although income distribution remained highly skewed. The US embargo on military aid was lifted, and negotiations for free trade agreements with the United States, Canada, and Mexico were begun.

The Aylwin government moved quickly in the area of human rights. To investigate human rights abuses Aylwin appointed a Commission on Truth and Reconciliation, headed by Raúl Rettig, a former Radical senator, and including Gonzalo Vial, a conservative historian and former education minister in the Pinochet government. The commission had no judicial powers and did not identify perpetrators, but it listed victims by name and called for moral and monetary reparations to the families of the victims. In April 1991 an additional politically inspired murder was added to the list with the assassination by the leftist Manuel Rodríguez Patriotic Front of Senator Jaime Guzmán, the founder of the rightist UDI party.

The Aylwin government was pressured by members of the Socialist and PPD parties, as well as by the Association of Families of the Detained and Disappeared (AFDD), to take further action in the human rights area. Political cases were moved from military to civilian courts, nonviolent political prisoners were released, and the Communist Party was legalized, but Pinochet continued to insist that he would protect "my people" (*mi gente*) from prosecution. In December 1991 he issued a low-level mobilization, or "call to quarters," that was intended to deliver a message to the government. Cases that involved murders and disappearances that had taken place after the amnesty declared by Pinochet in 1978, as well as the Letelier murder in Washington (which, at US insistence, had been exempted from that amnesty), proceeded at a slow pace through the court system.

The human rights cases were among the first problems of the new administration of Eduardo Frei Ruiz-Tagle, who took office on March 11, 1994, following a record win—with 58 percent of the votes—over Arturo Alessandri, a nephew of the former president. The jurisdiction of the civilian courts over human rights cases involving the military was finally established in November 1993 with the sentencing of retired general Manuel Contreras, the former head of the DINA intelligence agency, and his assistant, Pedro Espinoza, for their part in the Letelier assassination. After many months of resistance, including a stay at a military hospital by Contreras, the two former officers began in September and October 1994 to serve their sentences in a specially constructed jail for members of the military.

The Pinochet Case

In accordance with the 1980 constitution Pinochet went out of office as commander in chief of the army in March 1998 and decided to accept his seat as a senator for life. There were protests at his swearing-in, as well as an unsuccessful attempt by Socialist, PPD, and some Christian Democratic members of congress to deny him his seat. His only significant legislative activity was involvement in the resolution of a dispute over ending the status as a legal holiday of September 11, the anniversary of the coup, by replacing it with a Day of National Unity on the first Monday in September.

In October Pinochet went to London for back surgery, and on October 16, while he was recovering in a hospital, he was arrested by Scotland Yard in response to warrants issued by a Spanish judge requesting that he be extradited for trial for the murder of Spanish citizens, as well as for acts of "genocide, terrorism, and torture." The case went through many judicial bodies in Britain, including the House of Lords. On March 28, 1999, the Law Lords dismissed most of the charges on the grounds that they had not been crimes in Britain at the time they were committed but upheld the charges of torture for the acts carried out after December 18, 1988, the date that Britain had ratified the International Convention Against Torture. On October 8, 1999, the Magistrates' Court ruled that Pinochet could be extradited to Spain to stand trial on those charges.

In August and September Pinochet's health (he was now eighty-three) deteriorated with a series of minor strokes, and he was reported to be suffering as well from diabetes, asthma, circulatory problems, and depression. The Chilean government had already appealed to the British home secretary to return him to Chile on humanitarian grounds, and after a government-appointed board of doctors declared him in January 2000 unfit to stand trial, he was returned to Chile on March 4, 2000. Awaiting him were fifty-eight cases of human rights abuses being considered by a Chilean judge.

The Frei Ruiz-Tagle government, made up of Pinochet's opponents and in some cases his victims, had argued for his return, claiming that Chile, as the country in which the crimes had been committed, had original jurisdiction. That claim was initially unconvincing because of the slow pace of human rights cases in the Chilean courts, Pinochet's congressional immunity as a senator, and the amnesty that he had declared in March 1978 for crimes committed between 1973 and the date of the amnesty. However, during his detention in England there had been a turnaround in the personnel and decisions of the Chilean courts, as the Pinochet appointees began to retire. The judges began to take up more and more of the human rights cases, including those committed before 1978, which were now considered capable of being tried under the novel judicial doctrine that if the bodies of the disappeared had not been found, a crime of "ongoing kidnapping" (*secuestro permanente*) was still being committed. Cases such as the infamous "Caravan of Death" (the murders of political prisoners in central and northern Chile in October 1973, about which a best-selling book had been written), the assassination of a leading labor leader in 1982, and the 1974 murder of General Prats in Buenos Aires began to be pursued actively in the Chilean judicial system, and military commanders were called upon to testify.

Pinochet's successor as army commander protested against the new judicial activism and reinterpretations of the law, but took no further action. Frei Ruiz-Tagle's minister of defense organized a series of dialogues on human rights that included both members of the military and human rights activists, but there was no talk of military action. Clearly Pinochet's arrest and detention had changed the nature of politics in Chile.

The 1999–2000 Presidential Election

Proof that the Pinochet era had been left behind came with the presidential elections of December 1999 and January 2000. Ricardo Lagos, a Socialist who had served in the Allende government and had been education minister and public works minister in the Aylwin and Frei Ruiz-Tagle governments, won the Concertación primary election (a new feature of Chilean politics), resoundingly defeating the Christian Democratic candidate. The rightist Alliance for Chile, made up of the Party of National Renovation and the Independent Democratic Union, nominated Joaquín Lavín from the more conservative UDI. Neither Lavín's earlier association with the Pinochet government nor Lagos's participation in the Allende government was discussed in the campaign, which focused principally on issues of education, health care, public safety, and the economy. After a well-financed campaign in which he projected an image of youth, vigor, and charisma (and outspent the Concertación by a reported US$50 million to US$10 million), Lavín came within thirty-four thousand votes of defeating Lagos in the December 12, 1999, elections, winning a majority of the women's vote and carrying many of Chile's regions. He lost the January 16, 2000, runoff by 2.6 percent, and political observers attributed Lagos's margin to the votes of some or all of the 3 percent who had voted for the Communist candidate in the first round, and to a shift to Lagos in the women's vote as a result of the organization of women voters by the popular Christian Democratic minister of justice, Soledad Alvear.

The economy, adversely affected by the world crisis of the late 1990s, recovered dramatically, with growth rates around 6 percent in 2005 and 2006. Foreign investment poured in, copper prices rose to all-time highs, and Chile became the world's second-largest exporter of salmon. Chile signed free trade agreements with the European Union, South Korea, and the United States, adding them to those with Canada and Mexico concluded under the previous administration. While Chile's distribution of income remained among the most inequitable in the world, with the top 10 percent of the population receiving 42 percent of income and the bottom 20 percent only 3.3 percent, the expanding economy led to a decline in poverty to 13.7 percent in 2006 and to a reduction in unemployment. While other Latin American countries suffered inflation, government instability, and budget deficits, Chile's budgets and balance of payments remained in surplus, its price levels stable, and its level of corruption the lowest in Latin America.

The Lagos government modernized the judicial system, replacing the inefficient "inquisitorial" system, in which the judge also carries out the investigation and indictment, with the adversarial system in use in the United States and Britain. Augusto Pinochet's senatorial immunity was lifted after he returned from Great Britain; a number of judges ruled that he was fit to stand trial, despite his illnesses, and he was repeatedly placed under house arrest, but no actual trial took place.

In November 2004 the commander of the army accepted institutional responsibility for the human rights abuses of the Pinochet period. At the end of the month the Commission on Political Imprisonment and Torture, headed by Bishop Sergio Valech, gave gruesome and detailed accounts of the tortures inflicted by the Pinochet government as a matter of policy. Its reports demonstrated that more than twenty-eight thousand Chileans had been subjected to rape, torture, and physical abuse. It proposed that the victims receive health and education benefits as well as a pension equivalent to US$180 a month.

In 2004 and 2005 a subcommittee of the US Senate investigating money laundering found evidence that the Riggs Bank had assisted Pinochet in setting up fictitious accounts to hide dollar deposits. Further investigation revealed that the Pinochet family had more than US$17 million under false names in 125 bank accounts in nine American banks. Legal proceedings against the family included the arrest of Pinochet's wife and one of his sons, who were accused of involvement in the cover-up as well as income tax evasion.

The political and social consequences of these developments were considerable. The conservative vote was split as the center-right Party of National Renovation nominated as its presidential candidate Sebastián Piñera, a wealthy businessman who had voted against Pinochet in the 1988 plebiscite. In contrast, the Concertación avoided a primary fight when Soledad Alvear, the Christian Democratic candidate, bowed out in view of the commanding lead in the polls of Michelle Bachelet, the Socialist/PPD nominee. The fact that both Concertación candidates were women was an indication of the cultural liberalization that had taken place in Chile.

In August 2005 the congress passed a series of constitutional amendments removing the antidemocratic provisions of the 1988 constitution, such as the nonelected senators and the prohibition of presidential removal of military commanders without the consent of the military-dominated National Security Council, and returning the national police (*carabineros*) to the Ministry of the Interior. It also shortened the presidential term to four years, thus ensuring that henceforth the president, the Chamber of Deputies, and half the Senate would be elected simultaneously. However, it was not able to agree on abandoning the binominal congressional electoral system of two-member districts that had been designed by the outgoing Pinochet regime to ensure that the Communist Party would not be represented in the congress. (Its defenders argued that it promoted stability by encouraging the formation of two coalitions of the major parties.)

With the abolition of the appointed senators the Concertación secured a legislative majority in both houses of the congress in the December 2005 legislative elections. In the presidential race Michelle Bachelet secured 46 percent of the presidential vote against a divided opposition but, lacking a majority, was forced into a runoff against Piñera in January 2006, which she won handily.

As a relatively new figure in national politics, Bachelet promised to make significant changes. She named a cabinet that had women as 50 percent of its members. She worked with the parties of the Concertación, but her initial cabinet included many new faces. Her initial popularity was diminished by a nationwide strike of public school students, demanding improvements in the quality of their education. The "penguins," as they were called because of their uniform of dark jacket and white shirt, received wide support, and Bachelet responded by appointing a large study group to recommend reforms. A second problem that emerged in her first year was a badly planned and executed reform of public transportation in Santiago that substantially increased travel time to work. In other areas, however, promised reforms were carried out, including the establishment of a national system of day care centers, an extension of health care to many new ailments, new housing that effectively eliminated the shantytowns of Santiago, and an expansion of access to higher education. The most significant reform was the expansion of pension coverage to those who had not been able to participate in the contributory scheme initiated under the Pinochet regime—including for the first time housewives of retirement age.

In the last year of her term, Bachelet's approval rating rose to 72 percent, the highest of any Chilean president. Part of the improvement was related to Chile's response to the world economic crisis. At the beginning of her administration, the price of copper, one of Chile's principal sources of government revenue and foreign exchange, soared to unprecedented heights. Bachelet's finance minister, Andres Velasco, resisted pressures to spend the resulting surplus, arguing that it should be saved for periods when the price was low. When the worldwide financial crisis hit Chile, resulting in unemployment, a drop in the price of copper, and an increase in poverty, the government was able to draw on the surplus to support low-income and impoverished Chileans with monthly cash payments, and to finance stimulus programs in housing, education, and public investment. Chile thus was able to weather the crisis more successfully than other Latin American countries.

Yet the personal popularity of Bachelet, who was forbidden by the electoral law to succeed herself, could not be transferred to the Concertación government coalition. Partly because it wanted to appeal to centrist voters who were being wooed by Sebastián Piñera, the candidate of the right, the Concertación chose as its candidate former president Eduardo Frei Ruiz-Tagle from the Christian Democratic Party. Due to defections and expulsions, the Concertación had lost its legislative majority. It was further damaged by the sudden emergence as a presidential candidate of Marco Enríquez-Ominami, a thirty-six-year-old Socialist congressman who was the son of a guerrilla leader killed after the coup. Enríquez-Ominami appealed to previously apathetic young voters, and to those disillusioned with the government coalition after twenty years in power. Piñera was therefore able to win a plurality against a divided center-left in the first round of the presidential election and to defeat ex-president Frei Ruiz-Tagle in the runoff. However, the Concertación maintained a small majority in the congress, which meant that Chile would have a divided government for the next four years.

Two weeks before Piñera was sworn in, Chile suffered a major earthquake. Compared to the disaster in Haiti a month earlier, the quake did relatively little damage. But it was followed by a tsunami that inundated a section of the coast and killed 156 Chileans. The outgoing Bachelet government failed to give adequate warning of the destructive force of the tsunami, and it was slow to respond to the devastation that resulted—failures that were used against Bachelet when she ran again for president in 2013.

President Piñera appointed a cabinet largely made up of prominent business leaders with only a few representatives of the right-wing parties. Later in the year when 333 miners were rescued after being trapped in a cave-in for over two months, his popularity soared. In 2011, however, his approval rating in the polls dropped to 27 percent, the lowest level of any president since the return of democracy. The principal reason was his handling of another student strike, this one involving university students who repeated earlier demands for improvement of the quality of their education but now took a more militant position, denouncing the subsidized for-profit schools that had been established under the Pinochet government (they now enrolled half of secondary school students) and adding a further radical demand that the government provide free public higher education, rather than the existing system of student loans and mixed public and private universities. The Chilean public supported the students, and Piñera responded by negotiating with the students and promising more spending on education, but he did not give in to their more radical demands. The students continued to carry out demonstrations for the rest of his presidential term, some of them massive in scope and numbers.

The Chilean congress also suffered in the public opinion polls. The approval ratings of both the Concertación and the right-wing Alianza coalition dropped even further following what turned out to be an unsuccessful effort to increase citizen participation in politics. The congress replaced the compulsory voting system—which had led many Chileans not to register to vote—with a system of automatic registration at the age of eighteen and voluntary voting. In the municipal elections of October 2012, the number of eligible voters increased from 8.4 million to 12.8 million, but only 43 percent of them took the trouble to vote. (The Concertación made slight gains, most notably with the election of the daughter of an Allende cabinet minister as mayor of Santiago.)

Popular attitudes toward their political representatives were negative despite the fact that the figures for the Chilean economy were very positive. Inflation was low (about 1.5 percent), unemployment had dropped to 6 percent, and the economy was growing at an annual rate of 5.6 percent. On specific issues Chileans were not apathetic. Besides the student protests, there were frequent demonstrations and marches on issues as such as gay rights, threats to the environment, and the government crackdown on the Mapuche Indians (about 6 percent of the population, concentrated in southern Chile), who were burning houses and threatening farmers on what they regarded as their ancestral lands.

Michelle Bachelet was out of the country for most of Piñera's term, serving as head of a new UN agency on women. She continued to be very popular, both within and outside the Concertacion coalition. After her return to Chile in March 2013, it was widely assumed that the outcome of the presidential contest was already clear.

In a further effort to involve the citizenry, the government held primary elections on June 30 to select the candidates of the two major coalitions. Bachelet, running against the candidates of the other major parties of the coalition, easily won the Concertación nomination. The contest on the right between the RN candidate, Andrés Allamand, and Pablo Longueira, one of the founders of UDI, was won by Longueira, but he later withdrew and was replaced by Senator Evelyn Matthei, the daughter of an Air Force general who had been a member of Pinochet's junta at the time of the 1988 plebiscite.

THE POLITICAL PARTIES

The Right

Before 1973 the right was dominated by the National Party, which had been formed in 1966 by a fusion of the old Liberal and Conservative parties. The National Party declared itself dissolved after the coup, and during the 1980s two center-right parties were formed—the Independent Democratic Union, which was initially based on the anti-Allende *gremialista* movement at the Catholic University, and the Party of National Renovation, which is somewhat more secular in inspiration and less identified with the Pinochet regime. The electoral system, which favors both the largest and second-largest coalitions, has encouraged cooperation between the two parties and joint efforts to elect a rightist candidate in the presidential elections. Sebastián Piñera, the RN candidate in the 2005–2006 elections, proved to be a strong vote getter, and he became the undisputed leader of the right until his victory in January 2010. Under his presidency the two parties maintained their separate identities and they nominated separate candidates for the June 2013 presidential primary.

The Center

The most significant centrist party is the Christian Democratic Party of Chile. The government party in the 1960s, it maintained its internal structure and youth, student, labor, and women's branches during the period of military rule. Drawing its political philosophy (a welfare state, human rights, and a mixed economy) from Catholic social thought, the Christian Democrats were for many years the largest party in Chile, but their vote has declined in recent years, and the conservative UDI sometimes has a larger share of the vote. Having abandoned the policy of going it alone (*camino propio*) that it pursued in the 1960s, the party is strongly committed to working with other parties in order to maintain stable progressive governments in Chile.

The Christian Democratic Party is supported by the Chilean middle class, but it has an important labor component. The party has long since abandoned the communitarian socialism with which it briefly flirted during the Allende period, and it now recognizes the importance of the market as an allocator of resources, although it criticized the regressive social effects of the economic policies of the Pinochet regime. The Christian Democratic government of the 1960s adopted a strong agrarian reform law, but the party now advocates other means (e.g., technical assistance and access to credit) to raise living standards and production in the countryside. It favors the encouragement of foreign investment and the promotion of exports, but combines this with strong commitment to the expansion of educational opportunity, improved health care, and the reduction of poverty—what it calls the social market economy.

The Radical Party, now renamed the Radical Social Democratic Party, was once the fulcrum of the Chilean center, but it has been seriously weakened by frequent splits on the left and right. Although there are still Radical supporters in the provincial towns and rural areas, and the party has international recognition as, for example, a member of the Socialist International, it has received less than 5 percent of the vote in recent elections.

The Left

In the past the left has been dominated by the Socialist and Communist parties, which were allied in the Popular Action Front (FRAP) between 1957 and 1970 and formed the core of Allende's Popular Unity coalition between 1970 and 1973. In the late 1960s the Socialists adopted an increasingly radical position, so during the Allende period they represented the most revolutionary party in Allende's coalition, often taking positions to the left of Allende himself. After the coup most of the Socialist leaders went into exile in Europe. By the late 1970s a split had emerged between those (mainly in Western Europe) who favored a more moderate position similar to the positions of the French and Spanish Socialists and those (mainly in Eastern Europe and the Soviet Union) who favored continued close cooperation with the Communists and commitment to Marxism-Leninism. With the opening of politics in Chile the two groups united to reestablish the Chilean Socialist Party, which abandoned Marxism, becoming an important partner in the electoral coalitions and governments of Aylwin and Frei Ruiz-Tagle, and nominating the winning presidential candidates of the Concertación in 2000 and 2006.

Before the 1988 plebiscite, part of the more moderate wing of the Socialists decided to form the Party for Democracy (PPD) as an "instrumental" party to defeat Pinochet. The PPD identifies with the commitment of the left to social justice and emphasizes the need to modernize Chilean economics, politics, and society. It continues to field its own candidates but often cooperates with the Socialist Party.

Like the Christian Democrats, the Socialists have suffered from defections, most notably that of Marco Enríquez-Ominami, who received 20 percent of the vote as an independent in the first round of the 2009–2010 presidential elections. In 2013 the Socialists reunited and together with the PPD strongly supported the candidacy of Michelle Bachelet.

The Communist Party was outlawed after the coup and many of its leaders were persecuted and murdered, but it continued underground activity among workers and in the shantytowns. Although it endorsed the *via pacífica* to power between 1957 and 1973, in 1980 it began to advocate "all forms of struggle," including "acute forms of violence." For this reason the other parties were unwilling to ally with the Communists against Pinochet, although they supported its right to participate in the democratic process by nonviolent means. After the party was legalized in the 1990s it secured only 3 to 6 percent of the vote, compared with the 15 to 18 percent that it had received before 1973, although in alliance with other leftist groups it has received more votes in municipal elections. The Communists still have strength among the trade unions and in university student politics. The Manuel Rodríguez Patriotic Front, an offshoot of the party, carried out violent actions in the 1980s, but it split in the early 1990s on the issue of the continued use of violence, and it is no longer significant. The two-member district electoral system has been successful in preventing Communist candidates from being elected to the congress, but in 2013 the Concertación worked out a system of cooperation that was likely to ensure the election of one or more Communists to the congress in 2014.

After twenty years of democratic government the classic "three thirds" division of the Chilean parties into left, center, and right no longer describes the Chilean political scene. It has been replaced by a bipolar division between the governing Concertación, composed primarily of the Christian Democrats, the Socialists, and the PPD, and the conservative opposition, made up of the Party of National Renovation and the Independent Democratic Union. That division has been encouraged by the way representatives are elected to congress—in effect, the system only allots seats to the first- and second-ranking parties or coalitions. There is considerable support for abandoning the binominal system, but so far no alternative system has been able to secure the required two-thirds vote in the Senate. In the 2013 campaign Michelle Bachelet promised to give electoral reform a high priority in her presidential program. She also expressed support for drafting a new constitution to replace the 1980 document that, with significant changes, still governed Chile.

THE ARMED FORCES

It has been said that Chile has a British navy, a US air force, and a Prussian army. The navy has an aristocratic tradition, the army and air force draw many of their officers from the upper middle class, and members of the national police often come from lower-middle-class backgrounds. There were tensions among the services within the junta, especially over Pinochet's dominance and even concerning the advisability of his candidacy in 1988, but he was able to use his control of the army and, and after the adoption of the 1980 constitution, the military tradition of legalism and constitutionalism to maintain a facade of unity and support. He remained as army commander until March 1998, and when his intelligence agency, the National Information Center (CNI), was dissolved in January 1990, many of its members and activities were transferred to the army intelligence unit.

As long as Pinochet was army commander the threat of military action could not be discounted. After his arrest and detention in October 1998, however, a much younger group took power that accepted the legitimacy of civilian control of the military. With the official apology in 2004 by the army commander for the army's institutional involvement in human rights abuses during the dictatorship, the break from the Pinochet-dominated past was formalized. It was reinforced by the revelations in the same year that Pinochet and his family members had secret multimillion-dollar accounts in US banks.

BUSINESS AND AGRICULTURE

Chilean industry and business have long been formally organized into the Society for the Promotion of Manufacturing (SOFOFA) and the Confederation for Production and Commerce. Chilean industry was fundamentally altered by the policies of the Pinochet government. Inefficient companies protected by high tariffs went bankrupt, while new export-oriented businesses producing everything from kiwi fruit to rosehip tea flourished. Ownership became concentrated in a few financial-industrial *grupos* after the sell-off of state enterprises following the coup. Some of the largest groups went bankrupt and were taken over by the government in 1982. They and most other state enterprises (except the state-owned copper mines) were privatized later in the decade, sometimes through dubious transactions that enriched Pinochet supporters.

In agriculture too, a process of restructuring has taken place. Seized lands were returned to their owners after the 1973 coup, and the land that had been distributed into cooperatives under the 1967 agrarian reform law was divided into individual holdings. Many of the smallholdings were later sold to agribusiness entrepreneurs, resulting in a process of reconcentration—although often under owners different from the traditional landowning families. The landowners are organized into the National Agricultural Society (SNA), one of Chile's oldest interest groups. Other groups such as shopkeepers, truckers, and so on are represented by organized occupational groups, as are lawyers, doctors, nurses, and architects. However, their legal right to set rules for the professions was withdrawn in the late 1970s, and their influence has diminished since the return to democracy.

OTHER GROUPS

The Roman Catholic Church

More than 60 percent of Chileans claim to be Catholic, although the percentage of Chileans who actively practice that faith is much lower. Fifteen percent are

Protestants, many of them members of evangelical and fundamentalist churches. There are significant numbers of Lutherans descended from earlier German immigrants, a small Jewish colony, and an increasing number of Mormons. Although church and state have been separated since 1925, the Catholic Church retains considerable national influence. Several of the elite private secondary schools are church-affiliated, and the Catholic universities in Santiago and Valparaiso are important educational institutions that receive partial state support. Church publications are influential, and declarations by the Chilean Bishops' Conference are given wide publicity in the media. The bishops repeatedly criticized the human rights abuses of the Pinochet government, and the church-sponsored Vicariate of Solidarity actively assisted the victims of repression. In the past a progressive majority dominated the Bishops' Conference, but more recent Vatican appointments have substantially increased conservative influence. Opus Dei, the conservative lay Catholic group, has become influential, with its own university and secondary schools, as well as the nomination of an Opus Dei candidate in the 2000 presidential elections. The church opposed efforts initiated by Christian Democratic legislators to enact a divorce law to replace the existing fraudulent annulment procedure, but after many years of debate, legal divorce became possible in 2005. Abortion is illegal in Chile, and the church has opposed the government distribution of the morning-after pill as possibly abortive. As elsewhere, the moral influence of the Catholic Church has been diminished by a number of sensationalized cases of sexual abuse of minors by members of the clergy.

Labor Organizations

The Marxist-dominated Unitary Labor Central (CUT) was dissolved after the coup, and its leaders were persecuted, but the Christian Democratic labor leaders were treated less severely. In the late 1970s limited union activity was permitted, and in the early 1980s a National Labor Command (CNT) was organized, later renaming itself the CUT. With the return of democracy new legislation expanded the rights of labor, but the labor movement is much weaker than before 1973, with only 16 percent of workers enrolled as union members. The Lagos government reintroduced collective bargaining, but there are still limits on the right to strike.

Students and Intellectuals

Repeated highly organized and massive student strikes in 2006 and again from 2011 to 2013 made the students major players in Chilean politics, calling for radical reforms of the educational system, including the elimination of university tuition and a takeover of subsidized private schools. Many of their demands had public support, and police brutality in efforts to control the students gained them further sympathy.

Chilean intellectuals were highly critical of the Pinochet government. Two Chilean novels—*La Casa de los Espíritus* (The House of the Spirits), by Isabel Allende, the niece of the former president, and José Donoso's *Desesperanza* (Curfew)—were international bestsellers that attacked the dictatorship; Ariel Dorfman's play *Death and the Maiden*, concerning torture under the Pinochet regime, has been presented in many countries. *Machuca*, a fictionalized account of the impact of the Allende government on an exclusive private school, is the most successful Chilean film in recent years, and in 2012 *No,* a fictionalized account of the defeat of Pinochet in the 1988 plebiscite, was nominated for an Academy Award for Best Foreign Film.

FOREIGN INFLUENCES

Chileans have always tried to overcome their geographical isolation by keeping up with developments in Europe and the Americas through the media or, if they can afford it, foreign travel. There are significant foreign colonies in Chile as well as English, French, German, and American schools. With the opening of the Chilean economy foreign banks and financial institutions established branches in Chile, and foreign investment soared. Nearly all the economic technocrats of the Pinochet and Concertación governments were trained at American universities. There are major UN regional offices in Chile, the most important of which is the UN Economic Commission for Latin America and the Caribbean. The Chilean left was an active participant in the rethinking of radical, especially Marxist, ideology that occurred in Europe in the 1970s, and the Chilean right, also influenced by international ideological currents, has moved from a traditionalist hierarchical corporatism to more modern libertarian and economically oriented modes of thinking.

GOVERNMENT STRUCTURE

The 1980 constitution was clearly designed to limit the power of the congress. The president can call a plebiscite on constitutional amendments rejected by the congress. Presidential budgets must be voted on within sixty days or they automatically go into effect. New expenditures must be matched by new taxes, and the central bank may not borrow money. All takeovers of property must be compensated in cash at full value. The constitutional tribunal automatically reviews important legislation, and its decision is final. And, to reinforce the Pinochet government's intention to keep the congress out of the way, a new congress building was constructed in Valparaiso, an hour and a half from Santiago. (The congress will return to the capital in the near future.)

In addition, local government has been strengthened, taxing power has been given to the *comunas* (municipalities), education and health care have been partially privatized and decentralized (although some recentralization has taken place since the return of democracy), and social security has been turned over to private pension funds, although a public safety net has been considerably expanded for a large number of Chileans who were not financially able to participate. The number of state enterprises has been reduced from five hundred at the time of the coup to fewer than twenty, and even the state-owned copper mines have been opened to joint ventures with foreign capital.

TOWARD THE FUTURE: THE LESSONS OF CHILE

Many lessons have been drawn from the Chilean experience. An obvious conclusion is the importance of maintaining the institutional and constitutional consensus and the willingness to compromise that characterized Chile for so many years. Chile's civilian political leaders have learned from experience the desirability of avoiding the ideological dogmatism of the right, the left, and even the center that characterized the politics of the 1960s and early 1970s.

A second general lesson is the importance of maintaining a healthy growing economy that in recent years has meant opening Chile to foreign investment and integrating it economically into regional and global markets.

However, an open economy is not enough, Chile tells us. Both for ideological and pragmatic reasons it is necessary to improve education on all levels and to upgrade living standards through health, housing, and social security programs, often involving collaboration between the public and private sectors. Unemployment is still over 6 percent, educational opportunity has expanded but is still limited, and a regressive distribution of income remains the Achilles' heel of what appears to be a thriving economy.

In the twentieth century Chile experienced more than its share of political and economic upheavals. It became a laboratory for the application of the models of development proposed by Liberals, Radicals, and Conservatives, as often providing negative lessons as positive ones. It has modernized and globalized its economy, carried out a peaceful transition from military rule, and moved in the direction of greater social justice, tolerance, and democracy. No institutional model is perfect, but after many troubled decades Chile seems to have found a successful combination of democracy, economic growth, and social equity.

Suggestions for Further Reading

Angel, Alan. *Democracy After Pinochet: Politics, Parties, and Elections in Chile.* London: Institute for the Study of the Americas, 2007.

Arriagada, Genaro. *Pinochet: The Politics of Power.* Boston: Unwin Hyman, 1988.

Barahona de Brito, Alexandra. *Human Rights and Democratization in Latin America: Uruguay and Chile.* New York: Oxford University Press, 1997.

Barros, Robert. *Constitutionalism and Dictatorship: Pinochet, the Junta, and the 1980 Constitution.* New York: Cambridge University Press, 2002.

Borzutsky, Silvia, and Gregory Weeks, eds. *The Bachelet Government.* Gainesville: University Press of Florida, 2010.

Branch, Taylor, and Eugene M. Propper. *Labyrinth.* New York: Penguin, 1983.

Cavallo, Ascanio. *La historia oculta de la transicion: Chile 1990–1998.* Santiago: Ediciones Grijalbo, 1998.

Cavallo, Ascanio, et al. *La historia oculta del régimen militar.* 2nd ed. Santiago: Editorial Antártica, 1989.

Childress, Diana. *Augusto Pinochet's Chile.* Minneapolis: Twentieth Century Books, 2009.

Chile, Comisión Nacional Sobre Prisión Política y Tortura (Valech Commission). *Informe.* 2004. Available at www.gobiernodechile.cl/comisionvalech (a summary in English is at www.usip.org/publications/commission-of-inquiry-chile-03).

Chile, National Commission on Truth and Reconciliation. *Report.* Trans. Phillip E. Berryman. Notre Dame, IN: University of Notre Dame Press, 1994.

Collier, Simon. *Chile: The Making of the Republic, 1830–1865.* New York: Cambridge University Press, 2003.

Davis, Madeleine, ed. *The Pinochet Case.* London: Institute of Latin American Studies, 2003.

Davis, Nathaniel. *The Last Two Years of Salvador Allende.* Ithaca, NY: Cornell University Press, 1985.

Dinges, John. *The Condor Years: How Pinochet and His Allies Brought Terrorism to Three Continents*. New York: New Press, 2004.

Drake, Paul, and Ivan Jaksic, eds. *The Struggle for Democracy in Chile, 1982–1990*. Lincoln: University of Nebraska Press, 1995.

Franchischet, Susan. *Women in Politics in Chile*. Boulder, CO: Lynn Rienner, 2005.

Haughney, Diane. *Neoliberal Economics, Democratic Transition, and the Maphuche Struggle for Rights*. Gainesville: University of Florida Press, 2006.

Hauser, Thomas. *Missing: The Execution of Charles Horman*. New York: Touchstone Books, 1983.

Hilbink, Lisa. *Judges Beyond Politics in Democracy and Dictatorship: Lessons from Chile*. New York: Cambridge University Press, 2007.

Huneeus, Carlos. *The Pinochet Regime*. Boulder, CO: Lynne Rienner, 2007.

Kornbluh, Peter. *The Pinochet File*. New York: New Press, 2003.

Loveman, Brian. *Chile: The Legacy of Hispanic Capitalism*. 3rd ed. New York: Oxford University Press, 2001.

Meller, Patricio. *The Unidad Popular and the Pinochet Dictatorship: A Political Economy Analysis*. New York: St. Martin's Press, 2000.

Moran, Theodore. *Multinational Corporations and the Politics of Dependence: Copper in Chile*. Princeton, NJ: Princeton University Press, 1974.

Muñoz, Heraldo. *The Dictator's Shadow: Life Under Pinochet*. New York: Basic Books, 2008.

Pollack, Marcelo. *The New Right in Chile, 1973–97*. New York: St. Martin's Press, 1999.

Power, Margaret. *Feminine Power and the Struggle Against Allende*. University Park: Pennsylvania State University Press, 2002.

Roberts, Kenneth. *The Modern Left and Social Movements in Chile and Peru*. Stanford, CA: Stanford University Press, 1998.

Schamis, Hector. *Re-forming the State: The Politics of Privatization in Latin America and Europe*. Ann Arbor: University of Michigan Press, 2002.

Scully, Timothy. *Rethinking the Center: Politics in Nineteenth- and Twentieth-Century Chile*. Stanford, CA: Stanford University Press, 1992.

Sigmund, Paul E. *The Overthrow of Allende and the Politics of Chile, 1964–1976*. Pittsburgh: University of Pittsburgh Press, 1977.

———. *The United States and Democracy in Chile*. Baltimore: Johns Hopkins University Press, 1993.

———, ed. *Chile 1973–1998: The Coup and Its Consequences*. Princeton, NJ: Princeton University Program in Latin American Studies, 1999.

Spooner, Mary Helen. *The General's Slow Retreat: Chile After Pinochet*. Berkeley: University of California Press, 2011.

Stallings, Barbara. *Class Conflict and Economic Development in Chile, 1958–1973*. Stanford, CA: Stanford University Press, 1978.

United States Senate. *Staff Report of the Select Committee on Intelligence Activities: Covert Action in Chile*. Washington, DC: Government Printing Office, 1975.

Valdes, Juan Gabriel. *Pinochet's Economists: The Chicago School of Economics in Chile*. New York: Cambridge University Press, 1996.

Valenzuela, Arturo. *The Breakdown of Democratic Regimes: Chile*. Baltimore: Johns Hopkins University Press, 1978.

Verdugo, Patricia. *Chile, Pinochet and the Caravan of Death*. Miami: North-South Center Press, 2001.

Weeks, Gregory. *The Military and Politics in Postauthoritarian Chile*. Tuscaloosa: University of Alabama Press, 2003.

Whelan, James R. *Out of the Ashes: Life, Death, and Transfiguration of Democracy in Chile, 1833–1988*. Washington, DC: Regnery/Gateway, 1989.

9

COLOMBIA: UNFADING GLORY AND FURROWS OF PAIN

Vanessa Joan Gray

Since assuming office in August 2010, President Juan Manuel Santos has initiated a bold approach to Colombia's long-standing problems with armed insurgency and drug trafficking. His proposals—a negotiated settlement with the Revolutionary Armed Forces of Colombia (FARC) guerrillas and a rethinking of the criminalization of the drug trade—could have a huge positive impact if they succeed. Under the Santos government, Colombia enjoys a strong economy and improved relations with neighboring nations. It is possible that in the second decade of the twenty-first century, the nation may finally achieve the genuinely democratic and secure polity for which so many have worked and so many have died. The forces opposing the rule of law and the protection of basic rights in Colombia, however, are powerful and deeply entrenched.

Economic, social, and historical realities (including factors outside the nation's borders) fuel multiple forms of organized violence in Colombia. The violence is manifested in six general patterns. First, state security forces have periodically used large-scale, lethal violence to repress opposition groups since the founding of the republic. Second, property owners have used hired assassins and private armies to protect and expand their holdings since the colonial period, acting with impunity in jurisdictions where government officials are weak or complicit. Third, partisans of armed groups have dedicated themselves to annihilating their opponents, a tendency that emerged during a long century of intermittent civil war between the Liberal and Conservative political parties. Fourth, leftist guerrilla groups have been seeking to implement political goals via the force of arms since the early 1960s. Fifth, large, violent criminal organizations emerged in the 1970s with the proliferation of

COLOMBIA

drug trafficking in areas of Colombia with inadequate law enforcement and massive unemployment. Sixth, armed bands that start as instruments for protecting some group's financial interests and destroying its enemies become autonomous and then use violence for organizational goals of their own. All of these patterns remain in force today.

THE LAND

Geography is particularly important in the Colombian case. It is the fifth-largest Latin American nation and contains extraordinary natural abundance. Colombia has coasts on the Caribbean Sea and Pacific Ocean, three ranges of the Andes Mountains, expanses of tropical forest and savannah, and a network of rivers containing more fresh water than all the continent of Africa. Ranked as one of the three most biologically rich places on the planet, Colombia has more bird species than any other nation and the second-highest number of amphibian and plant species.

Colombia has five main regions: the Andean highlands and valleys, the Caribbean lowlands, the Pacific lowlands, the Orinoco plains (*llanos*), and the Amazon basin. Historically, population and economic and political activity were concentrated in the Andes and on the Caribbean coast. The capital, Bogotá, has more than seven million inhabitants, and four other cities—Medellín, Cali, Barranquilla, and Cartagena—contain millions of inhabitants each. Climate varies dramatically with altitude. Bogotá, at 8,628 feet (2,630 meters), has cold nights and abundant rain. In other Andean cities, temperatures are cooler or milder, depending on the elevation. Cities in low-lying regions can be extremely hot and humid.

Agricultural production also varies with elevation: grains and potatoes are cultivated at higher elevations, coffee and flowers are produced at middle altitudes, and tropical crops are grown in coastal and inland lowlands. Production in the *llanos* includes cattle ranches, rice and palm oil plantations, and petroleum extraction facilities. Commercial activity in the Amazon and the Chocó department in the Pacific lowlands has spread from limited rubber extraction and small-scale mining to intense logging, fishing, and wildlife trafficking. Emeralds are mined in the Andes and coal is extracted in the Guajira Peninsula. Coca cultivation is dispersed in the lowlands of the Orinoco, Amazon, and Pacific, and marijuana is cultivated mostly on the Caribbean coast. Natural gas and oil deposits are located in many regions, as are gold, nickel, platinum, silver, and copper.

The Colombian landscape poses difficulties for nation building. Relative to many countries at a similar level of development, Colombia's rich and dispersed resource endowment provides more opportunities for political rivals and illegal economies to prosper and avoid being eliminated. Topography also makes it more costly for the state to extend services and full citizenship rights throughout the territory. In less accessible regions, government representatives and programs are vulnerable to attacks from armed groups and corruption by local strongmen. Even before the Spanish conquest, the landscape hindered Bogotá's rule over other regions. Chronicles from colonial times to the present day note the deadly animals, insects, and diseases as well as the steep slopes, fast rivers, and impenetrable jungles and swamps that impede the central authority's administration of the territory. Today, trucking and aviation link population and production centers, but getting from Bogotá to some destinations still requires days of travel in a small boat or on foot.

Armed groups make it a priority to control areas where valuable resources are extracted, processed, or smuggled. Colombia's oil sector, drug production and agribusiness zones, and emerald, gold, and coal mining regions have been epicenters of violent activity. The conflict dynamics that scholars attribute to the presence of resource wealth are evident. Trust and discipline within armed groups is undermined, and the availability of financing prolongs the survival of groups that otherwise would be eliminated. Combatants—whether they are paramilitaries, guerrillas, or soldiers—tend to treat local residents as pawns or potential enemies. Civilians are injured in the crossfire between rival groups and they are also intentionally targeted as a tactic of war. The returns from resource operations, however, remain so high that business continues in spite of the security problems. Hence, the financial opportunities for armed groups persist.

Dedicated individuals and organizations are working to establish justice and accountability in Colombia's rural conflict zones, but progress is halting and the attrition rate is high. Some residents of these regions are rejecting the premise that laws can or should be imposed by force of arms and are developing community-based governing structures sanctioned by the constitutional court, sometimes drawing on indigenous traditions. The guiding principle for Colombia's rural "peace communities" is that the land and its natural resources should be owned and managed collectively by local residents.

SOCIETY

With almost forty-seven million inhabitants, Colombia has the third-largest population in Latin America and the twenty-seventh-largest in the world. About three-quarters reside in urban areas. The vast majority of Colombians are Christian; 80 percent identify as Roman Catholic, and around 10 percent of the population belong to a Protestant faith. Among the remaining tenth of the population are agnostics, Jews, Muslims, Hindus, Buddhists, and practitioners of indigenous religions.

Colombia's population has been ethnically diverse since the conquest, when consensual and forced unions of indigenous peoples, Africans, and Europeans were common. Though most Colombians have mixed European and indigenous ancestry, approximately 3 percent of the population are members of an indigenous group, and a 2005 World Bank report estimates that some 20 to 25 percent of Colombians have African ancestry. The many combinations of skin color, hair type, and facial features found in Colombia make it problematic to rely on phenotypes for discussions of race, but data on the number and the geographic location of citizens who consider their identity to be indigenous or Afro-Colombian have political and economic ramifications.

Before the arrival of the Spanish, Colombia had indigenous societies ranging from nomadic hunters to one of the largest civilizations of the Americas, the Muisca, also called the Chibcha. Colonial policies and disease caused massive loss of life and the nearly complete assimilation of many preconquest groups, but some eighty-seven indigenous cultures and sixty-four indigenous languages survive today. Government statistics in 2007 registered an indigenous population of 1.4 million people, more than half of whom live in the departments of Guajira, Nariño, Cauca, and Guainía. Almost all indigenous Colombians live in *resguardos,* of which there are more than seven hundred, covering approximately 30 percent of the national territory. In the *resguardos,* groups ranging from a hundred to more than ten thousand members practice specific forms of governance, worship, and food production.

Africans were brought to Colombia as slaves to labor on plantations and in mines during the colonial era. Their descendants constitute the majority of the population in coastal areas, a large portion of the people in the Cauca Valley, and a sizable minority in major cities. In some regions Afro-Colombians retain distinctive cultural practices, and throughout Colombia, African influences can be heard in the music and seen in popular forms of dance. An important milestone for Afro-Colombians is that in the 1990s the national government granted titles to 132 collective territories of traditional "black communities," most of which are located in the Pacific region and account for roughly 4 percent of the national territory.

Colombians of pure Spanish lineage take pride in their ancestry and together with the descendants of immigrants from other European countries and the Middle East constitute national economic and political elites. The Colombians who possess the most wealth and power almost never have dark skin or non-Caucasian features. Racial disparities in access to education also exist. According to a 2009 report on minorities by the UN refugee agency, Afro-descendant and indigenous Colombians have an illiteracy rate nearly three times that of the rest of the population, and 72 percent of indigenous people and 87 percent of Afro-Colombians over the age of eighteen have not completed primary school.

Indigenous and Afro-descendant Colombians are also disproportionately represented among the victims of armed conflict. In 2012 the UN refugee agency reported that in the previous eighteen months, 4,080 indigenous people were forcibly displaced and twenty-two indigenous leaders were assassinated. Organizations that advocate for Colombia's roughly three million internally displaced persons (IDPs) report that more than a third of all IDPs are Afro-Colombian.

THE ECONOMY

The Colombian economy occupies the upper middle tier globally and by some reports has replaced Argentina as Latin America's third-largest economy. World Bank statistics for 2011 rank Colombia's gross domestic product as the thirty-first-largest in the world, though its per capita GDP ranks lower (eighty-first), and income inequality as measured by the Gini coefficient (55.9 in 2010) is high by regional and international standards. Growth in 2011 was robust (5.9 percent) and inflation was low (3.1 percent). Strong economic performance continued in 2012, and forecasts for the future are upbeat. The main sources of Colombia's economic growth are exports, domestic consumption, and investment in the financial, commerce, and mining sectors. Overall, the Colombian economy has exhibited steady growth and macroeconomic stability since 1945.

In the last decade, the growth of Colombia's export sector has rivaled rates in Brazil and Chile. Colombia's main legal exports are petroleum products, coal, chemicals, gold, coffee, flowers, textiles, and bananas. For nearly a century Colombia was acutely dependent on coffee receipts, and in 1987 coffee still accounted for a third of the nation's exports. Since then, competition from coffee produced in other nations has been steep and global supply has driven down prices, adding to unemployment in Colombia's coffee regions.

Colombia's most important trade relationship continues to be with the United States. The European Union and China are growing markets for Colombian exports, and Colombia increasingly imports from China, Mexico, Brazil, and Germany. The US-Colombia Free Trade Agreement (FTA) was negotiated in 2006 and, after years of unsuccessful opposition from civil society groups in Colombia and the United States, went into effect in 2012. Colombia has free trade agreements with Chile, Mexico, Canada, South Korea, and Venezuela, and is pursuing FTAs with the EU, Switzerland, Turkey, Japan, and Israel, among other countries.

The illegal drug trade began drawing large amounts of foreign currency into the Colombian economy in the 1960s and has caused distortions ever since. By 1979 receipts from marijuana and cocaine brought in more foreign exchange than all of the nation's legal exports combined. The government has used a range of policies to curtail the drug industry: aerial spraying of herbicides and the manual eradication of plants, confiscating drug shipments, criminalizing production and commerce, extraditing high-level traffickers, and creating financial mechanisms to curb money laundering. After decades of vigorous antinarcotics policies with massive financial and military support from the United States, however, the industry remains strong in Colombia.

Since the 1990s, the government has offered incentives to foreign direct investment (FDI) by lifting capital controls, increasing protections for intellectual property, rewriting the mining and forestry codes, updating free trade zones, and pursuing bilateral trade agreements. From 2002 to 2007 new FDI to Colombia more than tripled, and in 2012 it reached US$15 billion. The United States is Colombia's largest source of FDI, and the petroleum and coal industries are the largest recipients of FDI.

Colombia has been a net oil exporter since 1986. The nation's refining capacity does not cover domestic demand, so some gasoline is imported. In the late 1990s, liberalizing reforms expanded petroleum exploration and the number of firms producing. New security policies and increased drilling during the Uribe years (2002–2010) kept petroleum production up, and Colombia is projected to continue to export oil through 2015.

Colombia is the world's fourth-largest exporter of coal. The country's biggest coal mining operation, Cerrejón in the department of Guajira, was developed by the government in a 1980s joint venture with a subsidiary of Exxon. In 2000 the government sold its stake in Cerrejón, now a massive rail, port, and mine complex. Today Colombia's coal sector has firms from the United States, Britain, Australia, Switzerland, Canada, and Brazil. High output from coal reserves is projected to last for decades.

Coal development was followed by the identification of large natural gas deposits. The government funded construction of pipelines from gas fields to cities and foreign markets, and links to Venezuela and Panama were inaugurated in 2007.

Colombia's gas reserves are expected to outlast coal as a source of energy and income. Hydroelectric dams are Colombia's main source of electricity generation. In 2004, Colombia began exporting electricity to Ecuador and later to Peru, Venezuela, and Panama. The final component of Colombia's burgeoning energy sector is agrofuel. Production of fuel from oil palm and sugarcane soared during the 2000s in response to European demand and incentives from US antinarcotics and energy policies.

Along with the energy sector, mining is crucial to Colombia both financially and politically. Nonfuel mineral exports are over a quarter of all exports. By volume, nickel and gold are the most important, but a variety of metals from platinum to molybdenum are mined. President Santos refers to mining as the nation's economic engine, and the sector is booming as a result of investment incentives, rising commodity prices, and reduced guerrilla activity in areas containing deposits.

Though many Colombians favor rapid development of the nation's mineral wealth, mining expansion has generated significant conflict. One reason is that minerals are sometimes located in lands designated as protected areas because they contain valuable biodiversity or are a critical buffer against water scarcity. Second, important deposits are located in indigenous *resguardos* and Afro-descendant territories. The constitution and legal code grant ownership of subsoil resources to the state, and the government has the authority to explore and extract the resources or grant concessions for private companies to do so. But at the same time, the constitution and Colombia's treaty obligations under the International Labor Organization's Convention 169 guarantee ethnic communities a role in decisions regarding resource development on their lands. In practice, the rights of communities to informed prior consultation are easily abrogated by incomplete information, bureaucratic inefficiency, corruption (including within the community itself), and the use of violent intimidation. Legal mechanisms exist for communities to block activities that do not comply with the law, to receive compensation for damages, and to claim a small portion of the earnings from resource ventures. But the stark reality is that tens of thousands of Colombians who invoked these rights have been victims of violent reprisal.

The third reason that mining expansion creates conflict is that hundreds of thousands of lower-income Colombians engage in small-scale mining on at least a part-time basis. Thus, many livelihoods are adversely affected when the government permits a large mining firm into a site already being worked by artisanal miners. Fourth, most mining operations either lack proper licenses or are outright illegal. Titling disputes abound. The government's capacity for enforcing laws and adjudicating disputes in the mining sector is woefully inadequate.

Under Santos's predecessor, Álvaro Uribe, the amount of land granted in mining concessions to national and international firms increased eightfold, affecting about 4 percent of the national territory. Hundreds of licenses were issued for mining in Afro-descendant territories and *resguardos*. Drug trafficking organizations increasingly used gold-mining operations for laundering funds. NGOs began a sophisticated public awareness campaign on mining abuses. Violent confrontations erupted between miners and government forces, activists and paramilitary groups, communities and guerrillas, and combinations of all of the above.

The Santos administration modified the approach. Its goal appears to be a modern, prosperous, regulated mining sector that avoids excessive disruption of critical ecosystems and discourages the blatant trampling of human rights. Government interventions in two high-profile gold-mining cases suggest a new tone: the government blocked an eviction of Afro-descendant miners and banned mining in a paramo watershed located in a concession belonging to a Canadian firm. Still, the government is pushing for legislation that favors capital-intensive operations at the expense of small domestic producers and more sustainable modes of use. Its initial proposals were struck down by the constitutional court for failing to properly consult with local communities in advance.

The Santos government also shows signs of trying to convert the mining sector from a source of conflict to an arena for strengthening government rule. It has renegotiated major mining contracts to obtain a higher percentage in royalties for the state, and completed a multiyear survey of all mining activity along with a socioeconomic census of mining zone populations. New agencies have been created not just to manage information and process the administrative backlog, but also to provide health, education, and other services to people employed in artisanal mining, particularly women and children. A moratorium on new concessions was issued and remained in effect in 2012.

Considering Colombia's economic policy in a comparative context, the country has never suffered the macroeconomic calamities seen in other Latin American countries. From the late 1940s to the 1980s, GDP grew on average 6 percent per year, and real gains in per capita growth were achieved. When recession devastated most of Latin America in the 1980s, Colombian growth rates declined, but avoided the reversals seen elsewhere. Similarly, the global crisis that began in 2007 slowed growth for a couple years, but the economy soon rebounded.

Colombia's strong and steady growth can be attributed to a relatively stable political regime less subject to the populist and military demands for government spending found in other Latin American nations. One can also credit Colombian technocrats who, in addition to being relatively insulated from political pressures, had the foresight and consensus to pursue policies that encouraged investment and growth while avoiding excessive indebtedness, extreme protectionism, or radical openness. Examples of policy successes are the early application of the crawling-peg devaluation, the export-led growth strategy, and the development of coal and petroleum through joint ventures.

Until the late 1980s, Colombian political elites took pride in a mixed economy in which the government played a muted statist role. During the administrations of Virgilio Barco (1986–1990) and César Gaviria (1990–1994), the government began implementing the neoliberal policies promoted by Washington and already adopted in most of Latin America. Privatization represented a less dramatic shift for Colombia than for some because fewer industries were state-owned in the first place. But over time the "economic opening" did reshape the political economy. As in the rest of the world, restructuring favored some groups (consumers with money to buy imports, and large national and foreign firms able to compete globally) and hurt others (producers in certain sectors, workers in formerly protected industries and public agencies, and lower-income groups who lost subsidies or lacked the skills or social connections to seize new opportunities).

What set Colombia's neoliberal restructuring apart was the degree to which criminal organizations and armed groups were able to take advantage of worsening unemployment and destitution to expand their ranks. In the late 1990s, the Colombian economy experienced its sharpest downturn since the Great Depression, just as the power of guerrilla groups was peaking and paramilitary organizations were growing exponentially. Government forces had dismantled the Medellín and Cali cartels, but the drug trade was flourishing due to robust external demand and the proliferation of smaller trafficking groups. Worse, guerrillas and paramilitaries moved into the sector and their coffers swelled with receipts from the drug trade.

When President Andrés Pastrana (1998–2002) took office, the violence had worsened to the point that the legitimacy of the political system and the solvency of the economy were in doubt. The country lost its investment-grade rating on sovereign debt in 1999, and Colombia had to borrow from the International Monetary Fund, devalue the currency, and allow the peso to float. The Pastrana administration deepened neoliberal reforms, and by the time Álvaro Uribe took office in 2002, the economy had improved.

The Uribe government continued the neoliberal orientation of its predecessors, invested some US$50 billion in the mining and oil sector, and, most of all, sought to reduce the security threat to those doing business in Colombia. Armed with billions of dollars in US aid and having imposed a new tax on wealth, the government achieved its goal by expanding the armed forces by half and striking the guerrilla hard. Tighter security in production and shipping areas fueled strong economic growth, which peaked at 8.2 percent in 2007.

Since Santos took office in 2010, the government has carried forward structural fiscal and tax reforms and focused on strengthening commercial ties in Latin America. In 2011 Colombia's credit rating was restored to investment grade and FDI in the energy sector hit a record high and was double that of Mexico and Argentina. For conventional economists, the elements of concern in Colombia's current profile are high inequality rates, unemployment in the double digits, and a national infrastructure that needs upgrading to be able to support future growth.

For the political economist, it is troubling that urban violence resurfaced toward the end of Uribe's second term and that paramilitary violence is resurgent. The Santos government is engaged in a multifaceted effort to avoid another wave of violence that would disrupt production and drive investors away. In 2012, the government entered into formal negotiations with the largest guerrilla group, FARC. President Santos also has taken on an international role as a proponent of reevaluating the costs of the drug war, joining former Brazilian and US presidents Fernando Henrique Cardoso, Lula, Bill Clinton, and Jimmy Carter in that endeavor. In the realm of social spending, the government has increased services for the poorest segment of the population.

To fail to address what Brazilians call a "social deficit" has dire consequences in the Colombian case. The legions of young people who come from troubled families and neighborhoods and lack a decent job or formal education constitute a ready pool of potential recruits for all the armed groups. Policies that do not reckon with this social reality can deliver only temporary results when it comes to promoting economic growth or defeating an armed group. Programs to mitigate the social dislocations caused by two decades of neoliberal reform, not to mention the ravages of armed conflict, are urgently needed. It is too soon to draw conclusions about the priorities of the Santos government, but if fewer resources were required for fighting the FARC and the drug trade, then the resulting "peace dividend" could perhaps be used to fund a major investment in human capital.

POLITICAL HISTORY

History to 1930

As a Spanish colony, Colombia was neither a backwater nor an administrative and economic hub like Mexico, Peru, and Cuba. Colombia was part of the viceroyalty of Peru until 1739, when Bogotá became the center of a new viceroyalty that included present-day Venezuela, Panama, and Ecuador. The war for independence from Spain was led by elites and won in 1819. Colombia's liberator, Simón Bolívar, went on to assist other republics to break away from Spain. Colombia was part of a postindependence confederation with Venezuela and Ecuador, but the union lasted only ten years. Panama was a province of Colombia until 1903, when the United States helped secessionist elites break away from Bogotá and form a separate republic.

The aftermath of Colombia's war for independence was marked by violence and political instability. By 1850, civilian rule emerged, with two political parties dominating: the Liberals and the Conservatives. Both parties were controlled by elites. The parties had differing positions on federalism, free trade, and power for the Roman Catholic hierarchy, but they shared the same ideology regarding the social and economic order.

A change of party in the presidential palace replaced one vertically integrated network of bosses and clients with the other, which led to fierce party competition that extended beyond the ballot box. There were six civil wars between the parties in the nineteenth century, some of which were long and bloody. The worst conflict, the Thousand Days' War (1899–1902), killed between 60,000 and 120,000 Colombians. Party bosses mobilized peasants (*campesinos*) who were economically and socially dependent on them, and some boys younger than twelve were conscripted. The wars instilled partisan hatred among lower-income groups, making other cleavages—social, economic, ethnic, and regional—less salient than party affiliation.

The Government and Organized Violence Since 1930

A long period of Conservative Party rule ended in 1930 due to divisions within the party and discord among elites over how to deal with a growing labor movement undeterred by government repression. When a Liberal president was elected in 1930, war broke out between Liberal and Conservative campesinos. Meanwhile, modernization in the agrarian sector generated conflict because land holdings were being consolidated, struggles over land and water rights intensified, and rural labor was displaced.

A faction of the Liberal Party that advocated an activist government role in development came to power with the election of President Alfonso López Pumarejo (1934–1938, 1942–1945). Social welfare, agrarian, and import substitution industrialization policies were implemented, and labor organization promoted. A faction of the Conservative Party joined with elements of the Liberal Party to block further reforms, and López left office before finishing his second term. In the next election the Liberals were divided and the Conservatives won the presidency.

In the mid-1940s partisan violence was instigated by Conservative Party bosses seeking to consolidate power and win a majority in the next congressional elections. Liberal followers fought to prevent those gains. Conservative farmers seized lands that had been taken by Liberals sixteen years earlier, believing correctly that the government in Bogotá would support them. The civil war that unfolded is known as *la violencia* and vastly exceeded previous wars in scope and cruelty. The 1948 assassination of Jorge Gaitán—a populist Liberal favored to win the presidency in 1950—triggered the largest spontaneous urban riot in world history, but the war was most intense in rural areas experiencing land conflicts. Over a period of twenty years more than two hundred thousand Colombians (in a country of ten million) were killed. In some parts of the country, such as the coffee-growing region, almost everyone became a victim, perpetrator, or firsthand witness to carnage. The violence took many forms: murder and plunder were carried out for personal gain, bandits of lower-class origins prospered, blood feuds cycled back and forth, and persecuted Liberals and Communists organized themselves into armed self-defense groups.

The period also witnessed Colombia's only military government in the twentieth century, headed by Gustavo Rojas Pinilla (1953–1957). He came to power supported by civilian leaders, and employed a combination of military force and populist spending that managed to pacify areas affected by partisan violence, banditry, and vendettas. But pockets of armed resistance survived where the peasantry had become radicalized. The government's public works projects, moreover, fell short of nation building. Much of Colombian territory remained isolated and without formal governance.

When Rojas grew more repressive and showed a reluctance to cede power, the leaders of the two parties joined forces to oust him and implement a power-sharing agreement called the National Front. The agreement dictated that from 1958 to 1974 the presidency would alternate every four years between the two parties, and representation in all legislative bodies, all cabinet positions, and all gubernatorial posts would be divided equally, regardless of how voters voted. Third parties were prohibited from participating.

The sixteen-year pact was a success in that it ended conflict between the traditional parties, but it had unintended political costs. Political institutions had the veneer of democracy without providing the benefits of democratic governance. At the same time, the government's capacity to implement change was more limited than in an openly authoritarian arrangement. It was a period of capitalist modernization, and so millions were migrating to cities and unemployment was rising, yet organizing within the system languished because there was little motivation for mobilizing voters or incorporating young people into formal politics. Ultimately, the parties' power-sharing arrangement resulted in political and socioeconomic conditions that favored the growth of guerrilla movements, the black-market economy, and the drug trade.

Over the years, there have been Colombian political leaders who recognized the dynamics fueling organized violence and attempted to address them, but they did not prevail over reactionary factions. For example, the two best attempts at land

reform (by Presidents Alfonso López Pumarejo in the 1930s and Carlos Lleras Restrepo in the 1960s) were defeated by intransigent elites.

Since then other Colombian governments have tried to curb organized violence
using a variety of policies, but none had comprehensive success. President Belisa-
rio Betancur (1982–1986) negotiated amnesties, offered truces, and reincorporated
guerrillas into society. One outcome was the founding of a political party, the Patriotic Union (UP, Unión Patriótica), by FARC insurgents who had laid down arms.
The UP garnered broad support from progressive civilian groups in many regions,
and five senators, fourteen representatives, and twenty-three mayors were elected.
The Betancur peace process was sabotaged by regional elites and military officials
who contracted with paramilitaries to assassinate thousands of UP members. Betancur also instituted democratization reforms, such as direct mayoral elections, that
went into effect under later administrations. But his efforts were financially constrained by unfavorable global economic trends, and his government lacked effective
means for mobilizing popular support.

President César Gaviria (1990–1994) negotiated with guerrillas and other armed
groups. Traffickers surrendered in exchange for plea bargains, and some paramilitaries turned themselves in. With US assistance, the government systematically eliminated the Medellín cartel. To broaden political participation, the government held
elections for a constituent assembly that debated and wrote a new constitution. The
constitutional court created in this period has become one of the stronger democratic institutions in Colombia. But at the end of Gaviria's term income inequality
had worsened, and the level of violence in Colombia was higher than before he took
office.

The Ernesto Samper government (1994–1998) did not pursue negotiations with
guerrilla groups, and as the guerrillas' numbers and territorial reach grew, they
bested the military in skirmishes. The Samper presidency was weakened by accusations that Cali drug traffickers had donated millions of dollars to his electoral
campaign. The scandal led the US government to impose sanctions that debilitated
the government further. Though almost all of the Cali cartel either surrendered or
were captured during the Samper years, other trafficking groups formed, production
rose, and the trade diversified to include heroin. Meanwhile, the number of rural
Colombians displaced by paramilitary violence soared.

By the late 1990s guerrilla forces were so powerful that analysts warned an insurgent victory was possible. Large firms, national and foreign, complained bitterly
about soaring security costs, and foreign investors shifted away from Colombia.
President Pastrana pursued negotiations, granting FARC forces control of an area
the size of Switzerland. FARC combatants, recalling the fate of comrades who demobilized during the Betancur years, were not inclined to disarm. Moreover, FARC
leaders were unwilling to cede much of anything at the bargaining table because
their power was on the rise and the FARC's main adversaries, the paramilitaries,
were multiplying their own forces and territory. The Pastrana government did not
pursue policies to rein in the paramilitaries. Rural massacres and mass displace-
ments reached levels that made Colombia a hotspot for global humanitarian relief
agencies. After the peace talks failed, guerrilla kidnappings and attacks on cities
intensified.

The Uribe government (2002–2010) built up the military with historic levels of assistance from the United States and pursued an all-out war against the guerrillas. Uribe also negotiated a cease-fire with the paramilitary umbrella organization, and thousands demobilized. The number of massacres tapered off and travel between urban areas became less dangerous. Many urban Colombians experienced a greater sense of security than they had felt in years. But paramilitary operations continued in many regions, as did impunity for crimes committed by paramilitaries.

In reality, the Uribe government was not well positioned to bring paramilitaries to justice. The paramilitaries demobilized voluntarily, not because they were weakened by force. They had close ties with influential politicians. It did not make sense for them to negotiate an accord that would result in their own prosecution. Meanwhile, drug production remained as robust as ever. As with its predecessors, the government's gains were but partial victories.

The problem that has plagued Colombia is that while the government tackles one or two forms of organized violence with negotiations or hard-line action, other forms of organized violence remain endemic or spike upward. Government policies to integrate former combatants into the legitimate economy are ineffective, and the "skills" employed by violent organizations remain in demand by other groups. Many former combatants find new violent occupations.

The feedback dynamics of organized violence are not uniquely Colombian. Studies of nations with protracted internal conflicts show that prior episodes of collective violence sharply raise the risk of recurrence in some form. The experience of large-scale conflict changes a society by creating economic incentives for violence and by increasing the supply of the materials and skills used for organized violence.

New types of organized violence are spawned in Colombia to interact with earlier forms without replacing them. This issue was identified decades ago by Colombian academics known as "violentologists," but only recently have Bogotá policy makers shown signs of trying to address the interconnectedness of the causes and manifestations of organized violence. The Santos government is trying to approach the problem from multiple angles, but unfortunately, sociological and economic forces favor the perpetuation of violence.

An account of the Colombian government's policies to grapple with organized violence would be incomplete without discussing the US role. On balance, US policies have not helped quell the dynamics of violence in Colombia. By pressing for a military response to issues that might be better addressed with social policies or political strategies, and by indirectly fueling violence in Colombia, the United States has reduced the prospects for nonviolent conflict resolution.

US involvement in the Colombian conflict dates back to the early 1950s, when Colombia was the only Latin American nation to send troops to assist the United States in the Korean War. In return for sending a battalion of professional soldiers, Colombia received equipment and training. The collaboration forged close ties between the two nations' armed forces and helped strengthen the Colombian military relative to civilian government agencies. The institutional partnership did not foist anti-Communist ideology upon the Colombian military, which had been battling a small Communist resistance since the 1940s, but its stridently antileftist stance was reinforced.

In the 1960s, US counterinsurgency aid to Colombia included helicopters, napalm, and advice on employing terrorist actions and paramilitary squads to fight guerrillas. The United States supported the Colombian elites who opposed the land reform efforts of President Lleras Restrepo, and worked closely with elites who supported the use of lethal force against a small leftist insurgency and a large, highly mobilized, and mostly nonviolent peasant movement. During the Cold War, the tendency of US policy makers was to treat any Latin American leader or group that advocated a redistribution of wealth and power as the enemy. A hallmark of this mind-set was to view state repression, even of civilians, as a lesser evil than allowing leftist political groups to gain political influence.

From the 1970s through the end of the century, the priority of the US government in Colombia was supply-side drug policies that criminalized and militarized the trade. In pursuit of the goal of making illicit drugs scarcer and costlier for US users, the US government applied intense diplomatic and economic pressure on Colombia to curb production and disrupt shipments. Drug war policies greatly expanded the mission of Colombian security forces and fortified them with advanced capabilities.

The absence of an effective US approach to consumption of drugs at home also contributed to Colombia's problems. US demand for illegal drugs fed the rise of Colombian traffickers in the first place, and decades later, purchases by US drug consumers had the effect of financing criminal, guerrilla, and paramilitary activity in Colombia. At the same time, the prohibitionist US stance on the issue truncated the policy options available to Colombian politicians for mitigating the violence, corruption, and social problems stemming from the illegality of the drug trade.

In 1998, the Clinton administration began implementing Plan Colombia, an aid package that ultimately spent US$9 billion to fumigate more cultivation areas, disrupt more processing operations, and supply more weapons, helicopters, and surveillance. It made Colombia the third-largest recipient of US military assistance in the world, intensified conflict in target areas, and drove drug-crop growers into new regions.

After September 11, 2001, the administration of George W. Bush shifted the rhetoric on policy toward Colombia to emphasize counterterrorism, but in the actual theater the distinction between counternarcotics and counterinsurgency had been moot for years. The key development during Bush's presidency was to focus more on Colombia's energy sector. Policy toward Colombia has continued in a similar direction under the Obama administration. In 2009 Colombian special operations troops, created and trained by the United States, were deployed in Afghanistan. Later that year a US-Colombian agreement expanded the use rights of US forces on Colombian military bases. The Santos government has not pressed forward with that particular accord, but all prior cooperative military ties with US forces remain fully intact.

ILLEGAL ARMED GROUPS

Three types of illegal combatant affect Colombia: guerrillas, drug traffickers, and paramilitaries. Each has very different goals—respectively, wresting power and wealth from foreign interests and national elites, the production and export of illegal drugs, and destroying guerrillas and leftist activism. All the groups use violence that includes assassinating government officials and community leaders; kidnapping, torturing, murdering, and extorting civilians; and aggressively recruiting lower-income youth. All three derive at least part of their funds from drug trafficking activities, sums that amount to hundreds of millions of dollars per year for each type of group.

Guerrilla Groups

In the early 1960s guerrillas began filling an institutional vacuum in remote parts of Colombia, performing statelike functions such as organizing the construction of roads and bridges and maintaining order (albeit an authoritarian and self-serving kind of order). In the 1980s four main guerrilla groups operated in Colombia: the Revolutionary Armed Forces of Colombia (FARC), the Army of National Liberation (ELN), the Nineteenth of April Movement (M-19), and the Popular Army of Liberation (EPL). The latter two groups demobilized and founded political parties in 1990; FARC, ELN, and fragments of EPL remain in arms, sometimes collaborating and sometimes facing off as lethal rivals.

FARC is the largest, wealthiest, and oldest guerrilla group in the history of Latin America. At its peak in the early 2000s it had more than twenty thousand trained combatants. FARC's strongholds originated in frontier regions and among small colonists and peasants growing illicit crops. From its roots in self-defense forces in the 1940s, FARC has had close ties with the Communist Party, and Marxist rhetoric is still found in FARC communiqués and interviews.

In the 1990s, popular support for FARC plummeted for a number of reasons. The dissolution of the Soviet Union ended a key source of financing, and the ideological appeal of Marxism was on the wane. FARC made up the shortfall in income by relying more on the cocaine and heroin sectors, kidnapping for ransom, and extorting ranches and other businesses in rural areas. Paramilitary groups and government forces stepped up attacks on FARC, and the guerrillas responded by shifting to tactics that harmed civilians. Using landmines and gas-cylinder bombs had the widest impact, but the FARC also kidnapped elected officials. When FARC bombed an upscale family recreation spot in the heart of Bogotá, the organization forfeited the battle for public sympathy.

FARC continued to gain territory and expand its troops through the early 2000s. The government of Andrés Pastrana (1998–2002) established a large cease-fire zone to facilitate peace talks with FARC, but the guerrillas used it for fortifying their strength. This enraged the military and raised alarm in Washington. Previous presidents had faced opposition for negotiating with guerrillas, but now there was widespread sentiment that FARC was acting in bad faith and had a shot at military victory. Pastrana called off the talks and the military invaded the cease-fire zone.

In the 2002 elections, the majority of voters chose Álvaro Uribe, who promised a hard line against the guerrillas and delivered the largest military campaign in Colombian history. According to Colombia's Institute of Legal Medicine and Forensic Science, more than seventy-five thousand people were killed as a direct result of Uribe's war. Guerrilla forces retreated from parts of the country and their ranks diminished. From 2008 on, FARC had more setbacks. The government bombed a

FARC encampment in Ecuador, killing a leader who was an international spokesman and obtaining his laptop for intelligence purposes. FARC's septuagenarian founder died of natural causes, and other commanders were felled by government forces. Desertions and defections rose. Government forces also rescued a group of politicians the FARC had held hostage for six years. It was a public relations coup for the government, and the guerrillas lost a valuable bargaining chip.

But when President Santos took office, the FARC still had more than ten thousand combatants in multiple regions. In 2012 Santos announced that negotiations with FARC for a permanent end to hostilities were under way in Havana. Rejecting language used by his predecessors, Santos refers to the FARC as armed political adversaries, not a group of criminals or terrorists. The formal agenda for the talks includes rights and protections for demobilized FARC combatants, land reform and rural development, reparations and justice for victims of conflict, and strategies for reducing the production of illicit drugs. Apart from the first item, the Santos government was already acting on this agenda, which seems to indicate a prudent interest in the peace-building dimensions of terminating conflict.

The second-largest guerrilla group in Colombia today is ELN, another Marxist group formed in the 1960s. It never matched the size of FARC and its ranks have dwindled since the late 1990s, but it still has several thousand combatants. ELN is distinctive for having former Catholic priests in its leadership and for its references to liberation theology in its communications. In the 1980s ELN extorted vast sums from oil and coal operations, enabling a dramatic expansion of its forces. ELN blew up hundreds of pipelines—damaging the national economy, ruining local ecosystems, and incinerating at least one village and its inhabitants. The shift of the national military toward prioritizing the energy sector put ELN on the defensive. The possibility of negotiating with ELN has been explored by the Pastrana, Uribe, and Santos governments, so far without fruition. In 2012 ELN leaders were calling on the Santos government for dialogue.

Drug Traffickers

Colombian drug-trafficking organizations are heirs to a contraband tradition dating back to colonial times. They emerged in the late 1960s and recruited couriers and assassins in slums filled with people displaced by rural violence and government counterinsurgency campaigns. The meteoric growth of trafficking groups went largely unchecked by the government until the mid-1980s, when a decade of intense combat ensued between government forces and traffickers based in the city of Medellín. Traffickers bombed the headquarters of the Colombian equivalent of the FBI, assassinated four presidential candidates and the minister of justice, waged car-bombing campaigns in major cities, and bombed a passenger jet. Their goal was to eliminate leaders who opposed their power and to terrorize the public into blocking extraditions to the United States.

The government defied the traffickers and worked in close cooperation with the US government. Hundreds of officials and tens of thousands of soldiers, policemen, and citizens in Colombia lost their lives in the struggle. The government emerged the victor, but it took major assistance—even from rival trafficking groups—for it to prevail. When the notorious drug lord Pablo Escobar was killed by government agents in 1993, it marked the end of the Medellín cartel, the most brazen, violent, and politically ambitious trafficking group. During this period President César Gaviria also employed a plea-bargaining arrangement that allowed traffickers who surrendered and confessed to receive reduced sentences, and the constituent assembly prohibited extradition (a provision that was subsequently reversed). Leaders of the Cali cartel either surrendered or were captured during the next administration.

The defeat of the two big cartels did not end the drug trade. Hundreds of small, mobile trafficking groups flourished, production diversified to include heroin, methamphetamines, and other drugs, and global demand rose. The worst development was that politically motivated groups—right-wing paramilitaries and leftist guerrillas—increased their involvement in the trade, giving them unprecedented access to cash. This ominous trend has persisted since then and constitutes an intractable facet of political violence in Colombia. The logic of the Santos proposal to rethink the war on drugs rests on the government's interest in denying these groups financing from the drug trade.

Paramilitaries

Paramilitaries have committed far more massacres and murders than any other armed group. They existed before the drug trade, but the phenomenon took on a new magnitude in the 1980s when drug traffickers allied themselves with emerald merchants to equip and train sophisticated armies. Traffickers in that era also collaborated with landowners and military officers to create a death squad whose mission was to kill the guerrilla kidnappers preying on landowners and ranchers. The group rarely confronted guerrillas directly, but instead killed thousands of leftist civilians, individuals suspected of associating with guerrillas, and street children, drug addicts, muggers, and prostitutes.

The paramilitary phenomenon originates partly in a self-defense tradition whereby rural Colombian communities organize and arm themselves in response to physical attack or threats to their livelihood. Paramilitary fighters sometimes claim they took up arms in reaction to guerrilla abuses or predation by criminal gangs. In the 1990s, paramilitary groups gained control of strategic corridors and resource extraction zones that previously had had a guerrilla presence. Their ranks soared to over fifteen thousand. In 1997 hundreds of paramilitary groups from around the country affiliated under the United Self-Defense Groups of Colombia (AUC), an organization founded by Carlos Castaño. Castaño was murdered by rivals in his fractious organization, but during his tenure paramilitaries greatly improved their public image. It was an impressive feat, given that their signature tactic was to depopulate rural areas by arriving in a town square with a list of names, torture and dismember targeted residents in public, and then threaten anyone who remained with the same.

Paramilitaries are not insurgents or rebels, because they rarely engage in combat with government forces and their aim is not to overthrow the government. They may attack specific government officials and agencies, but they function mainly as militias allied with elements of the armed forces and certain elites. In some regions, paramilitary groups have conducted joint operations with government forces while agencies of the same government were attempting to bring paramilitaries to justice.

Beyond acquiescing to groups using private militias, the government has on occasion actively relied on nonstate forces for fighting guerrillas. A 1964 counterinsurgency decree authorized self-defense units until 1989, when state-sponsored militias were declared unconstitutional after an outcry over the atrocities they committed. Since 1989, the government has legalized forms of paramilitarism on two other occasions.

During the first term of Álvaro Uribe, the government negotiated the demobilization of some thirty thousand paramilitaries. Though it was an achievement, the policy had troubling elements. High-level drug traffickers used the program for evading prosecution, and former paramilitaries were able to legalize property they acquired through violence. Despite the demobilization, civilians continued to be victimized by paramilitary-style groups, albeit with new names such as the *Águilas Negras* (Black Eagles).

In Uribe's second term, outright collusion between government officials and illegal rightwing paramilitaries came to light in a scandal known as *parapolítica*. The director of the national security agency (DAS) was arrested in 2007, and investigations showed that during his tenure DAS agents had worked with paramilitaries to assassinate union leaders and opposition figures, and also protected paramilitary drug-trafficking operations. Other investigations found that dozens of elected officials had received funding from paramilitaries, had assisted paramilitaries in evading justice, and had enlisted paramilitaries to intimidate and even kill political opponents.

By 2012 more than sixty politicians, many of whom were members of the senate and lower house of congress, were serving prison sentences for parapolítica crimes. Most of the jailed officials were close associates or allies of President Uribe, and even members of Uribe's extended family were implicated. For his part, President Uribe directed scathing attacks at the supreme court, the institution investigating senior political figures. The court responded by seeking and obtaining international oversight, and investigations are ongoing.

Under the Santos administration, Colombia continued to suffer from violence by criminal organizations and drug trafficking groups that had members who were former paramilitaries. The government refers to active groups such as the Urabeños as "emerging criminal bands" (BACRIM). The intimidation tactics, extremist politics, and territorial base of some new groups closely resemble that of former paramilitary groups of different names, making it clear that the paramilitary problem is not over.

THE GOVERNMENT

Few Latin American countries have had a longer tradition of civilian rule or elections held without incident than Colombia, but its democracy has clearly been a compromised one. Government efforts to make the political system more responsive include the 1991 popular election of governors (previously appointed by the president), and the popular election of mayors, which began in 1988. Institutional reform culminated in a constituent assembly in 1991 to rewrite the 1886 constitution. Seventy-four delegates, elected by proportional representation and including former guerrillas, indigenous representatives, and civil society activists, wrote the new charter.

Colombia's national government remains similar in structure to the US model of three branches with a separation of powers plus a system of checks and balances. The executive is the most powerful branch of government. The constitution of 1991 gives greater powers to congress than before, but this prerogative has yet to be exercised. Reforms that strengthened the judicial branch with the creation of a national prosecutor's office and provided for judicial review by the supreme court and constitutional court have produced substantive results. The higher courts have played a landmark role in events described in this chapter.

The new constitution decentralized administrative functions. Governments at the department and municipal level can levy taxes, and the national government disperses other revenues as well. Constitutional provisions allow for the recall of elected officials, citizen-initiated legislation, class action suits, and the collective rights of indigenous and other ethnic communities.

The Uribe government led a successful effort to change the constitution so that a sitting president can be reelected. The bill passed congress, the constitutional court approved the proposal, and it won a popular referendum. When Uribe won his second term in 2006, it was the first time since the nineteenth century that a president had been permitted to serve two consecutive terms. The president and his supporters then passed a bill to hold a referendum on whether a president could run for a third time, but the constitutional court declined to approve it, handing down the decision only three months before presidential elections were held in May 2010. Following the court ruling Juan Manuel Santos announced he would enter the race, and he won by a comfortable margin.

The current electoral system has proportional representation for both houses of congress, departmental assemblies, and municipal councils. An interesting feature is that the hundred-member senate is elected from a national constituency. Because of proportional representation, any party that receives 1 percent of the national vote has one senator. The change was intended to promote parties other than the Liberals and Conservatives, but so far the rule has not offset the many factors working against the formation of a strong party system.

In 2006 Colombia implemented new rules for congressional elections. With the old method, party lists were awarded seats according to the proportion of the vote received and winning candidates were chosen by the order in which the party placed them on the list. Under the new system, voters can choose any candidate on the party list they select. After officials determine how many seats a party list has received, votes for the individual candidates are counted, and those receiving the most votes are elected to congress. The provision appears to strengthen the trend toward personalist politics.

POLITICAL PARTIES

Two political parties, the Liberals and the Conservatives, dominated Colombian politics from the mid-nineteenth century through the end of the twentieth century. Though more of the electorate consistently identified with the Liberal Party, it did not prevent Conservatives from winning office almost half the time. Party leaders frequently split into factions, sometimes over policy and other times along personalist lines. The small degree of ideological difference between the Liberals and Conservatives is similar to that found between Democrats and Republicans in the United States. In the present century the Liberals and Conservatives continue to be dominant political organizations, but the two are rife with internal and personal divisions, and voter enthusiasm for the parties continues to decline. A legal change in 2009 made it easier for elected officials to change party affiliation, resulting in more politicians moving from one party to another and reinforcing personalist tendencies and fragmentation in the system.

Since the 1980s, third-party movements have gained importance in Colombian elections, at least in transitory fashion. The party created during Betancur's democratic opening, the Patriotic Union (UP), was founded by the Communist Party and demobilized FARC guerrillas but attracted a mass following. In the 1986 elections the UP presidential candidate received 4 percent of the vote, and the party elected twelve members to congress and scores of local officials throughout the country. In the presidential campaign of 1990 the UP candidate was assassinated. In that period paramilitaries carried out a politicide of the UP: thirteen members of Congress, eleven mayors, seventy municipal council members, and thousands of party members were killed. If not for the political violence, the UP might have developed as the Brazilian Workers Party did, gaining experience governing at the municipal level, developing a solid policy platform, and building a mass membership nationally.

The demobilization of the M-19 guerrilla group in 1990 produced another leftist party, the Nineteenth of April Democratic Alliance (AD M-19). Despite losing its own presidential candidate to assassination in 1990, the AD M-19 finished second in the elections for the constituent assembly later that year, winning nineteen delegates and playing a role in writing the new constitution. The party's showing in the 1990 presidential election (13 percent of the vote) was impressive, and some of its leaders became national political figures. The party itself, however, faded from relevance.

Disunity in the Liberal Party has fed third movements of a sort. In 2002 Liberal senator Álvaro Uribe failed to secure his party's nomination for the presidency. He resigned, ran as an independent, and won. It was the first time a candidate not backed by either of the traditional parties was elected president. Uribe constructed a coalition of Uribistas in Congress made up of Conservatives, dissident Liberals, and members of new parties, some of which were later implicated in the parapolítica scandal. To support Uribe's reelection in 2006, a coalition of Uribistas coalesced in a party called La U, which was headed by current president Juan Manuel Santos and has the largest number of seats in Congress. (La U's other cofounder, Senator Carlos García Orjuela, was jailed in 2008 for working with paramilitaries.) When Santos won the presidency in 2010 it was his first time as an electoral candidate, as his other posts had been appointments such as minister of defense and minister of finance. As president, Santos formed his own coalition among members of Congress, producing a group even larger than Uribe's was.

Outside the coalitions backing Uribe and Santos is the Alternative Democratic Pole (PDA), a party that formed in 2005 when two leftist parties joined forces. One of the parties was the Independent Democratic Pole (PDI), led by "Lucho" Garzón, a former Communist union leader elected mayor of Bogotá in 2003. Other PDI leaders were the mayor of the petroleum-refining city of Barrancabermeja, and the mayor of Bucaramanga, the capital of Santander. In the presidential elections of 2006, the PDA's candidate, Carlos Gaviria, came in second to Uribe with 22.04 percent of the vote. In the 2010 presidential elections, the Democratic Pole did not perform as well. The PDA's Gustavo Petro, formerly of the AD M-19, was elected mayor of Bogotá in 2011.

In the 2010 presidential elections, the center-left Green Party ran the iconoclastic former mayor of Bogotá, Antanas Mockus. In the second-round runoff, Mockus came in second to Santos. In 2013, more than a thousand social movement organizations founded a new organization that touted its alignment with leftist governments in South America. Led by personalities such as former UP mayor and former Liberal senator Piedad Córdoba and Iván Cepeda of the PDA, the group announced its intention to run in the 2014 elections as the National Patriotic Council.

Sectoral Organizations

Along with the political parties, groups representing economic elites have formal access to the political system. Associations of large landowners, industrialists, media interests, and financial groups are the most powerful. The National Association of Industrialists (ANDI), founded in 1944, counts more than five hundred of Colombia's largest enterprises as affiliates. It plays a key role in economic policy making and has influence in other policy areas as well. President Santos appointed a former president of ANDI to the government's five-person negotiating team for the peace talks with the FARC.

Also powerful is the National Federation of Coffee Growers (FEDECAFE). Founded in 1927, this private association is dominated by the larger coffee producers and exporters. Relations between the coffee growers and the government are close. Santos is former president of FEDECAFE, and a recent president of FEDECAFE served as ambassador to the United States under two presidents and was also minister of defense.

President Santos has close ties to Colombian firms that are major investors in Latin America. For example, Grupo Sura purchased US$3.6 billion worth of assets from ING to manage pensions, insurance, and mutual funds in Chile, Colombia, Mexico, Peru, and Uruguay in the largest acquisition in Latin America in 2011. Along with Grupo Sura, Sociedades Bolívar and Grupo Aval also have extensive investments in Latin America. These firms are backing the government's participation in the Pacific Alliance, a group of nations, formed in 2012 and linked by FTAs, that includes the United States, Mexico, Peru, Chile, and Colombia. The ambition is to pursue integration on the scale of the MERCOSUR trading bloc.

The Military

The Colombian military has been one of the least interventionist in Latin America, but on a few occasions it has taken actions that raise questions about the extent to which it is entirely under civilian control. In the 1930s President López Pumarejo, during his "Revolution on the March," transferred military officers who opposed him to remote posts and promoted those who supported him. He was briefly held prisoner in a coup attempt in his second, unfinished term. In November 1985, when M-19 guerrillas seized the Palace of Justice and took its occupants hostage, the military stormed the palace, defeating the takeover but also killing more than a hundred innocent people—including all the justices of the Supreme Court—and incinerating the contents of a building that housed a vital branch of government.

From the late 1990s on, the military grew more powerful than the national police, civilian government agencies, and other militaries in Latin America, except Brazil's. The Uribe government increased the armed forces by thirty thousand and the police forces by ten thousand, reorganized the structure of the armed forces, created new combat units, and integrated advanced technologies. During the Uribe years the military also began administering rural zones of "rehabilitation and consolidation" where civil liberties such as the right of assembly are restricted. Though US military aid and Colombian government spending on the armed forces have declined since 2010, it is too soon to assess trends in the military's power.

Recent evidence challenges the claim that the Colombian military is making progress in protecting human rights, but also attests to the vibrancy of the civilian justice apparatus. Criminal investigations in the Uribe years revealed that a number of innocent people were killed by soldiers whose superiors offered them economic incentives for every guerrilla killed. In the case known as the "false positives," members of the armed forces lured indigent youth with job offers, murdered them, and then disguised their corpses to make them look like guerrillas killed in combat. Some thirteen hundred cases of alleged homicide of this type are under investigation; more than a thousand implicated soldiers and officers have been discharged from service, and a couple of hundred cases have resulted in arrest warrants or convictions.

An issue of great concern to the military is the *fuero militar*, the right of military jurisdiction in cases where the military is accused of human rights violations. Despite intense lobbying by the military in favor of maintaining its exemption from rulings by civilian courts, recently four soldiers received sentences of thirty-four years in prison for a 2005 massacre. Another point of contention is that under the present legal framework for the peace talks with the FARC, only top leaders will be subject to prosecution. How these issues play out will shape future civil-military relations in Colombia.

Organized Labor

Unlike many countries in South America, Colombia does not have a history of mass mobilizations of workers or powerful unions. In the 1920s, strikes against the United Fruit Company were crushed with brutal force. In later decades labor organizations were divided along party lines: one confederation was founded in 1935 under the auspices of a Liberal government, and another was formed in 1946 with close links to the Conservative Party and the church. In 1986 the leftist United Workers Central Organization (CUT) was formed, and it soon became the largest and most influential trade union federation in Colombia. In addition to being fragmented, organized labor has never represented more than a third of formal wage earners. Repression has limited the growth of a workers' movement, and since the 1990s neoliberal restructuring has further diminished the ranks of organized labor.

In 2009 only about 4 percent of the Colombian workforce was unionized. Roughly 856,000 workers are members of 2,357 registered unions. Unions are most active in the public sector, education, health care, mining, and the petroleum industry. Organization in the agricultural sector is low, but SINTRAINAGRO, the largest banana workers' union in Latin America, represents eighteen thousand workers. Ideological orientations vary among Colombian trade unions, but they are unified in their opposition to privatization and efforts by the government and employers to weaken the labor code or change social security. Individual unionists may have ties to guerrilla organizations or, less frequently, paramilitary organizations, but the federations and larger unions emphatically condemn all the armed groups. They advocate greater state support for civil society participation in politics and an end to structural social inequality, which they contend is the root cause of the armed conflict.

Thousands of trade union activists have been killed in Colombia since 1991. During the Uribe years Colombia was ranked as having the highest rate of assassinations of trade unionists in the world. In 2012 the International Labor Organization reported a small decline in violence against labor activists. Labor activists also acknowledge that Colombia's high murder rate overall partly accounts for mortality among unionists, but the fact remains that members of labor unions are more likely to be killed than members of the general population. Colombian journalists are similarly at higher risk because of their profession.

Recent killings of trade unionists in Colombia have been carried out despite formal commitments made by Presidents Santos and Obama in April 2011 to take measures to reduce antiunion violence. The agreement was a condition imposed by the US Congress for the ratification of the free trade agreement. Colombia's main labor monitoring organization reported that in the eighteen months after the labor protection agreement went into effect, thirty-four trade unionists were assassinated and 485 leaders received death threats.

The Roman Catholic Church

Historically, the Roman Catholic Church in Colombia was among the most powerful in Latin America, partly because of the religiosity of the population and partly because of the church's extensive landholdings and formal alliance with elites. Until the National Front, ties between the church hierarchy and the Conservative Party were very close. During *la violencia,* bishops threatened to excommunicate anyone who voted for Liberal candidates, and some priests refused sacraments, even burial, to Liberals.

At the same time, there have been rare but dramatic instances of radical priests, such as Camilo Torres, in Colombia. Torres was a sociologist from an affluent Bogotá family who concluded that being a good Christian in Colombia required working for fundamental change. After frustrating experiences trying to promote land reform, first as a priest and then working for a government agency, Torres left the clergy and joined the guerrillas. He was killed in combat in the 1960s. Another example of a radical priest is Manuel Pérez Martínez, a defrocked Spaniard who from the 1970s until his death in 1998 was a leader of the ELN guerrillas.

Urbanization and secularization in the late twentieth century eroded the church's power, and the hierarchy became less emphatic in its support of the status quo. Under the leadership of Cardinal Alfonso López Trujillo, the church was considered the most hard-line in Latin America, but after he left for a post in Rome in the 1990s, church officials began to grapple with the cycle of violence afflicting the country. Members of the hierarchy critique the violence, but generally they refrain from condemning specific actors and are reticent about criticizing the government.

In contrast, since the late 1980s Colombian priests, religious workers, and laypeople have led efforts to document human rights atrocities, defend and assist victims, and promote nonviolence in high-conflict areas. These activities can and do involve confronting the government. Of the many faith-based organizations that promote human rights, social and economic development, nonviolence, and dialogue in Colombia, many of the most influential ones are either affiliated with the Catholic Church or founded by priests or church organizations. An NGO, the Center for Popular Education and Research (CINEP), runs the most comprehensive data bank on human rights violations and political violence statistics. Other Catholic organizations provide accompaniment to people in conflict and trafficking regions and act as intermediaries and information sources for international aid groups. Sometimes the Catholic Church is the only institution with a presence in a high-conflict rural area or IDP encampment, and through its social pastoral agency it provides critical services. The work is dangerous. According to the international nonprofit Catholic Relief Services, since the late 1980s some sixty Catholic priests, nuns, seminarians, and even bishops have been assassinated, and the number of pastoral agents and Protestant pastors killed is higher.

Rural Social Movements

Another type of organized political group is the social movements. The term encompasses a variety of forms of activism in Colombia, but one of the most interesting is nonviolent noncooperation by rural communities. Communities in regions where armed groups are active face difficult options. They can flee the area, cooperate with and seek protection from one armed group, and run the risk of reprisal by a rival group, or they can organize and use collective action to pressure all armed actors to stay away from their community. This strategy is used by peace communities or humanitarian zones, and also on many *resguardos*. One internationally renowned example is that of the movement led by the Nasa indigenous group in the department of Cauca. The community is 115,000 strong, and Nasa activists have chased down FARC guerrillas to rescue kidnapped members of their community, dismantled police stations and military barricades, and held trials to punish members of their community who work with armed groups. A standoff exists between Nasa leaders and government authorities over whether indigenous autonomy should mean that government forces can be excluded from indigenous lands.

A decade ago the Uribe government militarized Cauca, positioning soldiers in the Nasa town of Toribío, which brought more guerrilla attacks upon a community that has endured more than five hundred armed confrontations in the last twenty years. A fresh round of violence broke out between FARC guerrillas and government forces in July 2012, killing three people, injuring dozens, and destroying homes. Nasa leaders responded by stepping up their campaign to force government troops and guerrilla fighters to leave the area. In the wake of the incident, President Santos visited Toribío and told jeering residents that he would not order the military to vacate the nine towns that Nasa community leaders had requested be cleared. In subsequent protests another person was killed and twenty-three injured.

FUTURE PROSPECTS

There are five reasons for cautious optimism about the Santos peace talks. First, the government is in a stronger position for negotiating peace than the Pastrana government was, and is not offering a cease-fire until the talks conclude successfully. Not only is FARC weaker after eight years of Uribe, but also two of FARC's top leaders have been killed since Santos took office. Second, the military high command is aware that even a weak FARC can survive indefinitely in the jungles and mountains, which puts military victory out of reach for the foreseeable future. The military's formal participation in the negotiations should enhance the prospects for peace, just as a lack of military support doomed past peace efforts.

Third, Colombia's ascendant economic elites are invested in global finance and regional trade, and they seem inclined to view the guerrilla presence as a costly nuisance amenable to problem solving. Fourth, most Colombians support the peace process and there are presidential elections in 2014. Santos's bid for reelection will be favored if his government can keep the process on track, ideally producing results before voters go to the polls. Fifth, the regional context, sometimes called Latin America's "pink tide," offers a propitious climate for a settlement. Colombian firms are profiting from their commerce and investments in Latin America, particularly in neighboring countries that incur damage from Colombian military campaigns against the guerrilla. Moreover, FARC leaders may perceive the political climate in the region as favorable to the creation of a postdisarmament organization that can win elections.

The peace process is not without problems. Some FARC units may refuse to lay down arms or continue drug-trafficking activities. Resistance to land restitution will be intense from the powerful landholding sector, which has close links to paramilitaries and drug trafficking. Determining the rightful owners of contested lands will be tricky, and the implementation of land transfers may result in violence. Also, some of the victims of FARC violence expect guerrilla leaders to be held accountable for crimes such as murder and kidnapping. Since paramilitaries and soldiers have been prosecuted for human rights abuses (to a limited extent), groups sympathetic to those parties can be expected to oppose an amnesty for former guerrillas. Conversely, the guerrillas have little incentive to disarm without an amnesty. As the world has witnessed with the peace processes of other countries that eventually prevailed, the actors who stand to lose from the cessation of conflict often carry out attacks on leaders and engage in other violent actions to undermine the viability of a peaceful resolution. Overall, however, most observers see the Santos initiative as a welcome step in the right direction.

So far, the policies of President Juan Manuel Santos have brought positive change. His government restored good relations with Colombia's neighbors and is managing prosperous times well. He has emerged as an articulate proponent of a new global approach to drug trafficking and consumption. Colombia's international position has improved with the hosting of the Americas Summit in 2012 and taking a seat on the UN Security Council. Within this favorable climate the Santos government appears determined to pursue peace with guerrillas and invest in reducing inequality.

But since 1946 Colombia has experienced armed conflict involving atrocities against civilians. Millions have lost their homes and livelihoods, and hundreds of thousands have been killed. No country in the Americas has had to endure so much violence for so long. The idea that guerrillas are the main—and sometimes the only—culprits for the violence gained currency in the last fifteen years, but the truth is much more complicated. Colombia suffers from multiple types of organized conflict, and state weakness, unique landscape features, and external influences have aggravated the problem. The Santos government is taking crucial and possibly path-breaking steps, but the road is long and steep. Over the medium term it is possible that both significant reform and substantive peace will be achieved. A more responsive democracy and more effective judiciary have been emerging since the constitution of 1991, and without question, many Colombian leaders—in formal politics and civil society—aspire to transform their country via the rule of law.

Suggestions for Further Reading

Asher, Kiran. *Black and Green: Afro-Colombians, Development, and Nature in the Pacific Lowlands.* Durham, NC: Duke University Press, 2009.

Bagley, Bruce. "Drug Trafficking and Organized Crime in the Americas: Major Trends in the Twenty-First Century." *Woodrow Wilson Center Update on the Americas,* August 2012.

Bouvier, Virginia, ed. *Colombia: Building Peace in a Time of War.* Washington, DC: US Institute of Peace Press, 2009.

Carroll, Leah Anne. *Violent Democratization: Social Movements, Elites, and Politics in Colombia's Rural War Zones, 1984–2008.* Notre Dame, IN: Notre Dame University Press. 2011.

Kline, Harvey F. *Showing Teeth to the Dragons: State-Building by Colombian President Alvaro Uribe Vélez, 2002–2006.* Tuscaloosa: University of Alabama Press, 2009.

Molano, Alfredo. *The Dispossessed: Chronicles of the Desterrados of Colombia.* Chicago: Haymarket Books, 2005.

IO

PERU IN THE TWENTY-FIRST CENTURY: CONFRONTING THE PAST, CHARTING THE FUTURE

Julio F. Carrión and David Scott Palmer

Even in a region known for its diversity, Peru stands out. Within its borders are more subclimates than in any other Latin American country. A coastal desert gives way inland to imposing peaks of the Andes, high plains, and intermountain valleys, which in turn fall off to the dense tropical rain forest of the Amazon Basin. The population of thirty million is equally varied: large clusters of indigenous peoples in the highlands and scattered communities of jungle counterparts; descendants of the Spanish conquerors, colonists, and Afro-American slaves; European, Middle Eastern, Chinese, Japanese, and Korean immigrants; and a majority of mixed-race mestizos. The economy includes a significant export sector based on copper, gold, iron ore, zinc, and oil; fish and fish meal; and farm products from recently modernized, totally irrigated coastal agriculture. Politics may be characterized over Peru's more than 185 years of independence as alternating between one form of authoritarian rule and another, with occasional forays into formal democracy.

More than three decades have elapsed since the end of military rule in 1980. Yet Peru is still confronting the consequences of a succession of failed civilian governments, rampant economic mismanagement, and widespread political violence. In addition, Peruvians are still divided by a highly controversial elected regime that provided the benefits of pacification and economic stabilization, on one hand, but brought autocratic governance and pervasive corruption, on the other. At the same time, the dramatic improvement of sociodemographic indicators and rapid

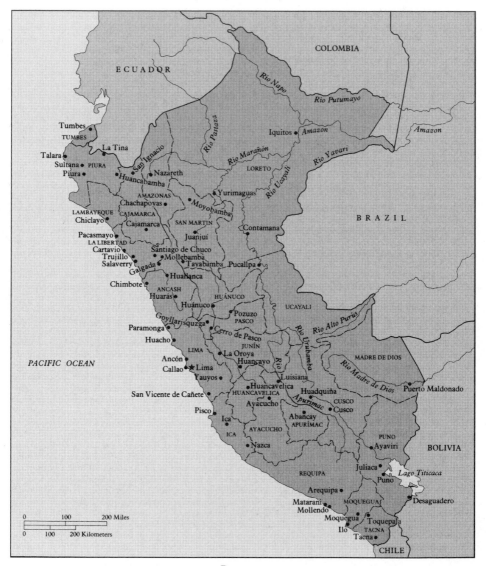

COLOMBIA

ECUADOR

Rio Napo

Rio Putumayo

Amazon

Tumbes
TUMBES
La Tina
Talara
Sultana • PIURA
Piura • Huancabamba
Nazareth

Rio Pastaza

Rio Marañón

Iquitos *Amazon*

LORETO

Rio Yavari

Rio Ucayali

AMAZONAS
Chachapoyas
Moyobamba
Yurimaguas

LAMBAYEQUE
Chiclayo
CAJAMARCA
Cajamarca
SAN MARTIN

Contamana

Pacasmayo
LA LIBERTAD
Cartavio
Trujillo
Salaverry
Galgada
Juanjuí
Santiago de Chuco
Mollebamba
Tayabamba
Pucallpa

BRAZIL

Huallanca
Chimbote
ANCASH
Huarás
Huánuco
HUÁNUCO

UCAYALI

Pozuzo
PASCO

Rio Alto Purús

Paramonga
Goyllarisquizga
Cerro de Pasco
JUNÍN
Huacho
LIMA
La Oroya
Huancayo

Ancón
Callao ★ Lima
Yauyos

Rio Urubamba

Luisiana

MADRE DE DIOS

Rio Madre de Dios

Puerto Maldonado

PACIFIC OCEAN

San Vicente de Cañete
Huancavelica
HUANCAVELICA
Ayacucho
Huadquiña
Apurimac
CUSCO
Cusco

Pisco
Ica
ICA
AYACUCHO
Abancay
APURÍMAC

Nazca

PUNO
Ayaviri

BOLIVIA

REQUIPA
Juliaca
Puno
Lago Titicaca

Arequipa
Matarani
Mollendo
MOQUEGUA
Desaguadero

Moquegua
Ilo
Toquepala
TACNA
Tacna

CHILE

0   100   200 Miles
0   100   200 Kilometers

PERU

economic expansion since the early 2000s have prompted many to wonder if Peru is on the brink of a significant developmental leap. Nevertheless, some also question the sustainability of an economic model that relies heavily on commodity exports. In addition, citizens bitterly complain about failing public schools, rampant citizen insecurity, corrupt state officials, ineffective political institutions, and an archaic and ineffectual judicial system. It seems that the challenges of charting the future cannot be properly addressed without first confronting the legacy of the past. In short, Peru's democracy is still a work in progress.

GOVERNMENTS BEFORE 1980:
AUTHORITARIANISM DOMINATES

Since Peru's independence in 1821, authoritarian regimes of one stripe or another have dominated the political landscape. There have been only brief interludes of elected civilian rule.

Early Years (1824–1895)

Because Peru had been the core part of a larger viceroyalty during the colonial period, it took some time simply to define the country's national territory. The boundaries were roughly hewn out between 1829 and 1841. Once the boundaries were more or less settled, there remained the key problem of establishing reasonable procedures for attaining and succeeding to political office. Peru had at least fifteen constitutions in its first forty years as an independent country, but force remained the normal route to political power. Of the thirty-five presidents during this period, only four were elected according to constitutional procedures, and no civilians held power for more than a few months. Regional caudillos often attempted to impose themselves on the government, which by the 1840s was becoming an important source of revenue because of the income from guano exports.

Unlike much of Latin America during the nineteenth century, Peru was divided politically less by a conservative-liberal cleavage and more by the issue of military or civilian rule. By the 1860s partisans of civilian rule were beginning to organize themselves into a *civilista* movement. The War of the Pacific (1879–1883), in which Chile fought against Peru and Bolivia, dramatically demonstrated the need for professionalization of the Peruvian military and helped provoke the formal establishment of the Civilista Party, as well as a number of more personalistic contenders. The eventual result was Peru's first extended period of civilian rule, starting in 1895.

The War of the Pacific also more firmly embedded the tendency to depend on foreign markets, entrepreneurship, and loans. War debts of more than US$200 million were canceled by British interests in 1889 in exchange for Peru's railroads, the Lake Titicaca steamship line, a large tract of jungle land, free use of major ports, a Peruvian government subsidy, and large quantities of guano.

Limited Civilian Democracy (1895–1919)

Peru's longest period of civilian rule began in 1895. Embracing neopositivist ideals of renovation, modernization, and innovation, the civilian elite also advanced the classic liberal precept of a government that would serve to enhance the capacity of the private sector. Their main political objective was modest: keeping civilians in power through increased government expenditures for communications, education, and health. These were financed by taxes on rapidly expanding exports, revenues from new foreign investments (largely US), and new foreign loans after Peru's international credit was restored in 1907.

The civilian democratic interlude did not last. Many factors explain its demise. First, the Civilista Party, although reasonably well organized, suffered periodic severe internal divisions. Other parties, such as the Liberal, Democratic, and Conservative parties, were personalistic, rising and falling with the fortunes of their individual leaders. Second, there was severe domestic inflation precipitated by the international economic crisis accompanying World War I. Third, elite-oriented parties were increasingly unwilling to respond to a wide array of demands from new groups entering the political system as the result of expanded government services, especially education. Also corrosive to civilian rule were the actions of some leaders themselves. In particular, Presidents Augusto B. Leguía (1908–1912, 1919–1930) and Guillermo Billinghurst (1912–1914) operated in self-serving and personalistic ways. Billinghurst, once elected, eschewed Civilista Party support to make populist appeals to the Lima masses.

Although he was beholden to the commercial elite, Billinghurst did not try to work within the party or the economic elite to try to bring about some quiet accommodation that might have avoided a confrontation. Growing dismay among elite members gradually drew them to the military, which intervened just long enough in 1914 to remove Billinghurst from office. Leguía, after ruling constitutionally during his first presidency, ended once and for all the shaky civilian democracy in 1919. Rather than work out a behind-the-scenes accommodation with opposition elements in 1919 after he won democratic election, he led his own successful coup and ruled without open elections until ousted by the military in 1930.

Populism, Mass Parties, and Veto Coups (1919–1968)

The populism of this period took two forms: civilian, exemplified by Leguía, and military, best illustrated by General Manuel Odría (1948–1956). Both forms were characterized by efforts to stymie political organizations and to encourage loyalty to the person of the president through favored treatment for the elites and by the distribution of goods, jobs, and services to politically aware nonelites. Both forms were also marked by favorable treatment for foreign investors and lenders, thereby maintaining external dependence relationships.

Both civilian and military populism had several important effects on the Peruvian political system. They permitted elites to retain control through their narrowly based interest group organizations (the National Agrarian Society, SNA; the National Mining Society, SNM; and the National Industrial Society, SNI) and their clubs (Nacional and La Unión). When confronted after 1930 with Peru's first mass-based political party, the American Popular Revolutionary Alliance (APRA), the elites were forced to rely on the military to carry out their political will because they had no comparable party to which they could turn. The military, in turn, found it could accomplish its own objectives through veto coups to keep APRA out of power. Thus populism, by discouraging political parties, contributed significantly to continued political instability.

Between 1914 and 1984, the only elected civilian to complete a term, his first, was Manuel Prado (1939–1945, 1956–1962). Why he did so is instructive. He was of the elite and accepted by it. He did not try to upset the status quo. He gained the military's favor by supporting its material and budget requirements. He reached an implicit modus vivendi with APRA. Finally, he happened to be president during a period when foreign market prices for Peruvian primary-product exports were relatively high and stable.

Perhaps the most important political event in pre-1968 Peru was the organization of APRA. Although founded in Mexico by exiled student leader Víctor Raúl Haya de la Torre in 1924, APRA soon became a genuinely mass-based political party in Peru with a fully articulated ideology. By most accounts APRA was strong enough to determine the outcome of all open elections held in Peru after 1931. For more than fifty years, however, the military ensured that the party would never rule directly.

Although APRA has had a strong popular appeal, the party's importance for Peruvian politics rests on its reformist ideology and its organizational capacity. APRA absorbed most of the newly emerging social forces in the more integrated parts of the country (with the exception of Lima) between the 1920s and the 1950s, most particularly labor, students, and the more marginal middle sectors of the north coast. The party's appeal thus helped prevent the emergence of a more radical alternative. Furthermore, even though APRA was an outsider for most of the period from its founding to 1956, it never overthrew the status quo. At key junctures the party leadership searched for accommodation and compromise to gain entry even while continuing to resort to assassinations and abortive putsches in trying to impress political insiders with its power. Between 1956 and 1982 APRA became a center-conservative party willing to make almost any compromise to gain greater formal political power. Although such actions discredited the party for many, APRA remained Peru's best-organized and most unified political force.

The Acción Popular Party (AP), founded in 1956 by Fernando Belaúnde, brought reformist elements into the system just as APRA had done before. AP's appeal was greater in the sierra and south, where APRA was weak. Thus the two parties complemented each other by region, and between them they channeled into the system virtually the entire next wave of newly mobilized popular forces.

Growing economic difficulties in 1967 and 1968 eroded public confidence, and a poorly handled International Petroleum Corporation nationalization agreement sealed Belaúnde's fate. On October 3, 1968, with a bloodless coup, the armed forces began long-term, institutionalized military rule in Peru.

Reformist Military Rule (1968–1980)

"The time has come," stated the new military regime's first manifesto, "to dedicate our national energies to the transformation of the economic, social, and cultural structures of Peru." Past governments had declared their intention to change Peru, but this one was prepared to act. What was surprising, given Peru's history of military intervention on behalf of the elites, was that a major reason for the 1968 coup occurred was the Belaúnde government's failure to deliver on promises of significant reform.

During this twelve-year period (the *docenio*) the military became an instrument for reform in Peru mostly because of developments related to the military itself.

One was the officers' educational experience after the mid-1950s in the Center for Higher Military Studies (CAEM). Another was a small but intense antiguerrilla campaign in 1965. Third was the effect on military institutional development of continuous US military training from the 1940s through the 1960s. Fourth was the US government's decision in 1967 not to sell jet fighter planes to Peru, which crystallized nationalist sentiment. Last was a vigorous and successful army-led civic action program after 1959. These factors prompted most of the officer corps, at least within the army, to conclude that the best protection for national security was national development. In their view, civilian politicians and political parties had failed to meet the development challenge in the 1960s. Many officers concluded that only the military, with its monopoly on legitimate force, was capable of leading Peru toward this goal.

Once in power, the military called itself revolutionary but practiced reform. Almost without exception, the 1968–1975 policy initiatives were based on the twin assumptions of continued economic growth, with improved distribution of this growth, and the willingness of economic elites to accept incentives to redirect their wealth toward new productive activities. Significant changes occurred. One of the most important was the rapid expansion of state influence and control. New ministries, agencies, and banks were established; basic services were nationalized, as were some large foreign companies in mining, fishing, and agriculture, with compensation and reinvestment incentives; and state enterprises or cooperatives were established in their place. Important areas of heavy industry were reserved for the state, new investment laws placed various controls on the private sector, and government employment mushroomed. At the same time Peru pursued the objective of enhancing development by diversifying its external relationships, thereby reducing the country's economic and political dependency.

Another significant initiative was a large-scale agrarian reform program, which effectively eliminated large private landholdings. About 360,000 farm families received land between 1969 and 1980, most as members of farm cooperatives. Commitment to cooperatives illustrated the regime's concern for popular participation at various levels. Neighborhood organizations, worker communities, and cooperatives of several types proliferated after 1970, as did various coordinating bodies. All of these changes represented substantial adjustments in past practices and for a time appeared likely to succeed.

A number of factors led to the regime's undoing. First and most fundamental was that the military's reform plans were much too ambitious. Leaders wanted to do too much in too many areas in too short a time. In addition, success was premised on continued economic growth, which stopped after 1974 when economic difficulties multiplied. With locally generated resources not available as expected, the military government turned to foreign loans, often short-term ones, to keep up the momentum, which produced a severe debt crisis by 1978. Also, those in power failed to consult with the citizenry, the presumed beneficiaries of the reforms. This neglect contributed to popular resentment and mistrust. Finally, the illness after 1973 of the head of state, General Juan Velasco Alvarado, contributed to a loss of the institutional unity of the armed forces themselves, which his dynamic and forceful leadership had helped to instill. The eventual result was a mixture of old and new programs in yet another overlay, which was increasingly ill-financed, confusing to citizens, and ultimately unsuccessful.

An August 29, 1975, coup, led by General Francisco Morales Bermúdez and supported by the military establishment, gently eased out the ill and increasingly erratic General Velasco. With the exception of the agrarian reform, initiatives were quietly abandoned or sharply curtailed. By 1977 mounting economic and political pressures prompted the military regime to initiate a gradual return to civilian rule.

THE TRANSITION TO DEMOCRACY IN 1980: ECONOMIC CRISIS AND POLITICAL VIOLENCE

The constituent assembly elections in 1978 opened the process of transition to democratic rule. They also represented another political milestone because they included participation by an array of leftist parties, which garnered an unprecedented 36 percent of the vote, although APRA won the most seats. The assembly itself was led by APRA founder Haya de la Torre—another first, given the long-term animosity of the military. These elections also marked the beginning of significant involvement in the system by the Marxist left. The assembly produced the constitution of 1979, which set up national elections every five years and municipal elections every three years, beginning in 1980. One irony of the elections was that they returned to the presidency the same person who had been so unceremoniously unseated in 1968.

This time Belaúnde's AP was able to forge a majority in congress, in coalition with the small Popular Christian Party (PPC), and won the first plurality in the municipal elections as well. However, events conspired once again to make life difficult for the governing authorities. Inflation continued to increase, reaching 60 percent in 1980 and exceeding 100 percent by 1984. The recession deepened, with GDP actually declining by over 10 percent in 1983 and real wages eroding during Belaúnde's second administration (1980–1985) by over 30 percent. World market prices for Peru's exports—copper, oil, sugar, fish meal, and minerals—remained low or declined even further. Devastating weather accompanied the arrival in 1982 of the El Niño ocean current, and crops and communications networks in the northern half of Peru were destroyed by rain and flood, while in the south crops withered as a result of drought.

Given such unfavorable economic developments, the foreign debt burden became even more onerous, increasing from US$8.4 billion in 1980 to over US$13 billion by 1985. International Monetary Fund (IMF) agreements provided new funds and debt refinancing, but they also imposed economic restrictions. With the domestic controversy that ensued, Belaúnde hedged on IMF strictures, which provoked a breakdown in the agreement and left a substantial burden for the next administration.

Another major challenge for the government and the democratic regime was the Shining Path guerrilla movement. Originally based in the isolated south-central sierra department of Ayacucho and headed by former professors and students from the local University of Huamanga, Shining Path advocated a peasant-based republic forged through revolution. The group's ideology was Marxist-Leninist, based on the principles of Mao and José Carlos Mariátegui, a leading Peruvian intellectual of the 1920s who founded what became the Communist Party of Peru. After some fifteen years of preparations—which included study groups, control of the University of Huamanga, leadership training in China, and work in the indigenous peasant-dominated local countryside—Shining Path launched its people's war on the very eve of the May 1980 national election that ended the military docenio.

The Belaúnde administration did not take the group seriously for almost three full years. Only in December 1982 did the government declare Ayacucho an emergency zone and send the military to deal with the problem. By the end of Belaúnde's term thousands had perished in the violence, human rights violations had skyrocketed, and more than US$1 billion in property damage had occurred. The emergence in 1984 of a new guerrilla group, the Túpac Amaru Revolutionary Movement (MRTA), added to popular concerns over the spreading political violence.

Such economic and political difficulties substantially weakened popular support for Belaúnde and the AP in the 1983 municipal elections. In the 1985 presidential vote the AP candidate was routed, gaining only 6 percent of the total. The largely Marxist United Left Party (IU) garnered 21 percent for its candidate, Alfonso Barrantes, and a rejuvenated APRA won with 46 percent with its youthful (thirty-six-year-old) standard-bearer Alan García Pérez (1985–1990).

The García victory was doubly historic: after a fifty-five-year struggle APRA had finally gained both the presidency and a majority in both houses of congress. Additionally, for the first time since 1945 and only the second time since 1912, an elected civilian president handed power over to an elected successor. The 1986 municipal elections also saw substantial APRA gains, including for the first time ever the mayorship of Lima.

Alan García's forceful, nationalistic leadership put the international banking community on notice that Peru would be limiting repayments on its debt (now over US$14 billion) to 10 percent of export earnings. Domestic initiatives, especially in agriculture, contributed to long-overdue economic growth at rates of 9 percent in 1985 and 7 percent in 1986. But the recovery ran out of steam in 1987. The economy never did recover from the president's surprise bank nationalization that year, even though this ill-considered attempt ultimately failed.

The second half of García's term was an unmitigated disaster. Peru suspended all foreign debt repayments, which resulted in international credit drying up. Inflation skyrocketed to 1,722 percent in 1988, 2,600 percent in 1989, and 7,650 percent in 1990. The economy declined by more than 20 percent during this period. Political violence, which had ebbed between 1985 and 1987, surged anew. By the end of the García government in 1990 casualties exceeded fifty thousand and direct and indirect damages were more than US$14 billion. Total foreign debt with arrearages was over US$23 billion. Not surprisingly, García's popularity plummeted from an 80 percent favorable rating early in his term to single digits near the end.

THE FUJIMORI ERA: THE AUTHORITARIAN
RECONSTITUTION OF THE STATE

In this challenging context, Peruvians went to the polls in 1990. From virtual oblivion, Peru's right reemerged, centered on the capacity of the novelist Mario Vargas Llosa to galvanize popular concern over President García's failures. A new coalition, the Democratic Front (FREDEMO), was formed among conservative and centrist parties, and it was able to win more mayoralties in 1989 than any other group.

In the run-up to the April 1990 national elections, opinion polls made Vargas Llosa the heavy favorite. Many were stunned when a political newcomer, National Agrarian University president Alberto Fujimori, came from less than 3 percent in the polls a month before the vote to finish second with 25 percent to Vargas Llosa's 28 percent. In June Fujimori won easily in the runoff between the top two contenders. His victory was explained as the product of popular frustration with politics as usual and Vargas Llosa's overidentification with politicians of the right.

Once in office President Fujimori launched an economic shock program even more severe than Vargas Llosa's proposal during the campaign. He argued that economic recovery could not be secured until Peru's economic mess had been straightened out and the country's international credit standing restored. In the short run, however, his drastic measures accelerated inflation to historic highs, further reduced domestic economic activity (28 percent in 1990), and pushed twelve million to fourteen million more Peruvians below the poverty line (60 to 70 percent of the population). Congress went along for the most part, even though Fujimori's party grouping, Cambio 90, held only about one-quarter of the seats. Surprisingly, most Peruvians also went along; Fujimori's support in opinion polls remained consistently above 50 percent.

By early 1992 such drastic measures began to produce results. Inflation was sharply reduced, running at only 139 percent in 1991. International economic reinsertion moved forward after foreign debt payments and negotiations with the international financial institutions were resumed in late 1990. Signs of economic recovery also began to appear. Beginning in October 1991, the United States increased bilateral economic assistance and initiated its first substantial military aid in over twenty years.

Peru's congress became more restive and assertive, particularly with human rights issues, but did authorize emergency executive-branch decree powers and approved most initiatives. Although political violence continued to be a serious problem, government forces had also had some successes against both Shining Path and the MRTA. Given such positive momentum, few were prepared for Fujimori's April 5, 1992, *autogolpe*—a coup d'état in which, despite having come to power through legal means, Fujimori dissolved the national legislature and assumed extraordinary powers.

This "temporary suspension" of democracy, dissolving congress and the judiciary with the backing of the armed forces, drew immediate and almost universal international condemnation. The United States immediately suspended assistance except humanitarian and counternarcotics aid. It also used its influence to ensure postponement of Peru's international economic reinstatement as well as of new aid by most of the dozen countries making up the Peru Support Group. The Organization of American States (OAS) pressed vigorously for democracy's reinstatement.

Fujimori, chastened by the intensity of the international response, agreed immediately to prompt electoral restoration. This was accomplished with national elections under OAS oversight for a new, smaller, one-house congress cum constitutional convention in November 1992 and municipal elections two months later. Results included marginalization of traditional parties, greater concentration of power in the presidency, and a congressional majority that supported Fujimori. Furthermore, former president García was forced into exile after the autogolpe and lost his leadership role in APRA. The new constitution was narrowly approved (52 to 48 percent) in an October 1993 referendum. It recentralized government authority, established the basis for privatization and economic liberalization, and allowed for the immediate reelection of the sitting president.

As the autogolpe worked out, Fujimori was very much the winner. However, his April 1992 action could easily have been disastrous. Suspension of economic assistance postponed economic recovery in Peru by at least a year. Shining Path expanded recruitment and violence and began to predict imminent revolutionary victory. What saved Fujimori's authoritarian gamble was the careful police work of a small, specialized antiterrorist group in the Ministry of the Interior, formed under García, which paid off with the dramatic capture of Shining Path leader Abimael Guzmán and key lieutenants on September 12, 1992. Several hundred other guerrilla operatives were rounded up in the following weeks, thwarting what was to have been a massive offensive to close out the year. Tougher antiterrorist decrees issued in the aftermath of the autogolpe permitted rapid trials in military courts and life terms without parole for some two hundred key figures. The fortuitous capture of Guzmán, however, was the major event that legitimated the autogolpe; not only did it help pacify the country but it also gave the Fujimori government the political space to pursue its ambitious national reconstruction agenda.

President Fujimori's government engaged in multiple machinations to remain in office, but he also had a broad base of popular support. Such approval stemmed largely from his government's ability to drastically reduce political violence and to restore economic and political stability. Inflation virtually ended (dropping from 57 percent in 1992 to 3 percent by 2000), and with economic liberalization and reinsertion into the international financial community, Peru's economic growth averaged over 7 percent from 1994 through 1997. Between 1993 and 1998, Peru received over US$10 billion in new investment and US$8 billion in new loans, and it restructured its foreign debt under the Brady Plan, reducing its debt by more than US$5 billion to just under US$19 billion by 1997. A variety of innovative local microdevelopment initiatives reduced extreme poverty by more than half from 1991 through 1998 (from 31 percent to 15 percent) while also creating hundreds of new community organizations to administer the projects.

Over the course of the Fujimori decade, political parties were further undermined by a combination of their own limitations and government actions. Independent groups, including the president's, proliferated, dominating the 1995 national elections and the 1995 and 1998 municipal votes. No traditional party except APRA received over 5 percent of the vote in the 1995 national elections—a dramatic turnaround from the 1980s.

After a clear mandate in 1995 (64 percent of the valid vote and a majority in congress) President Fujimori called for "direct democracy without parties or intermediaries" and increased expenditures for local development as well as initiating monthly stipends directly to municipal governments. However, his government also changed the political rules—often arbitrarily and unconstitutionally—to keep a robust political party system from reemerging and to undermine the opposition's electoral campaigns. Intimidation tactics included wiretaps, physical assault, and character assassination campaigns orchestrated by the Peruvian National Intelligence System (SIN), directed by Fujimori's closest ally and confidant, Vladimiro Montesinos. The regime also thwarted a 1998 national referendum on a third term (for which 1.4 million signatures had been secured) through a congressional vote denying its validity.

Having rigged the electoral machinery and procedures in his favor, President Fujimori surprised no one by deciding to run for a third, constitutionally dubious term in the 2000 elections. Unlike 1995, however, he did not secure an absolute majority in the first round, nor did his supporters win a congressional majority. He was forced into a runoff with second-place finisher Alejandro Toledo, a US-educated economist from a humble indigenous background—but without political experience. The best efforts of the international community, led by the OAS Election Observation Mission, to ensure a free and fair voting process for the runoff were not successful. Toledo withdrew in protest, and the incumbent won with just 52 percent of the valid vote (about one-third of all ballots cast were spoiled in protest).

THE END OF FUJIMORI AND THE CHALLENGES OF ESTABLISHING A STABLE DEMOCRACY

Events soon revealed the pyrrhic quality of Fujimori's 2000 electoral "victory." Inaugurated amid massive protest and tear gas in July, Fujimori was gone by November. Precipitating his downfall was the videotaped revelation that SIN director Montesinos was bribing elected representatives of the opposition to ensure a pro-Fujimori majority in congress. In spite of President Fujimori's desperate moves to maintain control—including firing Montesinos and forcing him into exile, and calling for early elections in which he would not be a candidate—popular indignation overwhelmed his maneuverings. By early November opposition parties had regained control of congress. They refused to accept Fujimori's letter of resignation from Japan, where he had fled in ignominy, but declared the presidency vacant instead on grounds of "moral incapacity."

A transitional government led by president of congress and longtime AP representative Valentín Paniagua took the oath of office on November 22. Fujimori's so-called direct democracy had ended in disgrace. The Paniagua interim presidency (2000–2001), though only nine months in duration, was surprisingly effective in righting the ship of state and putting it back on course. Amid multiple new revelations of official misdoing during the Fujimori years, hundreds of former high-level civilian and military leaders were tracked down and arrested for corruption and abuse of position, including Montesinos himself from his refuge in Venezuela. A Truth and Reconciliation Commission (CVR) was established in 2001 to document the human rights abuses committed during the "people's war." Attempts to bring Fujimori back from exile in Japan to face Peruvian justice were unsuccessful, however, as it turned out that he had Japanese citizenship and could not be extradited.

THE RETURN OF COMPETITIVE ELECTIONS

New elections in April 2001 were as free and fair as those of 2000 were tainted. A hard-fought first round between Lourdes Flores Nano of National Unity (UN) on the right and Toledo of Peru Possible (PP) and APRA's García on the center-left saw

Toledo (with 37 percent of the vote) and García (with 26 percent) edging out Flores (24 percent) in the first round. Here, García's efforts to cast himself as a wiser and more experienced leader fell short. Toledo, who had led the opposition to Fujimori in the aftermath of the 2000 electoral debacle, won with 54 percent of the vote, though without a majority in Congress.

The Toledo presidency (2001–2006) stumbled politically from the start. Upon taking office in July he faced a plethora of demands from an array of local organizations, including opposition to privatization, demands for a greater share of foreign corporation taxes, and an end to coca eradication programs. Toledo's government handled these issues badly in almost every case. Amid violence and property damage, promises were made and not kept, decisions reached and reversed, and new programs announced but not funded. The president's disorganization, his libertine personal life, his assertive if talented Belgian wife, and the controversial personal advisors and family members who surrounded him all contributed to growing popular disillusionment with his administration. Toledo's popularity declined to single digits for much of his five-year mandate. This occurred even in the context of renewed and sustained economic growth and a major decentralization initiative in 2003–2004 creating elected regional governments. However tainted Toledo's presidency, though, there was never a sense that Peruvian democracy itself would collapse.

As Peruvians returned to the polls to elect a new president in 2006, unresolved developmental problems, lingering issues of inequality and social exclusion, and political discontent were clearly manifested. At the same time, economic improvement, dispersion of the *fujimorista* vote, and past centrist voting appeared to favor Valentín Paniagua, widely respected for his successful provisional government. But his candidacy failed to take off, and for a short time Lourdes Flores Nano seemed poised to improve on her 2001 performance by making it to the runoff election. Although her appeal was particularly strong in Lima and she led in the polls for many months, she was displaced by the meteoric rise of Ollanta Humala, leader of the Nationalist Party (PN). Humala, a political outsider and former military officer, waged a left-populist campaign and secured first place, while Alan García would come from behind to finish second.

In the runoff, García won a much narrower victory over Humala than polls had predicted (53 to 47 percent) by convincing enough Peruvians that he had learned from the mistakes of his disastrous first presidency. In a graphic demonstration of the political center's neglect of the periphery, however, almost all sierra and jungle departments favored Humala, while the entire coast went for García. These were the first Peruvian elections to show such geographical polarization.

Although in his 2006 inaugural address President García proclaimed his determination to deliver a major "economic shock" to develop the sierra, his administration fell far short on actual delivery. He turned out to be genuinely "reinvented" in his second term as a promoter of continued economic liberalization, including the ratification of a free trade agreement with the United States in 2007. However, most of the highlands saw few benefits. One result was that local and regional social conflicts in both sierra and jungle almost doubled. As in the Toledo government, official responses were nearly always late, ineffective, and sometimes even disastrous. One dramatic example is the abortive police effort in June 2009 to dislodge jungle indigenous groups from a two-month highway blockade in the Amazonian town of Bagua, which resulted in at least thirty-five deaths, mostly police. In addition, regencrated Shining Path armed cadres in coca-growing regions of the Apurímac and Upper Huallaga valleys embarrassed Peruvian police and army operations on several occasions in 2008 and 2009; during this period guerrilla incidents rose to a fifteen-year high.

Another serious manifestation of the center's indifference to the sierra was the failure to implement the 2003 recommendations of the Truth and Reconciliation Commission for forensic identification of the victims of the violence in some forty-two hundred common graves, mostly in Ayacucho and most believed to be killings and interments by the military. Compensation was promised to surviving family members and to their communities. However, by the end of the García government in 2011 only the community payments had been made. For all of its success in the macroeconomic arena, the García government repeated the pattern of inattention and both inappropriate and belated responses to the multiple needs and demands of the population of Peru's periphery.

The decentralization initiatives that had begun in Fujimori's first term with funding of municipal (district) governments and which continued under Toledo with elections and funding for regional (department) governments, generating new opportunities for access by local political and social organizations, continued during the García years. These elections generated literally hundreds of local groups putting forth candidates for mayor, district council, or regional president, with a corresponding reduction in the historic concentration of political power at the national level. Although the quality and competence of such elected officials varies widely, the new array of district and regional governments with resources at their disposal offers many more opportunities for political access and for response to some local needs. At the same time, however, these elections have made the development of national parties more difficult.

THE 2011 PRESIDENTIAL ELECTIONS

Ollanta Humala ran a populist campaign in 2006, offering a radical departure from the economic model that Peru had followed since the 1990s. He proposed significant political reform as well, promising that if elected he would call for a constitutional assembly to draft a new constitution. His narrow defeat revealed worrisome undercurrents in Peruvian politics. As the new round of presidential elections approached and Humala declared his candidacy again, the question was whether additional years of economic growth had undermined his appeal among the poor and whether Peruvians would opt instead for a more moderate, democratic, and market-oriented figure.

For a while, it seemed that voters would indeed embrace such a candidate, in the figure of former president Alejandro Toledo. But a series of mistakes during the campaign deflated his candidacy and led people, especially in Lima, to take another look at Pedro Pablo Kuczynski. Known as PPK, he is an economist and technocrat who held ministerial positions during both the Belaúnde and Toledo governments. A seventy-three-year-old member of Peru's white elite, a naturalized citizen of the United States, and a successful financier and private equity investor, PPK was an unlikely candidate to attract the support of Peruvian voters. But his dramatic rise in the polls and victory in Lima deprived Toledo of the opportunity to make it to the runoff election. As Toledo's popularity fell, the fortunes of Humala and his electoral alliance, Gana Perú, rose. By early March 2011 Humala had cemented his lead and was widely considered the favorite to win a plurality of the vote in the April 10 contest.

The Humala of 2011 was quite a different candidate. Acknowledging that to have a credible chance at winning the runoff election he needed to appeal to the center, he decided to moderate both his image and message. Instead of praising the virtues of Hugo Chávez and his Bolivarian government, as he had done in 2006, Humala embraced the more moderate approach followed by Brazilian president Lula da Silva. In fact, Brazilian consultants closely associated with Lula and his party became Humala's main advisors. In 2006 Humala campaigned dressed in a red T-shirt and jeans; five years later, he opted for business suits and white shirts. Mixing a message of social inclusion, moderate economic reform, and social conservatism (he opposed gay marriage and abortion rights), he won first place in the first round but failed to obtain an absolute majority.

With the center-right vote split among three different candidates (Toledo, PPK, and Luis Castañeda, leader of National Solidarity [SN]), Keiko Fujimori, oldest daughter of the former president, was able to secure a place in the June 5 runoff. As the campaign for the runoff started, Humala further moderated his proposals, announcing a "road map" that would guide his government if elected. Decidedly different from his original platform, entitled "The Great Transformation," the new platform promised to respect the independence of the Central Bank, keep inflation low, and foster economic growth while embracing social inclusion rather than radical reform. After former president Toledo announced that he would support Humala in the second round, key members of his economic team became Humala's advisors. This further cemented Humala's move to the center.

With a few notable exceptions, most of Peru's establishment and media rallied behind Keiko Fujimori due to their concerns over the populist and antidemocratic elements of Humala's candidacy. The runoff polarized Peru once again, exposed the fault lines of its society, revealed the still prevalent racism, and unmasked the authoritarian predilections of some members of the establishment. For many voters the election posed an extremely difficult choice between a candidate who might restore the authoritarian practices of the Fujimori regime and another who might undo the significant gains made in the economy and the rule of law. When Peruvians finally went to the polls on June 5, they elected Humala with the slimmest margin of any presidential election since the return to civilian rule in 1980: 51.4 percent went for Humala and 48.6 percent supported Keiko Fujimori. Less than 500,000 votes, out of 16.5 million votes cast, separated the two. Humala was able to secure the presidency because he won in all the departments he carried in 2006 plus four in which he had not: Ancash, Ica, Pasco, and Ucayali. For the first time since 1980, the winning candidate was able to claim victory without carrying the capital.

It may be still too early for a definitive conclusion, but it seems that Humala is eschewing the wave of left-wing populism that afflicts most of the Andean countries. This is really remarkable, considering that Peru exhibits many elements that might favor such a development. First of all, it has a long tradition of populist rule.

Second, the crisis of the party system has created a vacuum that could easily be filled by a populist president. Third, there is widespread discontent with the political class and institutions, providing a fertile ground for an anti-political discourse. Finally, Peru's economic bonanza has enriched state coffers, making it easier to fund social programs to benefit a populist project. It is always unwise to try to provide reasons for a nonevent, but one can speculate that Humala is probably aware that despite their low levels of approval, political institutions in Peru are stronger than they were twenty years ago and thus could more easily derail any attempt to replicate the Fujimori years. Moreover, he has not encountered serious opposition to his government to date, thus making it less necessary to consider a strategy of political confrontation to pursue his platform.

RAPID SOCIAL CHANGE AND THE PAINS OF MODERNIZATION

Peruvian society began to change in the 1950s, but social and economic change has accelerated dramatically in the last thirty years. In the 1950s Peru experienced a dramatic surge in internal migration as people from the sierra moved to Lima. This mobilization had lasting consequences. From a primarily rural society in the early 1960s, Peru is now an urban society: almost 80 percent of the population lives in the cities. Many of them, in fact, live in large cities (about 50 percent of the total population resides in cities with at least 100,000 inhabitants). Migration has also changed the main geographical distribution of the population. Today the majority (57 percent) lives along the coast, and three out of ten Peruvians reside in Lima.

The demographic changes have been no less impressive. In three and a half decades, Peru has more than doubled its population, from thirteen million in 1972 to twenty-eight million in 2007, the year of the last census. According to the projections of Peru's National Office of Statistics and Informatics (INEI), Peru reached thirty million inhabitants in 2012. The rate of growth of the population was significant in the 1960s and 1970s and has slowed somewhat since then. Two significant demographic trends merit attention. First, life expectancy continues to rise. Between 1950 and 1955 life expectancy was 43.9 years; by 2007, Peruvians could hope to live, on average, around 76 years. Second, fertility has also declined, with women having fewer children than ever. In 1977–1978, women had on average 5.4 children. In 2004, the number had dropped by more than half, to 2.4. Likewise, while infant mortality continues to be high in comparison with countries such as Chile and Argentina, this indicator has improved dramatically in the last decade. In 2000, 40.6 of every 1,000 children born alive died before they reached their first birthday. In 2012, the rate dropped to 21.5 (only slightly higher than the rates found in Brazil, Ecuador, and Venezuela).

There are other indicators of the rapid process of modernization that Peru is undergoing. Almost all households in urban areas have electricity, and 91 percent of them have running water. In addition, 85 percent of urban households are connected to a sewage network. Possession of a television set is almost universal: 80 percent of all households, 91 percent in urban areas, and 96 percent in Lima. But perhaps the indicator that best illustrates the degree of modernization is the percent of Peruvian households with at least one member owning a cell phone: it went from

16.4 percent in 2004 to 75.2 percent in 2011. In early 2012, almost 90 percent of all households in Lima had a cell phone.

Since 2001, Peru has been experiencing a remarkable period of economic growth. The economy grew by 9.8 percent in 2008, the second-highest rate in Latin America that year, slowing to 0.9 percent the following year as a result of the global economic meltdown, but resuming its pace in 2010. The economy is on track for a full decade of average GDP growth close to 7 percent. Such growth is unprecedented and is based largely on the extended expansion of commodity exports at high international prices. Domestic results include increased tax revenues, public investment, and a rapidly growing internal market, along with growing domestic and foreign investor optimism. According to the Economic Commission for Latin America and the Caribbean (ECLAC), Peru's direct foreign investment levels more than doubled between 2003 and 2011, rising from US$3.5 million to US$7.7 million.

Sustained economic growth has improved key indicators of well-being. Total poverty has dropped from 58.5 percent in 2004 to 30.8 percent in 2010. Urban unemployment fell from 9.4 percent in 2002 to 7.2 percent in the first half of 2012. Average monthly incomes have also increased. INEI reports that the average urban income in the third quarter of 2012 (approximately US$515 per month) was over 7 percent higher than a year earlier. Public opinion polls also reflect more positive public perceptions of their economic situations. In 2006, 72.9 percent of respondents polled described their personal economic situation as either "good" or "fair." Six years later, that figure had improved to 84.9 percent. In the same 2006 poll, 27 percent described their personal economic situation as "bad" or "very bad"; by 2012, that figure had dropped to 15.1 percent. Even income inequality has shown modest improvement: the Gini coefficient fell from 53.2 in 2007 to 48.1 in 2010.

Peru exhibits today one of the most open economies in South America. This is largely the result of the adoption of market reforms in the 1990s during the Fujimori administration. Most state-owned enterprises were privatized, labor laws liberalized, tariffs reduced, exchange rate controls lifted, and import restrictions eliminated. The long-term modernization process and 1990s economic reforms have changed Peru's economic structure in important regards. Three changes in particular merit attention. First, agriculture's contribution to GDP has declined markedly over the past sixty years (from 14 percent in 1950 to 7.7 percent in 2008), more than replaced by expanding mining and oil production. Second, state participation in the economy has declined significantly in recent years, from a high of 21 percent in 1975 (during the reformist military government) to 6 percent in 2000 (even below the 1950 figure, 7 percent). Third, foreign capital has become much more important, contributing 28 percent of GDP in 2000 compared with 10 percent in 1950. Obviously Peru has abandoned the state capitalism of the 1970s and now embraces an economic model in which private investment, both domestic and foreign, plays a much larger role.

Despite such significant changes, Peru's economy continues to be dependent on the export of commodities and thus subject to the demands and vagaries of international markets. As a result, this recent economic growth is masking the structural weakness of relying too much on mining exports. Some economists argue that Peru is currently suffering a severe case of "Dutch disease," where the high profitability in mining discourages investment in other sectors of the economy that may be less profitable but which are also less vulnerable to external shocks. Moreover, the massive influx of dollars associated with mining and oil exports tends to overvalue the national currency, with deleterious effects for overall long-term economic prospects.

Recent instances of social conflict in Peru have been linked to mining areas, where local communities opposing the expansion of mining activities have resorted to violence to stop them. An emblematic example of these tensions is the Conga conflict in the northern department of Cajamarca. In late 2011, Newmont Mining Company announced that the Peruvian government had approved the company's plans for a US$4.8 billion investment in the Conga mines, which would be the largest single foreign investment in the country's history. Area residents, with the backing of the regional president, objected to the plan. They criticized the proposed investment's environmental impact and called for a regional strike. Soon the conflict gathered national attention, given the magnitude of the investment at risk and the death of five people in clashes between police and local residents in July 2012. This confrontation forced the Humala government to suspend constitutional guarantees in Cajamarca by declaring a state of emergency. These clashes undermined President Humala's promises as a candidate not to support the expansion of mining activity in the department.

Both the Conga conflict and the confrontation in the Amazonian town of Bagua are prime examples of the tensions associated with Peru's modernization process. Most urban respondents in a poll supported the Conga investment (56 percent) as long as environmental concerns were addressed. However, the local rural residents most directly affected, many in indigenous communities, were strongly opposed. Their opposition needs to be placed in the larger context of Peru's uneven modernization. The rural population is the one left behind, where all the indicators of modernization are still lagging. Their fierce resistance to the expansion of mining operations, perhaps incomprehensible to urbanites immersed in the globalization process, is a symptom of unresolved developmental issues.

Peru faces other important challenges as well as it tries to deepen its democracy. One is the deep distrust that citizens have in their political institutions and their skepticism toward democracy itself. Public opinion polls have documented the contradiction between sustained economic growth and widespread political discontent. A 2012 study places Peru among the bottom third in support for the political system among the Latin American countries where polls were carried out. In this same poll, Peru also ranks among the lowest four countries in support for the idea of democracy and for the judicial system. It is not surprising, then, that about 13 percent of those interviewed in Peru 2012 admitted to having participated in a protest the previous year, a percentage among the three highest in the region.

Another challenge is the inability of the state to provide security for its citizens. Between 1989 and 1993, homicides increased to a peak of 17.2 per 100,000 inhabitants, due largely to the Shining Path insurgency. This group's decline coincided with a sharp reduction in homicides, to 4.25 in 2002. Since then, however, violent crime has jumped significantly, to 18.58 homicides per 100,000 inhabitants in 2010, even higher than peak rates during the worst years of the political violence. In addition, Peruvians report high levels of crime victimization. A 2012 survey places Peru second in the region in the percentage of people who say they have been victims of delinquency in the previous year and first in their perceived levels of insecurity. Not surprisingly, then, Peruvians cite violence and insecurity as the country's most important issues in 2012, even above poverty, unemployment, and the economy. In fact, the proportion of respondents who say violence and insecurity are the most pressing problems tripled from 2006 to 2012, rising from 10.7 to 30.7 percent.

AN ELECTORAL DEMOCRACY WITHOUT PARTIES

As discussed above, the impressive performance of macroeconomic indicators obscures a deeper reality of a perilous overreliance on the prices of commodities exports, which generates economic distortions that may affect Peru's long-term development. As noted also, the rapid social change accompanying modernization, but over a longer period of time, has heightened tensions between urban and rural populations and has contributed to violence and perceptions of insecurity, among other challenges. Turning to the political arena, clearly the successful completion of three consecutive rounds of presidential elections in 2001, 2006, and 2011 needs to be celebrated, for it signals the return of free and fair elections in Peru. However, this positive development may also obscure some worrisome trends in the political arena, of which the most important may well be the virtual absence of established political parties.

Peru had a developing party system during the 1980s, with AP and PPC on the right, IU on the left, and APRA in the middle of the ideological spectrum. However, the continued development of a party system was cut short by several developments. First, the AP-PPC and APRA governments performed dismally when in office. Second, the rampant and prolonged economic crisis and the violence of Shining Path and the MRTA provoked a severe decline in civil society organizations. Third, the rise of Alberto Fujimori (1990–2000) as a hegemonic political actor in the 1990s and his administration's concerted effort to undermine any source of opposition to his regime fostered an antipolitical mentality that further undermined traditional parties. The 2000 presidential election saw the emergence of new political organizations to contest Fujimori's grip on power. However, the systematic smear campaign waged against the main candidates challenging his bid for a third term contributed to their inability to consolidate as full-fledged parties.

APRA continues to be the only functioning party worthy of that name; although it has become much weaker in recent years, it remains an important presence in Peru. The problem is that the new parties have trouble planting roots in society. PP had the greatest chance, but the shortcomings of the Toledo administration and Toledo's unsuccessful bid for reelection in 2011 have weakened the party. Other parties had even more difficult times. We Are Peru (SP) and its leader Alberto Andrade failed to develop a strong party after he finished his term as Lima's mayor and tried to enter national politics, with uneven success. After a dismal performance in the 2006 election and the death of Andrade in 2009 the party faded even further. Luis Castañeda, leader of National Solidarity (SN), was elected mayor of Lima in 2002 and then reelected in 2006. Despite success as mayor, Castañeda has been unable to expand the party nationally.

These organizations have not been able to consolidate into national parties in large part because they are essentially personalistic vehicles devoid of ideology, relying on the electoral fortune of their leaders and their potential access to state resources to support clientelistic and patronage networks. Deprived of political office, these parties struggle to survive. When Toledo finished his first term, he left the country and his party went into hibernation, only to be resurrected again in 2011 when he ran for reelection. Luis Castañeda basically initiated his political career from his position as a government bureaucrat, following his appointment by Fujimori as head of the National Institute of Public Health (1990–1996) and then as president of the Fishermen's Pension Fund (1997–1999), after which he founded SN. In short, Castañeda needs to be visible in office to continue his viability as a political figure. This may well have motivated him to spearhead an ill-advised recall election in 2013 against Susana Villarán, mayor of Lima, in the hope that he would be able to run again for the office himself and thus keep his party afloat.

There is an additional reason that might explain the inability of these three parties to develop into solid national organizations. In 2002 President Toledo organized regional elections for the first time. The objective was to elect twenty-three regional presidents (one for each of Peru's departments, with the exception of Lima and Callao) under an electoral law allowing participation by local and independent slates, which did not have to be registered as national political parties. Regional elections took place in 2002, 2006, and 2010 but further eroded national parties by facilitating the participation of independent lists. A conservative count of the electoral performance of these independent lists clearly illustrates the declining importance of national parties: in 2002, independent lists accounted for 21.9 percent of votes cast, steadily increasing to 40.2 percent in 2006 and 56.4 percent in 2010.

SOCIAL GROUPS

Organized social groups have played less of a role in Peruvian affairs than in most other Latin American countries until quite recently. The reasons may be traced in part to the strong patterns of Spanish domination that inhibited growth long after the formal Spanish presence was removed. What emerged instead was a strong sense of individualism within the context of region and family for that small portion of the total population that was actually included within the nation's political system.

With the establishment of limited civilian democracy between 1895 and 1919, some of what were to become the country's most important interest groups were founded, including the National Agrarian Society (SNA), the National Mining Society (SNM), and the National Industrial Society (SNI). For a long time, however, the important decisions affecting the country were usually made in the Club Nacional, formed much earlier (1855) and the lone survivor of post-1968 reforms. Even the military operated between 1914 and 1962 largely as the watchdog of the oligarchy. Thus elites could determine policy outside the electoral arena when necessary and had limited incentives to operate within any party system.

The changes produced by the reform military governments of 1968 to 1980 overturned the old elites and gave rise to opportunities for new sets of social actors through the rapid expansion of new forms of participation. These included various types of cooperatives in agriculture, neighborhood associations in the squatter settlements, and worker self-management communities in industry and mining. At their peak in the late 1970s such entities incorporated as many as eight hundred thousand workers.

With the restoration of civilian rule in 1980, parties and unions regained their pre-1968 roles, largely supplanting the military's model. Vigorous political participation through a score of parties covering the entire ideological spectrum characterized the 1980s, with power alternating between center-right and center-left groups at the national executive level and with substantial representation in congress by the Marxist left. In municipal elections political organizations won shares of district governments at different times, with pluralities shifting from AP to IU to APRA and back to IU. An unanticipated legacy of long-term reformist military rule, then, was to usher in a historically unprecedented level of partisan politics, institutionalized to a degree that few people foresaw and proceeding apace in spite of profound domestic economic difficulties and a substantial guerrilla movement.

However, with the breakup of IU in 1988–1989 and widespread popular disappointment with party politics as successive elected governments failed to respond to citizens' needs, political independents came to dominate national and local elections in the 1990s, and union membership declined. Fujimori's 1990 election and the 1992 autogolpe reflected the shift to antiparty politics, as did the independent-dominated 1992 congressional and constitutional assembly elections and the 1993 local elections. The result was a progressive deinstitutionalization of electoral politics and a return to more personalistic approaches at the center. Another outcome was a dramatic increase of popular organizations at the local level, as citizens sought to fill the newly available political space.

These new social actors included neighborhood/community improvement or environmental preservation groups, mothers' clubs, coca growers' associations, and school parents' organizations. Although they were usually focused on gaining official responses to immediate needs or perceived abuses, some also expressed concerns based on ethnic identification. With weakened parties and unions and new, locally directed government and nongovernmental organization programs, such newly mobilized groups filled an important role in articulating citizen demands to improve local conditions.

DOMESTIC AND FOREIGN POLICIES

Domestic Policy

Peruvian governments of most of the twentieth century can be characterized as small, centralized, and personalistic. Until the 1960s, government employees constituted a small proportion of the workforce and were usually selected on the basis of party affiliation, family ties, or friendship. Ministry bureaucracies were concentrated in Lima. Government presence in the provinces was limited to prefects and their staffs, military garrisons in border areas, small detachments of national police, schoolteachers, and a few judges, all appointed by authorities in Lima.

The government's size and scope increased considerably during the first Belaúnde administration with the establishment of new government agencies. Total government employment increased by almost 50 percent between 1960 and 1967 (from 179,000 to 270,000), and the public sector's share of GDP grew from 8 percent to 11 percent.

However, the most dramatic changes in the size and scope of the state machinery occurred between 1968 and 1980 under the reformist military regime, which dramatically expanded government involvement in order to accelerate development. Existing ministries were reorganized and new ministries and autonomous agencies were created. By 1975 total government employment had increased by almost 70 percent over 1967 (to 450,000), and the public sector's share of GDP had doubled to 22 percent. Even with such a rapid expansion of the state, however, central government activities remained concentrated in Lima. Official funding tended to go toward construction, equipment, and white-collar employment in the capital rather than for activities in the provinces.

The political and financial crises of 1975 and the change of government brought to an end the dynamic phase of public sector reforms. Resource limitations, growing popular opposition, and the inability of the military regime to act effectively to implement its own decrees prevented full implementation of the corporatist model articulated between 1971 and 1975. The 1979 constitution, however, drawn up by an APRA-IU majority, retained the statist orientation of the Peruvian political system even as it set the basis for civilian rule.

With the return to democracy in 1980 President Belaúnde announced his intention to restore the dynamism of the private sector and to reduce the role of government. However, continuing economic problems and substantial public resistance made these changes difficult to carry out. The García government moved quickly to implement long-standing APRA decentralization goals, including regional development corporations, expanded agricultural credit, and regional legislatures, while working simultaneously to win the confidence of domestic entrepreneurs. Initial successes were substantial, but by the end of García's term, they had been overwhelmed by an ill-advised nationalization of domestic banks, soon reversed, and by Peru's worst economic crisis in one hundred years. Central government employment expanded from six hundred thousand employees in 1985 to one million in 1990—but with half the budget.

The Fujimori administration, after implementing drastic shock measures to stop Peru's economic hemorrhaging, began to move the country toward economic liberalization. This process involved selling off state enterprises created or nationalized under the 1968–1980 military regimes, retiring many government employees and reorganizing ministries to be able to dismiss thousands more, and overhauling the legal framework to favor private property and investment. Tax collection was also reorganized so that government could begin to pay its own way again. Collections increased from less than 4 percent of GDP in 1989 to 14 percent by 1995. Over the course of the 1990s more than one hundred former state agencies were privatized, generating around US$8 billion in new foreign investment. The 1993 constitution incorporated these changes but also further concentrated power in the presidency and in central government. New government agencies, several designed to emphasize microdevelopment projects in Peru's poorest districts, began to operate in the early 1990s, as did a municipal fund to transfer resources to local governments.

Overall, the state did not become smaller during the Fujimori years, but was dramatically changed and reorganized.

The Toledo government ended some of the Fujimori regime's government agencies and reorganized others but also reduced their efficiency through political patronage. It also embarked on a new decentralization initiative in 2003–2004, which included regional elections. After 2006 the García administration engaged in further reorganization but also sustained the center's commitment to strengthen regional and local governments with additional funding and expansion of personnel. Nevertheless, even with such reinforcement and support, regional governments in particular were slow to implement meaningful development programs in their areas of responsibility. The Humala government, in pursuing the president's social inclusion agenda, has also reorganized some state agencies, most notably with the creation of the Ministry of Development and Social Inclusion. This new ministry is in charge of all social programs, including Humala's Pensión 65 (noncontributory pension support for the elderly in situations of extreme poverty), Cuna Más (provision of day care facilities for rural families), and the expansion of Juntos (a conditional cash transfer program primarily aimed at rural households).

Foreign Policy

The combination of deep domestic economic crisis and changing international realities contributed to a dramatic shift in Peru's foreign economic policies in the 1990s. Privatization and economic liberalization opened up the country once again to private investment. Economic nationalism receded rapidly as a cornerstone of Peru's foreign relations. Over the 1990s scores of public enterprises were privatized, tariffs slashed, foreign debt repayments resumed, and legal foundations for private investment restored. Foreign investment more than doubled, from about US$4 billion in 1993 to over US$9 billion in 1998. Peru led efforts to reconstitute the Andean Pact as the Andean Group on terms much more favorable to private sector activity. Finally, the international financial community became a major source of government development programs once again. Although foreign debt increased to over US$30 billion by 1998, with scheduled repayments running at about half of export earnings, most specialists continued to see Peru as a good credit risk.

Perhaps Peru's most significant foreign policy success in recent decades was the negotiation with Ecuador of a definitive border settlement in 1998. The Peru-Ecuador boundary dispute had been Latin America's longest-standing such conflict and had provoked almost two dozen armed clashes between the countries even after the issue was supposedly resolved by treaty (the Rio Protocol) in 1942. The most violent was the major confrontation between January and March 1995, which cost the two countries over US$1 billion and resulted in hundreds of casualties.

The role of US public and private participation in Peru has always been quite complex. Private investment grew rapidly in the early twentieth century but was almost exclusively in isolated enclaves on the north coast (oil and sugar, then later cotton and fish meal) and in the sierra (copper, other minerals, and later iron). Successive governments encouraged such investment. Even during the military docenio, in spite of some expropriations and a conscious attempt to diversify sources of foreign investment, substantial new US investment took place, particularly in copper

(Southern Peru Copper Company) and oil exploration and production (Occidental Petroleum Company).

The Belaúnde government's policy toward private investment was more open but only partly successful owing to international and domestic economic problems. The García administration's nationalistic posture in a context of growing economic and political difficulties discouraged most new investment, both domestic and foreign, between 1985 and 1990. Fujimori's shift to privatization and economic liberalization began slowly, given Peru's grave problems, but gathered momentum beginning in 1993 with several hundred million dollars in portfolio and direct investments. Between 1993 and 1998, more than one hundred public enterprises were privatized and over US$6 billion in new foreign investment generated. Spanish investment was the largest, with US$2.4 billion of the US$9.8 billion total as of 1998; US investment was second, with US$1.6 billion; and the British were third, with US$1.2 billion. Policies favorable to foreign investment continued during both the Toledo and the García governments, with the 2007 free trade agreement with the United States offering added incentives, even though among some sectors of the public there is growing concern over the negative environmental effects of some investments, especially those in mining.

The US role in counterdrug programs in Peru since the mid-1990s has been controversial. Funds for eradication and alternative development have had an impact on cocaine production, but interdiction of planes that appeared to be transporting drugs was suspended after a US missionary's plane was mistakenly shot down in 1999. During the latter years of the increasingly undemocratic Fujimori administration, US policy favored counterdrug activity over pressure to maintain democratic practice. With both the Toledo and the García governments, continuing counternarcotics activity contributed to significant increases in organized resistance by coca growers as well as new activity by a somewhat revitalized Shining Path, posing additional challenges for Peruvian authorities. There are indications that Humala's policies toward narcotics will not depart from those of previous governments.

CONCLUSIONS

As an independent nation, Peru has had great difficulty in overcoming its authoritarian legacy. For about three-fourths of its history nondemocratic governments have ruled the country. The legacy of Spanish colonial rule was an important factor impeding the evolution of liberal-democratic institutions in the nineteenth century, but additional considerations—including international market forces, the incorporation of more and more of the population into the national political and economic system, and political leadership perceptions and actions—prevented the emergence of a stable institutional structure in the twentieth century.

The reformist military governments of 1968 to 1980 tried but failed to construct a new participatory model of community-based politics and a new economic model based on a leading role for the state. Their failure had its origin in their inability to appreciate the boundaries within which reformers must operate in order to accomplish development objectives. In particular, they did not grasp the degree to which political leaders in a country such as Peru are hemmed in by forces largely beyond their control. Then, although full electoral democracy established in 1980 began with great enthusiasm and promise, it soon fell prey to some of the same problems that had undermined its authoritarian predecessors. It also had to cope with Latin America's most radical and violent guerrilla organization, Shining Path, and it handled that challenge poorly as well. Once again, a combination of circumstances and political leadership predispositions led to the dismantling of democracy in 1992 with Fujimori's autogolpe.

President Fujimori succeeded where his civilian predecessors had failed by pursuing a new strategy to deal with Shining Path and by implementing a new economic liberalization model that ended hyperinflation and restored economic growth. These successes gave him the popular support necessary to set up a new political system under the constitution of 1993. This system contained democratic forms and procedures, but it also included numerous mechanisms that gave untoward control to the head of state. Although many new government agencies and programs worked to benefit the less privileged at the periphery, the quality of democracy and democratic discourse in the center was progressively eroded. Most of the media were cowed, and opponents were often harassed and intimidated. Peru became a prime example in Latin America of a government that manipulates democratic procedures so as to ensure its own continuance in power. The result was democratic in form but authoritarian in substance—Peru's latest manifestation of its long authoritarian tradition.

Three presidencies have elapsed since the fall of Fujimori. Competitive democracy has returned with force, and the economy has been growing impressively. Sociodemographic changes and economic growth are transforming the nation in significant ways. Today, most Peruvians are healthier and live longer, reside in urban centers, enjoy smaller families, and are highly interconnected. But the process of modernization is uneven and has left unresolved long-standing issues of economic development and inequality. Peru is confronting, painfully and slowly, the legacy of an authoritarian past, an economic model that relies too heavily on the exports of primary products, and a state that frequently ignores the plight of the indigenous population. At the same time, the country is trying to chart a future of democracy and development in the midst of pent-up demands and unmet needs. Peru's democracy could become stronger and more inclusive, or it could succumb once again to the enormous size of the task. Although democratic practice under Toledo was chaotic and problematic, even in the midst of sustained economic growth, the second García administration surprised many by stabilizing the democratic process in spite of some continuing issues that have not been handled well. The trajectory of Humala so far indicates that he is reluctant to take his country down the path of authoritarian populism, to the surprise of many of his early detractors. He is polling well and seems to have escaped the curse of low approval rates that plagued his two predecessors. Though still incomplete, democracy in Peru seems finally to be replacing the country's authoritarian past.

Suggestions for Further Reading

Burt, Jo Marie. *Political Violence and the Authoritarian State in Peru: Silencing Civil Society.* Basingstoke: Palgrave Macmillan, 2008.

Carrión, Julio, ed. *The Fujimori Legacy: The Rise of Electoral Authoritarianism in Peru*. University Park: Pennsylvania State University Press, 2006.

Dietz, Henry A. *Urban Poverty, Political Participation, and the State: Lima 1970–1990*. Pittsburgh, PA: University of Pittsburgh Press, 1998.

Fumerton, Mario. *From Victims to Heroes: Peasant Counter-Rebellion and Civil War in Ayacucho, Peru, 1980–2000*. Amsterdam: Thela, 2002.

Levitt, Barry. *Power in the Balance: Presidents, Parties, and Legislators in Peru and Beyond*. South Bend, IN: University of Notre Dame Press, 2012.

Mares, David, and David Scott Palmer. *Power, Institutions, and Leadership in War and Peace: Lessons from Peru and Ecuador, 1995–1998*. Austin: University of Texas Press, 2012.

McClintock, Cynthia, and Fabian Vallas. *The United States and Peru: Cooperation—at a Cost*. New York: Routledge, 2003.

Palmer, David Scott, ed. *Shining Path of Peru*. 2nd ed. New York: St. Martin's Press, 1994.

Quiroz, Alfonso W. *Corrupt Circles: A History of Unbound Graft in Peru*. Baltimore: Johns Hopkins University Press, 2008.

Stern, Steve J., ed. *Shining and Other Paths: War and Society in Peru, 1980–1995*. Durham, NC: Duke University Press, 1998.

THE LEGACY OF CHARISMA: VENEZUELAN POLITICS AFTER HUGO CHÁVEZ

David Myers

INTRODUCTION

Nicolas Maduro's razor-thin margin of victory over challenger Henrique Capriles in the presidential election of April 14, 2013, came as a surprise. President Hugo Chávez Frías had anointed Maduro as his heir the previous December, prior to undergoing his fourth cancer surgery in Havana. Maduro became interim president when Chávez died on March 5, 2013. Maduro drew upon government resources to support his candidacy in the election that followed. His inner circle assumed that sympathy for their fallen leader would give Maduro a decisive victory. Thus the National Electoral Council's announcement that Maduro's advantage over challenger Henrique Capriles was only 1.5 percent stunned the government. It also emboldened opponents of Hugo Chávez's revolution.

On the day after the election Capriles enumerated multiple irregularities in the voting. He demanded an electoral audit and refused to recognize Maduro's victory until completion of the audit. Nevertheless, two days after the election Maduro was inaugurated in a ceremony boycotted by the opposition. Tensions escalated. Supporters of Capriles banged pans to protest what they deemed to be a stolen election. Violence erupted when supporters of Maduro and Capriles clashed in the streets. The National Electoral Council agreed to an audit, but not one that would extend to all ballots, the kind of in-depth probe that Capriles's supporters believed would show that their candidate had received 52 percent of the total votes cast.

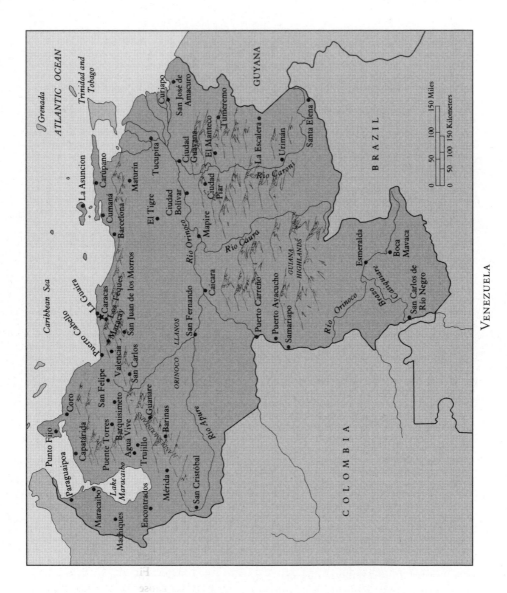

VENEZUELA

Most Latin American governments recognized Maduro's government, as did Iran, China, Russia, and other countries whose leaders had sympathized with Hugo Chávez. However, the United States and Canada argued that recognition should await the outcome of a thorough and impartial electoral audit. Resistance to an in-depth audit exacerbated concerns over the legitimacy of Maduro's election. However, the National Electoral Council stuck to its position that it would examine only a representative sample of ballot boxes. Capriles rejected this, arguing that anything less than a complete audit would not uncover the fraud he asserted had allowed Maduro to claim victory. The government took a hard line. The minister of prisons, Iris Valera, announced that she had a cell waiting for Capriles, and Diosdado Cabello, the Chavista president of the National Assembly, refused to allow opposition members to speak unless they recognized the legitimacy of Maduro's election. Tensions escalated.

The political order was subjected to greater stress following the April 2013 presidential election than following the presidential election of December 6, 1998. In the earlier contest Hugo Chávez ousted political and economic elites who had dominated Venezuela for more than two generations. He captured the presidency by promising change and attacking Democratic Action (Acción Democrática, AD) and the Social Christians (Partido Socialcristiano, COPEI), the political agents of that domination. By the end of the 1990s AD and COPEI were discredited and demoralized. Venezuelans, however, did not want a dictatorship. They preferred democracy, but a changed democracy, one with different political parties and leaders. Hugo Chávez Frías promised this. In 2013, by contrast, Venezuelans were politically polarized between supporters and opponents of Chávez's socialist revolution. Neither side was inclined to grant their rivals the status of "loyal opposition."

By and large governments between 1958 and 1998 spent oil income on domestic projects intended to modernize the country, make it attractive to foreign investors, and integrate Venezuela into the international capitalist system. President Chávez had other priorities. He favored centralized delegative democracy, initially labeling his transformation the "Bolivarian Revolution" and then "twenty-first-century socialism." By the time of the presidential election of April 14, 2013, Venezuela was looking increasingly like communist Cuba. Centralized control reduced the autonomy and influence of local and regional governments. Private enterprise had fallen out of favor. Media freedom was curtailed. Internationally, Venezuelan foreign policy gloried in confrontation with the United States, Western Europe, and institutions of the international capitalist economy. Chávez courted China by offering terms that encouraged Beijing to purchase Venezuela's petroleum. He reduced the amount of petroleum sold to the United States. Chávez's foreign policy also undercut the Organization of American States and pushed the formation of regional international organizations that excluded the United States. Finally, Chávez substituted the military doctrines of Middle East insurgents for those learned by an earlier generation of officers in the United States, purchased large quantities of Russian arms, and opened Venezuela to Iranian influence.

Venezuela's abandonment of liberal democracy and adoption of an activist, anticapitalist foreign policy are not the only reasons for interest in the country. Between 1945 and 1989 Venezuela changed from a rural society to an urban one while appearing to avoid chaos and soften the pain of modernization. Literacy rates rose dramatically, indigenous heavy industry took shape, and for a brief moment Venezuelans enjoyed one of Latin America's highest standards of living. Prosperity ended in the 1980s, however, when corruption and falling revenues from the international sale of petroleum undermined the political and economic institutions that nurtured liberal democracy. That regime, known as Punto Fijo, was the fruit of pacts between political and economic elites who united to prevent the return of traditional dictatorship. Initially Punto Fijo democracy allowed new actors to enter the ruling class, expanded the middle sectors, and improved living standards among the poor.[1] However, the regime's inability to consolidate and build upon these achievements in the 1980s led to bloody riots in 1988 and constitutional crises in 1992 and 1993.

Supporters of the Punto Fijo resisted Hugo Chávez's efforts at political transformation. They backed the failed coup attempt of April 2002, staged massive demonstrations to force him from office in the aftermath, and organized a recall referendum that took place in August 2004. President Chávez won the referendum, and subsequently his popularity surpassed that of any chief executive elected during the forty years of liberal democratic governments. Between 2005 and 2012 Chávez used his popularity to bring about one of the most profound political regime changes experienced by any Latin American polity since Fidel Castro openly embraced Communism in 1961.

BACKGROUND

Geography and history have shaped contemporary Venezuelan politics. Nestled in the northeastern quadrant of South America between 1 and 13 degrees north of the equator, Venezuela is hot and tropical. Cool temperatures predominate only at altitudes above 3,280 feet (1,000 meters). The country's thirty million inhabitants live in an area of 352,150 square miles (912,050 square kilometers), roughly the size of Texas and Oklahoma combined. Stretching some 1,750 miles (2,816 kilometers) along the Caribbean Sea and the Atlantic Ocean, Venezuela extends south into continental South America. It encompasses snow-covered mountains rising to 16,427 feet (5,007 meters, Pico Bolívar) and reaches into the Orinoco and Amazon jungles. Some 3,000 miles (4,800 kilometers) of continental borders form frontiers with Colombia, Brazil, and Guyana. The Orinoco River, one of the largest and most navigable in the world, drains four-fifths of the country. But the mountains, not the river or the plains, have historically been Venezuela's most influential geographical features. The dominant colonial settlements, agricultural estates, and urban centers are nestled in cool mountain valleys, and until 1925, when petroleum extraction became Venezuela's most important economic activity, these valleys formed the unchallenged economic, administrative, and social heartland of the nation.

Geographers divide Venezuela into five regions: the Guyana Highlands, the Orinoco Lowlands, the Northern Mountains, the Maracaibo Basin/Coastal Lowlands, and the numerous small islands along the Caribbean coast. These regions vary immensely in size, resources, climate, population, and historical input.

The Guyana Highlands, encompassing 45 percent of the national territory, is the largest region. Historically remote, poor, and sparsely populated, Guyana became a symbol in the 1950s of the nation's drive to industrialize. Guyana's industrial and mining centers remain oases of modern civilization surrounded by tropical forests. Until the 1950s Guyana exerted little influence on national affairs, but subsequent government investment in the region has made Guyana's industrial infrastructure central to Venezuela's development aspirations.[2]

Lying between the southernmost part of Venezuela and the coastal mountains are the great grassland prairies (*llanos*) of the Orinoco Lowlands. Occupying 33 percent of the national territory, the Llanos support 20 percent of the population. For six months of the year this vast, featureless plain, 620 miles (1,000 kilometers) long and 400 miles (645 kilometers) wide, is subject to rainfall so heavy that much of it lies under water. As the ensuing dry season progresses, the mud turns to deep layers of dust, the heat becomes intense, and streams dry up. Although the region is far from ideal for raising cattle, a type of culture based on that industry has grown there and continues to be managed by a rough—and for many years lawless—breed of man (*el llanero*) for whom cattle raising is a way of life.

The Northern Mountains constitute the third major geographical region. Although they encompass only 12 percent of Venezuela's land area, they support roughly two-thirds of the country's population. The principal mountain chain consists of the coastal range and the Sierra Nevada de Mérida. In the coastal range are found the capital city, Caracas, along with the Valencia-Maracay industrial center, large coffee holdings, sugar haciendas, and rich farmlands surrounding Lake Valencia. Although the coastal range's political leaders have played a central role in Venezuelan history, they have often lost to more aggressive rivals from less-favored regions.

The high and rugged Sierra Nevada de Mérida is a western spur of the Andes. With peaks rising to 16,400 feet (5,000 meters), its early inaccessibility discouraged great agricultural estates (*latifundios*). The Venezuelan Andes were thus characterized by medium-sized landholdings and populated by small clusters of people, both mestizos and Indians. Despite the presence of an influential university in the city of Mérida, Andean Venezuela remained isolated until the rise of coffee as a commercial crop.

Ten percent of Venezuela's national territory consists of a narrow, partly arid, partly swampy belt of lowland lying between the steeply rising coastal mountains and the Caribbean Sea. This region comprises the Maracaibo Basin and the Coastal Lowlands. Much of Venezuela's oil is found in the Maracaibo Basin, and the region's drained swampland has been transformed into rich farms and cattle ranches. However, over 80 percent of the basin's inhabitants are classified as urban. Most reside in Greater Maracaibo, the country's second-largest metropolitan region. Beginning in the 1920s, oil exploitation transformed the Maracaibo Basin into a thriving commercial, industrial, and educational center. In contrast, tourism is the most important economic activity of the eastern Coastal Lowlands. Here are located the best Caribbean beaches, and the climate is clear and dry. African influence is stronger in this region than anywhere else in Venezuela.

Most Venezuelans are an amalgam of Caucasian, Amerindian, and black. They have a common culture, predominantly Hispanic but with important Amerindian and African strands. Overwhelmingly Roman Catholic (85 percent) and Spanish-speaking, Venezuelans view themselves as members of a single ethnic mixture. The national census does not classify according to race or ethnicity (except for

Amerindians in the Orinoco and Amazon jungles), so it is only possible to make educated guesses. Pure Caucasians account for between 10 and 15 percent of the total population. Perhaps 10 percent of Venezuelans are pure black, less than 3 percent are pure Amerindian, and between 70 and 80 percent are of mixed ancestry. Ethnic mixing has occurred at all social levels, and ethnicity does not serve to distinguish either separate groups or classes. Nevertheless, Caucasian features are valued, and their predominance is greater among the higher social and economic strata.

Internal migration since World War II has transformed Venezuela from a rural society into one that is highly urbanized. Initially Caracas received a disproportionate number of these migrants, mushrooming from a metropolitan region of about five hundred thousand in 1945 to a diverse metropolis of over five million in 2010. Four other cities—Maracaibo, Valencia, Barquisimeto, and Barcelona/Puerto La Cruz—boast populations of more than one million. In contrast, large areas of rural Venezuela are depopulated.

SOCIAL STRUCTURE, SOCIAL CHANGES, CIVIL SOCIETY, INTEREST GROUPS

Historical and Political Economy

The history of Venezuela is one of progressive integration into the North Atlantic area. Crucial in this process were the pacification and development programs initiated by General Antonio Guzmán Blanco (1870–1888) and consolidated by General Juan Vicente Gómez (1908–1935). Over the final decade of Gómez's rule (1925–1935) the commercial bureaucratic system gave way to a petroleum-based technological imperium. This arrangement was and is the product of opportunities and complexities endemic to petroleum exploitation. Transformation involved creating modern systems of transportation and communication and diffusing industrial technology into the oilfields. It also facilitated the intervention of foreign interest groups and ideologies into Venezuela's internal politics.

Caracas, measured by any set of variables, gained disproportionately from the new economic regime, although not until after Juan Vicente Gómez passed from the scene. The long-lived dictator disliked and distrusted *caraqueños* (residents of Caracas) and ruled from Maracay, a small settlement some sixty miles to the west of Caracas. Gómez's successors then launched a major effort to bring standards of comfort in the capital up to those of urban North Atlantic countries. University education, art, culture, social services, architecture, urban grandeur—whatever the North Atlantic imitation, Caracas residents monopolized it to an ever-growing degree. Thus Venezuela's capital acquired the trappings of modernity while the rest of the country remained much the same. Caracas attracted the ambitious, the wealthy, and the young from other regions.

The petroleum-based technological imperium facilitated Venezuela's journey from primitive dictatorship (1935–1958) through party-centered democracy (1959–1999) to the current "twenty-first-century socialism." This journey began in the late 1920s, even before the passing of General Juan Vicente Gómez. At that time the demands of managing the new extractive economy exceeded the capabilities of the nineteenth-century commercial bureaucratic structures to broker social, economic, and political conflict. This prompted the search for new institutions, and growing US influence throughout the Caribbean led Gómez's successors to experiment with limited political democracy. The elitist tenor of this experiment proved its undoing.

On October 18, 1945, junior military officers joined with working- and middle-class reformers to seize power in a short but bloody coup d'état. Democracy for the few gave way to democracy for the masses. AD gained control of the government and passed legislation that began to redistribute wealth, power, and cultural authority. The upper and middle classes turned to the military for protection. On November 24, 1948, the armed forces overthrew the popularly elected government of Rómulo Gallegos, outlawed AD, and imposed a military junta to govern the country.

The military held power for a decade. After an initial economic boom fueled by revenue from petroleum the price of oil plummeted. The economic situation became critical in 1957, leading financial elites to criticize the military regime openly. General Marcos Pérez Jiménez, the president, attempted to counter declining support with increased repression. This only stiffened the resolve of his enemies, who received assistance from the US government. Early in the morning of January 23, 1958, after Pérez Jiménez lost control over Caracas, he fled the country.[3]

Fair and open elections occurred at the end of 1958. Rómulo Betancourt (AD) won the presidency, and AD gained control of Congress. The opportunistic Democratic Republican Union (URD), the Social Christian Party (COPEI), and the Venezuelan Communist Party (PCV) elected significant congressional delegations. The three major political parties (AD, URD, and COPEI) learned from their earlier failures and agreed to share power. The Pact of Punto Fijo gave bureaucratic positions and a place in the leadership of each major interest group organization (e.g., the Labor Confederation, the Peasant Federation, and professional associations such as the Engineering Guild) to each of the three political parties.[4] In addition to sharing power, the leaders of AD, URD, and COPEI agreed to build support for economic pluralism before undertaking far-reaching wealth redistribution. Agreement on this reformist agenda was a critical first step in building legitimacy for post-1958 liberal democracy. Supporters of Hugo Chávez Frias view adoption of the Pact of Punto Fijo as a betrayal of the 1958 revolution.

The Petroleum Roller Coaster and Institutional Stress

The flow of revenue from petroleum to Venezuela's central government between 1958 and the present has varied greatly. These ups and downs shaped the development of political institutions. Escalating petroleum revenue helped to consolidate liberal democracy in the 1970s, and declines in the 1980s contributed to its unraveling. Reductions of petroleum income in the 1990s dramatically reduced the distributive capability of the state and alienated most Venezuelans from Punto Fijo democracy.

The first government of the 1990s, the second presidency of Carlos Andrés Pérez, began on February 2, 1989. During his presidential campaign Pérez played on his image as the political leader who presided over boom times in the 1970s. Thus Venezuelans were stunned when three weeks after his inauguration Pérez announced that foreign reserves were severely depleted; that in 1988 the country had run a fiscal deficit exceeding 9 percent of GDP; that the current account of the balance of payments had its largest deficit in history; and that all prices in the economy, from interest rates and black beans to medicines and bus fares, were artificially low and impossible to maintain. The president warned that only bitter medicine could cure these maladies, but when he administered the first dose, three days of rioting and looting (an event known as the Caracazo) left more than three hundred dead. Fallout from the Caracazo weakened President Pérez, doomed efforts by his successor to restore the regime's legitimacy, and brought to power its most intractable enemies.

In the immediate aftermath of the February 1989 rioting there was reason to hope that Carlos Andrés Pérez might salvage liberal democracy. Venezuela settled into a deceptive calm even though conditions screamed that the petroleum-fueled distribution network could no longer sustain existing institutions.[5] President Pérez used this calm to initiate a neoliberal economic package, El Gran Viraje (The Great Turnaround). This radical departure from the past relied on four sets of policies: macroeconomic stabilization, trade liberalization, privatization, and deregulation.

The repercussions of Pérez's economic restructuring echoed throughout the 1990s. Early in the decade Venezuela's economy set world records. These records, however, masked the deterioration of state institutions, which became less capable of acting on the basis of technical and professional criteria. Carried into policy areas such as health care, transportation, housing, and agriculture, poor performance by the state further undermined the quality of life for most Venezuelans. Purchasing power also declined. Decay seemed pervasive, which damaged the government's legitimacy even more. The societal deterioration that eroded support for Pérez also extended to the armed forces. As early as the 1970s the professional military promotion system of the early democratic system was relaxed and politicized. This spurred partisan rivalries inside the officer corps, thereby intensifying incentives for aspiring officers and their protégés to block or even sabotage the career development and possibilities for promotion of their rivals. Until the fiscal crisis of the 1980s those who lost in this Byzantine competition received middle-level executive positions within the myriad of state enterprises. However, this became the exception as budgets tightened and the public sector contracted. Incentives then increased for the losers to overturn the political regime.

Another consequence of the fiscal crisis for the armed forces was that the daily needs of enlisted soldiers and junior officers became grossly underfunded. Tensions between junior and senior officers were also exacerbated by the fact that the former had received extensive opportunities to complement their military training with professional education at home and abroad, thus differentiating their experience in the profession from that of older officers. The latter belonged to a generation that came of age in the 1960s, when the fight against leftist insurgents was all-consuming.

The crisis broke on February 4, 1992, when a group of junior military officers calling themselves the Bolivarian Military Movement attempted a coup that almost succeeded. Although much in the Bolivarian Military Movement's program was confused, its call for the affluent and dishonest to be tried for crimes against the nation struck a responsive chord among the majority who had suffered during economic decline. Thus although the coup failed, it emboldened the opponents of President Pérez, his austerity plan, and even long-forgotten enemies of post-1958 liberal democracy.

The fifteen months that separated the February 1992 coup attempt from President Pérez's suspension from office in May 1993 proved remarkable for their turbulence and intensifying opposition to the government. Former president Rafael Caldera stopped just short of proclaiming that the Bolivarian Military Movement's cause was just, and former president Isaías Medina's last minister of the interior, Arturo Uslar Pietri, suggested that forcing Pérez from office before the end of his term might make amends for the revolution of 1945. In late November 1992 the military (this time the navy, air force, and marines) mounted a second unsuccessful coup, and Venezuela's once-robust macroeconomic indicators faded. The following May attorney general Ramón Escobar Salom presented evidence that President Pérez had misused government funds. The Supreme Court then found merit in these charges, and the senate suspended Pérez from office to face trial before the Supreme Court.

The eight months that followed raised more questions than they answered. After AD and COPEI came to an agreement, their senators selected one of their own, Ramón J. Velásquez, to serve as interim president. Velásquez, a political intellectual, oversaw free and open elections in December 1993 for president, congress, and the state legislatures. However, during his brief stewardship the economy failed to recover, privatization stalled, and bitterness over declining living standards intensified. The Velásquez legacy to his successor, Rafael Caldera (1994–1999), was perhaps an even chance of preserving Punto Fijo democracy.

For almost two years Rafael Caldera endeavored to set the clock back to a past that he viewed positively—the years of his first presidency (1969–1974). He blamed corruption and the neoliberal policies of Carlos Andrés Pérez for the country's ills. Soon after taking office Caldera moved against backers of Pérez in the financial community. The unintended consequence of that decision was the collapse of the entire banking system, a turn of events that severely damaged the government's capability to grow the economy.

In July 1996 President Caldera made a complete turnaround and negotiated an agreement with the International Monetary Fund that reinstated many of the neoliberal reforms (as a program called Agenda Venezuela) that he had previously criticized. The fruits of Caldera's earlier policies, despite their popularity when first announced, were an inflation rate of 103 percent (1996) and an increase in the foreign public debt to US $26.5 billion. In addition, the government had not built mechanisms of participation likely to generate support for the return to a more market-oriented development strategy. When it came to implementing Agenda Venezuela, President Caldera actually increased centralization. He and Luis Alfaro Ucero, the secretary general of AD, allied in the congress to give the national executive new powers to amend the consumer protection law and intervene in the foreign exchange market. This unmasked the AD as the silent partner in an unpopular government.

Blowback and Bolivarianism

Opportunity to change the political regime came with the national elections of 1998. Voters went to the polls to choose the president and members of congress. COPEI and AD nominated presidential candidates with fatal flaws. Just prior to the presidential voting, AD and COPEI abandoned their nominees and threw their support behind the promising but ultimately unsuccessful candidacy of Enrique

Salas Römer, the maverick governor of Carabobo. The real story of the presidential election campaign, however, was the meteoric rise of Hugo Chávez. He personified opposition to post-1958 liberal democracy, and on December 6 voters elected him president by a decisive margin.

Chávez rewrote the rules of Venezuelan politics. At his February 1999 inauguration he vowed to replace the existing "moribund" and "unjust" order with a new and responsive democracy. He quickly organized a referendum in which 85 percent of the voters authorized elections that would select delegates to a constituent assembly whose charge was to draft the new constitution. Delegates favorable to President Chávez dominated the constituent assembly, and on December 15, 1999, the government submitted the new constitution to voters for their approval. Seventy-two percent voted in favor.

Neither President Chávez nor his opponents were satisfied totally with the 1999 constitution. Opponents felt that it gave too much power to the national executive, especially after President Chávez implemented its provisions in ways that allowed his followers to dominate most of the state apparatus. The opposition claimed that this domination unfairly restricted their ability to compete in the political arena. Conflict between the opposition and the government intensified in November 2001 when President Chávez enacted a package of forty-nine special laws designed to reverse the neoliberal trends of the 1990s.

Seven months later opposition forces attempted an unsuccessful *golpe del estado* (April 11–13, 2002). In December 2002 and January 2003 the opposition attempted to force President Chávez from office through massive demonstrations. With the economy contracting and societal violence a real possibility, the government allowed the process to go forward whereby signatures would be collected to implement provisions in the 1999 constitution (Articles 72 and 233) that provided for a recall referendum. On June 8, 2004, following a contentious signature-collecting process that lasted for more than eight months, the National Electoral Council certified that the petition for a recall referendum had obtained the requisite number of signatures for the referendum to take place. The referendum was held on August 15, 2004, as the economy was beginning to turn around. More than 58 percent of voters expressed a preference for Hugo Chávez to remain as president. This defeat stunned the opposition and allowed President Chávez to increase his domination over the country.

Two subsequent referendums initiated by President Chávez reveal his dissatisfaction with the 1999 constitution. The first took place on December 2, 2007, a year after his election to a second six-year term as president. The paramount political change proposed by this referendum was the abolition of presidential term limits and the allowance of the indefinite reelection of the president (but this was not allowed for any other political post). Other important changes expanded social security benefits to workers in the informal economy, ended the autonomy of the central bank, prohibited large land estates while allowing the state to provisionally occupy property slated for expropriation before a court had ruled, reduced the maximum workweek from forty-four to thirty-six hours, prohibited foreign funding for political associations, and outlawed discrimination based on sexual orientation. In addition, the referendum provided for reorganization of the country's administrative districts and empowered the president to control elected state governors and mayors through an unelected "popular power."

Voters narrowly rejected the proposal (51 to 49 percent). It was Hugo Chávez's first major electoral defeat since his assumption of the presidency. Initially he conceded defeat and congratulated the opposition for this victory, while adding, "For now we could not do it." Two days later the president called the results a "victoria de mierda" (shitty victory). Manuel Rosales, the most important opposition candidate in the 2006 presidential election, had a different response. He proclaimed, "Tonight, Venezuela has won."

Defeat of the proposal to amend the constitution undercut President Chávez's power and authority. Inside the Chavista movement, speculation sprang up over who would succeed the president when his term expired in February 2013. The opposition waged vigorous campaigns in the subnational elections of November 23, 2008 and scored some surprising victories. Even more ominously, petroleum prices fell as the global recession deepened. Within the president's inner circle there was concern that economic decline would increase dissatisfaction with the government.

Seven days after the subnational elections President Chávez seized the initiative. He announced that he would open a new wave of discussion on the proposal for allowing postulation without limits for the presidential candidate. The initiative, however, received a mixed reception. Inside the Chavista camp, individuals with presidential aspirations grumbled. Opponents called the proposal "illegal and unconstitutional," pointing out that Article 345 of the 1999 constitution states that "a revised constitutional reform initiative may not be submitted during the same constitutional term of office of the National Assembly." Chávez finessed the constitutional issue by declaring that the change to the constitution would be in the form of an amendment instead of a constitutional reform. He defused reservations within his own movement by revising the amendment so it applied to all popularly elected positions (state governors, mayors, National Assembly deputies, and state legislators), not only to the president. The National Assembly overwhelmingly approved the proposal, which opened the way for the referendum.

On February 15, 2009, 54 percent of voters (abstention was 30 percent) backed the proposed amendment. Students and others took to the streets in protest, but the police quickly dispersed them. Most of the international observers found the voting to have been clean, transparent, and fair. Success strengthened Chávez's authority within his United Socialist Party of Venezuela (Partido Socialista Unido de Venezuela, PSUV) and the armed forces. It also disheartened the opposition. Following passage of this referendum President Chávez accelerated the implementation of "twenty-first-century socialism."

A series of laws passed by the National Assembly and signed into law by the president during December 2010 confirmed the acceleration. Especially significant was the law of socialist communes, which established communal development districts controlled by the minister of popular power for communes. The authority of the communes, of which there were 184 in 2010, blurred existing boundaries between local (*municipio*) and regional (state) governments. A related matter in need of clarification was the dividing line between the authority of the communes, local governments, and the community councils. On December 29, 2010, the revised Law of Communal Councils went into effect. The communal councils had been created in 2005 and had usurped some functions of local government. The 2010 legislation codified procedures for electing and replacing council members, increased the power of the councils to allocate resources, and established mechanisms for budgetary control. Finally, the National Assembly established the Federal Council of Government, giving it responsibility for defining relations between the communes, the community councils, the *municipios,* and regional governments.

As of June 2013 the institutional changes legislated in December 2010 have been implemented tentatively. This derives from the uncertainty produced by President Chávez's two-year struggle with cancer and the electoral calendar. For eighteen months after the president's first cancer surgery he insisted that he had become cancer free, but his physical appearance and additional cancer surgeries belied this assessment. Chávez grew weaker during the 2012 presidential election campaign and never appeared in public after he departed for Havana on December 10, 2012, to undergo a fourth cancer surgery. Between the presidential election of October 7 and the elections for governor and state legislators on December 16 government officials devoted most of their time to electioneering. This was also true of the period between Chávez's death (March 5, 2013) and the presidential election of April 14. The vigor with which the newly elected president, Nicolas Maduro, will implement the institutional changes legislated in 2010 is an open question.

Interest Groups and Civil Society

Venezuela under Bolivarian rule is less supportive of demands from organized interests than was Punto Fijo democracy. Chávez stated on more than one occasion that he viewed the checks and balances of liberal democracy as a smoke screen that allows the upper and middle classes to perpetuate their domination. Chávez's advocacy of direct democracy reflected his preference for populism and affinity for the political theory of Rousseau. Nevertheless, interest groups are not without influence after fourteen years of rule by Hugo Chávez.

The military, along with the church and the landed elite, dominated Venezuela from independence until General Pérez Jiménez fled the country on January 23, 1958. The provisional junta that replaced him faced nationwide strikes supported by business, labor, and other groups demanding civilian political rule. The armed forces, confused and dispirited, acquiesced to the election as president of its nemesis, Rómulo Betancourt. Betancourt's government endured threats from right-wing traditionalists and an insurgency mounted by leftists. The counterinsurgency effort that defeated the guerrillas forged a bond between the armed forces and civilian democratic leaders.

The affinity between liberal democrats and the military weakened after 1989. There are several reasons for this. First, the army was called out on numerous occasions to maintain order as demonstrations against the Pérez and Caldera governments became more frequent. Neither the officer corps nor the enlisted ranks saw this as one of their primary responsibilities. They were resentful over being asked to function as a police force. Second, the inability of the police to deal with demonstrations raised the issue of how law enforcement budgets were spent and increased suspicions of widespread corruption. In addition, the experience of using force against protesting civilians led many in the military to question their support of an unpopular, party-centered regime dominated by gerontocracies that appeared unscrupulous and isolated.

Finally, as suggested earlier, the opulent lifestyles of young politicians and businessmen during the 1990s, when contrasted with the economic difficulties experienced by junior officers, created resentments in the armed forces against the political and economic establishment. President Pérez sought to address these grievances after the unsuccessful coups of February and November 1992, and in early 1994 President Caldera made his own special overtures to the officer corps. Neither was able to return the armed forces to their earlier regime-supportive stance.

The military was divided into three factions during the first years of the Chávez era. One supported the Bolivarian Revolution, another was vehemently opposed, and a third argued that the armed forces should remain apolitical and focus on professional enhancement. President Chávez, however, wanted the military as a pillar of support for his regime. He launched Plan Bolívar 2000, a legally questionable program that funneled funds for infrastructure maintenance and development through regional military garrisons. Some officers opposed the policy, but many used the opportunities that accompany the construction of public works for personal enrichment.

By early 2002 factions in the military opposed to President Chávez viewed his leftward drift with concern. On April 11, a march through Caracas by hundreds of thousands of government opponents ended in shootings that killed or wounded more than fifteen individuals. Opposition leaders and government security forces blamed each other. This incident became an excuse for military officers opposed to President Chávez to remove him from office. They replaced Chávez with Pedro Carmona Estanga, president of the Venezuelan Federation of Chambers of Commerce (Federación de Cámaras y Asociaciones de Comercio y Producción de Venezuela, FEDECAMARAS), an umbrella business confederation. The perpetrators of the coup could not agree on how to organize a government. This gave supporters of President Chávez the opportunity to regroup. In less than forty-eight hours factions loyal to the president took control and returned him to the presidency.[6]

After the April 11 coup President Chávez never trusted the armed forces. He purged officers suspected of having sympathized with his removal and marginalized all who were not seen as active supporters. In addition, President Chávez organized militias of reserves among unemployed slum dwellers. On January 29, 2005, the secretary of the National Defense Council (Consejo de Defensa de la Nación) announced the adoption of a new military doctrine that gave priority to preparing for asymmetric warfare, an activity in which the militias would have an important role. This gave the government a national security rationale for strengthening forces composed of individuals from socioeconomic strata most supportive of the president.

On July 31, 2008, acting under authority given to him by the National Assembly, President Chávez promulgated a new Organic Law of the Armed Forces. The renamed Fuerza Armada Nacional Bolivariana (Bolivarian National Armed Forces) boasted a strengthened chain of command that allowed the president more direct control over all four services. The law also enshrined protection of the Bolivarian revolution as a primary obligation of the armed forces. Each service was now to be composed of three basic kinds of units: combat, logistics, and intelligence. In addition, the law gave formal recognition to the Bolivarian National Militia and subjected the entire population to mobilization at the discretion of the president.

The Roman Catholic Church has operated as a political interest group in Venezuela since independence, but the ecclesiastical hierarchy has had less influence than in most other Latin American countries. During the 1960s, after a two-decade conflict with the AD party over state control of education, the church reached an accommodation with AD.[7] Accommodation did not prevent church leaders from expressing their disapproval of corruption, decay in the judiciary, cronyism, inequality, and moral deterioration in the government. The Centro Guimilla, a Jesuit think tank, leveled especially biting criticism at AD and COPEI during the 1970s and 1980s. After the urban riots of February 1989 and two unsuccessful coups in 1992, the Episcopal Conference issued public statements intended to put distance between the church and the neoliberal policies of President Carlos Andrés Pérez. Church leaders gave strong backing to the second Caldera government and maneuvered behind the scenes to effect a reconciliation of the president and COPEI.

The bishops viewed the rise of Hugo Chávez with alarm, especially his reliance on militant leftists whose antagonism toward parochial education predated the revolution of October 1945. Nevertheless, the ecclesiastical hierarchy took no official position in the referendum that approved the 1999 constitution, even though it increased state power. After the unsuccessful coup of April 11, 2002, relations between the ecclesiastical hierarchy and the government deteriorated. President Chávez opined on more than one occasion that the church had supported the coup. Influential clerics condemned government policies for undermining democracy. This led President Chávez into a brief flirtation with evangelical Protestantism. However, his enthusiasm for this option cooled when Rev. Pat Robertson, a well-known fundamentalist preacher in the United States, suggested on his *700 Club* television program that President Bush should use the Central Intelligence Agency to "take out" the Venezuelan leader. President Chávez responded with a novel strategy to weaken established religious interests: he imported *babalaos*, or shamans of the Santería religion from Cuba, and installed them in the shantytowns. After the diagnosis of cancer Chávez returned to his Roman Catholic roots.

Private sector interests in Venezuela are diverse, ranging from local agribusinesses to multinational manufacturers. During the Trienio (1945–1948), the revolutionary interlude between military dictatorships, businesspeople were united in their opposition to AD because of its emphasis on regulation and state intervention in the economy. But after 1958 the business community adapted to Punto Fijo democracy and prospered.

Private sector leaders anticipated developing similarly profitable arrangements with the Chávez government. However, as the Bolivarians revealed their sympathy for socialist schemes, business relations cooled. When the leader of the most important private sector organization, FEDECAMARAS, agreed to serve as provisional president in the short-lived government of April 2002, relations turned frigid. In 2007, following his reelection to a second six-year term as president, Chávez nationalized a number of private enterprises, and the pace of nationalization accelerated.

Two hundred individual groups constitute FEDECAMARAS, but the institution is dominated by four pivotal interests: industry, trade, cattle raising, and agriculture. Each possesses its own chamber: CONINDUSTRIA for industry, CONSEC-OMERCIO for commerce, FENAGAN for cattle raising, and FEDEAGRO for agriculture. Because these key interests have different and sometimes conflicting priorities, the single-interest or intermediate chambers are as important as centers of political demands as FEDECAMARAS.

Multinational corporations have long been private sector players in Venezuelan politics. Exxon, Royal Dutch Shell, and Gulf invested massively in the twentieth century to make Venezuela one of the most important producers of petroleum. After President Carlos Andrés Pérez implemented the Great Turnaround in 1989, a torrent of foreign capital flowed into Venezuela from the United States and Western Europe. It left almost as rapidly following the unsuccessful coups in 1992. It returned in force in 1996, when the state petroleum company (Petróleos de Venezuela, PDVSA) signaled a willingness to accept overseas assistance to implement plans that would double Venezuela's oil production capability. Private foreign investment again fled in 1999 when the newly inaugurated President Hugo Chávez voiced criticisms of profit repatriation and multinational corporations in general. However, Chávez did sign contracts with selected multinationals to exploit reserves of viscous petroleum in the Orinoco tar belt. In matters of infrastructure development, such as the subways in Caracas, Maracaibo, and Valencia, President Chávez contracted engineering firms based in Brazil (Odebrecht), China, and France.

Organized labor and peasants, two associational interest groups, played pivotal roles in Punto Fijo democracy. As part of their strategy to wrest power from the entrenched Andean cabal in the 1940s, AD and COPEI organized workers and peasants.[8] A third interest group, professionals, fell under the domination of political parties in the 1970s. All three groups were subject to party discipline. AD and COPEI exercised decisive power and influence over unionized workers, peasants, and professionals until 1999.

After approval of the 1999 constitution the dominant labor organization, Confederación Venezolano de Trabajo (Venezuelan Confederation of Workers, CTV) opened negotiations with President Chávez. Its leaders offered to eliminate the influence of AD and COPEI in their unions in return for recognition by the national government. This was unacceptable to the president, who began organizing his own Bolivarian trade unions. Consequently, the CTV joined with FEDECAMARAS and other opponents of the government in the strikes that convulsed the country during 2002 and 2003. In March 2003, after breaking the final and most virulent strike, President Chávez discharged sixteen thousand workers belonging to the Federation of Petroleum Workers (FEDEPETROL), as well as six thousand of the petroleum company's elite staff. Contracts with other CTV unions were simply ignored. Still, the CTV persists. CTV and Bolivarian trade unions marched separately in the May Day parades of 2013, but the CTV is a shadow of its former self.

Until the early 1980s Venezuela's urban poor were only weakly integrated into the Punto Fijo system. This was largely because the political parties having the greatest appeal to slum dwellers during the decade of regime consolidation (the 1960s) lost out to AD and COPEI, both of which treated the shantytowns with benign neglect. The demand-making structures that eventually crystallized among shantytown inhabitants were different initially from the party-dominated associations of workers, peasants, and professionals. The most important organization to represent Venezuela's urban poor during the liberal democratic era was the Center at the Service of

Popular Action (CESAP). However, during the 1980s CESAP settled on the strategy of working within the existing partycentric regime. This choice undermined the legitimacy of CESAP when the second Pérez and Caldera governments adopted neoliberalism.

Feelings of abandonment by AD and COPEI, as well as reaction against neoliberal economic policies, drove the urban poor to Hugo Chávez Frías in the presidential elections of 1998 and 2000. Soon after taking office in 1999 Chávez began organizing shantytown residents into *círculos bolivarianos* (Bolivarian circles). These circles were multifaceted. On the one hand, they taught young women to sew, manage small businesses, and provide needed child care. On the other, they assisted the government in connecting with its supporters and identifying opponents.

Círculos bolivarianos remained active in most shantytowns during the first decade of Bolivarian rule. After 2004 other revolutionary organizations such as the electoral Comando Maisanta,[9] the irregular asymmetric warfare battalions, and the communal councils became the critical institutions facilitating government's hold over the urban poor.[10] In 2005 the addition of resource-allocating *misiones* (missions), administered directly by President Chávez, gave the government a broad range of programs to reward supporters and control shantytown activity. The *misiones* also played a major role in alleviating poverty, and no activity of the Bolivarian regime has been more popular among the urban poor than the *misiones*.

The institutions that allocate resources to the shantytowns, as indicated above, arose in an ad hoc manner. Their programs overlap. Often they are inefficient and wasteful. In July 2007 President Chávez appointed a commission that proposed constitutional reforms to merge the *misiones* and traditional bureaucracies into a unified socialist public sector. Despite approval by the National Assembly in December 2010, the implementation of these reforms has been hesitant and disjointed.

POLITICAL PARTIES AND ELECTIONS

Venezuela's contemporary political party system evolved from the antiparty consensus that predominated at the end of the 1990s. This consensus reflected disillusionment with the system of strong political parties that controlled the country between 1958 and 1998. Throughout the 1998 presidential campaign support for the once dominant AD and COPEI parties hovered in single digits. Hugo Chávez organized a loose grouping—the Fifth Republic Movement (Movimiento Quinto República, or MVR)—to coordinate his run for the presidency. Support for him mushroomed in the second quarter of 1998 after the early front-runner, beauty queen Irene Sáez, demonstrated that a single term as mayor does not prepare one for presidential leadership. Concern that a Chávez presidency would smash the structure of power led opponents of the surging candidate to unite behind the bid of Enrique Salas Römer, governor of the industrial state of Carabobo. Salas's campaign, like Chávez's, projected populism and opposition to established political parties. However, unlike Chávez, Salas had belonged to an influential political party (COPEI) before mounting his presidential campaign as an independent. To many he appeared as more of the same. Chávez swept the December 1998 presidential election, capturing roughly 57 percent of the total vote.

President Chávez began his term by demonizing the existing liberal democratic power structure. He drew upon abuses he ascribed to Punto Fijo institutions to justify rapid change. Political parties had been the linchpin of liberal democracy between 1958 and 1998, and the president's determination to weaken them led to the creation of the National Electoral Council, on which political parties had no representation. The new council was also prohibited from funding any political party. In addition, Chávez helped to embed in the 1999 constitution language that empowered civil society organizations and reduced the access to power of interest groups tied to AD and COPEI.

On July 31, 2000, Venezuela held elections for the first time under the 1999 constitution. In those elections voters chose the president, all governors and mayors, and all members of the new unicameral National Assembly. AD and COPEI declined to contest the presidency. President Chávez's only significant challenger was Lieutenant Colonel Francis Árias Cárdenas, his second in command during the unsuccessful military coup of February 4, 1992. In 1995, after being pardoned by then-president Rafael Caldera, Árias ran successfully for governor of Zulia as the candidate of the antiestablishment Radical Cause (Causa-R). He appeared to have split with Chávez over the president's anticlericalism and leftward drift. But the dour Árias was no match for the charismatic Chávez. The president captured 60 percent of the total vote, slightly more than in 1998. The MVR and its allies secured 46 percent of the seats in the National Assembly, while AD and COPEI together held only 21 percent. The remaining third of the seats were controlled either by allies of the MVR or by regional political parties.

Although Hugo Chávez and his allies controlled the National Assembly, they lacked the two-thirds majority necessary for modifying the constitution. This changed on December 4, 2005, when opposition political parties abstained from the National Assembly elections. Their decision in large part was a reaction to suspicions of fraud in the recall referendum of August 2004 and the municipal elections that followed in October. In addition, the opposition was demoralized because of the government's aggressive and successful patronage activities. Opposition leaders called for abstention in the hope of discrediting the National Assembly elections and forcing President Chávez to accept ones that would be internationally supervised. This proved a disastrous miscalculation. The rate of abstention approached 75 percent, but without opponents the Chavistas captured all 167 seats in the National Assembly.

There was never any doubt that Hugo Chávez would run in the presidential election of December 3, 2006. After much debate the opposition came together and participated. Their unity candidate was Manuel Rosales, governor of the oil-rich state of Zulia. Chávez portrayed the election as a choice between revolutionary progress and a return to discredited liberal democracy. Rosales attacked the government for its international giveaway programs, especially the discounted sales of petroleum to Cuba. He also promised to reduce crime, increase public safety, and replace much of the government social spending with direct grants to individuals. Rosales made a respectable showing, but Chávez won with almost 63 percent of the popular vote. The rate of abstention fell to 25 percent.

President Chávez moved quickly to advance his revolution after winning a new term. He created a new political party, the United Socialist Party of Venezuela

(Partido Unido Socialista de Venezuela, PSUV). He tasked the PSUV with organizing the masses, recruiting candidates for political office, and socializing citizens. These challenges were beyond the capabilities of the MVR, the protoparty that had run Chavista candidates for office since the 1998 elections.

The timeline for establishing the PSUV stretched from March through November 2007. The party was to be composed of "battalions," "platoons," and "squads" that had responsibility for organizing militants into a hierarchy of groups. Party leaders at the apex would choose candidates to run for governmental positions and mobilize militants. Eleven relatively insignificant political parties that backed President Chávez in the 2006 election quickly indicated that they would join. Three small supportive political parties with an identity that transcended that of the president—Fatherland for All (Patria Para Todos, PPT), For a Social Democracy (Podemos), and the Communist Party of Venezuela (Partido Comunista de Venezuela, PCV)—stated that they would remain autonomous until after the PSUV took shape. At that time, based on the party's program, they would decide on their membership. This reluctance led President Chávez to characterize the three as "almost in the opposition."

The PSUV coalesced in three phases. The first, which began on March 5, 2007, ended on June 10 with the announcement of a timetable for completing the process. Members of the MVR and the Frente Francisco Miranda (Francisco Miranda Front, President Chávez's personal enforcement organization) worked together in a membership drive that resulted in 5,696,305 signing up as "aspirants to become militants." This number was roughly 80 percent of the votes that Chávez received in the 2006 presidential election. The second phase began on July 31, 2007, when twenty-two thousand base organizations (known as *batallones socialistas*) held assemblies to organize and elect representatives to the Foundational Congress. The congress, attended by 1,681 delegates, met in Caracas on January 12, 2008. President Chávez subsequently approved a list of sixty-nine candidates for provisional posts in the party. Ninety-four thousand voted for fifteen from this list in elections held on March 9, 2008.[11]

The first electoral test for the PSUV came on November 23, 2008, when voters chose twenty-two regional (state) governors, the high mayor of metropolitan Caracas, and mayors of Venezuela's 265 *municipios*. The PSUV took seventeen governorships and roughly 80 percent of the mayoralties. Opposition candidates won governorships in several populous states (Zulia, Miranda, Carabobo, and Táchira) while also capturing the high mayorship of metropolitan Caracas. Manuel Rosales won the contest for mayor of Maracaibo, the country's second-largest city. Nevertheless, the PSUV gained a level of domination at the regional and local levels that had never been achieved by a single party during the forty years of Punto Fijo democracy.

Opposition to the PSUV in 2008 was concentrated in four small political parties, the residuals of AD and COPEI, and independents. The opposition parties were strongest in eastern Caracas and the relatively urbanized states of the west and the Andes. They were weakest in the small towns, rural areas, and the eastern region—precisely the locations where AD had been most dominant prior to 1998. After ten years of the Bolivarian revolution, however, voter identification with AD hovered around 5 percent. Less than 1 percent identified with COPEI and MAS (Movimiento al Socialismo), the other two political parties with significant followings during Punto Fijo.[12] Only when all opposition forces united behind a single candidate did the opposition candidate stand any chance of winning elections.

The three important post-1998 opposition political parties lack national followings. The middle-class Un Nuevo Tiempo (A New Time) exhibits some appeal to unionized workers, especially in the petroleum industry. It is strongest in the western state of Zulia. Manuel Rosales (the leader of Un Nuevo Tiempo) attempted to build the party into a national force following his defeat in the presidential election of 2006 but had little success. President Chávez forced him into exile soon after he was elected mayor of Maracaibo.

The second important opposition political party, Primero Justicia (Justice First), appealed to young Catholics who reacted against the ongoing internecine warfare between the second-generation leaders of COPEI and the party's founder, Rafael Caldera. Initially Primero Justicia attracted a broad spectrum of Catholic youth from the Caracas middle class and from some affluent urban neighborhoods in the central region. Before long, however, the party's elitist clerical orientation and bias toward Caracas reduced its appeal.

The third important opposition political party is Proyecto Venezuela (Project Venezuela). Proyecto Venezuela evolved out of the once-dominant COPEI party machine in the industrial state of Carabobo. After his unsuccessful run against Hugo Chávez in the 1998 presidential election, Proyecto Venezuela founder Governor Henrique Salas Römer passed control of the party to his son, Henrique Salas Feo. Salas Feo has had limited success in expanding Proyecto Venezuela beyond the boundaries of Carabobo.

Opposition political parties came together in the Unity Table (Mesa de la Unidad) to contest the National Assembly elections of September 26, 2010. They supported a single candidate for the National Assembly in each election district and agreed to unified party lists. Anticipating a strong challenge, the government modified the basic electoral law. Among the most important changes was the reduction of deputies elected by party lists to 30 percent. In addition, the new law completely separated the winner-take-all district vote and the party list votes, creating a mixed member majoritarian system. The electoral districts were redrawn in ways that critics of the government claimed would favor the PSUV, especially in giving more weight to votes in the countryside than to those in the city. Results supported this assessment. The PSUV received 48.2 percent of the total vote and the Unity Table obtained 47.2 percent, but the former captured 98 of 165 seats in the assembly while the latter gained only 65.

President Chávez campaigned hard for the PSUV candidates and framed the elections as a referendum on his leadership. He was disappointed even though the PSUV retained control of the National Assembly. The president was especially concerned that the PSUV had lost its two-thirds majority and thus would not be able to pass "organic legislation" without the support of at least some members of the opposition, the Democratic Unity Table (Mesa de la Unidad Democrática, MUD).[13] The opposition, however, remained implacably hostile. Its leaders felt empowered, as the closeness of the popular vote revealed an electorate that was almost evenly divided between supporters and opponents of the government. This suggested that President Chávez might find himself in a competitive race for reelection if the opposition united behind an attractive candidate. Still, no opposition leader emerged from the 2010 National Assembly elections with the stature to unilaterally mount a meaningful challenge to Hugo Chávez in the 2012 presidential elections.

Three elections in 2012 and 2013 configured the contemporary landscape of the political party system. The first, a contest for president, took place on October 7, 2012. Here Hugo Chávez notched an eleven-point victory over Henrique Capriles Radonski, candidate of the Unity Table. An election for regional governors followed on December 9. Candidates of the PSUV took twenty of the twenty-three governorships. This demoralized and disheartened the opposition. Three months later Hugo Chávez lost his struggle with cancer. In the presidential elections that followed, the opposition again put forward Henrique Capriles. The PSUV nominated interim president Nicolas Maduro, Chávez's choice to lead the Bolivarian revolution should he pass from the scene. This election, as we have seen, was unexpectedly close.

To summarize, the political parties and movements of the opposition in post-Chávez Venezuela are diverse. They control few major government offices and would have difficulty in governing should they gain power. As discussed earlier, the Unity Table that supported Henrique Capriles included parties that ranged from the center-right Primero Justicia to ones on the far left, such as Patria Para Todos. Madero begins his presidency with the PSUV in firm control. But factionalism lurks just below the surface of the PSUV. The most important structural cleavage feeding that factionalism is between the regional governors and the President. Table 11.1 suggests how results of the two recent presidential elections and the regional elections of December 2012 have strengthened the position of the regional governors.

The table reveals that in each state Maduro's margin of victory over Capriles was smaller than that achieved by Hugo Chávez in the election of October 7, 2012. Maduro's victory was by an even smaller margin in all states than that secured by the PSUV candidate for governor in December. This discrepancy is having a significant role in diluting the central control that characterized the PSUV during Chávez's lifetime. In other words, the divisions inside the PSUV, no less than those within the opposition, are likely to transform both the political party system and the individual political parties of post-Chávez Venezuela.

STATE ORGANIZATION AND POLICY

Government Structure

Venezuelan state organization has been in flux since 2000 when the shift toward institutions envisioned by the constitution of 1999 took shape. The 1999 constitution provides for a presidential system with five separate branches of government: the executive, the legislative, the judicial, the electoral, and the people's power. Twenty-three states and a capital district constitute the polity in which President Chávez recentralized many powers that in 1989 and 1993 had been allocated to regional and local governments. The 1999 constitution envisioned a Federal Council of Government, presided over by the vice president, which would oversee subnational governments. President Chávez delayed establishing the Federal Council of Government

Table 11.1: Sequential Elections That Strengthened PSUV Governors

	2012 Presidential Election Winner's Margin	Candidate	2012 Regional Election Winner's Margin	2013 Presidential Election Winner's Margin
Venezuela overall	11% Chávez			1.5% Maduro
Capital District	10% Chávez	— NA —		3% Maduro
Amazonas	6.2% Chávez	Liberio Guarulla	16% Mesa	6% Maduro
Anzoategui	3.9% Chávez	Aristóbulo Istúriz	14% PSUV	6% Capriles
Apure	30.7% Chávez	Ramón Carrizales	43% PSUV	24% Maduro
Aragua	17.8% Chávez	Tarek El Aissami	11% PSUV	8% Maduro
Barinas	18.3% Chávez	Adán Chávez	16% PSUV	4% Maduro
Bolivar	13.0% Chávez	Francisco Rangel G.	3% PSUV	4% Capriles
Carabobo	9.0% Chávez	Francisco Ameliach	7% PSUV	2% Maduro
Cojedes	30.1% Chávez	Erika Farías	27% PSUV	22% Maduro
Delta Amacuro	26.1% Chávez	Lizeta Hernández	66% PSUV	22% Maduro
Falcon	20.1% Chávez	Stella Lugo	16% PSUV	6% Maduro
Guarico	28.3% Chávez	Ramon Rodríguez C.	50% PSUV	18% Maduro
Lara	0.8% Chávez	Henr. Falcón	8% Mesa	4% Capriles
Merida	3.8% Capriles	Alexis Ramírez	11% PSUV	14% Capriles
Miranda	0.4% Chávez	Henrique Capriles R	4% Mesa	6% Capriles
Monagas	17.9% Chávez	Yelitze Santaella	13% PSUV	12% Maduro
Nueva Esparta	2.5% Chávez	Carlos Mata F.	8% PSUV	5% Capriles
Portuguesa	42.1% Chávez	Wilmar Castro S.	29% PSUV	32% Maduro
Sucre	20.9% Chávez	Luis Acuña	24% PSUV	16% Maduro
Tachira	13.3% Capriles	José G. Vielma M.	8% PSUV	27% Capriles
Trujillo	24.6% Chávez	Henry Rangel S.	66% PSUV	20% Maduro
Vargas	23.5% Chávez	Jorge García C.	48% PSUV	14% Maduro
Yaracuy	20.6% Chávez	Julio León Heredia	24% PSUV	14% Maduro
Zulia	7.0% Chávez	F. Árias C.	5% PSUV	4% Capriles
Voter turnout	81.00%		53.00%	80.00%

Source: Calculated by the author from CNE data

until April 2010. He expected that during a third term opposition in the regions would be marginalized and that the council could become a useful mechanism for exercising control from Caracas. This perspective is in keeping with the centralistic tradition of Hispanic and Roman Catholic constitutional development.

Venezuela's national executive is a presidential system. Hugo Chávez used his charisma to stretch presidential powers beyond what was envisioned by the framers of the 1999 constitution. Nicolas Maduro, because he began his presidency in a weakened position, will be unable to duplicate this style. The Venezuelan president is chosen by a plurality of the popular vote for a term of six years. The president names the vice president, who assumes the presidency should that office fall vacant. Presidents freely appoint and remove members of the cabinet, which numbered thirty-two as of May 2013. Cabinet positions can be created and eliminated at the pleasure of the president. He or she is commander in chief of the armed forces. Nicolas Maduro named his first cabinet on April 22, 2013. A majority of this cabinet were serving in President Chávez's cabinet at the time of his death. A notable exception was General Miguel Rodríguez Torres, whom Maduro moved from director of the Bolivarian Intelligence Service to the even more powerful position of minister of interior relations and justice.

The use of numerous *misiones* to allocate resources is a unique feature of Venezuela's national executive. In anticipation of the revocatory referendum of August 2004, President Chávez began establishing the *misiones,* which, as indicated earlier, he oversaw personally. For example, the Ministry of Education was bypassed to establish special programs for literacy (Misión Robinson), accelerated high school degree programs (Misión Ribas), and revolutionary Bolivarian universities (Misión Sucre). Other high-profile *misiones* include programs that provide public health services to the slums (Misión Barrio Adentro) and distribute food to the poor at subsidized prices in popular markets (Misión Mercal). There is even a mission to construct socialist cities, Misión Villanueva. In May 2013 the official website of the Venezuelan government listed thirty-six such *misiones.* The *misiones'* budgets are closely guarded, although to fund them the president can draw freely on the more than US $25 billion that the Venezuelan government is estimated to hold abroad.

The 1999 constitution substituted a unicameral National Assembly for the bicameral congress that under the 1961 constitution was the font of central government lawmaking. Legislation can be introduced into the National Assembly from seven sources: the national executive, the Delegative Commission of the National Assembly, any three members (deputies) of the National Assembly, the Supreme Tribunal, the Electoral Power, the Citizen Power, and petitions bearing the signature of 0.1 percent of registered voters. Deputies are elected in a mixed system for terms of five years, and following the referendum of February 15, 2009, they are eligible for indefinite reelection. Each state, regardless of population, has at least three deputies in the National Assembly. The Amerindian community, in a departure from tradition, elects three deputies. Sixty percent of each state's deputies come from single-member, winner-take-all districts, and 40 percent are elected on the basis of proportional representation by party list. The president can dissolve the National Assembly and call for new elections. Overall, the National Assembly has less autonomy and fewer prerogatives than did congress under the constitution of 1961. This reflects the disrepute into which congress had fallen at the end of the Punto Fijo era.

There have been three National Assemblies elected since the 1999 constitution entered into force. In the first (2000–2005), allies of President Chávez gained roughly 55 percent of the seats. The opposition boycotted the 2005 National Assembly election in 2005, and as we have seen, supporters of the Bolivarian revolution captured all 167 seats. The third election for National Assembly occurred on September 28, 2010. The opposition unified behind the candidates in each district who stood the best chance of defeating the government party. Changes made to the electoral law prior to the election favored the PSUV, which, as noted, won 98 seats (out of 165) while receiving 48.2 percent of the vote. The opposition Unity Table received 47.2 percent of the total vote but garnered only 65 seats. Nevertheless, the opposition had a sufficient number of seats to prevent the PSUV from passing *leyes orgánicas* (organic laws), which were capable of making more significant changes than regular legislation.

The 1999 constitution placed the Supreme Judicial Tribunal at the apex of the judicial system. Like its predecessor, the Supreme Court, the Supreme Judicial Tribunal meets in several kinds of chambers: plenary, political-administrative, electoral, and ones that deal with civil, penal, and social matters. The National Assembly elects justices to the Supreme Judicial Tribunal for terms of twelve years, and they cannot run for reelection. The constitution prohibits justices from engaging in partisan political activity during their term in office. Indeed, drafters of the 1999 constitution went to great length to shield the entire judiciary from the influence of political parties. Initially the twenty Supreme Judicial Tribunal justices enjoyed limited autonomy, and in several chambers opponents of President Chávez had the majority. After the 2004 recall referendum failed to remove Chávez, he increased the number of justices by twelve. Since then the National Assembly has elected as justices individuals who rubber-stamp government positions. Finally, the constitution of 1999 established separate courts for the military. This practice has its roots in the Castilian tradition of the military *fuero* (right), which shields members of the armed forces from being tried by civilian courts.

The 1999 constitution established the Electoral Power as a separate branch of government in reaction to domination of the Supreme Electoral Council (CSE) by political parties. During Punto Fijo the CSE funded the political parties and their election campaigns. The CSE also oversaw tabulation of the votes at local polling places prior to the transfer of ballots to a central location by the armed forces. In some polling centers only AD and COPEI had observers, and evidence exists that on occasion the two divided among themselves the votes of third parties where those parties had no observers. The worst excesses of this kind occurred in the 1993 national elections, but five years later the reorganized CSE eliminated these problems by mobilizing a random sample of citizens as poll watchers. Under the 1999 constitutional regime the Supreme Electoral Tribunal has supervised all elections, and most observers agree that voting has been generally free and ballots have been counted accurately. However, the tribunal has refrained from intervening in disputes during electoral campaigns when opposition parties charge the government with assisting the PSUV.

The Citizen Power, a second new branch of government, was established in reaction to the widely held perception that during Punto Fijo government had become abusive and corrupt. The Citizen Power is a kind of ombudsman and watchdog. The maximum authority of this branch of government is the Moral Republican Council, an institution composed of three individuals: the public prosecutor (*fiscal*), the national comptroller (*contralor general de la república*), and an official known as the People's Defender. The People's Defender "promotes, defends, and watches out for" constitutional rights and guarantees. By a two-thirds vote, the National Assembly designates the People's Defender, who serves for a single period of seven years. Like other institutions of the central government, the People's Defender is highly responsive to the president's desires.

Policy Making

In Venezuela policy making is personalistic and fluid. After President Chávez's reelection on December 3, 2006, he began the transformation to twenty-first-century socialism. Voter rejection in December 2007 of his constitutional reform proposals slowed the pace of change. But it picked up following voters' approval of indefinite reelection for the president and other elected officials on February 15, 2009. The pace of change slowed again in June 2011, after cancer debilitated Chávez.

The central issue areas of policy addressed in this context are service delivery, economic development, public order and safety, and foreign and national defense.

Service Delivery

Service delivery immediately and directly affects quality of life. Its diverse components include housing, infrastructure development, health, sanitation, food, environment, social security, education, urban development, culture, and transportation. Until the revolution of 1945 only the upper class enjoyed access to quality services, and one of the most attractive dimensions of the AD's early program was its promise to use the state so as to extend high-quality services to all. The making and implementation of service delivery policies as Venezuela transitions to twenty-first-century socialism is fluid and often confused. As of 2009 it was centered in five kinds of institutions: ministries of the national executive, regional governments, municipal bureaucracies, corporations managed by the state, and the *misiones*. Eliminating duplication in the area of service policy delivery is one of the most important challenges facing the Maduro government.

Economic Development Policy

Economic development policy encompasses activities that expand the capacity to produce goods and commodities for internal consumption as well as for export. Its impact on quality of life, although just as important as that of service delivery, is less immediate and direct. Like service delivery policy, economic development policy's issue areas are highly diverse, including mineral extraction, industry, commerce, finance, and planning. Venezuela's private sector coexisted with AD and COPEI governments between 1958 and 1990, even though suspicion existed between business leaders and the party elites. Punto Fijo governments reserved large areas of the economy for state enterprises. In the neoliberal decade of the 1990s Presidents Pérez and Caldera privatized many important public entities. Hugo Chávez's 1998 presidential campaign suggested that he would end the most flagrant abuses of the new economic order rather than merely change it. As of 2012, however, only three of Venezuela's top thirteen companies remained in private hands.

Venezuelan mineral extraction, despite the importance of gold, iron, and bauxite, revolves around petroleum. Nationalization of the multibillion-dollar oil industry, the product of a broad national consensus, occurred on January 1, 1976. To manage and coordinate the newly nationalized petroleum industry, the government created Petroleum of Venezuela (Petróleos de Venezuela, PDVSA), a state corporation attached to what is now the Ministry of Energy and Petroleum. One of President Chávez's first decisions was to replace the president of PDVSA with an individual from his inner circle. In early 2003, when PDVSA workers and executives sided with demonstrators seeking to remove the president, he discharged almost nineteen thousand PDVSA employees. PDVSA production of petroleum fell and has remained at almost 20 percent below the level attained prior to the dismissal.

With PDVSA in turmoil, the government looked increasingly to petroleum from the concessions given to multinational companies for exploitation of the Orinoco tar belt's heavy reserves. These concessions themselves became controversial when the soaring price of petroleum allowed the companies to profit mightily from their activities. In 2007, when the Venezuelan government increased the tax rate on these profits, ExxonMobil and ConocoPhillips rescinded their concessions. However, other multinationals remained, and in May 2013 PDVSA and Russia's Rosneft signed an agreement establishing a joint enterprise that anticipated extracting 2.1 million barrels of petroleum per day from the Orinoco tar belt.

Finance and commerce are issue areas that involve especially intensive interaction between the public sector and the private sector. The Ministry of the Treasury and the central bank set the broad financial parameters within which governments pursue economic development. The 1999 constitution gave the national executive limited authority to intervene in the central bank, but President Chávez has pushed intervention far beyond what was envisioned by the constitution's framers. On July 3, 2009, he assumed control of the influential Spanish-owned Banco de Venezuela. Combined with other state banks, this purchase gave the government control over about 21 percent of deposits, 16 percent of loans, a payroll of fifteen thousand employees, and 651 bank branches.

Public Order and Safety Policy

Public order and safety policy is the responsibility of the Ministry of Interior and Justice. The vice minister for the System of Integrated Policing directly oversees the National Bolivarian Police (Policía Nacional Bolivariana, PNB). President Chávez pressed for the creation of this national police force in 2009. The PNB assumed many of the policing functions that had been scattered throughout the national executive and some that had been the responsibility of regional and local police forces. In 2011, the Police Reform Commission established Citizen Police Oversight Committees (Comités Ciudadanos de Control Policial, CCCPs) to monitor the PNB. By the summer of 2012, forty-four committees had been formed. Additionally, twenty-two committees were monitoring state police forces and twenty-one oversaw municipal police forces. The other important national police force, the Bolivarian Intelligence Service (SERBIN), is also embedded in the Ministry of Interior and Justice. It focuses on counterterrorism, intelligence, counterintelligence, government investigations, and background investigations, and it provides protection and escort for high-ranking government officials, among other federally mandated duties. On occasion opposition leaders have accused SERBIN of harassing and intimidating opponents of the government.

Police reform has not increased personal security. With some fifteen thousand killings a year, Venezuela's homicide rate is the fifth-highest in the world, according to UN statistics. The murder rate doubled during the fourteen-year-rule of the late President Hugo Chávez, as cheap access to guns and an ineffective justice system fed a culture of violence in the shantytowns, parts of which have become no-go zones for outsiders, including police. Lack of security was a major issue in the April 2013 presidential election, and one of President Maduro's first initiatives was to dispatch the armed forces to the shantytowns to increase personal security.

Foreign and Defense Policy

Foreign and defense policy making is centered in the Ministries of Defense and Foreign Affairs as well as in the institutes and government entities attached to them. The Ministry of Energy and Petroleum, because of Venezuela's heavy dependence on international petroleum markets, also plays an important role in foreign policy. The focus here is on traditional national and foreign policy concerns: defense of the frontiers, control of the national territory, relations with foreign powers, and an array of nonpetroleum international economic issues.

Despite substantial overlap in the assigned tasks of the Ministries of Defense and Foreign Affairs, coordination between them was minimal until the 1980s. The most important explanation for this shortcoming is that historically the critical missions of the armed forces have been internal. Presidents Rómulo Betancourt (1959–1964) and Raúl Leoni (1963–1968) strengthened relations between AD and the military during their successful campaigns against leftist insurgents. Subsequently, until the ascent of Hugo Chávez, the primary mission of the military was to exercise control over the national territory in a manner that discouraged dissidents from waging guerrilla warfare. All four branches of the military (army, navy, air force, and national guard) provide a path for upward mobility. The officer corps attracted middle- and working-class youths, while peasants and shantytown residents filled the enlisted ranks.

On July 31, 2008, the new Organic Law of the National Bolivarian Armed Forces took effect. This law committed the military to defending the Bolivarian revolution and made the National Bolivarian Militia (Milicia Nacional Bolivariana) an integral part of the armed forces. The militias, acting with the defense committees of the communal councils, were empowered to determine which citizens were "patriotic." The law also increased the president's authority over maneuver units of the armed forces and gave him the power to order any citizen to serve in the military. In summary, the military was transformed from a professional force to a praetorian guard at the service of the president.

Foreign affairs, a constitutionally mandated presidential responsibility, center on the Ministry of Foreign Relations. During Punto Fijo presidents often selected prominent independents for the position of foreign minister as a way of building broad societal support. Over time AD and COPEI each formed a cadre of foreign policy experts. The professional foreign service was co-opted into these cadres, which also managed the Foreign Trade Institute (Instituto de Comercio Exterior, ICE).

Established in the early 1970s, ICE oversees and stimulates Venezuela's nonpetroleum exports. President Chávez appointed some of his most reliable collaborators to the position of minister of foreign affairs. One of the most important charges given early appointees was to purge the foreign service of diplomats with long-standing ties to AD and COPEI.

Venezuelan diplomacy during Punto Fijo gave lip service to reducing the importance of relations with North Atlantic countries, but successes were meager and fleeting. Cooperation within the Organization of Petroleum Exporting Countries (OPEC) to set the price of petroleum acquired great importance during the 1960s, and it gave Venezuela an influential voice among producers of petroleum. In the 1980s coordination with other debtor countries in negotiating repayment terms with banks in the Organization for Economic Co-operation and Development (OECD) countries became a priority. Membership in OPEC and coordination with debtor countries gave Caracas opportunities to resurrect rhetoric associated with such anti-European and anti-US themes as Latin American unity, international social justice, and Hispanic cultural superiority. As president, Chávez took these themes to new heights.

From the beginning Hugo Chávez voiced his unease with US influence over Latin America in general and Venezuela in particular. He clashed with President George W. Bush at the April 2001 Quebec summit over free trade in the Americas. He opposed the US invasion of Iraq in 2003 and took the lead in organizing UNASUR (Union of South American Nations), a regional organization designed to resolve political and military conflicts in South America, but without the United States.

Hugo Chávez excoriated Presidents Álvaro Uribe and Barack Obama for signing the treaty on July 16, 2009, which gave the United States access to three Colombian air bases. These bases were to facilitate efforts to stop the flow of drugs out of South America. They were a substitute for the Manta facility in Ecuador that President Rafael Correa closed. Chávez charged that US armed forces at Colombian bases could be used to invade Venezuela. He voiced his concern at the August 28 meeting of UNASUR in Bariloche, Argentina, but calls for sanctions against Colombia were rejected.

The final high concern of Venezuelan foreign policy is relations with Cuba. President Maduro has indicated he will continue supporting Cuba's Communist regime through sales of petroleum at deep discounts. These sales have freed the Castro brothers from accommodating to pressures intended to make Cuba more pluralistic as a condition for increased trade and investment from countries in the North Atlantic. Venezuela and Cuba also formed the trading group Bolivarian Alternative for the Americas (Alternativa Bolivariana para las Américas, ALBA), which provides an institutional home for states opposed to the US-supported Free Trade for the Americas Initiative. Other members of ALBA include Antigua, Bolivia, Cuba, Dominica, Ecuador, Nicaragua, and St. Vincent and the Grenadines.

Important but lesser foreign policy concerns include relations with Argentina, Brazil, and other countries of the Western Hemisphere.

THE FUTURE

Venezuelan politics changed dramatically when Hugo Chávez Frías died on March 5, 2013. He had come to power through elections when one of Latin America's

longest running liberal democracies unraveled due to economic deterioration, internecine conflict among its political elites, and corruption. Chávez gave voice to those
who had been impoverished and excluded from power. Once in control, Chávez de-
monized the liberal democratic system and those who continued to support it. Partisans of the Bolivarian revolution were those who counted—*el soberano*. Opponents
were *los escuálidos* (the squalid ones).

El soberano were the majority. In none of his runs for president did Chávez receive
less than 55 percent of the total vote, and his support reached 63 percent in 2006.
He was lucky, as the price of petroleum on the world market increased from roughly
US$10 a barrel at the time of his first inauguration to more than US$100 a barrel
when he ran for reelection in October 2012, giving President Chávez access to more
money than all the governments of the Punto Fijo era combined. Millions who had
fallen into poverty in the 1980s and 1990s benefited from programs initiated by
Hugo Chávez, and for them he embodied the general will of the people.

Opposition to the Bolivarian revolution was always intense and widespread. It
came from the middle class, many of whom had risen out of poverty during the
forty years of liberal democratic governments. It came from the political elites whose
power Chávez had taken. It came from domestic entrepreneurs and their foreign
associates whose businesses could not compete with imports sold in the country at
below cost. Merchants who supported the government received lucrative contracts
and prospered. They were known as the Bolivarian oligarchs. They purchased properties in exclusive neighborhoods that those who had lost their licenses to import
could no longer afford.

At the beginning of his presidency Nicolás Maduro finds himself governing a
country that is equally divided between partisans and opponents of twenty-first-century socialism. Venezuela's economy is stagnant following more than two years of
growth stimulated by the repatriation of funds held abroad. The physical infrastructure is deteriorated and needs extensive repair. State enterprises suffer from the kind
of rigidities and distortions that toppled the Soviet Union. In addition, post-Chávez
Venezuela has affirmed its obligations to assist its neighbors, especially Cuba, by
delivering oil at heavily discounted prices. Venezuela, however, sits atop extensive
petroleum reserves. Multinational corporations remain interested in extracting Venezuelan oil, as do state enterprises in Brazil, Russia, and China. Venezuela is likely
to receive substantial income from the sale of petroleum for the foreseeable future.

The heirs of Hugo Chávez will make important choices during the Maduro administration. On one hand, they can intensify the transition to twenty-first-century
socialism by expanding government programs, limiting the autonomy of subnational governments, taking greater control of political communication, and treat-
ing their opponents as *los escuálidos*. However, the Maduro government's financial
position is not as strong as that enjoyed by Chávez during most of his time in office.
Implementing hard-line partisanship, especially given the strength of the opposition, would likely require significant repression. The other option is to reintroduce
some tenets of liberal democracy. There could be greater toleration of private enterprise, more acceptance of regional and local autonomy, and conferral of the status of
"loyal opposition" upon opponents as long as they make demands through peaceful

channels. Advocates of both options exist within Chavismo. For its part, the opposition is unlikely to attempt a seizure of power by force given the disastrous outcome of this course of action in 2002 and 2003.

To summarize, the Venezuelan polity stands at a crossroads. It could become a militantly leftist democracy with overtones of Rousseau, a liberal democracy with a strong state sector, or even an authoritarian regime controlled by the military.

Notes

1. Venezuela's post-1958 democracy was popularly known as Punto Fijo democracy, the designation derived from the name of the house (belonging to Rafael Caldera) where party leaders signed a pact to share power in the wake of the overthrow of General Marcos Pérez Jiménez.

2. Lisa Peattie, *Rethinking Ciudad Guyana* (Ann Arbor: University of Michigan Press, 1987).

3. Judith Ewell, *Venezuela: A Century of Change* (Palo Alto, CA: Stanford University Press, 1984), 124–27.

4. Terry Lynn Karl, "Petroleum and Political Pacts: The Transition to Democracy in Venezuela," *Latin American Research Review* 22, no. 1 (1987): 63–94.

5. Moisés Naim, "The Launching of Radical Policy Changes, 1989–1991," in *Venezuela in the Wake of Radical Reform*, ed. Joseph S. Tulchin (Boulder, CO: Lynne Rienner, 1992), Chapter 4.

6. Brian A. Nelson, *The Silence and the Scorpion: The Coup Against Chávez and the Making of Modern Venezuela* (New York: Nation Books, 2009).

7. A more comprehensive discussion appears in Daniel H. Levine, *Popular Voices in Latin American Catholicism* (Princeton, NJ: Princeton University Press, 1992), 65–91.

8. Two rival labor confederations, the Unified Center of Venezuelan Workers (CUTV, estimated membership eighty thousand) and the Confederation of Autonomous Unions (CODESA, estimated membership sixty thousand), provided alternatives to the CTV during post-1958 democracy.

9. President Hugo Chávez swore in members of the newly created Comando Maisanta on June 9, 2004. The Comando's purpose was to organize the president's supporters and take them to the polls so they could vote against his removal in the recall election of August 15, 2004.

10. Steve Ellner, "A New Model with Rough Edges: Venezuela's Community Councils," *NACLA Report for the Americas,* May/June 2009, 11–14.

11. The official website of the PSUV is www.psuv.org.ve.

12. MAS (Movimiento al Socialismo) is a social-democratic political party in Venezuela. It began as a faction of the Communist Party of Venezuela that criticized the Soviet Union for its invasion of Czechoslovakia in 1968, and it was initially led by Teodoro Petkoff, holding its first congress on January 14, 1971. Between the 1970s and the 1990s, members of MAS hoped that the party would become the third-largest political force, challenging the dominant AD and COPEI parties. However, the party often won less than 5 percent of the vote. In the 1993 presidential election MAS supported the National Convergence coalition that elected Rafael Caldera, garnering 10.6 percent of the vote, a third of Caldera's total. In the parliamentary elections the same year it achieved a high-water mark of five senators and twenty-four deputies. MAS initially supported the government of Hugo Chávez in 1998. Petkoff disagreed with this decision and left the party. Disagreements between MAS and Chávez subsequently emerged, and MAS joined the opposition.

13. The Venezuelan "organic law" is halfway between regular legislation and a change to the constitution.

Suggestions for Further Reading

Carroll, Rory. *Comandante: Hugo Chávez's Venezuela*: New York: Penguin Press. 2013.

Corales, Javier, and Michael Penfold. *Dragon in the Tropics: Hugo Chávez and the Political Technology of Revolution in Venezuela.* Washington, DC: Brookings Latin America Initiative Books, 2010.

Coronil, Fernando. *The Magical State: Nature, Money, and Modernity in Venezuela.* Chicago: University of Chicago Press, 1997.

Ellner, Steve, and Miguel Tinker Salas, eds. *Venezuela: Hugo Chávez and the Decline of an "Exceptional Democracy."* Lanham, MD: Rowman and Littlefield, 2007.

Gates, Leslie C. *Electing Chávez: The Business of Anti-Neoliberal Politics in Venezuela.* Pittsburgh, PA. University of Pittsburgh Press, 2010.

Gil Yepes, José A. *The Challenge of Venezuelan Democracy.* New Brunswick, NJ: Transaction Books, 1981.

Hawkins, Kirk A. *Venezuela's Chavismo in Comparative Perspective.* New York: Cambridge University Press, 2010.

McCoy, Jennifer L., and David J. Myers. *The Unraveling of Representative Democracy in Venezuela.* Baltimore: Johns Hopkins University Press, 2005.

Morgan, Jana. *Bankrupt Representation and Party System Collapse.* University Park: Penn State University Press, 2011.

Myers, David J. "Venezuela: Politics, Urban Reform and the Challenges of Metropolitan Governance amid the Struggle for Democracy." In *Metropolitan Governance in the Federalist Americas*, ed. Peter Spink, Peter M. Ward, and Robert H. Wilson, 209–246. Notre Dame, IN: University of Notre Dame Press, 2012.

Nelson, Brian. *The Silence and the Scorpion: The Coup Against Chávez and the Making of Modern Venezuela.* New York: Nation Books, 2009.

Trinkunas, Harold A. *Crafting Civilian Control of the Military in Venezuela: A Comparative Perspective.* Chapel Hill: University of North Carolina Press, 2005.

Zúquete, Jose Pedro. "The Missionary Politics of Hugo Chávez." *Latin American Politics and Society* 50, no. 1 (2008): 91–122.

I2

URUGUAY: BALANCING
GROWTH AND DEMOCRACY

Ronald H. McDonald and Martin Weinstein

Uruguay is the smallest of the South American republics, but the distinctiveness of its political experience and innovations far transcends its size.[1] It is perhaps best known today as a long-standing democracy that "failed," one that is now struggling to reaffirm and redefine its democratic traditions. However, it is also a country that in the nineteenth century created democracy out of chaos and translated its traditional corporatist values and realities into democratic institutions. It experienced a profound disillusionment with the modern premises of economic growth and stability, as well as a period of escalating political instability and incremental military intervention. In 1985 Uruguay reestablished democratic government and politics, and since then it has been preoccupied with defining the meaning of "normalcy" in this new context.

Uruguay often has been viewed as a historical exception to the general pattern of politics in Latin America, an isolated instance of enlightened pluralistic politics in a region of corporatist authoritarianism. Uruguayans, in fact, have shared the same corporatist values as most of their neighbors but, almost uniquely, have shaped them into distinctive democratic processes and traditions. They have borrowed selectively from the experiences of Europe and the United States and, as necessary, made innovations to suit their own environment. Today Uruguay has reestablished its democratic heritage and revitalized its historical values, and in the process has cautiously explored new forms of organization and reevaluated the failed premises that previously eroded its traditional democracy.

The unique qualities of Uruguayan democracy have been little known, let alone understood, outside the country. Outwardly the country seems to have many

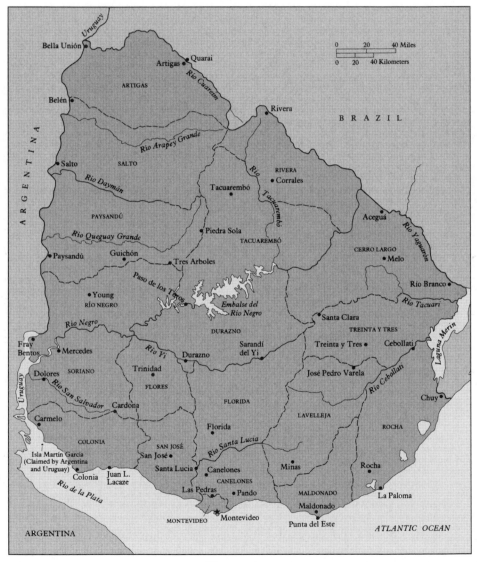

URUGUAY

similarities with other democracies, including regular and meaningful elections, a rule of law that respects and protects individual liberties and freedoms, and a policy-making process that is responsive to public opinion and scrutiny. Yet these qualities exist within a distinctively Latin American context, which recognizes and incorporates corporatist assumptions in the democratic processes, utilizing such familiar devices as co-optation, parity, coparticipation, and charismatic leadership. Many of the premises, which were the logic of the country's traditional democracy, proved unreliable, and in the mid-twentieth century Uruguay went through a period of sustained political and economic decay, violence, and ultimately authoritarian military rule.

The establishment of Uruguayan democracy originally was the result of an armistice between contentious landowners and provincial caudillos who came to recognize the potential for significant profits from increased exports. The politicians also saw democracy as a way to create political stability and gain political support from a rapidly expanding urban middle class committed to consumerism, consumption, and the benefits of state-provided services and welfare. Uruguayan democracy was based on an important economic assumption: economic growth was inevitable, irreversible, and largely a spontaneous process that could subsidize the expanding and increasingly costly demands of a democratic society.

The political ideas that underlay Uruguayan democracy were forcefully and explicitly articulated by its most influential statesman, José Batlle y Ordóñez. These included the belief that political stability was essential for prosperity and growth; that it would be achieved only by allowing free but balanced access to political power under a rule of law; that it could be sustained only by responding to the needs and demands of the masses; and that it must be protected from the pernicious influences of ambitious executives, politicians, and international opportunists while guaranteeing a strong role for the state. Batlle was also strongly anticlerical. He believed that the church and Catholicism were an organized threat to secular control and progress, and that church and state should be totally separated.

What is important about the Uruguayan experience is its relevance to other democracies whose processes, welfare, and stability are based on similar assumptions. The reexamination in Uruguay of fundamental democratic premises and values, particularly within a context of economic stress, was not an easy task; nor were the questions of blame and retribution for individuals and institutions that were culpable for the collapse of the democratic system. The concerns ultimately raised the issue of how normalcy would be defined within the new and reevaluated contemporary context. It is still unclear how much the result will borrow from the past, from neighboring societies in Latin America, or from new premises and new values. Uruguay has dealt with crises and dilemmas that would test any democracy, and for that reason its experience, both the universal and the parochial dimensions, merits careful evaluation.

ECONOMIC HISTORY AND SOCIAL CONTEXT

Uruguayan economic history is particularly important for understanding the country's politics and government. Early in the twentieth century Uruguay became a largely middle-class country with one of the highest standards of living in Latin America, but it subsequently experienced a protracted economic decline that challenged and eventually helped destroy its democratic politics. Uruguayan exports failed to remain viable and competitive internationally; its domestic economy became heavily dependent upon services rather than agricultural and industrial activities; its dependency on imports, particularly for energy, created massive financial problems; and its commitment to consumption rather than productivity distorted national priorities and created an escalating international debt and uncontrolled inflation. Uruguay's economic success and its subsequent decay were both influenced by international economic realities, most of them beyond the country's control.

Uruguay's wealth was generated by the export of traditional commodities, principally wool, mutton, lamb, cattle, and grains. The economy was too small to industrialize rationally or efficiently, and the effort to do so encouraged import substitution industrialization (ISI) and protectionist trade policies, which in turn created inefficient monopolies, both foreign and domestic, along with equally inefficient state-owned enterprises. The domestic economic situation was complicated by high production costs and profit expectations resulting from high-risk industrial ventures. It was also complicated by the modern but unrealistic economic expectations of workers, who effectively organized and created politically influential labor unions.

By the end of the nineteenth century the worldwide demand for Uruguayan exports had grown dramatically. Traditional fibers such as wool had not yet been challenged by synthetic ones, and by the mid-1870s the technology of refrigerated ships had made the export of fresh meat possible. The rural sector provided the capital on which the nation's development and wealth were based, thus subsidizing the industrial, commercial, and financial interests of the capital city, Montevideo. Export revenues allowed the importation of consumer goods demanded by urban dwellers and helped supply the capital for Montevideo's own inefficient industrialization. Because small-scale industrialization was inefficient, expensive, and monopolistic, Uruguay's industrial products could not compete in export markets or domestically either in quality or price with imports. However, the workers whom the industries employed, concentrated in and around the capital city, grew in number and became more highly organized and politically active than their rural counterparts. For them the process of industrialization was popular. There emerged an inevitable conflict between the rural and urban interests in the country, one in which the capital city eventually prevailed by virtue of its greater population. The situation was a corrosive and dangerous one in which the affluence, growth, and consumption of the urban area were being subsidized by the rural areas, whose economy was slowly deteriorating.

By the end of World War II the demand for Uruguayan exports had begun to decline. Other supplies of fresh meat were available in international markets, particularly for Uruguay's largest trading partner, Great Britain, and wool fibers were being replaced by synthetic ones. Rather than responding to these changes, the traditional rural economy continued producing the same export commodities, and so export revenues decreased within a context of shrinking demand.[2] Uruguay's failure to renovate its export economy and to recognize and respond to major shifts in international demand and new technologies set in motion a slow process of economic decay, which went largely unnoticed by the public until after decades its cumulative effects were clearly visible. The eventual political implications were disastrous.

At the end of World War II Argentina, Brazil, and Mexico were effectively industrializing at rapid rates, but industrial growth in Uruguay had slowed dramatically. The worsening imbalance between export revenues and import costs, an imbalance seriously aggravated by the sharp rise in the cost of imported energy in the 1970s, severely strained the country's financial solvency and encouraged two further and ultimately disastrous economic decisions. To sustain economic growth and financial liquidity the civilian governments expanded the money supply, inducing rapid and at times rampant inflation, and the country increasingly borrowed money from international sources to subsidize its worsening trade deficit.

The first policy eroded the confidence of Uruguayan investors and encouraged an acceleration in capital flight along with a decline in investment. It also destroyed the ability of the urban middle and working classes to save or maintain (not to mention improve) their living standards, which eventually alienated a substantial portion of the electorate and eroded confidence in the economic system. The second policy created a massive international debt, which by the mid-1980s was equal to about half the annual national per capita income. In the decade from 1977 to 1986 the level of international debt in Uruguay increased by more than 400 percent, one of the highest rates of increase in the hemisphere, and that was largely under a military government committed to economic austerity and willing to endure the response to unpopular policies.

However, economic decay was not an unpredictable, catastrophic experience that instantly devastated living standards and economic activity. It was slow, incremental, and entirely predictable, but the difficult political decisions required to reverse it were not or could not be made, even by a military government. As economic conditions deteriorated following World War II and a brief boom brought on by the Korean War, increasing demands were imposed on the government to provide jobs and to subsidize housing, which in turn created more public spending and inflation, further discouraged domestic and foreign investment, and ultimately reinforced the general pattern of economic decline and the political problems associated with it. Although the country had achieved one of the highest standards of living in Latin America, Uruguay began to face apparently unsolvable economic problems.

The country's economic performance in the 1990s was strong by historical standards, thanks for the most part to the creation of the Common Market of the South (MERCOSUR), which spurred a significant increase in intraregional trade. Gross domestic product grew by 7.9 percent in 1992, 3.0 percent in 1993, and 6.3 percent in 1994. It then slid to -1.8 percent in 1995 but moved back nicely in the following years to slightly above 5 percent before Brazil's currency crisis put Uruguay into recession in 1999. The big news on the economic front was that Uruguay's decades-old battle with inflation finally seemed to be coming to a victorious close. Inflation was only 4.5 percent for the first six months of 1998, making that year the first in memory with single-digit inflation. Low inflation continued until 2002, when it jumped to 14 percent and then rose even higher, to 19.4 percent, the next year. The rate of consumer price increases dropped steadily after that, reaching 6.7 percent in 2010. In December 2009 the government deficit had reached US$21.73 billion, which was

$5.2 billion higher than at the end of 2008, representing an increase of 31.5 percent. Private investment in machinery and equipment more than quadrupled (admittedly from very low levels) between 1986 and 1996. However, Uruguay continued to have a poor investment and savings rate and an unfortunate record of attracting foreign investment until the first decade of the new millennium. After US$8 billion of new investment in 2008, $12.5 billion in 2009, and $2.35 billion in 2010, total foreign direct investment reached US$14.4 billion in 2011, seven times the figure of eleven years before.

In 2012 Uruguay's exports, led by beef, soybeans, cellulose, rice, wheat, wood, dairy products, and wool, brought in US$9.907 billion, with Brazil (18.5 percent), China (17.9 percent), Argentina (6.8 percent), and Germany (4.3 percent) accounting for the largest share. In 2012 Uruguayan imports were US$12.22 billion, coming from China (16.1 percent), Argentina 15.8 percent, Brazil (14.6 percent), the United States (8.9 percent), and Paraguay (7.6 percent). Principal imported goods were refined oil, crude oil, passenger and other transportation vehicles, vehicle parts, and cellular phones.

Unemployment in this security-conscious country remained stubbornly high for some time, rising from 12 percent in 1999 to a high of 19 percent in 2002 before beginning a decline to 7 percent in 2010.

When all is said and done, the tiny Uruguayan economy, coupled with the state's historic commitment to welfare policies, allows a homogeneous population of some 3.2 million people to maintain one of the highest Physical Quality of Life Indexes (PQLI) in Latin America, according to the United Nations.

The Uruguayan people are themselves a distinctive mixture. During the colonial period the country had virtually no indigenous population. Most immigrants were from Spain and Italy, the latter primarily in the late nineteenth and early twentieth centuries. These were largely middle- and working-class people from urban areas, attracted to the prosperous and expanding Uruguayan economy, who remained in the capital city, Montevideo. They brought with them European political attitudes and economic expectations, which were absorbed into the country's party politics. Today about half the national population resides in the capital city. Rural life, perhaps because of its historical economic importance, spawned a mythology of its own centered around the gaucho, but the reality of rural life has little in common with the myths. During the period of economic decay following World War II and the Korean War there was a substantial migration of urban Uruguayans out of the country, many of them to Argentina and Brazil, a process that was reinforced by the turbulent political conditions of the 1960s and the subsequent military dictatorship.

Uruguay was one of the first nations in Latin America to make a major commitment to public education, with the result that a high level of literacy was achieved at a relatively early time historically. With literacy came high levels of political awareness and participation along with modern socioeconomic expectations.

POLITICAL ORGANIZATION IN URUGUAY

Uruguay is a highly organized society, with clearly defined interest groups and complex political parties, but the society is organized in organic rather than pluralistic ways. The framework for this organization was devised by José Batlle to achieve political stability out of the chaotic experience of civil wars, international intervention, and party-organized conflict.

The nineteenth century produced two political parties: the Colorado Party and the National Party, more commonly known as the Blanco Party (the parties originally were identified by the color of the brassards their adherents wore during armed confrontations). After generations of fighting for national hegemony, often with international provocation from Brazil, Argentina, and Great Britain, the possibility of economic prosperity, which came in the 1870s with the potential for a rapid expansion of exports, dramatized the advantages of cooperation rather than armed conflict for advancing the economic interests of both sides. The resolution of the civil conflict was promoted and eventually achieved by José Batlle.

Batlle was a descendant of a politically prominent and influential Uruguayan family who has produced many important political leaders. He was elected president twice, in 1903 and 1911, and he established the framework for modern Uruguayan politics and government. After defeating the Blancos in the last of the civil wars he established a political compromise with them based on the concepts of parity and coparticipation. Parity recognized the legitimate interests of the Blancos in the rural departments where they were strong, and Batlle all but ceded these departments to their control. He also accepted their participation in the national government, proportional to their share of the national vote, and allowed them a share of government patronage and revenues. The Blanco Party won only three subsequent national elections—in 1958, 1962, and 1989—and became virtually a permanent minority. Batlle's Colorado Party consistently attracted more voters nationally than the Blancos, but it was willing to share with the Blancos the exercise and benefits of power. The 1952 constitution went so far as to formalize coparticipation by awarding two of five positions on the boards of all state enterprises to the minority party.

Batlle designed an electoral system that incorporates parity and coparticipation both within and between the nation's political parties.[3] The Uruguayan electoral system regulates parties, elections, and the distribution of legislative seats, establishing *lemas* and *sublemas*, which are equivalent to parties and party factions. Lemas are composed of sublemas, factions that are the supporters or political machines of individual leaders. Anyone can form a sublema, acquire formal identification within a lema, and in effect create a personal political organization with a separate identity. The electoral strength of a sublema and its leader adds to the total vote of a lema, which in turn determines both lema and sublema legislative representation. From this process ambitious political leaders are thereby permitted into the political system and can exercise political influence proportional to their ability to attract votes. Their organizations are integrated into the larger lema, or party coalition, and they have a vested interest in the success of other sublemas, which they nonetheless campaign against because their representation is determined by their share of the cumulative vote for the lema. Presidential elections used to have the effect of combining a primary election with a general election.

Sublemas in Uruguay form the nucleus of political organization and encourage a clientele relationship between the party leaders and the voters. Constituents with problems can request help from sublema leaders and their organizations, and in

Montevideo sublemas maintain neighborhood clubs and organize campaigning. Through cross-endorsement, cross-listing, and a sharing of candidates, they form additional coalitions among themselves within the lemas, coalitions that constantly shift from one election to another.

The lema system is formalized by proportional representation, which allocates legislative representation according to the size of the popular vote. Campaign costs are also subsidized for sublemas according to the size of their vote. For the voter the system encourages a general identification with a lema and a personal identification with a sublema. The general electoral system also reinforces the Colorado and Blanco parties, which benefit principally from it, and restrains the growth and success of new or smaller parties.

José Batlle built the Colorado Party into the majority political organization by mobilizing the urban classes of Montevideo and appealing to their interests. He proposed—and while president implemented—vast public programs of education, culture, welfare, and social security. He encouraged industrialization and resisted foreign penetration of the country's economy. Batlle advocated abolishing the presidency as an institution and replacing it with a rotating collegial executive, an idea he borrowed from Switzerland. His reasoning was that the dictatorships that were so common in Latin America were the result of an inevitable greed for power, and because one could not change human nature, the only way to prevent dictatorships was to abolish the presidency and replace it with an institution that dispersed power. Batlle was by profession a journalist, and he used his journalistic interest to further his political objectives, a process that continues today in Uruguay. Opposition to his leadership arose within the Colorado Party, and anti-Batllista factions (sublemas) were formed.

Batlle's ideas were visionary for their time: he initiated a modern welfare state in Uruguay long before it had been tried elsewhere. He was a consummate politician, but his political pragmatism was tempered by his idealism. Batlle believed he could eliminate instability and turmoil by expanding and organizing the political base of the country and by responding to the basic needs of the Uruguayan people.

In spite of his influence and success Batlle's ideas were based on two vulnerable assumptions, both of which proved to be erroneous and eventually contributed to the decay of Uruguayan democracy. The first was the assumption of continued economic growth and prosperity, a common perspective among industrializing nations during the nineteenth century. This assumption was drawn from the experiences of large nations, specifically Great Britain, France, Germany, and the United States, and proved inappropriate for Uruguay. The second was the assumption that a collegial executive could prevent authoritarian governments. Uruguay did not experiment with a pure form of the collegial executive until the 1950s, perhaps the worst possible moment because the economy was declining and strong leadership was desperately needed. Ironically, for eight of the twelve collegial executive years the government was controlled by the Blanco Party, which was the first time in the twentieth century it had prevailed in national elections. The experiment with a collegial executive, combined with the economic dilemmas for which no answers could be found, contributed to the political paralysis that encouraged a revolutionary group known as the Tupamaros and, ultimately, military intervention. The

Tupamaros did not succeed in taking power, but they did provoke the military to do so.

There have always been minor political parties in Uruguay. One of the oldest was the Civic Union (UC), a conservative Catholic organization that provided an alternative to the prevailing tradition of anticlericalism that Batlle sponsored. By the 1960s several small parties combined with a dissident liberal sublema of the Colorado Party to form an electoral coalition, originally known as the Leftist Front of Freedom (FIDEL) and ultimately as the Broad Front. Included in the Broad Front were the Communist Party of Uruguay, the Christian Democratic Party, the Socialist Party, and List 99 of the Colorado Party, established by Zelmar Michelini. By combining the strengths of small parties in the 1971, 1984, and 1989 elections, the coalition posed a serious threat to the two traditional lemas, which in many ways are themselves political coalitions. Civic Union disappeared following redemocratization, having been replaced by New Space, an organization of radical Catholics and social democrats, some of whom had supported the Broad Front.

Like the political parties, economic interests have been well organized in Uruguay. The organizations include national associations of ranchers, business enterprises, and labor. Labor organizations emerged very early in Uruguay and were modeled after their European counterparts. The largest labor organization, the National Confederation of Workers (CNT), is Marxist, but its strength has not necessarily been translated into votes for Marxist parties. Organized workers were a principal target for Batlle's policies, and a large proportion has been Colorado Party supporters in spite of their union's orientation. The CNT was outlawed under the dictatorship, but a new organization, the Plenario Intersindical de Trabajadores (PIT), formed in the early 1980s and subsequently merged with the CNT after the reestablishment of democracy.

The political scenario that eventually produced a military dictatorship is a long and complex one. Military intervention occurred gradually, although by mid-1973 the military was fully in control of the government. The Tupamaro revolutionary movement, specializing in urban terrorism in the capital city, became a highly destabilizing influence during the 1960s. The government retaliated with a state of siege, massive arrests, torture, suppression of political leaders and groups, and censorship. Regardless, these actions were ineffective and even counterproductive. The military gradually assumed responsibility for the Tupamaro threat and brought the civilian institution under its control.

The military regime had both successes and failures in managing the economy, but the experience proved unpopular with Uruguayans and divisive for the military. No single military leader was able to consolidate his control, although one (Gregorio Álvarez) tried. The military response to the Tupamaros was brutal and, for Uruguay, unprecedented. The movement was crushed before the military took control of the government in June 1973, but at exceptionally high costs to Uruguayan legal and political values. The military ruled until 1985.

By the early 1980s the military leaders had begun to recognize the inevitability of restoring civilian rule and began looking for a way to maximize their continuing influence and minimize any retribution against them—individually and institutionally—after leaving power. They looked for inspiration to Brazil, whose officers were methodically and gradually returning that country's government to civilian control, and they were aware of the chaotic experience occurring in Argentina, where the military was leaving power in disgrace and facing civilian retribution.

The military regime decided to hold a referendum in 1980 on a new constitution that would protect the military's political influence, a referendum held under conditions of tight controls and censorship. The measure was so decisively defeated that the regime had no choice but to acknowledge its failure. At that point military officers began negotiating with civilian political leaders, at least those they were willing to talk with, about conditions for a return to civilian rule. This change was formally achieved in March 1985 after elections the preceding November in which two of the major presidential contenders, Wilson Ferreira Aldunate of the Blanco Party and Liber Seregni of the Broad Front, were prohibited from being candidates.

The victor in 1985 was a Colorado Party candidate, Julio María Sanguinetti. Party voting and the resulting legislative representation were very similar to what they had been in 1971, the last election before the total military takeover. The Colorado regime encountered difficulties and controversies in its quest for normalization, and in the 1989 elections the Blanco Party, for only the third time in history, prevailed, winning a plurality in the two legislative chambers and electing a president, the moderate Blanco leader Luis Alberto Lacalle. In 1994 the Colorados again won the presidency, but only barely, with the Blancos and the Broad Front close behind. National politics seemed to have been transformed by that election, perhaps permanently, to a three-party system.

GOVERNMENT STRUCTURE AND POLICIES

Uruguay has a centralized government and is divided into nineteen departments, including the capital city, Montevideo. Virtually all decisions in the country are made at the national level. The 1966 constitution allows departments to elect local legislatures comprising thirty-one members and an *intendente,* the departmental administrative officer.

The president is popularly elected for a five-year term, and all elections in the country are held simultaneously. The legislature is bicameral, with ninety-nine representatives in the chamber of deputies, elected from districts, and thirty-one in the senate, with the nation as a single district. All are elected by proportional representation. The current constitution was adopted in 1966 in the aftermath of the twelve-year experiment with a collegial executive. The legislature has considerable power and is organized through a system of committees.

In December 1996, after years of discussion, a reform was narrowly approved by the voters in a constitutional plebiscite. Under the new system each party can run only one presidential candidate, who will be chosen by primaries conducted in each party and ratified at a party convention. To be elected president the successful candidate must receive at least 50 percent of the total vote or face a runoff against his nearest competitor. Given the 1994 electoral results, such a runoff appeared all but a certainty for 1999, which in fact turned out to be the case, as discussed below.

This constitutional reform, which passed by the barest margin (50.3 percent) in a national referendum, represents a revolutionary change in the electoral system. In brief, the most significant features are as follows:

1. A primary system was established to determine each party's candidate. The successful candidate must obtain at least 40 percent of the primary vote, with a 10 percent difference between the winner and the nearest competitor. If not, a party convention chooses the candidate.
2. Local elections are now separated from national elections. Elections for intendentes of the nineteen departments and their local legislative bodies take place in May of the year following the presidential and congressional elections.

There are several major implications of these reforms. First, the elected president will be able to claim majority support, a result unheard of under the old system. Second, voters may have to choose from candidates not of their party, or even of their liking, in the second round. Third, the primary system may help produce a real party leader as opposed to the historical norm of leaders of party factions. Finally, local governments will be elected at a different time than the national government, allowing ticket splitting for the first time in history. This may help generate more power at the local level and with it more demands on the central government.

The Uruguayan economy is a distinctive mixture of private and public enterprises. Most of the economy is privately owned and managed, but about 20 percent of the gross domestic product comes from state-owned companies. The largest of the state-owned monopolies is the Asociación Nacional de Combustibles, Alcohol y Portland (ANCAP), which refines petroleum and manufactures alcohol and cement. That agency alone accounts for 4 percent of the GDP. In the 1970s there was an effort to encourage international banking in Uruguay in order to provide offshore benefits to foreign banks and investors and stimulate economic development by encouraging new investments in the country. The policy was partially successful and was supported by the military regimes and the subsequent civilian governments.

What has historically given Uruguay the appearance of a welfare state has been not so much the direct participation of the government in the economy but the benefits provided by the government. Nowhere is this situation more apparent than in the social security system, which partially supports over 350,000 retired Uruguayans, a number equal to almost one-third of the active workforce. Low population growth means Uruguay has the highest proportion of retired people of any Latin American nation, and this fact, combined with state-provided retirement benefits, creates an enormous financial burden on the people who are economically active.

The economic problems facing the Sanguinetti government in 1985 were formidable. The rural economy needed revitalization, both for export objectives and for food production; Uruguay had one of the highest per capita international debts in the region; national investment and economic growth were low; and the foreign trade situation was critical, with exports failing to provide sufficient revenues to pay for the energy, resources, and manufactured goods the country needed to import as well as to service its international debt. The only course the government had available was economic austerity, not a policy designed to cushion the return to civilian, democratic government. Besides these economic problems, the erosion of public services and programs and a decline in real income and savings during the twelve years of military control had stimulated new demands, which were difficult for political leaders to ignore in the restored democratic environment, but even more difficult for them to meet. Economic performance during the Colorado administration of President Julio Sanguinetti was better than most expected, based on a policy of economic liberalism.

The next president, Blanco leader Luis Alberto Lacalle, continued that policy, significantly reducing the foreign debt, renegotiating debt payments, attracting new investment, and repatriating fugitive capital. Efforts to privatize state corporations, however, met considerable opposition, resulting in another plebiscite in 1993 that overturned with 72 percent of the vote a legislative decision to sell the state telephone monopoly. Plans to privatize the state natural gas monopoly, the state fishing corporation, and the state electric utility seemed at least temporarily moribund. After the vote President Lacalle sarcastically observed, "Uruguay is a country that has been very happy for a very long time, and prefers a little with security rather than a lot with risk." Normalcy in Uruguay apparently meant public enterprises and service as usual, but Lacalle did cut Uruguay's high tariffs and joined the regional Common Market of the South, consisting of Argentina, Brazil, Paraguay, and Uruguay.

The Uruguayan military is professional by Latin American standards and, except for the recent dictatorship, it stayed out of politics for most of the twentieth century. During the dictatorship the size of the military grew at least 400 percent, and defense expenditures rose appreciably to a percentage of the GDP far exceeding that of Brazil, Argentina, or Mexico.

One of the principal objectives of normalization following redemocratization was to bring the military under the control of civilians, and the major issue was how to deal with military leaders who were responsible for human rights violations during the dictatorship. The issue plagued the Sanguinetti government, which was otherwise preoccupied with economic problems, and impeded the normalization of national politics. In late 1987 the legislature passed an amnesty bill that prevented prosecution of military and police personnel for human rights violations during the dictatorship. The legislation was very unpopular and provoked a petition campaign to hold a referendum on the legislation and the question of immunity. Public opinion polls showed that a majority of Uruguayans believed that military personnel did commit human rights violations during the dictatorship and that those who did should be punished. The petition campaign forced a referendum, which was held in April 1989, but the effort to overturn the immunity legislation failed by a negative vote of 53 percent. The majority of voters in Montevideo, however, voted in favor of the referendum. The fate of the disappeared continues to be an issue in Uruguayan politics.

The Uruguayan military never engaged in the mass killings for which their Argentine and Chilean comrades are so infamous. However, they did arrest thousands and subject them to torture while also imposing draconian rule on Uruguay's citizens from 1973 to 1985. The number of disappeared in Uruguay totaled a few dozen, with some 140 Uruguayans sharing the same fate in Argentina. The whereabouts of these individuals has never been clarified by the Uruguayan military. Children born to captive and subsequently disappeared Uruguayans are being sought by their relatives in much the same manner as the mothers and grandmothers of the Plaza de Mayo in

Argentina seek theirs. President Batlle was directly involved in this issue and planned to convene a commission to investigate and issue a report on the matter.

The first truly open national elections since the end of the military dictatorship were held on November 26, 1989. The Blanco Party won a plurality of the vote with 38 percent, and one of its leaders, Luis Alberto Lacalle, was elected president. Colorado candidates received less than one-third of the vote, and the Broad Front about one-fifth. The latter did, however, receive a plurality (34 percent) in the municipal elections for the city of Montevideo, electing a Socialist mayor, Dr. Tabaré Vázquez, and a majority of the municipal council. The failure of the Colorados to mobilize their traditional support in Montevideo was critical to their loss, but the results were ambiguous on the question of electoral realignment. At the least they seemed to imply a three-way party competition in the future.

National elections held in November 1994 confirmed that implication. Former president Julio Sanguinetti (1985–1989) barely won the election as the Colorado Party presidential candidate, and his party received only about 32 percent of the vote. The Blanco Party received somewhat more than 31 percent and the Broad Front, in a coalition known as the Progressive Front, only slightly less. The election signaled the end of the traditional two-party dominance of Uruguayan politics and a new balance between the three political forces. The Broad Front won the majority of Montevideo for the second consecutive time.

The 1999 party primaries proved no contest for the left, where Tabaré Vázquez easily won the nomination, and for the Blancos, whose former president, Luis Lacalle, also won handily but found himself with a bitterly divided party. The Colorado primary was hard fought, but in the end perennial candidate Jorge Batlle, son of one president and grandnephew of another, won the nomination.

In the first round of the elections the left, in a historic breakthrough, finished first with some 39 percent of the vote. The Colorado candidate finished second with 32 percent, and the Blancos finished a dismal third with only 22 percent. The Broad Front thus emerged as the single largest political force in the country, with high hopes of capturing the presidency in a runoff election with the Colorados. The Blanco leadership threw its support to Batlle, but no one could be sure that the rank and file would follow suit. Up until ten days before the second round all the polls showed Vázquez with a slight lead, but the final poll results showed that Batlle had pulled into a statistical dead heat. Uruguayans were both apprehensive and excited as election day approached. The undecided voters broke heavily for Batlle, who prevailed by 52 to 45 percent.

Uruguay began the new century with a wake-up call to its traditional parties. The voters indicated that although a majority still favored the rule of Colorados and Blancos, they wanted more creative solutions to the country's endemic problems of high unemployment and mediocre growth. They also wanted politicians who did not feel they were entitled to their power and got too comfortable as they shared its spoils with friends and family.

The year 2001 was a difficult one for Uruguay even before the events of September 11. President Batlle's first full calendar year in office confronted him with a worsening of Uruguay's economic situation exacerbated by an outbreak of foot-and-mouth disease that seriously disrupted Uruguay's meat exports. The government had hoped that 2001 would bring modest economic growth after two years of recession. Unfortunately, the continued devaluation of the Brazilian currency and the deepening economic and political crisis in Argentina had adverse effects on both Uruguayan exports and tourism. With these internal and external conditions unemployment skyrocketed to some 16 percent and the GDP fell 1.1 percent for the first half of the year. The only good news on the economic front was the continued low inflation rate of 4 to 5 percent.

Unfortunately, 2002 was a year of worsening economic crisis for Uruguay.[4] The financial meltdown in Argentina and the political and economic instability in Brazil caused by the election of the leftist candidate Luiz Inácio Lula da Silva (Lula) led to a deepening recession in Uruguay.

The most negative effect on the Uruguayan economy was produced by the freeze on deposits in Argentina caused by the collapse of the Argentine peso when that government abandoned its convertibility plan, which pegged its currency at one-to-one with the US dollar. This forced many Argentines to withdraw dollars from their bank accounts in the traditionally safe haven of Montevideo. The subsequent collapse of two banks in Uruguay had many Uruguayans fearing for the safety of their banking system, leading them also to withdraw funds. The result was that in the first seven months of the year Uruguay lost 81 percent of its foreign reserves. The country's sovereign debt abruptly declined from investment grade to junk status during the same period. The GDP fell 7.8 percent in the first half of the year and was expected to contract some 10 or 11 percent for the year as a whole. Uruguay's GDP then declined some 20 percent after the recession started in 1999 and unemployment climbed to a record 17 percent. Inflation, which was a mere 3.59 percent in 2001, hit 24 percent by September and was expected to go slightly higher by the end of the year.

President Jorge Batlle of the ruling Colorado Party tried to contain the damage but was obliged to accept the resignation of his minister of the economy, Albert Bensión, and replace him with the more highly respected Alejandro Atchugarry. The goodwill Batlle enjoyed in Washington helped him obtain a US$1.5 billion bridge loan from the United States in order to keep the banking system solvent until over US$3 billion in funds could arrive from the IMF, the World Bank, and the Inter-American Development Bank (IADB). Politically, the left appeared to be gaining strength as a result of the economic crisis. By October, polls showed that the leader of the leftist coalition, Tabaré Vázquez, would receive some 50 percent of the vote.

The following year proved no less difficult for the Uruguayan economy. In May Uruguay successfully renegotiated its private debt with an innovative bond exchange that stretched out the repayment schedule, thus giving some breathing room for the last two years of the Batlle administration and the first year of the next government. The banking system remained deeply depressed, with nonperforming loans running at 25 percent at private banks and a staggering 50 percent at such key public institutions as the Banco de la República and the Mortgage Bank (Banco Hipotecario). The latter institution lost US$1.1 billion in 2002.

The year 2004 was an exciting and pivotal time in Uruguay. After nearly four years of sharply negative growth, the economy—aided by recovery in Argentina, strong growth in Brazil, and excellent commodity prices—grew by a robust 13.6 percent in the first half of the year. Unfortunately for the ruling Colorado Party, little of this positive macroeconomic performance filtered down to Uruguay's poor or to the middle class. Unemployment remained above 13 percent, and more than one-third of Uruguayans lived in poverty.

In this context the presidential and congressional elections that took place on October 31 marked a sea change in Uruguayan politics. Throughout the year the polls showed that the leftist coalition known as the Broad Front–Progressive Encounter was the largest party in the country. The question that remained was whether it would secure the 50 percent plus one vote it needed in order to avoid a runoff with one of the traditional parties, the Blanco Party or the Colorados. In the last two weeks before the election all of Uruguay's polls agreed that the socialists had reached the magic number needed to avoid a second round and that Tabaré Vázquez, an oncologist who had been the political leader of the Broad Front leftist coalition since he was their presidential candidate in 1994, would be president. The photogenic and charismatic Vázquez, a Socialist Party militant, carefully juggled his coalition, which included social democrats, democratic socialists, socialists, Communists, and ex-Tupamaros.

In the election itself, the left received 50.4 percent of the vote, followed by the Blancos (34 percent) and the Colorados (10 percent). Vázquez assumed office on March 1, 2005. The historic victory by Vázquez and the left was seen by many to further strengthen the hand of Brazilian president Lula as he sought to turn MERCOSUR into the major voice for Latin American economic integration and the chief interlocutor with both the European Union and the United States in trade negotiations. Vázquez's victory was the latest example in South America of a move to the left and center-left.

Five years of leftist rule proved very positive for Uruguay. With the appointment of Danilo Astori as minister of finance, the Vázquez administration quickly signaled its willingness to accept the rules of international finance and investment. Early on Vázquez made it clear that he would keep an eye on budget deficits and inflation. The country enjoyed four years of exceptionally solid economic growth after the Broad Front victory, with average annual increases of some 7 percent. Inflation continued to be manageable during the same period. Exports boomed, due in no small measure to the voracious appetite of China and India for raw materials and foodstuffs, which propelled a hugely successful economic recovery in the emergence of Argentina and Brazil as major economic players. The good times enjoyed in the Southern Cone also translated into a tourist boom for Uruguay. Foreign investments grew exponentially, thanks in part to a US$1 billion investment in Uruguay's forestry and paper pulp industry. This latter project, however, proved a bone of contention between the Uruguayan and Argentine governments. Argentine president Nestor Kirchner fought the paper pulp plant all the way to the World Court. When Argentina lost there, its government continued to support environmental groups that closed the highways and bridges between the two countries, thereby causing an economic loss estimated at several hundred million dollars for Uruguay. In the end, however, the plant was completed and is functioning.

The Vázquez government took advantage of its majority in both houses of congress to pass legislation on same-sex partners' rights and health care coverage for poor children. The latter program was paid for by an increase in the minuscule personal income tax. This move proved deeply unpopular with the middle and upper classes, even those members of these groups who were supporters of the left. The 2009 presidential and parliamentary elections were an exciting affair. President Vázquez refused all entreaties to run again under a constitutional reform proposal permitting him to serve consecutive terms. A hard-fought primary in June 2009 resulted in the candidacy of the former Tupamaro leader José Mujica, head of the Movement of Popular Participation (MPP) faction of the Frente Amplio. Mujica turned to his main rival, Danilo Astori, as his vice presidential choice, but theirs was not a marriage made in heaven.

The Blancos saw their primary won by ex-president Luis Lacalle, who quickly asked his main competitor to join him on the ticket. The Colorado Party continued to fare incredibly poorly. Its standard-bearer, Pedro Bordaberry, received only 17 percent in the October election. Lacalle received 29 percent, while Mujica led with 48 percent. A second round took place the last Sunday in November to decide a winner between the top two vote getters. José Mujica won with 53 percent; hence the leftist government continued.

GLOBALIZATION, THE CHALLENGES FOR ECONOMIC GROWTH, AND THE CONSOLIDATION OF DEMOCRACY

Globalization and regionalization under MERCOSUR have shown mixed results for Uruguay. The neoliberal model adopted by Blanco president Luis Lacalle (1989–1994) and Colorado president Julio Sanguinetti (1994–1999) brought decent growth and an explosion of consumer credit in the mid- and late 1990s along with a boost in tourism and trade with Argentina and Brazil. Unfortunately, Jorge Batlle, Colorado president from 2000 to 2004, presided over the worst financial crisis since the Depression after the 1999 Brazilian devaluation led to a financial meltdown in Argentina that, not surprisingly, spread to Uruguay. The economic crisis in the first three years of the new millennium was a key factor in the left's electoral victory.

China and India may have an increasingly important role to play in Uruguay's future. Already the Indian software giant Tata Consultancy Services is guaranteeing jobs to all computer science graduates in Uruguay. Additionally, China's huge demand for food and raw materials is benefiting the Southern Cone, and Uruguay has enjoyed a piece of this export boom.

CONCLUSION

Uruguay has undoubtedly achieved democratic consolidation. The 2009 election was the seventh since democracy was restored. During that period all three major political forces have enjoyed at least one term in the presidential office. Elections are clean and fully contested, and voter fraud is virtually impossible. As we finish the third decade since the 1973–1984 dictatorship, it is clear that the sadly unpleasant rupture of constitutional democracy was an anomaly for Uruguay's proudly democratic political culture and political history.

In March 2010, Jose Mujica, a former Tupamaro guerrilla leader, was inaugurated as president of Uruguay, thus ensuring five more years of rule by the leftist coalition Progressive Encounter–Broad Front (EP-FA). The coalition enjoyed a majority in both houses of the Uruguayan congress. The left did lose, however, four governorships in the departmental elections in May. In the Mujica years the two major issues have been the economy and relations with neighboring countries.

In 2010 Uruguay continued to enjoy near-record economic growth. The economy grew 8.5 percent, as agricultural exports continued to boom and unemployment remained at its lowest levels in a quarter century, having fallen to 6.2 percent. Inflation was within the government target range of 6–8 percent.

In 2011, Uruguay continued to enjoy solid economic growth and international respect for its political stability. GDP was projected to increase by 5.7 percent, inflation was pegged at 6 percent for the year, and, most important, unemployment continued to remain at a historical low. Exports were at record levels. Tourism became the single greatest source of foreign exchange. Politically, two issues dominated. The first occurred in late October when both houses of the Uruguayan parliament passed contentious legislation to nullify the amnesty law that had been in effect since 1987. This law absolved the military for its crimes—especially human rights violations—during its dictatorial rule from 1973 to 1985. The original legislation had been upheld in two national referenda (1989 and 2009). New court cases were expected to begin almost immediately, but everyone anticipated that Uruguay's supreme court would ultimately determine whether the new legislation was constitutional.

The other major conflict erupted in November when the teachers' union and local school boards rejected a national pilot project for educational reform that had been painstakingly negotiated. President Mujica promised to take a firm stand to see that the reform project was implemented. Educational reform is long overdue in a country that, despite significant economic improvement and fiercely middle-class values, finds itself with a very high dropout rate in secondary school, especially among poorer students.

The Uruguayan economy continued to grow in 2012, but at a slower pace than in 2011. GDP grew at a 3.5 percent rate, while inflation ticked up slightly to 8.3 percent. The unemployment rate continued to be low. Exports continued to expand, due principally to the increased price for soy. Uruguay made international headlines over two issues in 2012. In June, President Mujica proposed that the government legalize marijuana and control its distribution in order to cut off revenue to drug dealers. The controversy and international coverage this proposal engendered made it clear that nothing would be decided for a long time. On September 25, Uruguay's house of representatives voted to decriminalize abortion during the first trimester. The senate followed suit in October, and the president indicated he would not veto the legislation. Thus Uruguay became the first country in South America to allow women to have abortions through the first twelve weeks of pregnancy.

Early in September, the Electoral Court confirmed that the requisite number of signatures (10 percent of registered voters) had been obtained to put a referendum on the ballot concurrently with the October 20, 2014, presidential elections that would lower the age of legal responsibility from eighteen to sixteen. This measure was promoted by both traditional parties as a response to the public's displeasure with rising crime rates in Montevideo, especially among juveniles.

Uruguayan-Argentine relations proved thorny in 2012, owing to President Kirchner's desire to prevent capital flight. Restrictions on imports from Uruguay were imposed despite MERCOSUR treaty obligations, and currency restrictions threatened to harm Argentine tourism to Uruguay.

Notes

1. The bulk of this chapter was coauthored with Ronald H. MacDonald. The material from 2001 on is Martin Weinstein's sole responsibility.

2. By comparison, Argentina has been reasonably successful in adjusting its rural exports—balancing cattle and grain exports—as international demand and prices have changed.

3. The discussion in the next several paragraphs is adopted from Martin Weinstein's entries on Uruguay in the 2002–2004 editions of *Britannica Book of the Year*.

4. For a more extensive discussion see Ronald H. McDonald and J. Mark Ruhl, *Political Parties and Elections in Latin America* (Boulder, CO: Westview Press, 1989), 91–110.

Suggestions for Further Reading

Campiglia, Nestor. *Los grupos de presión y el proceso político.* Montevideo: Arca, 1969.

Garcé, Adolfo. *Donde hubo el fuego: el proceso de adaptacion del MLN-Tupamaros a la legalidad y la competencia electoral (1985–2004).* Montevideo: Editorial Fin de Siglo, 2006.

Garcé, Adolfo, and Jaime Jaffe. *La era progresista.* Montevideo: Editorial Fin de Siglo, 2004.

Gillespie, Charles G. "Activists and Floating Voters: The Unheeded Lessons of Uruguay's 1982 Primaries." In *Elections and Democratization in Latin America, 1980–1985,* ed. P. W. Drake and E. Silva. San Diego, CA: Center for Iberian and Latin American Studies, Center for US-Mexican Studies, Institute of the Americas, 1986.

Gonzales, Luis E. *Political Structures and Democracy in Uruguay.* Notre Dame, IN: University of Notre Dame Press, 1991.

Handelman, Howard. "Prelude to Elections: The Military's Legitimacy Crisis and the 1980 Constitutional Plebiscite in Uruguay." In *Elections and Democratization in Latin America, 1980–1985,* ed. P. W. Drake and E. Silva. San Diego, CA: Center for Iberian and Latin American Studies, Center for US-Mexican Studies, Institute of the Americas, 1986.

———. "Uruguay." In *Military Government and the Movement Toward Democracy in South America,* ed. H. Handelman and T. G. Sanders. Bloomington: Indiana University Press, 1981.

Kaufman, Eli. *Uruguay in Transition.* New Brunswick, NJ: Transaction Books, 1978.

McDonald, Ronald H. "Legislative Politics in Uruguay: A Preliminary Analysis." In *Latin American Legislatures: Their Role and Influence,* ed. W. H. Agor. New York: Praeger, 1971.

———. "Redemocratization in Uruguay." In *Liberalization and Redemocratization in Latin America,* ed. G. Lopez and M. Stohl. Westport, CT: Greenwood, 1987.

———. "The Rise of Military Politics in Uruguay." *Inter-American Economic Affairs* 28 (1975): 25–43.

———. "Uruguay." In *Political Parties and Elections in Latin America,* ed. Ronald H. McDonald and J. Mark Ruhl. Boulder, CO: Westview Press, 1989.

Rial, Juan. "The Uruguayan Elections of 1984: A Triumph of the Center." In *Elections and Democratization in Latin America, 1980–1985,* ed. P. W. Drake and E. Silva. San Diego, CA: Center for Iberian and Latin American Studies, Center for US-Mexican Studies, Institute of the Americas, 1986.

Taylor, Philip B. "The Electoral System in Uruguay." *Journal of Politics* 17 (1955): 19–42.

———. "Interests and Institutional Dysfunction in Uruguay." *American Political Science Review* 58 (1963): 62–74.

Weinstein, Martin. *Uruguay: The Politics of Failure.* Westport, CT: Greenwood, 1975.

———. *Uruguay: Democracy at the Crossroads.* Boulder, CO: Westview Press, 1988.

13

PARAGUAY: THE PROBLEMS AND POLITICS OF DEMOCRATIC INSTITUTIONALIZATION

Paul C. Sondrol

The 2008 electoral defeat of the entrenched Colorado Party was a milestone in Paraguay's long trek toward democracy. After sixty-one years, Paraguay transitioned from a hegemonic party system to a multiparty one manifest in the coalition government of President Fernando Lugo. Undeniable positive changes have occurred in Paraguay since the 1989 coup that ended the thirty-five-year dictatorship of Alfredo Stroessner, including widespread acceptance of free elections, enhancement of civil and political rights, and greater press freedoms. Nonetheless, these newer democratic values coexist with remaining authoritarian and praetorian proclivities, rampant corruption, and impunity, all of which often prevail over justice and the rule of law. Democratizing Paraguay suggests many tasks yet undone.

Semitropical Paraguay is bordered by Argentina to the south and west, Bolivia to the north, and Brazil to the east. Slightly smaller than California (157,047 square miles [4,0675 square kilometers]) and located in the heart of South America, Paraguay, with seven million people, is one of the least densely populated countries on earth.

Paraguay, like Uruguay, is a buffer state, historically ensnared between the combined and conflicting ambitions of Argentina and Brazil. The history of Paraguayan foreign relations is one of attempts to maintain sovereignty by counterbalancing the covetous influences of its powerful neighbors. Like Bolivia, Paraguay is landlocked, and this status and remoteness as well as the problems that are a direct consequence of this isolation continue to impact foreign policy.

Paraguayans are the most racially and culturally homogeneous people in Latin America (95 percent of the population is mestizo), thus avoiding the racial/class

BOLIVIA

Fortín Ingaví

Fortín
Madrejón

Villazón

BRAZIL

GRAN CHACO

Fuerte Olimpo

Puerto Guaraní

Puerto Sastre

Mariscal
Estigarribia
Minas-cué

La
Esmeralda

Filadelfia

Puerto Casado

Bella Vista

Pedro Juan Caballero

Río Verde

Horqueta

Concepción

Río Paraguay

Puerto Ybapobó

San Pedro

Río Pilcomayo

Rosario

San Estanislao

Río Bermejo

Villa
Hayes

Asunción

Coacupé

Coronel
Oviedo

Hernandarias

Itaipu

Foz do
Iguaçu

Ciudad
del Este

ARGENTINA

Paraguarí

Villarrica

Caazapá

Boquerón

Corpus

Río Alto Paraná

San Juan
Bautista

Capitán Meza

Pilar
Desmochados

Yacireta

Encarnación

0   25   50   100 Miles

0 25 50   100 Kilometers

Río
Paraná

PARAGUAY

cleavages found in other Hispanic countries. Seventeen kinds of indigenous peoples constitute 3 percent of the population and remain the most marginalized sector of Paraguayan society. Paraguay is one of the few bilingual countries in the Western Hemisphere and the only one where an aboriginal language, Guaraní, is spoken more widely than a European tongue. Governmental affairs and most business matters are conducted in Spanish, but 90 percent of Paraguay's people speak Guaraní. The extremely arid Chaco region, bordering Bolivia, contains about 60 percent of Paraguay's territory but only 3 to 4 percent of the population. Most Paraguayans live east of the Paraguay River on isolated farms or in small villages or towns.

HISTORY AND POLITICAL CULTURE

In the early sixteenth century both Portuguese and Spaniards explored Paraguay, fruitlessly looking for gold. Asunción, the oldest city in the Rio de la Plata basin, was founded in 1537 by the Spanish explorer Juan de Salazar y Espinosa after hostile Indians forced the Spanish to abandon fortifications near present-day Buenos Aires. Asunción became the administrative center of Spanish colonial power over southern South America between 1537 and 1617, but the lack of precious metals and its remoteness soon relegated the town to little more than a fortified trading post and bulwark against the Portuguese in Brazil.

Spaniards in Paraguay quickly found that survival in such a poor, isolated place required independence, and they developed their own ways and resented interference by neglectful Spanish authorities. Overwhelmingly dependent on a subsistence agrarian economy that lacked easy access to markets, the colony lapsed into a stagnant backwater. With the transfer of colonial government to Buenos Aires in 1617, Spanish interest in Paraguay virtually ceased.

Spanish settlers in Paraguay developed a cordial relationship with the native Guaraní. Within a generation Spaniards were incorporated into the Indian lineage system on a kinship basis. The extensive polygamy influenced subsequent cultural developments in colonial Paraguay and produced a different social order than that elsewhere in South America. Acculturation, intermarriage, and racial miscegenation resulted within a few generations in a unique racial culture amalgamated from Spanish and indigenous influences, with few sociocultural distinctions separating rulers from the ruled. Paraguay evolved into a homogeneous, egalitarian society whose citizens claimed a higher degree of internal cultural unity than most other Latin American nations. This early sense of collective identity was a strong point in Paraguay's bid for independence and early nation building.

In 1776 Paraguay was placed under the larger jurisdiction of the newly created Viceroyalty of the Rio de la Plata, seated in Buenos Aires. In 1810 independent Paraguayans refused to give allegiance to Argentine leaders who were declaring independence from Spain. Paraguayans subsequently beat back invading Argentine armies in two decisive battles in early 1811, ending both Spanish and Argentine control over the country.

Nineteenth-Century Politics

Since its independence in 1811 Paraguay has experienced two protracted periods of extreme tyranny (1816–1870 and 1940–1989) sundered by one semidemocratic intermission (1871–1939). The dictatorships of three successive tyrants who ruled Paraguay for almost sixty years following independence are at least partially responsible for a political-cultural environment conducive to authoritarianism and militarism.

The dictatorship of José Gaspar Rodríguez de Francia (1814–1840) set the tyrannical tone. Although he ruthlessly quelled internal dissent, Francia also set Paraguay's finances on a sound basis and constructed a national army. He maintained Paraguayan independence by fending off blockades and border skirmishes from Argentina and Brazil. He further responded to these threats with a policy of isolation and autonomous development, sealing Paraguay's borders and restricting foreign contact. Francia created a socialist state from lands expropriated from his hated aristocratic Spanish and *criollo* enemies. From these lands he built state farms and factories for armaments and ships, while income from the land expropriations and state monopolies on yerba maté provided consistent profit.

Francia further eroded the Spanish colonial base by banning marriages between whites, thus accelerating *mestizaje*, or ethnic mixing and homogenization of the population. Via mass arrests and executions, the Spanish were obliterated as a ruling class in Paraguay. Francia managed to maintain Paraguay in peace and stability while other South American states were paralyzed by civil wars and political chaos in the early postindependence period, but the scope of his police-state control was far more pervasive and penetrative than brutal but chaotic caudillo governments elsewhere.

Francia's successors were the father-and-son dictatorships of Carlos Antonio López (1841–1862) and Francisco Solano López (1862–1870). Carlos Antonio López ended Francia's surreal solitude and reopened Paraguay to international trade and commerce. He established diplomatic relations with numerous countries, including the United States; built the first railroad in South America; and modernized the Paraguayan military. By the time López died in 1862 Paraguay was a regional power in southern South America.

Carlos Antonio's son Francisco Solano López became national dictator in 1862. Fancying himself as a Latin Napoleon, Solano López aimed to forge an alliance with Uruguay to counter the might of Argentina and Brazil in the Plata basin. However, Paraguay's meddling in the realm of these giants plunged the nation into the most savage war in the history of Latin America.

The Triple Alliance War (1865–1870) combined the armies of Argentina, Brazil, and Uruguay against Paraguay, which lost over half its prewar population of 525,000, of which only approximately 28,000 men survived. Paraguay also surrendered 25 percent of its national territory. After five years of slaughter, including the sacking of Asunción and Solano López's death in battle, Paraguay's utter defeat ended the nationalist era of autocratic development.

An extremely repressive brand of tyranny was ingrained into the national consciousness during those formative generations of Paraguay's history, perpetuating a tradition of intolerance to opposition and dissent and exaggerated adulation of strongman rule. But as unbridled as these three early autocrats were, they also brought Paraguay sovereignty, stability, and economic development during the first six decades of national life.

This experience stands in sharp contrast to the petty bosses and would-be democrats who dotted the next sixty years of the so-called Liberal Republic (1876–1936).

This era witnessed the reverberations of military defeat in the Triple Alliance War. The years between 1870 and 1932 saw political confusion, economic collapse, and foreign domination. A new, alien, liberal constitution, limiting the power of the state and expanding individual rights, was established by the occupying Brazilians, as was a provisional government representing neither the history nor the spirit of Paraguayan political culture. Novel notions of citizen participation and self-government lacked resonance in a nation unfamiliar with democracy and reeling from the demise of so many of its people and most of its male leadership. The chronic political instability of the postwar years in Paraguay reflected the jarring impact of one of the greatest military disasters in modern history.

After 1870 a dozen years of anarchy and violence involving various military chieftains precluded any real recovery from the war's devastation. In a climate of assassinations and intrigue, the political agenda of Paraguayan leaders who survived the war was rather basic: rebuild a shattered economy, settle boundary disputes and indemnification questions, get foreign troops off Paraguayan soil, and control the national government. Paraguay's party system began to take shape in 1887, when the political elite divided into two groupings. The Colorados, officially the National Republican Association (Asociación Nacional Republicana, ANR), dominated government between 1876 and 1904 and claimed lineage to the Francia and López dictatorships. The Liberals proclaimed themselves the vanguard of limited government and civil liberties but suffered an antipatriotic stigma via their collaboration with the occupying Brazilians.

Paraguay's traditional multiclass, two-party system is one of the oldest in the world. Yet despite the institutionalized nature of the traditional parties and their extreme partisanship, Colorados and Liberals are both personality-driven patronage machines of political bosses and supporters. For 140 years these parties have played an often violent game over national power and control, not necessarily ideology. Control of the national government means control of the few sources of wealth in an impoverished state such as Paraguay. As a result, the Colorado and Liberal parties remained malicious toward each other over generations.

As neither Colorados nor Liberals had much regard for democratic ideals, the net result after 1870 was a cycle of repression and revolt over decades of instability. Following thirty years of Colorado rule dominated by party founder General Bernardino Caballero, the Liberal "revolution" of 1904 wrested power, ruling for the next three decades in the most unstable era in Paraguayan history. Between 1870 and 1938 Paraguay had thirty-four presidents, two of whom were assassinated and three overthrown.

After 1870 Argentine, Brazilian, and British speculators were the main beneficiaries of Paraguay's bankrupt economy. Foreign capital bought up vast tracts of land sold by Paraguayan governments seeking revenue for the destitute nation. The old state-owned lands of the Franciata and vast tracts owned by the López family were parceled out in the land law sales of 1883 and 1885. By the time sales were curtailed in 1915 90,000 square miles (233,000 square kilometers) of land in Paraguay, comprising fully 35 percent of the area of the country, had been sold to foreigners. Prosperity was nurtured by the land sales, and by 1900 Paraguay finally began to recover from the devastation of the Triple Alliance War, regaining its prewar population of around five hundred thousand people living mainly in rural areas. At the beginning of the twentieth century, however, Paraguay remained a crude, insular, backward economy and polity.

The Twentieth Century

Although prosperity and trade increased in Paraguay after 1900, endemic political instability, notably civil wars in 1904, 1922, and most seriously 1947, hindered sustained economic and political development. By the mid-1920s Paraguay was again threatened from without, this time from the north. Bolivia, deprived of its Pacific coastline from its defeat in the War of the Pacific against Chile (1879–1883), now looked east to find an alternative outlet to the sea. Bolivia capitalized on Paraguay's political instability in the early 1900s in order to build a series of forts in the disputed territory of the Chaco desert, beginning a relentless thrust southward toward the Paraná River, running south through Argentina to the Atlantic. When war came in 1932 Bolivia's German-trained army held every statistical advantage. However, Bolivia sent an army of largely highland Indians into the mud, swamp, and tropical heat of the Chaco lowlands, where they were annihilated in battle against a highly mobilized Paraguayan military, fighting on its own terrain against a foreign aggressor. Over the next two years the Paraguayans won a string of bloody confrontations and were at the steppes of the Andes when a truce was signed in 1935.

The Gran Chaco War heightened social mobilization in Paraguay, generating demands by various classes and economic sectors that the existing Liberal regime could not meet. Standards of living in Paraguay in the mid-1930s were woefully low. Working conditions, especially in the yerba maté plantations, were atrocious, and Paraguay's educational system was the poorest in South America. In the 1930s Asunción remained a somnolent boondocks, largely lacking paved roads, running water, or even electricity in other than a handful of homes and government buildings. On February 17, 1936, a military coup led by war hero Colonel Rafael Franco removed Liberal president Eusebio Ayala. The "Febreristas" were a motley crew of Fascists, Social Democrats, and Marxists who revivified the old images of the Francia and López dictatorships, advocating an authoritarian, corporatist, one-party state modeled on Mussolini's Italy.

With the Febrerista coup of 1936, civilian supremacy in Paraguayan politics ended for the next half century. Another military uprising toppled the Febreristas in August 1937. Chaco War veteran General José F. Estigarribia seized power in 1940 and formally scrapped the 1870 Liberal constitution, replacing it with a new document enshrining presidential dictatorship and a powerful, regulatory state. When Estigarribia died in an airplane crash months after taking power, his successor, General Higinio Morínigo, became military dictator.

Morínigo's regime (1940–1948) was far more repressive than its predecessors. Morínigo outlawed the Liberal Party in 1942 and ruled over an openly pro-Nazi regime as Paraguay became a nest of Nazi intrigue during World War II. The war brought prosperity to Paraguay in response to world demand for agricultural exports, but the defeat of the Axis powers and pressure from the United States prompted Morínigo to liberalize his dictatorship in 1946. When Morínigo tried to reintroduce authoritarian controls in 1947 a military rebellion plunged Paraguay into a bloody, five-month-long civil war. Although 80 percent of the officer corps went over to the rebel side, Morínigo's outgunned forces nevertheless won. It was a Pyrrhic victory, as Morínigo was deposed by the ascendant Colorado Party in early 1948. Now civil service positions in the bureaucracy and promotion within the armed forces were contingent on Colorado Party affiliation. Meanwhile, the military, divided by factions loyal to various officers jockeying for power, revolted and seized control in 1948, three times in 1949, and finally in 1954, when General Alfredo Stroessner carried out his *golpe*.

The Stroessner Regime

Stroessner consolidated his dictatorship, becoming by 1989 the longest-ruling leader in Paraguayan history. Stroessner built his tyranny on the Colorado Party and the military, with himself as caudillo over both institutions. Unlike the more faceless military juntas surrounding Paraguay, Stroessner secured a popular base for his dictatorship, bringing the Colorado Party (the primary instrument of patronage) under his formal control and penetrating society via a national network of party branches and block wards. The Colorados acquired official status, sponsoring Stroessner's eight successive presidential candidacies, building a personality cult for the dictator, and providing a mass base to counterbalance the military. By 1967 Stroessner's dictatorship had immense grassroots support. To the preexisting ultranationalism of the Colorado Party, Stronismo added a demagogic, populist tone as well as a newer, maniacal, anti-Communist national security doctrine.

Along with the Colorados, the armed forces were the other key pillar—and ultimate guarantor—of the regime. A notorious web of corruption developed within the officer corps. Stroessner adroitly appealed to their corporate interests, reorienting their role and mission to one of protecting the regime against Communist insurgency. High military spending and public acclaim by Stroessner added luster to the armed forces. Unlike neighboring military regimes, Stroessner shielded his military from controversy, leaving most repression to the secret police. The Stronato continually utilized the shopworn menace of Communist subversion to move against any sign of independence or militancy among peasants, students, workers, or the church before these challenged the regime. The 1992 discovery of detailed documentation from the regime's intelligence agencies reveals the pervasiveness of regime control over almost all social institutions, belying stereotypes that Stroessner's was simply an old-fashioned, poorly organized autocracy.

By 1988 the dictator's sclerotic detachment from day-to-day decision making, a growing succession crisis, and a worsening economic situation had all served to rot the regime. Paraguayans themselves had also changed. They were a more mobilized, expectant population, no longer overwhelmingly rural and atomized. White-collar professionals chafed at the ongoing centralization of power and corruption. The international context was also different. Paraguay was now surrounded by new democracies in Argentina, Brazil, and Uruguay. Divisions emerged in the once-monolithic Colorado Party, threatening its symbiotic axis with the military. A militant faction remained fanatically devoted to Stroessner as president and ultimately to his son, Colonel Gustavo Stroessner. The traditionalist Colorados argued for a nonpersonalist transition after Stroessner to ensure continued Colorado Party hegemony. A violent coup d'état in early 1989, led by military rebels loyal to traditionalist General Andrés Rodríguez, deposed Stroessner, sending him into exile in Brazil.

PARAGUAY IN TRANSITION

General Rodríguez quickly consolidated power, purging the Colorados and army of high-ranking militants. Rodríguez released political prisoners, relaxed press restrictions, and allowed Paraguayan exiles to return. Snap elections in May 1989, three months following the coup, were won by Rodríguez and the Colorado juggernaut with a lopsided 74 percent of the vote. Rodríguez was inaugurated on May 15, 1989, for a four-year term.

Rodríguez initiated significant political reforms, taking remarkable steps toward rejoining the international community after decades of ostracism and isolation. The new 1992 constitution prohibited party membership for new military officers (but not those already serving). Corruption, integral to Stroessner's kleptocracy and deeply engrained in Paraguayan culture, skyrocketed after 1993, when the country entered a deep recession. Paraguay's enormous black market represents a large sector of the economy, and ranking military officers hold lucrative side interests in narcotics, contraband, prostitution, and money laundering. Rodríguez himself was reportedly involved during his career in parasitic rake-offs and graft.

Colorado divisions continued into 1993 over the party's presidential candidacy. Conservative construction magnate Juan Carlos Wasmosy ultimately prevailed, becoming the first civilian president in almost sixty years, but represented the continued alliance between the military, dominant economic groups, and Colorado politicians that formed the triad of the Stronato. Intimidation against opposition parties and open intervention by the military preceding national elections in May 1993 showed that party/military elites would only accept a Colorado victory.

In the "cleanest dirty" vote in forty-eight years, Wasmosy won the election on May 9, 1993, with 40 percent of the vote, beating Domingo Laíno of the Partido Liberal Radical Auténtico (PLRA or Liberal Party, 32 percent) and Guillermo Caballero Vargas of the new movement Encuentro Nacional (PEN, 23 percent). The failure of both opposition candidates to unite, unseat the ruling Colorados, and initiate a practice of party coparticipation was a historic opportunity lost.

With strong remnants of the military/Colorado alliance remaining, movement from authoritarianism to democracy was problematic in Paraguay. Citizen participation, in the form of strikes and protest marches by peasants, workers, and government employees, became more visible as social groups began to network and organize. Yet regime elites paid only lip service to polyarchy, remaining uncommitted beyond expediency to democracy.

Political crisis erupted in April 1996 when Wasmosy dismissed army commander General Lino Oviedo, who refused to step down. With Oviedo in revolt and threatening to kill the president, Wasmosy was temporarily forced to take refuge in the US embassy. Crucial to ending the crisis without bloodshed was the massive show of support he received from the Clinton administration, the Organization of American States, and Paraguay's trading partners Argentina, Brazil, and Uruguay, in the Common Market of the South (MERCOSUR). The renegade Oviedo was finally forced to resign. Paraguay's shaky electoral system triumphed, but Oviedo's barracks revolt was a dark reminder that ingrained praetorian tendencies do not suddenly disappear with liberalization.

Tension again mounted in September 1997 when the Colorados nominated Oviedo as their party candidate for the 1988 presidential elections, despite internal party opposition and negative reactions in Washington. When Wasmosy ordered Oviedo's arrest on charges of "insulting" the president, the general went into hiding, campaigning as a fugitive.

As Paraguay continued its madcap course to the May 1998 national elections, Oviedo surrendered and was sentenced to ten years in prison for his 1996 coup attempt but continued to campaign from jail, for a time leading in the polls. The MERCOSUR giants Argentina and Brazil again arbitrated Paraguayan politics by threatening the country's membership in the free trade bloc if Oviedo was elected, and the supreme court nullified his candidacy. Oviedo's running mate, Raul Cubas, then became the Colorado Party presidential candidate, and his archenemy, Luis María Argaña, an old Stronista, became the vice presidential nominee. Colorado upheaval was still not enough to help opposition Democratic Alliance (Liberal Party) candidate Domingo Laíno. But by February 1999 Cubas was locked in a power struggle with his vice president and faced impeachment for defying the supreme court and freeing Oviedo from prison as his very first act as president. The Colorado Party now extended its control over national government past a half century.

On March 23, 1999, Vice President Luis María Argaña was assassinated in downtown Asunción. Argaña's faction of the Colorados immediately blamed Cubas and his puppet master, Oviedo. Cubas was impeached by Congress a week later, after Asunción's central square became a battleground in response to Argaña's murder, with rooftop snipers killing six and wounding hundreds as rival blocs battled. Coup rumors swirled in the capital and prodemocracy demonstrations flooded the streets. The ambassadors of Brazil, the United States, and the Vatican met with Cubas, negotiating his resignation in the face of mounting demonstrations. A new Colorado-dominant coalition government, headed by former senate president Luis González Macchi, took power.

The August 2000 vice presidential elections resulted in a narrow, astounding victory for the PLRA—the first time a Liberal had been elected president since 1939 and the first time any opposition candidate had won an executive position via election since before the Colorado Party came to power in 1947. González Macchi's "national unity" administration soon fell apart when the PLRA withdrew from the government. The ruling Colorados remained split between Argañistas and Oviedistas.

The economic picture was equally murky. The government drastically downgraded Paraguay's growth estimates for 2001 from the original 3.5 percent to only 1.5 percent, and the country's fiscal deficit was a record US$257 million. The social deficit was worse. Proclaiming that Paraguay's economic and social crisis had reached extreme limits, the Catholic Church denounced the government's insensitivity and ineffectualness in addressing poverty. Waves of protest marches and highway blockings by peasant associations and trade unions were launched in March against the administration, increasingly seen as incompetent in the face of mounting land invasions by campesinos, a prolonged banking crisis and scandal, a police abduction and torture scandal, fiascos involving privatization of state monopolies and concomitant pressure from the International Monetary Fund, escalating crime (especially kidnappings), and pervasive corruption and cronyism.

In September 2002, the nongovernmental organization Transparency International rated Paraguay as the most corrupt country in Latin America and the third most corrupt in the world. This was no surprise to Paraguayans, 23 percent of whom in an opinion survey responded that the country was being run by the mafia. A 2001 UN study had already underlined "the absence of a culture of legality" in Paraguay.

In February 2003 President González Macchi survived his second impeachment attempt and prepared to wait out his unremarkable term, ending in August. The winner of the April 27 presidential election was no surprise: Nicanor Duarte of the Colorado Party, 14 percent ahead of the PLRA candidate. The Colorados, in power since 1947, seemed impervious to the collapse of the Stroessner dictatorship in 1989.

The new Duarte administration faced heightened expectations and growing demands to respond to Paraguay's social crisis. Colorado governments since 1989 fomented political liberalization but failed to address chronic economic and social concerns, especially corruption, thus displaying little difference from the Stroessner regime. Continuing Stroessner's model, Duarte, despite populist blandishments, supported the interests of large landowners, the business class, and the military in their dealings with peasants, workers, and civil society.

Duarte's presidency further splintered the Colorado Party, engaged in bitter infighting over the party's candidate in 2008. When his efforts to amend the constitution allowing him to seek reelection failed, Duarte's party faction endorsed education minister Blanca Ovelar over his own vice president, Luis Alberto Castiglioni. With the Colorados in civil war and coup-monger Lino Oviedo running under his Unión Nacional de Ciudadanos Eticos (UNACE) banner, the beneficiary was former Roman Catholic bishop Fernando Lugo, head of a disparate coalition of leftist parties termed the Frente Guasú (FG), who won the presidency on April 20, 2008, with nearly 41 percent of the vote compared to 31 percent for Blanca Ovelar. The era of Colorado Party domination in Paraguay was over—for the time being.

POLITICAL GROUPS

The Colorado Party clung to power for sixty-one years and was the official party of the Stroessner regime, only splintering in 1989 over the succession issue rather than any notions of democracy. Infighting among various factions clustering around political bosses led to its electoral defeat in 2008. President Fernando Lugo's coalition government had to deal with the Colorados, the largest party in both houses of congress, to push his legislative proposals.

The Liberal Party (PLRA), out of power since the end of the Chaco War, was illegal from 1942 to 1967. Despite claiming democratic ideals, during their years in power (1904–1936) the Liberals showed themselves to be the same elitist, exclusionary group as the Colorados. In exchange for recognition the Liberal Party provided token opposition during the dictatorship. The PLRA was the largest party in Lugo's Alianza Patriótica para el Cambio (APC) coalition, with competing factions expecting recognition and power after so many decades of repression and marginalization.

The Frente Guasú, a disparate coalition of nineteen leftist political parties and dozens of social movements headed by center-left President Lugo, has splintered because of political infighting. In his first year of office Lugo found it difficult to satisfy the often competing interests of the coalition, resulting in *imobilismo* in addressing Paraguay's staggering array of problems. With nothing concrete to show on campaign promises of land reform, tackling corruption, or renegotiating the terms of the Itaipú treaty with Brazil regarding the giant binational hydroelectric dam on the Paraguayan-Brazilian border, Lugo operated from an ever-weakening position.

Paraguay's two main peasant organizations, the Mesa Co-ordinadora Nacional de Organizaciones Campesinas (National Coordinating Table of Peasant Organizations, MCNOC) and the Federación Nacional Campesina (National Peasant Federation, FNC), pressured the government to improve access to credit, institute land reform, and put an end to official harassment of peasant activists. These groups have become radicalized in recent years, staging sporadic, sometimes violent land invasions, as Brazilian soybean farmers have bought up huge tracks of land in eastern Paraguay. Although production and export of soybeans and soy-related products has boomed over the past few years, the economic benefits have not trickled down to the more than 250,000 families who depend on subsistence farming, maintaining only marginal ties to the larger productive sector of the economy.

The Catholic Church and church-related groups constituted a moral challenge to the Stroessner dictatorship in the face of unbending repression, human rights abuses, corruption, and the extreme concentration of landholdings in the hands of regime elites. Following the 1989 coup a rapprochement developed between the government and the church, with the latter remaining a persistent voice for social justice in the new Paraguay. The clergy also remains the traditional defender of church prerogatives concerning abortion, education policy, and religious orthodoxy. President Lugo's confession of breaking his vow of celibacy and fathering an illegitimate child while still a bishop—along with other paternity suits (including statutory rape) pending—disillusioned Paraguayans and damaged Lugo's claim to morality and transparency in this still-traditional Catholic country.

Organized labor is scrawny in Paraguay. During the Great Depression Paraguayan governments never initiated import substitution industrialization (ISI), instead depending on the country's agricultural exports—mainly cotton, soybeans, tobacco, and yerba maté—for national income. Moreover, Stroessner reasoned that limited industrialization obviated the rise of an industrial working class and unions capable of threatening the regime. Therefore an urban proletariat with class consciousness never developed. Most economic enterprises, located in and around Asunción, are family-owned firms where personal, not professional, patron-client relations prevail. The Stroessner regime curtailed both the size and potential influence of labor by co-optation, repression, Colorado Party penetration of Paraguayan industry, and policies discouraging large enterprises. Fewer than fifty thousand of Paraguay's two million wage earners are confederated, and the small size of the domestic market ameliorates the demand to support a consequential industrialization program.

PUBLIC POLICY

The rise of newer social movements and of a free press publicizing group concerns illustrates both the changes and continuities in Paraguay. Given the durability of an authoritarian and patriarchal political culture, public policies designed to combat gender inequality and discrimination (domestic violence, reproductive rights) were nonexistent until 1992. Modernizing values are reflected in the notable increase in political participation by women and expansion of legal rights via reform of the civil code. As the Colorado Party's candidate for president, Blanca Ovelar is testament to how far women have come in Paraguay. Still, the women's movement remains a largely urban, middle-class affair.

The inequality of land ownership and pressures for landholdings by landless peasants (Paraguay's largest social group) remains another problem area of public policy. Peasants, believing that Stroessner's downfall entitled them to land, began an upsurge in land invasions after 1989. Successive Colorado governments, with strong links to landholding elites, responded with sometimes violent repression, rejecting demands for policies of redistribution and the amelioration of rural poverty. Agrarian reform, promised by Fernando Lugo when he was a candidate, took oblique shape in January 2009 with vague pronouncements about "rural development projects"—but not land distribution. The latter will be extremely difficult without alienating the big soybean producers in eastern Paraguay, primarily Brazilians. Paraguay's high birth rate, producing a population growth rate of 2.36 percent, has led to more landless peasants migrating to ever growing urban shantytowns.

Lugo's coalition government also faced growing demands by state and municipal governments and social movements to respond to the social deficit in health, public housing, and education. Also on Lugo's agenda was judicial reform away from the Colorado-politicized courts as well as reforming the military (merit promotion instead of seniority) and its image as a corrupt, repressive apparatus of the Colorados.

An extremely poor nation such as Paraguay pays a high price for the rampant corruption, sloppy organization, endemic patronage, and stifling inefficiency of its public sector, which absorbs scarce resources, wastes opportunities, and distorts market prices. Paraguay's membership in the MERCOSUR economic integration accord of two hundred million people is viewed, as was the giant binational Itaipú hydroelectric project a generation ago, as a panacea that would generate economic growth, but that growth has bypassed most Paraguayans.

THE INTERNATIONAL ARENA

In international affairs Paraguay negotiates from a weak position. Paraguay's landlocked isolation in the interior of the continent deprives it of strategic importance. Its small population is largely poor and uneducated. The economy is underdeveloped and bereft of important mineral resources. Paraguay possesses little in the way of vital financial, social, or natural attributes needed to give it some heft in international affairs.

Paraguay's history of violent conflict with threatening neighbor states imbues its foreign policy with a determination to maintain friendly relations with them, especially Argentina and Brazil. For a very long time Paraguay was overwhelmingly dependent on Argentina. As late as 1969, all of Paraguay's road, rail, and river links with the outside world passed through Argentine territory. Beginning in the 1950s, the Stroessner regime began to approach Brazil for developmental assistance and to counteract Argentine influences. Brazil built a bridge between the two countries over the Paraná River at the border town of Ciudad del Este that offered an alternative export route with a free trade port at Paranaguá, and it built a highway from Paraguay to the Brazilian coast. The enormous Itaipú project solidified the changed regional axis of power. By 1982 Argentina's share of Paraguayan exports fell to less than half, while Brazil's share rose from nothing to 58 percent.

By the early 1980s increased Brazilian economic penetration into Paraguay began to alarm the Paraguayan nation (as well as Argentina, Brazil's archrival) about the possibility of Paraguay becoming an economic satellite of Brazil. Paraguayans began to complain about Brazilian capital taking over Paraguayan firms and about Brazilian food, goods, and even music replacing Paraguayan products. Increasing immigration by Brazilian landowners into eastern Paraguay (so-called Brasiguayos) and economic domination by big Brazilian soybean-producing farms displacing small Paraguayan farmers added to the resentment.

The bedrock issue of Lugo's presidential campaign was vituperative criticism of and demands for renegotiation of the Itaipú treaty in order for Paraguay to receive more money for exportation of hydroelectric power to Brazil as well as freedom to export to other countries (prohibited by the treaty). Initially, Lugo's nationalist, anti-Brazilian rhetoric only hardened the administration of President Lula da Silva against any renegotiation. However, by 2011 Lugo had negotiated an agreement that tripled the price Brazil paid to Paraguay. It was one of his few successes in office.

Since World War II foreign relations between the United States and Paraguay have been conditioned by mutual interests involving national security, trade, and investment. After using economic and military aid to buy Paraguay's alignment with the United States against the Nazis in 1944, the United States continued to use leverage over Paraguay during the Cold War. In return for generous amounts of economic and military aid and political legitimacy, General Stroessner became a staunch defender of America's anti-Communist foreign policy, breaking diplomatic relations with Castro's Cuba, outlawing the Communist Party, and voting slavishly with the United States in the OAS and the UN.

Paraguayan-US relations during the Stroessner regime were cordial and reliable in the 1950s and 1960s but became more troubled over democracy and human rights issues from 1976 to the end of the regime in 1989. Relations deteriorated rapidly during the Carter administration, which announced it would no longer ignore human rights violations in Paraguay. With Ronald Reagan's election in 1980, expected improvement in bilateral relations did not materialize, as human rights policy had become an essential component of US foreign policy.

Rodríguez's political liberalization considerably improved US-Paraguayan relations after 1989. High-level US governmental and military officials visited Asunción, praising the positive changes in government and increasing US economic and technical assistance. The administration of George H. W. Bush pressured Paraguay to create an antidrug agency in Asunción, but Paraguay's fight against drug trafficking deteriorated as General Lino Oviedo's power increased and Paraguay verged on anarchy. The United States played an important role in defending democracy and helped to resolve the crisis. The culture of corruption in Paraguay hinders progress in antidrug operations. Paraguay partners with the United States in initiatives to combat money laundering, intellectual property rights, and counterterrorism. The United States is particularly concerned about terrorist financing by the influx of Arab-dominated mafiosi at the triple border where Paraguay, Argentina, and Brazil meet.

Paraguay's relations with Europe continue to expand. Contacts with France, Germany, Great Britain, Italy, and Spain focus on trade, technical assistance, and cultural exchange. After Argentina, Brazil, and the United States, Western European nations are the largest importers of Paraguayan goods, such as tobacco and tannin. Paraguayan contacts with Asia are also growing. Relations with Japan are of long standing, and Paraguay is increasing contact with China. Paraguayan-African relations are minimal except with South Africa and Egypt. Because of their shared pariah status, Stroessner's Paraguay and apartheid South Africa developed strong bilateral relations beginning in the 1970s. Aside from Egypt, Paraguay has little contact with the rest of the Arab world.

Regarding international organizations, by virtue of its last-minute declaration of war against the Axis powers in World War II, Paraguay was entitled to sign the Declaration of the United Nations, becoming a charter member. But Paraguay's small size and relative unimportance in international affairs work against much influence in the UN. In the Organization of American States Paraguay's status as a less-developed country has obtained it special trade and aid concessions, but all in all, Paraguay plays a minor role in hemispheric politics.

THE CONSOLIDATION OF DEMOCRACY

Until the defeat of the Colorado Party in 2008, Paraguay was a semiauthoritarian regime in which the Colorados claimed a commitment to democracy while attempting to perpetuate themselves in power indefinitely. Paraguay was neither a full-blown dictatorship nor fully democratic, instead displaying characteristics of each. It was a hybrid regime in that generally free elections were held and democratic institutions were in operation, but elections did not transfer substantive political power, and institutions operated weakly, providing the Colorados with a more elaborate and believable democratic disguise. If the Colorados had had their way, the system would have continued forever.

Lugo's election profoundly changed all that. For the first time in three generations an opposition defeated the entrenched Colorado Party, moving Paraguay along in its lengthy process of democratization. As President Lugo found, Paraguay today is a potpourri of upstart students, haranguing newspaper editors, and militant peasants in which *políticos* must wheel and deal in a more open political environment. However, Paraguay also remains praetorian with its continual involvement of the military in politics.

THE EFFECTS OF GLOBALIZATION

Post-Stroessner Colorado governments proved responsive to the advice of the US Agency for International Development, the World Bank, the International Monetary

Fund, and other external forces advocating more market-oriented policies (financing decisions conditioned, of course, on the government's economic policies). Following the 1989 coup President Rodríguez's technocratic economists privatized some money-draining public sector boondoggles, reduced government spending, simplified the tax code, eliminated controls on interest rates and foreign exchange transactions, and, portending participation in MERCOSUR, relaxed tariffs and other trade barriers. In recent years, Paraguay has also made steps toward greater fiscal transparency. The government also eliminated most tax exemptions.

But trade liberalization has hurt small and medium-sized domestic manufacturers of shoes, furniture, textiles, and clothing, forcing many to close. Despite Paraguay's submitting to neoliberal policies and enmeshing itself in the world economy, internal economic conditions continue to plague the middle and lower classes. The unemployment rate in 2011 was officially 7.9 percent but is considered by most experts to be much higher. Nevertheless, Paraguay in 2013 is in an economic boom from good harvests and high exports of corn and soybeans, despite the fact that 30 percent of the population remains mired in poverty. With a GDP per capita of US$4,000, Paraguay remains the second-poorest country in South America. The persistence of grinding poverty, gross inequality, and joblessness suggests that, twenty years on, the effects of the Washington Consensus's neoliberal economic policies on millions of Paraguayans are far less positive than promised.

This was the backdrop to Fernando Lugo's troubled presidency. Although his election signaled a shift away from neoliberal economic policies and a move toward introducing some redistributive and welfare policies, he had little concrete to show for it. Lugo's defeat of the interminable Colorado Party showed the progress of democratization in Paraguay, but the stability of the system remains threatened by gross socioeconomic inequities, weak political institutions, popular discontent, corruption, drug traffic, and lingering praetorian impulses that, with a few unexpected twists and turns, could result in political turmoil.

Lugo was impeached by congress in May 2012 for "poor performance of his duties," a result of his lack of progress in land reform, national security policy, and corruption, and also because he signed the Ushuaia II democracy clause of MERCOSUR without consulting congress. This clause was cited by the MERCOSUR countries that saw the sudden ouster of Lugo as a breach of democracy, outraging citizens and politicos alike, who argued that the suspension was a violation of Paraguay's sovereignty. By August, Lugo's vice president, Frederico Franco, said he was confident of Paraguay's readmission to MERCOSUR providing that democracy was fully functioning for the forthcoming presidential election in April 2013.

On February 2, 2013, presidential candidate Lino Oviedo died in a helicopter crash after a campaign rally. A retired general, Oviedo had been one of the most notorious and divisive political actors in Paraguay ever since his participation in the 1989 coup that ousted Stroessner. He was the personalist strongman of the Unión Nacional de Ciudadanos Éticos (UNACE), the party he founded in 2000 when he broke from the Colorado Party, and his death shocked the nation, even though he was lagging in the polls, placing him well behind the Colorado front-runner for the April election, banking and tobacco millionaire Horacio Cartes.

On April 21, 2013, Cartes won the presidency by a solid 46 percent of the vote against 37 percent for his strongest rival, Liberal Party candidate Efraín Alegre, returning the presidency to the Colorado Party, which had held such a tight grip on power for sixty years, until 2008. Unlike former president Fernando Lugo, business-friendly Cartes will be supported by a Colorado-dominated congress.

Institutionalization means that erratic, amorphous politics evolves into more stable and continuing political activity directed through established political institutions such as political parties, bureaucracies, courts, and legislatures via well established rules, pragmatism, bargaining, and conciliation. In this regard, Paraguay remains in the trial-and-error stage of democratic development.

Suggestions for Further Reading

Kelly, Phillip, and Thomas Wigham. "Democracy in Bolivia and Paraguay." In *Assessing Democracy in Latin America*, ed. Philip Kelly. Boulder, CO: Westview Press, 1998.

Lambert, Peter. "A Decade of Electoral Democracy: Continuity, Change and Crisis in Paraguay." *Bulletin of Latin American Research* 19 (2000): 379–396.

Lambert, Peter, and Andrew Nickson, eds. *The Transition to Democracy in Paraguay*. New York: St. Martin's Press, 1997.

Lewis, Paul H. *Political Parties and Generations in Paraguay's Liberal Era, 1869–1940*. Chapel Hill: University of North Carolina Press, 1993.

Mora, Frank O. "From Dictatorship to Democracy: The U.S. and Regime Change in Paraguay, 1954–1994." *Bulletin of Latin American Research* 17, no. 1 (1997): 59–79.

Sondrol, Paul. "Paraguay: A Semi-Authoritarian Regime?" *Armed Forces and Society* 34, no. 1 (2007): 46–66.

Zagorski, Paul W. "Democratic Breakdown in Paraguay and Venezuela: The Shape of Things to Come for Latin America?" *Armed Forces and Society* 30, no. 1 (2003): 87–116.

14

BOLIVIA: FROM NEOLIBERAL DEMOCRACY TO MULTIETHNIC, PLEBISCITARIAN POLITICS

Fabrice Lehoucq

INTRODUCTION

By the mid-1990s, appearances suggested that Bolivia had changed. Four presidents had come to power in competitive, multiparty elections. A decade earlier, there had been a transition to an elected government—that of Hernán Siles Suazo (1982–1985)—after decades of dictatorship and military coups. Bolivia, in fact, holds the distinction of being the most unstable country in Latin America, having experienced nineteen coups during the twentieth century.[1] And in 1952 Bolivia underwent a social revolution, prompted by the military's failure to recognize Víctor Paz's victory in the 1951 elections. In the ensuing years, the National Revolutionary Movement (MNR) and radicalized mineworkers spearheaded a revolution that enfranchised all adults and legalized the radical redistribution of rural property led by peasant unions.

Just as foreign observers noted the apparent change in political style, Bolivian politics began to revert to form. By the late 1990s, the number and intensity of street protests escalated as social movements and remnants of the country's left marched against the neoliberal consensus of established parties. They demanded the end of water privatization policies, the end of the US-sponsored war on Chapare-based coca growers, jobs, and a share of the proceeds from the country's growing gas exports. In 2003 and 2005, the groups—those opposed to the established parties—overthrew two presidencies, those of Gonzalo Sánchez de Lozada (2002–2003) and

BOLIVIA

Carlos Mesa (2003–2005). They also adroitly used the street and the ballot box to force changes in public policy, ones that had the state reassert its control over energy exports.

But the instability did not last. Multiparty, neoliberal democracy instead gave way to a new political order. In December 2005, 54 percent of the electorate voted for Evo Morales, the undisputed leader of the street protests and candidate of the Movement Toward Socialism (MAS). In early 2006, President Morales "nationalized" the administration of gas and oil deposits by nullifying existing contracts giving foreign companies ownership of such deposits (though not confiscating technology such as pipelines) and re-creating the state's energy corporation. By January 2009, MAS had succeeded in outflanking its rivals and held a referendum in which voters overwhelmingly approved its draft of a new constitution. This document sought to reverse centuries of ethnic discrimination and to promote nationalist and socialist policies. It has created a popular political order, one that allows MAS, in its capacity as the country's dominant party, to deactivate checks and balances on its exercise of political power.

GEOGRAPHY AND SOCIAL GROUPS

Bolivia's nine departments span the Andes mountain ranges in the west, the Amazon rain forest in the east, and the dry, sparsely populated, lowland Chaco region in the south. The lack of navigable rivers and the difficulty and expense of building highways and railroads across dramatic changes in elevation have impeded the country's economic and political integration. Bolivia's geography and climatic extremes presented barriers to European settlement, resulting in a small population for a large territory. Approximately ten million Bolivians (2011 estimate) are spread throughout a territory of 424,000 square miles (1.1 million square kilometers).

Bolivians belong to one of three social groups. The vast majority of Bolivians are descendants of the small number of indigenous peoples who survived the conquest. The 2001 population census indicated that thirty-three different native American languages are spoken, although 95 percent of the people who speak a language other than Spanish are either Aymará or Quechua. Until the late twentieth century, most indigenous peoples lived in rural areas. Being a peasant, in fact, has been synonymous with being Indian. Bolivians who speak a pre-Columbian language have been targets of discrimination and, until 1952, could not vote in national elections. The second group of Bolivians is of European descent, and because of their education and wealth they have monopolized positions of power. The third group consists of people of mixed ancestry or those belonging to a native American ethnic group that, for economic reasons, learned Spanish and adopted European customs. With time, *cholos* or mestizos gradually grew in number.

Ethnic identity is complex and fluid in Bolivia. The 2001 population census indicated that approximately half of Bolivians spoke a non-European language and that 63 percent identified themselves as members of an indigenous group. The 2008 AmericasBarometer survey found that the latter figure had risen to three-fourths of survey respondents.[2] This survey, however, suggests that 68 percent of adults also call themselves mestizos, 21.4 percent identify as indigenous or "original" peoples, and 8.2 percent identify as white. Depending on how questions about ethnicity are asked, Bolivians identify in different ways, suggesting that they have multiple identities.

INTEREST GROUPS

The Confederation of Private Entrepreneurs of Bolivia (CEPB) is the oldest business organization in the country. It includes importers, exporters, and firms producing for the domestic market. In recent years the CEPB has weakened; businesses in Santa Cruz no longer participate in the national confederation, and many of those businesses have diversified away from producing for the limited domestic market that was protected until trade liberalization in the mid-1980s. Since the 1980s, Santa Cruz–based businesses have invested in export of soybeans and grains. In the eastern lowland departments of Beni, Pando, Santa Cruz, and Tarija, businesses have gravitated to civic committees based in each of the cities to press for infrastructure improvements, fuel subsidies, and other policies. They have also used the civic committees to lobby the departmental and national governments to distribute royalties from mineral production in the departments where such resources are located.

The Bolivian Workers Central (COB) and the Confederation of Teachers of Bolivia (CMB) are two important labor groups, but the decline of employment in the formal sector has deprived both of membership. Gone are the days when mineworkers employed in state companies, which were privatized in 1985, helped to seat and unseat governments.

Since the late 1990s, social movements have become the dominant interest groups of Bolivian politics. In the Chapare, a tropical region in the Department of Cochabamba, coca growers organized powerful federations that not only raised taxes and provided, at their height, forty-five thousand coca-growing families with basic services but also battled the army in a US-financed war to eradicate the area's coca fields. It is widely recognized that coca grown in the Chapare is destined for the illegal trade in cocaine. By contrast, US government estimates suggest that the 30,000 hectares (74,000 acres) of coca in Los Yungas, a region outside of La Paz, are for domestic consumption; native Americans have chewed coca leaves, which have a mild stimulating effect, for centuries. President Morales remains the head of the coca federation and deploys its members in protest marches around the country. Political mobilization gradually ended the central government's eradication campaigns, and in 2008 the Morales administration expelled both the US Drug Enforcement Administration and the US ambassador from the country. As a result, there has been an expansion of coca-growing lands and the illegal trafficking of coca for cocaine production.[3]

Both highland and especially lowland indigenous peoples have organizations to mobilize on their behalf. The landless people's movement has occupied unused lands since the late 1990s. Neighborhood associations in the cities of Cochabamba and El Alto spawned a plethora of organized groups. In the case of El Alto, a city on the outskirts of La Paz that is located at 14,000 feet (6,100 meters) above sea level and filled with rural migrants, the groups organized to undo the privatization of their water resources in the late 1990s.

Social movements have become the vanguard of revolutionary change. Their power derives from leading protest marches, organizing blockades of highways, and threatening to topple elected governments. By occupying a handful of roads, protesters from El Alto can strangle access to La Paz, where the elected branches of government sit.[4] This is a peculiar piece of the country's political geography that empowers the social movements. The protesters also have support in the MAS congressional delegation and throughout the state apparatus.

POLITICAL PARTIES AND ELECTIONS

Since the 1952 revolution, three different party systems have existed in Bolivia. The first postrevolutionary party system was between 1952 and 1966, during which MNR tried to consolidate a one-party system by incorporating peasants, mineworkers, and leftists. MNR's bid for hegemony came to an end when Generals Alfredo Ovando and René Barrientos overthrew Víctor Paz's second government in 1964. Until the early 1980s, military dictatorships outlawed MNR and other leftist parties. After twenty-two years of military governments and fraud-tainted and/or inconclusive elections, Hernán Siles, of the left-wing United Democratic and Popular Unity (UDP) coalition, became president in 1982. The second party system existed between 1982 and 2002; this was the multiparty system known for its stability and its commitment to market-friendly policies. Since 2003, MAS has dominated a new party system.

Neoliberalism and Multiparty Politics

When Víctor Paz became president for the third and final time in 1985, inflation in Bolivia was more than 4,000 percent. The government had a fiscal deficit of 23.4 percent of GDP and the country had given up paying interest on its foreign debt. The collapse of Bolivia's tin-led export economy, along with the inability to forge stable governing coalitions, had forced Siles to cut his presidential term short by one year (October 1982–August 1985). If the revolution stood for nationalizing the means of production, establishing universal franchise rights, and radical agrarian reform, President Paz's final term in office initiated a series of reforms that would make Bolivia one of the model countries for neoliberal reform in the developing world.

Radical macroeconomic stabilization or shock therapy, advised by none other than economist Jeffrey Sachs, did eradicate inflation. First-generation reforms were followed by a wave of wide-ranging structural reforms during the presidencies of Jaime Paz (1989–1993) and Sánchez de Lozada (1993–1997). Under Jaime Paz, the government granted the central bank formal autonomy, reformed public administration, and began the privatization of small state-owned enterprises. In a concession to widespread support for nationalized industries, Sánchez de Lozada's administration did not privatize state corporations in petroleum and gas, the railroads, air transport, or any of the other areas that the Bolivian state had come to control. Instead, it created an innovative program whereby a private sector buyer would purchase a controlling share of a state company (originally Sánchez de Lozada's government had proposed that investors be granted 49 percent, but objections by bidding companies led to the change). Private pension funds would then become responsible for the remaining portion of the capitalized firm's stock, and they would end up paying dividends in the form of an annual pension (the Bonosol) to elderly Bolivians. His administration also obtained legislative support for ambitious social goals, including a bilingual education system; the creation of more than 310 municipalities, which would receive 20 percent of central state revenues; and administrative decentralization.[5]

The transformation of Bolivian politics not only made structural reform possible but also raised hopes that political instability was a thing of the past. Both left and right in the country's multiparty system agreed to abide by election results. When a congressional coalition between the rightist Democratic Action Party (ADN) and the Revolutionary Left Movement (MIR) made the latter's candidate, Jaime Paz, president in 1989 even though he came in third in the balloting, neither the MNR nor its candidate, Sánchez de Lozada (who came in first place), organized street protests or encouraged military factions to overthrow the government. The depth of the economic crisis and dependence on multilateral financial institutions had led to a convergence around market-friendly policies and liberal democratic institutions.

Two features of the political and party system made it possible to stabilize politics and to support structural reform. First, electoral laws reduced temptations to defect from the new policy equilibrium. The 1967 Bolivian constitution empowered congress to select the president should no candidate obtain an absolute majority of the popular vote. Equally important was the fused ballot system, which forced voters to cast ballots for the presidential and legislative candidates of the same party. Straight-ticket voting secured seemingly predictable shares of the vote, resulting in a stable number of parties (averaging 3.92 between 1985 and 2002). The balloting provisions also contributed to cooperative executive-legislative relations. The same congressional coalition of parties that elected a president also obtained seats in his cabinet, whose control of ministerial portfolios was contingent upon a complex bargain that allowed strong-minded and wily presidents to produce legislative majorities for their bills. To avoid getting locked out of the cabinet and a share of the spoils, parties learned to support the newfound policy consensus.

The Rise and Fall of Multiparty Politics

Several factors undermined the political foundations of the liberal policy consensus. First, the shift to a mixed member proportional (MMP) system from a closed-list proportional representation system in 1994 expanded voters' choices and thus fueled a market for antiestablishment parties. With the change to a German-style system, voters could select a representative in one of sixty single-member plurality districts (SMPDs) and still use fused ballots to select another sixty deputies in multiple-member proportional representation districts. First used in 1997, the MMP system allowed SMPD candidates to bypass the leadership of existing parties and appeal directly to voters. Morales's initial foray into electoral politics came from winning one of these seats, with the largest majority of any deputy in the 1997 elections.

Second, social movements throughout the country began to revive a nationalist and antiestablishment discourse by the late 1990s. As MAS began to organize, it built bridges between existing organizations to assemble a broader movement with revolutionary ambitions. MAS and its allies incorporated their specific demands into a common platform that targeted *neoliberalismo,* a catchall term of scorn that blamed fifteen years of economic and social reform for all of the country's economic and social ills.

Surveys indicate that a constituency exists for radical politics in Bolivia. AmericasBarometer's first, nationally representative poll of Bolivians in 1998 revealed that only slightly more than 10 percent of survey respondents were both highly supportive of the political system and highly tolerant of the political rights of individuals who make negative comments about the Bolivian system of government. Nearly half of those polled had low levels of both system support and political tolerance. This biennial poll revealed that these percentages barely changed between 1998 and 2006.[6]

Three structural conditions turned many Bolivians against the liberal policy consensus. First, macroeconomic facts did not help the established parties make their case before a skeptical electorate. Though inflation was low and social indicators were gradually improving, the Bolivian economy was growing very slowly. The country's per capita GDP had grown at an average annual rate of 0.6 percent between 1952 and 1982, and extensive structural reform since then had not done much to accelerate that anemic growth rate. Between 1985 and 2000, the economy only grew in per capita terms an average of 0.9 percent per year.[7]

The next structural condition, second-stage liberal reforms, had not overcome long-term political weaknesses. Daniel Kaufmann of the World Bank's Worldwide Governance Indicators project and two colleagues used sophisticated econometrics to understand the institutional roots of this tepid growth.[8] Their surveys of firms and of Bolivian public officials showed that cronyism, corruption, and general disregard for the rule of law reduced the profitability of companies and the transparency and effectiveness of the public sector. While there were pockets of excellence in the private and public sectors, firms had to be large and politically well connected to benefit from being part of the formal economy (and thus pay taxes). So even when inflation was low and the exchange rate was stable, a weak state did little to lift the country's growth rate and was not very successful at eliciting cooperation from society to pay taxes, stop purchasing contraband goods, and refrain from toppling governments.

Third, poverty and ethnic discrimination combined to turn many Bolivians against the state. Unimpressive growth rates meant that most Bolivians lived in poverty. Between 1990 and 2006, an average of 67.8 and 59.3 percent of Bolivians of the western and eastern lowlands, respectively, lived in poverty. Between 1990 and 2002, infant mortality rates had fallen from 109 to a still-high 77 per thousand live births, demonstrating that social conditions, at best, were only improving slowly. The AmericasBarometer showed that poor Bolivians were also more likely to be targets of ethnic prejudice: In the 2008 survey, 31 percent of Bolivians reported being discriminated against in the previous year, by the far the highest rate in the Western Hemisphere.[9] Respondents also indicated that government offices and public places were the two sites where they were most likely to be treated offensively.

Changing commodity markets created a golden political opportunity for social movements to appeal to a national-level audience. As the price of gas and oil began to climb with the start of the new millennium, foreign energy companies began to cash in on several years of investment that a liberalized energy policy regime had encouraged. By 2000, international energy markets realized that Bolivia had proven gas reserves second only to Venezuela's in South America. Since Bolivia has no coastline, the gas would have to be exported through another country; while Chile was the obvious choice, the absence of diplomatic relations between the two countries (stemming from Bolivia's loss to Chile in the 1879–1883 War of the Pacific) meant that gas exports would have to be routed through Argentina and Brazil. This issue stoked nationalist sensibilities, and increasingly larger numbers of Bolivians believed that the terms provided to foreign energy companies (under contracts made when the price for gas was low, a point often forgotten in domestic debates) were overly generous and depriving them of their rightful share of resource rents.[10]

Social protest began to escalate by the late 1990s. While there was an average of thirteen protest events per month during Sánchez de Lozada's first presidency (1993–1997), social movements organized an average of twenty-eight protest events per month during the second presidency of ADN's Hugo Banzer (1997–2002, though Vice President Jorge Quiroga became president after Banzer resigned for health reasons in 2001).[11] For the social movements, marches and blockades were a way to speak truth to power and part of a more general struggle to rid the country of neoliberalismo. For MAS's critics, these tactics revealed MAS's double-edged commitment to democracy. While participating in elections and taking seats in congress and on municipal councils, MAS was also forcing extraconstitutional changes in government and attempting to spark another social revolution.[12]

By October 2003, marches demanding the nationalization of gas deposits and the resignation of President Sánchez de Lozada turned violent, and the army killed more than fifty protesters. The government split on how to react to yet another regime crisis. Vice President Carlos Mesa, a popular television anchorman and published author, counseled negotiations, while Sánchez de Lozada holed up in a bunker known as the war room. Once the military, police, and congress abandoned the president, he resigned his post and turned power over to Mesa.

Bereft of congressional support, Mesa relied upon his high popularity ratings to achieve passage of constitutional amendments that would establish referendums. The first such referendum was held in 2003 and revealed that more than 90 percent of the voters wanted to renegotiate international energy contracts.[13] Street protests demanded that energy contracts be nationalized, which led legislators to hike taxes and royalties on gas companies. Despite efforts to find a middle ground, Mesa proved no more capable of navigating the daily marches and frequent blockades than his predecessor. Protest events soared, reaching an average of forty-nine per month during Mesa's presidency. In early June 2005 Mesa finally turned power over to Eduardo Rodríguez, chief justice of the supreme court. Even though the constitution mandated that the president of the senate, Hormondo Vaca Diez, assume the presidency upon the president's resignation, the social movements vetoed Vaca Diez's succession to that office.[14]

The December 2005 election of Evo Morales was the definitive end of the market-friendly multiparty system. Leftist and nationalist protest movements had managed to convert a plethora of local and regionally based sectoral movements into a political project that obtained the support of slightly more than half of all Bolivian voters. Former president Quiroga (2001–2002), representing a coalition of establishment parties known as the Democratic and Social Power Party (Podemos), obtained just 28.6 percent of the vote. The ability to appeal to voters from a variety of ethnic and class backgrounds indicated that MAS had outgrown its social movement and indigenous origins and had become a credible, national-level political force that appealed to an increasingly leftist electorate, one that was strongly in favor of asserting more sovereignty over the country's recently discovered gas reserves.[15]

Hegemonic Party Politics

The election of Morales to the presidency produced a new party system, one in which MAS is hegemonic. The December 2005 election gave the party 55 percent of the seats in the lower house of congress; it also gave it a plurality just two seats shy of controlling the twenty-seven-member senate. This was the closest thing to a unified party government that Bolivia had seen since the one-party governments of the immediate postrevolutionary period. The effective number of parties in the lower house of the legislature fell to 2.33 in 2005 from 4.76 in the 2002. The ideological pivot of the party system, as a result, moved substantially to the nationalist left.

In the constituent assembly elections of early July 2006, MAS came close to duplicating its performance in the general elections. It won 50.9 percent of the vote, which allowed it to obtain 137 of the assembly seats (53.7 percent), most of which were awarded to the plurality winner in three-member constituencies.[16] It could count upon the support of another dozen or so deputies, but still remained short of controlling a two-thirds majority in the assembly.

In an accompanying referendum, most citizens voted against granting more autonomy to the country's nine departments. However, the measure won overwhelming support in the eastern departments of Beni, Pando, Santa Cruz, and Tarija, where between 1990 and 2006 an average of 34.3 percent of the population resided and where 45.7 percent of the GDP was generated. Much of the country's (legal) agricultural exports are produced in the eastern lowlands. Most important, 80 percent of proven gas reserves are located in Tarija.[17]

A seven-month-long procedural struggle about the assembly's internal rules of order revealed not only the depth of distrust between MAS and its critics but also MAS's inability to decide whether to compromise or to overwhelm the opposition. The existing constitution stated that two-thirds of congressional members present during any session could convene a constituent assembly. The March 2006 law echoed the key phrase, that two-thirds of assembly members needed to approve a draft constitution. But in late November, after several months of arduous negotiations with Podemos, MAS managed to replace the two-thirds requirement in the assembly's internal rules manual with a requirement of merely an absolute majority, doing so in a midnight session and without the presence of opposition delegates. Opposition boycotts paralyzed assembly deliberations, held in Sucre (the country's capital), because a quorum could not be achieved. Opposition parties also organized hunger strikes and boycotted congressional deliberations in La Paz. In negotiations led by Vice President Álvaro García, MAS agreed to reinstate the two-thirds requirement in mid-February 2007.

In early August 2007 convention delegates agreed to postpone their deliberations so that the national congress (based in La Paz) could issue a new law granting assembly delegates a six-month extension on their work. Arguments about rules of order delayed substantive work on a new constitution, and the early August deadline was missed. MAS supporters concluded that the opposition's procedural objections meant that it was just stalling for time, reaffirming their belief that the opposition was little more than a creature of Santa Cruz–based oligarchic interests. For its part, the opposition interpreted the lack of progress on substantive questions as evidence that MAS was not interested in negotiation but rather wanted to impose a new constitutional order on the country. In exchange for accepting that an absolute majority of national voters (and not in each of the departments) would be sufficient to approve the draft constitution, the opposition got MAS to consent to holding two separate referendums on the assembly-approved draft constitution. While the first referendum would let voters decide, through majority vote, on measures that delegates could not agree on, the second would submit the final draft of the constitution (containing both the results of the first referendum and the convention-agreed articles) to the voters for final approval.

Disputes between MAS and its opponents deepened as the new deadline for drafting a constitution approached. Antigovernment groups, especially from the eastern departments, began to organize strikes and search for ways to become more autonomous of the central government. Demonstrations in Sucre became violent (ultimately resulting in two deaths and hundreds of injuries) as locals confronted MAS supporters over whether the executive and legislative branches of government should be moved from La Paz, where they had been relocated in 1898, back to Sucre, the de jure capital of Bolivia. Against this backdrop, MAS swiftly approved its preferred draft by availing itself of a procedure outlined in the August law extending assembly deliberations. The first article of this law stated that if the assembly could not achieve a two-thirds majority on controversial issues, it could submit such matters to congress, which could then, with a two-thirds vote, ask voters to settle them in a referendum. In assembly meetings that MAS had rescheduled in the city of Oruro in early December, pro-government delegates alleged that they had failed to reach consensus on one such issue, concerning whether the maximum size of agricultural properties should be 5,000 or 10,000 hectares. As a reporter for the daily *La Razón* confirmed in conversations with MAS delegates, this was a ruse to promulgate the MAS-preferred draft without having to satisfy the two-thirds requirement, for it was inconceivable that sessions filled with MAS delegates would split on this or any measure.[18]

The MAS-dominated assembly's vote created a constitutional controversy of enormous proportions. Under normal circumstances, the opposition would have appealed to the constitutional tribunal, created in 1994, to settle this conflict. But by late August 2007 the MAS-dominated lower house of congress had, in a stormy session, voted to begin impeachment trials against four of the five remaining magistrates on the tribunal because earlier that year they had ruled against Morales's use of a supreme (i.e., unilateral) decree to fill four vacancies on the supreme court while the congress was in recess. In response, these magistrates resigned, leaving the tribunal without a quorum. While an absolute majority of deputies was sufficient to suspend tribunal magistrates, only a two-thirds majority could approve their replacements.

Efforts to bridge the divide between MAS and the increasingly regionally based opposition proved fruitless. The early December 2007 congressional decision to reduce the share of gas and petroleum royalties received by departments only complicated these efforts. Even while reaffirming its commitment to "dialogue" with the prefects of the departments, Vice President Álvaro García Linera refused to reconsider the government's decisions. In late February, while progovernment protestors encircled the neoclassical legislative palace in La Paz and threatened opposition deputies, the MAS majority in the lower house of congress violated parliamentary procedures—and its agreement with the opposition—by approving bills to submit their party's draft constitution and one of its articles (fixing the maximum size of agricultural estates at 10,000 hectares) to the voters for their approval.

In response to this failure to honor agreements governing the production of a new constitution, between early April and late June 2008 the electorates of the opposition-dominated eastern lowlands approved several autonomy-seeking statutes that directly contradicted MAS's constitutional project and even the existing constitution on several key points. Santa Cruz's autonomy statute, for example, would make its legislative assembly and its governor (formerly prefect) responsible for administering national resources, education, citizen security, and tax collection. In the absence of a constitutional tribunal to arbitrate differences between the national and departmental government (and, by implication, the constitutionality of MAS's behavior), regional politicians implied, the eastern departments could increase their power and authority.

The opposition's effort to expand its autonomy put the national government on the defensive as it attempted to demonstrate the opposition's irrelevance in political competition. In early May 2008, Podemos senators unexpectedly joined forces with MAS to approve an (unconstitutional) recall referendum for the president and prefects (in December 2007 President Morales had submitted such a bill to break the logjam in the assembly, one that both he and opposition prefects gradually lost interest in enacting). The president rushed back to La Paz from Santa Cruz once he learned of the news. After midnight consultations with his advisors in early May 2008, the president accepted the challenge in what remains a perplexing series of events, one that illustrates the opposition's failure to unify even around a common strategic stance.

Even though the opposition won the August 2008 vote in the eastern lowlands, President Morales garnered more than two-thirds of the national vote—67.4 percent—in his own recall election. None of the opposition prefects did as well in their departments; two of them, José Luis of La Paz and Manfred Reyes of Cochabamba, lost their recall elections. The extent of the government's support demonstrated that it could indeed claim to speak on behalf of the overwhelming majority of Bolivians.

The government quickly acted upon its victory. When opposition prefects called for a strike to stop Congress from passing a law to hold a referendum on the draft constitution itself, the government sent the security forces to take over petroleum installations once opposition hard-liners cut off gas exports to Argentina. It arrested and (illegally) jailed the opposition prefect of Pando, Leopoldo Fernández, after a number of progovernment protestors were shot in an exchange of gunfire between MAS supporters and anti-MAS forces on departmental territory. After a series of high-level negotiations between government and opposition leaders, enough antigovernment legislators joined with government supporters to (illegally) amend the December 2007 draft constitution (illegally) promulgated by the constituent assembly.

The New Constitutional Order

In late January 2009, with 90 percent of registered voters turning out, 61.43 percent of voters approved the new constitution. It expands the state's control over the economy and promotes the rights of indigenous peoples and social movements. In the hands of a well-disciplined party, it promises to endow the executive with the ability to marginalize the opposition. In the absence of a dominant party, it threatens to fragment the state: the constitution divides power not only between the three branches of government and an array of semiautonomous institutions and oversight bodies, but also between the central, departmental, municipal, and autonomous indigenous communities.

The new constitution drops the legislative runoff system for selecting the chief executive. It opts for a modified Costa Rican approach to elect the president, one that would award the office to the candidate who both receives the most votes and receives at least 40 percent of the vote (and at least 10 percent more than the first runner-up). If that condition cannot be satisfied, there is a runoff between the top two candidates. The constitution creates a bicameral plurinational legislative assembly. Seventy of the 130 members of the lower house are elected in single-member districts. Another fifty-three are elected in multimember districts that award seats through proportional representation and whose ballots are headed by each party's presidential candidates. A final seven are elected in single-member districts reserved for indigenous peoples. The citizens of each department elect four senators through proportional representation. The president and legislators have five-year terms and can be consecutively reelected only once.

Having promulgated a new constitution, Bolivians returned to the polls to select leaders for a plethora of national and regional posts. In December 2009 Bolivians turned out to cast ballots in new, almost anticlimactic presidential and legislative elections. Both Evo Morales and Álvaro García Linera (the vice president) obtained 64 percent of the vote, beating their nearest rival, Manfred Reyes Villa, who won 26 percent of the vote. MAS also swept legislative races, winning almost three-fourths (96 of 130) of the lower house's seats and about the same proportion (26 of 36) of senate seats. In April 2010 the MAS did equally well in regional and municipal elections. In each of the country's nine departments, the MAS won popularly elected governorships and racked up comfortable majorities in newly created departmental assemblies.

The new constitution also calls upon citizens to select the magistrates on the supreme tribunal of justice, the plurinational constitutional court, the judicial council, and the agricultural court. Candidates for these fifty-six high judicial posts each received the endorsement of a two-thirds majority in the plurinational legislature, as stipulated by the new constitution. Each then ran in elections held in mid-October 2011, which did not allow for partisan affiliations or campaigning of any kind. But while 79.6 percent of voters turned out, only 42.1 percent of the total number of ballots cast were valid; the rest were invalid or blank.[19] MAS claims that these procedures will ensure the selection of only honest and impartial judges; its critics counter that this system is tailor-made to guarantee that only progovernment judges will be elected to the bench and thus not contest the majority's policies. The assembly has promised to amend conventional Bolivian laws so that the customary laws of many indigenous communities will have equal footing.

The new constitution also empowers both social movements and territorial interests to shape the design and implementation of central state policies. It stipulates the appointment of representatives of the social movements to oversee the institutions of "horizontal accountability" (a rough equivalent of checks and balance), including the National Electoral Court (CNE), the comptroller's office, and the central bank. While the president and the assembly select the governing boards of these institutions, "the sovereign people, by means of organized civil society," to quote the new constitution, "will participate in the design of public policies." For MAS, these oversight bodies and institutional fragmentation maximize the ability of its constituents to protect their interests, even should they lose their control of the two elected branches of government.

CONCLUSION

In less than a decade, MAS has built a new political system. It overthrew presidents in 2003 and 2004, decapitated the judiciary, curtailed regional autonomy, and marginalized the opposition in the national congress and constituent assembly—actions that have been ratified in successive referendums. MAS and its allies have erected a plebiscitarian regime privileging the relationship between the people and MAS, as mediated by Evo Morales.

Is the new political order democratic? It is undeniably popular, even if it was forged by using the power of the streets to subvert the previous constitutional order. No other party comes close to duplicating its levels of electoral support, even if the opposition complains that MAS uses public expenditures and public broadcasting for partisan advantage. There is no institution of horizontal accountability that it does not dominate. Moreover, key leaders of the regionally based opposition have been retired, exiled, or even jailed. In September 2010 President Morales announced that he would not rule out the possibility of seeking reelection in 2014, despite having promised in October 2008, in order to expedite legislative endorsement of MAS's draft constitution, not to run for reelection. In late April 2013 the refurbished constitutional court ruled that the constitutional ban on a third presidential term did not apply to Morales because his first term had occurred under the previous constitution, despite the fact that the 2009 charter contains a transitory clause saying the opposite. It is these facts that in 2012 allowed Bolivia to approach its precrisis (2003) rating on the Bertelsmann Foundation's Democratic Status Index (ranking it at the 60th percentile of the developing world's political systems); MAS's new political order, in other words, is approximating the status achieved by its predecessor.[20]

Like the 1952 revolution, MAS has created a one-party regime, one that will surely outlive its predecessor, which ended with the 1964 military coup and resulted in nearly two decades of instability. Unlike the 1952 revolution, MAS has consolidated a revolutionary project in the midst of a gas-induced export boom that has seen the value of the country's commodity exports increase by more than 150 percent between 2003 and 2010. GDP per capita has grown by an average annual rate of 2.9 percent during this period, which means economic growth during MAS's tenure in office has been three times the rate experienced during the neoliberal era. As a result, the poverty rate fell from 63.9 percent in 2004 to 42.4 percent in 2011, and the Gini coefficient of income inequality declined from 0.561 to 0.508 between 2004 and 2009.[21] Unprecedented growth has allowed MAS to reap the political benefits of noteworthy economic and social improvements. For the foreseeable future, MAS will remain in control of the Bolivian political system.

Notes

1. Fabrice Lehoucq and Aníbal Pérez-Liñán, "Breaking Out of the Coup Trap: Political Competition and Military Coups in Latin America," *Comparative Political Studies*, published online May 29, 2013, doi 10.1177/0010414013488561.

2. Daniel E. Moreno Morales et al., "The Political Culture of Democracy in Bolivia: The Impact of Governance," report prepared for the US Agency for International Development, La Paz, Bolivia, August 2008, xxx–xxxiii.

3. Eduardo A. Gamarra, "Bolivia: Evo Morales and Democracy," in *Constructing Democratic Governance in Latin America*, 3rd ed., ed. Jorge I. Domínguez and Michael Shifter (Baltimore: Johns Hopkins University Press, 2008), 141–147.

4. Before 2009 La Paz was the seat of the executive and legislative branches of the Bolivian government, and the judicial branch was in Sucre. But although the 2009 constitution states that Sucre is the capital, the president and the congress still operate in La Paz.

5. Useful overviews include Merilee S. Grindle, "Shadowing the Past? Policy Reform in Bolivia, 1985–2002," in *Proclaiming Revolution: Bolivia in Comparative Perspective,* ed. Merilee S. Grindle and Pilar Domingo (Cambridge, MA: DRCLAS, Harvard University, 2003), and Benjamin Kohl and Linda Farthing, *Impasse in Bolivia: Neoliberal Hegemony and Popular Resistance* (London: Zed Books, 2006).

6. Mitchell A. Seligson, "The Political Culture of Democracy in Bolivia: 1998," report prepared for the US Agency for International Development, La Paz, Bolivia, 1998, 90. The sample size is three thousand, with a margin of error of plus or minus 1.7 percent. Reports of subsequent poll results are available at http://sitemason.vanderbilt.edu/files/bVmbzq/The%20Political%20Culture%20of%20Democracy%20in%20Bolivia%201998.pdf.

7. "World Population, GDP and Per Capita GDP, 1-2003 AD," in J. Bolt and J. L. van Zanden, "The First Update of the Maddison Project; Re-Estimating Growth Before 1820," Maddison Project Working Paper 4 (2013), www.ggdc.net/maddison, accessed March 25, 2007.

8. Daniel Kaufmann, Massimo Mastruzzi, and Diego Zavaleta, "Sustained Macroeconomic Reforms, Tepid Growth: A Governance Puzzle in Bolivia?" in *In Search of Prosperity: Analytic Narratives on Economic Growth,* ed. Dani Rodrik (Princeton, NJ: Princeton University Press, 2003), 334–398.

9. Poverty figures are from Luis Carlos Jemio M., Fernando Candia C., and José Luis Evia V., "Reforms and Counter-Reforms in Bolivia," Research Network Working Paper, Research Department, Inter-American Development Bank, 2009. Infant mortality data are from Kohl and Farthing, *Impasse in Bolivia,* 197. Discrimination data are from Daniel E. Moreno Morales, "Los escenarios de la discriminación en Bolivia," *Nueva Crónica y Buen Gobierno* 27 (24 October–6 November 2008): 17.

10. Kurt Weyland, "The Rise of Latin America's Two Lefts: Insights from Rentier State Theory," *Comparative Politics* 41 (2009): 145–164.

11. Roberto Laserna and Miguel Villarroel, *38 años de conflictos sociales en Bolivia: descripción general y por periodos gubernamentales* (Cochabamba: CERES, COSUDE, and Instituto para la Democracia, 2008).

12. Álvaro García Linera, a former guerrilla and the current vice president, has written extensively about these movements. See García Linera et al., *Tiempos de rebelión* (La Paz: Muela del Diablo Editores, 2001) and García Linera et al., *Memorias de Octubre* (La Paz: Muela del Diablo Editores, 2004).

13. Anita Breuer, "The Problematic Relation Between Direct Democracy and Accountability in Latin America: Evidence from the Bolivian Case," *Bulletin of Latin American Research* 27 (2008): 1–23.

14. An insider's account of these months is Carlos D. Mesa Gisbert, *Presidencia sitiada: Memorias de mi gobierno* (La Paz: Editorial Plural, 2008), 51–116. A detailed chronology is Ricardo Sanjinés Ávila, *De la UDP al MAS* (La Paz: Hans Seidel Stiftung, 2006), 277–328.

15. Raúl Madrid, "The Rise of Ethno-Populism in Latin America: The Bolivian Case," *World Politics* 60 (April 2008): 484–486. Also see Salvador Romero Ballivián, *El tablero reordenado: análisis de la elección presidencial de 2005* (La Paz: Corte Nacional Electoral, 2006).

16. The plurality winner got two of the three seats in the three-member constituencies. Voters also cast ballots for an additional forty-five seats in nine departmental constituencies; the plurality winner received the first two seats in each five-member district. The subsequent runners-up would each receive one of the remaining three seats. See Ley No. 3364 (March 6, 2006, in *Compendio Electoral* (La Paz: CNE, 2007), 285–296.

17. George Gray-Molina, *La economía más allá del gas* (La Paz: PNUD, 2005), 155. The figures cited in the previous sentence are from Jemio, Candia, and Evia, "Reforms and Counter-Reforms in Bolivia."

18. "El oficialismo apruebe su CPE y la enviará a 2 referéndums," *La Razón* (La Paz), December 10, 2007. This article notes that 164 delegates—six fewer than the two-thirds required—were present during this session. I have been unable to confirm this with the assembly's records because its website has been down since late December 2007.

19. Amanda Driscoll and Michael J. Nelson, "The 2011 Judicial Elections in Bolivia," *Electoral Studies* 31 (2012): 628–632.

20. Bertelsmann Stiftung, Transformation Index, *BTI Scores, 2003–12*, www.bti-project.org/index, accessed April 28, 2013. Also see the essays in Tanja Ernst and Stefan Schmalz, eds., *El primer gobierno de Evo Morales: un balance retrospective* (La Paz: Editorial Plural, 2012).

21. Data on commodity export prices are from Ricardo Molero Simarro and María José Paz Antolín, "Development Strategy of the MAS in Bolivia: Characterization and an Early Assessment," *Development and Change* 43 (2012): 543. The other data stem from Comisión Económica para América Latina, *Anuario Estadístico 2012* (Santiago de Chile: CEPAL, 2013), 65, 70, 78, and this agency's *Panorama Social de América Latina 2013* (Santiago de Chile: CEPAL, 2012), anexo estadístico, cuadro 14.

Suggestions for Further Reading

Grindle, Merilee, and Pilar Domingo, eds. *Proclaiming Revolution: Bolivia in Comparative Perspective.* Cambridge, MA: Institute of Latin American Studies and David Rockefeller Center for Latin American Studies, Harvard University, 2003.

Klein, Herbert S. *A Concise History of Bolivia.* Cambridge: Cambridge University Press, 2003.

Kohl, Benjamin H., and Linda C. Farthing. *Impasse in Bolivia: Neoliberal Hegemony and Popular Resistance.* London: Zed Books, 2006.

Lazar, Sian. *El Alto, Rebel City: Self and Citizenship in Andean Bolivia*. Durham, NC: Duke University Press, 2008).

Moreno Morales, Daniel E., et al. *The Political Culture of Democracy in Bolivia: The Impact of Governance*. Report prepared for the US Agency for International Development, La Paz, Bolivia, August 2008. Available at http://sitemason.vanderbilt.edu/files/f8dPEI/Bolivia_2008_V3_English_final__doc.pdf.

Silva, Eduardo. *Challenging Neoliberalism in Latin America*. Cambridge: Cambridge University Press, 2009.

15

ECUADOR: FROM CRISIS
TO LEFT TURN

Jennifer N. Collins

INTRODUCTION

In February 2013, Ecuador's incumbent president, Rafael Correa, one of Latin America's "new left" leaders, was reelected for a third term. His party also swept legislative elections, winning more than two-thirds of the seats in the unicameral national assembly. Correa appears to have turned the page on more than two decades of political and economic instability in this small Andean nation and has made Ecuador a protagonist in the region's new left community.

For much of the twentieth century Ecuador was a seemingly sleepy country in which the dramatic winds of change that buffeted other countries arrived as faint gusts. However, by the end of the century new social forces had emerged and political struggle intensified, drawing more attention to this diverse and strikingly beautiful country. Of greatest significance have been two developments: the emergence of the indigenous movement as a national actor, and the country's entrance into the "pink tide" (the wave of elections of leftist presidents) with Correa's 2006 election and the implementation of his Citizens' Revolution.

Possessing significant oil reserves as well as a historically stratified society, Ecuador has struggled to develop economically and to modernize politically. The entrenched power of elites and long-ingrained traditions of racism and discrimination have meant that the struggles for inclusion and justice of those at the bottom of society—poor and nonwhite peoples, including indigenous peoples, Afro-Ecuadorians, and mestizos—have been long and difficult. However, in the three decades since the

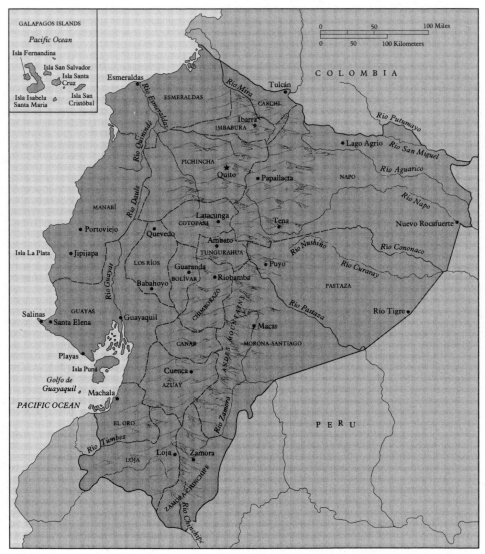

ECUADOR

country's democratic transition, cultural patterns of racism and elitism have been challenged, and formal politics, long the domain of white elites, have opened up and become increasingly inclusive as indigenous and other popular movements have organized and won some measure of political power.

Significantly, these dramatic social and political changes have occurred largely nonviolently. Taking a path different from that of its closest neighbors, Colombia and Peru, both of which have been plagued by guerrilla insurgencies and state violence, Ecuador has avoided large-scale internal violence. As a result, civil society and social movements have had greater freedom to organize and participate in the democratic process.

Ecuador offers an opportunity to examine politics in a developing country where struggles for citizenship rights and political inclusion by indigenous people and Afro-Ecuadorians have evidenced important successes, but where the goal of integral economic development capable of lifting all people out of poverty has yet to be realized. The contradictory and complex Citizens' Revolution showcases competing visions on the left for how to pursue this goal in the twenty-first century.

LAND, PEOPLE, AND ECONOMY

Ecuador takes its name from its location straddling the equator on the northern Pacific coast of South America. It is one of the smaller countries on the continent (roughly the size of Nevada), but it is the most densely populated, with a population of over fifteen million. Its diverse geography includes a coastal plain, a mountainous interior known as the Highlands, a flat jungle area to the east that forms part of the Amazon basin, and the Galápagos Islands, which lie approximately 600 miles (965 km) due west in the Pacific Ocean. Historically most Ecuadorians resided in the Highlands, but the growth of export agriculture and commerce on the coast led to demographic shifts, so today the coastal and Highlands populations are roughly equal. Ecuador's largest urban area is the port city Guayaquil.

Like its topography, Ecuador's population is diverse, having developed from three main groups: sizable indigenous populations, people of European ancestry, and a small population of African-descended people whose ancestors were brought over as slaves. Today, according to the most recent census of 2010, 70 percent of Ecuadorians self-identify as mestizos or people of mixed race, 7 percent as indigenous, another 7 percent as Afro-Ecuadorian, 7.4 percent as Montubios (a coastal culture), and 6.1 percent as white. While Ecuador's indigenous population appears small compared to that of Bolivia or Guatemala, the 7 percent figure belies the importance of issues relating to their place in the nation both historically and contemporaneously. By the end of the twentieth century Ecuador's indigenous movement had emerged as the country's most important social movement and as a leader among a wave of such movements regionally and globally. What seems clear is that while many Ecuadorians may have indigenous ancestry, sociodemographic change, economic development, migration, education, and expanding job opportunities are transforming indigenous reality and perhaps eroding indigenous identity.

Ecuador is a major oil exporter and a member of the Organization of Petroleum Exporting Countries (OPEC). In addition to being the world's top banana producer, it also exports flowers, shrimp, and cacao; tourism is another important sector. It is a middle-income country with a Human Development Index ranking in 2012 of 89, thus putting it in the category of high human development.

HISTORICAL BACKGROUND:
ELITE DOMINATION AND DEPENDENCE

During the colonial period the Real Audiencia de Quito, which comprised much of present-day Ecuador, was something of a backwater. It was not a source of gold or silver for the crown; instead its resource base lay in agriculture. The Highlands indigenous population became subject to forced labor on the landed estates (*haciendas*) and textile mills owned by the colonial elite. Thus, class and ethnicity were conjoined early in Ecuador's history, leaving a legacy of racism and discrimination that plagues the country to this day.

Gaining independence in 1822, Ecuador joined the ill-fated Gran Colombia Confederation. By 1830 the confederation collapsed and Ecuador began its life as an independent republic. Postindependence politics were marked by two features that had lasting effects on the country's political development: elite domination and elite fragmentation. Like most Latin American countries, the new republic was dominated by an elite minority, a propertied upper class uninterested in promoting a broad-based democratization of the political system. In Ecuador, however, the elite were divided by geography and had contending economic interests. In the highlands and around the capital city of Quito, large landowners lorded over traditional haciendas, exploiting Indian laborers who, in exchange for the right to farm a small subsistence plot, were subjected to working conditions reminiscent of medieval feudalism. Allied with the Roman Catholic Church, these landed oligarchs eventually formed the Conservative Party to defend their interests. On the coast, maritime commerce and tropical export agriculture produced a different, more entrepreneurial upper class. The coastal elite, interested in free trade and secularization, became the bedrock of the Liberal Party.

The nineteenth century witnessed violent conflicts between the two parties as they vied to control government. Conservatives ruled with an iron fist until the Liberal Revolution of 1895. Liberal caudillo Eloy Alfaro served as president for eleven years and brought important modernizing reforms to the country, including reducing the power of the Catholic Church, instituting the separation of church and state, and building the Trans-Andean railroad to connect the coast and the Highlands. He also established the first public high schools and universities. But ultimately Alfaro proved too liberal for his own party and was ousted from power. He met an ignominious death after he was jailed for trying to foment an antigovernment insurrection and then snatched from prison and lynched by an angry mob in 1912. Alfaro has been embraced by President Correa, who characterizes the Citizens' Revolution as the continuation of Alfaro's legacy.

The cacao boom in the early twentieth century brought wealth and social change to Guayaquil as new middle and working classes emerged. But economic prosperity and social differentiation did not do much to change elite attitudes: democratization was still of little interest to the Highlands landholders, who depended on controlling the indigenous labor force, or the cacao barons of the coast, who were determined to keep their political power intact. In 1922, when hundreds of workers were killed by police during Guayaquil's first general strike, Ecuador's incipient labor movement got its first taste of how far elites were willing to go to retain control.

When the export boom turned into a bust as worldwide prices for cacao declined and plant disease wreaked havoc, the economy unraveled and in 1925 young military officers seized power from the Liberals, who had accrued debt and failed to invest at home. Although the July Revolution failed to dismantle the power of traditional elites, it did succeed in establishing a state bureaucracy capable of governing with some autonomy from oligarchic interests. Moreover, it set an important precedent for the military itself. Rather than becoming a reactionary and oppressive force in public life, the armed forces identified themselves with reform and never resorted to the kind of brutal repression later practiced by militaries elsewhere in the region. It was the military junta of 1963–1966 that issued the country's first agrarian reform law, and the next military government (1972–1976) declared a Nationalist Revolution aimed at modernizing the economy, increasing the role of the state in economic development, and redistributing wealth through agrarian and labor reforms. However, as was often the case with would-be reformers in Ecuador, the nationalist generals proved unable or unwilling to take the steps needed to neutralize elite opposition, and as a result, the reforms were comparatively timid. By the end of the 1970s, facing increasing economic problems and public pressure to relinquish power, the military retreated peacefully from politics, handing over power to civilians in a negotiated transition in 1979.

Throughout the twentieth century Ecuador's elite demonstrated a remarkable capacity to regroup and reassert its political power when challenged by new leaders or movements. The career of Ecuador's foremost populist leader, José María Velasco Ibarra, offers a case in point. At various points during his long career Velasco attracted the support of elite-run parties when they found it expedient to ally with him. Velasco galvanized middle- and working-class audiences with his moralizing appeals and antioligarchic rhetoric: "Give me a balcony, and I will rule Ecuador," Velasco famously said. He did just that, albeit incompetently. Elected to the presidency five times, Velasco served only one complete term. The military removed him from office for his dismal public administration, not because he enacted policies that benefited the lower classes in any significant way. Without a strong party apparatus or roots in trade unionism, Velasco's personality-driven populism did nothing to undo the underlying dynamics of elite domination.

Ecuador's leftist parties never commanded a base sufficient to constitute an electoral threat. Nor was there a Cuban-inspired guerrilla insurgency in the style of those that appeared in other countries during the 1960s and 1970s. In short, though elites battled each other bitterly at times for the spoils of power, they also united periodically to make sure that would-be reformers or revolutionaries were co-opted or contained.

SOCIAL CHANGE AND THE RISE OF CIVIL SOCIETY

Given the weakness of nationalist, populist, and leftist challenges to elite rule, Ecuadorian society experienced evolutionary rather than revolutionary change, but change it has. The key factors propelling social change include agrarian reform, the oil boom of the 1970s, and urbanization.

While modest, the agrarian reforms that were carried out in 1964 and 1973 served to dismantle the feudalistic hacienda system on the Highlands estates, freeing up labor, prompting internal migration, and ultimately empowering indigenous communities. Greater access to land and eventually education, as well as the weakening of the historical tripartite power structure of the landowning families, the church, and the state, all contributed to the growth of autonomous indigenous organizing that would eventually culminate in the formation of the Confederation of Indigenous Nationalities of Ecuador (CONAIE) in 1986.

The discovery in 1972 of massive oil reserves in the Amazon transformed Ecuador into a petrostate—a nation in which public finances were extremely dependent on this single mineral export. During the 1970s, military governments used windfall profits from the oil sector to underwrite consumer spending and private sector expansion through policies that offered subsidies, cheap credit, and an overvalued exchange rate. Like other oil-producing countries, Ecuador fell victim to the "resource curse," which means that although the abundant natural resource generated extraordinary revenues, the boom failed to serve as a springboard to equilibrated and sustained economic growth. Instead, it invited corruption and wasteful spending in both the public and private sectors while fueling expectations of expanded consumption.

The oil boom helped to spur urbanization. Ecuador went from being a predominantly rural society—71 percent of the population lived in the countryside in 1950—to an urban one, where today 67 percent of Ecuadorians reside in cities. Oil also rapidly accelerated the integration of the vast Amazonian basin region into the nation. As part of the agrarian reform programs of the 1960s and 1970s, military governments opened up vast tracts of land in the Amazon to landless peasants in the Highlands, thus initiating a process of migration that continues today.

Ecuadorian civil society is quite vibrant, with a variety of social movements and civil society organizations representing an array of social sectors, including indigenous nationalities, students, neighborhood associations, labor unions, business associations, private media, women, environmentalists, and human rights activists, among others. Recent studies, however, indicate that membership in civil society groups has declined since a peak in the 1990s.

PARTIES AND ELECTORAL POLITICS: FROM PERPETUAL CRISIS TO ASCENDANCY OF THE ALIANZA PAIS

Ecuador achieved universal suffrage for the first time in 1979. While women had been granted the right to vote in 1929, literacy requirements disenfranchised the poor, particularly indigenous peoples and Afro-Ecuadorians. As late as 1968 the electorate was estimated to be as small as 15 percent of the population. In the decade after the 1978 constitution finally removed the old barriers, the size of the electorate doubled. However, most parties had shallow roots in society and instead relied on the popularity of their leader, as well as clientelism, to connect to voters. Ongoing economic austerity and crisis in the 1980s and 1990s made it difficult for incumbent parties to cement strong ties to those who elected them. Ecuador became a country noted for its high incidence of electoral volatility—voter preferences for parties swung, often dramatically, from one election to the next.

Ecuador has a presidential system and uses proportional representation to elect the unicameral legislature. The proportional electoral system produced a fragmented party system, which meant that every president previous to Correa came into office without a stable legislative majority. Complicating matters even further, parties were notoriously weak in terms of party discipline. Presidents often resorted to under-the-table payments or offers of political posts in order to win enough support for their legislative agendas. Rocky executive-legislative relations made it difficult to pass reforms and contributed to the public's perception of the political system as corrupt and inefficient.

During the 1980s and 1990s the major challenge faced by all governments was managing the troubled economy. Despite the country's oil wealth, military governments had borrowed freely from international lenders during the 1970s. When international interest rates shot up in 1980s and commodity prices plummeted, Ecuador was ensnared in the debt trap. In order to avoid defaulting, Ecuadorian presidents accepted International Monetary Fund (IMF) offers of new loans, and in exchange promised to apply austerity and neoliberal restructuring, including privatization, deregulation, and opening up to foreign investment. However, when they tried to implement these reforms they came up against stiff resistance from the public and even the business community. Comparatively, Ecuador was one of the region's shallowest reformers in areas such as deficit reduction and privatization.[1] Nonetheless, the episodic application of stabilization packages evoked the ire of labor unions and social movements, and fed public dissatisfaction with and mistrust of the political class. By the close of the 1990s, an estimated 63 percent of the population was living below the poverty line, and stagnant economic growth had given way to negative growth.[2]

Contentious Politics and Political Crisis

Between 1997 and 2005 public dissatisfaction with politics as usual and conflicts inside the political class turned Ecuador into the leader of a continentwide syndrome that political scientist Arturo Valenzuela dubbed "presidencies interrupted."[3] Within a ten-year period the country had seven different presidents, three of whom were forced to leave office before completing their terms.

The phenomenon began with Abdalá Bucaram (1996–1997), the founder and leader of the populist Roldosist Party (PRE). Known for his raucous campaign rallies in which he sang and danced to popular Ecuadorian music and vociferated against the "oligarchs," Bucaram promised to soak the rich and enact sweeping social assistance programs. However, once in office the faltering economy gave him little room to make good on his promises. Instead he resorted to a familiar recipe of reducing consumption subsidies and increasing taxes along with a convertibility plan aimed at curbing inflation by tying the value of Ecuador's currency to the US dollar. Bucaram's call for austerity and patience fell flat as accusations of corruption piled up, implicating the president and his family in schemes ranging from graft in the customs bureau to malfeasance in the handling of charitable donations.

By early 1997 a wide array of social sectors began to demand his resignation, including CONAIE and the Coordinator of Social Movements (CMS), but also business groups, the major opposition parties, and much of the private media. As thousands of protestors took to the streets in February 1997, opponents in congress looked for a way to remove Bucaram. Lacking the two-thirds majority necessary for impeachment, congressional deputies declared the president to be "mentally incapacitated." Without military backing, Bucaram had little choice but to flee the presidential palace and seek political asylum.

Bucaram's unceremonious removal from office set a precedent for resolving government crisis, although in a way that deviated from the rules prescribed in the constitution. The next elected president succumbed to a similar dynamic. Not long after taking office in 1998 Jamil Mahuad was faced with a massive banking crisis. Earlier in the decade, following neoliberal precepts, Ecuador's financial sector had been liberalized and deregulated. With scant and ineffective government oversight, Ecuadorian banks had engaged in risky, irresponsible, and corrupt practices, which ultimately led to the implosion of the whole sector. As major banks began to fail, Mahuad used government monies to bail them out, eventually spending somewhere between US$1.2 billion and $1.6 billion in the failed effort. This massive public bailout of the private banks, which involved printing huge quantities of money, quickly resulted in skyrocketing inflation, runs on the banks, and eventually the collapse of the currency—in other words, a full-blown economic crisis. As the banking crisis intensified, the government took the drastic step of freezing depositors' accounts. At first meant to be a stopgap measure, the freeze was kept in place for a year. As depositors were denied access to their savings, many bankers succeeded in escaping with their personal fortunes intact. The revelation that the owner of one of the major banks involved in the crisis had contributed over US$3 million to Mahuad's electoral campaign confirmed the public's sense that Mahuad had sold out the country to save the skin of the wealthy and corrupt bankers. Public support for the president plummeted to barely 7 percent.

The crisis took a devastating toll on the economy and ordinary citizens' pocketbooks: the economy contracted by 7–8 percent, unemployment nearly doubled, and poverty rates soared. Led largely by the CONAIE, social movements protested government austerity measures throughout 1999. In a last-ditch effort to stabilize the economy, Mahuad announced at the end of the year that he would adopt the US dollar as the country's official currency. The highly controversial dollarization decree triggered a new round of protests in January 2000. CONAIE leaders organized a march in Quito and supporters stormed the congress. Supported by dissident junior military officers, the protestors declared the formation of a new "government of national salvation." However, facing strong opposition from the US government and the rest of the military establishment, the new government lasted less than twenty-four hours. Nonetheless, the demonstrations were sufficient to force Mahuad's resignation; he was succeeded by Vice President Gustavo Noboa, who kept the controversial dollarization decree in place.

Colonel Lucio Gutiérrez, the leader of the rebellious officers, launched a bid for the presidency in 2003. He turned to the social movements with which he had joined forces to oust Mahuad, forming an electoral alliance with Pachakutik (PK), a political party founded in 1996 by the country's most important social movements, including CONAIE and CMS. Today Pachakutik is most closely associated with the indigenous movement and is often referred to as CONAIE's "political wing."

Gutiérrez won the election as the crusading anticorruption candidate of the left. Yet his left turn was short-lived. In a familiar sequence of events, Gutiérrez acquiesced to IMF pressures for debt repayments and public spending cuts. After CONAIE and PK withdrew their support, Gutiérrez struck political deals with right-wing parties, eventually making a devil's bargain with Bucaram's PRE. Facing accusations of corruption and the possibility of impeachment, Gutiérrez allowed the PRE to pack the court with new judges, who promptly cleared their leader, former president Abdalá Bucaram, of all criminal charges, thus paving the way for his triumphant return from exile. An unrepentant Bucaram arrived in Guayaquil in April 2005 pledging to run again for the presidency.

Bucaram's return unleashed mass demonstrations in Quito. This time CONAIE, CMS, and labor groups were not at the forefront of the protests; instead, it was students, housewives, businesspeople, and middle-class professionals who staged vigils and marches with an angry demand aimed at President Gutiérrez and the political class: "¡Que se vayan todos!" (throw them all out). Gutiérrez attempted to discredit the protestors by labeling them as *forajidos,* or "outlaws," but the protestors quickly appropriated this appellation and their revolt became known as the outlaw rebellion. When repeated attempts to quell the demonstrations failed, Gutiérrez too fled into exile.

As the 2006 presidential election approached, Ecuadorians were fed up with politicians and their crisis-prone political system. Public opinion polls showed that citizens had virtually no confidence in congress, political parties, or the government at large. Moreover, the poorly performing economy had torn families apart: an estimated three million Ecuadorians had left the country to seek work in the United States or Europe.

Correa and the Citizens' Revolution

Rafael Correa campaigned as a political outsider. Born to a modest middle-class family in Guayaquil, he earned scholarships that eventually led to a doctorate in economics from the University of Illinois and a professional career as a university professor in Quito. His only major stint in public service came after Gutiérrez's fall, when President Alfredo Palacio tapped him as finance minister. His tough stance toward foreign investors and the IMF helped establish his credentials as a fresh new leader on the left. Yet Correa had no formal ties to any party and no history of involvement with the social movements that had led the antineoliberal struggles of the 1990s. A devout Roman Catholic, Correa described himself as a "humanist Christian of the left." Tapping into the public's antiparty sentiment, Correa built an independent political movement, as opposed to a party, and enlisted the support of left-leaning intellectuals, technocrats, and leaders from Quito's outlaw rebellion.

Young, handsome, and charismatic, the forty-three-year-old Correa quickly proved to be an effective campaigner with a creative campaign team. He blamed the party establishment, the "partyarchy," for virtually all of the country's ills, ranging from malfunctioning governmental institutions to chronic economic crises and the flight of millions of Ecuadorians abroad. He promised to govern with "clean hands, lucid minds, and passionate hearts," sweeping away corruption, incompetence, and elitism and re-founding the country on the basis of a new constitution. Correa told voters that he would put an end to the "long and sad neoliberal night" by increasing social assistance, rejuvenating the role of the state in the economy, and putting foreign creditors and investors on notice that abuses would no longer be tolerated.[4]

As in previous elections, the fragmented multiparty system produced a crowded field of thirteen candidates and no first-round winner. Correa won 22.8 percent of the vote, thus securing his place in the second round, where he went head-to-head with Ecuador's richest man and perennial presidential candidate, banana magnate Álvaro Noboa. While Correa promised an end to neoliberalism, Noboa celebrated the merits of business and the free market.

Correa won the second round decisively, with 56.7 percent of the vote. Yet his victory was complicated by a crucial decision made during the campaign: in a daring gamble to prove his antiparty credentials, Correa ran without a slate of legislative candidates, arguing that the congress would be irrelevant since he was promising to convene a constituent assembly to draft an entirely new constitution. The gamble paid off during the campaign, as his popularity increased after the announcement; however, once elected he faced the dilemma of how to gain the needed consent of a recalcitrant legislature controlled by some of his bitterest enemies in order to convene the assembly.

Re-founding the Nation

Like former president Hugo Chávez of Venezuela and Bolivian president Evo Morales, Correa ran for office promising a radical restructuring of politics and economics, and the writing of a new constitution was the crucial mechanism to achieve this end. Correa proved determined to make good on this promise. His willingness to take risks and play political hardball early on in his presidency was supported by the social movements and served to dramatically increase his popularity, but it also led critics to accuse him of being a populist who was willing to bend the institutional rules of the game.

On his first day in office Correa signed Decree 002, which called for a referendum on convening a constituent assembly, but the legislature balked. Rather than back down in the face of congressional resistance, he directly appealed to the public to mobilize in support of the referendum and force the hand of the opposition. This led to a high-stakes showdown with congress that drew in the constitutional tribunal and the supreme electoral tribunal. Constitutionally questionable actions were taken by all parties, but ultimately intense public pressure, including massive demonstrations around the congressional building, forced the legislature to acquiesce to the referendum.

The referendum was held in April, and Correa won a huge victory, with 82 percent of voters supporting the call to convene an assembly that would be empowered not only to write a whole new constitution but also to dissolve the incumbent congress and assume legislative powers in the interim until the new constitution was completed. In September 2007 Correa's Alianza PAIS (Patria Altiva i Soberana [Proud and Sovereign Fatherland]) ticket won 80 of the 130 seats to the constituent assembly, thus giving them majority control and dealing a decisive blow to opposition parties. The new constitution was approved by popular referendum in September 2008 with 64 percent approving; this was followed by a general election in January 2009, under the new constitution, in which Correa was reelected, although without a party majority in the new legislature. In 2011 the president convened another referendum on a range of diverse proposals that included judicial reform, the establishment of a government agency to regulate press content, a law prohibiting banks and media conglomerates from diversifying their assets, and even new statutes outlawing bullfighting and gambling. On this occasion, while the president won public approval for all of the ten proposed changes, the margin of victory was narrower than in previous contests; in fact, the opposition emphasized the fact that if null and void votes were counted, the average of the yes votes did not reach 50 percent. However, in 2013 Correa and the Alianza PAIS regained their electoral predominance: Correa won 57 percent of the vote in the first round, trouncing the runner-up by nearly 35 percentage points, and his party swept the legislative elections. For the time being, Correa and the Alianza PAIS are clearly the dominant political force in the country.

GOVERNMENT, STATE POWER, AND INSTITUTIONS

Ecuador has a long history of constitution writing. The 2008 constitution is the country's twenty-first since its birth as an independent nation in 1830. Often referred to as the Montecristi constitution, for the coastal city where the assembly met and which was Eloy Alfaro's birthplace, Ecuador's newest Magna Carta is a very progressive, in some respects even revolutionary, document. It promises citizens an expansive array of political and socioeconomic rights, including a universal right to social security, free legal counsel and health care, rights to water and a clean environment, adequate housing, the use of public space, and even the practice of sports. With regard to the economy, it breaks with neoliberal orthodoxy by significantly increasing the power of the state to regulate and intervene in the market. It is nationalistic in its concern with protecting state sovereignty in interactions with more powerful states and actors, especially the United States. Finally, it has a strong ecological bent, being the first in the world to recognize nature and the environment as rights-bearing entities.

The result of a highly participatory process that involved extensive interaction between the assembly's working committees and civil society, the Montecristi constitution combines several strains of progressive and leftist thinking. It is social democratic in its vision of a state empowered to advance the public good and rein in and regulate the market. Postmodern ideas are reflected in its embrace of plurinationalism and collective rights for indigenous and other groups. Finally, the attention throughout to environmental sustainability reflects a postdevelopmentalist mindset. *Sumak kawsay,* a Kichwa term roughly translated as "to live well," is a central concept in the document; it emphasizes living in harmony and in balance with nature and other human beings and the rejection of consumerism and individualism in favor of sustainability and community.

The exercise of drafting the constitution evidenced the plurality of views within the Ecuadorian left and Correa's party itself. Correa did not fully respect the autonomy of the constitution-writing process and intervened when he disagreed with particular proposals. One of the key battles was over whether local communities would be able to veto state plans for large-scale mining in their territory. Most of Ecuador's natural resources, including oil and recently discovered deposits of precious minerals, are located in areas traditionally inhabited by indigenous peoples. CONAIE insisted that local communities should have the right not only to be consulted but also ultimately to stop extractive projects if they feared their communities would be negatively impacted by the environmental damage. Correa objected, arguing that local communities should not have the right to block projects that were in the national interest, and in the end the stronger language was removed. In the years since Montecristi the president has actively promoted large-scale mining projects against the strident objections of environmentalists and indigenous organizations.

In terms of state-market relations, the Montecristi constitution represents a sharp divergence from the previous one, clearly establishing the legal basis for expanding the state's role in the economy. No longer designated as market-based, the economy is now framed as "social and [one of] solidarity." In this new economy, the state is assigned rights to "administer, regulate, control and manage" the strategic sectors of the economy, which include energy, telecommunications, nonrenewable natural resources, transportation, hydrocarbon refining, biodiversity, and water. There are a number of provisions designed to protect small farmers and secure food sovereignty. The constitution specifically prohibits using public money to bail out large banks the way former president Mahuad did, and banks and financial institutions are barred from participating financially in other activities, in particular media ownership.

Restructuring institutions and intergovernmental relations was also part of the agenda of the new constitution. Presidential reelection for two successive four-year terms is now allowed. Moreover, if a president faces an uncooperative legislature, he or she has the power to dissolve the congress one time during the term and call for new elections. While the president would also have to run in the special election, the reform gives the president a powerful threat to wield in any executive-legislative conflict, making it less likely that the legislature would remove a president in the kind of legal maneuvers used against Bucaram and Gutiérrez.

STATE BUILDING AND PUBLIC POLICY

During the oil boom years of the 1970s the state dramatically expanded its functions and the services it provided to the population. However, during the neoliberal decades of the 1980s and 1990s the trend was reversed. Austerity and economic crisis forced governments to privatize, lay off government workers, and dramatically cut spending. During these years Ecuador had one of the lowest levels of public investment in the region. One of the most significant changes under Correa has been the dramatic expansion in the size and role of the state. Under his presidency public investment has increased by a factor of six, and now instead of one of the lowest levels of public investment in the region, Ecuador has one of the highest.

While Correa is often called a populist for his fiery rhetoric and direct appeals to the people, he is also a technocrat who surrounds himself and fills his administration with highly educated people from academia, NGOs, and business. He has sought to use this expertise to professionalize the government bureaucracy and policy making. Undoubtedly, the expansion of and improvement in state services has been crucial in maintaining popular support and consolidating his power.

Correa's government has invested heavily in road construction; newly paved highways crisscrossing Ecuador's difficult terrain have made transportation of goods and people faster and easier. Social spending has increased dramatically, with the largest increase for government programs that have built thousands of modest homes for low-income people in rural and urban areas. Spending on public education doubled between 2006 and 2009, and in the health care sector the government has spent significant amounts building and updating hospitals and clinics and equipping them with modern medical equipment. Ecuador's cash transfer program for the poor, the Human Development Stipend, reaches 44 percent of the population, one of the highest levels of coverage of any Latin American country. The public sector has expanded through the hiring of more public-school teachers, police, doctors and nurses, and government bureaucrats and administrators, and salaries have been raised. Lenin Moreno, Correa's vice president during his first two terms, is a paraplegic. He led efforts to increase government attention to the disabled. In addition to expanding access to services, professional assistance, and equipment, the government mandated that all leading employers set aside at least 4 percent of their jobs for disabled people. The significant expansion of the welfare state that Correa has spearheaded has helped reduce income inequality and the number of people living in poverty. According to the UN, since Correa took office Ecuador has seen the greatest reduction in income inequality of any Latin American country and has reduced the poverty rate by 5 percent.

The government has also spent vast sums on sophisticated media campaigns to tout its public works. The opposition has repeatedly criticized Correa for wasteful spending on government propaganda and for creating an unfair playing field at election time, as the government disposes of state-owned media outlets, as well as spending vast sums on paid advertising in the private media.

In 2012 the government budget was 160 percent greater than in 2004 and the largest in the country's history. However, unlike many early populists, Correa appears to have accomplished this feat without undermining macroeconomic health. Instead Ecuador has experienced solid economic growth, even weathering the 2008 international financial crisis despite the country's considerable vulnerability to international market forces as a result of its dependence on volatile oil prices and remittances, both of which were negatively impacted by the crisis. Additionally, dollarization means that the government does not have the option to use monetary policy to adjust to swings in the international economy.

Key to Correa's ability to expand government spending while maintaining a healthy economy has been the fact that government revenue has increased, going from 27 percent of GDP in 2006 to more than 40 percent in 2012. This has been accomplished through several key government initiatives: (1) raising the government's share of oil revenue through hard-nosed contract renegotiation with international oil companies; (2) reforming the tax code and significantly improving tax collection; (3) increasing regulation and taxation of the financial sector, including doing away with central bank autonomy and restricting capital flows; and (4) accepting long-term loans from China. Particularly interesting is the fact that the first three measures fly in the face of neoliberal policy prescriptions, which contend that these sorts of assertive measures by the state will drive away private investment. Ecuador under Correa's leadership appears to offer evidence that in fact there are alternatives to what Thomas L. Friedman has called the "golden straitjacket," or the imperative that supposedly all countries face to adopt the free market, neoliberal model if they are to thrive in a globalized marketplace.[5] For the moment, Correa's significant loosening of the straitjacket has generated positive economic results.

NATIONALISM AND INTERNATIONAL POLITICS

Restoring national pride, asserting the country's sovereignty, and fomenting regional integration are the key components of Correa's approach to foreign policy. In rhetoric and substance, Correa has demonstrated his readiness to distance Ecuador from its traditionally compliant relationships with the United States and international financial institutions such as the World Bank and IMF. Correa has also been a stalwart supporter of efforts to build new regional institutions that advance cooperation, integration, and a united voice for Latin America in international forums.

The Correa administration's willingness to assert its independence is evident in a number of actions over the years. Following through on a campaign promise, Correa refused to renew a lease to the US Air Force for a military base in the coastal city of Manta, forcing the US military to look for other countries willing to host its antinarcotics surveillance operations. In 2009 Ecuador withdrew from the International Centre for Settlement of Investment Disputes (ICSID), an international entity under the World Bank that arbitrates disputes between national governments and foreign investors. This action was in compliance with the Montecristi constitution, which prohibits ceding sovereignty to international tribunals in disputes with foreign companies, and also in anticipation of such disputes after the government raised taxes on foreign oil companies operating in Ecuador. Correa kicked out several high-ranking foreign diplomats, including a World Bank envoy and US ambassador Heather Hodges, over a WikiLeaks cable. In June 2012 the Ecuadorian embassy in London granted political asylum to WikiLeaks founder Julian Assange, thus blocking his extradition to Sweden for questioning on charges of sexual misconduct. By granting him asylum the Ecuadorian government accepted Assange's claim that the request for extradition was really an attempt to eventually have him transferred to the United States, where he would be prosecuted for divulging troves of classified government documents. Ecuador's support of Assange provoked the ire and frustration of the British and US governments.

Ecuador has played an active role in the recent development of new institutional infrastructure for regional integration, including the creation in 2008 of the Union of South American Nations (UNASUR), an intergovernmental union that aims to integrate the two existing customs unions in South America into a European Union–like structure. In 2010 UNASUR established its permanent headquarters in Quito. In July 2009 Correa announced Ecuador's entry into the Bolivarian Alliance for the Peoples of Our America (ALBA), which was Hugo Chávez's brainchild, and aims to develop an alternative model of solidary integration in contrast to that of neoliberal free trade regimes. Most recently, in 2011 Ecuador participated along with all thirty-three Latin American and Caribbean states in the founding of the Community of Latin American and Caribbean States (CELAC), which is a potential rival to the Organization of American States (OAS) and is notable for its inclusion of Cuba and exclusion of the United States and Canada.

UNASUR has helped to deescalate interstate tensions when conflicts have arisen between its member states. One such incident occurred in 2008 between Ecuador and Colombia after the Colombian military ordered a raid on a clandestine guerrilla camp of the Revolutionary Armed Forces of Colombia (FARC) inside Ecuadorian territory without informing the Ecuadorian government or asking permission. Correa took this as a grave affront to Ecuador's sovereignty; he broke off diplomatic relations and deployed troops to the northern border. Venezuela came to Ecuador's aid, raising the prospects of a military confrontation. In the end, with the help of UNASUR, all three countries backed away from military engagement. However, Ecuador's relations with Colombia remained tense as the Uribe administration accused Correa of having accepted campaign money from FARC. Relations between the two countries have improved and normalized under Colombia's current president, Juan Manuel Santos.

In addition to building ties with its Latin American neighbors, Ecuador has cultivated ties with extrahemispheric actors, in particular China. Estimates are that between 2005 and 2011 Ecuador received more than US$7 billion from China in exchange for commitments of oil shipments and another US$2 billion was negotiated at the end of 2013, making the country the fourth-largest Latin American recipient of Chinese loans after Venezuela, Argentina, and Brazil. Whereas in the past 75 percent of Ecuadorian oil was sold to the United States, today about 52 percent goes to China.

CORREA AND THE DEMOCRATIC DEBATE IN ECUADOR

Opinion polls previous to the 2013 election found that a large majority of Ecuadorians viewed the first five years under Correa very positively, and 60 percent were optimistic about the country's future. However, despite his popularity and achievements, Correa has also been a polarizing figure, with critics on both the left and the right. Much of the dissatisfaction stems from his aggressive—some would say authoritarian—political style and the way he has tended to concentrate power in the executive and use his substantial powers to sideline and intimidate critical and opposition voices. One of the main public battles has been with the private media. In one of the most widely publicized cases Correa sued *El Universo*, one of the country's leading newspapers, for libel after one of their columnists wrote an opinion piece accusing Correa of responsibility for civilian deaths that occurred during a 2010 police rebellion that the president argues constituted an attempted coup. Correa sued the columnist and the owners of the paper for US$80 million in damages. The courts, whose independence from the executive was questioned by the opposition, ruled in the president's favor, sentencing both owners and the journalist to three years in prison and a financial penalty of US$40 million. After the ruling, the president pardoned all three, thus releasing them from the prison terms as well as the fine, which surely would have bankrupted the newspaper. Nevertheless, this case and others like it have sent a strong signal to the private media that they need to carefully consider being too aggressive in their coverage and criticism of the president.

Correa has also clashed with social movements, particularly CONAIE. While his Citizens' Revolution has pursued an agenda that was shaped initially by Ecuador's dynamic social movements, Correa distanced himself from the postdevelopmentalist and environmental wing of the left. The main points of contention revolve around the president's insistence on large-scale mining, which environmentalists warn will have disastrous environmental impacts, as well as around water and land rights. About two hundred mostly indigenous activists who have publicly criticized the president or organized protest actions have been charged with crimes ranging from libel to sabotage and even terrorism. While so far these charges have not led to substantial jail time, they are viewed as a way of intimidating those who dare to challenge the president. Human rights organizations have accused the Correa administration of systematically "criminalizing social protest."

CONCLUSIONS

Correa's presidency has changed Ecuadorian politics in a number of crucial ways. First and foremost, it has produced stability after more than a decade of crisis. Under his leadership the country has experienced high levels of economic growth and has successfully weathered the international economic crisis that began in 2008. True to his promise to end the "long and sad neoliberal night," he has reempowered and rebuilt the state.

As successful as Correa has been thus far, however, there are real concerns with his belligerent tone toward those who disagree with him and his tendency to use his substantial powers to intimidate, ostracize, and silence opposition voices. Correa's plebiscitary presidency has eclipsed the powers of other institutions, tamped down groups in civil society, and defused the disruptive street politics that undid his predecessors. Although the consolidation of executive power means that Correa has resolved the problem of "presidencies interrupted," at least in the short to medium term, it comes at the cost of an executive branch that is not subject to the normal checks and balances of democracy. Under these circumstances, accountability is likely to be in short supply and the temptation to abuse executive power is substantial.

Critics on the left also argue that while Correa has increased social spending, he has not changed the country's underlying economic model, which is based on the unsustainable extraction of the country's abundant natural resources. His pursuit of large-scale mineral mining and continued development of oil will certainly help to maintain high levels of state funding for the short and medium terms, but it will most certainly have major environmental costs, as well as leave the country vulnerable to swings in international commodity prices. Whether Correa will succeed in using the country's mineral wealth to build a more diversified and modern economy remains to be seen.

While Correa is usually associated with the more radical wing of the Latin American new left, socialism is not a watchword of this political project. Correa has employed far fewer typical socialist-leaning policies, such as nationalization, when compared to Chávez or Morales. In statements after his 2013 reelection, he indicated that the emphasis would be on continuity as opposed to more-radical policies.

The Citizens' Revolution should be viewed as a national-popular project that has moved the country significantly away from neoliberalism without seeking to move in a socialist direction and without diverging dramatically from the traditional developmentalist path in terms of its reliance on natural resource extraction.

The chief fruits of this political project so far—and they are not insignificant— have been reductions in poverty and inequality, an improved standard of living for the poor, political and economic stability, and increased national sovereignty and independence.

Notes

1. Javier Corrales, "Market Reforms," in *Constructing Democratic Governance in Latin America*, 2nd ed., ed. Jorge I. Dominguez and Michael Shifter (Baltimore: Johns Hopkins University Press, 2003), 90–91.

2. Lisa North, "State Building, State Dismantling, and Financial Crises in Ecuador," in *Politics in the Andes: Identity, Conflict and Reform*, ed. Jo-Marie Burt and Philip Mauceri (Pittsburgh, PA: University of Pittsburgh Press, 2004), 202–203.

3. Arturo Valenzuela, "Presidencies Interrupted," *Journal of Democracy* 15, no. 2 (2004): 5–19.

4. "Presidente de Ecuador: 'Superaremos la triste noche neoliberal,'" *Prensa Latina,* December 9, 2006.

5. Thomas L. Friedman, *The Lexus and the Olive Tree: Understanding Globalization* (New York: Farrar Straus Giroux, 2000).

Suggestions for Further Reading

Becker, Marc. *Indians and Leftists in the Making of Ecuador's Modern Indigenous Movements.* Durham, NC: Duke University Press, 2008.

———. *¡Pachakutik!: Indigenous Movements and Electoral Politics in Ecuador.* Lanham, MD: Rowman and Littlefield, 2011.

Clark, A. Kim, and Marc Becker, eds. *Highland Indians and the State in Modern Ecuador.* Pittsburgh, PA: University of Pittsburgh Press, 2007.

De la Torre, Carlos, and Steven Strifler, eds. *The Ecuador Reader: History, Culture, Politics.* Durham, NC: Duke University Press, 2008.

Gerlach, Allen. *Indians, Oil, and Politics: A Recent History of Ecuador.* Wilmington, DE: SR Books, 2003.

Martin, Pamela L. *Oil in the Soil: The Politics of Paying to Preserve the Amazon.* Lanham, MD: Rowman and Littlefield, 2011.

Mijeski, Kenneth J., and Scott H. Beck. *Pachakutik and the Rise and Decline of the Ecuadorian Indigenous Movement.* Athens: Ohio University Press, 2011.

Pineo, Ronn. *Ecuador and the United States: Useful Strangers.* Athens: University of Georgia Press, 2007.

Roitman, Karem. *Race, Ethnicity, and Power in Ecuador: The Manipulation of Mestizaje.* Boulder, CO: Lynne Rienner, 2009.

Sawyer, Suzanne. *Crude Chronicle: Indigenous Politics, Multinational Oil and Neoliberalism in Ecuador.* Durham, NC: Duke University Press, 2004.

PART III

The Political Systems of Central and Middle America and the Caribbean

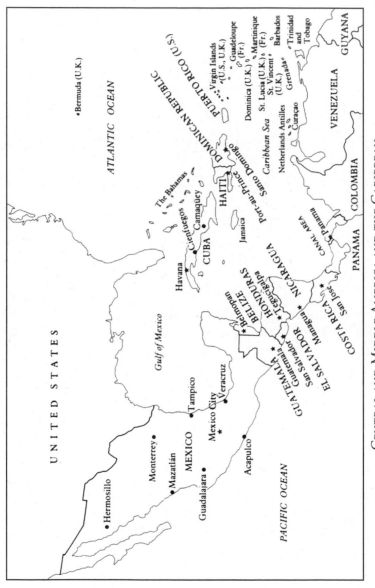

CENTRAL AND MIDDLE AMERICA AND THE CARIBBEAN

16

MEXICO: DEMOCRATIZATION, DEVELOPMENT, AND INTERNAL WAR

Judith A. Gentleman

Mexico's young democracy currently faces pressures from multiple forces that make governance and the continued development of the democratic order difficult. To begin with, Mexico's relationship with its neighbor to the north, the world's lone superpower, complicates the governing elite's political agenda—that of further opening Mexico's economic system—while at the same time honoring the cardinal political obligation of all Mexican national leaders to protect national sovereignty. Second, the Great Recession that emerged in 2008 in the United States and went on to engulf the world economy hurt the Mexican economy, in large part because of Mexico's extraordinary interdependence with the US economy. Finally, Mexico continues in the throes of an internal war that some have labeled a civil war. Criminal organizations battle each other and the Mexican state in order to maintain control of portions of Mexico's national territory to operate their drug trafficking and other criminal operations. To accomplish their objective, these criminal forces have succeeded in undermining already weak national and local institutions, including law enforcement and the judiciary.

Although Mexico doesn't begin to approach the "failed state" category that some have invoked in discussing the violence that has plagued the country, it nonetheless faces real peril to the core of its law enforcement, judicial, and political institutions. In many respects, Mexico's democracy is threatened. Enrique Krauze, one of Mexico's leading historians and political commentators, argues that Mexico has strong institutions that have shown ability to weather crisis. At the same time, he worries about the problems that Mexico now must deal with, warning that "this may be the

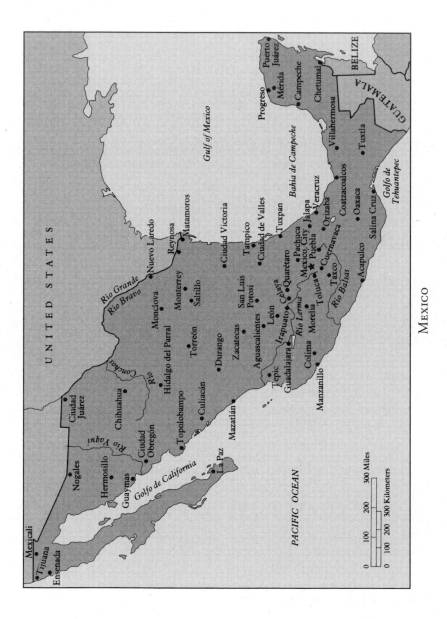

MEXICO

most serious crisis we have faced since the 1910 Mexican Revolution."[1] The concern over what to do in response to this threat has yielded divided opinion. Denise Dresser, another prominent Mexican political commentator, argues that Mexico is becoming a "lawless country" but fears that the strategy adopted in recent years to regain control is a flawed approach based chiefly on the "increased militarization of Mexico."[2]

Mexico is no longer the land of the peasant, although the campesino occupies an important place in the nation's core identity. It is now a middle-income country with nearly 80 percent of the population living in cities. Most Mexicans, 59 percent, are employed in the services sector, both formal and informal, representing 61 percent of the GDP. The industrial sector employs 25.7 percent of the workforce and produces 35.2 percent of GDP, while agricultural activities employ 15.1 percent of the workforce, accounting for 3.8 percent of national product. Only 12 percent of national territory is cultivated, and much of that area has been dependent on irrigation projects that date from several decades ago. Mexico's territory includes an arid northern area, coastal lowlands, a central high plateau, mountains, and tropical forested areas. Its coastline is extensive and presents a very considerable management challenge.

Mexico is rich in natural resources, including oil and gas and other mineral resources. It ranks ninth in world oil production and is the United States' third-largest supplier of imported oil after Canada and Saudi Arabia. Despite its natural gas reserves, Mexico still imports natural gas, as it has yet to develop sufficient domestic production. Important new discoveries of shale gas formations in northeast Mexico may transform Mexico's natural gas sector in the future. Other resource issues that call for increased attention in the future include intensifying water shortages, deforestation, and extensive soil destruction.

The population growth rate of 1.11 percent per annum has declined significantly from what were formerly much higher levels. Mexico's population is approximately 60 percent mestizo, 30 percent indigenous, and 9 percent Caucasian. Most Mexicans are Roman Catholics, although evangelical Protestantism increasingly has found appeal among the traditionally Catholic population. The population of the country is concentrated in the nation's major cities, including Mexico City and its metropolitan area, where an estimated twenty-two million citizens reside. Other major cities include Guadalajara, Monterrey, Puebla, Ciudad Júarez, Tijuana, Acapulco, Mérida, Leon, and Veracruz. Spanish is the predominant language, although there are also scores of indigenous languages spoken primarily in the southern states of the country.

Despite Mexico's ranking as the fourteenth-largest economy in the world based on GDP, fully half of the current estimated population of 111 million is considered poor. Fifteen percent of the population lives in extreme poverty. The World Bank estimates Mexico's 2011 GDP per capita at $10,047 calculated in US dollars. Approximately half of the forty-seven million Mexicans counted in the nation's economically active population (EAP) suffer employment problems and experience underemployment, unemployment, or employment only in the informal sector, where 30 percent of Mexico's laborers work. Eleven percent of Mexico's total population lives outside of the country, chiefly in the United States, having left in search of opportunity. The US Census bureau reported that in 2010 11.7 million people who were born in

Mexico resided in the United States. Although globalization generally and the 1994 North American Free Trade Agreement (NAFTA) specifically have generated an explosion in trade for Mexico, even workers in more advanced sectors still wait for the benefits to begin to pour in. In the automobile sector, where jobs have been arriving from other countries, new wage agreements provide for starting wages as low as US$1.50 per hour. According to officials at Volkswagen, workers may now take seven years to reach what was once a starting salary at their Puebla plant. Mexico admits to being in a race with China and that low-cost labor is a key to "victory."[3] Illustrative of the wage problem is the case of the auto workers employed at the DaimlerChrysler plant in Toluca who cannot afford to buy cars themselves.

Mexico suffers from an exceedingly unequal distribution of income and ranks as the eighteenth-most-unequal nation in the world. Although the per capita GDP figures may appear impressive, income and wealth are poorly distributed. The top 20 percent of the population owns 60 percent of income, while the bottom 20 percent owns 3 percent.[4] This inequality yields shortfalls in housing, health care, education, and opportunity. It is not surprising that despite Mexico's wealth, the country's educational deficit is significant, with Mexico's secondary school performance ranked the lowest of all countries in the Organization for Economic Co-operation and Development (OECD).[5] Mexicans over the age of fifteen now average eight years of schooling, although the problems of disruptions in attendance, poor teachers, and poor facilities leave students with achievement levels below a full eight years of education. Traditionally, the Mexican government has targeted higher education for substantial support at the expense of other educational levels, which then directly benefits elites whose children attend national public universities. Private universities have become more attractive in recent years, however, and this has led to some reconsideration of the financial emphasis placed by the state on public universities and higher education at the expense of support to other educational levels. Recognizing this problem, since 2000 the government has increased investment in basic education, but continues to devote substantial resources to universities as well. The government has developed innovative social support mechanisms to help families keep their children in school. Mexico's economic competitiveness is stymied both by its educational deficit and by the fact that only 35 percent of the population enjoys access to broadband Internet services, sometimes of substandard quality.

Mexico is an important country not only because of its economic prominence as one of the world's largest economies and as a major oil producer but also because it occupies a special place in world history. Together with France and Russia, Mexico's early twentieth-century revolution counts as one of the world's first modern revolutions. Mexico's revolution produced a modern, highly centralized state that, while nationalist and authoritarian, also embraced a corporatist formula that brought the broad Mexican population into relevance in the national political arena. Though not a democracy, this post revolutionary political order brought all sectors of Mexican society into the national political equation, thus differentiating the new order from traditional autocracies.

Mexico also occupies an important place on the world stage owing to its remarkable cultural and artistic tradition and national cultural inheritance. The pre-Columbian civilizations of the Teotihuacános, the Maya, the Aztecs, and numerous other indigenous peoples have influenced the tapestry of global society in numerous ways. From astronomy to religion, from art to foodstuffs, from administration to warfare—the contribution of Mexico's indigenous groups to our global social inheritance has been remarkable. Contemporary Mexico's influence on the study of archaeology and anthropology, reflecting the nation's rich cultural legacy, has been significant, as have been Mexico's art, music, and religious life. Mexico's artists, both in the fine arts and in folk art, have won world renown. In this time of global media and mass culture, one may even point to the financial success and worldwide appeal of Mexican-produced *telenovelas* (nighttime soap operas) as testament to Mexico's adaptive and continuing creative energy.

Although Mexico has played only a modest role in defense and security matters internationally, the current challenges it faces in combating drug-related crime have placed increased international attention on the Mexican state. For the United States and for Central America, there are few more direct, compelling problems than the threat posed by spillover effects from Mexico's drug war.

For the United States, Mexico's significance is heightened as both a market and a source of migratory labor. The flow of goods, services, and labor between the United States and Mexico constitutes one of the most dynamic and interdependent relationships that may be found anywhere in the world. So significant has the impact of this migratory labor flow been that the preponderance of population growth in the United States can now be traced to migrants, chiefly from Mexico.

The forces of globalization have led Mexico to significant levels of integration with the United States beyond the traditional arenas of trade and investment. The influence of culture and media from the United States and the push of cultural influences from Mexico into the United States via migrating populations have brought these two nations increasingly closer together. At the same time, both states actively—and even jealously—guard their own national prerogatives and sovereignty while pursuing economic and policy integration under the terms of NAFTA and the 2005 Security and Prosperity Partnership (SPP). These binding agreements also tie Canada, the third North American state, to its other North American neighbors. Mexico enjoys a close bilateral relationship with the United States, and for some foreign policy analysts on both sides of the border, there is no more important relationship for either state than the one they have with each other. Arguably, Mexico today has once again drawn as close to the United States as it was in the prerevolutionary period of President Porfirio Díaz's rule, when intense economic ties bound the two countries together.

Cultural integration between the United States and Mexico has been seen most especially in the borderlands region, which is increasingly viewed as a fully integrated and culturally distinct area. Cultural influences in both countries, however, also can be found far from the border. In the United States, the Cinco de Mayo holiday, popularized in the United States by the Corona beer company (its parent, Grupo Modelo, is now 50 percent owned by Anheuser-Busch), has become part of the routine of US cultural life. Baseball and soccer are followed passionately by millions on both sides of the border. Less known is the experimentation now taking place in some US communities with the *quinceaneara* tradition, a practice in which fifteen-year-old girls are introduced by family as now having reached the age of marriageability. Although feminists on both sides of the border may cringe at such practices, bilateral cultural exchanges and influences pose challenges for both societies. Conservative Mexican society may find distasteful the sensationalized and often offensive material produced by the US entertainment industry for television, movies, and the Internet, including violent video games. The construction of a Walmart within a mile (two kilometers) of the Teotihuacán pyramids provoked much opposition. On the other side of the border US animal rights groups confront the prospect of heightened interest in animal blood sports resulting from Mexican cultural influences, and environmentalists find few signs of progress in borderlands management on the Mexican side. For Mexico, the appetite for drugs and the gun culture on the US side of the border that arm Mexico's criminal syndicates are further evidence of the challenges of—and even the price to be paid for—globalization and interdependence.

Interdependence has extended the reach of Mexico's influence into traditional and growing Mexican communities in the United States via telecommunications (the US-based Spanish-language broadcaster Univision, for example) and by means of the rapidly growing system of Mexican government consulates in the United States, now numbering nearly fifty. Candidates for political office in Mexico routinely campaign in the United States in Mexican communities, some of which constitute larger regionally specific communities than exist in Mexico, where entire villages and regions have been all but depopulated as a result of migration to El Norte—the United States. Conversely, hundreds of thousands of US nationals now flock to Mexico to retire or have second homes in order to enjoy the weather, culture, and amenities. On a more ominous note, Mexico's drug cartels have aggressively infiltrated US society, where their customers are found, and have put down roots in major cities, with Atlanta and Los Angeles among the more prominent.

BACKGROUND: HISTORY, POLITICAL CULTURE

Mexico's pre-Columbian past was characterized by the spread of a host of nomadic indigenous groups who are believed to have made their way to the area from northern North America. Indications are that settlements were created as early as 20,000 BC. The development of permanent communities focused on agriculture dates to 1,500 BC. More advanced societies later came into existence between 200 BC and AD 900, and these included the sites known today as Teotihuacán in Central Mexico, Monte Albán in Oaxaca state, and the Mayan sites in Quintana Roo, Yucatán, Chiapas, and elsewhere. These settlements from the so-called Classic period were notable for their level of development in architecture, astronomy, language, and regional trade. Explanations for the collapse of these societies vary. Too often, however, the implicit suggestion is that the Maya or other indigenous groups "disappeared." This is hardly the case, however, as contemporary Mexican society is built upon the foundation of indigenous population groups that today remain present in one form or another.

Spain's conquest of Mexico, led by Hernán Cortés, led to the destruction of the Aztec empire by 1521. Spain imposed an order that sought to destroy all remnants of indigenous culture and to create a new religious and political authority. Building the new Spanish colonial order atop the central plaza of Aztec authority in Tenochtitlán, the Spanish even used the stones that had been part of Aztec construction to build their new cathedral. Mexico's population traded the old order of warrior-state oppression for a new political order that was also oppressive, harnessing the population to the economic interests of the Spanish mercantile state and to the ambitions of the Roman Catholic Church.

Mexico's war of independence was fought in the early nineteenth century, with independence recognized by the Spanish crown in 1821. The independence movement stemmed chiefly from the complaint of the *criollos* against the *peninsulares*. The criollos (many of whom were in fact mestizos), as native-born citizens in the colony, fought against what they viewed as discrimination. Opposition to continued Spanish rule was widespread, however, and both indigenous groups and mestizos fought against the crown. Following independence, the remainder of the nineteenth century was a time of remarkable upheaval and conflict. During this period, under the incompetent leadership of General Santa Ana, Mexico lost 55 percent of its national territory to the United States in exchange for compensation of US$15 million. This territory included what are now California, Arizona, New Mexico, Texas, and portions of Utah, Nevada, and Colorado. In addition, Mexico was forced to accept the loss of another sizable piece of territory in 1853 under the terms of the so-called Gadsden Purchase, which facilitated the construction of rail transport in the US Southwest. The Mexican-American War of 1848, which led to Mexico's catastrophic loss of territory, brought US troops to Mexican soil, ultimately leading to an eleven-month-long US military occupation of Mexico City and other parts of the country, including Chihuahua and Veracruz.

The weakness of the Mexican state and its susceptibility to external intervention were also reflected by France's invasion of Mexico in 1861 that led to the establishment of French rule under Maximilian from 1864 to 1867. Mexico's modern political system was built on a platform of convulsive revolutionary upheaval and authoritarian political values. Mexico's political culture has been traditionally characterized by conservative values derived from the Iberian culture of the Spanish colonial power. Order, hierarchy, respect for "natural" elites—especially the Roman Catholic Church, a political power in its own right—and governing authority were all principal features of postcolonial society. Although the revolution that was fought from 1910 to 1920 sought to overthrow the ruling authority and to eliminate the influence of the Roman Catholic Church, Mexico remained deeply traditional with respect to its inherited conservative religious traditions and subordination to autocratic rule.

The causes of Mexico's revolution are complex. Essentially, revolutionary forces emerged from different sectors of society in opposition to Porfirian rule. The dictator Porfirio Díaz governed Mexico from 1876 to 1910. His rural policies brought severe hunger to the countryside, triggered appeals for land reform, and ignited calls for the elimination of foreign control over natural resources and national production in addition to demands for the end of dictatorship. An array of insurgent forces eventually came into conflict, and civil war resulted, pitting rural and urban interests along with conservatively minded elites against each other. Ultimately, Mexico's revolutionary fires were doused with little agreement as to the direction that would be taken. Over many decades, national leaders would return to the still unsettled issues that had stirred the revolution, seeking to respond to grievances such as those of the landless peasantry. It was not until the government of General Lázaro Cárdenas in the 1930s that a serious land reform was initiated. The one enduring point of consensus among Mexico's postrevolutionary elite was the need to build a strong state, and in this sense Mexico's revolution paralleled other modern revolutions.

The new state was led by the military leaders who emerged as winners from the revolution. The losses suffered by Mexico during its revolution were devastating, with deaths estimated at 1.5 million—10 percent of the population. An estimated one million Mexicans also fled the country during the conflict, for the most part settling in the United States. The consolidation of the revolution continued from 1920 through 1940. Mexico's new leaders constructed a state that was led by a single official party that declared itself to be revolutionary in nature. This party would rule Mexico for seventy years and in time came to be known as the Institutional Revolutionary Party (Partido Institucional Revolucionario, PRI). The new government established full control of the military and in many ways was one with the military, as many of its early leaders were generals. In a departure from Latin American tradition, Mexico's military would serve as the instrument of the new revolutionary ruling elite rather than as an independent guarantor of the state. Although Mexico's political system evolved over time, moderating in some respects, it nonetheless remained highly authoritarian. The official party's political control of society was based on clientelism and a system of patrimonial relationships that flowed from the corporatist model of governance. Elections served the purpose of managing competing interests represented within the official party, thus forestalling the development of alternative political centers, and conferring legitimacy on the system. Elections were not designed to provide for political pluralism. Over time, despite the fundamentally fraudulent nature of Mexico's "elections"—until the 2000 election all successive presidents had been hand-picked by their predecessors—the system provided some veneer of international acceptability for Mexico. By the 1980s the government gradually had begun to take steps toward cooperating with the emerging international norms of democratic process.

The fact that Mexico turned inward in the twentieth century resulted not only from the country's revolutionary exhaustion but also from the rejection of the internationally focused commercial and investment patterns laid down during the Porfiriato. This inward orientation also stemmed from Mexico's experience of foreign interventions, including the Mexican-French War of 1862, the conflicts with the United States including the Mexican-American War of 1846–1848 that led to the loss of national territory, and the US interventions during the period 1914–1916 on behalf of the constitutionalist side in the revolution.

SOCIETY, ECONOMY, AND INTEREST GROUPS

In a dramatic shift from past political and economic practice, by the 1980s and 1990s Mexico had embraced globalization and pursued a very considerable opening of its economy. Not surprisingly, as a result of the close economic ties between Mexico and the United States, Mexico was hit hard by the global economic recession of

2008–2009. Mexico felt the pain of the US-based recession more than many other states in Latin America. Fully 85 percent of Mexico's exports were routinely destined for the United States, and as a result, the US recession had a devastating impact on Mexico's fortunes. Mexico's industrial production fell by over 13 percent and the economy shrank by over 11 percent. The automobile and electronics industries were badly hurt. Mexico's international trade declined by one-third in the first half of 2009. More than eight hundred thousand Mexicans lost their jobs by the first quarter of 2009. By contrast, Brazil and Chile were far more insulated from the effects of the global recession as a result of their more diversified trade profile.

Economic observers were impressed, however, by the speed of Mexico's recovery from the depths of the recession's impact. By the end of 2009, the GDP growth rate registered 6 percent, with growth continuing at 5.6 percent in 2010 and an estimated 3.9 percent in 2011. The manufacturing sector showed robust growth, with important international investment in aviation, for example. Bombardier's decision to build some of its new Learjet line in Mexico showed growing international confidence in Mexico's manufacturing platform. Strong performance in the export auto sector also signaled promise. Notably, the erosion of wage disparity between Mexico and China helped to promote investment in Mexico.

Yet the global recession highlighted features of the Mexican economy that contributed to limits on development. Although Mexico took important steps in the 1990s to liberalize its economy, some key sectors remain shielded from competition, including telecommunications and energy. Despite the success seen in some sectors of Mexico's economy as a result of NAFTA, and although Mexico initially saw a rising trade surplus following the treaty's implementation, the country now registers a significant trade deficit with the United States. The agricultural sector was particularly hard-pressed—it faced increasing competition from US producers as NAFTA reached full implementation, opening Mexico's economy further. This pressure generated increased unemployment among Mexico's rural poor, adding to migratory pressures on Mexico's cities.

Mexico's successful integration into the world economy was further impeded by the effects of corruption and the lack of public security. Mexico ranked at number 105, between Tanzania and Albania, in Transparency International's Corruption Perceptions Index for 2012, signifying a very substantial level of perceived corruption. The additional costs imposed on business by the public security problem are estimated to add roughly 25 percent to the costs of doing business. Finally, the failure to place sufficient emphasis on education, science, technology, and infrastructure development continued to plague the system, rendering Mexico less competitive in the process of globalization.

Any insulation that Mexico had from the US-induced recession derived from the oil revenues that had buoyed the economy from 2000 to 2008. During these years Mexico's oil revenues had risen dramatically, enabling the government to spend ambitiously. The petroleum sector generated 4 to 5 percent of Mexico's GDP and accounted for 40 percent of national government revenues. In 2009, however, oil revenues sank 24 percent. The Mexican government's diminishing ability to pump oil due to aging and inadequate infrastructure posed additional financial problems that required resolution down the road. Mexico's Petróleos de Mexico (PEMEX), the state petroleum monopoly, had plans to build its first new refinery in thirty years, but that facility would not open until 2015. Corruption also substantially undermined PEMEX's performance, with estimates from the mid-2000s of upward of US$1 billion per year lost. Not only did PEMEX serve as a leading source of revenue to the state, but it is also said to have provided illicit financial support for years to the PRI and the Petroleum Workers Union.

Major interest groups in Mexico include state workers, teachers, organized labor, rural workers, religious groups, professional groups, indigenous groups, women, law enforcement agencies, the military, private media, and of course business interests including foreign business and financial interests. Traditionally, state workers, organized labor, teachers, and peasants were organized under the umbrella of the state, and they exercised considerable leverage, with some groups enjoying considerable benefits so long as they operated within the confines of the system. Mexican labor confederations, including the Mexican Regional Labor Confederation (Confederación Regional Obrera Mexicana, CROM) and the Confederation of Mexican Workers (Confederación de Trabajadores de México, CTM), were among the more powerful interests. More recently an independent umbrella union, the National Union of Workers (Union Nacional de Trabajadores, UNT), formed to challenge the state's power in labor organization. Other powerful members of the PRI's organized labor system included the Petroleum Workers Union (Sindicato de Trabajadores Petroleros de la Republica Mexicana, STPRM), the Electrical Workers Union (Sindicato Mexicano Electrecistas, SME), the Teachers Union (Sindicato Nacional de Trabajadores de la Educación, SNTE), and the Peasant Confederation (Confederación Nacional Campesina, CNC).

Under the land reform introduced during the government of President Carlos Salinas, the dissolution of the *ejido* system (collective farms) diminished the power of the CNC, as its principal role had been to represent *ejidatorios*. Farmers are now more often represented by rural producers associations. Unions that were created and maintained within the state system remained powerful, in exchange for which their members were required to be members of the PRI. These workers understood that their jobs depended on their loyalty to the state and that any benefits they enjoyed would derive from their status as clients of the official party and the state.

For much of Mexico's modern history, civil society remained weak and dependent on the state. With the advance of economic liberalization beginning in the 1980s, with the privatization of significant areas of the economy and the end of many subsidies to workers, the private sector and civil society took on new importance. By no means has organized labor and its association with the state been eclipsed, however. Examples of the continued power of the state-labor association can be found in the energy sector, where reform efforts have been stymied by the opposition of major interests concentrated in these economic arenas, including unions. Another interest group that continues to enjoy enormous clout is the teachers union, which has been widely criticized for what some regard as its opposition to desperately needed reform. Recent testing by the federal government found that 75 percent of Mexico's aspiring teachers were unable to pass a skills exam, an indicator of the problem that plagues Mexico's educational system. Mexico's classrooms are too often staffed with unqualified but loyal union activists.

Economic liberalization, including privatization, deregulation, and the opening of the market to increased foreign investment, has also meant the growth of the influence of private sector organizations such as the Mexican Businessmen's Council along with the influence of independent business interests. With the privatization of hundreds of formerly state-owned enterprises, selected entrepreneurs who had been close to the Carlos Salinas group were enormously enriched. Carlos Helú Slim, now one of the world's richest individuals, benefited from the privatization arrangements governing the telecommunications sector. He and others who similarly grew enormously wealthy as a result of these opportunities, ballooning Mexico's new crop of billionaires, have come to wield great power in society and have been able to impede further decentralization and competitive reform within Mexico's economy in sectors where they hold overwhelming market power. The Televisa media empire has come to dominate televised news and entertainment in Mexico along with the much smaller Azteca national network. This concentration of media power (Televisa enjoys over a 70 percent share, in TV ratings parlance) raises concerns about media-government relations and news coverage, as it would in any society. Despite the fact that hundreds of newspapers are published throughout the country, their readership is low when compared to television viewership, thus reinforcing the problem of media concentration. Civil society has seen the growth of a host of new interest associations representing women, the environment, human rights, and others. As key actors in civil society, however, journalists have fallen victim to the violence themselves, including constant threats and an escalating number of homicides as they attempt to do their jobs. The pressure on media has been so intense that even major national broadcasters have sharply curtailed discussion of drug-related crime.

Within the government, the security sector has grown in influence as it has shouldered the task of responding to the continuing criminal threat to society. Although neither the military nor law enforcement is an independent actor, their resource requirements are such that their influence is likely to continue to grow. Mexico's military already stands as the second-largest military in Latin America, and its clout is likely to remain significant even as Mexico's government becomes the arena for more competitive political exchange among increasingly powerful actors.

PARTIES, ELECTIONS, AND DEMOCRACY

Mexico's democratization process developed out of the change in the society's system of values, beliefs, and political attitudes as support for the democratic ideal grew along with opposition to the old authoritarian order. Peru's prize-winning novelist and former presidential candidate, Mario Vargas Llosa, famously described Mexico's long-standing political system as "the perfect dictatorship." Mexico's political leaders had for years promoted the facade of pluralist democracy, particularly in its last decades of power, all the while maintaining a deeply authoritarian system. In power for nearly seventy years, the PRI ruled as the official party with strong-arm tactics, fraud, repression, and, importantly, financial incentives for cooperation. Embracing the mantle of revolutionary justice and social reform, governing elites placed great emphasis on their role as defenders of Mexico's national sovereignty and proclaimed their advocacy of social justice and of the rights of the downtrodden. In so doing, the system claimed popular legitimacy, enjoying the compliant support of co-opted social groups, including peasants, organized labor, teachers, and public sector employees. Once invested in the system, some within these groups became ardent supporters of the ruling party and the corporatist system. Many were directly employed in state bureaucracy or state enterprises and counted on the considerable security that the system offered. At the same time, the system was designed not to preclude private capital but to promote it, while the government often determined winners and losers in the market arena. Externally, the regime championed all manner of leftist causes, embracing Cuba among others, while simultaneously crushing all domestic opposition that challenged the rule of the official party and the regime.

The convulsive protests of 1968 and the government massacre of hundreds of student protesters in the Plaza of the Three Cultures at Tlatelólco in Mexico City seemed to mark a turning point, when governing elites began to lose popular legitimacy. A series of destabilizing developments further weakened support for the political system. Among these was the insurgency in Guerrero state during the 1960s and 1970s, led by Lucio Cabanes Barrientos, who headed the Party of the Poor. Cabanes was killed in 1974 by the Mexican military, but Guerrero remained under a de facto state of siege for years thereafter. In 1982, a devastating financial crisis engulfed Mexico soon after the government announced the presence of huge new oil reserves and had invested in massive new oil production facilities. The nation's financial collapse led to what was termed Mexico's "forgotten decade." The government's poor performance (the military was an exception here) in the aftermath of the catastrophic 1985 Mexico City earthquake further shook the public's confidence. Then in 1994 and 1995 the system was hit first by the January 1994 uprising by the Ejército Zapatista de Liberación Nacional (EZLN, or Zapatistas) in Chiapas, led by the charismatic Subcomandante Marcos, and then by the 1995 banking crisis that led to a US financial bailout.

The events in Chiapas and the banking crisis plus the US bailout were particularly problematic for Mexico's political leaders, as both involved the United States. The Zapatista attack was planned to coincide with the implementation of NAFTA and seemed to catch the government by surprise, in terms of both timing and the Zapatistas' brilliant use of media as the new weapon of choice. The uprising inevitably raised questions about the government's ability to function effectively in managing internal security. The military's incompetent performance in quelling the uprising further eroded the government's credibility. This criticism was added to the complaints leveled at the government over abuses perpetrated during the militarization of the nation's southern region to counter illegal entry from Guatemala and to control emergent insurgent forces in Chiapas and Oaxaca. Both the banking crisis and the bailout were humiliating to the government insofar as the United States was seen as having had to rescue Mexico's incompetent leadership. The assassination of the PRI's 1994 presidential candidate, Luis Donaldo Colosio, in March 1994 starkly exposed problems within the ruling elite itself. Although Colosio was executed at point-blank range, the investigation into his murder yielded only the conviction of the gunman himself, leaving a cold trail to the parties responsible for the political assassination. Furthermore, the suspicious death of a high-profile political leader had not been without precedent. One such incident involved the 1969 death of PRI elder Carlos Madrazo, father of 2006 PRI presidential candidate Roberto Madrazo. The mysterious crash of his airplane occurred soon after he announced that he was going to leave the PRI and form a new party in reaction to the events at Tlatelólco. Another case involved the 1989 single-car accident that killed the popular presidential candidate of the National Action Party (PAN), Manuel Clouthier. The accident aroused considerable suspicion at the time concerning the circumstances of the party leader's death. In November 2008 President Calderón's secretary of the interior, Juan Camilo Mourino (a probable choice to follow Calderón as the PAN candidate for the presidency), was in a bizarre aircraft accident over Mexico City. This raised substantial concern about the true nature of the accident that killed him and others on board who were involved in state security.

Competitive elections for the presidency had been taking place in Mexico since 1988, and multiparty races were held in state and local elections even earlier, but the first victory of an opposition presidential candidate was not until the election of the PAN candidate Vicente Fox in 2000. Fox had previously won the governorship of his home state, Guanajuato, but in the highly centralized Mexican presidential system, control of the presidency is critical. The question of whether the authoritarian system collapsed or was overthrown is frequently debated. The answer may be both. On one hand, the official party faltered as it confronted sequential votes that it appeared to lose. The old techniques of election rigging and intimidation no longer seemed to work in an environment of expanding communication and citizen mobilization. For a time PRI leaders sought to use the tactic of promising a political opening but then slow-rolling the rule making that would permit the opening. Then, with the passage of rules that permitted multiparty participation, the races would be rigged, with the use of elaborate schemes to steal votes. The PRI was the best in the business when it came to these operations.

When cameras began to film and election observers were present to bear witness to electoral malfeasance, however, the utility of such electoral fraud tactics as closed voting stations, *ratónlóco* (voters madly searching for a place to vote after their name disappeared from their local registry), or the "carousel," where vans carried would-be voters to multiple voting stations, diminished. The old dinosaurs of the party began to give way to modernizers who believed they could meet the competition head-on. On the other hand, the forces of democratization organized effectively, developed local citizen observer teams, enlisted international observers and assistance from nongovernmental organizations (NGOs) and intergovernmental organizations (IGOs) where possible, and appeared to offer the population a convincing alternative. Initially the PRI responded to the calls for change by permitting electoral competition at the local level. The floodgates had been opened, however, and citizens eventually demanded full democracy.

The government of Carlos Salinas, installed in power in 1988, introduced some degree of political reform as a complement to the major overhaul of the national economy that was one of the hallmarks of the Salinas period. The Salinas economic liberalization project brought with it costs to many who had been dependent on the state. To compensate for their losses, Salinas introduced the supremely corporatist National Solidarity Program (PRONASOL) in order to mend the tear in the political fabric that his economic reforms had created and to rebuild support for the party. He had absolutely no intention, however, of democratizing Mexico. As was said at the time, Salinismo meant perestroika (economic restructuring) without glasnost (openness), in a comparison often made between the Mexican and Soviet reform processes.[6] What the younger generation of PRI technocrats found was that market opening inevitably brought pressures for further political liberalization that were difficult to resist. Ultimately, both the old and new guards of the PRI, the politicos and the technocrats, learned how to compete in the new political game that had emerged in Mexico. The 2012 election of the PRI candidate Enrique Peña Nieto, which restored the PRI to the presidency after twelve years, demonstrated the PRI's impressive adaptive capacity.

The struggle to further expand and deepen democracy continues today. Mexico's political system boasts an array of strong, functioning parties with comparatively well-developed party cadres, all of whom now have considerable experience. In the initial years of electoral competition the Party of Democratic Revolution (PRD), the major left party, was significantly disadvantaged because it had not had a chance to develop its own party militants. Instead, it included a mix of refugees from the PRI who only knew the "old ways" and newcomers to electoral politics who were lacking in experience altogether. The National Action Party, by contrast, had had regional experience in electoral competition and was well funded. The PRI had experience, but all the wrong kind. Today, these parties of the left, right, and center are joined by the Workers Party (PT), an environmental party (PVEM), and the New Alliance Party (Partido Nueva Alianza).

The PRI finds support across the country, but especially in the southern states and among older voters. The PAN, the right-center, pro-business, and pro-church party, continues to find its stronghold of support chiefly in the northern states, but it has improved its position in the central region of the country. The PRD, the party of the left, finds support in Mexico City and in states across the center of the country. Some observers have argued that the PRI's resurgence in popularity is a result of the fact that voters remember the days when the government was able to maintain public order. The erosion of support for the PAN after twelve years of governance was hardly surprising owing to the nation's economic difficulties and the tremendous levels of violence and public insecurity that had overtaken the nation. Facing the 2012 electoral choice, analysts suggested that while voters recognized that the PRI had had its significant faults in the past, they credited the party with having had the capacity to keep the lid on crime and violence. Some believed that the PRI would be able to bring a level of public order back to society. Others feared, on the other hand, that the restoration of the PRI would pose challenges for Mexico's continued democratization.

Although Mexico now has a functioning democratic electoral system, the skepticism that many citizens express about democracy's performance reflects Mexico's deficit of good governance. When polled, only a minority of Mexicans agree that democracy is preferable to any other type of government. Despite the great efforts made to build democracy in their country, Mexicans are frustrated with what "democracy" has produced—and failed to produce. In the view of the majority, democracy has not created the public security, economic security, or opportunity for which they had hoped. Instead, Mexicans find themselves facing economic challenges and a public security crisis, leading many citizens to vote with their feet, by leaving for the United States. Although Mexicans do not support authoritarian solutions, Mexican citizens do feel deep disappointment with democracy's performance thus far and with politicians in general.

Although much has been accomplished in the past two decades to improve transparency and democratic performance in the electoral arena, many issues remain to be addressed. The role of highly concentrated private media in Mexico's national elections is of concern, as is the extraordinary cost of these elections, even compared to the extravagant spending that takes place in US national elections. Enormous controversy surrounded the defeat of the PRD candidate Andrés Manuel López Obrador in 2006 and again in 2012. In 2006 election results provoked demonstrations and López Obrador refused to accept Felipe Calderón's victory for the PAN. López Obrador claimed that the election had been stolen, and indeed, Calderón could claim only a razor-thin margin of victory. These elections raised again the question of whether Mexico's political and economic elites would ever tolerate the election to the presidency of a candidate from the left. That question had remained paramount in Mexico's politics since the outcome of the 1988 election, in which Carlos Salinas was declared the victor over the PRD candidate, Cuauhtémoc Cárdenas. In that election, the vote count was suspended for a week due to mysterious computer failures. Salinas was then declared the winner by the slimmest of margins.

Some worry that the PRI victory in the presidential election of 2012 may constitute a "restoration" of the old order, but arguably, President Enrique Peña Nieto's election signals considerable movement within the political system. In a significant departure from the past, the new government's agenda has won the endorsement of all major parties (even López Obrador's PRD). Initiatives for reform in telecommunications, energy, and education have, for now, won the support of many stakeholders. The selection of a presidential cabinet to include leading representatives from the PAN and the PRD has proved popular. Peña Nieto's plan to reform the security sector has also won support, and his emphases on building the economy and cooperation with the United States have won endorsement as well. His vision for the redesign of the political process at the state and local levels will face many challenges, as will his other plans, but he begins with considerable popular support and a successful if costly campaign behind him.

THE STATE, GOVERNMENT, AND BUREAUCRACY

Mexico's government is a federal republic built on a system of separation of powers. Its 1917 constitution guaranteed an array of citizen rights, both substantive and procedural. The federal system includes thirty-one states and the Federal District, where Mexico City is located. Currently the public sector accounts for 11 percent of the labor force. The government includes separate and independent executive, legislative, and judicial branches. Although the constitution provided for this arrangement, the true independence of these branches only materialized with the 2000 election. The system has always been characterized by a strong executive and a weak legislature and judicial system, as is typical throughout much of Latin America. The president is elected for a six-year period known as the *sexenio*. The congress, comprising a senate and a chamber of deputies, has become more powerful since opposition parties first won representation, beginning in 1997. With the advent of democracy congress has been in the process of becoming more professional, learning how to legislate in a constructive manner rather than either simply opposing executive initiative or compliantly affirming executive direction. The prohibition of consecutive reelection for the executive and for congress arguably diminishes the accountability of either of these institutions to the popular will. The judicial branch includes federal and state court systems as well as the supreme court. Justices are appointed by the senate after having been nominated by the president.

The judiciary is the weakest of the branches, although it, too, is undergoing considerable reform. Nonetheless, most citizens understand that with the current performance of the judicial branch and public security ministries, crime enjoys impunity in Mexico. An estimated 80 percent of crimes are never reported to authorities because citizens believe that nothing will be done, fear identifying themselves to relevant government officials, and/or fear law enforcement authorities themselves. Law enforcement agencies have been associated with kidnapping and extortion, inducing fear in the citizenry and leaving the public with a feeling of helplessness.

Mexico's state-level political systems are of considerable importance. State governors, legislatures, and local political leaders are important actors in the nation's political picture, and these arenas serve as platforms for many political leaders who later move to the national level. Recent presidential candidates from the three major parties, Vicente Fox (PAN), Enrique Peña Nieto (PRI), and Andrés Manuel López Obrador (PRD), all spent considerable time honing their skills at the regional level.

The national government's budget is substantially funded by oil revenues generated by PEMEX. As previously noted, taxes, royalties, and receipts from the petroleum sector constitute nearly 40 percent of the government's revenues. By hedging the price of oil per barrel the government managed to keep revenues steady through 2009, but the financial picture thereafter soured. By 2012 oil production had declined significantly, stabilizing at 2.5 million barrels per day, down from 3.4 million barrels per day in 2004. The two largest producing fields in the Mexican system, Cantarell and Ku-Maloob-Zaap (KMAZ), both suffered major declines in output.

Both Mexico's petroleum and electricity sectors are in need of major reform that would provide investment, technical expertise, and professional management that could diminish those political influences that have bled resources from the system and produced tremendous inefficiencies. The influence of the PRI-dominated unions in the energy sector and of the party itself represents a major impasse to the fundamental infrastructure modernization that Mexico so sorely needs. The dilemma concerning energy sector reform raises fundamental unresolved political questions concerning the role of the state and the further integration of the Mexican economy into the global system.

Oil receipts notwithstanding, the government faces a serious revenue problem. Like much of Latin America, Mexico's political culture has not been supportive of taxation or compliance with tax law. Admittedly, few people enjoy paying taxes, but the level of noncompliance in Mexico is such that the revenue stream from taxes alone is insufficient to support the government's operations. In part this problem stems from a record of significant corruption that has left many with the impression that tax receipts are simply siphoned off illegally by government officials and their cronies. Second, a tradition of noncompliance with tax law and ineffective tax collection procedures have bred a culture of tax evasion that is supported by impunity in the justice system. Third, the government has historically depended on state-sector-generated revenues, but with the privatization of so much state sector enterprise, these revenues have evaporated, thus requiring additional resources. It has been said often that no president of Mexico ever left office a poor man. In another widely circulated observation on the political practices prevalent during the years of the PRI's rule, a leading PRI figure remarked, "Only a poor politician is a poor politician." Corruption in this instance is defined not simply as stealing from state coffers directly, which certainly occurred, but also as managing public policy in such a manner as to pick financial and economic winners and losers. It also means payoffs to and from crooked businesses, public sector administrators, congressional representatives, senators, union leaders, and even criminal elements including drug traffickers. Corruption means protection from prosecution, impunity and the undermining of law enforcement institutions, special privilege, the abuse of average citizens, and the undermining of the public sector in the name of private interest. Some have argued that these methods were simply the necessary glue that preserved Mexico's long-running regime and thus ensured national stability and security. Others argue that this corruption has significantly slowed the development of the state and economy.

According to Transparency Mexico, an estimated US$2 billion is spent on bribes for public officials every year. The Calderón administration sought to tackle government corruption, and in his first year in office President Calderón announced on International Anti-Corruption Day that 11,500 public servants had been fined a total of US$300 million for corrupt practices. He set his sights most particularly on law enforcement agencies.[7] Illustrative of the problem faced by the Calderón government was the revelation in late 2008 that Mexico's drug czar, Noé Ramírez, had received US$450,000 in bribes from a drug cartel. In a related case, also at the end of 2008 the head of Mexico's Federal Preventative Police (PFP), Victor Gerardo Garay Cadena, resigned after being charged with having ties to organized crime.

Efforts to reform the state sector as the next step in the development of Mexico's democracy have been met with substantial resistance. During the years of PANista governance, Mexico suffered from divided government, thereby making change all but impossible. An area where reform efforts have begun to succeed, however, has been the judicial system. The government expects to see full implementation of this redesign of the system within eight years. Other areas targeted for future reform include fiscal affairs, pensions, energy, and labor law.

Some argue that it will take a social revolution to solve one of Mexico's major public policy problems, poverty, and that incremental reform will never lead to real change. The Ernesto Zedillo administration (1994–2000) initiated an antipoverty program known as Progresa, later renamed Oportunidades by the Fox administration. This cash transfer program for families was designed to tackle a variety of problems including family income, school attendance, and child health. The program provided for conditional cash support to families who would see to their children's health care and attendance at school.[8] Approximately five million families are enrolled in the program. The program appears to have had considerable success, but the problem of societywide poverty remains stubbornly entrenched. Several federal ministries manage programs to improve social health and welfare, but the development impasse that maintains poverty at very high levels has yet to be overcome.

The federal government bureaucracy consists of eighteen cabinet ministries and numerous additional agencies of significance at the subcabinet level. One growth area in the federal system is the security sector. Mexico's public security sector is managed by the president together with the "security cabinet," including the attorney general (PGR), the Interior Secretariat (SEGOB), Public Safety (SPP), and the military departments of National Defense (army and air force, SEDENA) and the Navy (SEMAR). Mexico's defense budget is currently estimated at US$5.26 billion for 2011 (compared, for example, to the fiscal year 2011 US defense budget of US$711 billion). The division of Mexico's military into two competing organizations, SEDENA and SEMAR, inevitably leads to competition over missions and resources. A host of political factors explain this division, but there is little prospect that a unified Defense Department under the direction of a civilian secretary of defense will emerge anytime soon.

In addition to the enormous problem faced by Mexico in its attempts to contend with the drug war and rising levels of crime, the country also faces significant environmental problems. To begin with, Mexico City is quite literally running out of water. Mexico's long-running dispute with the United States over the diversion of waters from the Colorado River is perhaps a problem better known to US citizens. Although that issue reached a resolution, however satisfactory or unsatisfactory, the problem of Mexico City's water is not subject to dispute resolution. The city was built in a region of lush lakes that have all but disappeared. That resource has been exploited to the point where the ground is now sinking under Mexico City, and even the floating gardens of Xochimilco are greatly diminished. In the spring of 2009 the government began rationing water, and more than five million residents were entirely cut off from water supplies. In addition to the water shortage itself, it is estimated that 40 percent of the water that is piped through the city's water system is lost through leaking pipes. The government has few options available to respond to these problems and even fewer plans in the works. Finally, the environmental devastation of the delicate northern territories, leading to increasing desertification, is paralleled by the rampant destruction of rain forest in the southern parts of the country. Mexico has had neither the political nor the administrative capacity to effectively respond to these desperate situations. Although a Green Party has emerged, it has acted primarily in alliance with the conservative PRI and has had limited impact on these issues.

FOREIGN POLICY

Mexico's postrevolutionary foreign policy and international relations have been shaped by the experience of invasion, a sense of the state's own weakness and vulnerability, and its desire to maintain internal stability. These priorities led Mexico's leaders to carve out several key principles in its approach to international relations. As a result of its catastrophic experiences with Spain, France, and especially the United States, it sought above all to protect its sovereignty and to insist on a policy of nonintervention in the affairs of other states and a posture of nonalignment. Above all, Mexico's foreign policy and international relations must be understood as a function of its relationship with its neighbor to the north. From Mexico's point of view, the United States historically has constituted Mexico's number one security problem. Although Mexico has chosen to focus on matters of internal security, this does not mean that it has ignored its neighbors or remained entirely uninvolved in international affairs. Mexico has succeeded in diversifying its relationships with other states despite its close relations with the United States, focusing on developing cooperative relations with politically like-minded states in Latin America. Mexico is actively engaged in a range of international institutions and takes very seriously its membership. Because Mexico is a state with little material power available to influence the behavior of other states, international organizations, law, and agreements are significant to any efforts it may make to influence world affairs.

One early exception to Mexico's decidedly noninterventionist approach to international relations was President Lázaro Cárdenas's decision to join the Soviet Union in supporting the Republican cause in the Spanish Civil War during the 1930s. Cárdenas sent rifles, ammunition, food, and even aircraft to the Republicans, although the matériel support was not significant to the war effort overall. Notably, only Mexico and the Soviet Union provided external support to the Republican side beyond the assistance provided by the International Brigades.

Mexico sought to maintain neutrality during World War II, but by January 1943 Mexico's president, Avila Camacho, concluded that Germany presented a threat, especially to shipping, and became a US ally in opposing the Axis powers. The government established a military draft and created a Pacific Security Zone under the command of General Lázaro Cárdenas, the country's former president. Mexico joined with the United States in creating a joint US-Mexico-North Defense Commission. In 1944 Mexico sent elements of what it called an aviation training group from its newly established 201st Mexican Air Force Expeditionary Squadron to San Antonio, Texas, for training. The squadron, known as the "Aztec Eagles," was sent to the Philippines in 1945 and flew fifty-nine missions in Luzon and Formosa. Seven pilots were killed.[9] Notably, nearly fifteen thousand Mexican citizens fought in the war under the US flag. At the time of the Korean War, Mexico had supported the UN's diplomatic approach to the problem. The United States sought to persuade Mexico to contribute troops to the war effort, but after some discussions and promises by the United States of matériel assistance, Mexico did not agree to support the troop request. This position was far more consistent with Mexico's overall position on international engagement, which emphasized engagement with international institutions and participation in international forums, with limited involvement in any issues not bearing directly on Mexico.

Mexico sought to avoid becoming a pawn in the Cold War struggle between the United States and the Soviet Union. Mexico had little to fear from Cuba, a Soviet ally, despite the fact that the Castro regime had supported insurgent groups in a number of other states in Latin America. Mexico enjoyed important ties with Cuba that dated to the 1950s, when Fidel Castro and Ernesto "Che" Guevara spent time at a guerrilla training camp in Mexico preparing for the Cuban Revolution. Mexico expended every effort to avoid appearing to take sides in the Cold War struggle, despite the fact that its internal security program succeeded in exterminating domestic forces that sought to pursue a Marxist or even reformist alternative. Mexico's intellectual elite had historically embraced Russian culture, especially art, film, and literature, and this too served to harmonize relations between the Soviet Union and Mexico.

Mexico's efforts to secure an independent foreign policy position largely succeeded and did so without jeopardizing its critical relationship with the United States. In the post–Cold War period, Mexico's foreign policy emphasized engagement with international organizations and postconflict resolution efforts. In the 1960s and 1970s Mexico did actively participate in and seek a leadership position within the nonaligned movement. Following his presidency, Luis Echeverría (1970–1976) competed for the post of secretary general of the UN, thus positioning himself as a Third World progressive leader even though, as Mexico's interior minister in the administration of President Díaz Ordaz (1964–1970), Echeverría had been responsible for the massacre at Tlatelólco in 1968. Mexico was a leader in efforts to bring about peace accords during the Central American wars of the 1980s and the Guatemalan civil war, which continued into the 1990s. It has also played a role in efforts to resolve the current conflict in Colombia, serving as a host for negotiations and for parties to the conflict. Furthermore, Mexico has been an eager and responsible participant in hemispheric intergovernmental organizations and a host of international organizations that function beyond the Western Hemisphere.

Beginning in the late 1980s Mexico warmed to the idea of increased international economic cooperation and exchange, particularly with the United States. In a remarkable overture, President Carlos Salinas initially approached the United States with the NAFTA concept. The United States responded favorably, understanding that NAFTA was both a good economic deal for some US sectors and a security hedge against potential instability in Mexico. With NAFTA, investment moving offshore from the United States, typically to Asia, would now be attracted increasingly to consider Mexico. From the US perspective, the agreement would provide enhanced employment and development for a close neighbor that the United States did not want to see destabilized. After the ratification of NAFTA, Mexico undertook a wide array of economic exchanges and free trade agreements, embracing globalization and interdependence as new operative concepts for Mexican society.

It was not until the Fox administration, beginning in 2000, that Mexico once again launched bold initiatives in the foreign policy realm. President Fox essentially gambled his presidency on reaching an immigration deal with the United States, having persuaded his friend and former border state governor, President George W. Bush, that Mexico needed such relief. For Fox, the 9/11 attacks by Al Qaeda on the United States destroyed the hopes on which he had bet his presidency, as the United States moved to seal its borders. Moreover, Fox's own silence in the immediate aftermath of 9/11 coupled with the anti-US sentiments being expressed in Mexico following the attacks did much to distance the two countries and chill relations. Further, the Mexican foreign minister's announcement that Mexico would withdraw from the Rio Treaty following 9/11 appeared to be a slap at the United States, especially when compared with the politically astute Brazilian invocation of the treaty in defense of the United States following the attacks.

Immigration remained a tremendous sore point for Mexico, particularly given the unilateral US decision to build a wall along the US-Mexico border. The offense taken in Mexico over the wall is difficult to exaggerate. That said, in the long run Mexico's cooperation with the United States regarding post-9/11 security proved to be robust and in some ways proactive. Mexico committed itself to tracking non-Mexicans who might be attempting to enter the United States from Mexican territory and to cooperate in a full program of antiterror actions. Officially, the Mexican government recognized terrorism as a global threat and partnered with the United States to take responsibility for monitoring the movement of identified targets in Mexican national territory. Mexico faced a significant challenge in controlling fifty-two ports of entry and monitoring extensive national territory that affords access by land or sea. The development of enhanced Mexico-US cooperation in border surveillance and intelligence sharing for counterterrorism purposes has been impressive. With respect to its overall approach to international relations, however, Mexico remained determined to refrain from overseas engagement of any kind other than support for humanitarian requirements. Mexico has refused to participate in peacekeeping operations sponsored by either the UN or the Organization of American States (OAS). Mexico did provide humanitarian support to victims of Hurricane Mitch, the horrific 1998 storm that pummeled Central America. Mexico also sent military elements to support humanitarian operations in Texas and Louisiana in the aftermath of Hurricane Katrina in 2005. Outside of this type of involvement, Mexico remained firmly committed to its noninterventionist posture and remained skeptical of international "values" regimes that challenge state sovereignty, for example in areas such as human rights, democracy promotion, and drug certification.[10]

With the election of center-right PANista presidents in Mexico, relations with both Cuba and Venezuela's Hugo Chávez soured. Although the PRI had always maintained its posture as a charter member of a community of international left-progressive states, the PANistas were no longer eager to play Fidel Castro's game and agreed that they would no longer protect the Castro regime from allegations of human rights violations in international bodies. Despite the fact that it had long been an ardent defender of its identity as a Latin American state, Mexico now began publicly to acknowledge its other identity, that of a North American partner to the United States and Canada. As a result, President Fox soon found himself branded a lapdog of the United States and a suspect member of the Latin American community of nations. Some of this rancor stemmed from the conflict that emerged between President Fox and President Hugo Chávez, while some stemmed from Brazil's emerging ambition to occupy the senior leadership position in Latin America. Brazil, for example, sought to promote a South American Free Trade Area (SAFTA) at the time that the Free Trade Agreement of the Americas (FTAA), promoted by the United States, was still a concept under discussion. SAFTA would have excluded Mexico from participation in the regional trade agreement along with the United States. Following this period of disagreement and with the election of Felipe Calderón, Mexico sought to moderate its relationships and once again build diplomatic bridges to both the north and the south, including Cuba and Venezuela.

Mexico maintains excellent relations with other states in the region, especially Chile, Colombia, and much of Central America. Mexico's relations with Colombia and Chile in particular have deepened over the past several years, reflecting these states' common perspectives on trade and economic values. Mexico and Colombia have seen a maturation of their collaboration in combating narcotrafficking, and representatives from their security agencies have engaged in exchanges to discuss common strategies and intelligence cooperation. In a dramatic move just after his election, President Peña Nieto named retired general Oscar Naranjo, former director of the Colombian National Police (CNP), as his senior security advisor. Naranjo comes to the job after decades of experience in counterdrug operations in Colombia. Mexico maintains close relations with the states of Central America, and in 2001 the Fox administration launched the ambitious Plan Puebla-Panama to promote development in southern Mexico and Central America. In part a reaction to the instability in Chiapas and Oaxaca and in part a reaction to Guatemala's and El Salvador's postconflict instability, the plan offered detailed development objectives, particularly for massive infrastructure projects, but the plan's sponsors never found the financing or popular support necessary to move the project forward.

Mexico's relations with the United States currently involve a host of difficult issues. At the August 2009 summit meeting that brought together the leaders of Mexico, the United States, and Canada, the issues on the agenda included economic recovery and competitiveness, citizen safety and security, and clean energy and climate change. For the Mexico-US relationship specifically, key issues currently on the table include security cooperation, immigration, and economic cooperation.

The United States and Mexico have exchanged numerous high-level visits, including Presidents Obama and Calderón and then president-elect Peña Nieto. These exchanges reflect the vital importance that each country represents for the other in terms of both economic and security issues. While Mexico's relations with the George W. Bush administration had been strained after the events of 9/11, relations improved dramatically at the end of that administration with the crafting of the Mérida Initiative, a binational plan for cooperative security. In a remarkable shift in approach, President Calderón proposed a strategic partnership between Mexico and the United States to fight the drug war and related crime. The United States responded positively and with remarkable speed to move a proposal forward. The initiative signaled that both parties would move beyond mutual recriminations as to who was at fault and would begin to partner in problem solving.

The complexity of the Mexico-US relationship is at least in part illustrated by the fact that there are 250 million legal crossings of the border per year. Tourism, family visits, and commerce account for the bulk of this traffic. At the same time, many Mexicans are pushed to enter the United States by the difficult circumstances at home, and are pulled by the attraction of wages that are many times greater in the United States than in Mexico. Mexico maintains that its citizens who enter the United States to work must be afforded protection of their human rights and should not be treated as a different class of workers only because they do not have papers. Mexico reasons that these workers are employed by US businesses and thus deserve to be treated with dignity and respect and should not be relegated to a dangerous and oppressive life in the underground. The 2012 US presidential election highlighted the continuing deep political divisions that exist in the United States over this issue. The election also underscored the growing importance of the Latino (largely Mexican) vote in the United States and its rising importance to US electoral politics. As such, the issue of immigration is likely to continue to be in the political forefront for both countries for the foreseeable future. Mexico has had its own difficulties with immigration pressure, as it has been faced with intense migration from Central America and the use of its national territory by human traffickers who are paid to bring people from all around the world to the United States. As an example of the problem Mexico faces, having waived the visa requirement for Brazilian travelers to Mexico in order to improve its relations with Brazil, Mexico later reimposed the visa requirement following a US request for assistance because so many Brazilians were using Mexico as a platform to illegally enter the United States. In another example, Mexico now also faces the growing problem of Chinese immigrant trafficking from Mexican territory into the United States.

DOMESTIC/INTERMESTIC POLICY: MEXICO'S DRUG WAR

The drug war and related public insecurity in Mexico became the immediate central focus of the Calderón administration. It is a policy concern that folds together domestic and foreign policy, and it is the domain of what has come to be called "intermestic" policy—a blend of the two. Although drug trafficking and associated criminality have plagued Mexico for decades, by the mid-2000s the level of violence had escalated, as drug-trafficking criminal organizations fought law enforcement and each other for prime access (*plazas*) to their market, the United States. These criminal syndicates had gained power in Mexico and elsewhere with the weakening of Colombian trafficking operations. In their new role Colombian traffickers became suppliers to Mexican operations, and Mexico's syndicates began to control an increasingly greater share of product development, transit, supply, and marketing into the United States. With the increase in operational responsibility and thus in the money involved, Mexico's syndicates grew in sophistication and firepower. Although the drug business was not new to Mexico and dated back as far as the early twentieth century, the stakes had grown more substantial, thus escalating the violence. Some observers suggested that what was transpiring was, in effect, the "Colombianization" of Mexico. While official Mexican pronouncements on the numbers vary greatly, reliable estimates put the total 2007–2012 death toll in Mexico from homicide at nearly one hundred thousand.

President Vicente Fox had declared the drug scourge to be Mexico's number one national security concern but was able to make little headway with the problem. Upon taking office, President Calderón launched a determined effort to address the growing violence in the country. With the success achieved in Colombia against Colombian drug-trafficking organizations, the Mexican cartels had grown in power, and the effects of their criminal enterprise were felt throughout the society. These organizations have been labeled by some as "mafias" and by others as "insurgents." Regardless of their precise designation, they have expanded their activities beyond drugs to include a broad menu of criminal activity, including extortion, robbery, assault, human trafficking, money laundering, counterfeiting, and so on.

President Calderón's number one problem in dealing with drug-related violence was the level of corruption in Mexican society. Some observers argued that when the society had been under the control of the former official party, the PRI, regional deals had been brokered with cartels throughout the Mexican state, therefore affording a certain amount of peace in the society. With the coming of the PAN to power under Presidents Fox and Calderón, observers argued that the old brokered deals had collapsed, thus opening up a new wave of violence and placing increased pressure on local law enforcement organizations and on local officials more generally. Mexico's cartels move cocaine, methamphetamine, heroin, and marijuana. Ninety percent of the cocaine entering the United States comes from Mexico, principally from coca grown in Colombia and Peru. President Calderón's initiation of a full-scale war against the cartels focused on targeting kingpins, whom the Mexican government has agreed to extradite to the United States. On the ground, forty-five thousand troops were deployed throughout the country, chiefly in the northern border states but also, for example, in the president's own home state, Michoacán, home of one of the most vicious of the cartels, La Familia Michoacana. The landscape of cartels constantly undergoes change as alliances shift and leaders are captured or killed. For now, in addition to La Familia, other major cartels include the Gulf Cartel, the Sinaloa Cartel, the Sonora Cartel, the Juárez Cartel, the Tijuana Cartel, and the Zetas. The Calderón counterdrug strategy ultimately led to the decentralization of drug-trafficking organizations and the proliferation of new groups; the number of such groups now ranges anywhere from thirty-seven to eighty, depending on the official source.

The Calderón government also focused on corrupt local police, taking them down on a selective basis and even arresting entire police forces. The government sought to create new, fully vetted law enforcement organizations at the national level. The use of the military to conduct not only anticartel operations but also antipolice operations led to an unprecedented level of conflict between the military and the police, leading to the execution of soldiers, including a retired general, by corrupt police officers. These killings have been extremely vicious and have involved displays of tortured, beheaded soldiers in order to terrorize the armed forces and the wider population. The armed forces have experienced desertions at the rate of thirty thousand per year, and those who remain in service are subject to threats and intimidation. Some of these deserters have been recruited by the cartels, who openly advertise for their services, especially those who have received training in special operations or intelligence. The military itself has not been immune to corruption, as was demonstrated by the notorious case of General Jesús Gutiérrez Rebollo, Mexico's former drug czar, who was arrested in 1997 for his ties to the Juárez cartel. At the time, allegations surfaced that both the Juárez and Tijuana cartels had negotiated protection with military commanders in the area in exchange for bribes.

The level of corruption in law enforcement organizations at both the local and national levels required a massive response by the government. As troops fanned out throughout the country to combat the traffickers, the violence escalated, and narcotrafficking organizations obtained increasingly powerful weaponry to battle government forces. Much of this weaponry poured into Mexico from the United States. According to the US Bureau of Alcohol, Tobacco, Firearms, and Explosives (ATF), since 2006 over 90 percent of the arms that were seized in Mexico and were traced had come from the United States.

It is estimated that more than five hundred thousand people are employed in the illegal drug industry. Although the path of the money is very difficult to trace, analysts suggest that half of the proceeds from the illegal drug trade are devoted to paying off government officials, including politicians and law enforcement entities. Unlike the case of Colombia, where huge swaths of legitimate business and large agricultural assets fell into the hands, legally or otherwise, of illegal armed groups, including drug traffickers, the orderly disposition of proceeds from trafficking in Mexico is still a work in progress.

The Mérida Initiative forged a new strategic partnership between Mexico and the United States to share responsibility for responding to the threat posed by the drug-trafficking organizations. Although initially some opposition to the plan surfaced in Mexico, once the United States agreed that there would be no true conditionality attached to the funding, such as to include human rights vetting, and once the Mexican government explained that the plan would not involve stationing US troops in Mexico, Mexican legislative and public opinion swung in favor of the plan. Under the terms of the agreement, the United States has poured US$2 billion into the program, significantly expanding security cooperation including training, systems development, equipment, intelligence sharing, and border protection (to include the use of drones).

The United States agreed to work on the demand side of the problem and to address illegal arms transfers to Mexico. For the United States, the issue of arms transfers presented a difficult challenge, as there were an estimated twelve thousand gun shops located along the US side of the border as well as numerous gun shows, thus providing easy access to weapons. US efforts to track weapons flowing south exploded in a partisan fireball as the US Justice Department's "Fast and Furious" program became the target of US election year politics in 2012. A more positive outcome was the agreement reached in August 2009 to join the US interagency efforts, including those by US Immigration and Customs Enforcement (ICE) and ATF, with those of Mexico's attorney general (PGR) to develop investigative methods for combating violence and following arms trafficking and other illegal activity along the border. Finally, the US administration ordered the creation of checkpoints by the US Department of Homeland Security to look for illegal arms smuggling and to conduct random inspections.

CONCLUSION

Mexico's elites have been able to avoid paying the real cost of their failure to bring full development to their population because they have relied for years on the safety valve of emigration to the United States. Porfirio Díaz is widely quoted as having said, "So far from God, so close to the United States," as he lamented the impact of the United States on Mexico's national development. Ultimately, he may have been correct in his assessment, as proximity to the United States has not only led to the loss of over half of Mexico's national territory but also permitted national elites to avoid taking responsibility for national development, particularly after World War II. As the Asian "dragons" and "tigers"—Taiwan, Korea, and Singapore, to say nothing of China—grew their economies and reshaped their destinies, leaders in those countries made important public policy decisions about the need to pursue education and to develop infrastructure and human capital. Unfortunately, the same cannot be said about Mexico's leaders.

In the 1960s and 1970s, when those key decisions could have been made, Mexico's ruling elites were consumed with preserving their power and amassing great wealth. Over time the system modernized and a market democracy did emerge, but it was one that was characterized by an untrained and comparatively uneducated labor force, little capacity for innovation, and an entrepreneurial class that had become complacent about its largely unfettered access to the US market. Unfortunately, poverty and inequality have bred the kind of opportunities that are destructive rather than productive: crime, drug trafficking, and social anarchy. While some economists point to the strengthening of the Mexican middle class, more than half the population still lives below the poverty line.

The Mexican state now faces a monumental challenge as it attempts to defeat the criminal forces that have put the society under siege. Unfortunately, Mexico cannot control the key factor that sets the condition for this situation: US demand for drugs. It may be that Mexico's best approach, under these circumstances, is to continue the sometimes agonizingly slow process of rebuilding its law enforcement and judicial institutions. In creating a new climate of security, significant additional resources will be needed in order to protect and insulate these new institutions from criminal influences. Mexico has begun this process, but this effort will require a broad and sustained political consensus within the society to continue the struggle over the long haul. Plans announced by Mexico's newly elected president, Peña Nieto, signal an intent to readdress the issue of domestic peace and security and to deemphasize kingpin capture. An emphasis on institutional development in law and justice administration, a new emphasis on intergovernmental cooperation to enhance state and local capacities, the reorganization of the federal police within the Interior Ministry, and the creation of a new forty-thousand-member *gendarmerie* to replace the presence of the military and the now largely discredited federal police all suggest a way ahead. The Mexican state will also need to commit to the use of force in a manner that respects human rights, and if it does not, any consensus achieved will be undermined. What is certain, however, is that without a reasonable level of safety and security for the citizenry, the consolidation of democracy and sustained, inclusive economic development will be difficult to accomplish.

Notes

1. Enrique Krauze, "The Mexican Evolution," *New York Times*, March 24, 2009.

2. Denise Dresser, "Reality Check for US-Mexico Relations," *Los Angeles Times*, January 15, 2009.

3. Mark Stevenson, "NAFTA Hasn't Proved a Vehicle for Prosperity," Associated Press, June 8, 2008.

4. Emily Edmonds-Poli and David A. Shirk, *Contemporary Mexican Politics* (Lanham, MD: Rowman and Littlefield, 2009), 270–271.

5. *Country Profile: Mexico* (Washington, DC: Library of Congress, Federal Research Division, July 2008), 12; US Department of State, *Background Note: Mexico,* May 2009, 1–12.

6. Michael Reid, *Forgotten Continent: The Battle for Latin America's Soul* (New Haven, CT: Yale University Press, 2007), 202–203.

7. Sara Miller Llana, "Setbacks in Mexico's War on Corruption," *Christian Science Monitor,* December 30, 2008.

8. Reid, *Forgotten Continent,* 233–234.

9. Monica Rankin, "Mexico: Industrialization Through Unity," in *Latin America During World War II,* ed. Thomas M. Leonard and John F. Bratzel (Lanham, MD: Rowman and Littlefield, 2006), 28.

10. Jorge I. Domínguez and Rafael Fernández de Castro, *The United States and Mexico: Between Partnership and Conflict,* 2nd ed. (New York: Routledge, 2009), 60.

Suggestions for Further Reading

Camp, Roderic Ai. *Mexico's Military on the Democratic Stage.* Westport, CT: Praeger Security International, 2005.

Castañeda, Jorge G. *Mañana Forever? Mexico and the Mexicans.* New York: Alfred A. Knopf, 2011.

Davidow, Jeffrey. *The US and Mexico: The Bear and the Porcupine.* Princeton, NJ: Marcus Wiener, 2004.

Domínguez, Jorge I., and Rafael Fernández de Castro. *The United States and Mexico: Between Partnership and Conflict.* 2nd ed. New York: Routledge, 2009.

Dresser, Denise. "Mexico: Dysfunctional Democracy." In *Constructing Democratic Governance in Latin America.* 3rd ed. Ed. Jorge I. Domínguez and Michael Shifter, 242–263. Baltimore: Johns Hopkins University Press, 2008.

Edmonds-Poli, Emily, and David A. Shirk. *Contemporary Mexican Politics.* Lanham, MD: Rowman and Littlefield, 2009.

Hamilton, Nora. *Mexico: Political, Social and Economic Evolution.* New York: Oxford University Press, 2010.

Morris, Stephen D. *Political Corruption in Mexico: The Impact of Democratization.* Boulder, CO: Lynne Rienner, 2009.

Preston, Julia, and Samuel Dillon. *Opening Mexico: The Making of a Democracy.* New York: Farrar, Straus and Giroux, 2004.

Selee, Andrew, and Jacqueline Peschard, eds. *Mexico's Democratic Challenges: Politics, Government and Society.* Stanford, CA: Stanford University Press, 2010.

Shorris, Earl. *The Life and Times of Mexico.* New York: W. W. Norton, 2004.

17

CUBA: REVOLUTION
IN THE BALANCE?

Juan M. del Aguila and Frank O. Mora

As the only nation in the Western Hemisphere that adopted revolutionary Communism for its model of political development, Cuba stands separate from other Latin American nations. The revolution of 1959 and its subsequent radicalization attracted the interest of students of politics as well as that of policy makers, journalists, intellectuals, and ordinary people, many of whom have been inspired by the Cuban example. In addition, the central role played by Fidel Castro from the beginning of the revolution is key to understanding developments in Cuba in the years since he and his followers came to power. Under his leadership Cuba became an influential actor in regional politics engaged in an unusual degree of revolutionary activism. Fidel personified his country to observers the world over, but his own transformation from an impetuous young revolutionary to an aging dictator parallels the course of the revolution itself, despite efforts by his brother and successor, President Raúl Castro, to "adjust" or "update" certain parts of the system.

The politics of revolutionary development have moved Cuba through periods of radical transformation in the economy and the social system, through phases when pragmatism and moderation shaped domestic priorities and affected social attitudes. In effect, the revolution and its consequences can be understood as an ongoing experiment in the process of achieving mature nationhood, but as with any experiment, Cuba's has been characterized by fits and starts, abrupt policy reversals, intense criticism of the real nature of socialism and revolution, and evident exhaustion. The defining characteristic of the Cuban Revolution in the two decades since the end of the Cold War and the collapse of the Communist bloc and the Soviet Union—a significant source of Cuba's economic sustainability—have been,

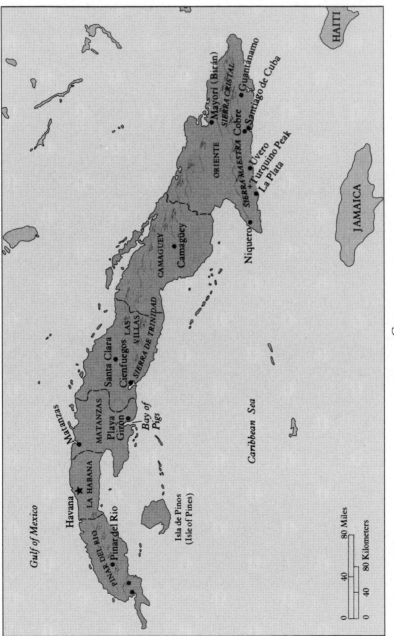

CUBA

as Eusebio Mujal-León notes, "chronic economic difficulty and remarkable political durability."[1] What explains this durability is a basic theme of this chapter.

HISTORY, POLITICAL CULTURE, AND EARLY DEVELOPMENT

Cuba, the largest of the Greater Antilles, is located at the entrance of the Gulf of Mexico, some 112 nautical miles (200 kilometers) from the United States. Its 44,218 square miles (114,525 square kilometers) of total surface stretch over a varied topography that includes mountain ranges, rolling hills, plains, and hundreds of rivers and streams. The principal mountain ranges lie in the eastern, central, and western provinces, and the highest mountain, Pico Turquino, rises to some 6,500 feet (1,981 meters) in the Sierra Maestra range.

Unlike many other developing countries, Cuba has not experienced a dramatic rise in population, and its demographic growth rates remain stable. Population growth averages around 1 percent, which alleviates the burden on employment and services that plagues many developing countries. Of the country's 11.2 million inhabitants in 2011, 73 percent reside in urban areas and the rest live in small towns and in the less densely populated rural areas. Since the 1930s most Cubans have lived in cities and large towns, and by the late 1980s over 20 percent of the population lived in the capital city, Havana, or its environs. Part of the infrastructure of some of Cuba's larger cities is deteriorating owing to neglect, scarce resources, and the sheer passage of time: Havana was founded by Spanish settlers in 1514, Santiago de Cuba, the second-largest city, in 1515.

Caucasians, mulattoes, and blacks are practically the only ethnic groups in the country. Whites account for 65 percent of the population, mulattoes and mestizos are nearly 25 percent, and blacks make up approximately 11 percent. Whites were the dominant ethnic group during the twentieth century, and many are descendants of the creole elite of colonial Cuba. No Indian subcultures exist because for all practical purposes the mostly primitive Indian communities that inhabited the island in precolonial times disappeared early in the colonial period.

Columbus initially encountered Cuba during his first trip to the New World in 1492, but because the island lacked substantial mineral wealth and had not developed an advanced indigenous civilization, it remained sparsely populated well into the eighteenth century. The fifty thousand or so native Indians at the time of the discovery were gradually subdued by Spanish settlers under the *encomienda* system. They were forced to search for precious minerals, work in agriculture, fish, and also engage in primitive forms of trade. Catholic missions were established and charged with propagating and maintaining the faith, so friars and priests played important roles in the early life of the colony. The Catholic Church subsequently grew in membership, wealth, and influence, and its notions of order, faith, spirituality, and salvation pervaded Cuba's cultural foundation.

Black slaves were brought to Cuba by the thousands from the 1700s to the middle of the nineteenth century, replacing Indians as laborers on sugarcane plantations, as servants in the larger towns and cities, and as manual laborers in service occupations. A census taken in 1791 showed that out of a total population of 273,000, 56 percent were white and that slaves made up the largest proportion of the black

population. A century later another census showed that over the entire colonial period, nearly 375,000 black slaves had been brought to Cuba. It is a fact that the slave
trade contributed to the wealth of many planters and traders.

Cuba's economy originally revolved around tobacco farming and subsequently
coffee cultivation, but it gradually became a plantation economy geared toward the
cultivation, production, and export of sugar. The island's geographical location offers the right temperatures as well as the necessary rainfall for sugar production, and
the terrain of the lowlands is suitable for harvesting cane. Indeed, economists and
historians maintain that the island's comparative advantage in sugar production was
soon realized and that earnings from sugar exports financed the imports of foodstuffs, textiles, machinery, and other capital goods.

The combination of sugar, slavery, and the plantation economy shaped the colonial social structure and laid the foundation for an economy geared to foreign commerce, but it did not produce a society of small landowners and rural proprietors.
Differences among *peninsulares, criollos,* slaves, and *libertos* (slaves who had obtained
their freedom) were evidence of a hierarchical system unmindful of any notion of
social equality. As depicted by popular novels, books, and documents of the time,
colonial Cuba remained unaffected by changes taking place elsewhere and therefore
stayed under the tight control of Spain. On the other hand, the benefits of free trade
were strongly felt during the English occupation of Havana in 1762–1763, as new
markets were found and the economy was further integrated into regional and international commercial networks. Geopolitical rivalries with Great Britain and the
United States in time forced Spain to modify the mercantilist regime, which gradually gave way to a more open trading system. Spain sought to reestablish political
control over its colonial domains, including Cuba, in the early nineteenth century,
but the impact of liberal ideas, in addition to the introduction of capital and new
technology, stimulated new thinking.

STRUGGLES FOR INDEPENDENCE, 1868–1901

The emergence of new political currents in the 1860s stemmed from the need to
challenge Spanish domination and to improve Cuba's economic position. On one
hand, a nationalistic and clearly separatist movement advocated confrontation and
war against Spain if those were the only means of achieving independence. More
moderate elements, represented by the Reformist Party, founded in 1862, advocated
representation for Cuba in the Spanish Cortes, administrative reforms, and liberal
trade policies. The issue of slavery often divided the creoles, as did class and economic differences between the eastern and western planters. The latter feared a social revolution and tended to be more conservative. Still, Spain's refusal to grant
meaningful concessions to the Cubans and its failure to satisfy legitimate political
demands led to rebellion in 1868 followed by a decade of bloody and destructive
warfare.

The rebels were led by Carlos Manuel de Céspedes, a patriot and moderately
wealthy planter from Oriente province. Other political and military leaders such as
Generals Antonio Maceo and Máximo Gómez fought bravely during the protracted
struggle, but latent political divisions among the rebels weakened their effort.

Nationalism fed the rebel cause, as did the commitment to emancipate Cuba from colonial domination. Spain poured thousands of troops into Cuba and sent one of its best generals, Arsenio Martínez Campos, to lead the Spanish forces. Yet the rebel cause was doomed by the failure to truly carry the war to the western provinces, by the deaths of Céspedes, Ignacio Agramonte, and other leaders, by the absence of external help, and by the lack of support on the part of many Cubans.

Nearly 250,000 people on both sides lost their lives in the struggle, and Cuba's infrastructure was devastated. The war cost Spain approximately US$300 million and was both a cause and a consequence of political quarrels among its own elites. Yet Spain and the rebels signed an armistice in 1878 that led to a tenuous peace and a period of self-criticism and questioning on the part of those Cubans who still advocated independence.

A growing dependence on the US market for trade, investment, technology, and industrial inputs characterized US Cuban relations in the 1880s and 1890s, even while Spain maintained political control. In 1896 US investments in Cuba were estimated at US$50 million, concentrated in mining and sugar holdings. Trade between the two countries was valued at US$27 million in 1897, and the composition of that trade showed that the United States exported to Cuba manufactured and industrial goods and imported sugar, molasses, tobacco, and a few nonmanufactured products.

There is little doubt that this growing penetration of a weak economy dominated by sugar and its derivative production by a growing capitalist, industrial power meant that the colonial regime was subjected to both internal and external pressures. Once again proindependence forces gathered to challenge Spanish authority and assert claims for independence and sovereignty, and this time they did so with a new and more compelling sense of unity and national purpose. New leaders, principally José Martí, had forged a more mature vision of political emancipation and nationalism, and the issue of slavery had been laid to rest since its abolition in the 1880s. In short, ideologically and organizationally, the separatists were in a stronger position than in the 1860s, whereas Spain vacillated between granting meaningful reforms and reimposing absolutist government.

As the founder of the Cuban Revolutionary Party (PRC) in exile and as the intellectual force and principal civilian organizer of the war effort, José Martí represented a younger generation of Cubans committed to the total liberation of the country. Martí believed that war was brutal but necessary—"a political process that would definitively resolve a situation in which fear of war is a paralyzing element"—and held that "patriotism is a sacred obligation when one struggles to create conditions in the motherland that would improve the lives of one's countrymen."

The war raged back and forth for three years, with the rebels fighting a guerrilla struggle and Spain following more of a scorched-earth strategy. A military stalemate between rebel and Spanish forces along with sensationalist accounts of the fighting published in the United States led to US military intervention in 1898. The Cuban question had become an important issue in US domestic politics, and Spain as well as the rebels had attempted to influence US public opinion. Spain rejected diplomatic entreaties and offers of mediation from European powers and obstinately refused to accept either military or political defeat. In April 1898 the US Congress passed a resolution granting President McKinley's request for authority to end hostilities in Cuba, but it also disavowed any interest in exercising sovereignty, jurisdiction, or control over Cuba once Spain had been driven out.

The US occupation of Cuba lasted until 1902, and many students of Cuban politics believe that it created a legacy of resentment and frustration because, in part, US intervention prevented the Cubans from achieving a complete victory over Spain. US military authorities partly rebuilt the nation's infrastructure and brought about significant improvements in public health, education, public administration, and finance, but Cuban nationalists and many intellectuals felt a sense of political impotence and frustration. Subsequently, the inclusion of the Platt Amendment, passed in 1901 by the US Congress, in the Cuban constitution meant that Cuba became a US protectorate rather than a sovereign nation because the amendment granted territorial concessions to the United States, placed financial restrictions on the Cuban government, and allowed the United States to intervene in Cuba's internal affairs.

Cuba's foreign economic relations were subsequently shaped by the Reciprocity Treaty (1903), which granted preferential treatment to Cuban sugar in the US market and reduced tariffs on US exports to Cuba. US investments in Cuba's sugar industry, cattle industry, public services, utilities, and other properties had reached US$200 million by 1909, nearly 50 percent of all foreign investment in Cuba. The Platt Amendment and the Reciprocity Treaty facilitated a growing US influence in Cuba and were often perceived as neocolonialist measures aimed at protecting US interests in the island. The US presence created a significant political cleavage, separating those people who felt it to be beneficial and necessary for Cuba's early development from nationalists who saw it as a direct infringement of genuine self-determination. The views of Ramón Ruiz illustrate a scholarly consensus on these matters, namely, that the Platt Amendment limited Cuba's first experience in self-government and "offered the Cubans a facile way out of domestic difficulties. Reliance on the United States eventually engendered among Cubans a loss of faith in their Republic and in their own nationality."[2]

THE POLITICAL DEVELOPMENT OF PREREVOLUTIONARY CUBA

Political competition during the early republican period existed predominantly between the Liberal and Conservative Parties. These parties—and others—were essentially controlled by the political caudillos José Miguel Gómez and Mario García Menocal, respectively, and did not articulate clear political philosophies or programs. The political system was based on client arrangements and patronage networks, so partisan loyalties were often exchanged for political favors. Electoral fraud and administrative corruption were common, and elections were often cynically viewed as attempts by manipulative politicians to preserve or expand personal power. Public office was held in disrepute, politics was used as a means of self-enrichment, and the democratic ideals that had motivated Martí and other revolutionary leaders remained little more than abstractions.

On the other hand, respected intellectuals such as Fernando Ortiz and Enrique José Varona formed part of an emerging democratic intelligentsia that rejected politics as a means to private gain and advocated civic-mindedness, cultural emancipation, and, above all, honest and democratic government. For instance, Varona attacked the evils of monoculture and the subordination of the economy to foreign capital, and he suggested that the revolutionary generation had betrayed principles articulated earlier. Reformist groups encouraged debate, much of it focused on the need to cleanse political culture and on appeals to the anti-imperialist principles of students, intellectuals and labor leaders.

Gerardo Machado was elected as a popular president in 1924, but he became a virtual dictator following his contrived reelection in 1928 and his violation of constitutional norms. From that point forward, politics took on a violent character. Government and opposition alike engaged in terrorism, shootings, and political assassinations, indicating that institutions were unable to resolve political conflicts and that force was seen as a legitimate arbiter of political disputes.

The Great Depression had a devastating effect on the economy. Plummeting sugar prices affected the livelihood of hundreds of thousands of families, and unemployment, social misery, and rural banditry reflected a deeper structural crisis. The government sought to alleviate the problems by acquiring new loans from US bankers, but the country's creditworthiness was shaky, and it had previously accumulated substantial debts. The economic picture deteriorated rapidly, helping stimulate and organize opposition to Machado.

Student protesters challenged the police in the streets, but resistance to Machado also involved professionals, middle-class elements, and labor leaders. One of the leading anti-Machado organizations was the University Students Directorate, through which a new generation of activists and revolutionaries advocated a complete and definitive change of regime. A diverse number of other anti-Machado groups with differentiated and often competing agendas emerged to confront the regime, often using violent means; they included the Popular Socialist Party (PSP, Communist Party) and the ABC, a secret organization made up of middle-sector individuals. In short, the opposition was unified in its commitment to driving Machado from power and ending the dictatorship, but it was also tactically and ideologically divided.

The army proved to be a critical contender because its support was essential for either keeping Machado in power or shifting the balance to his adversaries. The army was structured on parochial loyalties rather than merit, and its military competence was questionable. It remained the pillar of order and stability, but it also felt the violent political fragmentation that ultimately ousted Machado. Some lower-rank members, many of whom came from humble backgrounds, viewed the army as a vehicle for self-improvement and social mobility, and they demanded higher pay and an end to the politicization of promotions. Such internal pressure, at a time when a crisis of political authority affected the government's freedom of action and paralyzed decision making, opened the way for an internal revolt led by then-sergeant Fulgencio E. Batista y Zaldívar. Under his leadership the army sought to contain revolutionary outbursts and directly influence the selection of presidents. This would play a central role during the following decades.

Finally, as had been the case since 1898, the United States played the role of ultimate power broker. In 1933 the new Roosevelt administration, through Sumner

Welles as its special ambassador, shaped a resolution to Cuba's political crisis that preserved US interests and restored stability. Through Welles's efforts a weak government under Carlos Manuel de Céspedes succeeded Machado, but that regime was quickly overthrown. A five-member executive committee headed by Ramón Grau San Martín, a physician and university professor, took power briefly, but it too gave way to a more revolutionary government, still led by Grau. Jaime Suchlicki maintains that these events constitute a "turning point in Cuba's history," marking the "army's entrance as an organized force into the running of government and Batista's emergence as the self-appointed chief of the armed forces and the arbiter of Cuba's destiny for years to come."[3]

One cannot overestimate the impact of the truncated revolution of 1933 on the succeeding generation's psychological makeup, its social agenda, or the political determination of its most able leaders. The incomplete business of 1933 left a sense of frustration among the protagonists of reform and revolution, but in time the goals were rechristened. The failure to democratize politics, achieve economic sovereignty, and cohesively assert a national will shaped the ethos of future reformers and revolutionaries, for whom "the lessons of 1933" laid the foundation for new departures.

SOCIAL DEMOCRACY AND AUTHORITARIANISM
IN THE 1940S AND 1950S

After 1933, Cuba went through a period of realignment and moderate authoritarianism, characterized by the conservative domination of weak and undemocratic regimes supported by Batista and the army. Taking advantage of improved economic conditions and secure from military threats or revolutionary outbursts, the regimes governed by partially satisfying political demands and reintroducing client arrangements. On the other hand, electoral irregularities, corruption, episodic repression, and the subordination of civil authority to military pressures retarded the development of viable governing institutions, so the system remained personalist and moderately authoritarian.

Economic dependence on the United States meant that domestic capital played an increasingly important role, and Cuban interests gradually acquired a growing share of ownership in the sugar industry. Measures such as the Reciprocity Treaty and the Jones-Costigan Act, in addition to the policies of the Export-Import Bank, stabilized Cuba's economy and gave confidence to domestic producers, who always looked to the US market as the preferred outlet for Cuban products. US-mandated quotas for sugar guaranteed that Cuba's principal export would enter the United States under a preferential tariff and led to the expansion of acreage and production. The United States supplied 54 percent of Cuba's imports in 1933, a figure that increased to nearly 65 percent at the end of the decade and to some 81 percent by 1950. What Cuba bought was purchased in the United States, and although having a dynamic market close by proved to be convenient, it also retarded Cuba's industrial development.

A major threshold in the process of political development was reached in 1940 following the enactment of a democratic and progressive constitution, itself the result of political compromises among the democratic left, conservatives, and

Communists. This constitution established universal suffrage and freedom of political organization, recognized Western-style civil rights, and abolished the death penalty. Women, children, and workers received social protection, and racial and sexual discrimination was outlawed. Public education was mandated, and the needs of rural children in particular were identified. The state was charged with "orienting the national economy." Industrial development, agrarian reform, and greater rural-urban integration were set as national priorities, and the state was granted greater powers in national development, public administration, and fiscal and monetary policies. The constitution reflected a complex bargain between the rising middle sectors and traditional interests, and by explicitly framing a tutelary role for the state in economic and social affairs, it incorporated then-current ideas and political philosophies.

The Auténtico (authentic) administrations of Ramón Grau (1944–1948) and his successor Carlos Prío (1948–1952) initiated reforms in agriculture, fiscal management, labor, and education, while they also maintained respect for civil liberties. Public subsidies, bureaucratic employment, and the creation of new state agencies led to gains among middle-class and professional groups, but agricultural development lagged, and the power of foreign interests was not directly confronted. Worst of all, political violence and urban-based gangsterism threatened the integrity of the democratic regimes, and neither Grau nor Prío was able to stem the violence. Corruption was spawned by a vast system of patronage, payoffs, and bribes, and Grau's minister of education turned his office into a powerful political machine and an illegal financial network. Student activists turned the University of Havana into a haven for gun-toting thugs and criminal factions and often paralyzed the institution through intimidation and brutality. An entire system of nepotism, favoritism, and gangsterism predominated. Meanwhile, the reformist zeal of the Grau era degraded further, weakening and delegitimating democratic political institutions.

Modernization through reformism did not curb the power of vested interests or foreign capital, and central authority proved weak and incapable of eradicating violence and corruption. To the unfinished agenda of 1933 were added the unrealized promises of the democratic reformers, and scandals and internecine quarrels in Cuba's leadership class eroded public trust in government. The state, supported by neither a dominant class nor a traditional oligarchy, failed to convert diffuse support into legitimately accepted rule, so the nation simply drifted.

Batista's bloodless but effective coup in March 1952 ended the constitutional regime and restored order superficially through political authoritarianism. Cuba's political development was cut short by the coup, and the system proved vulnerable to force. Proclaiming that worry about the lack of guarantees for life and property had led him to accept "the imperious mandate" to usurp power, Batista and his supporters found little resistance to their actions. During his time in office Batista was unable to legitimate his regime through either elections, good relations with the United States, or negotiations with his opponents. Opposition to Batista included moderate, democratic elements sympathetic to the Auténticos but willing to entertain confrontational approaches.

Several revolutionary groups, including Fidel Castro's Twenty-Sixth of July Movement, participated in the struggle against the dictatorship. Among these, the

Revolutionary Directorate (DR) stood out because of its uncompromising ferocity and violent strategy aimed at assassinating Batista himself. Led by the charismatic student leader José Antonio Echeverría, the DR was not the vanguard of a social revolution but rather an organization committed to ending the dictatorship.

As one of the founders of the Twenty-Sixth of July Movement and its undisputed leader, Fidel Castro played a central role in the insurrection against Batista's dictatorship. A group led by Castro attacked the Moncada military garrison in the city of Santiago in 1953, but the attack failed and many of Castro's followers were either killed or subsequently arrested and shot. Castro himself was captured and tried for subversion, but as a trained lawyer with oratorical skills, he used the trial to issue an indictment of the government. Portraying his cause as just and inspired by patriotism and Martí's ideals, Castro called for a return to constitutional government, agrarian reform, profit-sharing arrangements between owners and workers, and social improvements in rural Cuba. He was convicted and sentenced to fifteen years in prison, but he was subsequently released in 1954 under an amnesty program.

Castro's political beliefs and true intentions before he came to power have been the focus of considerable debate. Some people argue that his commitment to armed struggle reflected the compelling facts that no compromise was possible with Batista and that rebellion itself is justified by lofty principles of Western political theory. Others maintain that Castro harbored Marxist beliefs during his days at the university but that he kept the Communists away from his movement so that it could appeal to the Cuban middle class. Some of his former close associates, such as Carlos Franqui, say that Castro's caudillo temperament and his egomaniacal pursuit of personal power raised unresolved questions among his followers.

It is thus unequivocally clear that before he came to power Castro was neither a member of the Communist Party nor a doctrinal Marxist. Rather, he was committed to a radical revolution whose final outcome could not have been foreseen but which placed him in the center of power. In addition, one of his top lieutenants, the Argentine revolutionary Ernesto "Che" Guevara, was a committed Marxist, as was Fidel's younger brother, Raúl Castro. Indeed, the Twenty-Sixth of July Movement itself was divided between moderates who rejected Communism and radicals such as Guevara who believed that the solution to the world's problems lay behind the Iron Curtain. A radical minority led by Castro saw themselves as the self-anointed vanguard of an epic political struggle against capitalism, the Cuban middle class, and US influence in Cuba, and this group launched a mass movement that created an unstoppable momentum.

The guerrilla phase of the insurrection ended successfully for the rebels in December 1958. Domestic isolation, rebel victories in eastern Cuba, and loss of support from Washington convinced Batista that his regime could survive only if the guerrillas were defeated. The army, however, was poorly led, partly because some of its top generals were corrupt and frightened; when a forty-thousand-man army disintegrated in the face of several popular uprisings, this demonstrated a profound loss of morale and an alarming unwillingness to fight a few hundred guerrillas. Cornered and without options, Batista and many of his closest allies fled at dawn on January 1, 1959, paving the way for a total victory by the guerrilla forces.

THE CUBAN REVOLUTION

Neither the insurrection against Batista nor the social revolution that the new regime began to carry out stemmed from deep-seated popular dissatisfaction with the development pattern of Cuba's dependent capitalism. The evidence shows that Cuba had reached a moderate degree of modernization by the late 1950s. Indicators such as literacy rate (75 percent), proportion of the population living in urban areas (around 57 percent), life expectancy (approximately sixty years), and the size of the middle class (between 25 and 30 percent of the population) suggest that Cuba's level of development was comparable to that of other, more advanced Latin American nations.

On the other hand, urban-rural contrasts were marked and the quality of life for the average *guajiro* (peasant) family was well below that of the average urbanite. Health services and educational opportunities were much better in Havana and other large cities than in the small provincial towns or isolated rural communities, and the best jobs and occupations were not available in rural Cuba. Seasonal unemployment also affected the rural areas disproportionately, and a rural proletariat dependent on the mills for employment saw its economic situation deteriorate once the sugar harvest ended. In effect, neither the model of Cuba as a chronically underdeveloped society nor that of an idyllic island characterized by social harmony, a sound economy, and a bustling population fits reality.

The success of the revolution can be better explained by political factors than by socioeconomic criteria. The failure of prerevolution governments to develop and nourish viable ruling institutions or to sustain a national ethos of civic-mindedness left those regimes vulnerable to force and strongman rule and to subversion from within. Legal and constitutional norms were not fully developed, and too many people viewed politics and public office as ways to obtain private, selfish gains. No idea of the public good had taken root, and the political culture revolved around traditional notions of order, loyalty, patrimony, and authority.

The new regime was originally divided among advocates of liberal democracy and a mixed economy and the more radical sectors around Castro and Guevara who called for a social revolution. The radicals believed that the basic capitalist system needed to be abolished and the social system uprooted so that the power of vested economic interests, some of them foreign-based, could be reduced. Policy making was shaped by statist practices, antimarket doctrines, and the goal of eradicating economic evils associated with a dependent capitalist system, and the revolutionary elite was fully aware that to increase state power meant to increase its own. The agrarian reform of 1959 satisfied the long-standing claims of peasants and rural workers, and it also made sense politically. The urban reform of 1960, which socialized Cuban-owned businesses and privately owned real estate, adversely affected the private sector's strength. By 1961 banking, wholesale trade, and foreign trade had been fully collectivized, as had 85 percent of industry and 80 percent of the construction business. This collectivization produced a massive transfer of power and resources from the private economy into the public sector, which was precisely the intended effect.

Structural changes combined with populist, redistributive measures signaled a willingness to incur domestic costs and foreign anger so as to accelerate the process of radicalizing the revolution. The revolutionary elite believed that to slow down was to court disaster; that momentum itself was proof that the masses supported the regime and enthusiastically joined the assault on capitalism and the private sector. Huge rallies commanded the attention of the populace, and during marathon speeches Castro often mesmerized crowds. The regime realized that social mobilization could serve as a form of explicit consent. For this purpose, it established mass organizations such as the Committees for the Defense of the Revolution, the Federation of Cuban Women, and the Union of Communist Youth to reach the grassroots.

Once it became evident that a radical social revolution committed to socialism was in the making—led by individuals seeking total power—an opposition emerged that attempted to restrain or defeat the revolutionary elite. As often happens in revolutionary situations, a decisive struggle between radicals and moderates ensued, between people committed to some form of democracy and those who would settle for radical socialism and nothing else. Both sides knew that only one would prevail, that no compromise was possible, and that personal risks were involved. The opposition included Catholic organizations, disaffected cadres from Castro's own ranks, respected democratic figures, and other anti-Communist elements.

Castro's relationship with the PSP stemmed from his desire to limit the damage inflicted on his regime by the defection of non-Communist revolutionaries as well as from the need to enlist Soviet support. The party shrewdly provided organization when Castro's own was being shaken up, and it offered a dialectical explanation for the society's troubles. Andrés Suárez believes that "the Communists played no role, neither in the political leadership of the country nor in the leadership of the students or of the trade unions," but that the party's discipline, support of "national unity," and foreign connections facilitated understandings with Castro.[4]

By the mid-1960s revolutionary changes restructuring class, property, political, and foreign policy relationships had eliminated a dependent capitalist order replete with US influence and moved the country toward radical socialism. The state took over the basic means of production as well as domestic and foreign commerce, industry, transportation, and utilities. Agriculture was reorganized into collective and state farms, but peasants could produce some goods on small, privately owned plots. The mass media were under state control, as was the national system of telecommunications. Party cadres supervised the information network, and Marxism-Leninism shaped the content of public discussion. Dissident intellectuals, nonconformists, and political opponents of the regime were arbitrarily imprisoned, scorned, or forced to leave the country.

The educational system was radically reorganized and centralized, and education was treated as a key to the process of political socialization. National literacy campaigns pushed literacy rates to the mid-90th percentile, but the quality of instruction left much to be desired. Much of Cuba's history was revised and rewritten, and patriotism and national virtues were highlighted. US influence over Cuba's destiny was made the root of many ills.

Considerable resources also were devoted to public health. Most basic medical services were provided free under a government-run health system that included preventive care, specialized services, and even advanced treatment for common or rare diseases. Over the years hundreds of clinics, hospitals, and specialized-care facilities were built and staffed by thousands of graduates in medicine, nursing, and health-related fields. As a result, life expectancy in the 2000s was about seventy-seven years of age, and Cuba's infant mortality rate of approximately ten per thousand ranks among the best for developing countries.

In conclusion, regime consolidation came about through sustained mobilization, direct exhortation, and a top-to-bottom direction of an ongoing revolutionary agenda rather than through elections. Rewards and sanctions were utilized to elicit compliance with revolutionary policies, but care was exercised not to alienate key sectors of the working class, peasantry, and urban proletariat. These sectors formed the class basis for the new regime once the middle class had been destroyed and the upper strata had either left the country or accepted a dramatic loss in privilege and status. Daily life became intensely political.

INSTITUTIONALIZATION AND CRISIS: ECONOMY, GOVERNMENT, AND SOCIETY, 1976–2006

Needing to regularize the political process and establish national ruling institutions through which stability could be preserved, the revolutionary elite succeeded in reorganizing the state and the Communist Party and created ruling councils at the local level. Fundamental changes in government became evident, especially in the manner in which central authority was exercised, in former President Fidel Castro's role as chief decision maker, in the critical role of the Revolutionary Armed Forces (FAR) and the Cuban Communist Party (PCC), and in the organization of social forces. A new socialist constitution was enacted in 1976 outlining the powers of a number of other key national and provincial institutions. This period of institutionalization, after more than a decade and a half of ad hocism and voluntarism, did not mean, however, that institutions gradually replaced the power and influence of Fidel Castro and his lieutenants.

Economy

A new economic model, the System of Direction and Economic Planning (SPDE), framed policies in the late 1970s and mid-1980s, taking into consideration criteria such as efficiency, rationality, prices, and other economic mechanisms. This framework accepted the validity of material incentives and market processes. From this, they introduced wage differentials, production norms, monetary controls, and taxes. Under the SPDE the emphasis would shift from building socialist consciousness through voluntarism and ideological appeals to the satisfaction of consumer demands through market mechanisms.

The collapse of orthodox Communism in the former Soviet Union and Eastern Europe prompted the Cuban leadership to declare a Special Period in Peacetime in the early 1990s. A strategy of economic survival took shape under conditions of severe austerity and hardship, largely because the US$5–6 billion subsidy from former Communist allies was no longer available. During the Special Period, consumption dropped dramatically, services and subsidies provided by the state were reduced or altogether eliminated, and the standard of living for the average individual or household fell precipitously.

Economic hardships multiplied under this strategy. Reliable studies show that Cuba's gross domestic product fell 35 to 50 percent between 1989 and the mid-1990s, plunging the economy into a depression. For the government, catastrophic losses meant downsizing the state bureaucracy, shutting down factories and industries, and reducing or eliminating subsidies to the transportation system, agriculture, construction, housing, and other sectors. Regardless, the authorities ruled out any prospect of a return to capitalism.

Unable to secure oil supplies due to lack of hard currency, the government imposed draconian measures throughout the economy, causing total or partial blackouts on a regular basis. Dwindling energy supplies forced households to burn wood or trash for fuel—a common practice in the least-developed countries of the world. Unemployment and partial unemployment rose as workers saw their jobs disappear and their schedules severely disrupted, all of which adversely affected the standard of living for millions of individuals and households.

As Cuba entered the new century, growth rates were erratic. Cuba's unproductive and uncompetitive economy was simply unable to generate the material or financial resources needed to sustain its eleven million people. The annual growth rate for 1990–2000 was 1.2 percent—the worst in Latin America. A very modest rebound started with 3.0 percent growth in 2001, 1.5 percent in 2002, 2.6 percent in 2003, and roughly 2.0–2.5 percent in 2004. Declines in the price of nickel and the failure to improve agricultural or industrial production lie at the root of the crisis, which has been further exacerbated by damaging hurricanes.

One explanation for the economy's abysmal performance is the catastrophic collapse of the sugar industry. The crown jewel of Cuba's political economy lies in ruins, no longer the dominant sector of the command economy. Total output in the 1990s stood at around four million metric tons per harvest, regularly falling short of planned targets and not generating adequate levels of hard currency. Precipitous declines in output forced the government to import sugar from Colombia and Brazil to meet export commitments and domestic demand. Output fell from 3.5 million metric tons in 2001 to 2.2 million in 2003 and 1.1 million in 2006–2007, the worst harvest in Cuba's history. Production in 2007–2008 and 2008–2009 came in at 1.4 million and 1.3 million metric tons, respectively. Nickel exports, revenue from services provided by Cuban professionals abroad, and tourist dollars have since replaced sugar exports as Cuba's main sources of hard currency during this decade.

An important source of revenue that compensated for austerity and the decline of the sugar industry is tourism, which generates badly needed hard currency. Nearly two million tourists reportedly visited Cuba in 2006, with net earnings estimated to be in the US$400–600 million range. Expanding tourist facilities is a top economic priority, requiring that long-held ideological prejudices against "contamination from capitalism" be overlooked.

Another source of hard currency are Cuban exiles, who during the second term of US president George W. Bush's administration sent anywhere from US$400 million to US$800 million annually in remittances to their relatives—although estimates vary greatly and some analysts put the total figure at around US$1 billion. A significant tightening of US policy toward Cuba under the George W. Bush administration made this more difficult, as the new restrictions limited visits to Cuba from Cuban Americans to one every three years. Furthermore, Bush's policy allowed remittances only to immediate family. Some restrictions were lifted under the Obama administration, making travel easier for Cuban Americans.

A central question faced by the Cuban regime regarding the economy is the degree to which the satisfaction of consumer demands is essential for regime legitimacy and stability. The economic crisis of the 1990s brought into focus the lack of resources and the adoption of ill-advised policies that deepened austerity. Promises that socialism would produce abundance and prosperity were not fulfilled; in fact, enormous scarcity of basic goods and services emerged. Such a dramatic deterioration in economic conditions inevitably produces resentment and political disaffection, weakening the social contract between the regime and the masses.

Revolutionary Armed Forces (FAR)

The small guerrilla force that Fidel Castro commanded in the Sierras in the late 1950s, known as the Rebel Army, quickly became the most dominant institution of the revolution after its triumph in 1959.[5] Scholars of Cuban politics generally agree that the Revolutionary Armed Forces (Fuerzas Armadas Revolucionarias, FAR) embodied the values associated with the struggle against the dictatorship of Fulgencio Batista. Unlike the socialist bloc in Europe, not only did the FAR predate the Communist Party, but it became the true vanguard of the revolution. Some analysts have argued the party was often subordinate to the FAR during the nearly fifty-four years of the revolution.

The revolutionary regime and leadership emerged from a military struggle that continued even after its triumph, when the level of societal militarization was enhanced. The FAR became the preeminent institution of the early stages of the revolutionary process by virtue of the important responsibilities it assumed. For the regime, the FAR has the highest degree of legitimacy and reliability in terms of historical background, prestige, honesty, and loyalty, all critical to guaranteeing the survival of the revolution.

During the early period of consolidation, the FAR played a pivotal role in providing internal and external defense as well in socialist development, working in the administrative and economic sectors. Until the 1980s, the FAR was at the vanguard of proletarian internationalism, serving as a critical instrument of the regime's foreign policy objectives in the Third World. By the mid-1980s, however, the political and economic costs of supporting revolutionary causes proved simply too great for Cuba and the FAR. In the late 1980s, as a result of a growing ideological and economic crisis brought on by Mikhail Gorbachev's reforms in the Soviet Union and the waning of the Cold War, the Cuban leadership announced a defensive campaign that led to deinstitutionalization and a return to the military-mobilization approach of the 1960s that placed the FAR at the center of the process. As the edifice of Cuban Communism seemed to begin to crumble, the response was for the trusted military to assume a greater role in areas considered by the government to be vital to its survival: the economy and state security.

The critical role played by the military in Cuba's bureaucracy and economy, particularly in the early years, produced what Jorge Dominguez described as "civic-soldiers": "military men who govern large segments of both military and civilian life . . . bearers of revolutionary tradition and ideology . . . who have educated themselves to become professional in political, economic, managerial, engineering, and educational as well as military affairs."[6] Frank Mora described this phenomenon in the post–Cold War era of the Special Period, when some special skills and revolutionary reliability were required, as "technocrat-soldiers": "a manager and administrator, in addition to being a soldier. He is implementing modern organizational and technical business practices and methods to enhance the efficiency and productivity of military and civilian industries, responding to market demands and relying on principles of financial engineering and complex telecommunications."[7]

The FAR was not spared the shock of the Special Period. The military budget was slashed by half, from US$2.2 billion in 1988 to US$1.35 billion at present, and expenditures as a percentage of GNP declined from 3.9 percent in 1987 to 1.6 percent in 1995. Troop strength and resources available for training, fuel, spare parts and other equipment were cut dramatically as a result.

In the late 1980s the military was once again given a decisive role in helping the regime weather a difficult period of crisis. The technical capabilities of a disciplined institution, under the unquestionable authority of the (then) longest-serving minister of the FAR (MINFAR) and first-generation revolutionary leader Raúl Castro, contributed to the regime's decision to rely on the FAR in implementing Raúl's proposal for economic modernization. The leadership had to rely on the FAR because all other institutions, the PCC above all, were failing to perform. The absence of a civil society and independent entrepreneurs placed the burden of the economy on the military.

The process of economic modernization was led by and largely implemented within the Cuban military. Through the *sistema de perfeccionamiento empresarial* (SPE, business improvement system), the regime sought to increase greater self-sufficiency within the FAR, increase the efficiency and productivity of military industries, and provide a model that could be adopted elsewhere in the economy.[8] By the early 2000s, as result of this new mission, the FAR's technocrat-soldiers controlled the most dynamic, strategic sectors or industries of the Cuban economy, such as tourism, retailing, and transportation. By one estimate, MINFAR's holding company, Grupo de Administracion Empresarial (GAESA), managed by the late General Julio Casas Regueiro, once a close confidant of Raúl's, is estimated to have invoiced US$1 billion in 2000.[9]

The Cuban Communist Party (PCC)

The PCC has undergone significant transformations since the early 1960s, when Castroites took effective control of its organization and eliminated political adversaries. Inaugurated in 1965, the party-building process went through a rocky process.[10] The party atrophied in the 1960s, and by 1969 membership was only fifty-five thousand. Lip service was paid to its leading role, but in fact the rambunctious politics of the period and the ad hoc manner in which policies were framed forced the party to the sidelines. The "microfaction affair" in 1968, in which orthodox former

PSP cadres led by Aníbal Escalante attempted to sow division in the ranks and provoke Castro's downfall, led to a bitter internal struggle. Purges followed and the guilty party members were sent to jail.

The PCC was never really the vanguard of the revolution, despite its legal standing and rhetorical pronouncements by Fidel and others in the ruling class of the party's role. The top Cuban leadership held high party positions, such as in the Political Bureau (Politburo), the highest body of the PCC, which directs the general orientation of the government and enacts policies, but their influence and power came from their relationship and loyalty to Fidel (and more recently Raúl) and not as a result of their standing in the party. Within this *partido fidelista*, "the PCC was responsible for administering the party-state bureaucracy and coordinating mass organizations that organized, directed and channeled participation in Cuban society"—often acting as a transmission belt for mobilizing and socializing the public.[11] Since the First Party Congress (December 1975), when the PCC was "institutionalized," there have been five congresses: Second (December 1980), Third (February 1986), Fourth (October 1991), Fifth (October 1997), and Sixth (April 2011).

In the mid-1980s, the PCC began to decline as a result of two key events: Fidel's rectification campaign, which dismantled SPDE and centralized economic decision making, and the end of the Cold War and collapse of the Communist bloc. Substantive questions emerged in the 1980s regarding the ideological rigor of the cadres, their discipline, and their willingness to lead through example and sacrifice. Instances of corruption in the party were common in the late 1980s. It suffered from scandals, poor leadership, careless management, lack of discipline, and other deficiencies. Many (perhaps thousands of) party leaders, members, and militants were purged in the late 1980s and early 1990s when the quality of their work was found wanting and abuses of authority and cases of personal corruption were discovered.

Some of the "negative tendencies" found in the party's performance stemmed from its failure to monitor the illegal activities of high officials—many of whom were party members—in the Ministry of the Interior, the armed forces, and elsewhere. In addition, party members were embroiled in the arrest, trial, and execution of division general Arnaldo Ochoa and three other officers in 1989. General Ochoa, a decorated veteran of the Angolan war and a "Hero of the Revolution," was found guilty of corruption and involvement in drug trafficking. Several officers received long sentences, while others, such as the powerful minister of the interior, General José Abrantes, were subsequently removed from their positions.

After much public debate (and internal wrangling), a series of limited economic reforms were approved during the Fourth Party Congress in order to make the party more responsive to popular concerns. It was clear to Fidel and his ruling cohort that Cuba had to tread very carefully in instituting deep economic reforms for fear that their "contaminating" social and political impact (i.e., the creation of dangerous islands of autonomy) could further weaken or even derail the regime, as it did in the Communist bloc. The strategy seemed to be just enough economic reform to weather the crisis but not so much as to threaten or question the political legitimacy of the revolutionary project. The Fifth Party Congress reaffirmed the limited economic reform strategy and its strong opposition to any political liberalization, as illustrated by its tough reaction against dissent inside and outside the regime. As far as Fidel and his lieutenants were concerned, by the end of the Fifth Party Congress they had weathered the storm without having to make structural market reforms.

Another party congress would not be held for another fourteen years. As the Cuban leadership could have predicted, economic reforms instituted in the early 1990s did weaken the PCC's monopoly, but it was a price that Fidel was prepared to pay because, in the end, the party was never the ultimate source of power and legitimacy in Cuba.

Governmental Framework

Cuba's highest-ranking executive organ is the Council of Ministers (CM), composed of the head of state and government, several vice presidents, and "others determined by law," as the constitution specifies. Raúl Castro formally succeeded his brother Fidel as its president in 2008; he also serves as first secretary of the Communist Party (since 2011) and commander in chief. In short, all lines of authority now converge on Raúl Castro.

The CM has the power to conduct foreign relations and foreign trade, maintain internal security, and draft bills for the National Assembly. It has an executive committee whose members control and coordinate the work of ministries and other central organizations. All of its members belong to the Communist Party, and some—such as the foreign minister, Bruno Rodriguez, and General Abelardo Colome, the minister of interior—also belong to the party's Politburo.

The Council of State (CS) functions as the executive committee of the National Assembly between legislative sessions. The CS issues decrees and exercises legislative initiative. Additionally, it can order general mobilization and replace ministers. It has some thirty-one members, including several of the fifteen members of the Political Bureau elected at the Sixth Congress of the PCC in April 2011. In addition to Raúl Castro, the CS includes influential party and military leaders such as Jose R. Machado Ventura, a vice president of the Council of Ministers and the Council of State, and second secretary of the PCC; vice president and former minister of economy and planning Marino Murillo Jorge; Salvador Mesa Valdes, secretary general of the Central Workers' Union; and General Álvaro López Miera, vice minister of MINFAR and chief of the General Staff of the FAR. As of the Sixth Party Congress, all four are members of the Politburo.

The National Assembly of People's Power (NA) is the national legislature. Deputies are elected for five-year terms, but the Assembly holds only two brief sessions per year. In the 2008–2013 *quinquenio* (five-year term) each of its 612 deputies stood for roughly nineteen thousand inhabitants. Deputies are directly elected by the people, but there is only one candidate for every seat. Among the NA's formal powers are deciding on constitutional reforms, discussing and approving (but not disapproving) the national budget, planning for economic and social development, and electing judges. In practice, legislative initiative is not exercised, the NA cannot challenge the political leadership, and it is, in fact, a rubber-stamp body.

At the conclusion of the National Assembly session in February 2012, Miguel Diaz Canel, former party provincial leader and minister of higher education, was elected to the post of first vice president of the CS. In his speech before the assembly, Raúl Castro announced his retirement in five years, anointing fifty-two-year-old

Table 17.1 Members of the Political Bureau of the Cuban Communist Party (PCC) (2008–2009)

Member	Office(s) Held
Fidel Castro (a)	First Secretary, PCC
Raúl Castro (b)	First Secretary, PCC
	President, Council of State
	President, Council of Ministers
	Commander in Chief
	Second Secretary, PCC
Juan Almeida (died 2009)	Vice President, Council of State
José R. Balaguer	Minister of Public Health
Concepción Campa	Director, Finlay General Institute
Julio Casas	Division General
	Minister of Defense
	Vice President, Council of State
José R. Machado	First Vice President, Council of State
Abelardo Colomé	Corps General
	Minister of Interior
	Vice President, Council of State
Ricardo Alarcón	President, National Assembly
	Member, Council of State
Carlos Lage (c)	Vice President, Council of State
	Executive Secretary, Council of Ministers
Felipe Pérez (d)	Member, Council of State
	Minister of Foreign Relations
Esteban Lazo	Vice President, Council of State
	PCC Secretariat
Ulises Rosales	Division General
	First Vice Minister, Armed Forces
	Minister of Agriculture
	Member, Council of State
Pedro Ross (e)	Member, Council of State
Abel Prieto	Minister of Culture
Leopoldo Cintra	Division General
	Chief, Western Army
Ramón Espinosa	Division General
	Chief, Eastern Army
Yadira García	Minister of Basic Industry
Pedro Sáez	PCC First Secretary, City of Havana
Jorge L. Sierra	Minister of Transportation
Misael Enamorado	PCC Secretariat
Miguel Díaz Canel	Minister of Higher Education
Ramiro Valdés (f)	Minister of Higher Education
	Commander of the Revolution
	Vice President, Council of State
	Minister of Information Technology and Communication
Alvaro López (f)	Corps General
	Vice Minister of Armed Forces
Salvador Mesa (f)	General Secretary of Cuban Workers Confederation

* The Fifth Congress of the PCC was held in 1997. The Sixth Congress has been postponed indefinitely.
  (a) Stepped down from presidency in 2006 due to serious illnesses.
  (b) Formally invested as President of Cuba in February 2008. Acted as Interim President from July 2006 until February 2008.
  (c) Dismissed from all his positions in government and PCC, March 2009.
  (d) Dismissed from all his positions in government and PCC, March 2009.
  (e) Ross was appointed Ambassador to Angola in 2007.
  (f) Joined Political Bureau in 2008. It is the second time around for Ramiro Valdés.

Diaz-Canel, an electrical engineer and former longtime member of the Youth Communist League (UJC), as his successor, signaling the start of a long and desperately awaited transition to a younger leadership in the Communist-ruled island.

THE INTERNATIONAL ARENA

The key factors framing Cuba's role in the world, particularly until the early 1990s, are revolutionary messianism, an anti-American and anti-imperialistic stance, a legacy of defiance, and Marxist-Leninist ideology. Fidel Castro's revolutionary convictions as well as his shrewdness and episodic demagogic outbursts—often in the midst of crisis and bipolar confrontations—made Cuba an influential actor in regional politics and in parts of the developing world, a pattern that, to a lesser extent, Raúl Castro has maintained.

In the 1960s Cuba's revolutionary messianism led it to support guerrilla movements in Venezuela, Bolivia, Guatemala, and Nicaragua. Cuba assisted groups such as M-19 in Colombia, MIR in Chile, the Tupamaros in Uruguay, the Montoneros in Argentina, and the Farabundo Martí National Liberation Front in El Salvador. Cuban support varied according to political circumstances and the country's own capabilities, but in practically all cases it involved either training guerrillas in Cuba and sending them out or supplying weapons and logistical assistance to such groups. Fidel Castro repeatedly stated that as a revolutionary country, Cuba was obliged to offer moral as well as material support to revolutionaries fighting their own wars of liberation.

Through a vigorous assertion of proletarian internationalism Cuba once maintained thousands of cadres abroad on various missions. The regime's view had been that through proletarian internationalism Cubans fulfilled their self-imposed revolutionary duties and advanced the cause of socialism and Marxism-Leninism. However, the policy has had explicit geopolitical aims. In the late 1980s approximately eighty-five thousand Cubans were stationed abroad either as combat troops (in Angola and Ethiopia) or as technical and economic advisors. Contingents included doctors, nurses, and other health care personnel as well as construction workers, teachers, agronomists, and other professionals. Intelligence people, political operatives, and security personnel also served abroad—often disguised as *internacionalistas* (internationalist workers). In some cases Cuba earned hard currency as a result of these missions, because countries such as Libya and Angola paid Cuba in dollars for its services, while the Cuban government paid its people's salaries in pesos.

On occasion, fulfillment of these international duties led to war or confrontation with status quo powers (such as in South Africa) or, as was the case in Grenada in 1983, direct clashes with US forces. In Angola Cuba supported the Marxist dictatorship, and in Ethiopia it backed a brutal Marxist regime. The Angolan war started in the wake of the Portuguese collapse in southwestern Africa in the mid-1970s, and Cuban forces helped turn the tide for Angola's Popular Movement for the Liberation of Angola (MPLA). Cuban troops were stationed in Angola until 1991 and fought against South African regulars and guerrillas connected with the Union for the Total Independence of Angola (UNITA).

As the late 1980s approached, changes began to surface in Cuban foreign policy. In the 1980s Cuba resumed diplomatic relations with influential Latin American states such as Argentina, Brazil, and Peru. Havana began to prefer normalization of state-to-state relations to active support for guerrilla movements. Meanwhile, key Latin American governments were seeking ways to bring Cuba back into the Latin American community. A process of reciprocity ensued that allowed Cuba to expand critical ties in exchange for pragmatic recognition on its part that democratic processes in Latin America are legitimate.

By the early 1990s, Cuba's once ambitious foreign policy of proletarian internationalism was considerably downsized as a result of economic hardships and the end of the Cold War. The government looked inward, focused on addressing the severe economic and social impacts of the Special Period. Cuba's foreign policy was quickly restructured to develop the greater political and especially economic space needed to help confront the two key challenges to the regime: continued US aggression and economic austerity.[12]

In the economic realm, Cuba sought to expand and diversify its economic relations by negotiating a number of bilateral agreements with Western Europe and Latin American and Caribbean countries, building upon the diplomatic inroads established in the 1980s. In the decade 1989–1999, trade with Western Europe and the Americas increased by 45 percent and 40 percent, respectively, while overseas investments expanded as a result of changes in Cuba's foreign investment laws. This broadening and deepening of economic ties, coupled with specific domestic economic adjustments, were enough to counter the more severe social effects of the Special Period. In short, international realignment and limited economic change were enough for the regime to muddle through.

One relationship that helped Cuba create the necessary economic and political space started in the late 1990s with President Hugo Chávez of Venezuela. Beginning in 2000, Venezuela provided Cuba with 53,000 barrels of oil per day; by 2005 the figure had reached nearly 100,000 barrels per day. This energy lifeline is considerable if one considers that Cuba consumes approximately 140,000 barrels per day, while it produces about 60,000 barrels per day, allowing it to reexport the surplus. Because payment terms are so favorable to Cuba, analysts estimate that Venezuela is providing Cuba with a total "gift" of US$6–$8 billion over the next fifteen years. In exchange, Cuba provides Venezuela with approximately thirty thousand technical staff, largely medical doctors, teachers, sports coaches, and a number of military, political, and intelligence advisors.[13] In short, the relationship goes beyond just ideological affinities and solidarity—there are real domestic material and political advantages, especially for Cuba.

In the 1990s and 2000s, Cuba continued to reach out in search of diplomatic allies, as Washington enhanced its efforts to pressure and isolate the island. Cuba established relations with the European Community in 1989 and resumed full diplomatic ties with Colombia (1993) and Chile (1995), and in 1998 the country welcomed a visit from Pope John Paul II. Fidel Castro established personal friendships with a number of leaders in the Americas, such as Brazilian president Luiz Inácio Lula da Silva, Venezuela's Hugo Chávez, and President Nestor Kirchner of Argentina, who were instrumental in "protecting" Castro from US and European criticisms of Cuba's human rights violations. Meanwhile, Cuba intensified its use of multilateral institutions, particularly emerging Latin American blocs such as the Bolivarian

Alliance for the Americas (ALBA) and the Community of Latin American and Caribbean States (CELAC), to oppose economic neoliberalism and US imperialism.

Finally, although US-Cuban relations fluctuate between hostility and tolerance, neither country was prepared to make the crucial political concessions that would lead to a genuine rapprochement. The failed Bay of Pigs invasion (1961)—undertaken by a counterrevolutionary militia trained and funded by the Central Intelligence Agency to spark the overthrow of the revolution—was a seminal event that shaped bilateral relations for decades to come.

Formal diplomatic relations were broken in 1961, but "interest sections" opened in Washington and Havana in 1977. Issues raised by the United States included Cuba's strategic relationship with the Soviet Union, its revolutionary activism in Africa and Latin America, and problems in the area of human rights. Historical grievances, nationalism, the US economic embargo, and Cuban insistence on sovereignty and on earning its powerful neighbor's respect have shaped Cuba's outlook.

The 1990s did not see much of an improvement after a period of open hostility during the 1980s when the Reagan administration tightened the economic embargo and called out Cuba as the source of instability in Central America and the Caribbean. Restoring relations with Cuba was not a high priority for the George H. W. Bush and William J. Clinton administrations. In fact, economic pressures were intensified in the form of the Cuba Democracy Act (1992) and the Democracy Solidarity Act (1996, known as the Helms-Burton Act) that prohibited foreign-based subsidiaries of US companies from trading with Cuba, travel to Cuba by US citizens, and family remittances to Cuba. Though largely driven by domestic political considerations, the objective of US policy was clear: regime change.

The means by which Washington pursued its policy objectives during the George W. Bush administration intensified. Three months into his first term President Bush expanded travel restrictions, and in 2003 he announced fresh measures designed to hasten the end of Communist rule in Cuba, including cracking down on illegal cash transfers and a more robust information campaign aimed at Cubans. Cuba's response followed the script it had consistently resorted to when confronted with intense pressure from Washington: mobilize the Cuban nation around nationalist and anti-imperialist measures and messages while rallying the international community against "determined efforts from the superpower to destroy a beacon of freedom and justice for the oppressed."

From Fidelismo to Raulismo: Change or Continuity?

In July 2006 Fidel Castro suddenly fell gravely ill from a severe intestinal ailment, probably diverticulitis, and delegated all executive functions to his brother Raúl on a provisional basis. Fidel recovered his health but not the same power and influence he had exercised before. In February 2008 Raúl assumed full authority within the government, becoming president of the Council of Ministers and Council of State, in addition to commander in chief of the FAR. Within a year, Raúl made a number of personnel changes, including naming several revolutionary leaders, such as Ramiro Valdes, the much-feared former minister of interior (and, many believe, Raúl's nemesis), to vice presidencies, while taking the more important step of removing young leaders associated with the hard-line ideological stance taken during the "battle of ideas" that Fidel had launched to mobilize youth. Raúl treaded carefully, so as not to seem like he was criticizing his brother, but it was clear that he was interested in charting a different course, one that emphasized pragmatism, efficiency and productivity, and accountability, specifically in the economic realm. As in the past, political liberalization was kept to a minimum; in fact, a campaign of low-intensity, arbitrary preventive detentions and violent suppression of dissidents and other opponents intensified. According to the dissident Cuban Human Rights and National Reconciliation Commission (CCDHRN), the number of arbitrary, temporary detentions rose from just over two thousand in 2010 to sixty-two hundred in 2012.

During the course of Raúl's presidency, a relatively extensive agenda of change was implemented. As described by Eusebio Mujal-León, the principal elements include:

> (1) Consolidating political control and preparing for an orderly transfer of power to successor generation; (2) shrinking the size and scope of the paternalistic state while enhancing its administrative efficiency and maintaining control over strategic economic sectors; (3) transforming state enterprises into autonomous holding companies that would no longer receive state subsidies and whose survival would depend on their ability to increase productivity and generate profits; and (4) expanding opportunities for self-employment (*cuentrapropismo*) with the goal of spurring agricultural production and providing additional jobs for laid off workers.[14]

Some key positions included a number of civilian and armed forces technocrats. In the words of Cuban historian Rafael Rojas, the Cuban government presided over by Raúl Castro resembles "an olive green oligarchy." The president is surrounded by loyal generals in control of key ministries and enterprises in strategic sectors of the economy administered by the armed forces. Several of these generals started out as guerrilla fighters under Raúl's command in the Second Front during the struggle against Batista.

In addition to its management of the economy, the FAR took control of the other key sector critical to ensuring durability: state security. After the Ochoa affair and the purging of the Ministry of the Interior (MININT) between 1989 and 1992, the ministry became a new, fully redesigned and restaffed institution serving the interests of MINFAR and its minister, Raúl Castro.[15] Raúl's most trusted friend and aide, General Abelardo Colome of the Army Corps, was named minister, and division general Carlos Fernández Gondín, longtime chief of FAR counterintelligence, took the post of vice minister. These two Raulistas were charged with not only restructuring the ministry but, more important, taking every measure necessary to subordinate the MININT to the MINFAR.

Although downsized, the armed forces as an institution remain loyal to the revolution and its historical leaders, occupying a larger presence in Communist Party organs following the Fifth and Sixth Party Congresses. By the end of the Sixth Party Congress, more than half the members of the Politburo and 30 percent of the Central Committee hailed from the armed forces. At the same time, high-ranking active and retired officers close to Raúl Castro expanded their presence in governmental institutions such as the Council of State and, more significant, in the economy, creating a web of relationships with foreign capital that led to the emergence of a new class of entrepreneurs who are well positioned to take advantage of economic opportunities.

Raúl began instituting the guidelines for economic reform in late 2010, culminating with its formal approval at the Sixth Party Congress (April 2011). However, the congress did not "settle the uncertainties regarding the pace and scope of the economic reforms," as conservative elements within the party and bureaucracy feared its impact on patronage. Raúl insisted on "order, discipline and exigency," but the bureaucracy slow-rolled the changes, guaranteeing its failure.[16]

The economic reforms of 2010 have not had their desired effect. Economic growth remains relatively low despite measures taken to incentivize small private enterprises and liberalize agricultural production. No other industry has seen as much liberalization as agriculture, with a steady rollout of incentives for farmers. Raúl Castro has been explicit in his reasoning: increasing efficiency and food production to replace imports that cost Cuba hundreds of millions of dollars a year is a matter "of national security." But, as the *New York Times* noted, "by most measures, the project has failed. Because of waste, poor management, policy constraints, transportation limits, theft and other problems, overall efficiency has dropped: many Cubans are actually seeing less food at private markets. That is the case despite an increase in the number of farmers and production gains for certain items."[17]

The nonagricultural sector has not fared better. The number of private sector jobs is not increasing at the pace required to hire the 500,000 to 1.3 million state sector employees the government is expected to slash by 2015. There are a number of reasons for the failure of these reforms, such as poor infrastructure, waste, inability to access capital, poor management, and policy constraints, but in the end it is politics that impeded economic modernization and progress. As in the past, the government continues to fear the emergence of independent, private economic activity that in other countries contributed to unleashing the forces of political liberalization. The Raúl Castro government remains committed to a pervasive system of social controls.

CONCLUSION

Cuba's political development following its independence was characterized by clientelism, strongman rule, and military intervention in politics. The legitimacy of these early regimes seldom rested on popular consent. In the 1940s and 1950s democratic reformism failed to develop viable ruling institutions, and as a result, corrupt governments undermined public support for political democracy. Authoritarian regimes alienated the rising middle sectors and relied on coercion rather than consent, thus seldom ruling with popular support. Economic dependency made national development difficult, resulting in a social system that lacked cohesion.

Radical structural transformation uprooted capitalism and reordered the political system through mobilization and charismatic rule because the revolutionary elite believed that development could be achieved only through political and economic centralization. Egalitarianism, unity, and social militancy became the supreme values of the new Marxist order. Private education was abolished, and the state reshaped the entire educational system, expanding health services as well. State control of industry, commerce, telecommunications, agriculture, and even small-scale production created a large bureaucracy, which in turn led to a new technocracy composed of administrators, planners, and managers, many from the Cuban military.

With the onset of the devastating Special Period, many predicted the collapse of Cuban socialism. These predictions about its demise or about the implementation of major transformations that would be necessary for the system to survive were not realized. Contrary to what many experts, social scientists, and regime opponents have held, the system has proved to be more resilient than anticipated. Limited economic reforms placed a bottom under what could have been an economic cataclysm, blunting the edge of social pressures that could have exploded into political disorder.

Broadly speaking, that resiliency is rooted in nationalism, not quite yet a spent force. The loyalty and relative cohesion of strategic elites such as the party apparatus, the armed forces, and younger, proven cadres involved in administration and management limit the probability that a reformist faction might shake up the system. A survival strategy of adaptation introduced in the early 1990s and intensified under President Raúl Castro—combining major ideological reversals with limited macroeconomic changes and a partial opening for foreign capital—generated sufficient resources to maintain social stability and elite cohesion, one of the crucial determinants of the regime's survival.

Notes

1. Eusebio Mujal-León, "Survival, Adaptation and Uncertainty: The Case of Cuba," *Journal of International Affairs* 65, no. 1 (Fall/Winter 2011): 150.

2. Ramón Ruiz, *Cuba: The Making of a Revolution* (New York: W. W. Norton, 1968), 31.

3. Jaime Suchlicki, *Cuba: From Columbus to Castro*, 5th ed. (Washington, DC: Pergamon-Brassey's, 2002), 114.

4. Andrés Suárez, *Cuba: Castroism and Communism 1959–1966* (Cambridge, MA: MIT Press, 1967).

5. Unless otherwise indicated, this section is taken from Frank Mora, "From Fidelismo to Raulismo: Civilian Control of the Military," *Problems of Post-Communism* 46, no. 2 (March-April 1999): 25–38; Frank Mora, "Military Business in Cuba, China and Vietnam," *Problems of Post-Communism* 51, no. 6 (November-December 2004): 44–63; Frank Mora, "The FAR and Its Economic Role: From Civic to Technocrat Soldier," ICCAS Occasional Paper Series, June 2004, University of Miami, Coral Gables, FL.

6. Jorge Dominguez, *Cuba: Order and Revolution* (Cambridge, MA: Belknap Press, 1978), 342.

7. For an excellent discussion of the FAR's restructuring during this period, see Domingo Amuchastegui, "Cuba's Armed Forces: Power and Reform," *Cuba in Transition* 9 (1999).

8. Brian Latell, "The Cuban Military and Transition Dynamics," 2003, Cuba Transition Project, Institute of Cuban and Cuban American Studies, University of Miami, Coral Gables, FL.

9. Gerardo Fernandez and M. Menendez, "The Economic Power of the Castro Brothers," *Diario 16* (Madrid), June 24, 2001.

10. William LeoGrande, *The Cuban Communist Party and Electoral Politics: Adaptation, Succession, and Transition*, 2002, Cuba Transition Project, Institute of Cuban and Cuban American Politics, University of Miami, Coral Gables, FL, 3.

11. Mujal-León, "Survival, Adaptation and Uncertainty," 154.

12. H. Michael Erisman and John M. Kirk, eds., *Redefining Cuban Foreign Policy: The Impact of the Special Period* (Gainesville: University Press of Florida, 2006).

13. Javier Corrales, "The Logic of Extremism: How Chávez Gains by Giving Cuba So Much," working paper presented at the meeting "Cuba, Venezuela, and the Americas: A Changing Landscape," Washington, DC, September 14, 2005.

14. Mujal-León, "Survival, Adaptation and Uncertainty," 155.

15. Frank Mora, "Cuba's Ministry of Interior: The FAR's Fifth Army," *Bulletin of Latin American Research* 26, no. 2 (April 2007): 222–237.

16. Mujal-León, "Survival, Adaptation and Uncertainty," 157.

17. Damien Cave, "Cuba's Free-Market Farm Experiment Yields a Meager Crop," *New York Times,* December 8, 2012.

Suggestions for Further Reading

Baloyra, Enrique, and James Morris, eds. *Conflict and Change in Cuba.* Albuquerque: University of New Mexico Press, 1993.

Del Aguila, Juan M. *Cuba: Dilemmas of a Revolution.* 3rd ed. Boulder, CO: Westview Press, 1994.

Dominguez, Jorge I. *To Make a World Safe for Revolution: Cuba's Foreign Policy.* Cambridge, MA: Harvard University Press, 1989.

Domínguez, Jorge I. *Cuba: Order and Revolution.* Cambridge, MA: Belknap Press, 1978.

Erikson, Daniel. *The Cuba Wars: Fidel Castro, the United States, and the Next Revolution.* New York: Bloomsbury, 2008.

Gonzalez, Edward. *Cuba Under Castro: The Limits of Charisma.* New York: Houghton Mifflin, 1974.

Horowitz, Irving L., and Jaime Suchlicki., eds. *Cuban Communism.* 11th ed. New Brunswick, NJ: Transaction, 2003.

Klepak, Hal. *Cuba's Military, 1990–2005: Revolutionary Soldiers During Counter-Revolutionary Times.* New York: Palgrave Macmillan, 2005.

Mesa-Lago, Carmelo. *The Economy of Socialist Cuba.* Albuquerque: University of New Mexico Press, 1981.

Oppenheimer, Andrés. *Castro's Final Hour.* New York: Simon and Schuster, 1992.

Pérez, Louis A. *Cuba: Between Reform and Revolution.* 4th ed. New York: Oxford University Press, 2010.

Pérez, Louis A. *Cuba and the United States: Ties of Singular Intimacy.* 3rd ed. Athens: University of Georgia Press, 2003.

Perez-Stable, Marifeli. *The Cuban Revolution: Origins, Causes and Legacy.* 3rd ed. New York: Oxford University Press, 2011.

Ritter, Archibald, ed. *The Cuban Economy.* Pittsburgh: University of Pittsburgh Press, 2004.

Schoultz, Lars. *That Infernal Little Cuban Republic: The United States and the Cuban Revolution.* Chapel Hill: University of North Carolina Press, 2011.

Smith, Wayne S. *The Closest of Enemies: A Personal and Diplomatic Account of US-Cuban Relations Since 1957.* New York: W. W. Norton, 1987.

Sweig, Julia. *Inside the Cuban Revolution: Fidel Castro and the Urban Underground.* Cambridge, MA: Harvard University Press, 2002.

Szulc, Tad. *Fidel: A Critical Portrait.* New York: Harper, 2000.

18

COSTA RICA

Mitchell A. Seligson

Virtually all the studies comparing Central American nations contain the phrase "with the exception of Costa Rica." Travelogues—and even many academic studies—refer to Costa Rica as the "Switzerland of Central America." The propagation of the notion of Costa Rican exceptionalism has become so widespread that the first-time tourist is likely to be surprised to find a Central American nation, not an alpine one. Yet, as with most stereotypes, there is more than a grain of truth in this one: Costa Rica is different from its neighbors in three very fundamental ways.

First, levels of social and economic development are far higher in Costa Rica than elsewhere in Central America.[1] Life expectancy at birth for Costa Ricans was seventy-nine years in 2011, exceeding by one year that of the United States, higher than any other country in Latin America, and substantially higher than the Latin American average of seventy-four years. The under-five infant mortality, a universally used measure for comparing development, stood at nine per one thousand live births in 2011, compared with twenty-six in Nicaragua and twenty-one in Honduras. In terms of the proportion of college-age students attending an institution of higher education, by 1989 Costa Rica surpassed even Switzerland, with 27 percent enrolled versus 26 percent in Switzerland. Costa Rica's rate also surpassed the United Kingdom's (24 percent) and was nearly twice as high as that for El Salvador (17 percent), its closest competitor in Central America in the area of college enrollments.

Second, Costa Rica has the longest and deepest tradition of democratic governance of any nation in Central America. Indeed, for many years experts have rated Costa Rica as the most democratic country in all of Latin America.[2] Civil liberties, including freedom of press, speech, and assembly, are widely respected and protected. Free and open elections have become the hallmark of Costa Rica's style of politics, with observers throughout the world seeking to copy elements of an electoral system

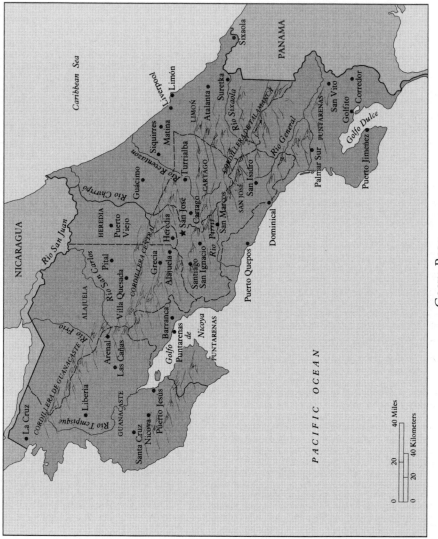

COSTA RICA

that faithfully guarantees against voting fraud and corruption. Human rights, so often brutally abused in other Central American nations, are carefully respected, and one rarely hears even of allegations of their violation.[3] Third, Costa Rica is a peaceful island in a violent region. It abolished its army more than fifty years ago and is constitutionally prohibited from forming another one. Although there have been minor incursions and incidents over the years along Costa Rica's northern and southern borders, border guards and paramilitary units have been adequate to cope with these international conflicts. Costa Rica would be incapable of mounting a credible defense against a determined aggressor, but Costa Rica's friends in Latin America have in the past made it clear that they would use their military forces to deter any such move. Strikes and protests are rarely violent, and negotiation is the most common mechanism for resolving disputes. Terrorism is almost unknown.

Costa Rica, then, stands out from its neighbors as being more advanced socially, economically, and politically and as more democratic and peaceful. There have been many attempts to determine why Costa Rica diverges from the regional pattern. Some studies have focused on historical accidents as an explanation, others on the mixture of resources (especially land and labor), and yet others on questions of ethnic homogeneity. To date, no comprehensive explanation has been established, yet partial explanations incorporating each of the mentioned features seem plausible. In this short introduction to Costa Rica these elements will be highlighted as factors that seem to explain Costa Rican distinctiveness.

HISTORY AND POLITICAL CULTURE

Costa Rica, the southernmost country in the group of five colonies that united into a loose federation shortly after gaining independence from Spain in the early 1820s, developed in isolation from its neighbors to the north. This isolation was partially a result of historical factors, since politics pivoted around Guatemala, the colonial seat of power. It was also partially the result of a geographic factor—namely, that the bulk of Costa Rica's population resided in San José, Cartago, and Heredia, towns located on the *meseta central* (central plateau), and thus was largely cut off from both the Pacific Ocean and the Caribbean Sea as well as from Nicaragua to the north and from Panama to the south.

Although Costa Rica can boast that it is more than twice the size of El Salvador, its 19,650 square miles (50,900 square kilometers) make it less than half the size of Guatemala and Honduras and only slightly more than one-third the size of Nicaragua. In US terms, it is tiny—about the size of West Virginia. The usable territory is further reduced by the presence of a mountain chain that cuts through the center of the country, running from north to south. The mountain chain is studded with active volcanoes, and the most recent eruption, in 1963, caused widespread damage to crops. The net effect of the mountains, volcanoes, and other natural formations is a reduction of arable land to an estimated 53 percent of the total land area.

Costa Rica was further weakened by the absence of large Indian populations widely found elsewhere in Central America. In Guatemala, for example, the conquering Spaniards were able to rely on a large supply of Indians to undertake heavy labor in the mines and in the fields. Although there is evidence that prior to the conquest there were perhaps as many as four hundred thousand Indians living in the territory that was to become Costa Rica, by the end of the sixteenth century there were fewer than twenty thousand, and according to some estimates as few as forty-five hundred by 1581.[4]

Isolation, mountains, volcanoes, and the absence of a sizable indigenous workforce do not seem to add up to a very promising basis for the impressive developments that Costa Rica was eventually to achieve. Paradoxically, however, what seemed like disadvantages turned out to be significant advantages. Isolation proved a blessing because it removed the country from the civil wars and violence that so rapidly came to characterize postindependence Central America. Later, the dictatorial rule and foreign invasions that plagued the rest of the region had little direct impact on Costa Rica. Hence, in contrast to its neighbors to both the north and the south (Nicaragua and Panama), Costa Rica has never experienced an invasion by US marines. The mountains provided the altitude and the volcanoes the rich soil, both of which were required for what was to prove to be a highly successful coffee industry. Finally, the absence of a large indigenous population meant that the repressive labor systems (especially the *encomienda* system) that predominated in much of the rest of Latin America could not prosper in Costa Rica.

The colonial period in Costa Rica was one of widespread poverty. Early explorers found little of the gold and silver that so strongly stimulated Spanish migration to the New World. Had they discovered major mines, no doubt they would have found ways of importing a labor force to work them. But significant mines were never found, the labor was not imported, and the flood of colonizers who settled elsewhere proved to be only a trickle in Costa Rica. There are reports that as late as 1675 there were only five hundred to seven hundred Spanish settlers in Costa Rica, and by 1720 the number barely exceeded three thousand. It was not until the mid-1850s that the total population of the country had grown to more than one hundred thousand.

The small population, both indigenous and immigrant, together with the absence of major gold and silver mines meant that agriculture became the principal source of economic activity throughout the colonial period. Although the soil was rich and a wide variety of crops grew well, farming was directed toward subsistence agriculture. As a result, Costa Rica had little to trade in exchange for needed goods that were not available locally. The initial poverty reinforced itself by placing beyond the reach of the settlers the farm tools and other implements needed for a more productive economy.

Throughout the colonial period efforts were made to add vitality to the fragile local economy. Attention was focused on export agriculture, especially cacao and tobacco. Both crops grew well and fetched high prices on the international market, but both eventually failed in Costa Rica. In the case of cacao, which was grown in the tropical lowlands bordering on the Caribbean Sea, marauding Indians from Nicaragua, in league with British pirates, systematically raided the plantations and stole the crop. Tobacco grew in the highlands and therefore was protected against such raids, but Spain declared a monopoly on tobacco exports and drove down profit margins for producers to the point where the cultivation of tobacco no longer proved worth the effort. By the end of the colonial period Costa Rica had not been able to find a way out of its poverty.

Independence was delivered as a gift to Costa Rica in 1821 when the isthmus, under the leadership of Guatemala, became independent from Spain. Although there was a brief period in which Costa Rica was joined with the other nations of Central America into a federation, shortly afterward independent political rule was established. Very early on in the postcolonial period the fledgling government took critical steps to help develop a stronger economic base for the country. One of these was the granting of land to all people who were willing to plant coffee on it. As a result, coffee cultivation increased dramatically in the first half of the nineteenth century, and by the 1840s direct exports of Costa Rican coffee to the markets in Europe had begun. The product was well received by buyers and quickly achieved recognition for its high quality.

Coffee exports soon became the principal engine of economic growth for Costa Rica. The income from these exports made it possible for coffee producers to import new tools and building materials, and the government was also able to invest funds in critical infrastructure projects, especially roads and ports to facilitate the production and export of coffee. One major project that grew out of the effort to facilitate coffee exports was the construction of a railroad to the Caribbean port of Limón. Until the completion of this project, virtually all coffee exports had been shipped to Europe via the Pacific coast port of Puntarenas, around the tip of South America, and then to Europe. The high shipping costs of the lengthy voyage, however, reduced profits for the producers. The railroad to the Caribbean therefore served to cut those costs. Its construction was financed by a series of foreign loans, which Costa Rica found itself unable to repay even before the railroad was completed. As a result, the US-owned firm that had contracted to build the railroad began to plant bananas to subsidize its construction. From this small start the United Fruit Company developed, and it became the major economic influence in the Caribbean tropical lowlands of Costa Rica up through the 1930s, after which time the company moved its operations to the Pacific coastal lowlands. Banana cultivation provided employment for the railroad workers who had migrated to Costa Rica from Jamaica and later for job seekers from Costa Rica's highlands. Jamaican blacks came to be the only demographically significant ethnic minority in the country, although today they account for less than 2 percent of the population.

Coffee and bananas proved to be the mainstays of the economy through the middle of the twentieth century. Over the years coffee fields were expanded to cover a wide area along the chain of mountains that runs through the country, an expansion caused by farmers in search of new land on which to grow coffee. As the territory suitable for coffee growing shrank, settlers moved to other areas where they planted basic grains, and in the higher mountain regions they grew vegetables or raised dairy cattle. In the province of Guanacaste the broad flatlands proved suitable for cattle raising, and a major export industry of fresh beef developed between Costa Rica and the United States. When the United Fruit Company left the Caribbean lowlands because of the onset of debilitating banana diseases there, those banana fields lay abandoned until the 1950s, when the discovery of new, resistant varieties allowed other companies to reinitiate the banana industry in that area. The economy of the 1980s, then, rested on the export of coffee, bananas, and beef. The recent introduction of nontraditional crops, such as pineapples, flowers, melons, tropical fruits, and vegetables, began to produce significant export earnings. The largest increase in income, however, has been from tourism, especially ecotourism, drawing on Costa Rica's natural beauty accompanied by a wise policy of establishing a large network of national parks. Tourists come from all over the world to visit Costa Rica's rain forests and enjoy its incomparable beaches. Today tourism earns more foreign exchange than bananas and coffee combined. The most recent expansion of the economy has been in the area of high technology, especially the manufacture of computer components for such giants as Intel as well as in the export of software.

Although agriculture has been the traditional base of the economy, when Costa Rica joined the Central American Common Market in the early 1960s it led to significant industrialization. By 1990 agriculture was producing only one-sixth of the gross domestic product and industry and manufacturing nearly one-half. The growth of industry has paralleled the growth of urbanization, and today over half of the population is urban. For many years Costa Rica's entry into the Central American Free Trade Agreement (CAFTA) with the United States was stalled by opposition in the legislature, but a national referendum held in 2007 gave a narrow edge to the proagreement side, and in late 2008 the final pieces of legislation were put in place for Costa Rica to join. This legislation paves the way for several market liberalization measures, including the introduction of competition into the telecommunications and insurance industries, which up until that point were closely held state monopolies.

POLITICS AND PARTIES

Poverty and the absence of a wealthy ruling class that derived its power from a slave or Indian population proved to be factors that favored the development of democracy in Costa Rica. Local government had its origins in colonial Costa Rica when local *cabildos* (city councils) were established in 1812. When independence was announced, a procedure was established that involved the popular election of delegates to a constitutional convention, and thus indirect, representative democracy was established in the first constitutional arrangements. A weak presidency was created, with the term of office limited to only three months, within a rotating directorate.

But all was not favorable for democratic rule. The system was weakened by regional rivalries between the two major population centers, San José and Cartago, and civil wars punctuated the first twenty years of independence—as did coups, assassinations, and invasions. In 1844 a new constitution was drafted and approved, dividing the government into three separate branches: legislative, executive, and judicial. Voting rights were established, but restrictions were many: to be eligible to vote, one had to be married, male, a property owner, and at least twenty-five years of age. Less than 3 percent of the population voted in the first elections under this new constitution. However, even this limited form of democracy was extinguished by a coup within two years.

Additional efforts at constitution making, more coups, and countercoups occurred until 1890. In that year a period of political stability and democratic rule was initiated, and this one lasted, virtually unbroken, until 1948. Direct elections were instituted in 1913, and a new constitution drafted in 1917 granted numerous social guarantees to the working population. Although this document was to be replaced in 1919, in the years that followed, Costa Ricans made continual improvements in the election laws and procedures. In 1925 the secret ballot was instituted, and in 1927 the Civil Registry, a verifiable voter registration system, was established.

Political parties were first organized in the nineteenth century, but until 1940 they were little more than loose, personalist coalitions built around the leading economic interests. In that year the coffee oligarchy elected Rafael Angel Calderón Guardia to power and was surprised when he quickly moved in a populist direction. Calderón, a physician who had developed a large following among the urban poor, embarked on a major program to introduce social legislation. In 1942 he began a social security program and approved a minimum wage law. He also established an eight-hour workday and legalized unions. In 1943, after the Nazi invasion of the Soviet Union, he formed an electoral alliance with the Costa Rican Communist Party, known as the Popular Vanguard Party. This party, organized in 1929, had attempted to run candidates for local office in the 1932 elections, but after it was barred from doing so it became increasingly involved in labor protests that took place during the Great Depression, especially among banana workers.

The alliance between Calderón and the Communists caused great concern and division within Costa Rica, but in the 1944 elections the alliance forces won, supporting a candidate of Calderón's choosing. With World War II over and the Cold War beginning, the wartime alliance of convenience with the Communists became the target of increasingly strong protests within Costa Rica, and in 1948 a coalition of the traditional coffee oligarchy in league with young reformist social democrats defeated Calderón, who was once again running for the presidency. The legislature, however, had the responsibility of declaring the results of the vote, and with Calderón's supporters in the majority, it annulled the election.

The reaction to the maneuver was swift and violent. An armed group led by José (Pepe) Figueres Ferrer organized in the mountains to the south of the capital and began a series of skirmishes with government forces, aided by unionized banana workers. After a brief but bloody civil war, Figueres triumphed. He took over the government and ran it for a year and a half, during which time a new constitution was drafted and approved. Although it was a modern constitution, guaranteeing a wide range of rights, it outlawed parties that were perceived as threatening to democratic rule, such as the Communists.

Four major consequences of the civil war of 1948 have served to shape Costa Rican politics ever since. First, the new constitution abolished the army and replaced it with a paramilitary force of civil guards. Without an army, it is far more difficult for dissenting forces to engineer a coup, and indeed, there have been no successful attempts to dislodge civilian rule since 1948. Second, Figueres did what no other successful leader of a coup in Latin America has ever done: he voluntarily turned the control of the government over to the victor of the annulled election. By doing so he firmly established a respect for elections that had been growing in Costa Rica since the turn of the century. Third, the civil war largely delegitimated the Communist Party, and since that time, even after the elimination of the constitutional prohibition on Communist candidates running for office, the voting strength of the Communist Party has not exceeded 3 percent of the total presidential vote. Fourth, Figueres ushered in with him a group of social reformers who, though in many ways merely expanded on programs begun by Calderón, sought to spur economic development and social progress without resorting to outright socialist schemes.

Once Figueres relinquished power he began to build a new party, called the National Liberation Party (PLN), to compete in the 1953 elections, which he won handily. From the moment of that election through 1998, the presidency oscillated between control by the PLN and control by a coalition of opposition forces.

Since 1998, however, party politics in Costa Rica have been shifting. New political parties, often forming coalitions with other minor parties, have entered the electoral arena in force. At the same time, electoral abstention has been increasing substantially. The result has been that the PLN has lost much of its firm grip on the presidency. In 2002, for the first time ever, elections went into a second round because of a strong run by a third party. In 2006 the election victory by Oscar Arias, allowed to run for office a second time as a result of a supreme court (Sala IV) decision, was by only a 1 percent margin. It was worrisome that abstention increased again, to almost 35 percent of registered voters. But in 2010 the PLN regained strength and elected Laura Chinchilla Miranda, Costa Rica's first female president, by a strong 46.9 percent vote total, followed by Ottón Solís of the Citizen Action Party (PAC) with 25.1 percent and Otto Gueverra of the Movimiento Libertario (ML) with 20.9 percent. The once powerful opposition party, the Unity Social Christian Party (PUSC), rocked by corruption scandals, received only 3.8 percent of the votes. Abstention declined somewhat from its high point in 2006 of 34.8 percent of the registered electorate to 30.9 percent, but was still far higher than the norm for the 1962–1994 period, where only about one-fifth of the registered voters stayed home. The PLN won twenty-three of the fifty-seven seats in the unicameral legislature, far exceeding PAC's twelve, but still necessitating coalition formation to achieve a majority. Women took nearly 37 percent of the seats, the highest total in history, and Chinchilla appointed women to two-fifths of ministerial positions.

Turnout at the local level (Costa Rican municipalities are called *cantónes*), where elections for mayor were held for the first time in 2002, has been far lower than for the presidential/legislative elections. Of the eighty mayoral spots, the PLN took fifty-eight, while the PUSC won nine.

One of the most serious problems to confront Costa Rica in recent history is the growing number of high-level incidents of corruption. Two former presidents have been convicted of taking bribes, and both were given five-year sentences. The Chinchilla government has been rocked by scandals among her ministers and principal advisors. Those scandals at the very top of the political system initially served to discredit the PUSC, the major opposition party, whose electoral alliance crumbled. But now it seems as though the political system as a whole is being tainted. The most recent AmericasBarometer surveys carried out by the Latin American Public Opinion Project (LAPOP) show declining support for the system and growing doubts about the legitimacy of the regime. Some observers are suggesting that Costa Rican exceptionalism is fast eroding and that in the not-too-distant future Costa Rica will look very much like its Central American cousins.

GOVERNMENT STRUCTURE

Since 1949 Costa Rica has operated under the constitution that grew out of the 1948 civil war. Power is shared among the president, a unicameral legislature, and the courts. Members of the legislature and the president are elected every four years. Candidates for the legislature, representing each of the seven provinces of the country, are selected by party conventions. The ability of a sitting president to implement programs has always depended on the strength of congressional support.

In order to implement the wide range of social and economic development programs envisioned by the leaders of the PLN, numerous autonomous and semiautonomous agencies have been created. Hence, one agency handles electric and telephone services, another water supply, and yet another automobile and home insurance. These agencies have been a positive force for development and have spawned many creative ideas. For example, the automobile and home insurance agency also runs the fire department, which guarantees that it is in the insurance agency's interest to have an efficient firefighting service. The autonomy of these agencies has helped to isolate them from partisan political pressure. Yet along with their autonomy has come the problem of an excessive decentralization of control. As a result, central planning and budgetary control have become extremely difficult as agencies and their functions have proliferated over the years. The free trade agreements, however, have served to reduce the power of these agencies.

POLICY MAKING

The modern state that Costa Rica has evolved into can be largely credited with the achievements that were noted at the beginning of this chapter. The high standard of living that has been attained, however, has been built on an economy that has limited industrial capacity. Most industrialization is of the assembly type, and as much as 90 cents of each dollar of output derives from imported materials. The continuously growing government and parastatal bureaucracies further increase costs without adding to production.

By the mid 1970s it was beginning to become clear that the growth model of the post-civil-war period was running out of steam and that the economy could no longer support the expense of a widespread social welfare net and a bloated public sector. Yet little was done to correct the system under successive PLN presidents. Then beginning in 1980, under the leadership of an opposition president, the system began to come apart. In order to shore up local production and consumption—and taking advantage of cheap loans being offered by foreign banks that were awash in petrodollars as a result of the dramatic rise in world petroleum prices—Costa Rica began to borrow wildly. Over a very short span of time the country's foreign debt grew to the point at which it exceeded the equivalent of the total annual national production, and by 1982 Costa Rica had one of the highest per capita foreign debts in the world. The local currency was devalued again and again, inflation and unemployment rose, and the system seemed headed for a crash.

By late 1981 the future seemed grim indeed. Yet while similar circumstances have led to coups in other Latin American countries, Costa Ricans waited patiently for the elections of 1982 and once again voted in the PLN. A dramatic plan for recovery was put in place by the victorious president, and the plan proved successful in stabilizing the economic picture. Inflation dropped, employment rose, the currency was revalued, and an effort was made to rationalize the foreign debt. These actions restored confidence in the system, but they did not return to the citizens the benefits of the growth that had been lost during the 1980–1982 period. Belts had to be tightened, taxes were increased, and prices rose. Economic growth picked up a bit, but there was no dramatic recovery.

Throughout the 1980s Costa Rica followed a slow path to economic recovery. Under the competent leadership of the central bank's president, Eduardo Lizano, the PLN conducted a strenuous and ultimately successful effort to renegotiate important components of the foreign debt. The recovery would have been stronger if it had not been for the precipitous decline in coffee prices brought on by the collapse of the International Coffee Organization's system of quotas and prices. Throughout the period and on into the 1990s, when the opposition again took office as a result of the 1990 election, Costa Rica operated under a strict International Monetary Fund (IMF) mandate to cut public expenditures and hold down inflation. Although the IMF goals have not always been met, by 1993 the economy had essentially recovered to its pre-1980 levels, and it enjoyed modest growth in the 1990s and strong growth, often over 6 percent a year, in the new millennium. The global financial meltdown that began in 2008, however, threatened to greatly weaken the economic outlook for Costa Rica, driving down tourism and threatening exports. Yet prudent anticyclical policies, including ones that reduced the cost of internal tourism to replace the decline in international tourism, helped restore the economy to reasonably good health.

THE INTERNATIONAL ARENA

In 1986 the PLN broke the pattern of electoral victory that had normally oscillated between the opposition party and itself by winning the election. It did so under the leadership of Oscar Arias Sánchez, and Arias took power in an increasingly threatening international environment brought on by crisis in Nicaragua.

When the Sandinista revolutionaries were fighting to overthrow the Somoza dictatorship in the late 1970s, they found extensive support in their neighbor to the south. Although Costa Rica remained officially neutral in that conflict, there was a long-standing antipathy for Somoza and the harsh dictatorial regime that he represented. Public support for a Sandinista victory was overwhelming, and there is much evidence that the government of Costa Rica did what it could to help.[5]

Once the Sandinistas took power, however, relations between Costa Rica and the new regime rapidly deteriorated. Costa Ricans perceived the revolution as having a Marxist-Leninist orientation, and as such, it presented two threats to Costa Rica. First, it was a threat because of the fear that Communist expansionism would mean an eventual attempt by Nicaragua to take over Costa Rica. Second, it presented a threat to internal stability because it was feared that disgruntled Costa Ricans, especially among the university youth, would turn to revolutionary activity. In fact, in a small way the second expectation was realized. Terrorism, which had been almost unknown in Costa Rica, erupted with a number of ugly incidents in which lives were lost, and several clandestine "people's prisons" were discovered that were apparently designed to hide victims of political kidnappings. With the Reagan administration in the White House, yet a third fear gripped Costa Ricans: that the United States would invade Nicaragua, possibly using Costa Rican territory as a base of operations. Such an event would have thrust Costa Rica into an international military conflict for which it was not prepared and that it did not want. Indeed, as the Iran-Contra hearings in the United States were later to demonstrate, a clandestine airstrip was built in Costa Rica to help ferry arms to the Contra rebels, and a plan was developed for a so-called southern strategy involving Costa Rican territory.

On top of all of these concerns was the growing problem of Nicaraguan refugees. As the Contra war grew in ferocity and the Nicaraguan economy deteriorated, waves of refugees joined those already in Costa Rica who had fled the initial takeover of the Sandinistas. In short, Costa Ricans mortally feared being caught up in an impossible international conflict that could only result in deep harm being done to their country's national economy and society.

Upon assuming office, Oscar Arias dedicated himself to bringing peace to the region. Doing so was not only appropriate for a country that had long been noted for its internal peace and lack of an army but also urgently needed if Costa Rica hoped to avoid the problems noted above. Arias managed to draw together the leaders of all of the Central American countries and develop a peace plan that not only would involve Nicaragua but also would serve to end the civil war in El Salvador and the guerrilla war in Guatemala. For his efforts Arias was awarded the Nobel Peace Prize.

Unfortunately, tensions between Costa Rica and its northern neighbor, Nicaragua, have boiled up in recent years. A long-standing dispute over navigation and other rights on the Río San Juan, which separates the two countries, reemerged as a flashpoint in Costa Rica's external relations. Heavily armed Costa Rican police forces have been sent to the northern border, while international diplomatic efforts have attempted to forestall violent clashes. Costa Rica has built an emergency access road near the border.

CONCLUSIONS

In the 1990 elections the PLN lost the presidency to an opposition coalition led by the son of Calderón Guardia. Within a few months of this loss, the Sandinistas in Nicaragua were defeated in an upset election. These two elections saw the new decade emerging with new leadership in these two Central American neighbors. The dominant parties of the decade of the 1980s, the PLN in Costa Rica and the Sandinista National Liberation Front in Nicaragua, were being asked by the voters to take a backseat in order to allow fresh faces to try their hand at economic development, democratization, and peace. The dramatic changes in the Soviet Union and Eastern Europe did not go unnoticed in Central America, as capitalism and democracy rapidly began to replace socialism and dictatorship. New elections in 2002 brought the opposition Social Christian Party (PUSC) to power with the election of Abel Pacheco, a physician who had participated in an attempt to overthrow Figueres in 1955. Elections in 2006 and 2010 returned the PLN to power.

In the region, however, youth gangs and narcotraffickers have produced an explosion of criminal violence. Costa Rica has not been immune to this new challenge, with crime rates at all-time highs. In this context, peaceful, democratic Costa Rica once again faces new challenges and opportunities for regional leadership as the one country in Central America with a long tradition of democracy. On the domestic scene, the ability of the economy to continue to grow remains a major challenge.

Nontraditional exports, computer chip manufacture, and tourism are critical factors in continued success.

New challenges face Costa Rica. Democratic rights were being expanded as a result of the creation of the Sala IV, a constitutional court, which has been augmenting individual liberties at a rapid pace. Yet many Costa Ricans wonder if this movement has gone too far, and there are signs of growing discontent. In the new century Costa Rica has had incidents of mass protest that it had not experienced before. As already noted, voting abstention, historically never very high, has increased markedly, a sign for some of growing disenchantment with the political system. Political leaders have been sensitive to this shift in voter sentiment and have begun a new process of institutional reform that promises to maintain Costa Rican politics are on an even keel, but many feel that the old parties are not capable of real democratization. Corruption scandals have become more widespread and have reached higher than ever before, implicating several former presidents.

Costa Rica's open, democratic style of governance has enabled the country to withstand crises that would cause others to wilt. If the past is any guide to the future, Costa Rica will rise to the test and overcome its problems.

Notes

1. The data in this paragraph are drawn from World Bank data available online.

2. See the various years of the Freedom House index.

3. The Latin American Studies Association reports that the National Reconciliation Commission, established as part of the Central American peace accord of 1987, found that "no one in Costa Rica claimed that there were systematic violations of human rights or denial of freedom of expression in the country." Latin American Studies Association, "Final Report of the LASA Commission on Compliance with the Central America Peace Accord," Pittsburgh, PA, March 15, 1988, 8.

4. This section draws on Mitchell A. Seligson, "Costa Rica and Jamaica," in *Competitive Elections in Developing Countries,* ed. Myron Weiner and Ergun Ozbudun (Durham, NC: Duke University Press, 1987).

5. See Mitchell A. Seligson and William Carroll, "The Costa Rican Role in the Sandinista Victory," in *Nicaragua in Revolution,* ed. Thomas W. Walker (New York: Praeger, 1982), 331–344.

Suggestions for Further Reading

Bell, John Patrick. *Crisis in Costa Rica.* Austin: University of Texas Press, 1971.

Biesanz, Richard, Karen Zubris Biesanz, and Mavis Hiltunen Biesanz. *The Costa Ricans.* Englewood Cliffs, NJ: Prentice Hall, 1982.

Booth, John A. *Costa Rica: Quest for Democracy.* Boulder, CO: Westview Press, 1999.

Booth, John A., and Mitchell A. Seligson. *The Legitimacy Puzzle in Latin America: Democracy and Political Support in Eight Nations.* Cambridge: Cambridge University Press, 2009.

Cruz, Consuelo. *Political Culture and Institutional Development in Costa Rica and Nicaragua: World-making in the Tropics.* New York: Cambridge University Press, 2005.

Edelman, Marc, and Joanne Kenan, eds. *The Costa Rica Reader.* New York: Grove Weidenfeld, 1989.

Gudmundson, Lowell. *Costa Rica Before Coffee: Society and Economy on the Eve of the Export Boom.* Baton Rouge: Louisiana State University Press, 1986.

Hall, Carolyn. *Costa Rica: A Geographical Interpretation in Historical Perspective.* Boulder, CO: Westview Press, 1985.

Hall, Carolyn, and Héctor Pérez Brignoli. *Historical Atlas of Central America.* Norman: University of Oklahoma Press, 2003.

Lehoucq, Fabrice Édouard, and Iván Molina Jiménez. *Stuffing the Ballot Box: Fraud, Electoral Reform, and Democratization in Costa Rica.* Cambridge Studies in Comparative Politics. New York: Cambridge University Press, 2002.

Seligson, Mitchell A. *Peasants of Costa Rica and the Development of Agrarian Capitalism.* Madison: University of Wisconsin Press, 1980.

————. "Ordinary Elections in Extraordinary Times: The Political Economy of Voting in Costa Rica." In *Elections and Democracy in Central America,* ed. John A. Booth and Mitchell A. Seligson, 158–184. Chapel Hill: University of North Carolina Press, 1989.

Seligson, Mitchell A., and Edward N. Muller. "Democratic Stability and Economic Crisis: Costa Rica, 1978–1983." *International Studies Quarterly* 31 (September 1987): 301–326.

Vargas-Cullell, Jorge, Luis Rosero-Bixby, and Mitchell A. Seligson. *La Cultura política de la democracia en Costa Rica, 2004.* San José, Costa Rica: Centro Centroamericano de Población, 2005.

Wilson, Bruce M. *Costa Rica: Politics, Economics and Democracy.* Boulder, CO: Lynne Rienner, 1998.

Yashar, Deborah J. *Demanding Democracy: Reform and Reaction in Costa Rica and Guatemala, 1870s–1950s.* Stanford, CA: Stanford University Press, 1997.

NICARAGUA: THE POLITICS OF FRUSTRATION

Richard L. Millett

Nicaragua, largest in area of the Central American republics, has a history marked by unfulfilled promises, frustrated hopes, and violent internal conflicts and external interventions. The Sandinista revolution of 1979–1990 now seems to be yet another episode in this dreary history. Obsessed with the past and dominated by conflicting personal ambitions, Nicaragua's political system offers few solutions to the nation's overwhelming social and economic problems.

Despite—or perhaps because of—this history, Nicaragua has enjoyed disproportionate attention from US scholars and political activists. Ruled briefly in the nineteenth century by an American named William Walker (a filibuster, or irregular military adventurer), occupied twice by US Marines in the first third of the twentieth century, and the scene of a nearly decade-long conflict between a Marxist regime and US-sponsored counterrevolutionary insurgents in the 1980s, the nation has frequently been the subject of fierce policy debates within the United States. The United States and other nations have also been interested in Nicaragua's potential as an interoceanic canal route. In addition, the Sandinista revolution in 1979 seemed to present an opportunity to test both the potential for social revolution in Central America and the possibility of creating a less dogmatic socialist state. Such hopes, like Nicaragua's aspirations to be the site of a canal, would remain unfulfilled.

HISTORY

From the colonial period until the present Nicaragua has been the scene of international rivalries. Its indigenous population was decimated in part to provide labor

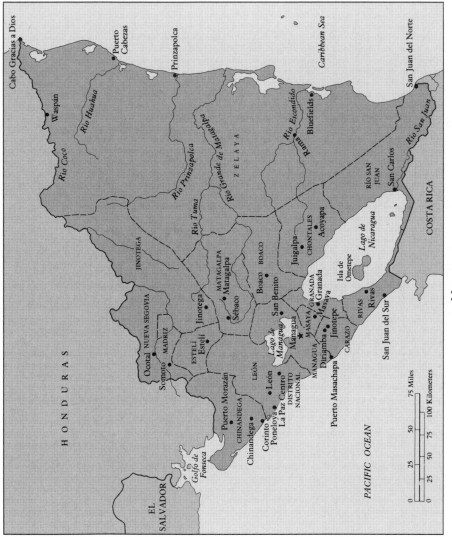

NICARAGUA

for the mines of Peru. The British waged a prolonged conflict over the rule of the Caribbean coast and competed with the United States for control over the potential transisthmian canal route. The nineteenth-century filibustering expedition of William Walker reflected rivalries over control of the isthmian transit route as well as plans to annex lands for the expansion of slavery. It also was a product of the interminable civil conflicts between the Liberal Party and the Conservative Party, both of which at times preferred foreign intervention to defeat at the hands of their domestic opponent. Ultimately, fear of reviving the slavery issue led the Pierce administration to cut off supplies and reinforcements to Walker, thereby thwarting his ambition to rule Central America and underscoring the US tendency to determine regional polices based on domestic political issues. Washington's decision to build a canal through Panama rather than Nicaragua damaged relations and led to the 1912 Marine intervention. Fearing that Nicaragua's Liberals might grant a canal concession to some other nation, the United States entered into a de facto alliance with the Conservatives, with the presence of a small Marine unit ensuring Conservative rule until the mid-1920s.

The United States then attempted to withdraw the Marines and promote honest elections and a professional military, but these efforts only contributed to another civil conflict and a much larger intervention in 1927. Washington imposed a peace settlement on Nicaragua's warring factions, providing for general disarmament, US supervision of the next two presidential elections, and the creation of a US-officered and -trained constabulary force to be known as the National Guard.

One Liberal general, Augusto César Sandino, rejected these terms and launched a guerrilla war against the Marines and the National Guard. Although never able to seriously threaten the government, Sandino's resistance endured until the last Marines departed at the start of 1933. Sandino then negotiated peace terms, but a year later he was murdered by the National Guard.

That force's commander, General Anastasio Somoza García, used the National Guard to propel himself into the presidency in 1936, inaugurating over forty-two years of Somoza family rule. The Somozas used three basic instruments—control of the National Guard, manipulation of the Liberal Party, and the image of a close alliance with the United States—to perpetuate themselves in power. In the process they amassed vast personal wealth and established a network of corruption. The dynasty's founder was assassinated in 1956, but his sons Luís and Anastasio Somoza Debayle managed to hold on to power. They provided the United States with the launching pad for the abortive 1961 Bay of Pigs invasion of Cuba, and in turn, Fidel Castro supported the creation of an anti-Somoza insurgency. When the Somozas used the devastating 1971 earthquake that leveled Managua to further enrich themselves and their cronies, popular discontent increased dramatically. A Marxist guerrilla movement, the Sandinista Liberation Front (FSLN), had been in existence since the early 1960s, but now it began to attract support from wider elements of society. When opposition newspaper editor and political leader Pedro Joaquín Chamorro was murdered in early 1978, popular discontent exploded. Political and economic pressures exerted by business leaders, with some support from the Carter administration, failed to oust President Anastasio Somoza Debayle, and national and international support increasingly coalesced around the Sandinistas. After a prolonged and bloody struggle, the Sandinistas forced Somoza into exile and occupied the capital in July 1979.

Sandinista leaders initially convinced non-FSLN politicians and business leaders to cooperate with the FSLN in forming a broad-based government. However, it soon became clear that real power lay with the nine-member Sandinista national directorate, which was intent on creating a controlled economy, supporting other Central American insurgency movements, and establishing close ties with Cuba and the Soviet Union. Internal political conflict increased, and with the inauguration of the Reagan administration in 1981, the United States began to support armed resistance to Sandinista rule. Known as Contras, these forces inflicted significant economic damage, but they were never able to seriously challenge Sandinista power. Elections were held in 1984, but, protesting conditions that they claimed made effective participation impossible, major elements of the internal political opposition boycotted the process. The FSLN used these elections to consolidate control, installing party leader Daniel Ortega as president and adopting a new constitution that incorporated the aims and principles of a socialist revolution. However, a combination of the costs of the ongoing Contra war, the impact of a US economic boycott, and the FSLN's own economic mismanagement ultimately devastated the economy and undermined FSLN efforts to consolidate their control.

A combination of mediation by Central America's presidents and a decision by the George H. W. Bush administration to pursue negotiated solutions to Central America's conflicts led to internationally supervised elections in 1990. To the surprise of the FSLN, these were won decisively by a fourteen-party coalition headed by Violetta Barrios de Chamorro, widow of Pedro Joaquín Chamorro. The FSLN, however, remained the largest bloc in the legislature. To govern effectively, the Chamorro administration made working agreements with the FSLN, including leaving General Humberto Ortega, brother of ex-president Daniel Ortega, in command of the military. This, however, broke up Chamorro's own coalition and created new problems with the US Congress.

Under the Chamorro administration Nicaragua experienced six years of political turmoil, economic crisis, and citizen insecurity. Determined to "govern from below," the FSLN promoted strikes, obstructed legislation, and resisted military reforms. Conservative elements ultimately gained control of the legislature and engaged in a fierce battle with the administration over constitutional amendments. Jobless and landless, former members of both the Contra and Sandinista forces again took up arms, returning some rural areas to a virtual state of war. Despite all this, some progress was made. Annual inflation, which under FSLN rule had surpassed 30,000 percent, fell to under 20 percent. The strength of the military was greatly reduced, the police were brought under government control, and the draft was ended. Most contras disarmed and some refugees returned. Humberto Ortega was eventually replaced as military commander, demonstrating a loss of FSLN control over the armed forces.

After a bitter fight the constitution was amended to reduce executive powers, protect private property, depoliticize the military, and bar the reelection of the president or any close relative. Finally, the Chamorro administration conducted reasonably fair—if far from perfect—elections in 1996 and peacefully transferred power to another party. The 1996 elections produced more than twenty candidates but quickly became a race between Daniel Ortega of the FSLN and an alliance of Nicaragua's factionalized Liberals, headed by Managua mayor José Arnaldo Alemán. Alemán was elected president with 51 percent of the vote to 37.7 percent for Ortega. The Alemán administration managed to improve relations with the United States, but the economy remained a disaster and charges of corruption threatened to engulf the regime. In addition, the devastation caused by Hurricane Mitch in 1998 further undermined efforts at economic recovery. By the end of his term Alemán was seeking means to ensure his immunity from future prosecution. Constitutional amendments approved by the legislature at the start of 2000 reduced the role of smaller parties, undercut the independence of the comptroller general's office, and made it more difficult to convict a president.

A combination of the changes in the electoral system and fears of a Sandinista return to power ensured the victory in the 2001 elections of Alemán's hand-picked candidate, his vice president, Enrique Bolaños Geyer. Once in office, however, President Bolaños turned on his predecessor, actively seeking his prosecution for massive corruption. He succeeded in getting Alemán convicted and imprisoned, but it cost him the support of the Liberal Party, leaving him with only a small minority of support in congress and producing efforts by the Liberals to form an alliance with the FSLN to force him from office. Alemán continued to control the party even while under house arrest and, in alliance with the FSLN, gained control of the legislature and used it against Bolaños. Nicaragua entered into a prolonged period of political paralysis as various factions maneuvered to gain an advantage in the scheduled 2006 elections.

A deeply divided opposition opened the way for a return to power by Daniel Ortega and the FSLN in the 2006 elections. The Liberals split between pro- and anti-Alemán factions. A dissident group of Sandinistas formed their own party, the Sandinista Renewal Movement (MRS), and for a time appeared to be a major factor. Their candidate, however, Managua mayor Herty Lewites, suffered a fatal heart attack a few months before the election. The Nicaraguan constitution had been amended to give victory to anyone with a plurality in excess of 35 percent, and in the election Ortega and the FSLN won 38 percent to 28.3 percent for the anti-Alemán Liberals; the Alemán faction received 27.1 percent and the MRS 6.3 percent. The FSLN also won thirty-eight of the ninety-two seats in the National Assembly.

President Ortega governed by making deals with Alemán and by manipulating the courts and local and legislative elections. He benefited from close ties with the Venezuelan government of Hugo Chávez, obtaining petroleum on favorable terms and receiving other assistance. As the 2011 elections approached, the Nicaraguan supreme court, packed with his supporters, ruled that the constitutional ban on reelection did not apply to Daniel Ortega, setting the stage for him to win another term. Aided by a divided opposition and an improving economy, Ortega won reelection with over 60 percent of the vote, and his supporters gained a majority of the seats in the National Assembly. He further consolidated his political power in the 2012 municipal elections, when the FSLN gained control of almost every major town.

SOCIAL STRUCTURE

At the beginning of the twenty-first century Nicaragua had a population of approximately 4.5 million, most of whom are mestizos. Some Indians along the Caribbean coast do remain ethnically distinct, and there is also a strong Afro-Caribbean influence on that coast, where much of the population emigrated from the British Caribbean. Because of its ethnic makeup and its isolation from the rest of the nation, the Caribbean coast was granted a measure of political and cultural autonomy in 1987.

The majority of Nicaraguans are Roman Catholic, but Protestant groups have made major inroads, so the nation today is perhaps 20 percent evangelical, and an evangelical political party finished third in the 1996 elections.

Nicaragua is the largest Central American nation in area, and its economy is heavily dependent on agriculture. Nevertheless, it is also the region's most urbanized nation. Flows of refugees from conflict in the countryside exacerbated this situation in the 1980s and 1990s, and today the nation is over 60 percent urban. Unemployment and underemployment often run above 50 percent in urban areas. Nicaragua has the hemisphere's second-lowest GNP per capita and Central America's highest infant mortality rate.

Both business and labor are relatively well organized in Nicaragua. Many of the largest labor and peasant organizations are controlled by the FSLN. The major business group, the Superior Council of Private Enterprise (COSEP), was a center of anti-Sandinista opposition. Its former president, Enrique Bolaños, served as Nicaragua's president, succeeded by Daniel Ortega.

In contrast to most of the hemisphere, the military has never been a truly autonomous actor in Nicaraguan politics. It was first the tool of traditional parties, then the instrument of a foreign intervention, then the guardian of a prolonged family dynasty, and finally the bulwark of support for a revolutionary political project. Today, its ties to the FSLN have considerably weakened, and it is becoming more like a traditional Central American military. Several regular changes of command have taken place, any fears that it would intervene in the political process have largely evaporated, and its size has been greatly reduced. It even sent a contingent to Iraq in 2003. Today the greatest remaining issue is disposal of its aging surface-to-air missiles, which Washington fears might find their way into terrorist hands.

Nicaragua's mass media have always been highly politicized. Under the Somozas and then again under the Sandinistas the newspaper *La Prensa,* controlled by the Chamorro family, became a symbol of resistance to the regime in power. Over the last forty years radio has become even more important than print media in efforts to boost support for or mobilize opposition to a particular regime. Television, too, has steadily increased its influence. Television was largely government-controlled until the 1990s, but today both national channels and widely available foreign programming reflect a broad variety of views.

POLITICAL INSTITUTIONS AND PARTIES

Nicaragua is governed under the Sandinista-authored constitution of 1987, but this was significantly altered by a series of amendments adopted in 1995 and by others added in this century. In many ways the government structure follows traditional Central American patterns, with a unicameral legislature, a prohibition on immediate presidential reelection, an independent electoral authority, a supreme court, and numerous autonomous agencies. Local government consists of two levels, departmental and municipal. There are fifteen departments plus the two semi-autonomous regions along the Caribbean coast. Outside of these coastal regions, departments are generally dominated by the central government, but municipal governments have had a growing degree of autonomy.

Beginning in 1990 Nicaraguans elected municipal officials directly. The powers of municipal government were strengthened, and mayors became the most important local political figures. At least fifteen Nicaraguan cities have populations over fifty thousand, and metropolitan Managua's population is about two million.

Under the rule of the Somoza family the executive branch was totally dominant, and the legislature and courts generally rubber-stamped whatever the president wanted. The FSLN's 1987 constitution then strengthened executive authority even further. In both cases there was an extraconstitutional power that controlled the government. Under the Somozas this was the Somoza family and the National Guard. Under the Sandinistas it was the FSLN's nine-member national directorate. Today, political power is largely in the hands of elected officials. The president and vice president are elected for five-year terms and, along with close family members, are barred from immediate reelection. Presidential powers have been broad, including the right to propose a budget, appoint cabinet members and other high officials, and, prior to 1995, to rule by decree. These powers were significantly reduced by recent amendments, but the president still retains considerable independent authority, especially if a state of national emergency is declared.

Nicaragua's unicameral legislature has ninety-three members. Complex constitutional provisions provide that twenty seats be elected from national party lists and seventy be elected departmentally under a system of proportional representation. In addition, defeated presidential candidates who win over 1 percent of the vote are given a seat. This encouraged a proliferation of parties, with eleven winning one or more seats in 1996. However, in 2001 only the Liberal alliance, the FSLN, and the Conservatives (who won just one seat) gained seats in the legislature. Electoral law reforms in 2000 had changed the system, curbing the proliferation of smaller parties but also concentrating power in the hands of the two dominant parties. The revised constitution gives the Assembly broad powers, including the ability to enact laws, override presidential vetoes with a simple majority vote, and amend the constitution with a 60 percent majority. This became a real possibility following the 2011 elections.

As in much of Latin America, a weak judicial system presents a significant obstacle to efforts at democratic consolidation. Nicaragua has little tradition of an independent judiciary, and partisan efforts to manipulate the supreme court are constant. As a result, the court at times is unable to function. Lower courts are poorly staffed and overwhelmed by the rising crime rate. Conviction rates in criminal cases have run under 5 percent. One result is that prisoners are often incarcerated for prolonged periods before coming to trial. Prisons are badly overcrowded and conditions fall well below minimal international standards. Despite such problems, Nicaragua still has a much lower crime rate than Guatemala, Honduras, or El Salvador and has significantly fewer issues with youth gangs and/or international organized crime.

A fourth power is the Supreme Electoral Council (CSE), which not only runs elections and certifies the results but also controls the Civil Register and issues citizens their identity cards (*cédulas*). In January 2000 an agreement between the

Liberals and the FSLN reformed the electoral law, eliminating provisions requiring broad representation of political parties in the administration of local polling stations and giving the CSE virtual carte blanche in the appointment of these officials. The seven members of the CSE would be appointed by the Assembly and would need the approval of 60 percent of those voting. This ensured that the FSLN and the Liberals would have to agree on members and that smaller parties would have no effective voice in the process. To gain a place on the ballot, any party that failed to win 3 percent of the vote in the previous general election must obtain the signatures of 3 percent of eligible voters. Only the Liberal alliance, the FSLN, and the Nicaraguan Christian Way (CCN) qualified for exemption from this provision. Nicaragua's Conservative Party managed to gain a spot on the 2001 ballot, but its presidential candidate garnered only 1.4 percent of the vote. Municipal elections in 2004 gave control of most of Nicaragua's cities to the FSLN. Elections for president, vice president, and Assembly members were again held in late 2006. Suffrage is universal for those sixteen and older. In presidential elections there will be a second round of voting between the two leading candidates if the leading candidate does not obtain 40 percent of the vote or 35 percent or more with a margin of 5 percent over the second-place candidate. The CSE will set the date for this election, but it must be within forty-five days of the general election.

Among the most important of the autonomous governmental institutions are the central bank and the office of the comptroller. The central bank controls the currency, disburses government funds, and exercises some control over private banks. The comptroller oversees the disbursement of government funds and audits government accounts. Both have been the scene of bitter partisan fights.

Nicaragua has dozens of political parties, many of which exist only to promote individual ambitions and have no national structure. The political scene is dominated by the two major Liberal factions and the FSLN. The Constitutional Liberal Party is dominated by former president Alemán and merges three elements of Nicaragua's traditional Liberal Party. Because this party was long the vehicle of the Somoza dynasty, it is frequently accused of having ties with elements of that regime. The party has support among Nicaragua's upper and middle classes. It is pro-business and generally supportive of the United States in international affairs, and it has traditionally been strongly anti-Sandinista. Its strength has, however, significantly declined in recent elections. Together with the FSLN it forged a pact to inhibit efforts by other parties and/or political alliances to gain legal status, though the pact has since largely collapsed, with a dissident Liberal faction, the PLI, emerging as Nicaragua's major opposition party.

The FSLN has somewhat modified its Marxist rhetoric and now portrays itself as more of a social democratic party. It has strong support within the labor movement and in other mass popular organizations. It advocates increased government control over the economy, expanded social welfare policies, and an independent foreign policy. Its support has been damaged by a reputation for corruption derived from the massive looting of state resources at the end of its period in power, by deep internal divisions that resulted in the defection of some of the leadership before the 1996 elections, and by personal scandals revolving around the party's leader, former president Daniel Ortega, and his common-law wife, Rosario Murillo. Many of the party's original leaders have defected, including former vice president Sergio Ramírez, former culture minister Ernesto Cardenal, and former official newspaper editor Carlos Chamorro. None of this, however, has reduced Daniel Ortega's control over the party. Several smaller parties, including Christian Democrats and the remnants of the traditional Conservative Party, retain legal status but have little if any power and must seek alliances with one of the two Liberal factions to compete in elections.

PUBLIC POLICY

Nicaragua's public policies are a strange mixture of the revolutionary heritage of the Sandinistas and the personal ambition of Daniel Ortega. Efforts to keep inflation under control have been undermined by persistent budget deficits. In addition, the decline in coffee prices has badly hurt export earnings. The prevailing climate of corruption has jeopardized many international aid sources and held up agreements with the International Monetary Fund. Industry has lagged behind other sectors in the limited economic recovery that has occurred, thus further exacerbating the high rate of urban unemployment. Economic growth in 2004 was the best in many years, but rising petroleum prices and domestic political turmoil combined with global economic problems have largely undone this. Foreign investment in real estate grew under Bolaños, but it has largely stopped and in some cases even reversed under Ortega. This loss of foreign assistance has been somewhat compensated for by aid from Venezuela, but falling petroleum prices may reduce this.

The Bolaños administration had made some efforts to deal with the crisis in social welfare, health, and education, but its lack of support in the Assembly crippled its efforts. Privatization efforts had begun, but the combined effects of a lack of investor confidence, continued concerns over Sandinista influence, and high-level corruption have produced disappointing results. Ortega has largely abandoned such efforts.

Nicaragua's external debt totals over US$6 billion. Prospects for debt forgiveness by foreign governments and international financial organizations seemed significantly enhanced, however, in the wake of Hurricane Mitch. Nicaragua was included in the World Bank's Highly Indebted Poor Countries program, thus making it eligible for the forgiveness of up to 80 percent of its debt, but this has been limited by the ongoing political crisis. The nation consistently runs a high deficit in its current accounts and depends on external aid to cover this. It even depends on foreign assistance for such basic programs as conducting elections.

Nicaragua has little in the way of a regular civil service. Most government positions, at both the national and local levels, are seen as rewards for political support. The bureaucracy has been reduced from the massive levels it reached in the 1980s, but it is still inefficient and widely viewed as corrupt. Disputes over political patronage are a constant theme because apportioning positions is both a major motivation for and a constant source of tension in the formation and maintenance of political alliances.

FOREIGN POLICY

Nicaragua's foreign policy revolves around four principal foci: relations with the United States; an alliance with other left-wing governments in Latin America, notably Venezuela; the constant search for foreign assistance and debt relief; and relations with other Central American nations, notably Honduras and Costa Rica.

Initiatives in these areas are, at times, openly contradictory. The Bolaños administration was a strong supporter of free trade arrangements with the United States (CAFTA), but the Ortega administration has abandoned this track, instead joining the Venezuelan-sponsored ALBA group. Relations with Costa Rica have been complicated by disputes over rights along the San Juan River and by issues involving Nicaraguan immigrants to Costa Rica. The Honduran political crisis has further polarized regional politics, with Nicaragua taking the most extreme position in support of ousted President Zelaya. Foreign policy is further hampered by the tendency to make major appointments on the basis of domestic political considerations rather than competency, by the deteriorating international image of the Ortega regime, and by persistent property disputes dating back to the 1979 revolution.

Despite open US efforts in the 1980s to topple the Sandinista regime, formal diplomatic relations were never broken off. The inauguration of President Chamorro ended these tensions, but other issues soon arose. Conservative circles in the United States opposed the Chamorro administration's working arrangements with the FSLN and made a constant issue of property claims against the government advanced by Nicaraguans living in the United States. Aid and loans were delayed, contacts with the Nicaraguan military were blocked, and investment was discouraged. Relations improved somewhat under the Alemán administration. Progress was made in resolving the property issue, and military-to-military contacts were established. The Bolaños administration attempted to improve relations with the United States, even sending troops to Iraq in 2003, but its efforts were handicapped by domestic political turmoil and by the emerging issue of disposal of the surface-to-air missiles. The United States openly opposed Ortega in the 2006 elections, but initially relations with the Ortega administration were not hostile. However, the fraud in the 2008 municipal elections, combined with evidence of massive corruption and increased efforts at political repression, has led to increasing conflict.

Nicaraguan governments over the past decade had generally good relations with Europe and with some of the international financial institutions. The Scandinavian nations were especially forthcoming with assistance. Spain and other members of the European Union also provided vital assistance. Hurricane Mitch did produce a new outpouring of assistance, but increased evidence of corruption, the failure of the government to undertake needed economic reforms, and constant political conflict caused nations such as Denmark and Sweden to end aid disbursements, and in 2008 the European Union likewise suspended its assistance. Nicaragua's decision to recognize the tiny Russian puppet states taken from Georgia then further damaged relations with Europe. The European Union's observer mission to the 2011 Nicaraguan elections was strongly critical of the political system.

Relations with other Central American states were very tense during the Sandinista years. Nicaragua's support for regional revolutionary movements created constant problems with El Salvador. The Contras' use of Honduras and Costa Rica as bases for actions against the Sandinistas led to a series of bitter clashes that, in the Honduran case, frequently spilled over the border. For a time fears of a regional war were quite real. Ultimately, however, a regional initiative, led by Costa Rican president Oscar Arias, helped resolve the tensions and end the Contra war.

Relations under the Chamorro and Bolaños administrations were largely quiet. Many of the refugees returned home, and the emphasis was on rebuilding regional cooperation rather than preparing for armed conflict. Regional presidents met frequently, and fears of regional war vanished.

Under the Alemán administration a series of border disputes with both Costa Rica and Honduras, combined with Nicaraguan anger over Honduran recognition of Colombia's claim to disputed areas in the Caribbean, produced renewed tensions, which the Bolaños administration was unable to resolve. In addition, Nicaragua's continued economic crisis has provided a major obstacle to regional growth and development. Under Ortega, relations with Honduras and El Salvador improved as those nations moved more to the left, but the Honduran crisis over the ouster of President Zelaya has undone much of this. A recent World Court decision confirmed Colombian sovereignty over its Caribbean islands but significantly expanded the maritime areas under Nicaraguan control.

AN UNCERTAIN FUTURE

Nicaragua's future is uncertain. On the positive side, the economy has grown steadily, with annual increases between 4 and 5 percent over the past four years. Exports have risen at a constant pace, debt has been reduced, and reserves have grown. There seems little danger of a return to the open violence of previous decades, although the Ortega administration is increasingly inclined to use force against its opponents. Politics remain mired in bitter conflicts, reflecting both personal rivalries and past disputes. The population seems increasingly cynical about the entire process, as they see little hope offered by any party. The nation's reservoir of international sympathy and goodwill, generated by the events of the 1970s and 1980s and reinforced by the impact of Hurricane Mitch, seems exhausted, and both the United States and the European Union have suspended most assistance. Despite some recent improvements poverty is endemic, much of the infrastructure is inadequate and worn out, and both human and financial capital tends to seek foreign prospects. The uncertain political future in Venezuela could imperil the assistance from that nation, which has helped fuel recent economic growth.

Nicaragua is not without important assets. Rural areas are generally not overpopulated, and the nation has some of the best soils in the hemisphere. Its geographic position offers several advantages, especially if a project to improve traffic to the Atlantic via the San Juan River reaches fruition. There is even talk of building a canal across the nation with Chinese assistance. International contacts forged in the past two decades, along with the considerable resources of the Nicaraguan diaspora, notably those in Miami, are significant potential assets.

The situation is far from hopeless, but the key will be in developing competent political and economic leadership concerned more with national well-being than with personal aggrandizement. Unfortunately, the nation has little tradition of such leadership, and the most likely prospect seems to be continued suffering for the bulk of the population.

Suggestions for Further Reading

Literature on Nicaragua is extensive, but much of that produced in recent decades is highly partisan and of limited value. There has also been a sharp drop-off in scholarly work on Nicaragua in the past decade. The following are recommended as starting points for a fuller understanding of Nicaragua's past and present.

Booth, John A. *The End and the Beginning: The Nicaraguan Revolution*. Boulder, CO: Westview Press, 1985.

Cajina, Roberto. "Security in Nicaragua: Central America's Exception." Inter-American Dialogue working paper, Washington, DC, January 2013.

Christian, Shirley. *Revolution in the Family*. New York: Vintage, 1986.

Close, David. *Nicaragua: The Chamorro Years*. Boulder, CO: Lynne Rienner, 1999.

Colburn, Forrest D. *Post-Revolutionary Nicaragua*. Berkeley: University of California Press, 1986.

European Union Election Observation Mission. "Nicaragua: Final Report: General Election and Parlacen Elections 2011." Available at www.eueom.eu/files/dmfile/moeue-nicaragua-final-report-22022012_en.pdf.

Gilbert, Dennis. *Sandinistas: The Party and the Revolution*. Malden, MA: Basil Blackwell, 1988.

Kirk, John M. *Politics and the Catholic Church in Nicaragua*. Gainesville: University Press of Florida, 1992.

Lean, Sharon. "The Presidential and Parliamentary Elections in Nicaragua, November, 2006." *Electoral Studies* 26 (December 2007): 828–832.

Macaulay, Neill. *The Sandino Affair*. Durham, NC: Duke University Press, 1985.

Merrill, Tim L., ed. *Nicaragua: A Country Study*. Washington, DC: Government Printing Office, 1994.

Millett, Richard. *Guardians of the Dynasty*. New York: Orbis, 1977.

Pastor, Robert. *Condemned to Repetition: The United States and Nicaragua*. Princeton, NJ: Princeton University Press, 1987.

Seligson, Mitchell, and John Booth, eds. *Elections and Democracy in Central America Revisited*. Pittsburgh, PA: University of Pittsburgh Press, 1995.

Spalding, Rose. *Capitalists and Revolution in Nicaragua: Opposition and Accommodation, 1979–1993*. Chapel Hill: University of North Carolina Press, 1995.

Walter, Knut. *The Regime of Anastasio Somoza, 1936–1956*. Chapel Hill: University of North Carolina Press, 1993.

20

EL SALVADOR: CIVIL WAR
TO UNCIVIL PEACE

Christine J. Wade

In 1992 El Salvador experienced one of the region's most profound political and social transformations. Years of war and violent oppression that killed more than seventy-five thousand people and displaced one million more gave way to peace and democracy in one of the United Nations' most successful peacekeeping endeavors. The sweeping institutional reforms included the creation of a new civilian police force, a functioning judiciary, an apolitical army, and a competitive electoral system. In 1994 El Salvador held the first truly democratic elections in its history. In 2009 the country witnessed the first peaceful transfer of power from one party to another when Mauricio Funes became the first elected leftist president. Many heralded his election as a milestone in the consolidation of democracy.

Yet El Salvador's peace has been an uneasy one for most Salvadorans. Institutions remain highly politicized, as battleground rivalries have been transferred to the ballot box. While many socioeconomic indicators have improved, more than two decades of neoliberal policies have failed to invigorate the Salvadoran economy, now deeply dependent on remittances from abroad. The country suffers from a legacy of impunity and excessively high levels of social violence. For the past decade, "peacetime" El Salvador has had one of the highest homicide rates in the world. Some Salvadorans refer to the current situation as "not war," and public opinion polls frequently reveal that many believe that conditions are worse than during the war.[1] While much progress has been made, the story of El Salvador is a cautionary reminder about the limitations of peace building and democratization in postwar societies.

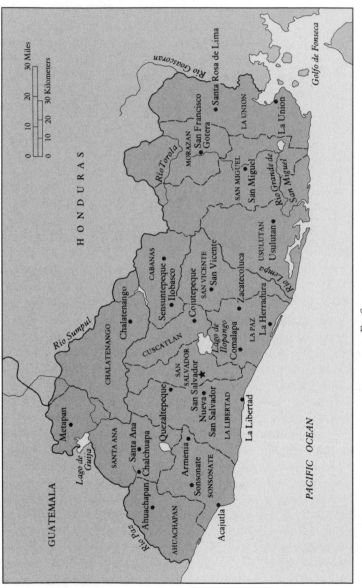

EL SALVADOR

HISTORICAL BACKGROUND

Called Cuzcatlán by its indigenous inhabitants, El Salvador is the smallest and most densely populated country in Central America.[2] The only country in the region without a Caribbean coast, El Salvador had few natural resources, unlike Bolivia and Mexico with their gold and silver mines. Instead, El Salvador's early economic development was characterized by the development of a monocrop economy with repeating patterns of development and decline. This pattern had a significant, negative impact on the distribution of resources and created conflict between communal lands and private property.

Cacao, which was being cultivated by the Indians when the Spanish arrived—and was usurped and converted into an export crop by the conquerors—was followed by indigo in the eighteenth century and coffee in the nineteenth. Not until the mid-twentieth century would there be any significant effort at crop diversification. As each cycle unfolded, more and more communal land—which was the indigenous pattern of land tenure throughout Latin America—was taken over by the Europeans and turned into private property.

The development of haciendas led, in turn, to the creation of new relationships between landowners and indigenous folk or peasants that could be characterized, for the most part, as feudal. The eighteenth-century expansion of haciendas, which grew in number with each succeeding depression, had the added effect of concentrating land in a decreasing number of hands, primarily through usurpation of communal lands without compensation to the former owners. Meanwhile, the *hacendados* (landowners) had come to exercise increasingly firm control over the political life of the colony by the late eighteenth century, establishing a pattern of economic and political control that would continue for 150 years.

Independence and the Repressive, Exclusionary State

The struggle for independence in El Salvador coincided with movements elsewhere in Central America during the second decade of the nineteenth century. In July 1823 the Federal Republic of Central America was created by the five former Central American colonies, and a year later Manuel José Arce, a Salvadoran, was elected its first president. This experiment lasted for fifteen years, then broke apart in the wake of a liberal-conservative struggle that was exacerbated by regional economic woes.[3]

The principles on which the new Salvadoran republic was founded were those of classical liberalism—namely, that the role of the state was to maintain order, and economic policy was strictly laissez-faire with the sanctity of private property its guiding principle. During this period emerged the basic policies that would shape the Salvadoran nation: encouragement of coffee production, construction of railroads to the ports, elimination of communal lands, laws against vagrancy that permitted the state to force peasants to work for hacendados at low wages, and repression of rural unrest. From the latter part of the nineteenth century into the early twentieth century most Salvadoran presidents were both generals and major coffee growers.

Periodic indigenous revolts increased after independence, largely in response to the growing concentration of land and the elimination of communal lands. A major revolt occurred in 1832 and lasted a year until its indigenous leader, Anastacio

Aquino, was captured, shot, decapitated, and had his head publicly displayed as a warning to other would-be rebels. The unrest in the countryside required the creation of local and then state "security forces," which were in the pay of the landowners and always at their beck and call.

The 1886 constitution guaranteed that the liberals' policies would be pursued without obstacle. It established a secular state, decentralized state authority by allowing for the popular election of municipal authorities, and confirmed the inviolability of private property. The notion that the state has some responsibility for the health, education, and general well-being of the people it governs was not a part of Salvadoran political culture. For example, the idea of collecting taxes to pay for roads, sewers, and schools was not on the radar screen of the Salvadoran elite, even into the late twentieth century.

The problem of dealing with peasants who periodically rebelled against their patrons was solved by employing private armies for which the patrons paid. Elements of these armies would become the Rural Police and the Mounted Police, created by decrees in 1884 and 1889, respectively, in the western coffee growing departments. An 1895 decree extended these two forces over the entire country, and the Rural Police eventually became the National Police. In 1912 the National Guard was created to eliminate the hacendados' private armies and their excesses. Within a few years, however, the National Guard gained a reputation for being the "most cruel, most barbaric" security force.[4] A third security force, the Treasury Police (Policía de Hacienda), was created in 1936.

By the late 1920s coffee was central to the economic life of the country. Production of *el grano de oro* (the gold grain) expanded rapidly, while other crops and industries stagnated. This, coupled with growing business acumen and sophistication, moved the national economy from depression to boom. Coffee averaged between 75 and 80 percent of all exports between 1900 and 1922, then soared to 92 percent during the remainder of the 1920s. Similarly, land use increased dramatically. In 1919 70,000 hectares were planted in coffee; by 1932 the figure had increased 34 percent to 106,000 hectares.[5]

Despite the boom, the average Salvadoran's living conditions deteriorated during this period. This resulted in an increasingly militant labor union movement, which had begun as World War I ended, and a flirtation with authentic electoral democracy at the beginning of the 1930s that ended in a coup d'état, stolen local elections, a disastrous peasant uprising known as La Mantanza that left thirty thousand dead, and a political division of labor under which the army assumed control of the state for the next sixty years while the oligarchy continued to control the economy.

Between 1932 and 1948 El Salvador was ruled by a succession of generals whose chief concern was to maintain order and protect elite interests. The ouster of General Salvador Castañeda Castro in the 1948 coup led to an extended period of institutionalized military rule from 1948 to 1979, wherein a cycle of alternating liberalizing and repressive regimes dominated the political landscape. The political system opened significantly following a reformist coup in 1960, allowing for the growth of popular organizations and opposition parties, most notably the Christian Democrats (Partido Demócrata Cristiano, PDC), a social democratic party. The Christian Democrats won increasing numbers of seats in the assembly during the

1960s followed by the mayoralties of the three largest cities, including San Salvador, in 1968. These gains, together with smaller gains by other opposition parties, presented a growing challenge to traditional interests. In 1972 the PDC coalition ticket, headed by José Napoleón Duarte, was denied electoral victory by the army.

This event, and subsequent fraud in the 1977 elections, led many Salvadorans to conclude that electoral politics would get them nowhere, and so they opted for a revolutionary alternative that included political (mass, grassroots organizing) and military (armed struggle) dimensions. During the 1970s five revolutionary organizations, which had their roots in peasant uprisings of the previous century, in labor organizations of the 1920s, and in the PCS, began working among urban laborers and peasants. Divided over ideology and strategy for a decade, the five came together in the Farabundo Martí National Liberation Front (Frente Farabundo Martí para la Liberación Nacional, FMLN) in October 1980. In January 1981 the FMLN initiated military operations that would plunge El Salvador into eleven years of civil war.

The Civil War

In October 1979 a group of junior officers in the armed forces overthrew Carlos Humberto Romero, who had come to power in the fraudulent 1977 elections. The goal of the coup was to remove military conservatives, derail the revolutionary movement, and institute long-overdue socioeconomic reforms. A number of prominent civilians who had been leaders of opposition parties and were forced into exile after 1972 returned to participate in the new government. It soon became clear, however, that a group of extremely conservative officers had displaced the progressive coup leaders, and two months after the coup most of the civilians resigned. The United States encouraged the Christian Democrats to join the military in a new government. This, however, split the party, as some leaders—notably José Napoleón Duarte, the former mayor and exiled presidential candidate—accepted the military's offer while others left the party and created the Popular Social Christian Movement (MPSC), which allied itself with other center-left opposition parties, labor unions, and nongovernmental organizations (NGOs) to create the Democratic Revolutionary Front (FDR) in the spring of 1980. The FDR formed a political alliance with the FMLN and served as its international political voice for much of the next decade.

The United States, fearing another revolution in Central America, increased its involvement via a two-track policy. Politically, reforms and elections were emphasized; militarily, the Salvadoran armed forces were trained in counterinsurgency. Meanwhile, in May 1979 the generals informed their old allies in the oligarchy that they had to begin taking care of themselves.[6] This had two effects. One was the creation of paramilitary death squads, funded by wealthy members of the oligarchy in collaboration with sympathetic elements in the armed forces. The second was the creation in 1981 by some of these same oligarchs of their own political party, the Nationalist Republican Alliance (Alianza Republicana Nacionalista, ARENA).

Elections for a constituent assembly that would write a new constitution were held in 1982, and to everyone's shock, ARENA won a plurality of the seats and effective control of the assembly. Only intervention by the US ambassador prevented ARENA from electing its founder, Roberto D'Aubuisson—a man closely tied to the death squads and identified ten years later by the United Nations' Truth

Commission as the intellectual author of Archbishop Oscar Romero's assassination in March 1980—as interim president of the country.

In the 1984 presidential elections the man who had been denied in 1972, José Napoleón Duarte, defeated D'Aubuisson. This and subsequent elections in the next decade—for the legislative assembly in 1985, 1988, and 1991 and for president in 1989—provided a "democratic government" that rarely exhibited the conditions of a functioning democracy: freedom of speech, the media, and party organization; freedom for interest groups; the absence of state-sponsored terror; the absence of fear and coercion among the population; and subordination of the military to civilian rule. Indeed, the armed forces, formally removed from power, continued to wield effective political control of the country. Duarte, elected on a platform of economic reform and peace negotiations with the FMLN, delivered neither while presiding over one of the most corrupt governments in Salvadoran history. The PDC, rent by internal squabbles, split again in 1988, and they then lost the 1989 presidential election to ARENA's Alfredo Cristiani.

Peace

Leading a country that was demonstrably fatigued by war, President Cristiani pledged in his June 1989 inaugural address to pursue peace negotiations with the FMLN. The flaw was that ARENA and the US government, now headed by President George H. W. Bush, who wanted to extract the United States from Central America as expeditiously as possible, assumed that the only thing to negotiate with the FMLN was its surrender. The government's failure to negotiate in good faith and several assassinations of leftist political leaders in the fall of 1989 convinced the FMLN that it had to demonstrate its power. The most significant offensive since 1981, launched on November 11, 1989, brought the war to San Salvador for the first time. It revealed both the FMLN's inability to provoke a general uprising and the army's incompetence. It also exposed the bankruptcy of US policy: despite nine years of training and more than US$2 billion in US military aid, the army could not rout the FMLN from the capital. The army's murder of six Jesuits and two other people in San Salvador during that struggle had an impact at least as great as the offensive itself. Together they marked the beginning of the end of the war.

At the behest of both parties, the United Nations served as mediator of the negotiations. The negotiations, which began in 1989 and ended in 1991, culminated in the Chapultepec accords, which sought to end the armed conflict as quickly as possible and to deal with the fundamental causes of the war by promoting democratization, guaranteeing absolute respect for human rights, and reunifying Salvadoran society. These objectives were unprecedented: no previous civil war had ended with an agreement not simply to stop shooting but to restructure society. The accords established a precise calendar for implementation during the cease-fire period. They mandated demilitarization, including halving the size of the armed forces, eliminating the state security forces and the FMLN's guerrilla army; legalizing the FMLN as a political party; amending the constitution; reforming the electoral and judicial systems; settling the land distribution issue, one of the root causes of the war; and establishing independent commissions to identify those responsible for major human rights abuses and to purge the army of its most serious human rights violators.

The United Nations Observer Mission in El Salvador (ONUSAL) was created to verify the implementation of the agreements, and its mission was later expanded to observe the 1994 elections.

To the credit of both sides, the cease-fire was never broken. By 1993 a new police force, the National Civilian Police (Policía Nacional Civil, PNC), had replaced the old security forces; a new governmental institution, the National Council for Human Rights (Procuraduría de Derechos Humanos, PDDH), was created so that citizens could bring complaints about governmental abuses; the army was reduced in size and sent to its barracks, with all its special units disbanded and its officer corps purged; the virtually nonfunctioning judicial system was experiencing the first steps toward reform; and the FMLN was a legal political party. Perhaps most significant, there was a sea change in El Salvador's political culture: it was no longer acceptable to kill people for political reasons.

ETHNICITY, SOCIAL AND CLASS STRUCTURE, AND INTEREST GROUPS

Ethnic Patterns

As land ownership became increasingly concentrated in fewer hands during the eighteenth and nineteenth centuries, the ethnic composition of the country also changed. At the beginning of the seventeenth century the country was about 85 percent indigenous, 10 percent mestizo, and 5 percent white. To this were added four to five thousand African slaves who were imported to work the cacao plantations as the indigenous population died out. That the country was well on its way to becoming a mestizo nation was evident by 1780, and that it had become one was clear thirty years later. By the twentieth century the slaves, who were freed in 1823, had been assimilated and officially ceased to exist as a separate racial group.[7] At the beginning of the twenty-first century El Salvador's six million inhabitants were 94 percent mestizo, 5 percent indigenous, and 1 percent white.

Social and Class Structure

El Salvador has produced great wealth since the conquest, yet 43 percent of its people live below the poverty line, with 12 percent in extreme poverty. Poverty in rural areas is more acute, with close to 50 percent living below the poverty line and nearly 20 percent in extreme poverty. Though El Salvador ranks below the Latin American average in human development, there have been significant improvements in various development indicators in recent years. With a per capita gross national income in 2011 of US$3,480, El Salvador ranked second-highest in Central America. In 2010 fourteen infants died for every thousand live births, and the death rate for children under five was seventeen per thousand live births. The average Salvadoran completes seven and a half years of education. The literacy rate, at 87 percent nationwide and 79 percent in the countryside, is one of the lowest in Latin America. Inequality has persisted in El Salvador despite overall reductions in poverty in recent years. In 2009 the richest 10 percent of the population consumed 37 percent of national income, while the poorest 10 percent consumed a mere 1 percent. El Salvador's Gini coefficient was 44.[8]

The Churches and Social Change

The development of Christian Base Communities (Comunidades Eclesiales de Base, CEBs) in the late 1960s and 1970s throughout the region was a reflection of and a means of teaching the tenets of liberation theology to people. Key documents, including those originating in the Second Vatican Council (1962) and the 1968 bishops' conference at Medellín, Colombia, called on the church to denounce injustice and established a "preferential option for the poor." In El Salvador the message of social justice offered through CEBs was labeled "Communist" and "subversive" by the right. Between 1972 and 1989 eighteen Catholic priests, one seminary student, one Lutheran minister, three nuns, and a lay worker from the United States were murdered or disappeared for their work in defense of the poor and human rights.

Although he was selected in 1977 by the Vatican for the post because he was thought to be conservative, San Salvador's new archbishop, Oscar Arnulfo Romero, soon became a champion of social justice and called for an end to the violence that was consuming the country. His assassination while delivering mass on March 24, 1980, served as a catalyst for many to join the guerrillas. The murder of three Maryknoll nuns and a lay worker in December reiterated the danger faced by religious workers. After Romero's death dozens more priests and nuns were driven into exile, while a handful continued their ministries in guerrilla-controlled areas. Despite the violence, the Catholic Church, along with the Anglicans and Lutherans, pushed for a negotiated end to the war throughout the 1980s. Ironically, it was this targeted violence against the Church that ultimately helped end the war. On November 16, 1989, the US-trained Atlacatl Battalion entered the grounds of the Jesuit Universidad Centroamericana José Simeón Cañas and killed six Jesuit professors (including the rector), their housekeeper, and her daughter. The murders caused the United States to suspend military aid, and El Salvador's new president, Alfredo Cristiani, was forced to the negotiating table.

Many of the CEBs disrupted by the violence have not recovered, and a change in archbishops has hindered their regrowth. The 1994 appointment of Spanish-born Fernando Sáenz Lacalle, a member of Opus Dei, following the death of Romero's successor, Archbishop Arturo Rivera Damas, was seen as a blow to human rights and social justice. In December 2008 José Luis Escobar Alas was appointed to replace Sáenz Lacalle as archbishop.

Evangelical Protestants came to play an increasingly important role in politics. The evangelical movement, which gained momentum during the war, represented a conservative social counterpoint to the Catholic lay community. Powerful figures, such as Edgar López Bertrand (Brother Toby), of the Baptist Biblical Tabernacle Friends of Israel, drew considerable crowds to their services. They also had increasing political clout. President Tony Saca, himself an evangelical Protestant, invited Brother Toby to deliver the prayer at his inauguration. Presidential candidates for the 2009 elections, both Catholic, aggressively courted evangelical congregations, which broke for ARENA in 2004.

Elites and Business

During the 1990s significant disagreement emerged among the economic elite over economic policy as well as between important parts of the elite and the government.[9]

El Salvador's once monolithic oligarchy disappeared. A generation earlier the mono-lith had two parts: the traditional agricultural sector, whose wealth was exclusively in the land—coffee, cotton, and/or sugar cane—and the landowners who had diver-sified into finance and industry. By the middle of the decade there were four clearly identifiable sectors: financial, commercial, industrial, and agricultural. In each of the first three sectors there was a small subsector that controlled the overwhelming majority of the capital within that sector. The result was not only intersector con-flicts but intrasectional disputes, as smaller players battled to stay in the game.

Two of the most prominent NGOs in El Salvador came to represent the tri-umph of new industrial and commercial elites over the traditional agrarian sector. The National Association of Private Enterprise (ANEP), established in 1966, has played a very influential role in economic and public policy. Its membership com-prises the country's most prominent businesspeople and associations, transnational corporations, and public servants. Former Salvadoran president Tony Saca served as president of ANEP from 2001 to 2003. The group has been very critical of the Funes administration. The Salvadoran Foundation for Economic and Social Devel-opment (FUSADES) was created in 1983 with a large grant from the United States Agency for International Development (USAID) to promote neoliberal reforms. Like ANEP, the think tank has also enjoyed significant influence over economic policy. When Cristiani, one of the original members of the board of directors, was elected president in 1989 he appointed several members of FUSADES to his cabinet and other positions.

Women

Women's participation in public life grew from near zero in the 1970s to an in-creasing number of women in government a decade later. During the Cristiani ad-ministration, two of his most competent ministers, those heading the planning and education ministries, were women. Two women were members of the FMLN's ne-gotiating team at the peace talks, and the party later adopted a rule that one-third of all its candidates for office must be women. In 1999 the FMLN's vice presidential nominee was a woman, and in 2004 the vice presidential nominees of ARENA and the CDU-PDC coalition tickets were women. The ARENA victory in 2004 gave El Salvador its first female vice president. Neither ARENA nor the FMLN had women on their presidential or vice presidential tickets in 2009. After the 2003 elections, seventeen of 262 mayors were women, down from twenty-nine after 2000. All but six belonged to ARENA: four FMLN and two PCN. In 2009, however, once again twenty-nine women were elected mayors. In the legislative assembly eighteen of eighty-four deputies were women.

In preparation for the 1994 elections a broad coalition of women's organizations hammered out an agenda called Mujeres '94 (Women '94), which it asked every party to adopt as part of its platform. Only the FMLN agreed, thanks to the pres-sure of its women members. By the mid-1990s women's organizations had formu-lated legislative bills to guarantee workers' rights in the *maquiladoras*, make rape a public crime and no longer require a witness (other than the victim) to the rape in order to press charges, require men to prove they are *not* the father of a given child, and ensure inclusion of articles that protect women in the new penal code.

A new education law guaranteed equal access for girls, barred discrimination based on gender, and proscribed sexist stereotypes in textbooks. In 2009 President Funes introduced the Cuidad Mujer (City for Women) project, which creates safe zones in urban areas for women to access social services. In 2011 the assembly passed the Law of Equality, Equity and the Eradication of Violence Against Women, which guarantees equal access to education, equal pay, and various protections against discrimination. Despite this, violence against women, both public and domestic, remains high. The ban against abortion, which provides for no exceptions, is the most stringent in the region. Beyond simply banning the procedure, El Salvador's law criminalizes it, imposing harsh jail sentences for both the provider and the woman. The ban has led to the rise of back-alley abortions, mostly among poor women.[10]

POLITICAL PARTIES AND ELECTIONS

Presidential elections are held every five years, while elections for the eighty-four deputies in the legislative assembly and the 262 mayors are held every three years. Elections and electoral reforms are overseen by the Supreme Electoral Tribunal (TSE), an electoral commission created by the peace process. Though no election cycle has been without some irregularities and many necessary reforms still linger, elections since 1994 have generally been considered free and fair.

Political parties did not emerge in El Salvador until the 1920s. The first modern party was the Communist Party (PCS), which was banned following the 1932 uprising. From 1932 until 1944 General Maximiliano Hernández Martínez governed through the Pro-Patria National Party, the only legal party at that time. The party changed its name to the National Conciliation Party (PCN) in 1961, dominating elections until 1982. The PCN and the center-right Christian Democratic Party (PDC), founded in 1960, were disbanded in 2011 for failing to meet the required minimum vote threshold in the 2004 elections.

The current Salvadoran party system is dominated by the right-wing ARENA and the left-wing FMLN, effectively transferring wartime rivalries to the ballot box. While smaller right-wing parties have at times benefited from ARENA's declining vote share, centrist parties struggle to survive. Parties must win 3 percent of the vote (or 6 percent in coalition races) to remain registered political parties. Electoral reforms permitted independent candidates to run for office for the first time in 2012.

The 1994 elections were hyperbolically dubbed the "elections of the century" because they were the first to occur after the war's end, because the FMLN was participating for the first time as a legal party, and because a president (who serves for five years), assembly deputies, and mayors (groups that serve three-year terms) were all being elected. While ARENA won the largest vote share in the 1994 elections and its candidate, Armando Calderón Sol, won the presidency, the FMLN's fortunes increased significantly in the coming years. In the 2000 elections, the FMLN won more seats than ARENA in the legislative assembly.

While the FMLN steadily increased its vote share in legislative and municipal elections in 1997, 2000, and 2003, it struggled in presidential contests. Internecine political battles within the party created the impression that the party could not govern at the presidential level and resulted in candidates without broad national appeal. As a result, ARENA handily won presidential contests in 1999 and 2004.

The 2009 elections were the first time since 1994 that elections for all offices would be held during the same year. However, the TSE implemented reforms that separated polling days for the legislative and municipal and presidential elections by more than a month. It was a contentious campaign, pitting ARENA's Rodrigo Avila, a former PNC director, against popular television journalist Mauricio Funes for the FMLN. Twenty years of failed ARENA policies left it vulnerable to the FMLN's moderate candidate. Funes, who had not been a guerrilla and was not a member of the FMLN, carved out a centrist position and easily rebuffed ARENA's fear campaign of previous election cycles. Unlike prior US administrations, the new Obama administration vowed to work with the victorious party.

The January legislative and municipal elections promised to be a preview of the presidential elections. The FMLN won thirty-five seats, ARENA thirty-two, PCN eleven, PDC five, CD one, and FDR none. The FMLN also increased its share of mayoralties from fifty-eight to ninety-six (seventy-five on its own and twenty-one in coalitions), although it lost San Salvador. ARENA, which won San Salvador for the first time since its loss in 1997, suffered a number of losses, dropping from 148 to 122 municipalities. The PCN and PDC lost fourteen and sixteen municipalities, respectively. Following the legislative and municipal elections, the PDC and PCN withdrew their presidential candidates and lent their support to ARENA. Most of the FDR, which failed to win any seats in the legislative assembly, supported the FMLN.[11]

Funes defeated Avila, 51 to 48 percent. On June 1, 2009, Tony Saca transferred power to Mauricio Funes, the first transfer of power from one party to another since the signing of the peace accords. In the aftermath of the election, former president Alfredo Cristiani, who initiated ARENA's dominance in 1989, returned to head the party—a clear sign that the party was regrouping.

ARENA's electoral fortunes improved in the March 2012 legislative and municipal elections, capturing the most seats in the assembly, 33, and the most municipalities, 116. The FMLN won thirty-one seats in the Assembly and ninety-five municipalities, ten of those in coalitions. Smaller parties picked up the remainder of the seats, but the most prominent of these was the new Grand Alliance for National Unity (GANA). GANA was created by former members of ARENA, including former president Tony Saca, following the 2009 elections. The defections, which included more than a dozen deputies, shifted the balance of power in the assembly away from ARENA. The party, which had been working in coalition with the FMLN since the 2009 defections, won eleven seats in the assembly and eighteen municipalities in its first electoral contest. In December 2012 former president Tony Saca announced his intention to run for president in the 2014 election on the GANA ticket, making him the first democratically elected president to run for a second term.

POSTWAR GOVERNMENT AND PUBLIC POLICY

The Cristiani and Calderón Sol administrations implemented most of the key elements of the peace accords, though not always with transparency or as intended by the accords. Electoral and judicial reforms must be approved through the legislative assembly under the auspices of the 1983 constitution, which gave ARENA significant control over the content and implementation of the reforms. The Cristiani administration failed to accept the findings or implement the recommendations of the Truth Commission, which assigned most of the blame for abuses during the war to the state. The 1993 amnesty law ensured that victims would never have access to justice in El Salvador.

Beginning with the Cristiani administration, four successive ARENA administrations pursued neoliberal economic policies as recommended by international financial institutions. Much of these reforms focused on the privatization of state-owned enterprise, tariff reduction and elimination, a new value-added tax (IVA), and the liberalization of monetary policy. The banks, coffee, and sugar were privatized under Cristiani, who became a major stakeholder in Banco Cuscatlán as a result of the sale. Armando Calderón Sol, the first president elected after the signing of the peace accords, oversaw the privatization of the state-owned telephone and electric companies and an increase in the IVA to 13 percent, which disproportionately affected the poor and working class. Between December 1991 and August 1999 minimum daily salaries declined from 28.18 to 27.37 colones.[12] In another measure, GDP per inhabitant grew dramatically over the decade, from US$1,002 in 1991 to US$2,258 in 2003. Most of that increase, however, was lost to inflation. Running as high as 19.9 percent in 1992, the cumulative inflation rate was 186 percent by 1998. By the turn of the century the government had inflation under control, although it continued to exceed growth.

Calderón Sol's successor, Francisco Flores, demonstrated an unwavering commitment to the neoliberal model, as well as an unwillingness to engage in dialogue with civic groups or members of the opposition. Objecting to government plans to privatize the health system, the Social Security Institute Union (STISSS) began a strike in November 1999. President Flores refused to negotiate, and the strike continued until thirty-six hours before the March 2000 elections, when a marathon session resulted in an agreement to return to work. It was a political fiasco for Flores. A second major health care strike, collectively referred to as the "white marches," erupted in October 2002 over the privatization of services. The strike ended nine months later following government assurances that the health care system would not be privatized.

By 2000, El Salvador's economy was in deep trouble. GDP growth declined throughout Flores's tenure, from 3.4 percent in 1999 to 2.2 percent in 2002 and to 1.8 percent in 2003. In 2003 the annual rate of inflation was 2.5 percent, with less than 2 percent growth. Inflation doubled in 2004 while growth lagged at a mere 1.5 percent. In January 2001 Flores's Law of Monetary Integration, which dollarized the economy, was passed by the legislature. The policy has had a disproportionate impact on the standard of living of the poor, as rounding up prices from the conversion became a common practice among vendors in the informal sector.[13] Thus, inflation for the poor was higher than for the general population.

The Flores government was also confronted with growing public insecurity. In 1999 El Salvador's murder rate was sixty-five per hundred thousand, the highest in the hemisphere. Flores cited the influx of criminal street gangs from the United States, such as Mara Salvatrucha and MS-18, as the reason for El Salvador's insecurity. Flores's *mano dura* (iron fist) legislation targeted gang activity, but it did little to address the growing problem of social violence.

ARENA's fourth consecutive president, Antonio Elías Saca, promised to promote social and economic security. Shortly after taking office, Saca imposed *super mano dura* in a further effort to crack down on gang violence. Although mano dura and its successor were very popular with the public, they did little to stem the violence. In fact, violence increased as a result of the policies. The judicial system refused to cooperate with Saca's policy of arresting and jailing young men who sport the identifying tattoos of gang members, arguing that individuals must be arrested for doing something, not for how they look. By July 2005—more than a year after super mano dura went into effect—El Salvador's murder rate climbed to twelve per day, nearly double that of the previous year. The government continued to blame gangs for a majority of the homicides, but the level of impunity in the country made any statistics dubious. Saca also sought to control social protest through the 2006 Special Anti-Terrorism Law (Ley Especial Contra Actos de Terrorismo). The law criminalized common means of protest, including demonstrations and marches. More than a dozen prominent social activists were arrested in the town of Suchitoto in July 2007 en route to the town to protest water privatization. Although the charges were ultimately dropped, the arrests revealed the government's intention to quash its opposition.

Economic growth (the GDP increased 4.2 percent in 2006 and 4.7 percent in 2007) was insufficient to keep pace with the rising cost of living. Despite increases in the minimum wage for industrial and agricultural workers in 2006, real wages were still lower than their 1996 levels—and lower than they had been before the war. A 20 percent increase in bus fares and 14 percent increase in electricity rates exacerbated the problem. Saca also announced the creation of a multipoint poverty reduction program. Part of the program, Red Solidaria, entailed a plan to reduce extreme poverty by one-half, focusing on providing nutrition, education, and health care in some of El Salvador's poorest communities. The plan targeted twenty thousand families its first year, growing to one hundred thousand families within four years.

Mauricio Funes inherited a myriad of problems, but nothing was of greater concern than the growing criminal violence. In 2009 El Salvador had one of the highest homicide rates in the world, at seventy-one per hundred thousand. While murders decreased slightly in 2010, they rose by almost 10 percent in 2011. Authorities continued to cite gang violence, though it was increasingly clear that organized crime and drug cartels were also responsible for the violence. In 2010 the assembly passed a controversial law criminalizing gang membership, reminiscent of the initial mano dura policy. Funes continued to allow joint patrols by the police and military, and in 2011 he named retired general and former minister of national defense David Munguía Payés as the minister of justice and public security and then in 2012 retired general Francisco Ramón Salinas Rivera as the director of the PNC. The appointments were widely criticized for breaking the spirit, if not the letter, of the peace accords.

In March 2012 members of MS-13 and the 18th Street Gang agreed to a truce in exchange for better prison conditions for incarcerated members. Though the truce was mediated by a Catholic bishop and former FMLN legislator, it was later revealed that Funes and Munguía Payés had played a significant role in the truce. In December 2012 the truce was expanded to include "safe cities" in ten municipalities where the gangs would cease operations. While the most dramatic result of the truce has been a significant decrease in homicides, the truce's long-term viability remains to be seen.

Funes, consistently ranked as one of the most popular presidents in Latin America, faced additional challenges. A crisis erupted in June 2011 in response to a decree that required unanimity among the five judges on the constitutional chamber of the supreme court to approve decisions. Decree 743 was repealed the following month after significant public protest. A second constitutional crisis emerged in June 2012 when members of the constitutional chamber ruled that the elections of supreme court magistrates in 2006 and 2009 were invalid because the assembly had voted on the composition multiple times rather than once per cycle, as permitted. The subsequent order that new elections be held for two-thirds of the appointed judges led to a standoff between the judiciary and the legislature, which was ultimately mediated by President Funes.

Additionally, the Salvadoran economy, which had grown heavily dependent on the United States, was affected by the global recession. Growth fell more than 3 percent in 2009 and increased only 1.4 percent in both 2010 and 2011.

Despite the difficulties, there were some positive developments in the area of reconciliation. In November 2009, Funes awarded the National Order of José Matías Delgado to the Universidad Centroamericana Jesuits in a public act of atonement for mistakes by past governments. He also pledged that El Salvador would investigate the 1980 assassination of Archbishop Oscar Romero, determine culpability, and make reparations. At a ceremony in January 2010 celebrating the eighteenth anniversary of the peace accords, Funes offered the first formal apology for the war by a Salvadoran president. In his apology he acknowledged the human rights abuses that had occurred during the war and asked the Salvadoran people for forgiveness.

GLOBALIZATION AND INTERDEPENDENCE

Unlike other Central American countries, the United States demonstrated relatively little interest in El Salvador until the 1979 military coup. US interest in the country accelerated under the Reagan administration, which saw the civil war in El Salvador as an extension of the revolution in Nicaragua and Soviet expansion in the hemisphere. Soon El Salvador became one of the most important countries in the US sphere of influence. El Salvador has remained one of the United States' strongest allies in the region, committing troops to the US-led coalition in Iraq and participating in CAFTA and the Partnership for Growth initiative.

El Salvador has become a transnational society. More than one million Salvadorans fled the country during the war, at least half of them to the United States, though they were not eligible for asylum during that time. Salvadoran migration to the United States has increased dramatically in recent years. As much as 20 percent of the Salvadoran-born population lives in the United States: according to the 2000 US Census, there were 817,336 Salvadoran-born Salvadorans living in the United States. In 2010, the Census Bureau estimated that there were 1.8 million people of Salvadoran origin in the United States, making it the fourth-largest Latino population in the United States. Approximately 250,000 of the Salvadorans in the United

States were under temporary protected status (TPS), a special program that allowed individuals from specified countries to register to work legally in the United States.

The steady flow of Salvadoran emigrants has been vital to sustaining the Salvadoran economy. In 1991 US$790 million was sent to families in El Salvador; by 2004 that figure had increased to US$2.5 billion, or 17 percent of El Salvador's GDP. In 2008 remittances totaled US$3.8 billion, nearly 20 percent of GDP. Though remittances declined in 2009 as a result of the global economic recession, they soon returned to previous levels and even showed prospects for growth in 2012. Approximately one-third of Salvadoran households received remittances, which were commonly used for housing, education, and consumer goods.

The Salvadoran community in the United States is very active in promoting transnational issues, including immigration reform, labor rights, and the right of Salvadorans living abroad to participate in overseas voting.

CONCLUSIONS

As El Salvador prepares for the 2014 presidential elections, it is clear that it has made significant progress toward the consolidation of democracy in the twenty years since the "elections of the century." That said, many challenges remain on El Salvador's road to lasting peace and democracy. High rates of social violence, corruption, poverty, inequality, impunity, and political polarization have challenged successive governments and continue to undermine the quality of peace. Many Salvadorans, devoid of economic opportunity and security, make their way to the United States in even greater numbers than during the war.

The Funes administration has demonstrated significant political will in addressing a wide variety of problems, though not without controversy. Funes's support for the anti-gang law, Decree 743, and appointments of former generals to civilian security positions drew criticism from many, including his own party. His public apologies for crimes committed by the state during the war and his criticism of the amnesty law, though welcomed by the human rights community, have been rebuked by some in the army and ARENA. The gang truce, which appears to have resulted in a 40 percent decrease in homicides for 2012, has been met with skepticism by the public, who question its sustainability. Finally, successive constitutional crises have underscored both the fragility and the resilience of Salvadoran institutions. In future years Salvadorans will once again find themselves at a major crossroads, selecting new leadership to lead them into a third decade of peace—whatever that means.

Notes

1. For a discussion of postwar violence and attitudes toward peace, see Ellen Moodie, *El Salvador in the Aftermath of Peace* (Philadelphia: University of Pennsylvania Press, 2010).

2. Portions of this section are drawn from Tommie Sue Montgomery, *Revolution in El Salvador: From Civil Strife to Civil Peace* (Boulder, CO: Westview Press, 1995), 25–28, 30–32, and Tommie Sue Montgomery, "El Salvador," in *Political Parties of the Americas 1980s to 1990s*, ed. Charles Ameringer (Westport, CT: Greenwood Press, 1992), 281–301.

3. Latin American conservatives and liberals bear little resemblance to liberals and

conservatives in the Anglo-American political tradition. Conservatives were aristocrats and monarchists who wished to keep church and state tied closely together and were dedicated to preserving the church's wealth and privileges. Liberals were anticlerical and often antireligious. They were inclined to support free trade, while conservatives preferred to erect tariff barriers to protect local textile production. Within El Salvador the differences were smaller than in other countries because the church did not have much wealth that could be confiscated. The liberals succeeded in abolishing monastic orders, establishing civil marriage, and taking some initial steps toward removing education from control by the clergy and creating a state education system.

4. Robert Varney Elam, "Appeal to Arms: The Army and Politics in El Salvador 1931–1964," Ph.D. dissertation, University of New Mexico, 1968, 9.

5. Max P. Brannon, *El Salvador: Esquema estadística de la vida nacional* (San Salvador: n.p., 1936), 22–24. By 1950 there were 115,429 hectares, or 75 percent of the total land, under cultivation; in 1961, the figure was 139,000 hectares, or 87 percent of the total. Eduardo Colindres, *Fundamentos económicos de la burguesía salvadoreña* (San Salvador: UCA Editores, 1978), 72.

6. Laurie Becklund, "Death Squads: Deadly 'Other War,'" *Los Angeles Times*, December 18, 1983.

7. Blacks were officially barred from living in El Salvador for many years, although this broke down in the 1980s as African American diplomats and military trainers were posted to the US embassy and US military group, respectively. Other blacks came as journalists, human rights workers, and staff members of nongovernmental organizations and the United Nations. Still, racism is an ugly fact, particularly among the white (European) elite. In the early 1990s, for example, a very senior Salvadoran political official informed a senior official of the UN peacemaking mission (ONUSAL) that one of his aides, a female Jamaican political officer, was not welcome at their meetings. The African heritage of many Salvadorans is, however, apparent in a stroll down any street, especially in the capital. There seems to be no societal discrimination because of this. Rather, discrimination stems more from class than from ethnic background.

8. The GINI coefficient measures inequality of income distribution on a scale of 1 (perfect equality) to 100 (perfect inequality).

9. This paragraph is adapted from Tommie Sue Montgomery, "Constructing Democracy in El Salvador," *Current History*, February 1997, 62–63.

10. Jack Hitt, "Pro-Life Nation," *New York Times*, April 9, 2006.

11. Salvadoran election law requires that parties receive a minimum of 3 percent of the national vote to be officially registered. As such, the FDR will cease to exist in the aftermath of the 2009 elections.

12. Ibid. In the late 1990s the colon was stable at 8.8 to the dollar.

13. Marcia Towers and Silvia Borzutzky, "The Socioeconomic Implications of Dollarization in El Salvador," *Latin American Politics and Society* 46, no. 3 (Autumn 2004): 29–54.

Suggestions for Further Reading

Boyce, James K., ed. *Economic Policy for Building Peace: The Lesson of El Salvador*. Boulder, CO: Lynne Rienner, 1996.

Ladutke, Larry. *Freedom of Expression in El Salvador: The Struggle for Human Rights and Democracy*. Jefferson, NC: MacFarland, 2004.

Montgomery, Tommie Sue. *Revolution in El Salvador: Origins and Evolution*. Boulder, CO: Westview Press, 1995.

Moodie, Ellen. *El Salvador in the Aftermath of Peace*. Philadelphia: University of Pennsylvania Press, 2010.

Popkin, Margaret. *Peace Without Justice: Obstacles to Building Rule of Law in El Salvador.* University Park: Pennsylvania State University Press, 2000.

Stanley, William. *The Protection Racket State: Elite Politics, Military Extortion, and Civil War in El Salvador.* Philadelphia: Temple University Press, 1996.

Wood, Elizabeth Jean. *Insurgent Collective Action and Civil War In El Salvador.* New York: Cambridge University Press, 2003.

21

GUATEMALA: PROGRESS AND PERIL IN AN AGE OF GLOBALIZATION

Dwight Wilson

In the second decade of the twenty-first century the political situation in Guatemala is reasonably upbeat. Scarred by ethnic and class divisions from its very beginnings, Guatemala's history has been one of oppression and upheaval. A tumultuous twentieth century saw dictatorship, revolution, coups, and civil war. Since a transition to democracy in the 1980s and a peace agreement in 1996, Guatemala's democratic institutions have proven durable, if not impeccable. After many decades of polarization and conflict there is consensus, for the most part, around the most important goals of the state: democratic governance, the rule of law, a market economy, and free trade. By embracing democracy and globalization, the country has thus settled on the most widely recommended contemporary prescription for development.

Guatemala nonetheless faces problems old and new. A variety of corrosive forces buffet the country. Poverty burdens much of the population, corruption remains deeply embedded, and violent crime rages uncontrolled by authorities. Compounding these problems, new threats have emerged from outside the nation's borders. Transnational criminal networks engaged in the drug trade, human trafficking, arms sales, and money laundering threaten to overwhelm a weak state. As Guatemala consolidates its democratic institutions and is further embedded in the global economy, the greatest threats to the country appear no longer to be ideological division or elites contesting for power over the state, but persistent lawlessness that has only been exacerbated by globalization itself.

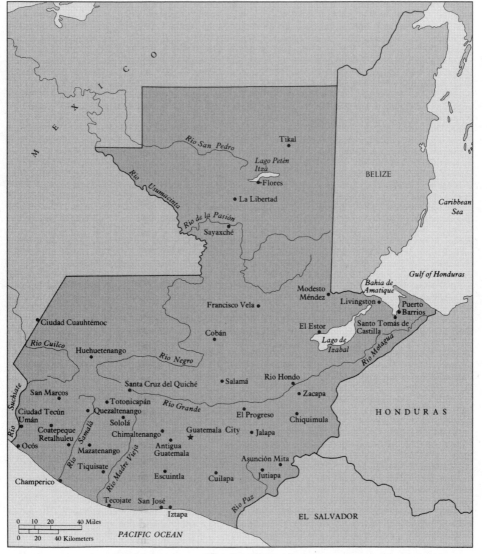

GUATEMALA

HISTORY

The conquistador Pedro de Alvarado arrived in the western highlands of modern Guatemala in 1524 leading an expedition of a few hundred Spaniards and an auxiliary army of recently defeated Aztecs. Whereas the Aztecs in Mexico were united under Tenochtitlán, the Mayans lived in independent and squabbling city-states. Alvarado walked in on a war between the Quiché and Cakchiquel Indians that divided the cities into competing alliances. The conquest required separate attention for each of the decentralized cities; Indians in the northern forests of Petén beat back the invading Spanish until the 1690s. Eventually Hispanization proceeded by conversion to Catholicism, the priestly hierarchy and rituals of which mirrored indigenous religion. Uniquely in Central America, though, the majority Indian population stayed largely autonomous and unassimilated, a fact only beginning to change in recent generations.

The area eventually developed into the Kingdom of Guatemala, the seat of colonial government for all Central America, which stretched from Chiapas to Costa Rica. It was the spiritual, cultural, and economic heart of the isthmus as well, but next to Mexico and Peru, the colonial jewels in the royal crown, Guatemala was a backwater. The precious metals prized by Spain dried up early there, and the colony languished in relative obscurity, supplying the monarchy with mahogany, cacao, and dyes. Eighteenth-century revolutions in Europe, however—political and intellectual—could not escape notice even in the farthest corners of the empire.

Independence and Liberal Dictatorship

The independence movements agitating for separation from Spain in Mexico and South America were greeted in Central America with confusion and indecision, with many municipalities acting separately from the central government in Guatemala. Most Central Americans resolved in favor of separation from Spain, but the question remained whether to form a separate country or append to Mexico. In the end Mexico itself decided in favor of the second alternative, swallowing Guatemala as a part of the short-lived empire of Augustín Iturbide. After he was deposed, Central Americans went their own way, and Guatemala declared its sovereignty (minus Chiapas, which stuck with Mexico).

Initially the former kingdom stayed together, proclaiming itself the United Provinces of Central America in 1823. Under Liberal leadership the government set out to erase the Hispanic past in order to fashion the new nation according to Enlightenment ideals. Hopes ran high that its location and prospects for an interoceanic canal would propel the federation into the ranks of the wealthiest nations on earth. In fact, the factional strife between anticlerical Liberals and traditionalist Conservatives that burned across the continent doomed the arrangement from the outset. The federation was pulled apart by dissension, jealousies, and rebellions, and by 1837 it was a dead letter.

After the federation crumbled, Guatemala's leadership swung from Liberal to Conservative and back to Liberal again. In the 1870s Liberal presidents managed to consolidate power and reigned supreme. Many were elected, and most served their country until they died or were forcibly ejected. Executives enjoyed wide latitude, and constitutional niceties were easily amended to extend presidential terms and powers, making the presidency essentially an elective dictatorship. Liberal reforms rotated the membership of the ruling class—the Catholic Church was the big loser—but did not drastically change living conditions for the multitudes of Guatemalans.

The last of the long-term Liberal dictatorships was that of General Jorge Ubico y Castañeda. Taking power in 1931, he oversaw the modernization of national infrastructure, professionalized the military, encouraged commerce, and expanded the bureaucracy. In doing so he also let loose a new and implacable political force: a frustrated and politically minded middle class. During his third term in office Ubico managed to alienate much of the citizenry, whose condition had been made worse by the deplorable economic conditions of the Great Depression. Student protests in June 1944 sparked a chain reaction of popular unrest that led to the general's resignation that same month and an uprising in October that ousted the military from the government altogether.

The Revolutionary Decade

The democratic revolution of 1944 lasted for ten years and came to be known as the Decade of Spring. The movement that installed the new regime was a modern one in which the mobilized middle classes cast out the outdated nineteenth-century-style despotism. The budding popular sectors demanded an opening of the political sphere and participation in the affairs of state—a new development in Guatemala. Until now, the multitudes had been unorganized and pliant, requiring periodic, forceful correction. The revolution opened unprecedented avenues of communication and participation for the excluded classes. Pluralism and liberal democracy could not so painlessly penetrate traditional Guatemala, however. The revolutionary period polarized Guatemalan society over progressive reforms, and all the while the threat of violence, a familiar political tool, loomed darkly.

Juan José Arévalo, a "spiritual socialist" known as the philosopher of the revolution, headed the first administration, from 1945 to 1951. His moderately progressive government created channels of participation for the previously disenfranchised—a kind of New Deal for Guatemala. The relatively mild changes upset the traditional balance of interests, but Arévalo carefully sidestepped any radical impulses, such as serious agrarian reform, that could have sent conservative forces over the edge. He failed, however, to establish a coherent party that would secure the future of the revolution after his tenure, and the following administration did not imitate his tact.

Jacobo Arbenz Guzmán, a colonel who took part in the revolution, was elected in 1950 after his chief opponent, another revolutionary leader, met an untimely end at the hands of assassins. The Arbenz regime sought to further level the playing field for Indian peasants and urban laborers, funneled state resources to education and health, and broached the taboo subject of redistributing the highly concentrated land. In this way Arbenz collected no few enemies among conservative forces in the military, business, and the Catholic Church.

An increasingly radical Arbenz regime also alarmed an Eisenhower administration on the lookout for Communist infiltration in the West. Arbenz stepped up fiery nationalist rhetoric toward the United States, looked benignly on the participation of Communists in the government and labor unions, expropriated land owned by the United Fruit Company (the largest landholder in the country), and imported weapons from Czechoslovakia—the arms merchant of the Soviet bloc—to arm peasant and labor groups. Convinced Arbenz was intent on bolting to the Soviets, Eisenhower could swallow no more and threw his lot in with the armed opposition. The CIA lent financial and material support to disaffected members of the military, led by Colonel Carlos Castillo Armas, who were plotting to overthrow Arbenz.

The coup of June 18, 1954, has been hailed as a smashing success against creeping international Communism in some quarters, and in others it is remembered bitterly as the imperialist overthrow of a popularly elected reformer. Though the long civil war that would follow had its immediate catalyst in these events, social divisions and oppression had planted the seeds of discord long before the Cold War.

The Counterinsurgency State and Democratization

The post-1954 military government was confronted with a disintegrating society. Officers viewed the military as the last bastion of order and felt compelled to take extraordinary measures to defend against chaos and Communism. To restore a semblance of order, the Armas and succeeding regimes set out to forcibly quell the activity of popular organizations let loose during the revolution. Economic indicators were upbeat in the 1960s and 1970s, contributing to middle- and upper-class satisfaction, but the improvement also fed the restiveness of peasant and labor sectors anxious for the right to organize and share the wealth. Military governors allied with civilian technocrats who attempted to manage economic and social diversification while also guarding security as a revolutionary crisis gripped all of Central America.

A variety of leftist insurgents, including Communists and Indian peasant groups, took up arms around the country beginning in the early 1960s. The fighting waxed and waned with the strength of the guerrillas, who were twice nearly crushed—in the late 1960s and again in the early 1980s—only to regroup later and continue their campaign of attrition. Four of the principal groups banded together in 1982 to form the Guatemalan National Revolutionary Unity (URNG). The war reached its low point in the early 1980s during the rule of General Efraín Ríos Montt, a Protestant evangelical with a penchant for messianic imagery. During Ríos Montt's eighteen-month dictatorship he implemented his vision for securing peace and development, a plan of *frijoles y fusiles* (beans and guns) that combined populist redistributive measures with a merciless counterinsurgency campaign. The toll of the internecine war fell most heavily on the Indian population, thus provoking charges of a systematic campaign of genocide that invited international attention and sparked political fires in the United States and Europe.

An elongated process of democratic transition began with the promulgation of a new constitution in 1984. Elections in 1985 then ushered in the first civilian government since 1969, and the URNG and the government finally signed peace accords in December 1996. During the war the military fended off rebellion and social conflict with systematic repression. Now elected civilians try to maintain the integrity of the same fractious nation as disillusionment and discontent seethe. The frustrations of governing provoked President Jorge Serrano Elías to attempt to remain in power via a Fujimori-style *autogolpe* in 1993, in which he illegally suspended the constitution and dismissed the legislature and supreme court. The maneuver failed and ended with his fleeing the country. The fragile democracy seems to lurch from one crisis to the next, but it has nevertheless lived to see successive elections and orderly administrative turnover.

SOCIAL STRUCTURE AND CIVIL SOCIETY

Around fourteen million Guatemalans live in a land of renowned natural splendor that has promised—and delivered—easy riches, but only to a select few colonists, adventurers, and investors. Sixty percent of the population is Indian, situated primarily in the western highlands; they speak twenty-four different languages, and many are ignorant of Spanish. Half of the population lives below the national poverty line, and the majority of the poor are Indians. More than four million inhabitants crowd the only major urban center, Guatemala City. It is a young country; close to 40 percent of its population is younger than fifteen.

The hierarchical system of exploitative labor familiar to most of Latin America characterizes centuries of Guatemalan political and social history. The Spanish adventurers of the sixteenth century coming to the new world on a civilizing and Christianizing crusade (one that might also prove quite profitable) formed the core of a feudal society of landowners and state authorities squeezing labor out of Indians and poor ladinos in the hinterland, thus entrenching a strict observance of race and class that persists even now. A pyramidal power structure sent orders down and services up, first to the monarch and later to a president. Participation by the masses, when it occurred at all, was usually limited to rubber-stamping preselected candidates in safely mediated elections.

The mixture of blood between Europeans and Indians did not create understanding through living together. Liberal, Conservative, and military regimes varied in their policy approaches toward Indians, but all shared a haughty disdain for the indigenous peoples. Conquerors crusaded to civilize the savage, which was usually limited to promising to Christianize their subjects while pressing them into semislavery. Europeanized ladino elites have also viewed Indians with contempt, but this is mixed with an enthusiasm for assimilation into Guatemalan national society. Curiously, this can be accomplished within a single generation: racial identity is supplied through language and dress rather than genetics. An Indian who picks up Spanish and moves to the city becomes a ladino. Mayan communities have nonetheless demonstrated remarkable resilience in maintaining distinctive cultural patterns, unlike in Mexico and its sister republics, where Hispanic hegemony was more complete. Though their cultures are unavoidably modified through synthesis, Indians stayed outside the national structure, identifying with their parochial communities rather than an abstract Guatemala. The culture of the conquest was particularly strong in the old colonial capital. Strong currents of personalism, patrimonialism, militarism, and traditional Catholicism ran deep here and radiated outward to the rest of Central America.

Iberian organic corporatism (reinforced by group-centered Indian traditions) has sharply conditioned state-society relations in Guatemala. Accordingly, the

Guatemalan state has always kept a watchful eye on social segments, maintaining special laws for the formation and oversight of political parties and interest groups. As Guatemala has been exposed to the global norms of democracy and free trade, of course, currents have shifted, working a striking shift in social and political relationships. Independent political opposition and civil society have been solidifying ever since democratic procedure began operating in the 1980s; Indians have continued a trend from the war years of greater organization and participation in national politics; the military has receded from outright domination of the political process. In perhaps the most striking social evolution to date, the Catholic Church has watched half the church-going population embrace Protestantism.

Given the underdeveloped state of most parties (see below), organized interest groups have offered the most energetic representation for social sectors. Established interest groups are older, better organized, and more stable than most parties. The term "interest group" can be extended to embrace a wide range of sectors, including the old feudalistic corporate bodies as well as newer power contenders such as business, urban labor, and human rights groups. Lobbying in the halls of government is frequent, but because politics was a closed affair among tightly knit elites for so long, many groups, particularly among the popular sectors, have been pushed into confrontational tactics. Rather than orderly, consensus-driven bargaining, competition often assumes a zero-sum character. Groups often resort to direct action over official channels, each threatening to use its own trump card—strikes, lockouts, demonstrations, or, before democratization, coups. Pluralism is a brute fact of social life in Guatemala, but it is not a part of public culture.

POLITICAL PARTIES AND ELECTIONS

Political parties, usually considered the driving force in political competition, are weakly institutionalized in Guatemala. In an elite-directed despotism, without the political space to breathe, ideological parties offering alternative platforms to voters were scarcely known. The Liberal and Conservative Parties that battled for total political domination in the nineteenth century engaged in machine politics, dispensing patronage in return for loyalty. Family and social ties normally determined party membership, and the factions took turns ruthlessly punishing each other when in power. Modern parties, on the other hand, are fluid—a group of erratic coalitions and constantly shifting alliances, often fashioned to serve the personal ambitions of political bosses or military factions, only to fizzle with the death or irrelevance of their leaders.

Since the latest constitution took effect, a multitude of new parties and coalitions across the political spectrum have crowded the ballot—including the former armed guerrillas. Most of the main players in the old party system have reorganized or splintered into obscurity. In current elections voters choose from around fifteen parties, many of which will not survive to see the next election. Politicians regularly change party identification, and parties that contested elections as adversaries in one election might act as a coalition in the next. The Grand National Alliance (GANA), a coalition of several center-right parties, is the only political organization that has managed to elect more than one president since democratization.

The conduct of elections reveals that democratic consolidation does not come easily. Guatemalan elections are not a sham; citizens have a choice among manifold parties, and in large measure their votes are counted and the results respected. As was the case during the civil war, though, electoral season in Guatemala is often attended by unruly protests, intimidation, and assassinations. The elections of 2011, like those of the past, were marred by assassinations of political candidates and other political figures.

THE STATE AND GOVERNMENT INSTITUTIONS

Historically reliant on simple force, the state has suffered from low legitimacy, and a lack of resources contributes to low effectiveness. A modern, centralized state structure began to emerge in the Liberal reform period, but many of the significant powers of the state authorities remained outside the definitions provided in the constitution and laws. Strong presidents and military dictators found it easy to give legal sanction to this or that preferred policy option through parliamentary fig leaves, decrees, and constitutional amendments or suspensions. State power hardly projected itself outside the capital, however, so large planters and political bosses acted with impunity in their rural domains. The fact of power has thus traditionally beaten out the rule of law.

Guatemala's constitutions have separated powers, as in the tripartite US model, but in practice servile legislatures and judiciaries have respected the Hispanic tradition of strong executives. In addition to the three branches, modern constitutions have created an independent Supreme Electoral Tribunal (TSE) to monitor elections. The unicameral congress consists of 158 members elected for four-year terms. Parties that cannot muster 4 percent of the vote lose their registration and cannot compete in the next election. The president and vice president are also elected to four-year terms without the possibility of reelection.[1]

A Supreme Court of Justice sits at the top of the judicial branch, to which thirteen justices are elected by congress for five-year terms, and a Constitutional Court exercises judicial review of legislative acts to ensure their conformity to the constitution. The constitution guarantees the independence of the judiciary, but the courts are weak, and they are criticized for the appearance of openness to political manipulation and threats.

Few radical changes are evident in the new fundamental law, but there is evidence that democratic practices are becoming more fully institutionalized. Perhaps most dramatically, the military appears satisfied that it need no longer control the political system. It has thus accepted deep cuts in its budget and subordinated itself to civilian command. Positive signs, no doubt, but it bears remembering that legal prohibitions have always proved parchment barriers to political participation by the military, and a coup in neighboring Honduras in 2009 clearly showed that the era of military intervention in Central America was not only a phenomenon of the twentieth century.

DEMOCRACY IN THE TWENTY-FIRST CENTURY

In spite of radical changes in the last century, and maybe unsurprisingly in this divided country with no history of limited government, liberal democracy has not met with immediate success. Some commitment to the rule of law manifested itself during Serrano's autogolpe, when massive civil condemnation and even military disapproval forced his resignation. Nevertheless, the annual Latinobarómetro opinion polls show that the percentage of Guatemalans who prefer democracy to any other regime has been consistently low and in 2011 limped in at a dismal 36 percent, dead last among Latin American countries and barely above the percentage who think there is no difference between democracy and authoritarianism.[2]

Freedom House, an organization that measures civil rights and political freedoms around the world, rates Guatemala as "partly free," a designation that calls attention to the complex character of democracy. Even the freest and fairest elections do not guard against corruption, crime, and destitution. All of these permeate Guatemalan society, demonstrating that the democratic political process is not sufficient for a peaceful and prosperous society. Since the transition to democracy we have witnessed two seemingly contradictory trends: the stabilization of electoral democracy and a continuing atmosphere of public crisis.

For the first time since democratization, a military figure occupies the presidency. Otto Pérez Molina, a retired army general, won the 2011 presidential election as the candidate of the center-right Patriotic Party. Pérez Molina campaigned on promises to get tough on crime, a message attractive to many Guatemalans wearied by public insecurity, but feared by those with vivid memories of the unrestrained violence of the civil war. That fear is only intensified by accusations that Pérez Molina murdered and tortured civilians during war. Despite his hard-line stance and the cloud over his past career, Pérez Molina has not simply advocated further militarization of the country. As a member of the government in the 1990s, he advocated negotiating an end to the civil war, and later he was instrumental in forcing President Serrano from office after his autogolpe. As president, he has labeled the war against drugs a failure, and he has called for an international dialogue on drug legalization as an alternative method for dealing with drug violence. Though drug liberalization is unlikely in the near future, this former general's surprising stand may contribute to a shift in the terms of debate on how best to address transnational crime.

PUBLIC POLICY

Though material progress since has given rise to a growing middle class and improved the conditions of many Guatemalans, many major policy challenges facing the country would have been familiar to governments of decades past: boosting economic growth, improving education, increasing employment opportunities, and providing health care. Center-left president Álvaro Colom took strides during his tenure to expand access to social services, and during the 2011 elections candidates of all ideological stripes promised to build on his initiative. But for the weak institutions of a relatively poor country, these challenges are daunting enough. In addition to these—and exacerbating them—is a more recent crisis of public insecurity.

Availability of guns and human desperation fuel an epidemic of violent street crime in both the cities and the countryside. The enormity of the violence has made it impossible for the state to exercise full control over its territory and has infected already frail institutions. Police have proven inadequate in dealing with the crisis and are often charged with complicity in organized crime, and the large majority of crimes go unpunished. Street gangs known as *maras,* exported from Los Angeles to Central America, have overrun swaths of the country and stretch the already thin resources of law enforcement. The government declared war on the gangs but is entirely ill-equipped to wage it.

Effects of such violence on the provision of public goods are manifold. Crime consumes the attention, robbing resources from other areas of public importance. Insecurity also corrodes public confidence in the state (which, according to opinion polls, stands at 18 percent in Guatemala, again the lowest number in Latin America), further contributing to the debility of institutions that makes combating crime difficult in the first place.[3]

INTERNATIONAL RELATIONS AND GLOBALIZATION

As a colony, Guatemala was kept isolated from the world around it, lest exotic ideologies infect a safely Iberian colony. After independence its foreign relations were limited mainly to securing foreign investment and disputing boundaries with neighbors Mexico and Belize.[4] Just as the old feudal order crumbled away under the forces of economic and social modernization, Guatemala in the twenty-first century is ineluctably drawn further into a global web of trade, communication, and migration. Further, an international ethos celebrating democracy means that Guatemala must contend with constant scrutiny by foreign governments and international human rights organizations in addition to domestic civil and political groups.

The opportunities afforded by globalization have proven beneficial to the Guatemalan economy but have not proven an easy route to development and greater equality. Further, international integration in some cases exposes Guatemala to greater risk. Guatemala has always been deeply sensitive to conditions in the United States, for that country has at least partly determined the fates of a number of political leaders besides Arbenz. The Guatemalan economy is heavily dependent on aid from the United States, primarily provided through USAID. Assistance is tied to achievement of political and economic reforms aimed at democratic institutionalization and transparent government. Remittances from migrant Guatemalan workers in the United States funnel around US$4.5 billion into Guatemalan homes—a figure representing 12 percent of the country's economy.

As have most Latin American governments, successive administrations have pursued economic liberalization and diversification. Free trade agreements govern commerce with the Central American states and Mexico, and Guatemala joined the World Trade Organization in 1995. Political and business leaders hope a new free trade agreement passed in 2006, the Central America–Dominican Republic Free Trade Agreement (CAFTA-DR), will reinforce commercial growth, while detractors, echoing the dependency school, fear that it will only compound already gross inequalities. The overall economic outlook of the country has improved dramatically in recent years, but the risks of economic integration were on display in 2008; though rates have since rebounded, in the aftermath of the financial crisis starting in that year remittances dropped and exports slowed due to the slowing of the US economy.

Inevitably, globalization brings less salutary trends as well. Improvements in transportation, underresourced authorities, and a central location combine to make Guatemala prime real estate for international crime syndicates doing business throughout Central America, Mexico, and the United States. Drugs, humans, and arms are all trafficked through the country, adding a transnational dimension to an already intractable crime scourge. The Kaibiles, an elite military force created to fight insurgents, have been enlisted to fight the drug war, but some members have gone renegade and made common cause with Los Zetas, the infamously savage drug cartel in Mexico. At the same time, the maras have also been enlisted by Los Zetas, lending greater manpower to the cartel and enormous firepower and training to the gangs. Already overwhelmed by local crime, it is unlikely the government will soon find the power to meet the challenge of criminal syndicates that even much larger Mexico cannot eradicate.

CONCLUSIONS

During the Cold War, Guatemala was the scene of intervention and ideological division that appeared to doom the country to continuous conflict. Encouragingly, Guatemala's nascent democracy has survived for more than a quarter century. No longer is there conflict over the basic direction the state should take, but all mainstream political actors endorse democratization and globalization. Nonetheless, liberal democracy requires more than free and fair elections, and formal democratic freedoms are undermined by persistent insecurity, corruption, and poverty. Furthermore, though proximity to its larger neighbors offers potential advantages through integration, this proximity has also subjected the country to the sinister phenomenon of the globalization of crime. As a relatively small country with weakly consolidated institutions, this likely represents the greatest current threat to Guatemala's long-sought but elusive development and democratic consolidation.

Notes

1. Amendments changed the original length of terms served by elected officials, in addition to other changes.

2. Figure from the Latinobarómetro 2011 *Informe*, 38. Available on the Web at www.latinobarometro.org.

3. Ibid., 51.

4. The British colony was considered a violation of Spanish and Guatemalan sovereignty. President Serrano surprised—and angered—many when he unilaterally recognized Belize in 1991.

Suggestions for Further Reading

Brett, Roderick. *Social Movements, Indigenous Politics, and Democratization in Guatemala, 1985–1996.* Boston: Brill, 2008.

Cullather, Nick. *Secret History: The CIA's Classified Account of Its Operations in Guatemala, 1952–1954.* 2nd ed. Stanford, CA: Stanford University Press, 2006.

Grandin, Greg. *The Blood of Guatemala: A History of Race and Nation.* Durham, NC: Duke University Press, 2000.

Menchú, Rigoberta. *I Rigoberta Menchú: An Indian Woman in Guatemala*. Edited by Elisabeth Burgos-Debray. Translated by Ann Wright. 2nd ed. New York: Verso, 2009.

O'Neill, Kevin Lewis. *City of God: Christian Citizenship in Postwar Guatemala*. Berkeley: University of California Press, 2009.

Schlesinger, Stephen, and Stephen Kinzer. *Bitter Fruit: The Story of the American Coup in Guatemala*. Revised ed. Cambridge, MA : Harvard University, David Rockefeller Center for Latin American Studies, 2005.

Stoll, David. *Rigoberta Menchú and the Story of All Poor Guatemalans*. Expanded ed. Boulder, CO : Westview Press, 2007.

Woodward, Ralph Lee Jr. *Central America: A Nation Divided*. 3rd ed. New York: Oxford University Press, 1999.

22

HONDURAS: FRAGILE DEMOCRACY

J. Mark Ruhl

INTRODUCTION

Honduras seems an unlikely candidate for democracy. The nation has been ruled throughout most of its history either by dictatorial political bosses or by military strongmen. After the power of the armed forces finally receded in the 1990s, Honduras did become a procedurally democratic country for more than a decade. However, its democratic progress was abruptly halted in June 2009 when a constitutional crisis that set leftist president Manuel "Mel" Zelaya against most of the rest of the Honduran civilian political elite sparked a military coup. Elections a few months later restored democratic government and placed conservative National Party leader Porfirio "Pepe" Lobo in the presidency. The 2011 Cartagena Accord he negotiated stabilized the political situation by allowing former president Zelaya to return from exile and form a new political party. Nonetheless, Honduras's democracy remained polarized and fragile.

The consolidation of democracy requires that both political elites and the mass public accept the democratic process as legitimate and as the only game in town. Honduran civilian and military elites had appeared, at last, to have learned to abide by democratic rules by the late 1990s, but the 2009 coup and the illegal actions by President Zelaya that precipitated it proved otherwise. Most ordinary Hondurans had, by this time, already found democratic governance to be a great disappointment. Neoliberal economic reforms required by international financial institutions have only modestly reduced poverty in a country where nearly two-thirds of the population still lives below the poverty line. Moreover, widespread embezzlement and bribery have discredited one democratically chosen government after another.

417

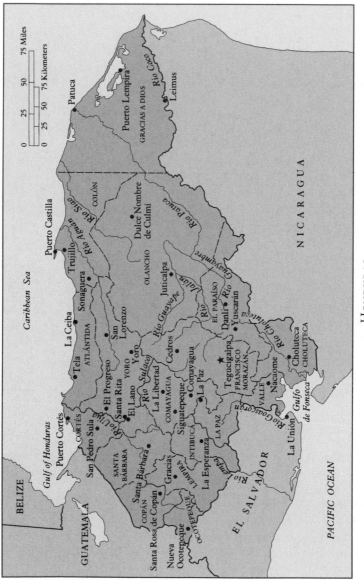

HONDURAS

Elected leaders also have proven unable to stem a frightening expansion of organized crime and gang violence that has placed all Hondurans at risk. Democracy's future is in doubt in Honduras.

HISTORY AND POLITICAL CULTURE

Honduras is a mountainous, Pennsylvania-sized country of over eight million people. About half of the population lives in rural areas, where illiteracy is common (20 percent of all adults are illiterate). Nearly 90 percent of Hondurans are mestizos, but there are significant African Honduran concentrations on the north coast as well as some remaining indigenous communities. A majority of Hondurans are Roman Catholics, although evangelical Protestants have made important inroads. With a per capita GDP of US$4,200 at purchasing power parity, Honduras is one of Latin America's three poorest countries. Its economy is dependent upon remittances from more than nine hundred thousand Hondurans working in the United States (US$ 2.9 billion in 2011) and on the export of bananas, coffee, and products assembled in *maquiladoras*.

Authoritarian governments have traditionally ruled Honduras. However, Honduran rulers and political elites were less repressive of popular-sector groups than their more violent counterparts in neighboring El Salvador, Guatemala, or Nicaragua. While many powerful families in other Central American countries made their fortunes as members of an arrogant coffee oligarchy, Honduran elites of the late nineteenth and early twentieth centuries focused on small-scale cattle ranching, silver mining ventures, or small banana export enterprises.[1] None of these activities posed a threat to the peasantry in an underpopulated country where agricultural land was widely available. Later, when coffee did become important in Honduras, small and medium-sized farms produced most of the crop. Although there was little friction between peasants and large landowners, constant battles for power among rival landed caudillos rendered the nation chronically unstable. These warring political bosses fought over the spoils of office rather than public policy. They promoted a clientelist political tradition in which constitutional and electoral rules were regularly violated.

At the beginning of the twentieth century, the United Fruit Company and other US banana enterprises established large plantations on the sparsely populated north coast. Hondurans who went to work for the banana giants eventually formed the strongest trade union movement in Central America. Longtime dictator Tiburcio Carías Andino (1932–1949) of the National Party was a loyal ally of United Fruit, but some leaders of the weaker Liberal Party were closer to labor. In addition, a commercial-industrial elite with an important Arab-Honduran (*turco*) element formed on the north coast; it often backed the banana workers.[2]

Created with US assistance in the 1940s, the armed forces became an important political actor independent of the feuding Liberal and National parties. The Honduran military first intervened in politics in 1956 to depose an unpopular provisional president. Before relinquishing control, senior officers demanded constitutional guarantees of the armed forces' political autonomy. Elected with the support of unions and reformist business elements, Liberal president Ramón Villeda Morales (1957–1963) introduced an urban social security system, a progressive labor code, and a limited agrarian reform that upset new agricultural export elites as well as traditional rural political bosses. When the Liberal candidate to succeed Villeda also threatened to end the military's autonomy, the armed forces staged a preemptive coup in 1963 in alliance with the National Party.

Armed forces commander General Oswaldo López Arellano dominated Honduran politics from 1963 to 1975. During the López era, peasants organized to press for land reform in response to land scarcity caused by rapid population growth and the post–World War II expansion of commercial agriculture. Although López initially repressed these organizations, he later evicted about eighty thousand Salvadoran peasants living in Honduras in order to make more land available to them. During the subsequent 1969 war with El Salvador, Honduran peasants, trade unionists, and the north coast business community rallied around the armed forces despite their previous differences with General López. Shortly thereafter, the air force general broke with the National Party to form a progressive political alliance with these groups. López's more conservative military successors in the presidency, however, re-allied with the National Party and large landowners. Nonetheless, some land redistribution continued, and trade unions remained important political players. The Honduran military's more accommodative stance encouraged popular-sector organizations to continue to press their demands within established political channels. While highly repressive, intransigent governments in El Salvador, Nicaragua, and Guatemala drifted into civil war, Honduras remained stable.

Democratic Elections and the Decline of the Military

With encouragement from the United States, the Honduran armed forces permitted an elected civilian, Liberal Roberto Suazo Córdova (1982–1986), to assume the presidency. In spite of the new democratic veneer, the armed forces grew larger than ever as the United States raised military aid to unprecedented levels in return for permission to base anti-Sandinista Nicaraguan guerrillas in Honduras. President Suazo became the junior partner in an unsavory alliance with right-wing armed forces chief General Gustavo Álvarez Martínez. General Álvarez conducted a short but brutal "dirty war" of torture and assassination against suspected revolutionaries and used the army and police to infiltrate unions, student organizations, and peasant groups. After Álvarez's fall from power in a 1984 internal coup, the military continued to maintain its supremacy over elected civilian authorities. Corruption within the armed forces reached new extremes as some officers became rich by protecting drug traffickers.

The democratic electoral process was strengthened in 1990 when Suazo's Liberal successor José Azcona (1986–1990) passed the presidential sash to freely elected National Party leader Rafael Callejas. This ceremony marked the first democratic turnover of power between competing Honduran political parties in nearly sixty years. During the rest of the decade, the electoral process became institutionalized with regular presidential and legislative elections every four years. Yet in spite of Honduras's free elections and expanded civil and political liberties, the military continued to be the strongest political actor.

With the end of the Cold War and the Central American civil wars, however, the United States no longer needed the Honduran military as an ally against

Communism. By 1993, US military aid had been reduced to almost nothing, and the US embassy had become a strident critic of the armed forces. Honduran human rights organizations, student groups, unions, the Catholic Church, and even many business groups joined forces in an attack on the military's power and prerogatives. The unusual strength and breadth of this antimilitary movement within civil society persuaded Honduran political party leaders to challenge the armed forces on a range of issues.

The political decline of the military accelerated under Liberals Carlos Roberto Reina (1994–1998) and Carlos Flores (1998–2002). Reina passed constitutional reforms that ended obligatory military service and stripped the armed forces of control over the national police. He also trimmed the military budget and removed the Honduran telecommunications system and other sources of illicit funding from armed forces management. The military shrank dramatically in size. In early 1999, President Flores passed a constitutional reform that formally ended the military's political autonomy, placing the armed forces under a civilian defense minister for the first time since 1957. By the time National Party leader Ricardo Maduro (2002–2006) assumed the presidency, the subordination of the armed forces to civilian control appeared to be an accomplished fact.

The 2009 Military Coup and the Breakdown of Democracy

Unfortunately, the polarization of civilian elite politics during the tenure of Liberal president Manuel Zelaya (2006–2009) ushered the armed forces back onto the political stage.[3] Although a centrist politician throughout his career, President Zelaya unexpectedly allied himself with radical populist Hugo Chávez of Venezuela and brought Honduras into the Bolivarian Alternative for the Americas (ALBA). Zelaya's sudden shift to the left alienated most of the nation's civilian political class, including other Liberal politicians. When the Honduran chief executive began to campaign for a constituent assembly to revise the constitution, his opponents suspected that he intended to abolish the ban on presidential reelection and remain in power beyond the conclusion of his term in 2010 (or return to office in 2014). The national congress, the supreme court, the Supreme Electoral Tribunal, and the attorney general united in ruling his actions illegal and unconstitutional. President Zelaya nevertheless continued with preparations to hold a nonbinding referendum on adding the constituent assembly issue to the upcoming November 2009 ballot. When the president ordered the armed forces to assist with the referendum, the chief of the Joint General Staff, General Romeo Vásquez, refused, citing the poll's illegality. President Zelaya immediately dismissed Vásquez and personally led a crowd of supporters onto an air force base to take possession of referendum materials stored there. The supreme court, which had quickly reinstated General Vásquez, ordered him to arrest the president. Military units deposed Zelaya on the day the referendum was to take place (June 28) and expelled him from the country. National congress president Roberto Micheletti, a Liberal, became head of a de facto civilian government with wide congressional support.

The Organization of American States (OAS) immediately suspended Honduras, and an outraged international community clamored for Zelaya's reinstatement. For several months, crowds of Zelaya supporters competed with pro-Micheletti partisans for control of the streets. Repressive measures by the security forces caused the deaths of twenty Zelaya activists. Ultimately, neither external nor internal pressures proved sufficient to put the ousted president back in office. Despite its initial support for his return, the United States later recognized the results of the previously scheduled November 2009 presidential elections, which transferred power to National Party leader Porfirio Lobo.

Although his actions were condemned by the extreme right, Lobo stabilized the political situation by negotiating the political reintegration of Zelaya and followers via the 2011 Cartagena Accord with the assistance of Colombia's president, Juan Manual Santos, and Venezuela's Hugo Chávez. Lobo also appointed a balanced Truth and Reconciliation Commission that blamed both Zelaya and his opponents for the coup. Nevertheless, the country remained polarized, and serious political difficulties continued. A new constitutional confrontation broke out in December 2012 when the national congress, with President Lobo's blessing, illegally dismissed four supreme court justices who had blocked parts of a law intended to purge the country's corrupt police force.

INTEREST GROUPS AND CIVIL SOCIETY

The fragmented Honduran private business sector encompasses several competing financial groups that contribute to political campaigns and vie for influence over government economic decisions. The business community is also split by region (those enterprises based around San Pedro Sula, on the north coast, versus those based in Tegucigalpa), ethnicity (Arab Honduran–owned companies versus others), and economic sector. The principal umbrella organization for the private sector is the Honduran Private Enterprise Council (COHEP). Foreign investors in the maquiladoras, the banana industry, and elsewhere also seek to influence government policy. Most of the private sector and its mass media organs fiercely opposed President Zelaya's swing to the left.

The armed forces regained political influence in 2009 when the clash between President Zelaya and his civilian opponents prompted both sides to try to enlist military support. Internal factional squabbling among *promociones* (military academy graduating classes) has divided the officer corps in the past, but the military was unified behind the 2009 coup. The armed forces also still control the nation's only intelligence-gathering agency and play a key internal security role in collaboration with the police to patrol Honduras's crime-plagued cities and combat drug trafficking.

Honduras once was home to the strongest independent labor movement in Central America, but its unions have suffered from ideological divisions and internal leadership conflicts. Less than 10 percent of the workforce is unionized today. The moderate, AFL-CIO-linked Honduran Workers' Confederation (CTH), which includes most banana workers, is the country's leading labor federation. The other major national labor organizations are the social-Christian (Christan democratic) General Confederation of Workers (CGT) and the leftist Unitary Confederation of Honduran Workers (CUTH). Some organizations within the fragmented peasant movement are affiliated with these three labor confederations, while others exist independently. Labor unions that organize public sector employees, particularly teachers and health care workers, have been successful in using strikes to win economic concessions from the government despite external demands for fiscal austerity. Most trade unionists backed President Zelaya before and after the 2009 coup because of his enactment of generous minimum wage increases and other policies that benefited labor.

Honduran civil society has expanded in the last two decades as indigenous and environmental groups have joined existing human rights proponents such as the Committee for the Defense of Human Rights in Honduras (CODEH) and traditional actors such as the Catholic Church to pressure government officials on a range of issues. In addition, student groups and women's organizations as well as organized urban slum dwellers have become more active. Since the late 1990s, unions, peasant organizations, and indigenous groups have increasingly resorted to direct action (road blockages, protest marches on the capital) to press their demands.

POLITICAL PARTIES AND ELECTIONS

Relatively few Hondurans enter politics to serve the public interest. The traditional Liberal Party and National Party are both patron-client political machines primarily organized to compete for state jobs, contracts, and other resources. Each party is divided into competing personalist factions. Both parties choose their presidential candidate in a national primary election that pits factional contenders against one another. The Nationals and the Liberals are centrist, multiclass parties that traditionally have benefited from widespread, hereditary party affiliation that is now weakening. In 2011, former Liberal president Manuel Zelaya established a new radical populist Liberty and Refoundation Party (LIBRE), which attracted almost one-quarter of the voters who participated in the 2012 primary elections. Several minor political parties, including the centrist Innovation and National Unity Party (PINU), the center-left Christian Democrats (PDCH), and the socialist Democratic Unification Party (PUD), also participate in Honduran elections.

The Honduran president is elected by plurality to a single four-year term. The unicameral national congress is selected at the same time by open-list proportional representation (PR). Honduran elections are supervised by a Supreme Electoral Tribunal (TSE) chosen by the national congress. Beginning in the early 1980s, Honduras held seven consecutive democratic general elections, four of which produced peaceful turnovers in party control (1989, 1993, 2001, and 2005). The 2009 presidential election, however, took place in the midst of the crisis precipitated by the overthrow of President Zelaya, who urged his supporters to boycott the contest. Wealthy rancher Porfirio "Pepe" Lobo of the National Party, with 57 percent of the vote, won easily over former vice president Elvin Santos, an anti-Zelaya Liberal, in an election for which the TSE reported a disputed 50 percent turnout rate. The Nationals also won 71 of 128 congressional seats, compared to the Liberals' 45. Minor parties captured the remaining 12 seats.

The next electoral cycle began with the November 2012 primary elections, which involved three Liberal Party presidential candidates, seven National Party candidates, and Zelaya's social activist wife, Xiomara Castro de Zelaya, as the single LIBRE contender. Attorney Mauricio Villeda Bermúdez, son of reformist president

Ramón Villeda, won the Liberal nomination for the November 2013 election, while the president of the national congress, Juan Orlando Hernández, emerged as the National Party's standard-bearer. The primary elections were marred by allegations of vote buying and other irregularities that further undermined trust in the TSE and the electoral process.

GOVERNMENTAL INSTITUTIONS

The Honduran governmental system is highly centralized, with power traditionally concentrated in the presidency. The president directs the activities of executive branch agencies and usually introduces most legislation. If the president heads a majority coalition of party factions in the national congress, his policy initiatives generally become law. However, the making of public policy is often not the president's highest priority. The chief executive typically spends much of his time protecting his personal power base by distributing patronage and other material payoffs to supporters in his own and allied party factions and by countering the moves of his political enemies. The National Congress historically did not play a significant policy-making role; congressional seats traditionally have been viewed as rewards for factional loyalty rather than as opportunities for public service. However, the national congress has become much more important in policy making and executive oversight of late. This has been true especially when the national congress has been controlled by party factions not affiliated with the president (as under Zelaya in 2008–2009) or when the president of the national congress has harbored ambitions to become chief executive. President Lobo collaborated closely with congressional leader Juan Orlando Hernández and backed his successful campaign for the 2013 National Party presidential nomination.

The Honduran judiciary is highly politicized, and judicial corruption and incompetence are widespread. Few high-ranking officials or major drug traffickers have been prosecuted successfully. The national congress appoints the fifteen justices of the Honduran supreme court for seven-year terms from a list of forty-five candidates approved by a nominating committee composed of civil society representatives. The supreme court justices then appoint the judges of the lower courts. The high court played a decisive role in the ouster of President Zelaya in 2009, but its future significance was placed in doubt when, in late 2012, the national congress claimed the authority to oust supreme court justices at will.

DEMOCRACY: SUCCESS OR FAILURE?

Honduras made important democratic strides after formal civilian rule was restored in the 1980s. Four turnover elections appeared to demonstrate that the electoral system had become institutionalized. By the late 1990s, the long dominant military also seemed to have returned to the barracks for good. But the 2009 coup showed how fragile these achievements actually were. When President Zelaya violated basic democratic rules by moving ahead with an illegal referendum and appeared to pursue an unconstitutional second term, his opponents felt justified in using whatever means they could find to stop him. They conspired with the military to oust the president, and not even opposition from the United States could dissuade them. Although the Cartagena Accord permitted Zelaya to again compete for power via his new party, LIBRE, it was not clear if Honduras's polarized democracy could survive an electoral victory by his wife in 2013 if that should occur. LIBRE's current radical populist platform and the Zelayas' continued insistence on a constituent assembly to rewrite the constitution pose major threats to established political and economic interests.

Long before the 2009 coup took place, the performance of elected democratic leaders had fallen far short of the general public's expectations. Most public officials have concentrated on capturing the legal and illegal spoils of office for themselves and their political networks rather than on addressing the needs of one of the poorest populations in the Americas. Neoliberal economic reforms have yet to substantially improve the lives of the underprivileged majority. Crime continues to rage out of control. Too many young Hondurans have come to believe that only emigration to the United States will solve their problems. The mass public's unhappiness with the quality of democratic governance in Honduras was clearly indicated in a 2011 Latinobarómetro survey in which only 29 percent of Hondurans expressed satisfaction with the functioning of democracy in their country.[4] Just 43 percent of Honduran respondents preferred democracy to any other type of political system.

PUBLIC POLICY

Effective policy making is difficult in Honduras Resources are scarce, the state bureaucracy is notoriously inefficient, and the political class is driven by spoils rather than policy goals. Some Honduran presidents, such as Liberal reformer Carlos Reina, have come into office with clear policy objectives; however, the enactment of public policies to address national problems more often is driven by external pressure or by an acute internal crisis. The fundamental changes in Honduran economic policy that led to the adoption of neoliberalism in the 1990s, for example, were forced by an international credit boycott orchestrated by international financial institutions and the United States.

President Rafael Callejas (1990–1994) began orthodox structural economic reform in 1990. He cut the size of the nation's chronically high fiscal deficit by shrinking the bureaucracy and increasing taxes. He also liberalized trade, devalued the currency, and persuaded foreign investors to establish new maquiladoras. His successors, with the notable exception of leftist Manuel Zelaya, have largely maintained these IMF-mandated neoliberal policies, although many presidents have made more concessions to organized labor than the IMF recommended. President Ricardo Maduro (2002–2006), a Stanford-educated economist, signed the Central America Free Trade Agreement (CAFTA) with the United States, and his fidelity to neoliberal principles won the country more than US$4 billion in debt relief. GDP growth accelerated to over 6 percent in the last year of his term.

President Zelaya's alliance with Venezuelan populist leader Chávez initially stimulated the Honduran economy with low-interest loans, reduced oil import costs, and generous development assistance, although it raised investors' suspicions. Zelaya granted hefty wage increases to public sector employees and generally demonstrated less financial discipline than Maduro as inflation climbed to over 11 percent. The

Honduran economy continued to grow at a rate of more than 6 percent through 2007 but slowed to 4 percent in 2008 with the onset of the global recession, then began to contract sharply with the 2009 constitutional crisis. Remittances from the United States, exports, foreign aid, and investment all declined, and tens of thousands of Hondurans were thrown out of work. GDP fell 2.1 percent.

President Lobo's return to neoliberal orthodoxy and his political reconciliation efforts helped engineer a modest economic recovery during 2010–2012 (3 percent average GDP growth rate). He reduced energy subsidies, public pension obligations, and teachers' salary increases. Levels of foreign aid and investment returned to precoup levels, and inflation subsided to under 6 percent. Unfortunately, public spending again pushed the fiscal deficit to a dangerous level in 2012, as several ministries overspent their budgets.

Although Lobo and most of his predecessors have won praise from international financial institutions for their efforts to reform and expand the nation's economy, most ordinary Hondurans have seen only small improvements in their miserable living conditions. The poverty rate did decrease from 75 percent to 63 percent of the population between 1990 and 1998, but it has remained at about the same high level for more than a decade. Reforms to combat tax evasion by the nation's well-to-do might have helped to better fund social programs to reduce deep inequalities, but few of those with political influence are interested in paying more taxes. Small conditional cash transfer (CCT) programs of income subsidies to poor families have been in place since 2000, but only because of international assistance. Recent governments, including Zelaya's, also have not revived the agrarian reform program that came to a halt during the Callejas administration. In April 2012 more than thirty-five hundred landless and land-poor peasant families mobilized to occupy almost thirty thousand acres (twelve thousand hectares) of agricultural land before being evicted by the police and army.

Hondurans have also been deeply disillusioned by the high level of government corruption. In 2012, Transparency International rated Honduras as one of the three most corrupt countries in Latin America.[5] Yet for many, the greatest disappointment has been their democratically elected leaders' inability to control the crime wave that has enveloped the country. Bank robberies, homicides, car thefts, kidnappings, and muggings have exploded since the 1990s, and criminal organizations have proliferated. President Ricardo Maduro, whose own son was killed by kidnappers, made attacking crime his highest priority, but his zero-tolerance policies directed against Mara Salvatrucha (MS-13), Mara 18 (18th Street), and other youth gangs had limited success. Estimates of youth gang membership range up to thirty thousand. By 2011, the Honduran homicide rate (eighty-six murders per hundred thousand people) became the highest in the world. Both President Zelaya and interim chief executive Micheletti largely ignored the rapid expansion of drug trafficking by the Mexican Sinaloa and Los Zetas cartels after the Mexican government's increased counternarcotics efforts beginning in 2007 pushed more of their operations into Central America. By 2011, an estimated two hundred metric tons of cocaine from South America moved through Honduras on its way to the US market every year. President Lobo belatedly addressed the growing internal security crisis with assistance from the United States, but his attempts to purge the corrupt and inefficient national police force were complicated by the supreme court's insistence that accused officers receive due process.

Few Hondurans base their opinions about government performance on foreign policy, although this is an area of major concern to Honduran presidents and the nation's political elite. Honduran foreign policy officials traditionally have devoted more attention to their relations with the United States than to their ties with the rest of the world combined. Their principal goal has been to secure economic resources, trade preferences, and favorable immigration policies by demonstrating loyalty to the United States. President Zelaya broke with this tradition by joining the anti-US ALBA alliance, but President Lobo returned to the US fold.

GLOBALIZATION

Honduras is highly integrated into the global economic and cultural network. According to the KOF Index of Globalization, the country ranked in the most globalized third of the world's nations in 2012.[6] The Honduran economy depends heavily on exports to the United States and the European Union and on remittances from the more than 10 percent of its citizens who work legally or illegally in the United States. Moreover, the nation's current internal security crisis has been driven by the high demand for cocaine in the United States and the deportation by the US government of thousands of youth gang members back to Central America since the 1990s. Hondurans are also fully integrated within US popular culture via US television programs and the Honduran news media, which extensively cover events in the United States. In contrast, Honduras has little impact on the global community. The nation is too small and poor even to attract much international media attention except in cases of unusual political instability (such as the 2009 military coup) or extreme natural disaster (1998's Hurricane Mitch).

FUTURE PROSPECTS

A constitutional crisis caused Honduras's democracy to collapse in 2009. Although the semblance of a democratic political process has since been reestablished, its roots are shallow. Neither the political and economic elites who control the traditional National and Liberal Parties nor the radical populists who lead LIBRE can be trusted to respect democratic rules when their interests are in jeopardy. The National Party congressional leadership recently ousted supreme court justices in clear violation of the constitution, and after the 2012 primaries LIBRE leader Manuel Zelaya warned that his movement would consider taking power by force if the electoral route failed. In addition, the Honduran mass public's attachment to democracy and its values is tenuous because democracy has done little to tangibly improve the lives of ordinary people. The next major challenge for Honduras's fragile democracy will be the 2013 general elections. As long as one of the two traditional parties' candidates wins the presidency, the democratic system will likely persist despite all of its defects. However, Honduran democratic institutions will be sorely tested if LIBRE increases its support among the nation's discontented poor enough to return the Zelayas to power in 2013 or after.

Notes

1. The historical section of this chapter draws extensively on J. Mark Ruhl, "Honduras: Militarism and Democratization in Troubled Seas," in *Repression, Resistance, and Democratic Transition in Central America*, ed. Thomas Walker and Ariel Armony (Wilmington, DE: Scholarly Resources, 2000).

2. Darío A. Euraque, *Reinterpreting the Banana Republic: Region and State in Honduras, 1870–1972* (Chapel Hill: University of North Carolina Press, 1996), 96–97.

3. For a fuller discussion of the 2009 military coup, see J. Mark Ruhl, "Honduras Unravels," *Journal of Democracy* 21, 2 (2010): 93–107.

4. "The Latinobarometro Poll: The Discontents of Progress," *Economist*, October 29, 2011, 48.

5. Transparency International Corruption Perceptions Index, 2012; www.transparency.org.

6. Axel Dreher, Noel Gaston, and Pim Martens, *Measuring Globalization* (New York: Springer, 2008).

Suggestions for Further Reading

Euraque, Darío A. *Reinterpreting the Banana Republic: Region and State in Honduras, 1870–1972*. Chapel Hill: University of North Carolina Press, 1996.

Mahoney, James. *The Legacies of Liberalism: Path Dependence and Political Regimes in Central America*. Baltimore: Johns Hopkins University Press, 2001.

Morris, James A. *Honduras: Caudillo Politics and Military Rulers*. Boulder, CO: Westview Press, 1984.

Reichman, Daniel R. *The Broken Village: Coffee, Migration, and Globalization in Honduras*. Ithaca, NY: Cornell University Press, 2011.

Schulz, Donald E., and Deborah S. Schulz. *The United States, Honduras, and the Crisis in Central America*. Boulder, CO: Westview Press, 1994.

23

PANAMA: THE CHALLENGE
OF GOVERNANCE IN BOOM TIMES

Steve C. Ropp

Panama's fifth civilian president since the end of military authoritarian rule in 1989 governs during a critical period of both political and economic transition. President Ricardo Martinelli is a businessman who owns not only Panama's largest supermarket chain but also a host of associated enterprises. Educated in the United States, he is thoroughly familiar with the country that used to control Panama's destiny as well as with the world of multinational business and banking. In terms of politics, it will be important to see how his managerial (some say authoritarian) style of governance serves the country during the upcoming 2014 electoral cycle. It will be equally important to see how Martinelli manages matters related to the booming economy and anticipated grand opening of the newly expanded canal—events that will determine the country's economic future for decades to come.

Precisely because presidential leadership plays such an important role in Latin America, it is instructive to compare President Martinelli's background to that of his two immediate predecessors. Former president Mireya Moscoso (1999–2004) is the daughter of a poor schoolteacher from Panama. At a very young age she joined the Panamenista Party (PP), which was founded and led by her future husband, Dr. Arnulfo Arias. Dr. Arias, who was elected president in 1940, 1949, and 1968, espoused a brand of nationalist and racially exclusionary populism that won him few friends in either the racially mixed police force or in the United States. He was never allowed to complete a full term in office, and his third and final overthrow in 1968 led directly to two decades of military rule. Following the US invasion of Panama in 1989 and the death of Dr. Arias, Mireya Moscoso became the standard-bearer for his particular brand of nationalist politics.

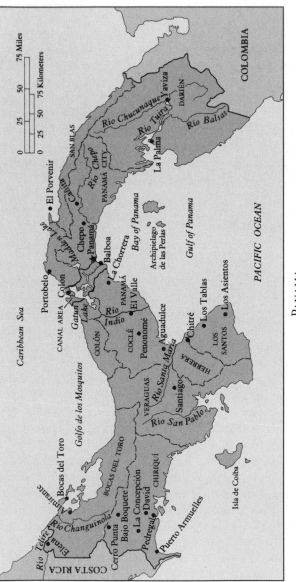

PANAMA

President Martinelli's immediate predecessor represented a second variant of Panama's national populist tradition. Former president Martín Torrijos (2004–2009) is the son of the late General Omar Torrijos, who helped lead the military coup that ousted Dr. Arias in 1968. The elder Torrijos founded the Democratic Revolutionary Party (PRD) and espoused his own brand of nationalist populism, though it was more racially inclusive. Best known for having successfully negotiated new Panama Canal treaties with US president Jimmy Carter in 1977, he played a central role in the canal's eventual transfer to Panama in the year 2000. It was this critical role that allowed his son Martín to become one of the PRD's standard-bearers following the transition from military authoritarianism to democratic rule.

Although these two nationally based movements and their associated political parties differed in many respects, they both suggest the enduring presence of the political phenomenon known as populism. Populism is simply the direct and unmediated personal relationship that a charismatic leader establishes with his or her people. As a result of its long and tortured history of authoritarian populist politics, Panama's contemporary democratic political scene resembles nothing more than a landscape dominated by two dormant volcanoes.

The first of these populist volcanoes erupted in the 1930s, when the followers of Dr. Arias rebelled against a rising tide of uncontrolled immigration and against an elitist urban commercial class that was perceived as too closely aligned with the United States. The second erupted in the late 1960s when officers within Panama's emerging military institution rebelled against the inept antimilitary populism of Dr. Arias and the continued presence on Panamanian soil (in the Panama Canal Zone) of the United States. Although these two populist volcanoes have lain dormant since the US military invasion of 1989, they sometimes still show signs of life in this supposedly postpopulist age of liberal representative democracy and market economy.

Representing the Democratic Change Party (CD), President Martinelli leads a country that has experienced twenty years of civilian democratic governance following twenty years of military authoritarian rule.[1] Military rule came to an end in December 1989 when President George H. W. Bush sent US troops into Panama to destroy the Panamanian Defense Forces (PDF) and capture its commander, General Manuel Antonio Noriega.[2] During the ensuing years, democratic government was reestablished and four general elections were successfully held (1994, 1999, 2004, and 2009). For assessing the quality of Panama's current democracy, it is important to note that the two largest political parties (the PP and PRD) have demonstrated a willingness to relinquish power when defeated in an electoral process that was perceived to be both free and fair.

However, any meaningful assessment of Panama's continuing prospects for democracy must also rest on an understanding of the forces that lie just below the country's political surface. Most fundamentally, Panama's two dormant populist volcanoes lie among rigid social and economic "tectonic plates" that have historically kept Panama's rich very rich and its poor very poor. Although the end of military rule and four successive elections have created the impression that democracy has been consolidated, underlying social and economic realities suggest that serious problems still remain. Can Panama's political leaders successfully deal with the continuing challenges presented by severe income inequalities? Will they prove willing to more equitably distribute the new wealth that will be generated through canal expansion and its many attendant economic spin-offs? And, most important, will the political parties and their leaders prove willing to work together and to control their ambitions in order to limit the possibilities for an eventual return to some form of authoritarian rule?

HISTORY AND POLITICAL CULTURE

The Republic of Panama is a small, narrow country that joins Central America to South America. Shaped like a giant S and some 420 miles (675 kilometers) long, it winds from the border of Costa Rica in the west to Colombia in the east. In total area Panama encompasses some 29,209 square miles (75,651 square kilometers), making it slightly larger than the state of West Virginia. The population of 3.5 million is largely composed of mestizos and mulattos, together with black West Indians brought to Panama in the late nineteenth century to help construct the canal. Small numbers of native Indians occupy some of the interior provinces as well as the San Blas Islands along the northern coast.

Panama is as much a location as it is a country. Its lack of significant size and its position between the Atlantic and Pacific Oceans make Panama a vital strategic bridge. Although geography is not always destiny, the enduring legacy of the country's location has been to constantly reinforce a particular kind of laissez-faire economic thought and open economic practices.

Faith in the benefits of an open economy developed during colonial times, when the isthmus served as a major transit point linking Spain to its most important colonial possessions along the west coast of South America. Legal trade with the Spanish colonies was supplemented by contraband trade in slaves and other "commodities." These illicit activities, particularly critical to the isthmian economy in hard times, served as a precursor to the more recent traffic under both military and civilian rule in merchandise such as arms and cocaine.

The result of Panama's early role as a strategic bridge was to concentrate economic resources in the hands of a small white urban commercial elite. The politicians who assumed leadership positions in Panama following independence in 1903 did not have ties to the traditional agricultural sector. Panama had never developed an *encomienda* system because of a lack of a large indigenous population, and unlike its Central American neighbors, Panama never experienced a nineteenth-century coffee boom.[3]

Throughout the twentieth century Panamanian politics was dominated by a struggle for power between the largely white urban commercial class and largely nonwhite (mestizo and black) groups who felt themselves excluded from the full benefits of nationhood. During the period of French and US canal construction (1878–1914), large numbers of black workers were imported from Caribbean islands such as Jamaica and Barbados. These workers spoke English and were physically incorporated as an underclass into the US-controlled Canal Zone. Although their wages were low compared to those for white workers from the United States, they constituted an urban labor elite when compared with Panama's mestizo and black Spanish-speaking population.

During the 1920s and 1930s the Panamanian economy deteriorated owing to the termination of canal construction activities and, later, the Great Depression. Resentment began to grow, particularly among mestizos from the interior provinces, against West Indian blacks and members of the urban commercial elite, who were viewed as natural allies of the United States. This resentment crystallized in 1923 with the formation of Community Action, a movement whose intent was to gain access for mestizo professionals and urban day laborers to the more lucrative jobs associated with the canal.

In the 1930s Dr. Arnulfo Arias emerged as the leader of this highly nationalistic popular movement. Elected president in 1940, he quickly promulgated a new constitution that contained discriminatory provisions against West Indians and Chinese. The political crisis precipitated by this constitutional change was resolved when the United States, upset with Arias's apparent sympathy with Italian Fascism, helped remove him from office. Although the political crisis associated with the rise of Community Action became more attenuated with the passage of time, Arnulfo Arias remained a major fixture in Panamanian politics until his death in 1988.

From the 1940s on, the struggle for political power between urban elites and populists such as Dr. Arias was increasingly influenced by the reemergence of the Panamanian military as a political force. The army was disbanded for the first time shortly after independence in 1903 because it was viewed as a threat to both the political hegemony of the commercial class and to the United States. Through a slow evolutionary process, however, it was reconstituted out of the small police force that had taken its place.[4] By the early 1950s the national police had been turned into a national guard and a colonel had been elected president with military backing.

After a turbulent period of civilian elitist democracy during the late 1950s and early 1960s, a military coup against Arnulfo Arias brought Omar Torrijos to power. Torrijos then built a populist political base among marginal groups in both Panama City and the countryside. Farm collectives were formed, labor unions organized, and the government expanded dramatically to accommodate popular needs. In this regard Panama's military government looked much like the one that emerged in Peru at the same time, and for much the same reasons.

When General Torrijos and the military first seized power from President Arias in 1968, they did so as agents of change. Although some significant changes were made during the earliest years of military rule, the military's social reform agenda slowly fell by the wayside as top officers became increasingly concerned with their own well-being. This in turn led them to become involved in a variety of illicit activities such as arms trafficking and drug smuggling.

The military's increasingly repressive and corrupt behavior created a backlash in the mid-1980s. Precipitating this backlash was the death of General Torrijos in 1981 and his eventual replacement by General Manuel Antonio Noriega. As head of the intelligence branch within the PDF, Noriega was in a position not only to spy on his fellow officers but also to control the most lucrative of the military's illicit activities. The rapidly growing Medellín drug cartel (headquartered in neighboring Colombia) found his services useful for the laundering of their cocaine profits, and by the mid-1980s the PDF had become a drug-trafficking mafia masquerading as a formal military institution.

Panama's crisis of military rule became so intense that it eventually drew the attention of the Reagan administration in the United States. For a variety of complex reasons having to do with General Noriega's stance on regional issues, his corruption, and increasing repression of domestic dissent, the Reagan administration applied economic sanctions in 1988. At the same time, it supported the domestic political opposition that was now to be found not only within Arnulfo Arias's Panamenista Party but also among portions of the urban commercial class who had previously supported the military government.

Beneath its surface complexities we can thus see the workings of the underlying tectonic plates in Panamanian politics. Historically, they produced a consistent tension that pitted urban elites against poverty-stricken groups who were excluded from the full benefits of Panama's strategic location. The result was cycles of elitist democracy and authoritarian populism that occurred in slightly different form at various points in time, depending on the strength of various domestic political forces, the state of the global economy, and the level of involvement of the United States.

During the 1930s and 1940s Arias led a civilian popular movement aimed at increasing the political voice of rural mestizos and urban day laborers. In the 1970s the military then spearheaded attempts to include additional marginalized rural and urban groups. Both of these authoritarian populist movements were eventually challenged and displaced by traditional urban forces acting in collaboration with the United States. Thus, the successful effort to restore civilian democratic rule in Panama, which resulted from the US military invasion in 1989, was not particularly unique but rather reflective of a long-standing cyclical historical process.

POLITICAL PARTIES AND INTEREST GROUPS

Panama's pattern of civilian elitist democracy followed by periods of populist authoritarian rule influenced the development of the country's twentieth-century party system. During periods of elitist rule, political parties reflected divisions within the urban commercial class based on personality clashes between individual leaders. There was a general lack of real differences in the policy agendas of these parties, extreme fragmentation (reflected in their relatively large numbers), and an absence of party structures that survived any given election.

Although Panama's party system historically has been fragmented and elitist, the sporadic emergence of both civilian (Arias) and military (Torrijos) populist leaders led on occasion to efforts to create dominant parties through outright elimination or manipulation of the competition. The urban commercial elite's power resources have been primarily its private sector financial assets, whereas those of the populists have been their control of the government apparatus itself. Thus, when populist leaders came to power, they attempted to create dominant political parties largely based on their supporters in the various government bureaucracies.

During the period of elitist democracy that immediately preceded the military coup of 1968, approximately twenty small political parties vied for power. These parties were banned when General Torrijos assumed dictatorial control in the name of popular reform. However, deteriorating economic conditions in the mid-1970s led Torrijos to reassess the costs and benefits of direct military rule, and in 1978 he formed the Democratic Revolutionary Party (PRD) to incorporate various groups who supported his military regime. Formation of the PRD suggested that the military wished to give permanent institutional form to its reformist ideals through the establishment of a new political party that would regularly win elections with military backing. When presidential elections were held in 1984 and 1989, the military had to resort to fraud in order to ensure a victory for the PRD candidate.

Following the US invasion, Panamanian politics appeared to be returning to its normal pattern, in which civilian elitist democracy is associated with a highly fragmented and personality-based party system. However, Panama's "new normal" since 1989 has turned out to be something a bit different. Now what we see is the emergence of a political party system that combines the fragmentation and transience associated with elitist democracy with the more enduring party structures and loyalties associated with historically mass-based populist movements. This new system now contains several large and enduring pools of voters (associated with the populist PP and PRD) who have served since 1989 as the base either for winning elections themselves or for helping another party (Martinelli's CD) to do so.

For a variety of reasons, Panamanian political parties, the party system itself, and interest groups have undergone significant change over the past several decades. Party leaders are aging and increasingly out of touch with the realities of a new generation of Panamanians whose aspirations they have not been fully able to ascertain. Continued movement of rural dwellers to Panama City has created an electorate that is more detached from the combination of self-interest and coercion that determined its vote in the past. All of these changes were reflected in Martinelli's victory in the 2009 presidential elections, and they will surely be reflected in the 2014 electoral cycle and beyond.

FORMAL GOVERNMENT STRUCTURES

Panama's formal government structures are delineated in the country's four constitutions, those of 1904, 1941, 1946, and 1972. All of these constitutions assigned a predominant role to the president within a centralized unitary form of government that included executive, legislative, and judicial branches. Thus Panama's formal government structures have historically been very much within the Iberian tradition, with the executive branch intended to dominate the other two. The president appointed provincial governors, so his power extended directly down to the regional level, and although local municipalities theoretically possessed some autonomy, this idea was rarely honored in practice.

Although all four of these constitutions created governments in which the president was the dominant figure, Panama's populist governments assigned greater powers to the executive branch than did ones dominated by the urban commercial class. The constitution of 1941, promulgated during the presidency of Arnulfo Arias, and the 1972 constitution, promulgated under military rule, are more expansive in terms of the president's prerogatives than those of 1904 or 1946.

When the Panamanian military seized power in 1968, it considerably altered traditional formal government structures. The National Assembly, which had come to be viewed by the military as an elite-dominated institution, was replaced with a much larger legislature, whose members were elected from the country's 505 municipal subdistricts. The traditional political parties were banned from electoral participation, and short legislative sessions ensured that there would be no time to mount meaningful challenges to military executive authority.

The 1972 constitution, which created this new popular legislature, also recognized the central role within the executive branch of General Torrijos and the defense forces. Although there was still a civilian president, real power was given to Torrijos as "maximum leader" of the Panamanian Revolution. The impotence of the president within this new constitutional structure was best expressed by the fact that he could neither appoint nor remove military personnel. The military legally became a fourth branch of government, and the other three branches were constitutionally required to act in "harmonic collaboration" with the military.

When civilian democrats replaced populist authoritarians in 1989, they continued to govern according to the provisions of the military's constitution. Under the terms of this constitution, political power resides largely in the executive branch and, more specifically, in the office of the president. President Ricardo Martinelli thus governs with the help of a cabinet council comprising the various ministers of state. The legislative assembly is limited in its general powers and has little control over the national budget. Although a supreme court does exist, it has historically demonstrated minimal independence from the executive branch, and various presidents (including Martinelli) have attempted to pack it with their followers. Perhaps the most significant change in formal government structures during the 1990s was a provision for the independent election of mayors. Because Panama City and Colón are major metropolitan areas, this change from appointment to election created several potentially important new centers of political power.

GOVERNMENT POLICIES

As in most countries, government policies in Panama have varied depending on the administration in power. The primary factor determining the general content of policy has been whether any particular administration fundamentally represented the interests of the urban commercial class or those of urban and rural middle- and lower-class groups.

When populist leaders have controlled the government, there has been a tendency to alter the constitution in such a way as to allow for a broader role of government in public policy formation and implementation. For example, Arnulfo Arias's 1941 constitution mentioned the "social function" of private property for the first time, and the government was granted the right to intervene in conflicts between business and labor. New government agencies were also created to pursue expanded goals and objectives.

Then, during the 1950s and 1960s, presidential administrations dominated by the urban commercial class pursued social and economic policies that relied somewhat less on the central government. Their policies were reformist within the context of the US-sponsored Alliance for Progress. Economic growth strategies were aimed at simultaneously expanding the dynamic, outwardly oriented service sector and encouraging continued growth of the domestically oriented industrial sector.

The military coup of 1968 initiated another wave of populist policy making. Observers of politics under military rule noted a curious blend of populist development policies mixed with more conventional ones. Populist policies that were intended to redistribute goods to the popular sectors were the natural result of the military's disdain for the urban commercial class. The simultaneous pursuit of more conventional developmental policies, emphasizing continued growth of the more dynamic areas of the private sector, reflected the permanent historical reality of Panama's open service economy.

Major components of the military's populist policies included the implementation of land reform, enactment of a progressive labor code, and efforts to gain control of the Panama Canal. General Torrijos worked hard during the early 1970s to create an international support group that would help speed negotiations with the United States for a new treaty. Through such international coalition building as well as support for changes in the treaty arrangements on the part of several US presidential administrations, Torrijos was able to achieve his goal. In 1978 a treaty was ratified that returned the Canal Zone to Panama and stipulated that Panama would gain full control of the canal in the year 2000.

When Panama's thoroughly corrupt but populist military regime was overthrown in 1989, government policy underwent a radical reorientation, which was partly due to the fact that the commercial elite once again exercised considerable influence. However, this reorientation also resulted from a sea change in global thinking concerning strategies of economic growth. In the post–Cold War world, a new economic model emerged that stressed reduction of the size of the public sector through privatization of state corporations and a shift from the traditional economic growth strategy of import substitution industrialization to one of export-oriented industrialization.

Since 1989, five successive Panamanian governments have largely restored the country's financial credibility. President Guillermo Endara (1989–1994) made some progress in reorienting Panama toward an export-oriented growth strategy. Additional changes came during the administration of Ernesto Pérez Balladares (1994–1999). More strenuous efforts were made to attract foreign investment by selling off state-run companies and reverted properties in the former Canal Zone, thus curbing the power of organized labor. President Moscoso's economic policies were aimed at mitigating some of the negative side effects of these various neoliberal economic reforms, particularly as they impacted her core constituencies within agriculture and the government bureaucracy. When Martín Torrijos succeeded her in 2004, however, he returned again to policies that placed more emphasis on fiscal responsibility.

Defying the odds presented to him by the 2007 global financial crisis, President Ricardo Martinelli has governed during a period of explosive economic growth. Most of his success has been due to his enthusiastic support for a number of internationally funded public works projects, including but not limited to expansion of the Panama Canal (see below). These projects have aimed at transforming the larger transit area around the canal and its terminal cities of Panama and Colón into a world-class hub for maritime and corporate activity on a par with city-states such as Singapore and Dubai. In support of this transformation, Martinelli backed the building of additional transportation infrastructure including highways and an underground metro system in Panama City. The Special Economic Area created at an old US Air Force base now houses a number of new regional corporate headquarters, and there has been fevered construction activity in the tourism sector, including the opening of a Trump Ocean Club.

Still, it is not clear that all of the breathless attention that is currently being given to Panama's "economic miracle" is fully warranted. The government has incurred substantial new financial obligations. While somewhat attenuated during recent good economic times, the historical gap between Panama's very rich and very poor remains large, and poverty is particularly pronounced in the rural interior provinces. In addition, corruption is rampant in sectors that have experienced the economic boom, criminal gangs operate with impunity in Panama's largest cities, and cocaine trafficking is having an impact everywhere. Only time will tell whether Martinelli's policies have resulted in the normal growing pains associated with any major structural transformation or are leading to something far worse.

PANAMA IN A TWENTY-FIRST CENTURY WORLD

During the twentieth century Panama's place in the world was largely defined by its relationship with a single great power: the United States. This key bilateral relationship long determined the overall nature of Panama's global involvement because US diplomats made sure during World War II and the subsequent Cold War years that relationships with adversarial great powers either were not allowed to develop in the first place or were subsequently minimized.

Panama's international contacts, however, did multiply rapidly during the 1970s and 1980s due to a number of factors, including the progressive ideological stance of the country's military regime, its growing importance as a global service center, and the conflict in Central America. Despite these developments, Panama's pattern of global involvement during those decades can still largely be seen as resulting from the continued dominance of the United States. Efforts to expand international contacts were a reaction to such dominance and part of a national strategy designed to gain diplomatic leverage in the battle to negotiate new canal treaties.

During the Cold War years (1947–1989) the United States treated Panama as a constant in a relatively simple global security equation. With troops on the ground and planes in the air, the Panama Canal Zone could be used as a platform from which known quantities of US power could be projected in order to deal with various global or regional security and humanitarian contingencies. Even during the years of the populist military rule (1968–1989), the United States was able to treat Panama as a constant in dealing with the civil wars then raging in Central America. When Panama itself became a problem during the Noriega years, the same simple calculus applied.

Now all of that has changed. Following the departure of US troops from the isthmus and transfer of the canal in the year 2000, Panama has become more of an unknown in the global security equation. This equation has become more complex largely because of the reemergence of a multipolar international system following the end of the Cold War. As a result of this growing multipolarity, the influence of the Asian great powers of Japan and China has grown significantly. Asian shipping firms control three of the country's four major ports and a significant proportion of foreign investment comes from that region.[5]

In addition to the return of multipolarity, Panama's future position in the world will also be affected by ongoing political and economic developments in neighboring countries. Most important, Colombia remains engaged in a seemingly endless civil war that pits several guerrilla groups against the central government. This civil war has been spilling over into Panama in the form of heightened tensions in the border area associated with illicit flows of drugs, arms, people, and money. Also, Venezuela continues to contribute a measure of unpredictability to Panama's South American neighborhood.

Many of Panama's current problems are due to the increasing ties that have developed between guerrilla groups and drug suppliers in South America (particularly Colombia) and drug trafficking cartels based in Mexico. Mexican cartels have partially displaced their South American rivals and view Panama as a critical link in the supply chain. Here, in relative tranquility, they can strike deals with their Colombian counterparts, store cocaine and prepare it for transshipment to the United States, launder drug money, and recuperate from the stresses associated with their risky business. The difficulty for Panama in this regard is that its use as a transit point in the drug business threatens to at some point turn it into just another Central American country constantly racked by drug-related violence.

Finally, Panama's future role will continue to be shaped by the presence on its territory of one of the most important transportation arteries in the world—the Panama Canal. The canal was run by the United States government from its grand opening in 1914 until the year 2000, when its management became the responsibility of an autonomous Panamanian agency called the Panama Canal Authority.[6] During the intervening years, this agency and its leadership have proven its doubters wrong by providing professional and farsighted leadership that has so far remained largely immune to domestic political and economic pressure.

While the original existing canal served the international shipping community well, Panama is now engaged in a major expansion project that will accommodate twenty-first-century changes in the industry. Since an increasing number of the world's giant container ships have become too large to transit the existing canal, the country's leaders decided that new channels would have to be dug and more sophisticated gates constructed. The Panama Canal Authority's new US$5 billion expansion project is being undertaken by an international consortium of firms and financed through the sale of bonds that are backed by future toll revenues. [7]

There can be little doubt that the completion of the canal's expansion, anticipated for 2015, will be a transformational event not only for Panama but also for world trade in general. For example, US West Coast ports currently handle some 70 percent of all cargo reaching the country from Asia due to the inability of the canal to accommodate large so-called post-Panamax ships. With completion of the canal expansion project and the attendant upgrading of port facilities such as those in Miami, the US East Coast should receive a much larger share of the US-Asia trade. [8]

CONCLUSIONS

As is the case in most countries, Panamanian politics exhibit a number of recurrent themes as well as subsequent variations on these themes. The first of these is the enduring presence of populism and a populist style of governance by Panamanian presidents of all political persuasions. Because of major economic and racial inequalities that have persisted since the founding of the republic in 1903, there have been cycles of elitist democracy and authoritarian populism associated with prominent political figures such as former president Arnulfo Arias and General Omar Torrijos. A second and closely related phenomenon is cycles of violent repression of the Panamanian police/military followed by its slow restructuring and rebirth along nationalist lines.

Perhaps the most important current variation on these themes is a significant change in the nature of the political party system. Historically (prior to 1989) periods of elitist democracy and authoritarian populism were associated with relatively distinct types of party systems—highly fragmented ones and single-party-dominant ones, respectively. As noted earlier, these two different cyclically recurring types of party systems have been replaced by a single more inclusive one that has for more than two decades incorporated characteristics of both.

Looking ahead, a key question is whether this party system and the democracy with which it is associated will prove resilient enough to meet the twin challenges to governance that they will face in the near future. The first of these challenges is to ensure that the next elections are both free and fair. This will be no easy task in light of the fact that President Martinelli's governing coalition has collapsed and that he is perceived as wanting to retain power by either direct or indirect means. The second challenge is to manage Panama's economic boom in such a way that it does not exacerbate existing class and racial tensions. Recent riots among marginalized groups show that there are hidden perils associated with this boom, and committed leadership will be needed to ensure that the poor have greater access in the future to the economic benefits associated with canal expansion and other government-controlled projects.

Depending on how well these challenges are met, Panamanian politics could take several distinct paths. The first (and most likely) is that politicians of both elitist and populist persuasions will continue to find ways to settle their differences and to govern effectively. This best-case outcome would further solidify the democratic gains of the past several decades. The second path would lead in the direction of some form of new elitist managerial or populist authoritarianism. With the canal's expansion and hence increased importance to world commerce, there will be a growing demand in global multinational circles for the type of strong managerial leadership that civilian entrepreneurs such as Martinelli can provide. On the other hand, in light of widespread discontent among Panama's marginalized population, one cannot discount the possibility of the third wave of populism. And given the rapid militarization of certain units within Panama's Public Forces, this third wave could once more take a security-enabled form.[9]

Notes

1. This was one of the longest periods of military rule in the modern-day history of Latin America. See Steve C. Ropp, "Explaining the Long-Term Maintenance of a Military Regime: Panama Before the US Invasion," *World Politics* 44, no. 2 (January 1992): 210–234.

2. Noriega was subsequently tried in the United States and sentenced to forty years in prison. He was extradited from the United States to France in 2010 and from France to Panama in 2011. In Panama, he is currently serving time for a number of crimes committed during the years of military rule.

3. For an overview of Panama's early economic development and its implications for the distribution of political power, see Andrew Zimbalist and John Weeks, *Panama at the Crossroads: Economic Development and Political Change in the Twentieth Century* (Berkeley: University of California Press, 1991), 1–19.

4. Thomas L. Pearcy, *We Answer Only to God: Politics and the Military in Panama 1903–1937* (Albuquerque: University of New Mexico Press, 1998).

5. This is not to say that Panama's economic relationship with the United States is now unimportant. For example, the new Panama–United States Trade Promotion Agreement suggests continuing strong economic ties between the two countries in the future.

6. Actually, the canal's official grand opening on August 15, 1914, was something less than grand. Completely overshadowed by the onset of World War I, there were no foreign dignitaries in attendance and the event hardly made the international news. Indeed, the lack of commercial traffic during the war and frequent mudslides in the Culebra Cut rendered the canal largely irrelevant from a global economic standpoint until the 1920s. See David McCullough, *The Path Between the Seas* (New York: Simon and Schuster, 1977), 607–611.

7. Mark P. Sullivan, *Panama: Political and Economic Conditions and US Relations* (Washington, DC: Congressional Research Service, 2011), 25–26.

8. Keith Wallis, "Port Miami Delegation in Beijing to Woo Asian Cargo," *South China Morning Post*, December 5, 2012.

9. In this regard, it is important to note the degree to which units such as the National Frontier Service (SENAFRONT) have become professionalized and militarized in recent years. It was precisely this type of unit within the old National Guard that produced the leadership for the 1968 military coup. See, for example, Eric Jackson, "Police Pay, Power and Profile Rising," in *Panama News*, December 8, 2012.

Suggestions for Further Reading

Conniff, Michael. *Panama and the United States: The End of the Alliance*. 3rd ed. Athens: University of Georgia Press, 2012.

Greene, Julie. *The Canal Builders: Making America's Empire at the Panama Canal*. New York: Penguin Press, 2009.

Guevara Mann, Carlos. *Political Careers, Corruption, and Impunity: Panama's Assembly 1984–2009*. Notre Dame, IN: University of Notre Dame Press, 2011.

Maurer, Noel, and Carlos Yu. *The Big Ditch: How America Took, Built, Ran, and Ultimately Gave Away the Panama Canal*. Princeton, NJ: Princeton University Press, 2011.

Parker, Matthew. *Panama Fever: The Epic Story of One of the Greatest Human Achievements of All Time—The Building of the Panama Canal*. New York: Doubleday, 2007.

Perez, Orlando J. *Political Culture in Panama: Democracy After Invasion*. New York: Palgrave Macmillan, 2012.

Sanchez, Peter M. *Panama Lost? US Hegemony, Democracy, and the Canal*. Gainesville: University of Florida Press, 2007.

Szok, Peter. *Wolf Tracks: Popular Art and Re-africanization in Twentieth-Century Panama*. Jackson: University Press of Mississippi, 2012.

24

THE DOMINICAN REPUBLIC:
A WINDING ROAD TO DEMOCRACY
AND DEVELOPMENT

Esther Skelley Jordan

The story of the Dominican Republic is one of resilience. It is a little country of about ten million people and 49,000 square miles (127,000 square kilometers) on the island of Hispaniola. It has suffered multiple dictatorships, foreign invasions, natural disasters, and economic crises, yet it has emerged triumphant. Dominicans are proceeding along a winding road to democracy and development. The road is paved with patronage and great inequality, but it is headed in the right direction. The country has integrated into the globalized world, experienced multiple spans of record economic growth, and become a key trading partner of the United States. It recovered strongly from the domestic economic crisis of 2003 and the global economic crisis of 2008 and 2009.

The Dominican Republic has experienced tremendous change over the last several decades. It long followed Latin American tradition with a triumvirate of power (oligarchy, church, and military). That is no longer so. After two US interventions and many decades of dictatorship and authoritarian "democracy," the Dominican Republic is maturing into a unique democratic state. Economic diversification has diminished the once-dominant agricultural sector to less than 6 percent of the national gross domestic product.[1] The land-holding oligarchs have gone into business and maintained a position at the top of society—albeit a somewhat diminished one. Meanwhile, the church and military have declined in power, but they continue to act as arbiter and counterbalance to the state, respectively.

Although much has changed, Dominicans continue to live in a society characterized by family connections, patronage, and strict class divisions based on race and

444

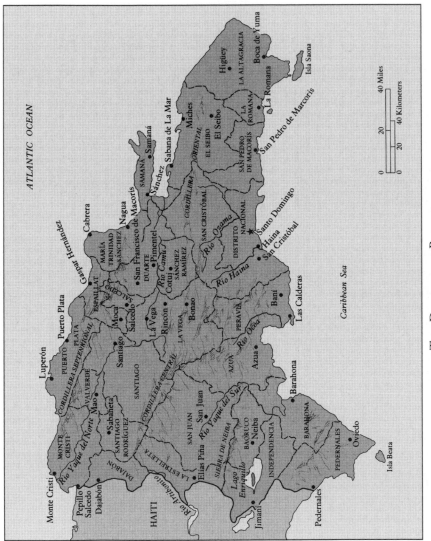

THE DOMINICAN REPUBLIC

socioeconomic status. Despite great leaps in economic growth, a severe income gap remains, as a very large segment of the population still does not have access to even the most basic necessities of life. Although the country at this time appears on an upward trajectory of democratic development in many regards, corruption remains rampant. After all, patronage is the grease that lubricates the institutions of the Dominican Republic. It remains to be seen whether a society that has long preferred public handouts to public service is ready for drastic change in this regard.

BACKGROUND

Columbus first encountered Hispaniola in 1492. The Spanish soon established Santo Domingo (now the Dominican capital) as their first capital in the New World. As agriculture and mining took off, Spain built churches, schools, and hospitals. Through disease as well as arms the Spanish quickly eliminated most natives on the island and then imported slaves from Africa. Over the next fifty years the colony received an influx of Spaniards and built a racially based, two-class authoritarian system.

The early years of a state-run extraction economy quickly depleted the colony's mineral supply. The next two hundred years were marked by economic decline and social and political disarray as the Spanish, the French, the British, and pirates from the Netherlands competed for control of the island. The Spanish ceded the western third of the island to the French in 1697.

At the outset of the nineteenth century Santo Domingo's economy lagged far behind that of its western neighbor, Saint-Dominique (now Haiti), then the largest sugar producer in the world. The French colony's large slave population began to revolt in 1793. Soon thereafter former slaves from Saint-Dominique invaded Santo Domingo. In response Spain sent forces in 1809 to occupy Santo Domingo and prevent a slave revolt there. After several years of weak Spanish rule the colony declared independence in 1821. No sooner did the Dominican Republic break free than the newly independent Haiti invaded and seized control. The Haitians began to modernize the sugar industry and freed the slaves. They also redistributed the land and drove out the Spanish elites. These moves greatly upset the Catholic Church, which owned most of the former colony's land, and led Santo Domingo to declare independence from Haiti in 1844.

The first two decades of Dominican independence were marked by repeated coups and Haitian invasions. Then in 1861 the Spanish reannexed their former colony. The Dominican Republic declared independence again in 1865, and power shifted between parties until Ulises Heureaux's dictatorship in 1882 provided stability and modernization. This modernization, however, also put the country into great debt.

After Heureaux's assassination in 1899 the United States feared a European intervention aimed at collecting debts. Consequently, the United States took control of Dominican customs receipts in 1905 and began economic restructuring in 1915. One year later US Marines invaded to quell increasing political instability and depose the anti-American faction in power. Until their 1924 departure the marines built infrastructure, trained a Dominican army, and established the procedures for democratic government. The US troops brought great advances in many areas, from health and sanitation to roads and education. They left behind a nation obsessed with baseball, one that in time produced major-league greats such as Juan Marichal, Pedro Martínez, Manny Ramírez, Sammy Sosa, and Albert Pujols. They also left behind a fledgling electoral democracy and a well-trained army under General Rafael Trujillo.

In 1930, soon after the United States withdrew, Trujillo wrested power from the weak democratic government of President Horacio Vásquez. Trujillo immediately established a semifascist, totalitarian dictatorship that is widely regarded as the most repressive in Latin American history. He wielded a heavy and often brutal hand in all aspects of Dominican society for thirty years. He controlled the food supply and was responsible for sordid crimes ranging from forced prostitution to murder. In 1937 he ordered the massacre of thousands of Haitians along the Dominican border. This massacre marked the beginning of an anti-African and anti-animist nationalist ideology, which the leading intellectuals of the day, Joaquín Balaguer and Manuel Arturo Peña Battle, contended was essential for the maintenance of independence and protection of the Haitian border. These same intellectuals helped Trujillo construct a corporatist system in which the government created state-sponsored, -regulated, and -controlled business, labor, and other groups to help regiment the citizenry.

The 1959 Castro revolution in Cuba sparked fear in the United States that rising opposition against Trujillo would culminate in another socialist revolution in the Dominican Republic. With US support, a group of assassins killed Trujillo in 1961. However, there was no contingency plan in place and the political system spun into crisis.

Trujillo's puppet president, Joaquín Balaguer, assumed control of the state following the dictator's assassination but was replaced by elected leftist Juan Bosch in 1962. A military coup removed Bosch from power, which quickly led to civil war. The United States' fear that a socialist government would emerge victorious prompted another US invasion of the Dominican Republic in 1965. Leading scholars contend that this fear was unfounded given that the rebels heading the revolt supported both democracy and the United States.[2] After a year of fighting, the US peacekeepers and the Dominican factions reached an agreement that called for elections. This imposed reconciliation between Dominicans and led to US withdrawal.

Balaguer, a conservative, was elected in a 1966 violence-ridden election. He did, however, bring stability to the country. The United States contributed millions of dollars to his administration while turning a blind eye to his practices of clientelism and political repression. The 1978 election then replaced Balaguer's corrupt government with the candidate favored by the Carter administration, Antonio Guzmán. Four years later Jorge Blanco won on an anticorruption message, but he did not follow through. He also failed to make good on his promise to never accept an IMF package: in 1984 he reached an agreement with the IMF that brought on mass riots and subsequent police brutality.

Balaguer was consequently returned to power in the 1986 election. He then won the next two elections amid accusations of electoral fraud. This time his still-authoritarian regime governed with less violence. He closed the economy despite the trend of liberalization spreading throughout Latin America. He invested in infrastructure and espoused an anti-Haitian nationalist ideology characterized by consistent police harassment of Haitian workers. Despite his authoritarian rule and election fraud, Balaguer was considered by many to be a strong leader and father figure. Not only did he establish stability and promote modernization, he was known to garner support in the countryside by handing out money to passersby. In the end the 1994 election irregularities aroused so much domestic and international opposition that a constitutional amendment was passed to prevent the president from seeking reelection. Nonagenarian Balaguer was also forced to serve only two years of his term.

The 1996 election that followed brought Leonel Fernández to power. Already on an upward path, the Dominican economy took off under the Fernández administration through diversification. The undeveloped and traditional sugar-dependent economy gave way to a sustained average growth rate of over 7 percent. It even surpassed the growth rates of the newly industrialized countries of East Asia. The constitution, however, prevented Fernández from seeking reelection for a second term in 2000. Despite the candidacy of an aging Balaguer, power was yielded to the opposition party of Hipólito Mejía. Growth was sustained for two years under the new administration, although at a lower rate of 3 to 4 percent.

However, a devastating banking crisis brought this positive trend to a halt in 2003. It was discovered that the country's largest banks were engaged in rampant fraudulent activity that involved government officials and members of competing political parties alike. The Mejía administration's failure to prosecute those involved evoked widespread public protest. A government bailout of the banks that diverted a huge share of the national budget began a sharp economic decline. Inflation soared, business confidence dropped, and capital flight began. The cost of living increased exponentially as salaries decreased. Public unrest ensued. In response Mejía took control of several media outlets. He also amended the constitution to allow himself to seek a second consecutive term, doubled the size of the military, reinstated and increased the pensions of retired officers, and issued large numbers of motorcycles, helicopters, and cars to the military.

Despite Mejía's apparent attempts to buy off the armed forces and limit negative press as he campaigned for reelection, he conceded defeat in the 2004 election and transferred power peacefully. This third consecutive peaceful transfer of power in as many elections placed the Dominican Republic in the company of maturing democracies.

Leonel Fernández was elected in 2004 to a second, nonconsecutive term on promises to increase government transparency and restore the prosperity of the 1990s. He was reelected to a third (second consecutive) term in 2008. He made good on his economic promises, despite the international financial crisis of 2008 and 2009. By 2006 he had returned the country to significant growth, at 10.7 percent GDP growth. He managed the effects of the international economic crisis, multiple tropical storms and hurricanes, and the refugee influx and cholera outbreak that followed the 2010 earthquake in neighboring Haiti.

By 2010 the country had returned to growth at a rate of 7.75 percent GDP and, as of late 2013, has maintained growth at a rate hovering around 4 percent GDP ever since. However, President Fernández's efforts to alleviate suffering during the multiple crises placed great strains on a government budget already stretched thin with decreased revenues. He led the country in its internationally lauded first-response efforts to aid Haiti following the earthquake. He also increased food, electric and natural gas subsidies throughout his time in office, and continued to increase public handouts in the lead-up to the 2012 election. Meanwhile, he doled out ever increasing numbers of positions in his administration as favors. This led to an exceptionally bloated bureaucracy, ranked worst among 144 countries in favoritism and wasteful spending by the World Economic Forum.[3] Although prospects for economic growth remain promising and inflation decreased under his watch from 50 percent to 8 percent, the Dominican fiscal deficit increased from 2.6 percent to 8 percent in his last year in office.[4]

President Fernández's longtime chief of staff and former president of the House of Representatives, Danilo Medina, was elected president in May 2012, with former first lady Margarita Cedeño de Fernández as his running mate. Medina campaigned on promises to reduce the deficit, enlarge the middle class, increase spending on education, and get tough on rising crime and corruption. After assuming office in August 2012, he has taken steps in this direction. He immediately increased taxes amid popular protest and appointed Gustavo Motalvo—well known for his anti-corruption stance—as his chief of staff. However, given Medina's campaign slogan, "The best change is safe change," and his predecessor's wife as his vice president, many people predict little significant change. Given Fernández's success in getting a new constitution passed in 2010 that would allow him to seek the presidency again in a nonconsecutive term, he may run for president yet again in 2016.

Here we have a case of a country that since independence in 1844 has experienced weak institutions, great instability, and only about twelve years of relatively effective government. If we consider Trujillo's assassination in 1961 and the subsequent political opening as the beginning of the Dominican Republic's transition to democracy, then that transition has been a very long one—fifty-one years so far—and it is still incomplete and nonconsolidated. The Dominican case shows that transitions to democracy in countries based on clan rivalries, patronage politics, and weak civil society and institutions can be very long indeed.

STATE-SOCIETY RELATIONS

State-society relations in the Dominican Republic are characterized by class divisions, personality politics, and clientelism. The primary interest groups include extended family groups, the military, the Catholic Church, economic elites, the middle class, students, and organized labor. In addition to these domestic groups, the United States has tremendous influence on public policy.[5]

Class relations are based not only on socioeconomic status but also on race. The upper class comprises primarily Dominicans of white or European descent. Mulattos form the middle class, and the lowest class includes black Dominicans descended from African slaves as well as Haitian immigrants. Those of European descent have historically dominated society, politics, and the economy. However, some black Dominicans have been able to work their way up, primarily through the military.

While the lowest 20 percent of the population earns only about 5 percent of the nation's income, the highest 20 percent earns 53 percent.[6] This income gap translates into a deep divide between the political interests of the upper class and those of the lower classes. The interests of the upper class include trade, relations with the United States, the tourism industry, and social connections. In stark contrast, and despite significant improvements since the 1990s, the lower class is interested primarily in basic quality-of-life improvements. Although the urban poor are more likely to participate in the political process, it is the rural poor who are much worse off, with significantly lower literacy rates, life expectancies, and income.

It is important to also note the emerging middle class, which has grown to nearly 43 percent of the population since the economic boom of the 1990s. This group is politically divided. The upper middle class comprises businesspeople and high-ranking military officers who tend to be politically conservative. The middle of the middle class includes professionals, military officers, university students, and government midlevel managers, who also tend to be conservative, albeit less so. The lower middle class comprises workers whose political leanings fluctuate between conservative and reformist politics, depending on the economic climate of the day.

Another defining characteristic of state-society relations is the centrality of extended family groups in politics and economics. Old family rivalries and clientelistic exchanges of favors shape even the most far-reaching national policies. This is facilitated by the reality that those in power are usually interrelated on one level or another. From political parties to civil-military relations, family ties play an even greater role than policy issues and political ideology.

The oligarch-church-military triumvirate no longer holds the reins of power as it did in times past. The power of the Dominican military has decreased drastically in recent decades. It does, however, continue to ensure that its interests are served by the civilians in power. Given the Dominican history of military occupation, those civilians are always conscious of the military's ability to take the reins of power by force. Contrary to that of Western armed forces, the role of the Dominican military is not one of national defense. Instead, it serves as a political apparatus for its own self-preservation and self-enrichment and for the maintenance of social order. Once active in the foreground, its political machinations now take place primarily in the background. Further, the military's support of democracy is highly dependent on their satisfaction with salaries and perks, and officers have been known to facilitate drug trafficking through the Haitian border.

The Dominican Catholic Church has also traditionally been a power broker in Dominican politics. For many years the church supported the brutal Trujillo regime and told parishioners how to vote. However, a lack of resources and personnel has diminished the church's current influence on voting and public policy. Although the church's strength has declined significantly in recent decades, the Dominican Republic is still a Catholic country and the church still plays a significant role in education and society. Successful church mediation of election irregularities and political disputes and the recent passage of a new constitution that bans abortion and same-sex marriage are but two examples.

Just as the military and Church have declined in power, so too has the oligarchic pillar of the power triumvirate. The small landed oligarchy that once governed the Dominican Republic does so no more. The oligarchs did, however, go into business and consequently continue to have significant influence on the affairs of state. It was the business groups they formed that played a central role in the 1963 overthrow of Bosch's democratic government. Their influence has only grown since then, as they have organized into a chamber of commerce and various business associations. Not only are they well connected and wealthy, but the well-being of the Dominican economy depends on their success.

Organized labor seeks to influence public policy, but it is far less influential than it was in days past. The labor movement was long kept at bay under the authoritarian dictatorship of Trujillo. Following his assassination, however, it became an important player in Dominican politics. Another period of suppression followed the revolution, but the booming economy of the 1990s reestablished the opportunity for organized labor to become a significant political player. The effectiveness of the eight confederations that constitute the labor movement is now diminished, not from external forces but rather through internal division and competition.

The once-prominent political role played by students has likewise lessened in recent years. After contributing significantly to the political transformation of the 1960s and the establishment of a more competitive democracy in the late 1970s, students have become decreasingly involved in politics and more oriented toward moving up the social and economic ladder. The major universities still serve as a platform for debate, and students still participate in political protests on occasion. However, students are now far more focused on economic advancement than they were in the long-gone 1970s, when they incited political violence in protest against the repressive Balaguer regime. In late 2012 they turned out in large numbers to protest President Medina's tax hikes.

As the political influence of the above groups has decreased over time, that of civil society has risen. Despite a conflict-ridden lead-up to the 1998 and 2000 elections—as well as the economic crisis that preceded the 2004 election and the tropical storms and cholera outbreak that wreaked havoc before the 2008 and 2012 elections, respectively—all recent elections went off without major incident. However, accusations of electoral fraud are common. The prominent Dominican watchdog group Participación Ciudadana as well as the Organization of American States and other international observer groups contend that both major parties engaged in voter fraud in the 2012 election.[7]

In recent decades Dominican nongovernmental organizations have secured the attention and responsiveness of the country's leadership, and they have done so in a very creative way. Although the Dominican Republic is progressing toward democratic maturity, it still runs largely on patronage and clientelism. Consequently, Dominican civil society stimulates grassroots activism, then when either local or national institutions serve as impediments to change, it employs the old patronage practices to secure its aims. Although this may be criticized as only partial democracy, it works. New social groups now have more of a say because they have found the way to catch the ear of the leadership, first through mobilization and then through patronage.[8] They continue to grow in strength, funded largely by foreign assistance.

Finally, the United States plays a major role in domestic Dominican policy making. Although some anti-American sentiment followed the long military occupations, many Dominicans view the United States as a protector and benefactor. The

Dominican Republic is one of the few countries where the Washington Consensus has proven a successful approach to development. The who's who of Dominican society frequent American embassy parties, and the US ambassador has tremendous access to and influence over Dominican policy makers. It must also be noted, however, that the Dominican Republic has likewise learned how to secure its interests from the United States. This small Caribbean state is a large market for US products, with US$7.3 billion in imports from the United States in 2011.[9] There are also hundreds of thousands of Dominican citizens who live in the United States and send remittances home each year, accounting for one-tenth of the Dominican GDP.[10]

In sum, power still rests in the hands of the few. The economic elites, the military, well-connected civil society groups, and the United States have the greatest influence. The church, university students, and organized labor play a significant albeit lesser role. Unfortunately, the impoverished masses are still excluded from the equation. Perhaps the emerging civil society will take on the plight of and make a difference for the least fortunate in Dominican society. In fact, a couple of organizations have attempted to do so in recent years in the education and health care arenas. However, net secondary school enrollment remains just above 62 percent, and infant mortality rates average approximately twenty-two deaths per one thousand births (as compared to deaths in the low single digits in Western Europe and North America).[11] There is still much to be done.

POLITICAL PARTIES AND ELECTIONS

The political parties of the Dominican Republic contrast sharply with those of the developed nations. Many have arisen over the years, but three main parties have withstood the test of time. Each was formed in the caudillo tradition around the personality of one dynamic individual as opposed to a particular political ideology. Despite the recent passing of all three founding fathers, election campaigns continue to extol the legacies of their deceased leaders and pay minimal attention to policy platforms.

Social democrat Juan Bosch established the Dominican Revolutionary Party (PRD) in exile in the 1930s in support of social justice for the poor. However, it was not until Trujillo's 1961 assassination that the PRD became a significant player in Dominican politics, with close ties to the left wing of the US Democratic Party and socialist parties in Europe and Latin America. Bosch was elected president in 1962, but he was thrown out of office by a military coup after only seven months in office. Following the US intervention in 1965 he lost the 1966 election to Balaguer.

The party suffered repression under the Balaguer administration and boycotted the elections of 1970 and 1974. Soon thereafter Bosch left the PRD to form the Party of Dominican Liberation. The party he left behind successfully united under Antonio Guzmán to become a formidable contender in the elections of 1978, 1982, and 2000. Guzmán won the 1978 election and another PRD candidate, Salvador Jorge Blanco, won the 1982 election. Both administrations were rife with corruption but allowed far more freedom than did earlier repressive regimes. PRD candidate Hipólito Mejía won the election in 2000. He then amended the constitution to allow his own reelection to an immediate second term, but his 2004 reelection campaign struggled to a defeat that resulted in yet another party split. It is currently the minority in congress and has not won a presidential election since 2000. That said, Mejía received a respectable 46.95 percent of the vote when he ran for president yet again in 2012.

The Party of Dominican Liberation (PLD) was formed by Juan Bosch following his split from the PRD in 1973. He contended that both US policy and democratization had failed. On this basis he sought a "dictatorship with popular support" in the likeness of the then populist revolutionary regime in Peru. The PLD, however, did not win popularity until discontent mounted with Balaguer's corrupt regime in the late 1980s. Bosch then lost the fraudulent election of 1990 and lost again in 1994, with young and charismatic running mate Leonel Fernández. Upon Bosch's retirement Fernández redirected the party to advocate for economic liberalization and foreign investment, à la the Washington Consensus. His victory in the 1996 election put an end to the Balaguer era. Following in Balaguer's steps toward modernization, Fernández oversaw a period of record economic growth. Despite his success, the constitution forbade him from seeking a second term. Further, corruption charges led to waning support for the party and a loss in the 2000 election. It was not until the economic crisis of 2003 that the PLD regained its footing. The charismatic Fernández returned to the presidency in 2004, with promises to restore economic stability and progress, which he fulfilled. He was then reelected in 2008 after securing public approval through grocery and cooking gas subsidies in the wake of two severe tropical storms and a subsequent food crisis. Although he was constitutionally barred from running again in 2012, the PLD ran his longtime chief of staff and ally, Danilo Medina, at the top of the ticket. With former first lady Margarita Cedeño de Fernández as the vice presidential nominee, Medina secured 51.21 percent of the vote and won the election for the PLD with a campaign that promised "safe change."

The center-right Reformist Party (PR) was established by Balaguer upon his return to the Dominican Republic in 1965. From 1966 through 1978 the PR served as his personal political apparatus. It mobilized voters, doled out favors, secured support, and repressed his opposition. Always savvy about the evolving political climate, Balaguer was quick to recognize that the PR in that form would no longer be acceptable to an increasingly democratic society. He therefore merged his party with the Social Christian Party to form the Social Christian Reform Party (PRSC), which still exists today. This was a smart move, as the PRSC won all three elections from 1986 through 1994, albeit amidst allegations of electoral fraud in 1990 and 1994. After the constitutional amendment was passed to prohibit Balaguer from seeking reelection, PRSC support declined. It garnered only 15 percent of the vote in 1996. Balaguer was allowed to run again in 2000, but he lost to the PRD. In a surprising move he waived his right to participate in a second round of voting against Mejía. The 2004 PRSC ticket was led by Eduardo Estrella in an attempt to honor the legacy of Balaguer. However, Estrella did not fare well in 2004, and the party went on to win a mere 4 percent of the vote in the 2008 presidential elections. Internal divisions have since plagued the PRSC and popular support has waned. The party won only a handful of seats in the 2010 legislative elections. Party president

Carlos Morales, who was President Fernandez's foreign relations minister, led the PRSC to align with the PLD in the 2012 election. It ran no candidate of its own, leaving the PRD and PLD to win a combined 98 percent of the popular vote. The PRSC's position as one of the three major parties is now in question.

GOVERNMENT INSTITUTIONS

Dominican government institutions were built in the likeness of the three-branch US system. However, the executive, legislative, and judiciary branches have yet to function together as the system of checks and balances they were intended to be. The first two decades following the second (1965) US intervention were characterized by a very weak and patronage-based legislature, judicial system, and bureaucracy that were dominated by the authoritarian Balaguer regime. This was then briefly interrupted by the Guzmán and Blanco administrations of the late 1970s and early 1980s, both of which were significantly less authoritarian. Their regimes allowed a significant degree of conflict and debate between parties as well as branches. But this small step toward greater independence of the other branches of government as well as greater accountability was reversed with the return of the Balaguer regime in 1986. The 1996 election of Leonel Fernández ushered in a new era, as he formed coalitions with competing factions and negotiated with the legislature. Although congress served as a check on his administration for several years, this was not the case in his most recent term, when his party secured a two-thirds majority of the legislature.

The judiciary also has more power now than in earlier years, but it is plagued with corruption. The Mejía administration did little to prosecute those in the government and private sector who held responsibility for the banking scandal. Despite advocacy by groups such as the Foundation of Institutionality and Justice (Fundación Institucionalidad y Justicia) as well as efforts by the second Fernández administration to implement reforms that increase judicial independence, the system is still deeply flawed. Its inability to decrease police violence (especially toward Haitians and the poorest Dominicans) is but one example.

The military has also played a central role in the affairs of the state. However, its role has decreased over time as democracy has advanced and military repression has become less the norm. Military force has not been used against political opponents or social protestors for quite a few years.

Finally, family ties and clientelist governance are so entrenched in the Dominican system that they combine to form an institution of their own. Every administration has worked this institution to its advantage. So too has much of the Dominican public. As noted earlier, even civil society groups have figured out how to work within this framework in order to achieve their goals. The continuance of corrupt practices by all sectors is confirmed by the World Bank's governance indicators, which assigned the Dominican Republic a score in the 22nd percentile on the 2011 Control of Corruption index, a 32 percent decline since 1996. This is in contrast to ever increasingly better performers in the region, such as Chile in the 92nd percentile and Costa Rica in the 72nd percent.[12]

MAIN PUBLIC POLICY ISSUE AREAS

At the top of the Dominican public policy agenda are continued economic growth and stability, with a new focus on deficit reduction. While under the helm of the Fernández administration for twelve of the last sixteen years, the Dominican Republic weathered domestic and international economic crises to experience record growth. This was accomplished by bringing rampant inflation under control, increasing transparency to some extent, liberalizing trade, attracting foreign direct investment, and maintaining a commitment to partnership with the United States through the Central America–Dominican Republic Free Trade Agreement (CAFTA-DR), the Caribbean Basin Security Initiative, and beyond.

The electricity sector continues to be an area of concern. Despite rhetoric espousing change, the Dominican Corporation of State-Owned Electrical Enterprises (CDEEE) remains bloated with far more staff than it needs, while nearly a third of all electricity is consistently stolen and rolling blackouts are the norm. In response to the energy crisis the government has subsidized nearly 90 percent of consumers' power supply and has taken measures to improve the financial administration of the electricity sector (by improving bill collection, reducing operating costs, etc.). However, many blamed President Fernández for not holding his friends who run the company accountable for their mismanagement. It remains to be seen if President Medina will continue with business as usual in this regard.

Also on the public policy agenda are social issues such as drug trafficking, human trafficking, organized crime, and immigration across the Haitian border. In addition, the country suffers from high levels of youth unemployment and a deficient education system. This has only been exacerbated by the numerous schools that were destroyed or damaged by tropical storms and hurricanes in recent years. As a result of persistent challenges in all of these areas, crime rates are on the rise and race-based human rights violations continue. Promises to increase education spending and get tough on crime and police corruption were central tenets of President Medina's campaign. It is too early to tell the extent to which these promises will square with his commitment to deficit reduction and a Dominican culture of clientelism.

GLOBALIZATION

The Dominican Republic is an active participant in the world system, albeit a primarily dependent one. The evolution from an agricultural export economy to a diversified economy has decreased Dominican dependence on some levels. However, the export of goods and services still accounts for about a quarter of the country's gross domestic product.[13] Reliance on IMF loans, financing assurances from the Paris Club of rich countries, and foreign direct investment make dependence a continuing state of affairs.

The Dominican Republic has much at stake in its relations with the United States. To that end, Dominicans continually seek American favor. Recent examples of engagement with the United States include the Mejía administration's contribution of troops to Operation Iraqi Freedom as well as President Fernández' frequent trips to the United States, ardent support for CAFTA-DR, and cooperation with United States via the Caribbean Security Initiative and the United States Drug Enforcement Administration's Sensitive Intelligence Unit. President Fernández also maintained an unprecedented presence in policy conferences and support for US policy priorities. Although President Medina has expressed an interest in emphasizing stronger regional partnerships in Latin America and the Caribbean, it is expected that he will continue his predecessor's pro-US stance.

Finally, the forces of globalization are apparent in many aspects of Dominican life, albeit with great discrepancies between classes. Cable television, the Internet, and SUVs are common only among the upper classes. From the tourist industry to fast food and shopping malls, affluent Dominicans have kept in step with the globalization trend, while the poor lag far behind.

CONCLUSIONS

Dominican politics and development have taken many twists and turns, but this small Caribbean nation appears to be slowly progressing toward democratic consolidation, economic development, modernization, and global integration. Despite two American interventions, the brutal thirty-year Trujillo dictatorship, frequent election irregularities, and multiple administrations under the authoritarian Balaguer, the Dominicans have built a democracy that is well on its way toward maturity. Following the modernization efforts of Balaguer and the diversification of its economy, the unprecedented economic growth of the past two decades under Fernández ushered in a new era for the Dominican people. Full consolidation of democracy, however, is still a distant goal.

A severe income gap remains, and a majority of the population is still stuck in the lower class, isolated from many benefits of globalization. The recent international economic crisis, the banking fiasco of 2003, a continuing energy crisis, and the influx of Haitian refugees after the 2010 earthquake placed great strains on the economy. However, with international support and the leadership of Leonel Fernández, both the Dominican economy and democracy have emerged triumphant and are expected to continue under President Medina. All indicators point to continued economic growth, and Medina has already taken steps to reduce the high federal deficit. Corruption and patronage still characterize the Dominican political system, but civil society is emerging as a force to be reckoned with. Despite media restrictions and threats of violence in the 2004 presidential election and allegations of voter fraud in more recent elections, the electoral process has been remarkably free and relatively fair. Additionally, President Medina has promised to take the country in the direction of greater transparency and accountability. These changes are likely to proceed in a characteristically inconsistent, sometimes chaotic, and particularly Dominican way. Nevertheless, the Dominican Republic has weathered the storm of economic crises and natural disasters. At present the political and economic future of the Dominican Republic looms bright on the horizon despite the great challenges it continues to face.

Notes

1. World Bank, *World Development Indicators 2012* (Washington, DC: World Bank Group, 2012).

2. See Michael J. Kryzanek, *U.S.-Latin American Relations* (Westport, CT: Praeger, 1996).

3. World Economic Forum, *Global Competitiveness Index 2012–2013,* www3.weforum.org/docs/GCR2011–12/CountryProfiles/DominicanRepublic.pdf, accessed March 2013.

4. "After Leonel," *Economist,* May 26, 2012; Central Intelligence Agency, *World Factbook 2013,* /www.cia.gov/library/publications/the-world-factbook/geos/dr.html, accessed March 2013.

5. See Howard J. Wiarda and Michael J. Kryzanek, *The Dominican Republic: A Caribbean Crucible,* 2nd ed. (Boulder, CO: Westview Press, 1992).

6. World Bank, *World Development Indicators 2012.*

7. "After Leonel."

8. See Anne Marie Choup, "Limits to Democratic Development in Civil Society and the State: The Case of Santo Domingo," *Development and Change* 34, no.1 (2003): 25–44.

9. US Trade Representative, "Dominican Republic," www.ustr.gov/countries-regions/americas/dominican-republic, accessed March 2013.

10. Central Intelligence Agency, *World Factbook* 2013.

11. World Bank, *World Development Indicators 2012.*

12. World Bank, Worldwide Governance Indicators 1996–2011, http://info.worldbank.org/governance/wgi/index.asp, accessed March 2013.

13. World Bank, *World Development Indicators 2012.*

Suggestions for Further Reading

Atkins, G. Pope, and Larman C. Wilson. *The Dominican Republic and the United States: From Imperialism to Transnationalism.* Athens: University of Georgia Press, 1998.

Betances, Emilio. *The Catholic Church and Power Politics In Latin America: The Dominican Case in Comparative Perspective.* Plymouth, UK: Rowman and Littlefield, 2007.

Choup, Anne Marie. "Limits to Democratic Development in Civil Society and the State: The Case of Santo Domingo." *Development and Change* 34, no. 1 (2003): 25–44.

Fernández, Leonel. *Años de formación, escritos políticos de vanguardia.* Santo Domingo: FUNGLODE, 2012.

Hartlyn, Jonathan. *The Struggle for Democratic Politics in the Dominican Republic.* Chapel Hill: University of North Carolina Press, 1998.

Kryzanek, Michael J. *U.S.-Latin American Relations.* Westport, CT: Praeger, 1996.

Mendelson Forman, Johanna, and Stacey White, *The Dominican Response to the Haiti Earthquake: A Neighbor's Journey.* Washington, DC: Center for Strategic and International Studies, 2011.

Moya Pons, Frank. *The Dominican Republic: A National History.* New Rochelle, NY: Hispaniola Books, 1995.

Oostindie, Gert, ed. *Ethnicity in the Caribbean.* London: Macmillan Caribbean, 1996.

Pomeroy, Carlton, and Steve Jacob. "From Mangos to Manufacturing: Uneven Development and its Impact on Social Well-Being in the Dominican Republic." *Social Indicators Research* 65 (2004): 73–107.

Soderland, Walter C. *Mass Media and Foreign Policy: Post–Cold War Crises in the Caribbean.* Westport, CT: Praeger, 2003.

Vargas-Lundius, Rosemary. *Peasants in Distress: Poverty and Unemployment in the Dominican Republic.* Boulder, CO: Westview Press, 1991.

Vega, Bernardo. *Dominican Cultures: The Making of a Caribbean Society.* Princeton, NJ: Markus Wiener, 2007.

Wiarda, Howard J., and Michael J. Kryzanek. *The Dominican Republic: A Caribbean Crucible.* 2nd ed. Boulder, CO: Westview Press, 1992.

Wiarda, Howard J., and Esther Skelley. *The 2004 Dominican Republic Elections: Post-Election Report.* Washington, DC: Center for Strategic and International Studies, 2004.

25

HAITI: CONFLICT AND THE SEARCH FOR DEMOCRATIC GOVERNANCE

Georges A. Fauriol

Haiti celebrated the bicentenary of its independence from France on January 1, 2004. Born of the excesses of slavery and the political violence of the French Revolution, Haiti had emerged in 1804 as an independent nation in ruin. Two centuries later, the sometimes bitter and dysfunctional character of its polity was in evidence. On February 29, barely two months after the bicentennial celebrations, Haiti's president, Jean-Bertrand Aristide, fled the country under pressure from a ragtag assortment of gangs, renegade former police and military, and a loose coalition of the country's urbanized civil society. Shadowing these developments were Haiti's traditional international interlocutors, notably the United States.

Few factors have had a more dramatic impact on today's Haitian and neighboring Caribbean societies than their transitions from colonial dependencies of European powers to initially little more than nominal independence. Haiti's early status as an outcast among the community of nations further increased its vulnerability to both internal and external threats. At the beginning of the twentieth century this overlap of factors ultimately generated direct US military and political administration (1915–1934), and in the follow-up to the Duvalier dictatorships, after 1986 Haiti's political crises triggered enduring engagement from the international community.

This multivariant legacy of instability has generated a frustrating search for political change and democratic governance—framed by weak political institutions, an absence of coherent economic policy making, and an overburdened social infrastructure. Arguably, Haitian institutional independence is now commingled with extensive participation from the nongovernmental (NGO) and humanitarian communities, and since 2004 a quasi-permanent multinational presence anchored by United Nations

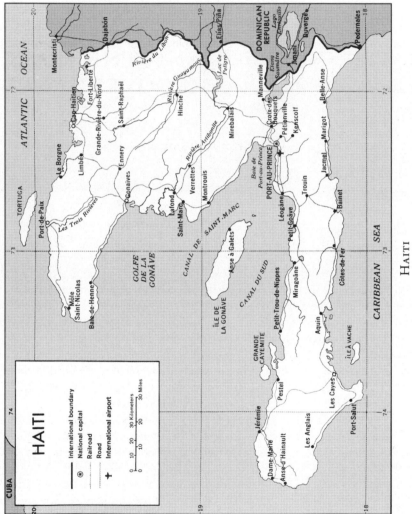

HAITI

peacekeeping forces. The January 2010 earthquake that destroyed much of the national capital's infrastructure only reinforced this trend line for the immediate future.

Despite these misfortunes, Haiti has not lost the basic fabric of its national character. Its roots lie in a hybrid of African ethnicity and culture, French eighteenth-century colonialism, an evolving brand of Catholicism, and the aftereffects of the United States' strategic sweep in the Caribbean region. The African cultural and spiritual features are foundational for a majority of the population since they were first imported in the seventeenth century. Haiti remains ethnically and culturally distinct, with about 85 percent of its people of direct African descent, and the only independent French-speaking nation in the Caribbean region. These characteristics have survived despite economic adversity and the extraordinary failures of political leadership in advancing national development.

Approximately the size of the state of Maryland, Haiti lies at a crossroads of historical trading passages and strategic interests: Cuba is to the immediate west across the Windward Passage, the open waters of the Atlantic Ocean bound Haiti on the north, and the Caribbean Sea lies to the south. Haiti is the poorest country in the Western Hemisphere, with a GDP estimate in the US$700 range, a ranking that places Haiti 144th out of 182 countries in the UN Human Development Index, an estimated population of 9.8 million with a life expectancy that ranks 156th out of 198 in UN data, and a mountainous topography coupled with failing agriculture and land-management neglect that have reduced further the negligibly fertile 28 percent of arable land. Revenues from a few odd agricultural and mineral exports as well as apparel manufacturing and offshore assembly have limited economic impact, leaving much of the workforce on the margins of economic life; the estimated unemployment of 40 percent of the labor force is compounded by the probable underemployment of two-thirds of those who are working. As a result, Haiti's surplus talent keeps leaving for other shores. The current US population of Haitian origin is estimated to be over 1.5 million, and their remittances and other economic flows contribute, by some accounts, nearly half of Haiti's GDP. An indeterminate portion of the economy is dependent on drug trafficking and contraband trade.

Characterizing the Haitian polity is a challenge and opinions have varied. Baseline analyses generally reference urbanized political and economic elites, often at odds with each other in maintaining a fragile status quo and in exploiting a limited enclave of export-oriented commercial activity. Some have described the environment as "kleptocracy," a "predatory state," and the "politics of squalor." Some allude to the "colonial" or "self-colonized" character of Haitian society. Others borrow from development literature and assess Haiti in the context of a "transitional society." The arrival on the political scene in the late 1980s of Jean-Bertrand Aristide, a Roman Catholic priest espousing liberation theology and populist politics, gave currency to notions of "deliberative" democracy. More recent characterizations draw attention to Haiti's status as a "failed state."[1]

THE DECAY OF THE STATE

The challenges facing the Haitian state arc back to a flourishing plantation colony characterized by extraordinary wealth and deep social and racial divisions.

Saint-Domingue, as Haiti was then known, was the crown jewel of France's overseas empire, fueled by the importation of more than eight hundred thousand African slaves. This untenable socioeconomic mix of slaves and sugar came crashing down after 1789, triggered partly by the explosions of the French Revolution. What followed was Haiti's own revolution and war of independence (1789–1804). In the ensuing confrontation blacks, lighter-skinned mulattoes, and whites built shifting alliances, intermittently supported by the intervention of warring British, Spanish, and, naturally, French forces.

After independence Haiti faced the traditional threat patterns of nineteenth-century power politics regarding small states, and as a spiritual heir to the French Revolution, it provided a serious challenge as the first non-European postcolonial state in the modern world. According to diplomatic historian Rayford Logan's characterization, Haiti started out as a "power and enigma," turned into an "anomaly," became a "threat," and ultimately was an "outcast" among the nations of the earth.[2] Haiti initially evolved a remarkable collection of powerful personalities who shaped the nation's style of governance—authoritarian figures anchored to coercive power: Jean-Jacques Dessalines (1804–1806), Haiti's first emperor and efficient exterminator of the colonial white power structure; Henri Christophe (1807–1820), Haiti's first crowned king; Alexandre Pétion (1807–1818), Haiti's first president for life; and Jean-Pierre Boyer (1818–1843), who ruled over an increasingly crippled nation.

At midcentury another extraordinary figure emerged—Faustin Soulouque (1847–1859), later Emperor Faustin I. He ordered a general massacre of the mulattoes, led the country in several abortive campaigns into the neighboring Dominican Republic, and further precipitated Haiti's decline. Of the twenty-two presidents who served between 1843 and 1915, one finished his term in office, three died a natural death while in office, one was blown up with the presidential palace, another one was probably poisoned, one was hacked to pieces, and one resigned. The fourteen others were overthrown.

The effects of nineteenth-century economic imperialism did not mix well with Haiti's instability. France had underwritten all external loans between 1825 and 1896 and owned the national bank. The Germans controlled the trading sector. Increasingly, most imports came from the United States, and after 1900 US influence expanded into banking. Ultimately, in a pattern seen elsewhere in the region at the time, the sorry state of Haitian finances was perceived by Washington as a Trojan horse for European interference in the Caribbean. Without any clearly defined endgame, in 1915 US Marines landed in Haiti following political violence in the capital, Port-au-Prince. The initial security rationale for the landing mutated into a policy to promote Haitian political stability, financial rehabilitation, and economic development.

Instead, Haiti became one of the United States' least successful interventions. Although a minimum of financial order was established, debt was reduced, and the administrative infrastructure was improved, the US presence did not lead to the emergence of democratic political virtues or national development coherency. Ultimately, nationalist backlash, some violent, forced a review of US policy in 1930. Faced with similar problems in Nicaragua, President Herbert Hoover and his successor, Franklin D. Roosevelt, were determined that the United States would exit from Haiti's tropical imbroglio as quickly as possible, and did so in 1934.

What ensued was initially hopeful, anchored to an energized political and cultural effort to institutionalize the foundations of a modern nation. Ironically, the most visible product of the US occupation—the Garde d'Haiti, trained by US Marines—later transformed into Haiti's armed forces, undermined these hopes, and gave way to the decaying weight of presidential excesses. This period came to an uninspired end with the 1957 elections that brought François Duvalier to power in a period of brutal family rule that was to last until his son's downfall in 1986.

INSTITUTIONAL PATTERNS
AND THE CHARACTER OF SOCIETY

Born out of revolutionary violence, Haiti never succeeded in establishing the structures of a civilian society capable of minimizing conflict. Instead, the rule of force through the consolidation of political power in the hands of strongmen has been the baseline institutional characteristic. Part of Haiti's history is the story of competing mercenary bands (*cacos*) and peasant groups (*piquets*) fighting an unreliable government military. This changed with the US occupation's legacy, the Garde d'Haiti, and its subsequent transition into Haiti's armed forces. Although weakened somewhat during the Duvalier dictatorships, until the 1990s they remained by default the only organization with a national political reach and a semblance of institutional continuity.

With the Duvalier regime's collapse in 1986 the military inherited political control and promptly failed the test. The army was ultimately disbanded by Aristide in late 1994 and, in a return to the past, replaced by a national police. The rapid politicization of the police in the late 1990s began to fuel the return of intimidation and corruption. Worse yet, the intersection of a politicized police and the impact of drug trafficking created new pressures of their own and was a factor in the downfall of the second Aristide presidency (2001–2004). The reintroduction of a professional military force has remained a sensitive topic and received some attention in the 2010–2011 presidential elections that brought Michel Martelly to office.

Haiti's low level of political participation has therefore generated few alternative institutions. Not only has the overall poverty of the nation centralized national authority into a minute urban constituency, but the cumulative ravages of crises since the 1980s have also undermined the reservoir of political leadership. The political party structure, anchored more by personalities than by viable agendas, remains weak. In order to appeal to a wider public, national leadership has been tempted by populist solutions that often lack any practical policy deliverables. In contrast, more-traditional political parties have oscillated between legalistic political platforms and well-intentioned technocratic proposals—often appropriate solutions for Haiti's challenges but devoid of any contextual meaning for the average citizen.

Modern social or political pressure groups typical of democratic environments (for example, human rights organizations, local community interests, women's groups, students, labor unions, and the media) have found some space to prosper. Many of these are tied to an expanding multinational network of donors and an NGO community. This was exacerbated by the 2010 earthquake, and in its wake has broadened a long-lasting debate about who actually controls Haitian economic and social policies. Unionization, paralyzed under the Duvaliers, has not been a factor despite limited efforts to energize an urban workers' rights movement in recent years. For its part, the small modern business community—often living a life very different from that of the average Haitian citizen—remains cautious or is sometimes co-opted by changing political winds. Significantly, a politicized civil society and business community played a salient role in the collapse of the Aristide presidency in 2004. Another pressure group is Haiti's large US-based exile community, a source of remittances and also a potential basis of political influence, as was the case in the 2010–2011 round of national elections.

What in the past made life somewhat bearable for the average Haitian was the fact that government had historically not intruded too much into their lives. After 1957 the Duvalier regimes modernized notions of "government" by introducing a more formal and occasionally brutal local presence. Neither modern law enforcement nor much of an effective local administrative structure emerged. Nonetheless, government administration has constituted a center of influence, if for no other reason than that it has represented the source of jobs, money, and patronage, if not outright access to the national treasury. At its most senior echelon are the lucky few whose authority is derived from ties to the presidential palace. This dysfunctional structure is not only inefficient and corrupt but also further weakened by the absence of a capable second or even tertiary layer of public administration. This is a serious factor in how Haiti's international development assistance is managed—or, some argue, wasted.

The Catholic Church's influence has at times rivaled that of the government. After the 1860s the church fulfilled an important educational mission and provided isolated communities with the rudiments of continuity and linkage to the outside world. As elsewhere in the region, the clergy has in recent times split between conservative and liberal contingents. As a result, the church has played decisive roles in modern Haiti's political transitions. Pope John Paul II's 1983 visit to Haiti legitimized opposition to and the ultimate demise in 1986 of the Jean-Claude Duvalier regime. Under pressure from the Vatican, the church subsequently pulled back from a formal political role, but its engagement continued to be the conduit through which human rights and sociopolitical concerns were exposed. The grassroots or "Ti Legliz" movement in the 1980s that was the basis for Aristide's arrival to power in 1990 highlighted splits within the church hierarchy and more generally within Haitian society. More recently the expanding grassroots involvement of evangelical Protestant denominations has translated into political movements with national presence.

Religious institutions are numerically and culturally important in the Caribbean, but in Haiti established churches also coexist with indigenous cults and practices derived from tradition and folklore. Voodoo has a deeply engrained national persona, enriched by both ancestral African rites and Christianity. It is socioculturally relevant in the contemporary environment by providing a link to an ancestral past. From it derives a certain fatalism that is perceived as not leaving much room for shaping the present or the future. Although exaggerated, for some observers this begins to explain Haiti's frustratingly difficult historical experience.

A more direct explanation of Haiti's experience points to the historically exploitative features of Haiti's elites: the mulatto (lighter-skinned) minority, generally associated with the country's commercial activity, and the black elite, representing the political governing class. Paradoxically, despite the modernizing sociopolitical influences of the urbanized elites, the emotional heart of Haiti remains in its inner country—rural, poor, dedicated to basic agricultural production, and living in socioeconomic conditions often reminiscent of past centuries. Long periods of isolation have made this part of Haiti a conservator of African traditions, and it is in this milieu that traditional spiritual influences remain strong.

This duality is exacerbated by geographical separation of the elite from the masses and of the urban population from the rural one, with significant political and social implications. The peasantry and rural populations until recently played no formal role in national decision making. Language use underscores the point: the lingua franca is Creole, yet national debates take place partly in French, a language that the vast majority of the population does not speak or read. Significantly, the use of English is expanding due to the growing influence of the Haitian diaspora and proximity to the United States.

The dysfunctional character of socioeconomic development has triggered a movement of populations to larger cities, particularly Port-au-Prince. The nation's capital is now an unsightly, crowded, and chaotic urban region that encompasses by some estimates almost one-third of Haiti's population. This demographic urbanization has created an expanding universe of slumlike communities and a subculture with its own political and social dynamics. Arguably, in the past twenty years a new paradigm has therefore emerged, at the heart of which is a political contest to determine the direction and control of these communities. The relative success of populist leaders such as Aristide after 1990 was based in part on the mobilization of these urban constituencies, and a related appeal to Haiti's peasant heartland.

HOPING FOR CHANGE: FROM DUVALIER TO ARISTIDE

The Duvalier era began in 1957 and was paradoxically the product of a movement toward political resurgence and even democratic governance that took hold during the US occupation (1915–1934). The intellectual class that emerged in the 1920s was nationalist in character, subscribed to varying forms of progressive social change later tinged with Marxism, and was anchored to the reevaluation of the country's African tradition—*noirisme* or black nationalism. This somewhat messy ideological brew also held hope for a potentially vibrant environment of political change, an incipient modern civil society, a labor movement, political party development, and cultural revival. The high point of these hopes was the Dumarsais Estimé presidency (1946–1950), which, however, floundered under conflicting ideological tensions and radicalization. The real tragedy of the period following the end of the US occupation was that it provided the backdrop for François Duvalier's sinister regime (1957–1971). With the hindsight of what was to follow with his son's tenure (1971–1986) and the Aristide presidencies (1990–1995, 2001–2004), it was "at best a missed opportunity, and at worst a complete failure."[3]

In practice, the Duvalier years were characterized by brutal political control, corruption, and economic decline, all compounded by brain drain. Unlike many of his predecessors, François Duvalier ("Papa Doc" became president for life in 1964) was never a military man and shrewdly played up his image as a soft-spoken physician and part-time ethnologist. Significantly, he also successfully cultivated US concerns with Communism in the Caribbean, which generated somewhat reluctant support from Washington. He ruthlessly suppressed opponents who were challenging or appeared to challenge his authority. The influence of the mulatto elite was eroded, the political power of the Roman Catholic Church was reduced, and the army was purged and brought into line. A powerful paramilitary organization (Volontaires de la Securité Nationale, or VSN—the infamous Tonton Macoutes) was established to protect the regime and enforce its directives.

Confounding most predictions, Jean-Claude "Baby Doc" Duvalier, who was an unknown quantity when he assumed office in April 1971, at age nineteen, following his father's death, began to show some potential. What was ultimately termed an "economic revolution" operationally implied greater solicitation of economic assistance from major donor countries (notably the United States) and lending agencies. Yet the aimless nature of Haitian governance ultimately led to Duvalier's downfall in 1986 after facing hardened Catholic Church militancy and declining support from Washington, which had had a change of heart regarding "friendly" dictators.

Pope John Paul II's references to "injustices" and the need for a more equitable society during his 1983 visit were seen as an indication of the church's intent to champion change and take on an active political role. US policy also shifted, beginning with the Carter administration's emphasis on human rights followed by a broader global theme of freedom and democracy under the Ronald Reagan presidency. Likewise, Haiti became a matter of interest in the halls of the US Congress, driven by public awareness resulting from the drama of Haitian refugee flows in the early 1980s. These factors mobilized segments of the African American political community on behalf of Haiti's struggles. The regime's political weakness coupled with the army's reluctance to confront with deadly force street demonstrations erupting throughout the country led to the government's collapse. Duvalier left on board a US military transport plane for exile in France on February 6, 1986. What followed was not, however, what either Haitians or the international community had hoped for.

Governmental authority passed to the military-led Council of National Government, led initially by General Henri Namphy. The ensuing near-anarchy subsided temporarily when it appeared that the interim regime was planning for elections. US foreign aid flows then increased, as did support from other donors. Some progress was even achieved in stabilizing the economy. However, the foundations upon which this stability was constructed were flawed. International policy designs were tied to notions of democratic consolidation, when the reality on the ground visibly lacked the political consensus to achieve that objective. The first casualty was the bloody elections of November 1987, halted in the first hour of balloting by armed thugs linked to the army and Duvalierist allies. A truncated election in January 1988 brought to power an exiled academic turned politician, Leslie Manigat. He received little international support and was overthrown by the military in June. The political situation unraveled further with a succession of intramilitary coups; under international pressure this process gave way to an interim consensus government that in turn led to elections in December 1990.

By an overwhelming majority, Haitians chose a charismatic ordained priest, Jean-Bertrand Aristide, as president in what was regarded by most observers as the nation's first modern election. The 1990 elections presaged a fifteen-year period of intermittent euphoria as well as a succession of spectacular failures during which Aristide was the principal political variable. His capacity to speak the social and political language of Haiti's overwhelmingly poor population and to appear to convey an almost mystical message of hope were powerful attributes. This was encapsulated most vividly by Aristide's signature concept, "Lavalas," the cleansing flood that would lead Haiti's masses "from misery to poverty with dignity."

What began as a liberation-theology-based political movement anchored in Port-au-Prince's slums was catapulted into national prominence in the late 1980s at a time when the nation's military leadership was providing neither stability nor hope. Aristide was chosen by the Haitian electorate to achieve justice, address the concerns of Haiti's poor, and provide a clear break with the recent Duvalier era. Often accused of holding a questionable commitment to Western-based notions of representative democracy, Aristide sustained a political marathon lasting through two presidencies, two constitutional interruptions, and periods of exiles.

Within eight months of his 1990 election he was ousted in a coup. Whether it was a result of the army's paranoia, Aristide's inflammatory rhetoric, or the reaction to violence directed at Aristide's political opposition, the crisis that ensued endured through interim military regimes and only concluded with an international intervention that returned Aristide to power in October 1994. He was succeeded in 1995 by his protégé, René Préval, whose singular achievement was to be able to complete his five-year mandate. His term (1996–2001) was highlighted by increasing distrust between Aristide's Lavalas movement and the rest of the political community, let alone portions of the international community. By the late 1990s some of Aristide's early allies had become his opponents. A practical impediment was the inability of the government and the national assembly to work together to pass laws, approve budgets, and sign off on appointments (notably for prime minister), all of which led to political paralysis.

Aristide returned to office in early 2001 following local and national elections the previous year, the credibility of which was questioned by the international community. What was a serious but manageable technical dispute regarding the May 2000 parliamentary races instead triggered a deepening mistrust among Haitian political actors as well as in the international community. Diplomatic mediation by the OAS failed, and by 2003 the political atmosphere between the Aristide government and multiple opponents had deteriorated close to the point of no return. Pockets of violence erupted, generated by loose coalitions of Aristide's tactical allies turning against him along with an assortment of gangs, former military, and renegade police. Increasingly large segments of Haiti's urban civil society also began to mobilize against Aristide. In the increasingly violent standoff, and under pressure from Washington and Paris, Aristide left the country (some argue was forced out) in late February 2004 for exile in South Africa.

THE SEARCH FOR STABILITY

An interim government oversaw a difficult transition that ultimately brought Préval back to office in 2006. Akin to his tenure in the 1990s, he governed weakly and was able to complete his presidential term, but not without drama. Two events came to overshadow the end of his presidency, one natural, the other man-made. The first was the catastrophic January 12, 2010, earthquake whose epicenter in the Port-au-Prince region devastated the nation's core infrastructure, killed about three hundred thousand people, and left another one million or more homeless. The dysfunctional nature of Haitian governance and its overwhelming inadequacies were compounded by the material and human damage that also affected the UN and other parts of Haiti's international development apparatus.

In the aftermath of the earthquake the country's dependence on foreign assistance increased further to a combined multiyear commitment of about US$10 billion, in addition to the significant public and private international aid immediately following the earthquake. To add insult to injury, within a follow-on two-year period Haiti was hit by additional tragedies. A cholera epidemic, originating from within the UN peacekeeping contingent, emerged in late 2010 and easily spread in a vulnerable postearthquake environment. In 2012 two unusually destructive hurricanes (Isaac and Sandy) flooded much of the country's agricultural regions and damaged an already weakened infrastructure.

The conclusion of Préval's tenure was overshadowed by a second crisis, this one political. The 2010–2011 electoral calendar was delayed by the earthquake, initially triggering violence and overall uncertainty. A national elections machinery partially destroyed by the earthquake was hard-pressed to contain controversies surrounding the results of the first round of presidential elections in late 2011. The ensuing political standoff pitted Préval's heir apparent, Jude Célestin, against his two most significant electoral opponents, Mirlande Manigat (wife of former president Leslie Manigat) and Michel Martelli, with confirmations of widespread fraud serving as the backdrop. This lasted for several tense weeks and was only resolved through direct engagement from the international community, which essentially imposed the analytical results and political implications of a multinational team brought in to do a partial vote recount. This resulted in a change among the two contenders making it into the presidential runoff, pushing aside Célestin and ensuring a spot for Michel Martelli, who was ultimately elected president in March 2011.

A popular musician with no formal political background, "Sweet Mickey" was perceived probably prematurely as a game changer following the turbulent Aristide and Préval presidencies. Generally mainstream, less of an ideologue and politically more conservative than his immediate predecessors, Martelli has demonstrated a populist streak and mass appeal, notably among youth, and an approach to governance whose effectiveness remains to be determined. In a strange twist of history, in the final run-up to Martelli's election former presidents Aristide and Jean-Claude Duvalier returned from exile with motivations open to much speculation.

OVERCOMING EXPANDING CHALLENGES

The search to establish a modicum of good, let alone democratic, governance has turned out to be a frustrating campaign, and the timeline of recent transitions speaks for itself: 1987, 1990, 1995, 1997, 2000, 2004, 2010, and 2011. Remarkably, the international community has midwifed this calendar of crises without really consolidating democracy or improving the socioeconomic well-being of most Haitians. Alarmingly, approximately two decades after Aristide's first election, a quasi-permanent international peacekeeping presence, led by Latin American countries, sheds light on the character of the international community's continued commitment to Haiti's political and economic development process.

Haiti's contemporary experience has been built on domestic political foundations lacking a working consensus and featuring conflicting expectations among international actors. Those expectations are built from a mosaic of initiatives that includes the Haitian Hemispheric Opportunity Through Partnership Encouragement Act (HOPE), passed in 2006 by the US Congress, and Venezuela's regional Petro-Caribe oil discount program, not to mention Cuba's intermittent rural health initiatives in Haiti. In varying ways these all bear the hallmark of political promises with few returns, economic activity with little growth, and sustained international support undermined by either misuse or misallocation of foreign assistance. Arguably, the January 2010 earthquake deepened the quasi-permanent internationalization of the country's challenges. Yet was the damage so severe that it could serve as the basis for a makeover of Haiti's political and economic map? And would it be led by Haiti's leadership?

A critical element of this makeover is human capital. Haiti retains a reservoir of individual skills and political acumen, but the challenge lies in the pooling of these human resources and the development of relevant economic and political organizations. There may be egalitarian and cooperative features in the nation's peasant environment, yet Haiti's traditional political culture and linguistic bifurcation are profound obstacles to the development of a modern democratic government. Likewise, while the components of a modern civil society have emerged, its effectiveness has been squeezed by the absence of credible governance interlocutors at both the national and local levels, and undermined by intermittent layers of corruption and violence. The historically dubious interest of some elites in collaborating in the economic, political, and cultural integration of the nation has been an additional disappointment. Still, the multiple crises of the last two decades have also generated a more mature universe of competing political and economic elites, a potentially salient development if channeled in a constructive direction.

Another component in Haiti's makeover might lie in the mobilization of its diaspora, notably in the United States. More than just a source of remittances, this community has begun to successfully participate in the US political process, suggesting points of contact, interest, and influence regarding Haitian affairs. While the potentially beneficial impact of the diaspora on Haiti's politics has so far been unsubstantiated, it is beginning to emerge as a measurable variable. This was the case during the 2005–2006 elections and even more so during the 2010–2011 electoral contests, when personalities from the diaspora (accompanied by funding from those places) surfaced as potential candidates.

These factors represent a fragile basis upon which Haiti's future is to be built. With the nation's catastrophic social and ecological collapse—worsened by almost yearly hurricanes—any Haitian government therefore faces a daunting task. This has now been heightened even further by the 2010 earthquake. Fears of political crisis will continue to attract external interest, exacerbated by concerns with their humanitarian implications. This is particularly true for Washington, whose vision of regional strategic interest is amplified by a concern that any crisis in Haiti will affect the United States directly. The tensions between Haitian political leadership, Haiti's fragile civil society, and the international community in determining who actually governs the country and sets priorities will need to be addressed.[4] This will define Haiti's continuing search for what has so far been an elusive national consensus toward generating politically democratic governance and socially measurable economic development.

Notes

1. Compare, among others, David Nicholls, *From Dessalines to Duvalier: Race, Colour, and National Independence in Haiti* (Cambridge: Cambridge University Press, 1979); Robert I. Rotberg, *Haiti: The Politics of Squalor* (Boston: Houghton Mifflin, 1971); Robert Fatton, *The Roots of Haitian Despotism* (Boulder, CO: Lynne Rienner, 2007); and Laurent Dubois, *Haiti: The Aftershocks of History* (New York: Metropolitan Books, 2012).

2. Rayford W. Logan, *The Diplomatic Relations of the United States with Haiti, 1776–1891* (Chapel Hill: University of North Carolina Press, 1971).

3. Smith, Matthew J. *Red and Black in Haiti: Radicalism, Conflict, and Political Change, 1934–1957.* Chapel Hill: University of North Carolina Press, 2009.

4. In one of many assessments of this issue following the 2010 earthquake, see Jonathan M. Katz, *The Big Truck That Went By: How the World Came to Save Haiti and Left Behind a Disaster* (New York: Palgrave Macmillan, 2013).

Suggestions for Further Reading

Abbot, Elizabeth. *Haiti: The Duvaliers and Their Legacy.* New York: McGraw-Hill, 1988.

Deibert, Michael. *Notes from the Last Testament: The Struggle for Haiti.* New York: Seven Stories Press, 2005.

Fauriol, Georges A., ed. *Haitian Frustrations: Dilemmas for U.S. Policy.* Washington, DC: Center for Strategic and International Studies, 1995.

Gibbons, Elizabeth D. *Sanctions in Haiti: Human Rights and Democracy Under Assault.* Westport, CT: Praeger, 1999.

Girard, Philippe R. *Clinton in Haiti: The 1994 U.S. Invasion of Haiti.* New York: Palgrave Macmillan, 2004.

Heinl, Gordon Debs Jr., Nancy Gordon Heinl, and Michael Heinl. *Written in Blood: The Story of the Haitian People 1492–1995.* Rev. ed. Lanham, MD: University Press of America, 1996.

Schmidt, Hans. *The United States Occupation of Haiti, 1915–1934.* New Brunswick, NJ: Rutgers University Press, 1971.

Stotzky, Irwin P. *Silencing the Guns in Haiti: The Promise of Deliberative Democracy.* Chicago: University of Chicago Press, 1997.

Trouillot, Michel-Rolph. *Haiti, State Against Nation: The Origins and Legacy of Duvalierism.* New York: Monthly Review Press, 1990.

Wilentz, Amy. *The Rainy Season.* New York: Simon and Schuster, 1989.

PART IV

Conclusion

26

LATIN AMERICA AND THE FUTURE

Howard J. Wiarda

Harvey F. Kline

A LIVING LABORATORY

Latin America has long been one of the world's most exciting living laboratories of economic, social, and political change. Historically it has been a hotbed of conflict between democracy and authoritarianism; mercantilism, capitalism, and socialism; First and Third World perceptions; changes and continuity; the traditional and the modern. These conflicts have often torn Latin America apart and hindered its progress.

By now some of these earlier conflicts have faded, although they have not disappeared. Beginning in the early 1990s and continuing into the new millennium a new consensus seemed to have emerged between the United States and Latin America on the desirability of (1) democracy in the political sphere, (2) open markets and liberalization mixed with state regulation and social policy in the economic sphere, and (3) an international order focused on openness and free trade. Under this rubric a large number of changes have occurred in Latin America and much of the area is freer and more democratic than it was a decade or two ago. But the various chapters of this book also make clear how limited, incomplete, and perhaps even reversible these changes are. History has not yet ended in Latin America.

It is both the common trends and the differences among the countries that make Latin America such a fertile laboratory for studying comparative economic, social, and political change. Few areas of the world offer such rich conditions for study and research on the processes of comparative change and modernization. Here we have countries with a common historical background, colonial experience, law, language, religion, sociology, and politics. All were cast five hundred years ago in a common feudal and medieval setting and a colonial, subservient relationship to the mother countries of Spain and Portugal. Yet because of geography, topography, resources, ethnic mix, and history, each country has developed differently and now has its own system of values, sociology, politics, and national identity. Moreover, the countries of the area, although retaining many common traits, are becoming more and more unlike rather than alike. As President Ronald Reagan once told the reporters who accompanied him on a trip to Latin America (and knew no more about the area than he did): "There really are different countries down here."

These common background features, combined with increasingly diverging trends among the countries of the area, are what make Latin America such an interesting place for comparative study. Here we have countries with similar backgrounds and yet very different developmental patterns. How do we explain why some countries have become democratic, others remain authoritarian, still others feature a mixture of authoritarianism and democracy, and Cuba pursues a Marxist-Leninist course? How can we account for why some countries have developed economically while others remain mired in poverty? Once again the living laboratory metaphor comes into play. Latin America is like a laboratory in which we can hold some variables constant (law, language, religion, colonial experience) while we examine other variables (such as resources, social structure, or political institutions and policy) to help account for why and how some countries succeed and develop economically and politically while others do not. There is probably no other area in the world that offers both so many individual country cases combined with such a clear delineation of converging/diverging variables as does Latin America.

Looking at Latin America comparatively, it is clear that almost all the countries conform more or less closely to the general model set forth in the introductory chapters of this book. There were colonial experiences and institutions common to most of the countries, similar patterns (as well as differences) in the interrelations of the races, and common problems of organization and underdevelopment to overcome. All the countries remained locked in a medieval and semifeudal colonial experience for three centuries; all had common problems of instability, rigid class structure, lack of viable political institutions, and economic underdevelopment in the nineteenth century. All were colonial possessions, exploited, isolated, and dependent. However, the strength of the Spanish model was stronger in some places (Mexico and Peru) than in others (Costa Rica, Chile, Uruguay), and accordingly their developmental patterns were different. It is no accident that the latter group of countries is more democratic.

In the twentieth century all the countries experienced accelerated economic development, greater social change, industrialization, and more rapid political change. Yet even in colonial times the differences (in geography, resources, ethnic makeup, and value to the monarchy) among the several colonies were apparent, differences that were accentuated in the nineteenth and twentieth centuries. It is in this context of similarities and widening differences that we can begin to explain today's national variations, developmental success or the relative lack thereof, and why some countries became democratic and others did not. Hence the imperative in studying Latin America is that we must know and understand the general pattern of the region as a whole while comprehending the individual country variations. That is what this book, with the substantive general introduction followed by detailed treatment of all the countries, seeks to provide.

CHANGE AND CONTINUITY

Although the main structures and institutions of Latin American society and politics remained remarkably stable through three centuries of colonial rule and even on into the postindependence nineteenth and early twentieth centuries (the "twilight of the Middle Ages"), in recent decades the process of change has been greatly accelerated. In the introduction we identified six broad areas of change and asked the authors of our individual country chapters to assess these as well: changes in the political culture and values, changes in the economy, changes in social and class structure, changes in political groups and organizations, changes in public policy, and changes in the international environment. Now it is time to assess and pull all these themes together, linking the general propositions set forth in the introduction to the concrete cases provided in the individual chapters, to see what general trends and conclusions apply.

The country chapters make clear the degree to which Latin American political culture is undergoing transformation. New values and ideologies—democracy, participation, liberalism, capitalism, and socialism—have challenged the traditional belief system of fatalism, elitism, hierarchy, authority, and resignation. New communications and transportation networks are increasingly breaking down traditional beliefs and isolation. The hold of the traditional Catholic Church and religion on Latin America is also decreasing as Protestantism, secularism, a changed Catholic Church, and other belief systems make serious inroads. Although varying from country to country, the older authoritarian assumptions are being questioned and the older bases of legitimacy are being undermined. Latin American political culture is rapidly changing.

However, many of the old beliefs linger on, particularly in the backward rural areas and in the more traditional and poorer countries, but by no means exclusively there. For example, although Latin America prefers democratic rule, it tends to define that as "strong government." It wants regular democratic elections but often wants spoils, patronage, and government favors in return for the vote. It believes in separation of powers but still vests strong authority in an all-powerful executive. Hence, although formal democracy has been established throughout the region (except in Cuba), a genuinely egalitarian and participatory democracy is still weak in most countries. Most of the countries lack a well-developed "civil society"—a network of independent interest groups that mediate between the citizen and the government.

The economic structure has also been dramatically changed in recent decades even while many problems remain. These are no longer sleepy, traditional, backward "banana republics"; rather, the Latin American economies have become much more dynamic and diversified. The older subsistence agriculture and one-crop economies are increasingly giving way to industry, manufacturing, commerce, business, tourism, technology, and services. Latin America is now far more integrated into the world economy; feudalism and semifeudalism have given way to capitalism, neoliberalism, and in some cases socialism. All these changes have put more money into the economies of the area; provided new jobs, including jobs for women; quickened the way of life; and increased general prosperity.

Yet these changes are very uneven. Much of Latin America remains poor, backward, and Third World. Some countries and some people are making it into the developed world, but others lag behind. Moreover, even with the new wealth, Latin America has the worst distribution of income of any area in the world. In addition, although some markets have been freed up, the temptation to return to the older mercantilism and statism is still powerful. So although there has been economic progress, many problems remain.

One of the most serious is the continuing social dualism that exists, with a few very wealthy people and a large number of abjectly poor ones. This led to Brazil sometimes being referred to as "Belindia": one part modern and wealthy like Belgium and another part traditional and poor like India. This dualism exists in all Latin American countries, with the possible exception of Cuba, and in some countries—Peru, Bolivia, and Guatemala, most notably—the dualism is accentuated by the fact that the traditional, poor sector also contains poverty-stricken Indians who are outside the money economy. Hugo Chávez in Venezuela claimed to speak and govern for the marginalized sectors of the population.

Economic development has given rise to widespread social changes in all the countries. Latin America has gone from 70 percent rural to 70 percent urban and from 70 percent illiterate to 70 percent literate, life expectancy is up from sixty to seventy years, and per capita income has significantly increased. In addition, the formerly feudal, two-class societies of Latin America now have business, industrial, commercial, banking, and other elites along with the traditional landholding oligarchy. All the societies now have sizable middle classes ranging from 20 to 50 percent of the population. Trade union movements, peasants, women, indigenous elements, and the urban poor are all being organized for the first time. There are new community groups, social movements, and NGOs—civil society. These social changes have made Latin America far more pluralistic than in the past and have thus provided a more solid base for democracy.

However, these gross figures are often deceiving. Poverty, malnutrition, illiteracy, and disease are still often endemic in Latin America in both the rural and urban areas. Most of the wealth has remained in the hands of the elites and middle classes, with little having trickled down to the poor. In most countries these same elites still rule; despite elections, power is still mainly in the hands of the social, economic, and political elites. The social system is still unbalanced: compared with the elites, the trade unions, peasant leagues, women's groups, indigenous movements, and other mass organizations tend to be weak, divided, and with limited power.

As pointed out in Chapter 3, traditionally interest groups could exist only if given permission by the elite. Today there seems to be a change in this, as new groups and civil society can survive even if the government does not grant them recognition. Yet it is unclear to what extent the change from a system of corporatism or government regulation and sanction of groups to a new one of de facto liberal, pluralist legitimacy has been made. In addition, although Latin America is undoubtedly more pluralist than before, the mass of the population is still excluded from effective participation in decisions that affect them most closely. Nor does Latin America, despite the greater pluralism, have the kind of counterbalancing interest group competition and lobbying characteristics of US democracy.

Many of the same problems are characteristic of political institutions. Nineteen of the twenty Latin American countries hold elections regularly and are at least formally democratic, and that is encouraging. Similarly, the human rights situation is significantly better in most countries than it was thirty years ago. But the cultural and institutional bases of many of these new democracies are still fragile. Polls indicate that democracy's popularity is actually declining in some countries of Latin America, as the public doesn't think democracy has delivered on its promise. Cronyism and patrimonialism are still widely practiced rather than egalitarianism and advancement based on merit. Corruption, violence, and crime are increasing. At the same time political parties, local governments, and political institutions in general are not held in high esteem by the public. Latin America seems to practice democracy at election time but in the intervening years presidents rule almost as constitutional dictators, in a phenomenon known as delegative democracy.

If we look at public policy, many of the same disclaimers apply. Economic growth is occurring, but the gap between rich and poor in too many countries is widening. Liberalization, privatization, and economic reform are going forward, but ever so slowly. Agrarian reform is all but dead as an issue, and where there is urban reform, the problems seem to mount faster than the solutions. There are new social reforms, but they seldom seem to reach those most in need. In the areas of education, housing, health care, and employment, important steps have been taken, but the difficulties seem often to outstrip government's capacity to cope with them. At the same time some countries are succeeding in reducing poverty.

The final area of major change in Latin America is the international realm. It is clear that Latin America no longer lives in isolation. Globalization has come to the area. Global television and movies bring in new styles of taste and comportment: blue jeans, dating, McDonald's, Coca-Cola, freedom, consumerism. Globalization also brings with it the requirements of democracy and human rights, and if these are abused, international sanctions on the country involved are likely to follow. Globalization also means economic competition, requiring that Latin America lower its protective tariffs and be prepared to compete with the world's most efficient economies. Competition has major political implications as well, requiring downsizing, privatization, lessened patronage, and the likely going out of business of thousands of small, inefficient mom-and-pop stores and businesses. The Internet and social media connect Latin America to the world.

So the balance sheet on Latin America politics and development is still a mixed one: lots of progress on economic growth, social change, and democratization, but all of these with major weaknesses and problems as well. The gross figures sound wonderful—nineteen of twenty countries democratic—but the deeper we probe into the individual countries, the more problems we see.

What overall conclusions emerge from these considerations? First, most of Latin America is now in a transitional stage: it is in the process of breaking the back of the past but is not yet fully modern or developed. Second, we need to recognize that sustained development, whether in Africa, Russia, or Latin America, requires several generations, not just a few years. Third, modernization is uneven: urban areas are affected more rapidly than rural ones. Fourth, the benefits of development are also uneven: some groups benefit more than others, and there is always a trade-off between growth and equity. Fifth, it is clear that those countries that have ample resources, strong institutions, and good public policy—Brazil, Chile, Colombia, Costa Rica, Mexico, and Uruguay—are doing better than those that lack these features.

Latin America today represents a dynamic, ever-changing mix of traditional and modern. Abject poverty exists alongside gleaming skyscrapers and the most modern, high-tech industry. Widespread corruption and patronage coexist with efficient firms and new public policy agencies. Latin America has embraced democracy, but it is sufficiently concerned about instability, chaos, and ungovernability to retain authoritarian features. The countries, their businesses, their governments, and their unions all recognize the need to streamline and eliminate waste, but that is hard to do if a job, business, agency, or family will be hurt in the process. Given these conditions, it is probably no accident that we have seen such leaders as Chávez in Venezuela, Morales in Bolivia, Fujimori in Peru, the Kirchners in Argentina, and the Revolutionary Institutional Party (PRI) in Mexico, which appear to combine democratic tendencies with authoritarian and populist ones. It is in the bridging of these gaps between traditional and modern, authoritarian and democratic, and statism or mercantilism and liberalism that the genius of Latin America politics and politicians often shines through.

The future now looks brighter in Latin America than it has previously. On both the political (democracy) and economic (development) fronts, even with all the problems here enumerated, Latin America seems to be doing better than at any other time in its history. Although there may be reversions to authoritarianism in some of the poorer, weakly institutionalized countries, the possibility of a continentwide reversion to authoritarianism as occurred in the 1960s and 1970s seems unlikely. Over time the social, economic, and political base for authoritarianism is being eroded by greater literacy, affluence, middle-classness, and democracy, but its attractiveness in some countries has not yet entirely disappeared.

Among the most important questions remaining to be answered are which Latin American countries can succeed in consolidating and institutionalizing their still-fragile political systems, whether they can adapt rapidly enough to globalization, and whether they can reconcile their recently renewed democratic precepts with their own past historical traditions, which are often authoritarian, corporatist, and patrimonialist. On the answers to these and other important questions hang not only the possibilities for Latin America's future success but also why Latin America remains such a fascinating area.

COMMON CURRENTS AND DISTINCTIVE SITUATIONS

Although the Latin American countries have become increasingly diverse over time, the common currents that emerge from this book remain equally interesting. These include the continued decline of the traditional semifeudal order in all countries, the emergence throughout the region of greater social and political pluralism, the continued weakness of modern institutions including those necessary for democracy, and the ongoing power of elite groups. The balance of power within Latin American politics is changing as the Roman Catholic Church, the armed forces, and the landed oligarchy lose power relative to the expanded influence of commercial, banking, manufacturing, and political elites and middle classes. Similar changes are occurring at the international level, with the United States being less interested in the domestic politics of Latin America but more interested in trade and commercial relations.

Although Latin America as a whole is undoubtedly more democratic than it was three or four decades ago, democracy is often limited, partial, and blended with authoritarian and corporatist features. Similarly, in the economic sphere greater liberalization has occurred but with persistent mercantilist and statist features. If we were to rank-order the twenty Latin American countries in terms of the strength of democracy, the list at the end of the first decade of the new millennium would be as follows:

1. Most democratic: Chile, Costa Rica, and Uruguay
2. Democratic but not fully consolidated: Argentina, Brazil, Colombia, Dominican Republic, Mexico, and Panama
3. Democratic in the past but now threatened: Venezuela
4. Formally democratic but with weak institutions: Bolivia, Ecuador, El Salvador, Guatemala, Honduras, Nicaragua, Paraguay, and Peru
5. Having some fragile democratic institutions but lacking a democratic base: Haiti
6. Marxist-Leninist, undemocratic: Cuba

Note that very few of the countries are fully consolidated democracies; most are in transition, where democracy is still weak and may still be precarious. Remember the injunctions of the introduction: elections are a good start on the route to democracy, but many other criteria—human rights, civil liberties, genuine pluralism, freedom and equality, civic consciousness and participation, civilian supremacy over the military, separation of powers, social justice—must also be met before a country can be considered fully democratic.

Most of Latin America made an impressive transition to electoral democracy during the 1980s, when the region's economies were in severe recession and plagued by foreign debt. In the 1990s most of the economies of the area began to recover, to show positive growth, and to begin a process of economic reform to go with the earlier political reforms. In the twenty-first century, with commodity prices high, growth continued. Economic reform helped to free up what had been overly statist and inefficient economic systems just as democratization had challenged the older authoritarianism; increasingly liberalism, social reform, and a mixed public-private partnership in the economic sphere were seen as related to democracy in the political sphere. More recently globalization has laid down the imperative that Latin America must continue with both political and economic reform if it wishes to be competitive and a significant player in the world of the twenty-first century.

Latin America has made great strides in recent decades, but many problems and uncertainties remain. Both the progress and the problems provide good reason for students of the area to remain fascinated by it. We hope that some of our enthusiasm for the area has rubbed off on you.

ABOUT THE EDITORS
AND CONTRIBUTORS

CO-EDITORS

HOWARD J. WIARDA is the Dean Rusk Professor of International Relations and Founding Head of the Department of International Affairs at the University of Georgia. He is also a Senior Scholar at the Center for Strategic and International Studies (CSIS) and a Public Policy Scholar at the Wood row Wilson Center in Washington, DC. He is co-author with Harvey Kline of *A Concise Introduction to Latin American Politics and Development* (Westview Press, 2007) and author of *Civil Society: The American Model and Third World Development* (Westview Press, 2003).

HARVEY F. KLINE is Professor Emeritus at the University of Alabama. He has studied Colombia for fifty years, during which time he received three Fulbright fellowships to research and to teach there. He has written eight books on Colombian politics, including *Colombia: Democracy Under Assault* (Westview Press, 1995), *State-Building and Conflict Resolution in Colombia* (University of Alabama Press, 1999, Choice Outstanding Academic Book for 1999), *Chronicle of a Failure Foretold* (University of Alabama Press, 2007), *Showing Teeth to the Dragons* (University of Alabama Press, 2009) and *Historical Dictionary of Colombia* (Scarecrow Press, 2012).

CONTRIBUTORS

JULIO F. CARRIÓN is Associate Professor of Political Science and International Relations and Director of the Center for Global and Area Studies at the University of Delaware. He previously held positions at Troy State University (Alabama) and the Facultad Latinoamericana de Ciencias Sociales in Ecuador (FLACSO-Ecuador). He is the editor of *The Fujimori Legacy: The Rise of Electoral Authoritarianism in Peru* (Penn State University Press, 2006) and his most recent publication is *Cultura política de la democracia en el Perú* (co-authored with Patricia Zárate [Lima: IEP-Vanderbilt University, 2012]). He is currently working on a book manuscript on populist governance in the Andes.

LINDA CHEN is Professor of Political Science at Indiana University, South Bend, where she teaches courses on Latin American politics, politics of the developing world, and women and global politics. She has published on democratic transition in Argentina and currently works on issues related to gender and politics. She currently directs the Master of Public Affairs program.

JENNIFER N. COLLINS is Associate Professor of Political Science at the University of Wisconsin-Stevens Point. Her work focuses on social and indigenous movements and parties in the Andes. Currently she is finishing a book on social movements and the new left in Ecuador and Bolivia.

JUAN M. DEL AGUILA received his doctorate from the University of North Carolina at Chapel Hill in 1979 and subsequently taught and carried out research as an Associate Professor of Political Science at Emory University in Atlanta for thirty-two years. He is now retired and living in South Florida. During his career, he authored one book and many articles and chapters on Cuban politics and Latin American politics. He also published dozens of book reviews and served as the Book Review Editor for *Cuban Affairs*, an online, academic journal.

GEORGES A. FAURIOL is Vice President of Programs-Planning, Grants Management, Compliance, and Evaluation at the National Endowment for Democracy, and Senior Associate at the Center for Strategic and International Studies. He has extensive cross-regional field experience with a focus on democracy assistance and political party development, and leadership roles in electoral observation and assessment missions. He is the author or co-author of more than seventy publications, including *Haitian Frustrations* (CSIS, 1995), and editor of *Public Opinion Research and Democracy Promotion* (IRI, 2006).

JUDITH A. GENTLEMAN is Professor Emeritus at Air University. Before she retired, she was Professor and previously Chair of the Department of International Security Studies of the Air War College. She also served as Associate Dean at AWC and served as an adjunct instructor in the USAF Special Operations School at Hurlburt. Her research focused primarily on Mexico and the Andean states.

VANESSA JOAN GRAY teaches political science at the University of Massachusetts, Lowell. She specializes in rural conflict issues in Colombia and is researching a book on communities that have resisted dispossession by practicing nonviolence and sustainable resource use.

ESTHER SKELLEY JORDAN received her doctorate at the School of Public and International Affairs at the University of Georgia. She teaches international relations and empirical research methods at the Georgia Institute of Technology and holds a master's degree in political science from the University of Georgia. She has contributed chapters to or co-authored numerous publications, including: *The Window of Favor: Public Opinion and the Urgency of Reformation in Transitioning Democracies* (IRI, 2009); *Globalization: Universal Trends, Regional Implications* (The University

Press of New England, 2008); *The 2004 Dominican Republic Elections: Post Election Report* (CSIS, 2004); and "Communism in Latin America" (Charles Scribner and Sons, 2004).

FABRICE LEHOUCQ is Associate Professor, Department of Political Science, University of North Carolina, Greensboro. A specialist in comparative politics, democratic politics, and political economy, his books include *Stuffing the Ballot Box: Fraud, Democratization, and Electoral Reform in Costa Rica* (Cambridge University Press, 2002) and *The Politics of Modern Central America: Civil War, Democratization, and Underdevelopment* (Cambridge University Press, 2012).

RONALD H. MCDONALD was Professor Emeritus of Political Science in the Maxwell School, Syracuse University, and was former chair of the department. He was the author of *Party Systems and Elections in Latin America* (Markham, 1971) and co-author with J. Mark Ruhl of *Party Politics and Elections in Latin America* (Westview Press, 1989).

RICHARD L. MILLETT is adjunct professor at the Defense Institute of Security Assistance Management and is a Senior Advisor for Political Risk to the PRS Group. He is co-editor with Jennifer S. Holmes and Orlando J. Pérez of *Latin American Democracy: Emerging Reality or Endangered Species?* (Routledge, 2009).

FRANK O. MORA is director of the Latin American and Caribbean Center and Professor of Politics and International Relations at Florida International University. He is the author of several articles and edited volume contributions on Cuban politics and military. Dr. Mora served as Deputy Assistant Secretary of Defense for the Western Hemisphere (2009–2013).

DAVID MYERS is Associate Professor of Political Science at Penn State University. His primary research interests are in comparative politics with special attention to Latin America (emphasis on the Andean South America and Brazil), political parties, elections, and comparative urbanism. He has published more than fifty articles and book chapters, some of which have appeared in *Comparative Politics, Comparative Political Studies*, the *Latin American Research Review*, and *Latin American Politics and Society*. He has authored, edited, or co-edited eight books, most recently (with Jennifer McCoy) *The Unraveling of Representative Democracy in Venezuela* (Johns Hopkins University Press, 2005).

DAVID SCOTT PALMER is Professor Emeritus of International Relations and Political Science and was the Founding Director of Latin American Studies at Boston University.

STEVE C. ROPP is Distinguished Emeritus Professor of Political Science at the University of Wyoming and an Honorary Research Fellow at the University of Queensland, Australia. He has written widely on Panamanian and Central American politics, and also on global human rights. Among his current research projects is one that explores the question of where the current canal expansion fits in the sequence of technological events that have traditionally shaped and reshaped Panamanian politics.

J. MARK RUHL is the Glenn E. and Mary L. Todd Professor of Political Science and the Chair of the Department of Latin American, Latino, and Caribbean Studies at Dickinson College in Carlisle, Pennsylvania. He has written extensively on the problems of democratization in Latin America with special emphasis on the Central American countries. His most recent articles have appeared in *Journal of Democracy*, *Latin American Politics and Society*, and *Security and Defense Studies Review*.

MITCHELL A. SELIGSON is the Centennial Professor of Political Science and Professor of Sociology (by courtesy) at Vanderbilt University. He founded and directs the Latin American Public Opinion Project (LAPOP), which carries out the AmericasBarometer democracy surveys in twenty-six countries. He is an elected member of the General Assembly of the Inter-American Institute of Human Rights, an appointed member of the Organization of American States (OAS) Advisory Board of Inter-American Program on Education for Democratic Values and Practices, and is a founding member of the International Advisory Board (IAB) of the AfroBarometer. His most recent books are *The Legitimacy Puzzle in Latin America: Democracy and Political Support in Eight Nations* (Cambridge University Press, 2009), and *Development and Underdevelopment: The Political Economy of Global Inequality, Fifth Edition* (Lynne Rienner, 2014).

PAUL E. SIGMUND is Professor Emeritus of Politics at Princeton University, specializing in political theory and Latin American politics. He has published many books, including *The Overthrow of Allende and the Politics of Chile, 1964–1976* (University of Pittsburgh Press, 1977), *The United States and Democracy in Chile* (Johns Hopkins University Press, 1993), and *Chile 1973–1998: The Coup and Its Consequences* (Program in Latin American Studies, Princeton University, 1999) as well as over one hundred articles and chapters in books on Chilean politics.

PAUL C. SONDROL is Associate Professor of Political Science at the University of Colorado–Colorado Springs. He has published in the United States and Europe on Paraguay, Uruguay, Chile, Cuba, militarism, and authoritarianism.

CHRISTINE J. WADE is Associate Professor of Political Science and International Studies at Washington College in Chestertown, Maryland. She is the co-author of *Understanding Central America: Global Forces, Rebellion and Change* (Westview Press, 2009), *Nicaragua: Living in the Shadow of the Eagle* (Westview Press, 2011), and *A Revolução Salvadorenha (The Salvadoran Revolution)* as part of the Revolutions of the Twentieth Century Collection at São Paulo: Fundação Editora Da *UNESP* (2006). She is also the author of several publications on the FMLN, peace building, and postwar politics in El Salvador and Central America.

MARTIN WEINSTEIN is Professor Emeritus of Political Science at William Paterson University. During his four-decade career he authored two books, *Uruguay: The Politics of Failure* (Greenwood Press, 1975) and *Uruguay: Democracy at the Crossroads* (Westview Press, 1988), as well as dozens of book chapters, encyclopedia entries, and articles on Uruguay's political, economic, and social development and US-Latin American relations, especially in regard to human rights.

IÊDA SIQUEIRA WIARDA is Luso-Brazilian Specialist at the Library of Congress and Professor of International Relations and Comparative Government at the University of Georgia. She is a consultant to various governmental and nongovernmental institutions, such as the State Department, and on the Board of Directors of various organizations, such as the International Women's Health Coalition. She has authored and co-authored many books, articles, and papers and is a lecturer in the United States, Latin America, Europe, and Asia.

DWIGHT WILSON is Professor of Political Science and International Affairs at the University of North Georgia. His research interests include the ideas and ideologies of Latin America and the intersection of culture and democratization. Currently his research focuses on the challenges to democracy posed by organized crime in Central America and Mexico.

INDEX